THE LANDMARK

A TOUCHSTONE BOOK
Published by Simon & Schuster

THUCYDIDES

A COMPREHENSIVE GUIDE TO
THE PELOPONNESIAN WAR

A Newly Revised Edition of the Richard Crawley Translation
with Maps, Annotations, Appendices, and Encyclopedic Index

Edited by Robert B. Strassler

With an Introduction by Victor Davis Hanson

The editor gratefully acknowledges permission to use illustrations from various sources, as follow: 1.1: Courtesy of the Royal Ontario Museum, Toronto. 1.90: Ostia Museum. Photo Gabinetto Fotografico. 1.132: Deutsches Archäologisches Institut, Istanbul. 1.135: American School of Classical Studies at Athens, Agora Excavations. 1.144: Copyright British Museum. 2.22: Photograph by David Finn. 2.44: Alinari/Art Resources. 2.69: Epigraphic Museum, Athens. 2.84: Paul Lipke/The Trireme Trust. 3.48: American School of Classical Studies at Athens, Agora Excavations. 3.86: Copyright British Museum. 4.41: American School of Classical Studies at Athens, Agora Excavations. 5.47: Epigraphic Museum, Athens. 6.54: Epigraphic Museum, Athens. 6.61: American School of Classical Studies at Athens, Agora Excavations. 8.7: Copyright British Museum. 8.8: Courtesy of Thames & Hudson Ltd. Photograph by Peter A. Clayton. Appendix G: The Trireme Trust. Illustration by John F. Coates.

TOUCHSTONE
Rockefeller Center
1230 Avenue of the Americas
New York, NY 10020

First Touchstone edition 1998

TOUCHSTONE and colophon are registered trademarks of Simon & Schuster Inc.

Designed by Kim Llewellyn
Maps by Anne Gibson

Manufactured in the United States of America

10 9 8 7 6 5 4 3 2

Library of Congress Cataloging-in-Publication Data

Thucydides.
    [History of the Peloponnesian War. English]
    The landmark Thucydides : a comprehensive guide to the Peloponnesian War / edited by Robert B. Strassler; introduction by Victor Davis Hanson.
       p. cm.
    "This edition uses the translation by Richard Crawley (1840–93) published in 1874"—CIP front matter.
    Includes bibliographical references and index.
    1. Greece—History—Peloponnesian War, 431–404 B.C. I. Strassler, Robert B., 1937– .
II. Crawley, Richard, 1840–1893. III. Title.
DF229.T55C7   1996
938'.05—dc20   96-24555
ISBN 0-684-82815-4
ISBN 0-684-82790-5 (Pbk.)

TO THE MEMORY OF
SAMUEL A. STRASSLER

CONTENTS

INTRODUCTION

I. Life

i.

"Thucydides, an Athenian, wrote the history of the war" is the first pronouncement of *The Peloponnesian War* (1.1.1). Unfortunately, the merest glimpses of our author's life follow this promising initial revelation of his name, nationality, and calling. Only at a very few unexpected places in his chronicle does Thucydides disclose somewhat more about himself. He announces, for example, that he once suffered from the great plague that struck Athens between 430 and 427 (2.48.3),[a] the scourge that killed Pericles and thousands of his fellow Athenians (3.87.3).

Once more Thucydides, in the third person, matter-of-factly enters his own narrative during the account of the successful Spartan attack on the northern Greek city of Amphipolis (424). He tells us that:

> "The general, who had come from Athens to defend the place, sent to the other commander in Thrace, Thucydides son of Olorus, the author of this history, who was at the isle of Thasos, a Parian colony, half a day's sail from Amphipolis." (4.104.4)

His father's name, "Olorus," is probably Thracian and royal, suggesting both a foreign and a wealthy pedigree. Thucydides confirms that standing and prestige when he explains that he was called to Amphipolis precisely because "he possessed the right of working the gold mines in that part of Thrace, and thus had great influence with the inhabitants of the mainland" (4.105.1).

For his failure to save Amphipolis from the shrewd Spartan general Brasidas Thucydides bore the full brunt of Athenian popular indignation:

> "It was also my fate to be an exile from my country for twenty years after my command at Amphipolis; and being present with both parties, and more especially with the Peloponnesians by reason of my exile, I had leisure to observe affairs more closely" (5.26.5).

I.i.a   All dates in this edition are B.C. Numbers in paren-
theses refer to the book, chapter, and section
number in Thucydides' text.

Later Roman and Byzantine biographies, their anecdotes and gossip unproved but not necessarily always fanciful, add a few more intriguing personal details about Thucydides' life: formal philosophical and rhetorical training, aristocratic connections, a violent death, and burial at Athens. But beyond his own admitted survival of disease, battle, and exile, Thucydides tells us little else about his experience in the war years other than that he lived "through the whole of it, being of an age to comprehend events" (5.26.5). We should conclude that he was near thirty when the fighting broke out (431) and probably died in his sixties or early seventies in the mid-390s, with his history apparently left uncompleted.

ii.

Besides an intrinsic interest in learning more about the author of the finest history of the ancient world, we search for the elusive historical Thucydides in hopes of learning something of the man's outlook, his role in the events of his time, his association with the eminent figures of the fifth century—indeed, anything that might shed some additional light upon the intention, disposition, and outlook of the author of *The Peloponnesian War*. Given that he was an Athenian during the city's greatest age; a man of some wealth, property, and important family connections; and once an official of the government with a sizable command, important friends, and apparently numerous enemies at Athens, a few inferences are in order.

Like his contemporary the Athenian playwright Euripides, Thucydides was familiar with, but did not necessarily approve of, the sophistic and rhetorical movements that were spawned by the bounty of this Athenian century. Nor does Thucydides' own participation in the expanding regime of Athens suggest his agreement with an imperial democratic culture that grew out from the vast possession of subject states. Despite opportunity for profitable overseas concessions and military repute, wealthier Athenians like Thucydides probably felt more at home with a past timocratic[a] government that had once been the private domain of property owners. As moderate oligarchs, then, they were skeptical of unpredictable democrats and any others who championed a more radically egalitarian agenda that might diminish the power of Athens' upper classes (8.97.2).

For a man of Thucydides' experience and upbringing, democracy worked best when nominal and under the control of a single great man like Pericles (2.65.6–13). Less responsible demagogues and politicians, like Cleon and Hyberbolus, were both unpredictable and unreliable and so to be feared (3.36.6; 8.73.3). Their stock-in-trade was the agitation of the Athenian *demos*, an always fickle and sometimes quite dangerous rabble (2.65.4; 2.65.10–11; 3.36.4; 6.24.2–4).

In contrast, by the latter fifth century conservative Athenians of piety and virtue were odd men out. A particular Thucydidean example of this is the very rich Athenian statesman Nicias, who failed to arrest the folly of the Athenian mob, and for his troubles ended up dead at the end of the ill-fated Athenian expedition to Sicily (7.86.2–5). It is no accident that there is little naïveté, much less idealism and inno-

---

I.ii.a   A timocratic government is one in which political
         power is directly proportional to property ownership.

cence, to be found in the black-and-white history of Thucydides (2.35.2; 3.44.4; 5.89). Its author, we must remember, was above all a man of action, an elected official, a captain, a traveler, and a pragmatic intellectual, a successful combatant against warrior and disease alike, hardbitten and intimate with both privilege and disgrace, a man who suffered with and outlived most of the greatest men of his age.

II. The Peloponnesian War

i.

"Not as an essay which is to win applause of the moment, but as a possession for all time . . . " (1.22.4).

So Thucydides confidently writes of his own historical aims. We are warned early on that the "history"—Thucydides gives us no exact title of his work—is to be more than an accurate account of the events of his age, momentous and portentous as they were (1.1.1). Clearly, he believed that the war between Athens and Sparta offered a unique look at the poles of human and not just Greek experience, at contrasting ideologies and assumptions for a brief time ripped open by organized savagery (1.23.2–3) and left exposed for autopsy by the bewildered but curious who were eager for explanation and instruction. For the diagnostician Thucydides, the nature of humankind was constant and predictable, the story of civilized man somewhat continuous and repetitive, and thus his account of these events surely of educational value to sober and reflective men not yet born (1.22.4–5; 2.48.3).

Most often this message "for all time" appears in elaborate antitheses of thought and expression: individual words, entire sentences, even whole episodes. Nature and culture, word and deed, pretext and candor lead to larger corollaries of land power and sea power, oligarchy and democracy, commerce and agriculture, wealth and poverty—all for a purpose. The war between Athens and Sparta offers profound human knowledge in the extreme variance between what a man says and what he does (3.82.4–84.3), between the jealousy of ambition and the contempt for docility (2.35.2; 2.61.4), between the dream of a people and the reality of their experience (6.31.5–6; 7.75.6–7; 7.87), between innate discomfiture with the good and the human attraction toward the base (2.64.4–65.11; 3.36.6; 4.21.2–22.2; 6.24.2–4), between the burdens and responsibilities of power and the necessary acknowledgment of impotence (5.85–116), between democracy at home and imperialism abroad (2.62.2–64.3; 6.17.2–18.7), between the Athenian thesis that they are powerful but reluctant players in a brutal cosmic order, and the Spartan notion of free will, which hinges on the gods' punishment of the guilty and aid of the virtuous (1.69; 1.121–124; 2.60–62; 5.104–106). Athens and Sparta are states in a real war, but they are also metaphysical representations of opposite ways of looking at the universe, whose corollaries are often emphasized in a variety of contexts.

So the majestic Funeral Oration of Pericles (2.35.1–46.2) is to be placed immediately before the horrific plague (2.47.3–54.3), in the same manner as the Athenians' butchery of the hapless Melians (5.116.2–4) is a formal prelude for their own brutal extermination to come in Sicily (7.84.2–85.2). More concretely, the magnificent navy of Athens is to be contrasted with the invincible hoplites of Sparta (1.18.2–3; 1.142.5–8). The capital of Athenian imperialism is a match for the agrarian industriousness of the Peloponnesians (1.141.2–6), as the majestic Pericles towers over subsequent weaker successors (2.65.8–12) like Cleon and Alcibiades.

In his interest in formal polarities of thought and action, Thucydides is not always, I think, a more astute recorder than Herodotus (who lived c. 484–25), a near-contemporary historian, and therefore our most natural object of comparison. That Herodotus was less critical of sources and motive, more interested in ethnography, anthropology, myth, and yarn does not make him any less of a historian—or in turn Thucydides any more the biased theoretician, eager to select, omit, manipulate, and distort data according to his own preconceived and refined notion of what constitutes important and unimportant lessons of human behavior.

Rather, the differences between the two historians lie more in approach, method, and the generations in which they lived. Herodotus' travel mosaics of exotic tales, alien characters, and oddities of experience are all to be sorted out by the reader himself to form an overall picture of why a past generation of free Greeks triumphs over an oppressive and autocratic Persia, of who lies and who tells the truth, of what is believable and what not, of what is wisdom and what folly. So Herodotus, the itinerant Dorian, relies mostly on and is comfortable with an oral tradition. He feels no need to assess—at least in any systematic or formal way—the accuracy of what he hears, and provides little idea how all these reports join and fit into a unified whole. In some ways Herodotus is the most modern of historians, providing raw data and documentation without the intrusion of personal interpretation or explication.

In contrast, the younger Thucydides lives the history of the war that he writes, an account verifiable by eyewitnesses still alive (1.22.1–3). His prose is to be accepted or rejected by contemporaries in Athens with keen interests in rhetoric and style, a generation well acquainted with the logic of Socrates, the realism of Euripides, and the arguments of the Sophists. The influence of contemporary medical writers also offered to Thucydides the methodology of symptomatology, diagnosis, and prognosis that could be applied outside the realm of pure science: history is also a scientific discipline with its own proper set of rules and procedures (1.21–22; 2.48–49; 3.82–84). He cannot often, then, like Herodotus, say simply, "It is said . . . ," because the late-fifth-century Athenian audience of his history knows better and wants more. In any case, Thucydides feels the way to understanding is not through the sheer aggregate of examples, from which a few great notions of fate and chance might be freely deduced. The historian instead believes that the truth requires his own interpretation of the events he presents. It demands that he deem some occurrences not worthy of inclusion into his narrative, while others must take on unusual importance. If Thucydides' historical material is less rich and enchanting than *The Persian Wars* of Herodotus, his carefully chosen military episodes and political speeches by themselves explicitly reveal cause and effect (1.97.2), follow a discernible chronology (5.20.2–3), and often lead to more profound and general truths about human experience (3.82–84; 5.85–116). And perhaps most importantly, Thucydides suffered through a war (5.26.5) far more lengthy, brutal, and horrific than the allied Greeks' noble defense of their country a half century earlier, an experience that must in some part account for his bleaker conclusions that human conflict was both uncontrollable and inevitable.

ii.

Very different from Herodotus also are the composition, style, and organization of Thucydides' history. How Thucydides assembled *The Peloponnesian War* and arranged his material is not really ascertainable. His history has come down to us divided into eight books, but we do not know whether these divisions, or the chapter and section divisions, derive from Thucydides himself or (far more likely) from editors and publishers who worked centuries after his death. He seems instead to have envisioned his story more as a chronicle of consecutive yearly military campaigns (2.1) than chapters of related episodes. So after Book 1 has set the stage, the narrative commences with the spring warring season of the first year of the war, 431, and proceeds to relate events in sequence through midwinter of 411. But then in Book 8 (which alone has no speeches), the history ends abruptly in midsentence (8.109). Seven years of his proposed twenty-seven-year account (5.26.1) are left unrecorded.

Thucydides must have either (1) composed his history without revision year by year as the fighting progressed; (2) begun writing the narrative from his notes only after the war was completed in 404; or (3) written and revised on and off from 431 to the early 390s, when his death—or perhaps simple frustration—cut short his narrative-in-progress in the summer of the year 411, and prevented completion of an ongoing reworking of the whole. The third possibility seems most likely, for here and there throughout the entire account Thucydides reveals knowledge of the war's outcome (2.65.12–13), and thus the approximate role his characters and events would play in the general unity and theme of his work—if it had been completed.

Still, the history quite clearly divides into roughly two parts. The initial half (Books 1–5.25.2) covers the first ten years, the so-called Archidamian War from 431 to 421. It contains a formal preface (1.1–118.3) and seems to conclude with the notion that the Peloponnesian War ended in stalemate with the Peace of Nicias in 421 (5.18.1–24.2).

But with the abrupt resumption of hostilities in a variety of theaters in 421 (5.32.1–7), and the subsequent Athenian disaster at Sicily (415–13), Thucydides seems to have inserted something like a second introduction at 5.26. At some point in his research, he must have envisioned an integral and continuous twenty-seven-year war, one whose cohesive chronicle might now be brought all the way down to the destruction of Athens' Long Walls in 404. This continuation, clearly incomplete and less revised, is extant from 415 to 411 (from Book 5.26 to Book 8.109).

iii.

There is little argument that Thucydides' prose is difficult, and at times nearly incomprehensible. Yet its inherent abstruseness, its lengthy clauses and antitheses, and its deliberate understatement can still be moving. Thucydidean language often translates into English in a way more memorable than the direct and accessible expression of near-contemporary writers such as Xenophon or Lysias:

> "Revolution thus ran its course from city to city, and the places where it arrived at last, from having heard what had been done before carried to a still greater excess the refinement of their inventions, as manifested in the cunning of their enterprises and the atrocity of their reprisals. Words had to change their ordinary meanings and to take those which were now given them. Reckless audacity came to be considered the courage of a loyal supporter; prudent hesitation, specious cowardice; moderation was held to be a cloak for unmanliness; ability to see all sides of a question incapacity to act on any. Frantic violence became the attribute of manliness; cautious plotting a justifiable means of self-defense. The advocate of extreme measures was always trustworthy; his opponent a man to be suspected. To succeed in a plot was to have a shrewd head, to divine a plot a still shrewder; but to try to provide against having to do either was to break up your party and to be afraid of your adversaries" (3.82.3–5).

Thucydides' use of abstract nouns, his preference for constant variety in vocabulary, his fondness for archaic and even poetic expressions, and his often dramatic inversion of normal word order all ensure that his Greek is as complex as is his method of historical inquiry. Yet bear in mind that very little Attic prose was written before Thucydides. Nearly all of what was composed has been lost. Therefore we are not sure whether Thucydides' perplexing language is unique or typical, whether it reveals an entirely original method of expression, or simply mirrors the spirited intellectual ferment and experimentation of the times. Does the need to create ex nihilo words and phrases to match the depth of his abstract and conceptual thinking explain his singular literary technique? Or is Thucydidean style simply one with a peculiar, mostly lost, and now unrecoverable Athenian rhetorical florescence?

iv.

At Book 1.21–22 Thucydides clearly outlined his own methods of historical inquiry, offering a self-conscious candor rare in ancient narrative writing. He did not trust first impressions, he says, not even his own. But through inquiry and cross-examination of witnesses ("tried by the most severe and detailed tests possible"), autopsy, and apparent inspection of written documents, Thucydides claims an objective inquiry that has "cost me some labor." His later admission that his own exile allowed him time for careful investigation, "especially with the Peloponnesians" (5.26.5), suggests the image of a careful and nonpartisan note taker, eager to hunt down the principals themselves—both Athenian and Spartan—who took part in the war. His keen knowledge of Spartan custom and tradition (1.20.3; 4.80; 5.66.2–72.4) bears out this confident assertion.

While it is once again fashionable to see this statement of principles at 1.21–22 as a clever smokescreen of sorts, a sham to hide biased fiction packaged as "objective history," such modern cynicism rings mostly false for a variety of reasons. Although some of Thucydides' narrative is highly stylized and focused deliberately on just a few individuals who best illustrate the author's own ideas about fate, chance, and human experience, elsewhere he is clearly aiming to be accurate, objective, and comprehensive.

Anonymous men are questioned (6.55.1), oracular pronouncements investigated (2.17.1; 2.54.2–5; 5.16), poets and prose authors both consulted and rejected (1.97.3; 3.104.4), inscriptions on stone noted and copied (5.18.2–19.2; 6.54.7; 6.59.3), and the material remains of buildings and walls explored and analyzed (1.10.2; 1.93.2; 2.15.4–6). Even the contents of graves are examined and marshalled to support historical hypotheses (1.8.1). Often such detail can appear to the reader as digressive (6.2.1–5.3), near-trivial (6.54.1–59.4), or even irrelevant, as if the historian means to follow up on his earlier promises of completeness, regardless of the tedium involved. Thucydides himself said such research "cost me some labor" (1.22.3). No wonder he despaired that "the absence of romance in my history will, I fear, detract somewhat from its interest" (1.22.4).

v.

There are one hundred forty-one speeches in the history, presented in both direct and indirect discourse. Because of the sheer number and variety of these addresses, the problematic use in general of formal speeches in ancient historical and rhetorical writing, and Thucydides' own enigmatic comments about his rules of usage (1.22.1), debate persists over their degree of veracity. There are, I think, four possible interpretations: (1) the speeches are accurate and nearly verbatim reproductions of what Thucydides either read, himself heard, or was told by others; (2) they are entirely fictitious and made up by the author himself; (3) they are greatly elaborated, modified, or refined versions of what men probably said; or (4) the one hundred forty-one addresses are not uniform and so vary according to the above categories.

Before Thucydides, both the historians Herodotus and Hecataeus, like the Greek poets, used speeches mostly as literary and dramatic fictions to interrupt and vividly illustrate the argument of the narrative. But Thucydides' own characterization of his speeches at 1.22.1 suggests a much different approach, one that warns his audience of his departure from past practice, and so should solve for us the problem of their historicity:

"With reference to the speeches in this history, some were delivered before the war began, others while it was going on; some I heard myself, others I got from various quarters; it was in all cases difficult to carry them word for word in one's memory, so my habit has been to make the speakers say what was in my opinion demanded of them by the various occasions, of course adhering as closely as possible to the general sense of what they really said."

This careful declaration, however, has led only to more controversy. Does not Thucydides admit to two contrary agendas: contrivance ("to make the speakers say what was in my opinion demanded of them") and historical exactitude ("adhering as closely as possible to the general sense of what they really said")? Has he not entered that most controversial and irreconcilable of arguments—so popular once again now in academic circles—the cleft between "objective" and "subjective" truth?

Apparently, Thucydides is envisioning two very different circumstances for setting down speeches in his history: well-known addresses in which he was more or less able to find out what was really said, and other instances in which something probably was spoken, but went unrecorded or was forgotten. The latter orations had to be reconstructed more or less according to Thucydides' own particular historical sense of what was likely, appropriate, and necessary. How, then, can the exasperated reader determine the degree of authenticity of any given speech in the history?

He cannot. But surely he can rely on common sense to learn which addresses are more likely to have been spoken as recorded in the text of the history. Is there evidence—a large audience, an annual festive occasion, an official government proceeding—to suggest a speech was actually communicated, recorded, and subject to verification by Thucydides' readership? How conceivable is it (considering the place and time) that Thucydides could have either heard a speech himself or learned of its contents from others? Does an oration confirm a personal imprint, in line with the speaker's apparent nature and personality? Or does it seem instead stereotyped, designed by the historian himself to illustrate general and universal themes and so sometimes attributed to minor and otherwise unknown if not anonymous characters? And what are the preface and the reaction to a speech? Does an oration logically follow a course of events and in turn have an immediate effect on the conduct of subsequent actions in the narrative?

vi.

Succeeding generations of Greeks and Romans credited Thucydides with establishing objective history. His considerable skill in presenting that doctrine in formal prose left an undeniable mark even on his immediate literary successors, who likewise saw history as largely the unromantic story of political and military affairs. Indeed, many inquirers—Xenophon, Cratippus, and Theopompus—began their accounts where Thucydides had left off in 411. It is no surprise, then, that subsequent ancient historians were judged largely by the degree to which they followed the canons of accuracy and integrity established by Thucydides. Xenophon (428–354), therefore, is faulted for his failure to consult sources other than his own Spartan confidants, his blindness to the larger meaning of the very events he describes, and his view that his histories were not much more than one personal memoir. The fourth-century chronicler Ephorus (405–330), also unlike Thucydides, appears too credible and naive in his uses of sources, and lacks a workable chronology. Even the more erudite Theopompus (b. 378) is found too bitter in his judgments, without the distance and even the presumed air of objectivity of Thucydides in *The Peloponnesian War*.

In contrast, the anonymous Oxyrhynchus Historian, the mostly lost Hieronymus of Cardia (d. 250), and the later and extant Polybius (200–c. 118) have often won praise as "Thucydidean" precisely because they are didactic and strive to teach the reader larger and more abstract lessons from the near-endless wars and coups they relate. An awareness of cause and effect, the employment of a strict chronology, and evidence of a unity of purpose predominate. And like Thucydides these historians appear skeptical of what they hear and read. Often they must outline formally the mechanisms they employ to sort out rumor from fact. Even their speeches, embroidered and contrived as they are, lend explication and sense to larger issues beyond the drama at hand, and thus appear as "Thucydidean" rather than as mere fancies or as exhibitions of rhetorical expertise.

III. The Conflict between Athens and Sparta

i.

Thucydides wrote his history while confidently believing that

> "it would be a great war, and more worthy of relation than any that had preceded it. This belief was not without its grounds. The preparations of both the combatants were in every department in the last state of perfection; and he could see the rest of the Hellenic race taking sides in the quarrel; those who delayed doing so at once having it in contemplation. Indeed this was the greatest movement yet known in history, not only of the Hellenes, but of a large part of the barbarian world—I had almost said of mankind." (1.1.1–2)

The later history of the classical culture bears out Thucydides' judgment that the Peloponnesian War was a twenty-seven-year nightmare that wrecked Greece.

Before the fifth century, the Greek *poleis* (city-states) had been unusually isolated from the turbulence of Mediterranean history. Free to form their own customs and traditions, the many hundreds of poleis nevertheless shared a common and venerable religious, linguistic, and political culture. Most were broad-based oligarchies that had evolved out of landed aristocracies or had inherited power from intermediary tyrannies. The citizenry of hoplite yeomen, each owning and farming about ten acres of land, formed up as heavily armed infantry (*hoplites*) in the phalanx to battle neighboring Greek communities over disputed strips of borderland (1.15.2). From the seventh to the fifth centuries, there was a steady, if sometimes slow, advancement of Greek material and intellectual culture (1.13.1), as the protective practice of timocratic government and near-ritual infantry fighting prevented most political upheavals and limited the damage caused by frequent wars. The fifth century changed all that (1.1.2–3; 1.18.2–3; 1.23.1–6).

After the repulse of the Persians (in 490 and again in 480–79), the insular Greeks were faced with unforeseen military and political responsibilities in the Aegean and the Mediterranean at large, which were largely antithetical to the landed capital, infantry exclusivity, and smug isolationism of the traditional city-state (*polis*) (1.91.4–7; 1.93.3–7; 1.96.1). Unfortunately, as early as 478, the two most atypical and powerful of the city-states, Athens and Sparta, could not agree on joint leadership of the Greek alliance that had been so successful against the Persians (1.18.2–3; 1.95.7–97.1). Oddly, both poleis, although in diametrically opposite ways, rejected much of the traditional culture of the city-state—pitched battle by amateur militias, government by yeomen peers, economic reliance on citizen-worked farms, absence of satellites and tributaries. The antagonism set the stage, as Thucydides saw, for a horrific war like none other in the Greek past (1.1.1–3; 1.23.1–2).

The leadership of the maritime Greek federation against Persia fell to the Athenian navy (1.18.2; 1.73.4–75.3). Far from dismantling an oppressive imperial hierarchy, the Athenians throughout the mid-fifth century refined the Persian system of empire, and channeled the tribute to solidify and enlarge their own democratic culture at home while seeking tyrannical aggrandizement abroad (1.89.1–1.117.3). The enfranchisement and enrichment of those Athenians without money and land (2.37.1), together with the freedom and capital to wage war both imaginatively and continuously (2.39.2–3), meant that the past limiting protocols of the polis did not apply to an increasingly restive Athens (1.80.3–81.6; 1.142.1–144.3) In the process, Thucydides says, Pericles and the Athenian intelligentsia craft an apology for their oppression. It becomes a determinist, Hobbesian doctrine which explains that power—and hence justice—always and rightly accrues to the strong (2.64; 5.97).

Sparta offers both a material and a philosophical contrast. Her unique enslavement of nearly a quarter of a million rural indentured servants, the Helots, excused an armed elite from working their own plots. Rejecting the traditional Greek practice of free agriculture, Spartan society gradually institutionalized a complicated and harsh system of apartheid that called for constant surveillance of an enormous productive underclass (1.101.2–103.3; 1.132.4–5; 4.41.3). The result was the creation of the first true militaristic culture in the West, where all Spartiate males from the age of seven embarked on a vigorous course of military training (2.39.1–2; 5.66.2–4). The ensuing expertise would ensure a professional army (1.18.2; 4.40.2; 5.66.2–72.4), able to put down murderously at a moment's notice any hint of domestic insurrection (4.80.2–4) or, if need be, to march out to absorb and consolidate nearby territory in the Peloponnesus (1.19.1; 1.76.1). Inward, blinkered, reluctant to venture on the sea, Sparta's self-interested conservatism takes on the appearance of an anti-Athenian philosophical system, in which most Greek states should be left alone to practice justice under absolute canons of Hellenic law (1.83–85; 4.86–87).

ii.

Thucydides saw that the ultimate confrontation between these two remarkable societies would be both inevitable and terrible (1.23.2; 2.11.6–9; 2.12.3); inevitable, because of their remarkable antitheses between land and sea, autocracy and liberality, narrow Dorian gentry and broader Ionian commerce; terrible, because there existed between the two powers neither an adherence to the past restrictions on Greek warmaking nor sufficient common political ground to negotiate a lasting peace. The battlefield once and for all might arbitrate their contrasting views of human and divine justice.

Athens, with its huge navy fueled by overseas tribute, had no need to engage grim Spartan hoplites in pitched battle (1.143.4–5; 2.13.3–8). Athens' biggest worry was the sheer recklessness of its own democratic government (1.144.1). A simple majority of the citizenry, urged on and incensed by clever demagogues, might capriciously send out military forces in unnecessary and exhausting adventures (2.65.11–12; 6.31.1–5).

Sparta might continually invade Athens (2.21.1–23.3). But for what purpose? Her narrow and conservative policy of simple challenges to pitched battle, coupled with the unimaginative agricultural devastation of Attica, could never bring a maritime Athens to her knees (1.143.4–144.3; 2.65.11–13). Peloponnesian victory required innovative thinking and a veritable change in Spartan character itself (1.81.1–6), if she were to cut off the tribute of Athens, spread insurrection among Athenian allies, and so acquire a navy of her own (1.121.2–5; 1.142.2–143.3)—all steps counter to her own reactionary and inbred culture (1.69.4–70.8; 1.84.1–4), and to her professed notion that there are gods who punish an imperial power's wanton destruction of Greek states.

So, for Thucydides, the struggle between a sea power and a land power meant not a short, decisive conflict like the border fights of the past, but a long-drawn-out and murderous affair: Eventually it became apparent that Sparta must man ships and Athens must fight on land. Maritime states loyal to Athens through contributions of tribute and manpower were to be lured away (1.81.3–4; 1.122.1); members of Sparta's Peloponnesian League must know that war by land might be brought to their very doorstep (1.142.4; 2.25.1–5). Homicidal revolution (3.82.1–84.3), the mobilization of serfs and slaves (4.80.5; 7.57.8), drawn-out sieges (3.20.1–24.3; 5.84–116), mass murder and execution (5.116.3–4), and random, senseless killing (7.29.4–30.3)—all these were for Thucydides the expected cargo of a war between opposites, who would become ever more desperate and barbaric as the fighting progressed, as they learned that innovative and murderous responses were required for absolute victory.

Thucydides suggests, I think, that the legacy of the Peloponnesian War would not be the victory of Spartan authoritarianism and the repudiation of the imperial democratic culture of Athens. No, it would be the irrevocable exhaustion and bankruptcy of the Greek city-state itself. The polis was, after all, an egalitarian but closed and static institution that could not adapt well to the military, economic, and political challenges of the wider Mediterranean world, changes initiated by the Persian invasion at the beginning of the fifth century, but dramatically and tragically elaborated by the virulent war between its most distinctive representatives, Athens and Sparta. And even if the Athenians are right about the universal relativity of justice and the amorality of power, we sense that such belief is nevertheless explicatory of their own destruction—and the demise of the *polis* itself. Our historian, it seems, does not necessarily like what he knows may be true.

IV. The Credibility of Thucydides

i.

Naturally, when the careful political and military tenets of centuries were cast out, Greeks turned toward superstition and religious fervor to explain both natural (earthquake, flood, eclipse, volcanic eruption, plague) and human (war, political extremism, revolution) calamity. This rise of concern with supernatural exegesis during the fighting held an obvious psychological interest for Thucydides. The gods and the haunts of the gods—Delphi, Delos, Olympia—appear frequently within *The Peloponnesian War* (1.25.1; 1.103.2; 1.134.4–135.1; 3.104.1–4; 5.1.1; 5.105.1–3; 5.49.1–50.4). But this fascination with the divine or unusual (1.23.3) does not seem to have clouded the author's own historical objectivity (2.28.1; 3.89.5). Nor does it suggest that Thucydides himself held deep religious beliefs, much less approved of the proliferation of oracles and prophecies. Again unlike Herodotus, he does not detect a divine motif in the unfolding of human events and surely does not write his history to confirm the sins of irreverence, hubris, and impiety.

On the contrary, Thucydides seems to see popular religion as more a social institution, valuable for inculcating and maintaining traditional conservative values. In that regard, superstition bereft of formal religious piety and restraint could only cloud human reason (2.8.2–3; 2.54.3–5; 7.50.4), and so add to the general cultural and intellectual decay unleashed by the war.

ii.

Of more interest are the occasional discrepancies and inconsistencies of Thucydides. They have caused alarm, understandable given the historian's vaunted pledge of accuracy. As in any great history, there are a few omissions (see note 8.5.5b), distortions, and mistakes in *The Peloponnesian War,* and they must be understood both in the context of the times and in light of the author's own historical aims and particular political outlook. Yet to perceive a personally engaged and emotional Thucydides, with clear preferences in his selection of material, is not necessarily to dispense with the notion of objectivity. An historian, remember, can (and should) be judgmental and opinionated, but he is not necessarily unfair or biased—if, as in the case of Thucydides, his evidence and method of inquiry are stated candidly for review and rebuttal.

Thucydides does not give an economic and social history of the Peloponnesian War, and provides, for example, only an abbreviated list of Athenian financial resources (2.13.2–7). More lamentably, only occasional glimpses are given of the countryside during the constant fighting (2.16.1–2.17.1; 4.84.1–4), for this was the area where the majority of the Greek population lived and suffered during the war. The drain, both psychologically and emotionally, on the people who provided the wherewithal to wage war is omitted, primarily because Thucydides is writing a strictly military chronicle of the Peloponnesian War, not a cultural or agrarian history of late-fifth-century Greece. In this regard, Herodotus is by far the more inquisitive recorder of ethnography and anthropology, and proves the more sensitive to the role that culture plays in a people's political and military conduct.

There are also clear heroes and villains in Thucydides' history. To a modern audience steeped in the behavioral and social sciences, Thucydides can appear to miss nuances in human temperament, concentrating instead on "objective" and absolute criteria such as timidity and heroism or recklessness versus self-control. In his eyes, human behavior is not predicated on or explained by one's specific environment or upbringing, but instead directed by the play of chance, fate, and hope upon innate character—conditions universal to all and particular to no man.

The ambiguity of a man's thought and intent is scarcely appreciated in the historian's effort to paint broad strokes of character. Intention counts for little; action is everything. Pericles is thoroughly majestic (2.65.5–9), and Cleon is violent and mean-spirited (3.36.6; 4.21.3–4.22.2)—period. Most Spartans predictably conform to their conservative and unimaginative stereotypes (1.86.1–1.87.6; 5.105.4), as if better to contrast a few Spartans of unquestioned dash and audacity, like Gylippus (7.1.1–7.7.2) and Brasidas especially (2.25.2; 4.11.4–4.12.1; 4.81; 5.6.3–5.11.5). The rash and amoral Alcibiades is as un-Periclean (6.15.2–4) as the conventional, cautious, and ineffective Nicias. Admiration for men of action like Hermocrates of Syracuse (5.32.3–5.35.1; 6.72.2–5) and the Athenian general Demosthenes (7.42.3–5) often outweighs their occasional failures and errors in judgment (6.103.4; 8.85.3; 3.98.5; 7.44.1–8).

More curious is Thucydides' very limited angle of vision. Slaves and women are scarcely mentioned. Yet from snippets in Thucydides' own text it is clear that women played crucial roles during times of sieges (2.4.2; 3.74.2), and must have suffered inordinately from the loss of male providers and especially during the great plague inside the walls of Athens (2.45.2; 2.51.2–5). From Thucydides and other sources we know that slaves provided at least some of the power for the triremes on both sides. Their flight in numbers was felt by all to have deleterious effects on their host cities (1.139.2; 7.27.5; 8.40.2). More mundanely, no hoplite army could easily march without a servile baggage corps, who carried both equipment and supplies

(7.75.5). Yet again, both the unfree and the women remain virtually unknown, as Thucydides' history deals almost exclusively with the free male citizenry of the Greek city-states, a group that constituted perhaps no more than a quarter of the adult resident population.

Thucydides' concentration on political and military affairs is not to suggest that even he could possibly have given a comprehensive account of those events during the twenty-seven-year war (3.90.1). Both Plutarch and Diodorus, and extant official documents written on stone, all suggest that more went on than what we are told by Thucydides. No inkling, for example, is given about the transference of the Delian treasury to Athens (454), which marked the formal rise of Athenian imperialism. The purported "Peace of Callias" between Persia and Greece (449),[a] the important Athenian colony at Brea (445), and the reassessment of the Athenian tribute[b] (425) all help explain the rise and nature of Athenian power but are ignored by Thucydides. Events critical to an understanding of war itself are often scarcely mentioned or absent altogether, such as the "Megarian Decree" (the Athenian sanctions against Megara in 432) and the important treaties between Athens and Sicilian Egesta (418–417?).[c] Yet even that list of oversights is small, and it pales beside the information found only in *The Peloponnesian War*, completely unknown to later sources and undiscoverable from extant archaeological and epigraphic remains.

iii.

In the final analysis, what stands out about Thucydides is not his weaknesses but his strengths as a historian. We note his omissions, but no account of the Peloponnesian War or of fifth-century Greece in general is more complete. Some scholars worry over his cut-and-dried heroes and villains. But is there much evidence to suggest that these assessments were fundamentally wrong? Others argue that his speeches are biased distortions, but no one can prove that any are outright fabrications. At times Thucydides may be clearly mistaken in both detail and interpretation, but the extent of his accuracy and analysis astounds in a world where travel was difficult, written sources rarely available, and the physical obstacles to the writing of history substantial. For all the contributions of archaeology, epigraphy, and the wealth of Athenian literature, without Thucydides' singular history we would know very little about fifth-century Greece

Even more extraordinary is Thucydides' ability to use that knowledge to reach a higher wisdom about the nature of human behavior, whether it be unveiled by plague (2.53), revolution (3.82–84), or war (5.103). And never forget that Thucydides was much more than an accurate recorder, more even than a keen judge of human character and the role that natural law and chance play in men's affairs (3.45.5–7; 3.84.1–3). He was a profound literary artist as well, emotional and

---

IV.iia See Appendix E, The Persians, §5, and Appendix B, The Athenian Empire, §8.
IV.iib See Appendix B, The Athenian Empire, §11.
IV.iic If the correct date for this treaty is 418/7. Thu-

cydides was either unaware of the recent treaty or felt it unnecessary or even antithetical to his explanation (6.6.8) of of the relationship between Athens and Egesta.

poignant on so many surprising occasions. The trapped Athenians who died in the wilds of Aetolia were not anonymous unfortunates, but irreplaceable patriots "all in the prime of life, by far the best men in the city of Athens that fell during this war" (3.98.4). The boys at Mycalessus are tragically and ironically butchered in their school by Thracian barbarians hired by democratic Athens to fight in Sicily, but who, having arrived late, were sent home for reasons of economy and instructed almost capriciously "to injure the enemy" on the way. The disaster on Sicily was more than a grievous loss of triremes and infantry, more even than a warning about the dangers of national chauvinism and intellectual arrogance. It becomes in the end a human tragedy after all,

> "most glorious to the victors, and most calamitous to the conquered. They were beaten at all points and altogether; all that they suffered was great; they were destroyed, as the saying is, with a total destruction, their fleet, their army—everything was destroyed, and few out of many returned home." (7.87)

And while Thucydides, a man of empathy and passion, was proud that he had written his history "not as an essay which is to win the applause of the moment, but as a possession for all time (1.22.4)," *The Peloponnesian War* turns out to be no dry chronicle of abstract cause and effect. No, it is above all an intense, riveting, and timeless story of strong and weak men, of heroes and scoundrels and innocents too, all caught in the fateful circumstances of rebellion, plague, and war that always strip away the veneer of culture and show us for what we really are.

Victor Davis Hanson
Professor of Greek
Department of Foreign Languages
and Literatures
California State University, Fresno

EDITOR'S NOTE

The survival of Thucydides' history over the last two thousand four hundred years is all the more remarkable in that his text has long been characterized by those who have read it (or have been assigned to read it) as difficult, complex, and occasionally obscure. Scholars have written detailed commentaries—and excellent ones too—to assist readers in comprehending its compressed and abstruse Greek, to discuss interpretations of certain problematic sections, and to clarify the sometimes confusing parallel structure with which Thucydides describes simultaneous events. Yet almost all these guides presume a knowledge of the ancient Greek language and a familiarity with many practices and mechanisms of Thucydides' world that today's student or general reader cannot be expected to bring to the text. Some very fine translations of Thucydides are available, but in unhelpful editions that contain little besides the text itself; they have uneven appendices, sparse indices, few if any explanatory footnotes, and maps of such poor quality as to be downright useless. As one reads them, it becomes difficult to remember what year it is at any given point in the narrative (even in the work's own system of consecutive year dating). Since Thucydides' work is a complex political and military history of a protracted war that took place long ago over a wide expanse of territory, it is not surprising that the general reader—in the absence of maps, specific dates, or knowledge of many practices, beliefs, or technical conditions of the time—is often puzzled by the text and unable to draw pleasure or instruction from it. Indeed, without the guidance of a teacher, or the acquisition of background knowledge from other sources, most readers simply cannot comprehend—let alone appreciate—many of Thucydides' observations or the intentions and actions of his characters.

The goal of this edition is to fill that lacuna: to develop and employ a set of helpful features that can be used with any text of Thucydides—the original Greek version or a translation in any language—so that students or general readers will always be able to orient themselves both geographically and temporally, and thus more easily understand the narrative. Beyond an introduction to Thucydides and his work, this edition includes over one hundred maps embedded in the text, a running header providing information on the date and location of the narrative, marginal summaries of the text of each chapter, explanatory footnotes, a thorough and encyclopedic index, an epilogue, a glossary of terms, a regional and chronological outline of events by book and chapter, and a few relevant illustrations. Finally, it contains a number of short technical appendices that provide background information about those aspects of life in ancient Greece that Thucydides did not think required explanation for readers of his time, but that will not be commonly known by readers today. This edition attempts by itself to provide sufficient textual assistance, geographic information, and background material for the general reader to understand and enjoy the marvelous work of one of humanity's first, and very best, historians.

Some elaboration is needed on a few of the important features mentioned above.

Maps of every significant episode are located in the text within that episode. Thus, every city, town, river, mountain, or other geographic feature that is important to the narrative and mentioned in a given episode is referenced to a location on a map found nearby in the text. For complex maps with many labels, a simple grid system permits footnotes to identify sites with map coordinates so that readers will know where to direct their attention on the map and thus minimize the time and effort required to locate a specific site. In the interest of clarity, each map displays the names of only those features that appear in the surrounding text: thus the reader is not forced to turn to a map section elsewhere in the book or a general map crowded with names drawn from the entire work. If the location of a place is unknown, the footnote admits this. If we moderns are not sure of its location, our uncertainty is mentioned in the footnote and indicated on the map with a question mark.

To orient the reader, a locator map with longitude and latitude coordinates appears in the outside margin of the page. It identifies the location of the main map by a rectangular outline placed in the larger, more easily recognizable regional setting. A few locator maps show outlines of two main maps to illustrate action occurring in widely separated locations. Some of the main maps show outlines of an additional inset map that displays particularly relevant areas at an enlarged scale. In the example on the following page, the area of the main map (Boeotia and Attica) is outlined on the locator map to the right, and the main map itself displays the outline of a detailed inset map of the Athens-Piraeus area, which is placed to the left. Figures containing more than one map are usually designed to be read from the outside inward on the page as map scales increase.

All maps display rudimentary scales in miles and kilometers and depict major topographical or cultural features cited in the text, such as mountains, rivers, roads, temples, defensive walls, and the like. A key to all map symbols used in this volume is located on page xxxii. The basemap used displays the modern positions of coastlines, major rivers, and major inland bodies of water, but the location and even the existence of some of these current features may be quite different from what existed in classical times. Significant differences in ancient and modern coastlines and bodies of water have been approximated using a narrow vertical stripe pattern.

Three reference maps showing all important sites named in the text are placed after the Index, at the very end of the book, where the reader can easily find them.

Main Map   Locator Map

Inset Map

MAP 2.19 ATHENS AND ITS DEFENSES

Following cartographic convention, water and other natural features, such as islands and peninsulas, are labeled with italics to distinguish them from cultural features labeled in roman type. Centers of population are indicated using small dots and upper- and lower-case lettering, while regions are labeled using several sizes of upper-case lettering designed to approximate their relative sizes and degrees of importance. With a few exceptions, specific regional boundaries have not been indicated because exact borders are not known or at best only partially known, and most of them tended to fluctuate over time. This lack of precision sometimes makes it difficult to arrange regions in a hierarchy of importance, or to classify certain sites as a village, a city, a fortress, a battle site, or a religious center, because a specific location might fit one or more of these categories at any given time, or over a period of time.

Footnotes not only refer place-names in the text to nearby maps, but also connect sequential episodes of regional narrative that are separated by Thucydides' treatment of historical simultaneity. Since his method is to describe all the events that take place in a given season throughout the Greek world before moving on to the events of the next season, he cannot provide the reader with any sustained or continuous regional narratives. Events of the winter of 426/5,[1] for example, are described serially for such regions as Sicily, Acarnania, and Attica, and this set of episodes is then followed by another sequence of regional episodes for the next time frame: the summer of 425. Thus regional narratives are broken up and extremely difficult for the reader to follow. This edition connects the regional episodes by footnote, specifying at the end of one such episode the book and chapter where the narrative returns to that region and, at that return, citing the location of the previous episode. Readers are thereby assisted to pursue a continuous regional narrative if they so wish. Footnotes are also used to mention and to discuss briefly some of the major points of scholarly controversy over interpretation, translation, or corruption of the text, and to indicate some of the more important connections of Thucydides' narrative with other ancient sources.

The reader who reads discontinuously, who casually dips into the history as time permits, is well served by the repetition of certain useful footnotes, usually at least once in each of the eight books. Map data are also frequently repeated for the same reason.

A **running header** is placed at the top of each page in order to help the same intermittent reader to reorient himself each time he returns to the work. The sample header displayed below identifies the book to which the particular page belongs (BOOK SIX), the date by our calendar (416/5), the date by Thucydides' own system (16th Year/Winter), the location where the action takes place (SICILY), and a brief description of the narrative (*Settlement of Other Hellenic Cities*).

BOOK SIX	416/5	16th Year/Winter	SICILY	*Settlement of Other Hellenic Cities*

More information is displayed in notes placed in the outside page margin at the beginnings of the hundred or so chapters into which each of the books is divided. In the sample marginal note shown on the next page, the first line identifies the book and chapter number (Book Four, Chapter 67). This identification is always aligned with the beginning of the new chapter, which usually, but not always, occurs at a new paragraph. The second line in the sample note, 424, is the date by our calendar; the line below that gives the date by Thucydides' own system (8th Year/Summer).[2] The fourth line describes where the action is taking place (MEGARA), and the final section briefly describes the action covered in the adjacent narrative. The text of each chapter contains section numbers in square brackets [2] to mark the divisions into which scholars have traditionally divided the text for ease of search, analysis, and discussion.

1 Classicists today use the virgule (/) to denote the winter season that crosses our year terminations—e.g., 426/5 is the winter season that begins after the Fall of 426 and ends before the Spring of 425. The numbers 426–25 would signify the entire span of the two years 426 and 425. All dates in this edition are B.C., unless otherwise specified.

2 Note that Thucydides' dating system is not included in the running headers and the marginal side notes of Book One because the war, whose years it measures, did not begin until the opening of the war in Book Two.

4.67
424
8th Year/Summer
MEGARA
The Athenians attack from ambush and gain entrance by a gate that has been opened by a stratagem of their Megarian confederates.

The Athenians, after plans had been arranged between themselves and their correspondents both as to words and actions, sailed by night to Minoa, the island off Megara, with six hundred hoplites under the command of Hippocrates, and took a position in a ditch not far off, out of which bricks used to be taken for the walls; while [2] Demosthenes, the other commander, with a detachment of Plataean light troops and another of *peripoli,* placed himself in ambush in the precinct of Enyalius, which was still nearer. No one knew of it, except those whose business it was to know that night. [3] A little before daybreak, the traitors in Megara began to act. Every night for a long time back, under pretense of marauding, and in order to have a means of opening the gates, they had been used, with the consent of the officer in command, to carry by night a rowboat upon a cart along the ditch to the sea and to sail out, bringing it back again before day upon the cart and taking it within the wall through the gates in order, as they pretended, to baffle . . .

Since Thucydides' history ends abruptly in mid-war, mid-episode, and almost mid-sentence, I have written a short **Epilogue** in an attempt to satisfy the general reader's curiosity as to how the war ended. It addresses the often-asked question of who really won what advantage from it and outlines what happened to the main protagonists during the next eighty years until the rise of Macedon ended this historical epoch.

A series of **Appendices** written by a number of scholars is intended to provide just the specific background information that would be necessary or useful to understanding the text. These essays provide limited discussions of such topics as the Athenian government, the Athenian Empire, the Spartan government, the Peloponnesian League, the Persians in Thucydides, hoplite warfare, trireme warfare, dialects and ethnic groups in Thucydides, religious festivals, classical Greek money, and classical Greek calendars and dating systems. The introduction by Victor Davis Hanson discusses what is known of Thucydides' life, aspects of his work, and his place among ancient historians. Where appropriate, the introduction and the appendices are cross-referenced by footnote to relevant places in the text.

To assist the reader in finding passages or subjects within the text, this edition offers a more thorough and full **Index** than can be found accompanying any other translation. As a quick reference tool, and to display more clearly the relationship between many simultaneous but serially described events, the reader can also consult a matrix **Theaters of Operation in the Peloponnesian War.** There are, in addition, a **Glossary** and two **Bibliographies,** one concerned with ancient sources (more or less contemporary with Thucydides) and the other addressing modern books about Thucydides and his work. Finally, a number of **illustrations** have been chosen that bring to life places and objects that are contemporary with or prominent in the text: for example, Illustration 4.41 (located in Book Four, Chapter 41)[3] is a picture of the Spartan shield (now on display in the Agora Museum at Athens) that was captured by the Athenians at Pylos and taken to Athens, where it was discovered some years ago in an abandoned well in the Athenian *agora* (central square and marketplace).

This edition uses the translation by Richard Crawley (1840–93) published in 1874, which remains one of the two most widely read translations today—a testament to its fidelity to the text and its power as English prose. It was necessary, however, to update some of Crawley's Victorian English usages, to revise his outdated punctuation, and to replace terms he used whose meaning has shifted or been lost entirely. For example, I have substituted "trireme" (with an explanation of that term) for Crawley's "galley," a word that no longer means an oared warship so much as a nautical kitchen or a publisher's proof. After much deliberation, I decided in the interests of clarity to break up a few of Crawley's longest and most complex sentences (which often mirror the original Greek). I have also discarded the artificial and unhelpful titled segments into which Crawley divided his text.

On the whole, however, other than to americanize Crawley's British spelling, revisions are few and minor. Almost no changes were made to the speeches themselves, as these are the most outstanding and powerful feature of Crawley's work. Perhaps because he was educated at a time when oratory was still valued as a useful skill, and was systematically studied and taught in the schools, his translated speeches employ rhetorical devices in an expert and natural manner akin to the Greek usage itself. In this way, he achieves an eloquent rhythm and cadence that far surpass the speeches in all other translations that I have read—and which, sad to say, we rarely find in speakers today. Crawley's Pericles, for example, is truly grandiloquent and perhaps even purposefully a bit pompous, but never commonplace, wordy, or banal. Indeed, it has been a pleasure to work with Crawley's prose, and during the compilation of this edition my admiration and respect for his writing and diction skills have grown immensely.

Many of the best elements of this edition derive directly from the wonderful counsel and assistance I consistently received from many friends and colleagues,

3 This is the chapter in which Thucydides completes his description of the battle of Pylos.

whom I try to acknowledge elsewhere. But since I did not in every case follow the advice of others, I must stand behind and be responsible for all errors of omission and commission, of which I can only hope that there are not too many. At the least, I hope to have designed and assembled the useful features of this edition, so that the basic task needs never be undertaken again. There is an unbroken string of readers stretching back from us to Thucydides himself—more than one hundred generations of humans who, despite many obstacles, have derived pleasure and instruction from the text sufficient to ensure that it did not become lost, as were so many literary works of the ancient world. It is thanks to these readers that Thucydides is still here for us to enjoy—and there must have been moments in time when there were precious few of them.

The Landmark Edition is intended to increase the number of general readers of Thucydides, both now and in the future, by assisting them to appreciate his great value as a historian, to consider the nature of historiography itself, and to learn about the extraordinary world of ancient Greece—from which our own still derives so much. Despite the edition's focus on the non-scholar, I believe that the scholar too will find this work's unique set of features quite useful. If this edition expands the number of general readers who tackle Thucydides and extends their grasp and appreciation of the text, or if it even marginally increases the number of professors and teachers who decide to incorporate Thucydides in their curriculum and to enlarge the amount of his text that they include in their course work, I will rest content. For if I may be permitted "to compare small things with great" (4.36.3), it is my hope that this array of maps, notes, appendices, and indices will also become "a possession for all time" (1.22.4)—admittedly a minor and derivative one, but one that will nevertheless prove useful to future readers of this marvelous history for as long as Thucydides is read.

R.B.S.

Key to Map Symbols

◻ **Area of greater detail**

Cultural features

•● settlements

⚑ fortified place

⌂ temple

⚔ battle site

× miscellaneous place

⚓ anchorage

═ road

▤ walls

▦ urbanized area (larger scale)

◟◞ regional boundary or extent (approximate)

Natural features

⌃ mountain; mountain range

⌃ cliff

◡ river

◍ area of water in Classical period (approximate)

⚮ marsh

Calendar of the Peloponnesian War

Thucydides' Date of the War	Modern Date	Season	Location by Book and Chapter
1st year	431	End of summer	2.33
1st year	431/0	End of winter	2.47
2nd year	430	End of summer	2.69
2nd year	430/29	End of winter	2.70
3rd year	429	End of summer	2.93
3rd year	429/8	End of winter	2.103
4th year	428	End of summer	3.19
4th year	428/7	End of winter	3.25
5th year	427	End of summer	3.87
5th year	427/6	End of winter	3.88
6th year	426	End of summer	3.103
6th year	426/5	End of winter	3.116
7th year	425	End of summer	4.50
7th year	425/4	End of winter	4.51
8th year	424	End of summer	4.88
8th year	424/3	End of winter	4.116
9th year	423	End of summer	4.133
9th year	423/2	End of winter	4.135
10th year	422	End of summer	5.12
10th year	422/1	End of winter	5.25
11th year	421	End of summer	5.36
11th year	421/0	End of winter	5.39
12th year	420	End of summer	5.51
12th year	420/19	End of winter	5.51
13th year	419	End of summer	5.55
13th year	419/8	End of winter	5.56
14th year	418	End of summer	5.76
14th year	418/7	End of winter	5.81
15th year	417	End of summer	5.82
15th year	417/6	End of winter	5.83
16th year	416	End of summer	5.115
16th year	416/5	End of winter	6.7
17th year	415	End of summer	6.62
17th year	415/4	End of winter	6.93
18th year	414	End of summer	7.9
18th year	414/3	End of winter	7.19
19th year	413	End of summer	8.1
19th year	413/2	End of winter	8.6
20th year	412	End of summer	8.29
20th year	412/1	End of winter	8.60
21st year	411	End of summer	8.109

BOOK ONE

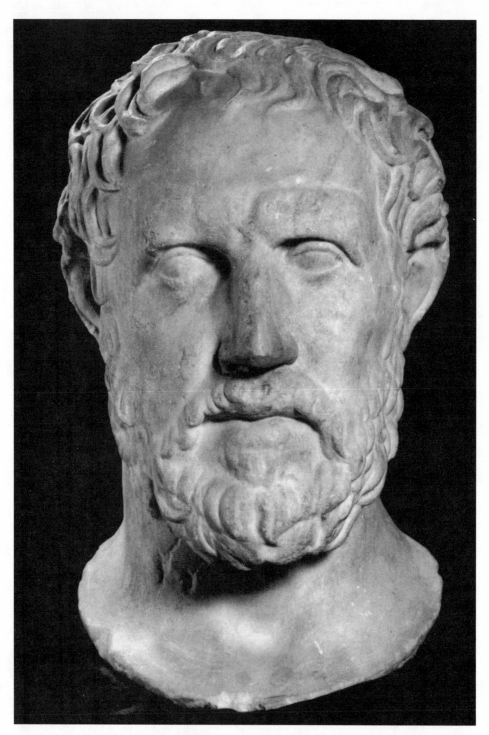

ILLUSTRATION 1.1 BUST OF THUCYDIDES

Thucydides,[1a] an Athenian, wrote the history of the war between the Peloponnesians and the Athenians, beginning at the moment that it broke out, and believing that it would be a great war, and more worthy of relation than any that had preceded it. This belief was not without its grounds. The preparations of both the combatants were in every department in the last state of perfection; and he could see the rest of the Hellenic race taking sides in the quarrel; those who delayed doing so at once having it in contemplation. [2] Indeed this was the greatest movement yet known in history, not only of the Hellenes, but of a large part of the barbarian world—I had almost said of mankind. [3] For though the events of remote antiquity, and even those that more immediately precede the war, could not from lapse of time be clearly ascertained, yet the evidences which an inquiry carried as far back as was practicable lead me to trust, all point to the conclusion that there was nothing on a greater scale, either in war or in other matters.

For instance, it is evident that the country now called Hellas had in ancient times no settled population; on the contrary, migrations were of frequent occurrence, the several tribes readily abandoning their homes under the pressure of superior numbers. [2] Without commerce, without freedom of communication either by land or sea, cultivating no more of their territory than the necessities of life required, destitute of capital, never planting their land (for they could not tell when an invader might not come and take it all away, and when he did come they had no walls to stop him), thinking that the necessities of daily sustenance could be supplied at one place as well as another, they cared little about shifting their habitation, and consequently neither built large cities nor attained to any other form of

1.1
ATHENS
Thucydides explains why he decided to write his history.

1.2
The Archaeology[1a]
HELLAS
Thucydides offers an anthropological analysis of primitive life, noting that Attica's poor soil led to overcrowding and the establishment of colonies.

1.1.1a   See the Introduction (sec. I) for a discussion of what is known about the life of Thucydides the historian.
1.2.1a   "The Archaeology" is the term commonly used for the opening chapters of

Book 1 (2–23) in which Thucydides seeks to contrast the greatness of the Peloponnesian War with the pettiness of previous history.

greatness. [3] The richest soils were always most subject to this change of masters; such as the district now called Thessaly,[3a] Boeotia,[3b] most of the Peloponnesus[3c] (Arcadia excepted),[3d] and the most fertile parts of the rest of Hellas. [4] The goodness of the land favored the enrichment of particular individuals, and thus created faction which proved a fertile source of ruin. It also invited invasion. [5] Accordingly Attica,[5a] from the poverty of its soil enjoying from a very remote period freedom from faction, [6] never changed its inhabitants. And here is no minor example of my assertion that the migrations were the cause of there being no correspondent growth in other parts. The most powerful victims of war or faction from the rest of Hellas took refuge with the Athenians as a safe retreat; and at an early period, becoming naturalized, swelled the already large population of the city to such a height that Attica became at last too small to hold them, and they had to send out colonies to Ionia.[6a]

There is also another circumstance that contributes not a little to my conviction of the weakness of ancient times. Before the Trojan war[1a] there is no indication of any common action in Hellas, [2] nor indeed of the universal prevalence of the name; on the contrary, before the time of Hellen son of Deucalion, no such name existed, but the country went by the names of the different tribes, in particular of the Pelasgian. It was not till Hellen and his sons grew strong in Phthiotis,[2a] and were invited as allies into the other cities, that one by one they gradually acquired from the connection the name of Hellenes; though a long time elapsed before that name could fasten itself upon all. [3] The best proof of this is furnished by Homer. Born long after the Trojan war, he nowhere calls all of them by that name, nor indeed any of them except the followers of Achilles from Phthiotis, who were the original Hellenes: in his poems they are called Danaans, Argives, and Achaeans. He does not even use the term barbarian, probably because the Hellenes had not yet been marked off from the rest of the world by one distinctive name. [4] It appears therefore that the several Hellenic communities, comprising not only those who first acquired the name, city by city, as they came to understand each other, but also those who assumed it afterwards as the name of the whole people, were before the Trojan war prevented by their want of strength and the absence of mutual intercourse from displaying any collective action.

Indeed, they could not unite for this expedition till they had gained increased familiarity with the sea.

And the first person known to us by tradition as having established a navy is Minos.[1a] He made himself master of what is now called the Hellenic

---

1.2.3a	Thessaly: Map 1.3, AX.	1.3.1a	Troy, site of the Trojan war: Map 1.3, AY.
1.2.3b	Boeotia: Map 1.3, AX.		
1.2.3c	Peloponnesus: Map 1.3, BX.	1.3.2a	Phthiotis: Map 1.3, AX.
1.2.3d	Arcadia: Map 1.3, BX.	1.4.1a	Minos is the probably mythical ruler of
1.2.5a	Attica: Map 1.3, BX.		Minoa, a legendary seafaring culture
1.2.6a	Ionia: Map 1.3, AY. See Appendix H,		based on the island of Crete; see Map
	Dialects and Ethnic Groups, §4–5, 7–8,		1.3, BY.
	for information on the Ionians and the		
	colonization of Ionia.		

MAP 1.3 EARLY HELLAS

sea, and ruled over the Cyclades,[1b] into most of which he sent the first colonies, expelling the Carians[1c] and appointing his own sons governors; and thus did his best to put down piracy in those waters, a necessary step to secure revenues for his own use.

For in early times the Hellenes and the barbarians of the coast and islands, as communication by sea became more common, were tempted to turn pirates, under the conduct of their most powerful men; the motives being to serve their own greed and to support the needy. They would fall upon a town unprotected by walls, and consisting of a mere collection of villages, and would plunder it; indeed, this came to be the main source of their livelihood, no disgrace being yet attached to such an achievement, but even some glory. [2] An illustration of this is furnished by the honor with which some of the inhabitants of the continent still regard a successful marauder, and by the question we find the old poets everywhere representing the people as asking of voyagers—"Are they pirates?"—as if those who are asked the question would have no idea of disclaiming the imputation, or their interrogators of reproaching them for it. [3] The same pillaging prevailed also on land.

And even at the present day many parts of Hellas still follow the old fashion, amongst the Ozolian Locrians[3a] and the Aetolians,[3b] for instance, and the Acarnanians[3c] and that region of the continent; and the custom of carrying arms is still kept up among these mainland peoples from the old piratical habits.

The whole of Hellas used once to carry arms, their habitations being unprotected, and their communication with each other unsafe; indeed, to wear arms was as much a part of everyday life with them as with the barbarians. [2] And the fact that the people in these parts of Hellas are still living in the old way points to a time when the same mode of life was once equally common to all. [3] The Athenians[3a] were the first to lay aside their weapons, and to adopt an easier and more luxurious mode of life; indeed, it is only lately that their rich old men left off the luxury of wearing undergarments of linen, and fastening a knot of their hair with a tie of golden grasshoppers, a fashion which spread to their Ionian kindred,[3b] and long prevailed among the old men there. [4] On the contrary a modest style of dressing, more in conformity with modern ideas, was first adopted by the Spartans,[4a] the rich doing their best to assimilate their way of life to that of the common people. [5] They also set the example of contending naked, publicly stripping and anointing themselves with oil in their gymnastic exercises. Formerly, even in the Olympic games,[5a] the athletes who con-

---

1.4.1b	Cyclades, Aegean islands: Map 1.3, BY.	1.6.4a	Sparta: Map 1.3, BX.
1.4.1c	Caria: Map 1.3, BY.	1.6.5a	These contests, the ancestor of the modern "Olympic Games," took place at the shrine of Olympia (Map 1.3, BX); see Appendix I, Religious Festivals, §5. Such festivals often included athletic and cultural contests.
1.5.3a	Ozolian Locris: Map 1.3, AX.		
1.5.3b	Aetolia: Map 1.3, AX.		
1.5.3c	Acarnania: Map 1.3, AX.		
1.6.3a	Athens: Map 1.3, BX.		
1.6.3b	See Appendix H, Dialects and Ethnic Groups, §4–5, 7–8, for more on the Ionians.		

tended wore belts across their middles; and it is but a few years since that the practice ceased. To this day among some of the barbarians, especially in Asia, when prizes for boxing and wrestling are offered, belts are worn by the combatants. [6] And there are many other points in which a likeness might be shown between the life of the Hellenic world of old and the barbarian of today.

With respect to their cities, later on, at an era of increased facilities of navigation and a greater supply of capital, we find the shores becoming the site of walled cities, and the isthmuses being occupied for the purposes of commerce and defense against a neighbor. But the old cities, on account of the great prevalence of piracy, were built away from the sea, whether on the islands or the continent, and still remain in their old sites. For the pirates used to plunder one another, and indeed all coast populations, whether seafaring or not.

The islanders, too, were great pirates. These islanders were Carians[1a] and Phoenicians,[1b] by whom most of the islands were colonized, as was proved by the following fact. During the purification of Delos[1c] by Athens in this war all the graves in the island were taken up, and it was found that above half their inmates were Carians: they were identified by the fashion of the arms buried with them, and by the method of interment, which was the same as the Carians still follow. [2] But as soon as Minos had formed his navy, communication by sea became easier, [3] as he colonized most of the islands, and thus expelled the evildoers. The coast populations now began to apply themselves more closely to the acquisition of wealth, and their life became more settled; some even began to build themselves walls on the strength of their newly acquired riches. For the love of gain would reconcile the weaker to the dominion of the stronger, and the possession of capital enabled the more powerful to reduce the smaller cities to subjection. [4] And it was at a somewhat later stage of this development that they went on the expedition against Troy.[4a]

What enabled Agamemnon to raise the armament was more, in my opinion, his superiority in strength, than the oaths of Tyndareus, which bound the Suitors to follow him. [2] Indeed, the account given by those Peloponnesians who have been the recipients of the most credible tradition is this. First of all Pelops, arriving from Asia[2a] with vast wealth among a needy population, acquired such power that, stranger though he was, the country was called after him; and this power fortune saw fit materially to increase in the hands of his descendants. Eurystheus had been killed in

1.7
HELLAS
Because of piracy, cities were first built away from the sea.

1.8
AEGEAN ISLANDS
Thucydides cites evidence from graves that early islanders were Carians. After Minos expelled the pirates, cities expanded, accumulated capital, and built walls to protect themselves.

1.9
PELOPONNESUS
Thucydides describes how Agamemnon inherited his great power, which included naval power.

1.8.1a Caria: Map 1.3, BY, and Map 1.11, BY.
1.8.1b Phoenicia: Map 1.14.
1.8.1c Delos: Map 1.11, BY. This purification is described by Thucydides in 3.104.
1.8.4a Troy: Map 1.11, AY.
1.9.2a "Asia" here means Asia Minor, corresponding to the Asian territory of modern Turkey; see Map 1.11, locator.

Attica[2b] by the Heraclids. When Eurystheus set out on his expedition (to Attica), he committed Mycenae and its government to Atreus, his mother's brother, who had left his father on account of the death of Chrysippus. As time went on and Eurystheus did not return, Atreus complied with the wishes of the Mycenaeans, who were influenced by fear of the Heraclids—besides, his powers seemed considerable and he had not neglected to seek the favor of the populace—and assumed the rule of Mycenae and of the rest of the dominions of Eurystheus. And so the power of the descendants of Pelops came to be greater than that of the descendants of Perseus. [3] To all this Agamemnon succeeded. He had also a navy far stronger than his contemporaries, so that, in my opinion, fear was quite as strong an element as love in the formation of the expedition. [4] The strength of his navy is shown by the fact that his own was the largest contingent, and that of the Arcadians was furnished by him; this at least is what Homer says, if his testimony is deemed sufficient. Besides, in his account of the transmission of the scepter, he calls him

Of many an isle, and of all Argos[4a] king.

Now Agamemnon's was a continental power; and he could not have been master of any except the adjacent islands (and these would not be many), if he had not possessed a fleet.

And from this expedition we may infer the character of earlier enterprises. [1.10.1] Now Mycenae[1a] may have been a small place, and many of the cities of that age may appear comparatively insignificant, but no exact observer would therefore feel justified in rejecting the estimate given by the poets and by tradition of the magnitude of the armament. [2] For I suppose that if Sparta[2a] were to become desolate, and only the temples and the foundations of the public buildings were left, that as time went on there would be a strong disposition with posterity to refuse to accept her fame as a true exponent of her power. And yet they occupy two-fifths of the Peloponnesus[2b] and lead the whole, not to speak of their numerous allies outside. Still, as the city is neither built in a compact form nor adorned with magnificent temples and public edifices, but composed of villages after the old fashion of Hellas, there would be an impression of inadequacy. Whereas, if Athens were to suffer the same misfortune, I suppose that any inference from the appearance presented to the eye would make her power to have been twice as great as it is. [3] We have therefore no right to be skeptical, nor to content ourselves with an inspection of a city without con-

1.10
HELLAS
The size and magnificence of a city's ruins do not necessarily indicate its power: witness Sparta and Athens. Homer's description of the armada against Troy indicates its small size relative to current fleets.

1.9.2b　Attica: Map. 1.11, BY.
1.9.4a　Argos: Map 1.11, BX.
1.10.1a　Mycenae: Map 1.11, BX.

1.10.2a　Sparta: Map 1.11, BX.
1.10.2b　Peloponnesus: Map 1.11, BX.

sidering its power; but we may safely conclude that the armament in question surpassed all before it, just as it fell short of modern efforts; if we can here also accept the testimony of Homer's poems in which, without allowing for the exaggeration which a poet would feel himself licensed to employ, we can see that it was far from equaling ours. [4] He has represented it as consisting of twelve hundred vessels; the Boeotian[4a] complement of each ship being a hundred and twenty men, that of the ships of Philoctetes fifty. By this, I conceive, he meant to convey the maximum and the minimum complement: at any rate he does not specify the amount of any others in his catalogue of the ships. That they were all rowers as well as warriors we see from his account of the ships of Philoctetes, in which all the men at the oar are bowmen. Now it is improbable that many who were not members of the crew sailed if we except the kings and high officers; especially as they had to cross the open sea with munitions of war, in ships, moreover, that had no decks, but were equipped in the old piratical fashion. [5] So that if we strike the average of the largest and smallest ships, the number of those who sailed will appear inconsiderable, representing as they did, the whole force of Hellas.

And this was due not so much to scarcity of men as of money. Difficulty of subsistence made the invaders reduce the numbers of the army to a point at which it might live on the country during the prosecution of the war. Even after the victory they obtained on their arrival—and a victory there must have been, or the fortifications of the naval camp could never have been built—there is no indication of their whole force having been employed; on the contrary, they seem to have turned to cultivation of the Chersonese[1a] and to piracy from want of supplies. This was what really enabled the Trojans to keep the field for ten years against them; the dispersion of the enemy making them always a match for the detachment left behind. [2] If they had brought plenty of supplies with them, and had persevered in the war without scattering for piracy and agriculture, they would have easily defeated the Trojans in the field; since they could hold their own against them with the division on service. In short, if they had stuck to the siege, the capture of Troy[2a] would have cost them less time and less trouble. But as want of money proved the weakness of earlier expeditions, so from the same cause even the one in question, more famous than its predecessors, may be pronounced on the evidence of what it accomplished, to have been inferior to its renown and to the current opinion about it formed under the tuition of the poets.

1.11
TROY
A lack of money forced the Greeks at Troy to disperse their force, reduce siege efforts, and forego a quick victory.

1.10.4a Boeotia: Map 1.11, BX.
1.11.1a Chersonese: Map 1.11, AY.
1.11.2a Troy: Map 1.11, AY.

MAP 1.11 THE AEGEAN BASIN

Even after the Trojan war Hellas was still engaged in removing and settling, and thus could not attain to the quiet which must precede growth. [2] The late return of the Hellenes from Ilium[2a] caused many revolutions, and factions ensued almost everywhere; and it was the citizens thus driven into exile who founded the cities. [3] Sixty years after the capture of Ilium the modern Boeotians[3a] were driven out of Arne[3b] by the Thessalians,[3c] and settled in the present Boeotia, the former Cadmeian land; though there was a division of them there before, some of whom joined the expedition to Ilium. Twenty years later the Dorians and the Heraclids became masters of the Peloponnesus; so that much had to be done [4] and many years had to elapse before Hellas could attain to a durable tranquillity undisturbed by removals, and could begin to send out colonies, as Athens[4a] did to Ionia[4b] and most of the islands, and the Peloponnesians to most of Italy[4c] and Sicily[4d] and some places in the rest of Hellas. All these places were founded subsequently to the war with Troy.

But as the power of Hellas grew, and the acquisition of wealth became more an objective, the revenues of the states increasing, tyrannies were established almost everywhere—the old form of government being hereditary monarchy with definite prerogatives—and Hellas began to fit out fleets and apply herself more closely to the sea. [2] It is said that the Corinthians were the first to approach the modern style of naval architecture, and that Corinth[2a] was the first place in Hellas where *triremes*[2b] were built; [3] and we have Ameinocles, a Corinthian shipwright, making four ships for the Samians. Dating from the end of this war, it is nearly three hundred years ago that Ameinocles went to Samos.[3a] [4] Again, the earliest sea fight in history was between the Corinthians and Corcyraeans;[4a] this was about two hundred and sixty years ago, dating from the same time. [5] Planted on an isthmus, Corinth had always been a commercial emporium; as formerly almost all communication between the Hellenes within and without the Peloponnesus was carried on overland, and the Corinthian territory was the highway through which it traveled. She had consequently great money resources, as is shown by the epithet "wealthy" bestowed by the old poets on the place, and this enabled her, when traffic by sea became more common, to procure her navy and put down piracy; and as she could offer a market for both branches of the trade, she acquired for herself all the power which a large revenue affords. [6] Subsequently the Ionians[6a] attained to great naval strength in the reign of Cyrus, the first king of the Persians, and of his son Cambyses,[6b] and while they were at war with the former com-

1.12
HELLAS
Migration and turmoil occurred in Hellas after the Trojan war. When tranquillity returned, Ionia, the islands, Italy, and Sicily were colonized.

1.13
HELLAS
As the cities of Hellas grew in wealth and power, traditional monarchies gave way to tyrannies. Corinth developed triremes.

1.12.2a "Ilium" is another name for Troy: Map 1.11, AY.
1.12.3a Boeotia: Map 1.11, BX.
1.12.3b Arne in Thessaly: Map 1.11, AX.
1.12.3c Thessaly: Map 1.11, AX.
1.12.4a Athens: Map 1.11, BX.
1.12.4b Ionia: Map 1.11, BY. See Appendix H, Dialects and Ethnic Groups, §5, 7–8, for more on the Dorians and the Ionians.
1.12.4c Italy: Map 1.14.
1.12.4d Sicily: Map 1.14.

1.13.2a Corinth: Map 1.11, BX.
1.13.2b *Triremes* were the standard warships of this period; see Appendix G, §4–7.
1.13.3a Samos: Map 1.11, BY.
1.13.4a Corcyra: Map 1.11, AX.
1.13.6a Ionia: Map 1.11, BY.
1.13.6b Cyrus the Great founded the Persian kingdom and ruled from 550 to 530. Cambyses ruled from 530 till 521. See Appendix E, The Persians, §1–2.

manded for a while the seas around Ionia. Polycrates also, the tyrant of Samos, had a powerful navy in the reign of Cambyses with which he reduced many of the islands, and among them Rhenea,[6c] which he consecrated to the Delian Apollo. About this time also the Phocaeans,[6d] while they were founding Marseilles,[6e] defeated the Carthaginians[6f] in a sea fight.

These were the most powerful navies. And even these, although so many generations had elapsed since the Trojan war, seem to have been principally composed of the old fifty-oars and long-boats, and to have counted few triremes among their ranks. [2] Indeed it was only shortly before the Persian war and the death of Darius the successor of Cambyses, that the Sicilian tyrants and the Corcyraeans acquired any large number of triremes. For after these there were no navies of any account in Hellas till the expedition of Xerxes; [3] Aegina,[3a] Athens, and others may have possessed a few vessels, but they were principally fifty-oars. It was quite at the end of this period that the war with Aegina and the prospect of the barbarian invasion enabled Themistocles to persuade the Athenians to build the fleet with which they fought at Salamis;[3b] and even these vessels had not complete decks.

The navies, then, of the Hellenes during the period we have traversed were what I have described. All their insignificance did not prevent their being an element of the greatest power to those who cultivated them, alike in revenue and in dominion. They were the means by which the islands were reached and reduced, those of the smallest area falling the easiest prey. [2] Wars by land there were none, none at least by which power was acquired; we have the usual border contests, but of distant expeditions with conquest the object we hear nothing among the Hellenes. There was no union of subject cities round a great state, no spontaneous combination of equals for confederate expeditions; what fighting there was consisted merely of local warfare between rival neighbors. [3] The nearest approach to a coalition took place in the old war between Chalcis[3a] and Eretria;[3b] this was a quarrel in which the rest of the Hellenic world did to some extent take sides.[3c]

Various, too, were the obstacles which the national growth encountered in various localities. The power of the Ionians[1a] was advancing with rapid strides, when it came into collision with Persia, under King Cyrus, who, after having dethroned Croesus[1b] and overrun everything between the Halys[1c] and the sea, stopped not till he had reduced the cities of the coast; the islands only being left to be subdued by Darius and the Phoenician[1d] navy.

1.13.6c   Rhenea: Map 1.11, BY.
1.13.6d   Phocaea: Map 1.11, AY.
1.13.6e   Marseilles: Map 1.14.
1.13.6f   Carthage: Map 1.14.
1.14.3a   Aegina: Map 1.11, BX.
1.14.3b   Salamis: site of the decisive naval battle between the Greeks and Persians in 480; see Map 1.11, BX, and Appendix E, The Persians, §4.
1.15.3a   Chalcis, Euboea: Map 1.11, BX.
1.15.3b   Eretria, Euboea: Map 1.11, BX.
1.15.3c   Thucydides here refers to the "Lelantine

war" of the late eighth century B.C. between Chalcis and Eretria of Euboea (Map 1.11, AX).
1.16.1a   Ionia: Map 1.11, BY.
1.16.1b   Croesus, king of Lydia (Map 1.14), conquered by the Persians in 546. See Appendix E, The Persians, §2–3.
1.16.1c   Halys River: Map 1.14.
1.16.1d   Phoenicia: Map 1.14. The Phoenician fleet was a major component of Persian naval power.

MAP 1.14 THE MEDITERRANEAN SEA

Again, wherever there were tyrants, their habit of providing simply for themselves, of looking solely to their personal comfort and family aggrandizement, made safety the great aim of their policy, and prevented anything great proceeding from them; though they would each have their affairs with their immediate neighbors. All this is only true of the mother country, for in Sicily they attained to very great power. Thus for a long time everywhere in Hellas do we find causes which make the states alike incapable of combination for great and national ends, or of any vigorous action of their own.

But at last a time came when the tyrants of Athens and the far older tyrannies of the rest of Hellas were, with the exception of those in Sicily, once and for all put down by Sparta;[1a] for this city, though after the settlement of the Dorians, its present inhabitants, it suffered from factions for an unparalleled length of time, still at a very early period obtained good laws, and enjoyed a freedom from tyrants which was unbroken; it has possessed the same form of government for more than four hundred years, reckoning

1.17
HELLAS
Tyrants in Hellas itself, unlike those in Sicily, did not greatly extend their power.

1.18
HELLAS
Sparta put down Hellenic tyrants and led Greek resistance to Persia. After the Persians' defeat Athens and Sparta quarreled.

1.18.1a Sparta: Map 1.11, BX.

to the end of the late war, and has thus been in a position to arrange the affairs of the other states.[1b] Not many years after the deposition of the tyrants, the battle of Marathon was fought between the Medes[1c] and the Athenians. [2] Ten years afterwards the barbarian returned with the armada for the subjugation of Hellas. In the face of this great danger the command of the confederate Hellenes was assumed by the Spartans in virtue of their superior power; and the Athenians having made up their minds to abandon their city, broke up their homes, threw themselves into their ships, and became a naval people. This coalition, after repulsing the barbarian, soon afterwards split into two sections, which included the Hellenes who had revolted from the King,[2a] as well as those who had shared in the war. At the head of the one stood Athens, at the head of the other Sparta, one the first naval, the other the first military power in Hellas. [3] For a short time the league held together, till the Spartans and Athenians quarreled, and made war upon each other with their allies, a duel into which all the Hellenes sooner or later were drawn, though some might at first remain neutral. So that the whole period from the Median war to this, with some peaceful intervals, was spent by each power in war, either with its rival, or with its own revolted allies, and consequently afforded them constant practice in military matters, and that experience which is learnt in the school of danger.

1.19
HELLAS
Thucydides describes the different policies of the Spartan and Athenian alliances.

The policy of Sparta was not to exact tribute from her allies, but merely to secure their subservience to her interests by establishing oligarchies among them;[1a] Athens, on the contrary, had by degrees deprived hers of their ships, and imposed instead contributions in money on all except Chios[1b] and Lesbos.[1c] Both found their resources for this war separately to exceed the sum of their strength when the alliance flourished intact.

1.20
ATHENS
Thucydides notes that people accept traditions that are clearly in error, for example, the tale about Harmodius and Aristogiton.

Having now given the result of my inquiries into early times, I grant that there will be a difficulty in believing every particular detail. The way that most men deal with traditions, even traditions of their own country, is to receive them all alike as they are delivered, without applying any critical test whatever. [2] The Athenian public generally believe that Hipparchus was tyrant when he fell by the hands of Harmodius and Aristogiton. They do not know that Hippias, the eldest of the sons of Pisistratus, was really supreme; that Hipparchus and Thessalus were his brothers; and that Harmodius and Aristogiton, suspecting on the very day—indeed at the very moment fixed for the deed—that information had been conveyed to Hippias by their accomplices, concluded that he had been warned. They did

---

1.18.1b See Appendix D, The Peloponnesian League, §6.
1.18.1c The battle of Marathon (Map 1.11, BY) was fought in 490. See Appendix E, The Persians, §4. The Greeks regularly referred to the Persians as "the Mede," or "the Medes," and to the Persian wars as the "Median wars," although the Medes and Persians were distinct peoples. See Appendix E, The Persians, §1.

1.18.2a The term "King" is capitalized throughout this edition when it signifies the great King of Persia to distinguish him from all others carrying that title. See Appendix E, The Persians, §2.
1.19.1a See Appendix D, The Peloponnesian League, §6.
1.19.1b Chios: Map 1.11, BY. See Appendix B, The Athenian Empire, §2, 5.
1.19.1c Lesbos: Map 1.11, AY.

not attack Hippias but, not liking to risk their lives and be apprehended for
nothing, they fell upon Hipparchus near the temple of the daughters of
Leos and slew him as he was arranging the Panathenaic procession.[2a] [3]
There are many other unfounded ideas current among the rest of the Hellenes, even on matters of contemporary history which have not been
obscured by time. For instance, there is the notion that the Spartan kings
have two votes each, the fact being that they have only one; and that there
is a military company of Pitane, there being simply no such thing. So little
pains do the vulgar take in the investigation of truth, accepting readily the
first story that comes to hand.

On the whole, however, the conclusions I have drawn from the proofs
quoted may, I believe, safely be relied upon. Assuredly they will not be disturbed either by the verses of a poet displaying the exaggeration of his craft,
or by the compositions of the chroniclers that are attractive at truth's
expense; the subjects they treat of being out of the reach of evidence, and
time having robbed most of them of historical value by enthroning them in
the region of legend. Turning from these, we can rest satisfied with having
proceeded upon the clearest data, and having arrived at conclusions as
exact as can be expected in matters of such antiquity. [2] To come to this
war; despite the known disposition of the actors in a struggle to overrate its
importance, and when it is over to return to their admiration of earlier
events, yet an examination of the facts will show that it was much greater
than the wars which preceded it.

With reference to the speeches in this history, some were delivered
before the war began, others while it was going on; some I heard myself,
others I got from various quarters; it was in all cases difficult to carry them
word for word in one's memory, so my habit has been to make the speakers
say what was in my opinion demanded of them by the various occasions, of
course adhering as closely as possible to the general sense of what they
really said.[1a] [2] And with reference to the narrative of events, far from permitting myself to derive it from the first source that came to hand, I did
not even trust my own impressions, but it rests partly on what I saw myself,
partly on what others saw for me, the accuracy of the report being always
tried by the most severe and detailed tests possible. [3] My conclusions
have cost me some labor from the want of coincidence between accounts of
the same occurrences by different eyewitnesses, arising sometimes from
imperfect memory, sometimes from undue partiality for one side or the

1.21
HELLAS
Thucydides believes his conclusions to be reliable, and
notes that this war was much
greater than earlier ones.

1.22
HELLAS
Thucydides discusses the
speeches in his text. He says
it lacks romance because he
intends it to be "a possession
for all time."

1.20.2a The assassination of Hipparchus is
described at greater length in 6.54–59.
1.22.1a See the Introduction (sec. II.v) for discussion of the speeches in Thucydides.

other. [4] The absence of romance in my history will, I fear, detract somewhat from its interest; but if it be judged useful by those inquirers who desire an exact knowledge of the past as an aid to the understanding of the future, which in the course of human things must resemble if it does not reflect it, I shall be content. In fine, I have written my work, not as an essay which is to win the applause of the moment, but as a possession for all time.

The Median war, the greatest achievement of past times, yet found a speedy decision in two actions by sea and two by land. The Peloponnesian War went on for a very long time and there occurred during it disasters of a kind and number that no other similar period of time could match. [2] Never had so many cities been taken and laid desolate, here by the barbarians, here by the parties contending (the old inhabitants being sometimes removed to make room for others); never was there so much banishing and bloodshedding, now on the field of battle, now in political strife. [3] Old stories of occurrences handed down by tradition, but scantily confirmed by experience, suddenly ceased to be incredible; there were earthquakes of unparalleled extent and violence; eclipses of the sun occurred with a frequency unrecorded in previous history; there were great droughts in sundry places and consequent famines, and that most calamitous and awfully fatal visitation, the plague.[3a] All this came upon them with the late war, [4] which was begun by the Athenians and Peloponnesians with the dissolution of the Thirty Years' Peace[4a] made after the conquest of Euboea. [5] To the question why they broke the treaty, I answer by placing first an account of their grounds of complaint and points of difference, that no one may ever have to ask the immediate cause which plunged the Hellenes into a war of such magnitude. [6] The real cause, however, I consider to be the one which was formally most kept out of sight. The growth of the power of Athens, and the alarm which this inspired in Sparta, made war inevitable. Still it is well to give the grounds alleged by either side, which led to the dissolution of the treaty and the breaking out of the war.[6a]

The city of Epidamnus[1a] stands on the right of the entrance of the Ionic gulf.[1b] Its vicinity is inhabited by the Taulantians, an Illyrian[1c] people. [2] The place is a colony from Corcyra,[2a] founded by Phalius son of Eratocleides, of the family of the Heraclids, who had according to ancient usage been summoned for the purpose from Corinth,[2b] the mother country. The colonists were joined by some Corinthians, and

1.23
HELLAS
Thucydides compares the Persian war and the much longer Peloponnesian War, and states that the latter's true cause was Spartan fear of the growth of Athenian power.

1.24
435
IONIAN GULF
Beset by civil strife, the commons of Epidamnus solicit aid from their "mother city," Corcyra, but she refuses them.

1.23.3a   This is a much debated passage for what it indicates about Thucydides' attitude toward religion. See the Introduction (sec. IV.i).

1.23.4a   The Thirty Years' Peace treaty of 446; see 1.115.1.

1.23.6a   It has been argued that section 6 here was written by Thucydides at a substantially later time than section 5, and may

represent a radical change of mind about the causes of the war.

1.24.1a   Epidamnus: Map 1.26, AX.
1.24.1b   Ionic (Ionian) Gulf (the modern Adriatic Sea): Map 1.26, locator.
1.24.1c   Illyria: Map 1.26, locator.
1.24.2a   Corcyra: Map 1.26, AX.
1.24.2b   Corinth: Map 1.26, BY.

others of the Dorian race. [3] Now, as time went on, the city of Epidamnus became great and populous; [4] but falling a prey to factions arising, it is said, from a war with neighboring barbarians, she became much enfeebled, and lost a considerable amount of her power. [5] The last act before the war was the expulsion of those in power by The People. The exiled party joined the barbarians, and proceeded to plunder those in the city by sea and land; [6] and the Epidamnians finding themselves hard pressed, sent ambassadors to Corcyra beseeching their mother country not to allow them to perish, but to make up matters between them and the exiles, and to rid them of the war with the barbarians. [7] The ambassadors seated themselves in the temple of Hera[7a] as suppliants, and made the above requests to the Corcyraeans. But the Corcyraeans refused to accept their supplication, and they were dismissed without having effected anything.

When the Epidamnians found that no help could be expected from Corcyra, they were in a quandary about what to do next. So they sent to Delphi[1a] and inquired of the god, whether they should deliver their city to the Corinthians, and endeavor to obtain some assistance from their founders. The answer he gave them was to deliver the city, and place themselves under Corinthian protection. [2] So the Epidamnians went to Corinth, and delivered over the colony in obedience to the commands of the oracle. They showed that their founder came from Corinth, and revealed the answer of the god; and they begged them not to allow them to perish, but to assist them. [3] This the Corinthians consented to do. Believing the colony to belong as much to themselves as to the Corcyraeans, they felt it to be a kind of duty to undertake their protection. Besides, they hated the Corcyraeans for their contempt of the mother country. [4] Instead of meeting with the usual honors accorded to the parent city by every other colony at public assemblies, such as precedence at sacrifices, Corinth found herself treated with contempt by a power, which in point of wealth could stand comparison with any state, even the richest in Hellas, which possessed great military strength, and which sometimes could not repress a pride in the high naval position of an island whose nautical renown dated from the days of its old inhabitants, the Phaeacians.[4a] This was one reason for the care that they lavished on their fleet, which became very efficient; indeed they began the war with a force of a hundred and twenty triremes.

All these grievances made Corinth eager to send the promised aid to Epidamnus. Advertisement was made for volunteer settlers, and a force of

1.25
435
IONIAN GULF
After consulting the oracle at Delphi, Epidamnus seeks and obtains promises of Corinthian help. Corinth had long resented Corcyra's contempt for her.

1.26
435
IONIAN GULF
When Corinthian settlers arrive at Epidamnus, Corcyra decides to support the Epidamnian exiles and besieges Epidamnus.

1.24.7a   Presumably the temple of Hera (Map
          3.76, inset) where Corcyraean oligarchs
          were suppliants. See 3.75.4.
1.25.1a   Delphi: Map 1.26, BY.
1.25.4a   For the Phaeacians, see Homer's *Odyssey*,
          Books 6–8.

Map 1.26 The Corinthian Expedition

Ambraciots,[1a] Leucadians,[1b] and Corinthians was despatched. [2] They marched by land to Apollonia,[2a] a Corinthian colony, the route by sea being avoided from fear of Corcyraean interruption. [3] When the Corcyraeans heard of the arrival of the settlers and troops in Epidamnus, and the surrender of the colony to Corinth, they took fire. Instantly putting to sea with five-and-twenty ships, which were quickly followed by others, they insolently commanded the Epidamnians to receive back the banished party (it must be premised that the Epidamnian exiles had come to Corcyra, and pointing to the sepulchers of their ancestors, had appealed to their kindred to restore them)—and to dismiss the Corinthian garrison and settlers. [4] But to all this the Epidamnians turned a deaf ear. Upon this the Corcyraeans commenced operations against them with a fleet of forty ships. They took with them the exiles, with a view to their restoration, and also secured the services of the Illyrians. Sitting down before the city, they issued a proclamation to the effect that any of the Epidamnians that chose, and of the foreigners, might depart unharmed, with the alternative of being treated as enemies. On their refusal the Corcyraeans proceeded to besiege the city, which stands on an isthmus; [1.27.1] and the Corinthians, receiving intelligence of the investment of Epidamnus, got together an armament and called for volunteers to go to a colony at Epidamnus,[1a] complete political equality being guaranteed to all who chose to go. Any who were not prepared to sail at once might by paying down the sum of fifty Corinthian *drachmae*[1b] have a share in the colony without leaving Corinth. Great numbers took advantage of this proclamation, some being ready to start directly, others paying the requisite forfeit. [2] In case of their passage being disputed by the Corcyraeans, several cities were asked to lend them a convoy. Megara[2a] prepared to accompany them with eight ships, Pale in Cephallenia[2b] with four; Epidaurus[2c] furnished five, Hermione[2d] one, Troezen[2e] two, Leucas ten, and Ambracia eight. The Thebans[2f] and Phliasians[2g] were asked for money, the Eleans[2h] for unmanned hulls as well; while Corinth herself furnished thirty ships and three thousand *hoplites*.[2i]

When the Corcyraeans heard of their preparations they came to Corinth with envoys from Sparta and Sicyon,[1a] whom they persuaded to accompany them, and bade her recall the garrison and settlers, as she had nothing to do with Epidamnus. [2] If, however, she had any claims to make, they were willing to submit the matter to the arbitration of such of the cities in the Peloponnesus as should be chosen by mutual agreement, and to accept that the colony should remain with the city to whom the arbitrators might

1.27
435
IONIAN GULF
Corinth organizes a large force to colonize and rescue Epidamnus from Corcyra.

1.28
435
IONIAN GULF
Corcyra offers to submit the dispute to arbitration or to the god at Delphi.

1.26.1a   Ambracia: Map 1.26, AX.
1.26.1b   Leucas: Map 1.26, BX.
1.26.2a   Apollonia: Map 1.26, AX.
1.27.1a   Epidamnus: Map 1.26, AX.
1.27.1b   The *drachma* is a monetary unit. See
          Appendix J, Classical Greek Currency, §3.
1.27.2a   Megara: Map 1.26, BY.
1.27.2b   Cephallenia and the city of Pale on that
          island: Map 1.26, BX.
1.27.2c   Epidaurus: Map 1.26, BY.

1.27.2d   Hermione: Map 1.26, BY.
1.27.2e   Troezen: Map 1.26, BY.
1.27.2f   Thebes: Map 1.26, BY.
1.27.2g   Phlius: Map 1.26, BY.
1.27.2h   Elis: Map 1.26, BX.
1.27.2i   *Hoplite* is the Greek word for a heavily
          armed infantryman; see Appendix F,
          Land Warfare, §2.
1.28.1a   Sicyon: Map 1.26, BY.

assign it. They were also willing to refer the matter to the oracle at Delphi. [3] If, in defiance of their protestations, war was resorted to, they should be themselves compelled by this violence to seek friends in quarters where they had no desire to seek them, and to make even old ties give way to the necessity of assistance. [4] The answer they got from Corinth was, that if they would withdraw their fleet and the barbarians from Epidamnus, negotiation might be possible; but, while the city was still being besieged, going before arbitrators was out of the question. [5] The Corcyraeans retorted that if Corinth would withdraw her troops from Epidamnus they would withdraw theirs, or they were ready to let both parties remain where they were, an armistice being concluded till judgment could be given.

Turning a deaf ear to all these proposals, when their ships were manned and their allies had come in, the Corinthians sent a herald[1a] before them to declare war, and getting under weigh with seventy-five ships and two thousand hoplites, sailed for Epidamnus to give battle to the Corcyraeans. [2] The fleet was under the command of Aristeus son of Pellichas, Callicrates son of Callias, and Timanor son of Timanthes; the troops under that of Archetimus son of Eurytimus, and Isarchidas son of Isarchus. [3] When they had reached Actium[3a] in the territory of Anactorium,[3b] at the mouth of the gulf of Ambracia,[3c] where the temple of Apollo stands, the Corcyraeans sent on a herald in a light boat to warn them not to sail against them. Meanwhile they proceeded to man their ships, all of which had been equipped for action, the old vessels being tightened[3d] to make them seaworthy. [4] On the return of the herald without any peaceful answer from the Corinthians, their ships being now manned, they put out to sea to meet the enemy with a fleet of eighty sail (forty were engaged in the siege of Epidamnus), formed line and went into action, and gained a decisive victory, [5] and destroyed fifteen of the Corinthian vessels. The same day had seen Epidamnus compelled by its besiegers to capitulate; the conditions being that the foreigners should be sold, and the Corinthians kept as prisoners of war, till their fate should be otherwise decided.

After the engagement the Corcyraeans set up a *trophy* on Leukimme,[1a] a headland of Corcyra, and slew all their captives except the Corinthians, whom they kept as prisoners of war. [2] Defeated at sea, the Corinthians and their allies returned home and left the Corcyraeans masters of all the sea about those parts. Sailing to Leucas,[2a] a Corinthian colony, they ravaged

---

1.29.1a   Heralds, already a venerable Greek institution in Thucydides' day, operated under the protection of the god Hermes and were easily identified by the staff they carried. They alone could travel unmolested between states or armies during wartime in order to deliver messages, take back replies, and make perfunctory arrangements.
1.29.3a   Actium: Map 1.26, AX.
1.29.3b   Anactorium: Map 1.26, AX.
1.29.3c   Gulf of Ambracia: Map 1.26, AX.
1.29.3d   Like all triremes, these older ships required internal torsion ropes that pulled

the bow and stern of the vessel together, strengthening the ship against wave action by tension and preventing joints from opening. For more information about naval battles, see Appendix G, Trireme Warfare.
1.30.1a   Cape Leukimme: Map 1.26, AX. After a battle in ancient Greece, the victorious side raised a *trophy*, usually a set of captured armor, arranged on a pole at or near the battlefield; see Appendix F, Land Warfare, §6.
1.30.2a   Leucas: Map 1.26, BX.

their territory, and burnt Cyllene,[2b] the harbor of the Eleans, because they had furnished ships and money to Corinth. [3] For almost the whole of the period that followed the battle they remained masters of the sea, and the allies of Corinth were harassed by Corcyraean vessels. At last Corinth, roused by the sufferings of her allies, sent out ships and troops in the fall of the summer, who formed an encampment at Actium[3a] and about Chimerium, in Thesprotis,[3b] for the protection of Leucas and the rest of the friendly cities. [4] The Corcyraeans for their part formed a similar station on Leukimme. Neither party made any movement, but they remained confronting each other till the end of the summer, and winter was at hand before either of them returned home.

Corinth, exasperated by the war with the Corcyraeans, spent the whole of the year after the engagement and that succeeding it in building ships, and in straining every nerve to form an efficient fleet; rowers being drawn from the Peloponnesus and the rest of Hellas by the inducement of large bounties.[1a] [2] The Corcyraeans, alarmed at the news of their preparations, being without a single ally in Hellas (for they had not enrolled themselves either in the Athenian or in the Spartan confederacy), decided to appeal to Athens in order to enter into alliance, and to endeavor to procure support from her. [3] Corinth also, hearing of their intentions, sent an embassy to Athens to prevent the Corcyraean navy being joined by the Athenian and her prospect of ordering the war according to her wishes being thus impeded. An assembly[3a] was convoked, and the rival advocates appeared: the Corcyraeans spoke as follows:

1.31
433
ATHENS
Alarmed by Corinthian threats, Corcyra sends envoys to Athens to ask for help. Corinth also sends envoys to Athens to present her position.

"Athenians! when a people that have not rendered any important service or support to their neighbors in times past, for which they might claim to be repaid, appear before them as we now appear before you to solicit their assistance, they may fairly be required to satisfy certain preliminary conditions. They should show, first, that it is expedient or at least safe to grant their request; next, that they will retain a lasting sense of the kindness. But if they cannot clearly establish any of these points, they must not be annoyed if they meet with a rebuff. [2] Now the Corcyraeans believe that with their petition for assistance they can also give you a satisfactory answer on these points, and they have therefore despatched us hither. [3] It has so

1.32
433
ATHENS
Speaking to the Athenian assembly, the Corcyraeans acknowledge that their past policy of avoiding alliances has now left them dangerously isolated.

1.30.2b Cyllene: Map 1.26, BX.
1.30.3a Actium: Map 1.26, AX.
1.30.3b Chimerium and Thesprotis: Map 1.26, AX (according to N.G.L. Hammond, "Naval Operations in the South Channel of Corcyra, 435–433," *Journal of Hellenic Studies*, 65:26–37).
1.31.1a Generally, rowers were paid one drachma per day, i.e., the standard wage for a day's labor. Experienced rowers, especially *thranites* (see Glossary) were highly sought after and could demand a bonus;

see note 6.31.3b. Also see Appendix G, Trireme Warfare, §12.
1.31.3a Assembly: see Appendix A, The Athenian Government, §5–8.

happened that our policy as regards you, with respect to this request, turns out to be inconsistent, and as regards our interests, to be at the present crisis inexpedient. [4] We say inconsistent, because a power which has never in the whole of her past history been willing to ally herself with any of her neighbors, is now found asking them to ally themselves with her. And we say inexpedient, because in our present war with Corinth it has left us in a position of entire isolation, and what once seemed the wise precaution of refusing to involve ourselves in alliances with other powers, lest we should also involve ourselves in risks of their choosing, has now proved to be folly and weakness. [5] It is true that in the late naval engagement we drove back the Corinthians from our shores single-handed. But they have now got together a still larger armament from the Peloponnesus and the rest of Hellas; and we, seeing our utter inability to cope with them without foreign aid, and the magnitude of the danger which subjection to them implies, find it necessary to ask help from you and from every other power. And we hope to be excused if we forswear our old principle of complete political isolation, a principle which was not adopted with any sinister intention, but was rather the consequence of an error in judgment."

1.33
433
ATHENS
The Corcyraeans argue that because they are the second greatest naval power in Greece, their offer of alliance is an extraordinary opportunity for Athens, particularly since Sparta will surely start a war against Athens soon.

"Now there are many reasons why in the event of your compliance you will congratulate yourselves on this request having been made to you. First, because your assistance will be rendered to a power which, herself inoffensive, is a victim to the injustice of others. Secondly, because all that we most value is at stake in the present contest, and by acceding to our request under these circumstances you will give unforgettable proof of your goodwill and create in us a lasting sense of gratitude. [2] Thirdly, yourselves excepted, we are the greatest naval power in Hellas. Can you conceive a stroke of good fortune more rare in itself, or more disheartening to your enemies, than that the power whose adhesion you would have valued above much material and moral strength, should present herself self-invited, should deliver herself into your hands without danger and without expense, and should lastly put you in the way of gaining a high character in the eyes of the world, the gratitude of those whom you shall assist, and a great accession of strength for yourselves? You may search all history without finding many instances of a people gaining all these advantages at once, or many instances of a power that comes in quest of assistance being in a position to give to the people whose alliance she solicits as much safety and honor as she will receive. [3] But it will be urged that it is only in the case of a war that we shall be found useful. To this we answer that if any of you imagine that the war is far off, he is grievously mistaken, and is blind to the fact that the Spartans out of fear of you want war, and that Corinth is influential with them—the same, remember, that is your enemy, and is even now trying to subdue us as a preliminary to attacking you. And this she does to prevent our becoming united by a common enmity, and her having us both on her hands, and also to insure getting the jump on you in one of two ways, either by crippling our power or by making its strength her own. [4] Now it is our policy to preempt her—that is, for Corcyra to make an offer of alliance and for you to accept it; in fact, we ought to form plans against her instead of waiting to defeat the plans she forms against us."

"If she asserts that for you to receive a colony of hers into alliance is not right, let her know that every colony that is well treated honors its parent state, but becomes estranged from it by injustice. For colonists are not sent forth on the understanding that they are to be the slaves of those that remain behind, but that they are to be their equals. [2] And that Corinth was injuring us is clear. Invited to refer the dispute about Epidamnus to arbitration, they chose to prosecute their complaints by war rather than by a fair trial. [3] And let their conduct toward us who are their kindred be a warning to you not to be misled by their deceit, nor to yield to their direct requests; concessions to adversaries only end in self-reproach, and the more strictly they are avoided the greater will be the chance of security."

"If it be urged that your reception of us will be a breach of the treaty existing between you and Sparta, the answer is that we are a neutral state, [2] and that one of the express provisions of that treaty is that it shall be open to any Hellenic state that is neutral to join whichever side it pleases.[2a] [3] And it is intolerable for Corinth to be allowed to obtain men for her navy not only from her allies, but also from the rest of Hellas, no small number being furnished by your own subjects; while we are to be excluded both from the alliance left open to us by treaty, and from any assistance that we might get from other quarters, and you are to be accused of political immorality if you comply with our request. [4] On the other hand, we shall have much greater cause to complain of you, if you do not comply with it; if we, who are in peril, and are no enemies of yours, meet with a repulse at your hands, while Corinth, who is the aggressor and your enemy, not only meets with no hindrance from you, but is even allowed to draw material for war from your dependencies. This ought not to be, but you should either forbid her enlisting men in your dominions, or you should lend us too what help you may think advisable."

[5] "But your real policy is to afford us open approval and support. The advantages of this course, as we premised in the beginning of our speech, are many. We mention one that is perhaps the chief.

1.34
433
ATHENS
The Corcyraeans report that Corinth has attempted to dominate Corcyra and refuses Corcyra's offer of arbitration.

1.35
433
ATHENS
Claiming that their alliance with Athens will not breach existing treaties, the Corcyraeans argue that Athens should prevent their naval power from becoming subject to a potential enemy of Athens.

1.35.2a For the Thirty Years' Peace Treaty of
          446, see 1.115.1.

Could there be a clearer guarantee of our good faith than is offered by the fact that the power which is at enmity with you, is also at enmity with us, and that power is fully able to punish defection. And there is a wide difference between declining the alliance of an inland and of a maritime power. For your first endeavor should be to prevent, if possible, the existence of any naval power except your own; failing this, to secure the friendship of the strongest that does exist."

"And if any of you believe that what we urge is expedient, but fear to act upon this belief, lest it should lead to a breach of the treaty, you must remember that on the one hand, whatever your fears, your strength will be formidable to your antagonists; on the other, whatever the confidence you derive from refusing to receive us, you will be the weaker and less terrifying to a strengthened enemy. You must also remember that your decision is for Athens no less than for Corcyra, and that you are not making the best provision for her interests if, at a time when you are anxiously scanning the horizon that you may be in readiness for the breaking out of the war which is all but upon you, you hesitate to attach to your side a place whose adhesion or estrangement is alike pregnant with the most vital consequences. [2] For it lies conveniently for the coast navigation in the direction of Italy and Sicily,[2a] being able to bar the passage of naval reinforcements from there to the Peloponnesus, and from the Peloponnesus to there; and it is in other respects most suitably positioned. [3] To sum up as shortly as possible, embracing both general and particular considerations, let this show you the folly of sacrificing us. Remember that there are but three considerable naval powers in Hellas, Athens, Corcyra, and Corinth, and that if you allow two of these three to become one, and Corinth to secure us for herself, you will have to hold the sea against the united fleets of Corcyra and the Peloponnesus. But if you receive us, you will have our ships to reinforce you in the struggle."

[4] Such were the words of the Corcyraeans. After they had finished, the Corinthians spoke as follows:

"These Corcyraeans in the speech we have just heard do not confine themselves to the question of their reception into your alliance. They also talk of our being guilty of injustice, and their being the victims of an unjustifiable war. It becomes necessary for us to touch upon both these points before we proceed to the rest of what we have to say, that you may have a more correct idea of the grounds of

Margin notes

1.36
433
ATHENS
Reminding the Athenians of Corcyra's strategic location on the route to Italy and Sicily, the Corcyraeans conclude by warning that if Athens refuses alliance now, she may well confront combined Corcyraean and Peloponnesian fleets in a future war.

1.37
433
ATHENS
The Corinthians accuse Corcyra of having pursued a policy of isolation so as to use their geographic position to abuse the many ships forced to put into Corcyra.

Footnotes

1.36.2a　The geographical relation between Corcyra and Italy–Sicily is displayed in Map 1.14. See Appendix G, Trireme Warfare, §7, for an explanation of why military vessels (triremes) were forced to follow coastlines and rarely ventured, like merchant vessels, into the open sea.

our claim, and have good cause to reject their petition. [2] According to them, their old policy of refusing all offers of alliance was a policy of moderation. It was in fact adopted for bad ends, not for good; indeed their conduct is such as to make them by no means desirous of having allies present to witness it, or of having the shame of asking their concurrence. [3] Besides, their geographical situation makes them independent of others, and consequently the decision in cases where they injure any lies not with judges appointed by mutual agreement, but with themselves, because while they seldom make voyages to their neighbors, they are constantly being visited by foreign vessels which are compelled to put in to Corcyra. [4] In short, the object that they propose to themselves in their specious policy of complete isolation, is not to avoid sharing in the crimes of others, but to secure a monopoly of crime to themselves—the license of outrage wherever they can compel, and of fraud wherever they can elude, and the enjoyment of their gains without shame. [5] And yet if they were the honest men they pretend to be, the less hold that others had upon them, the stronger would be the light in which they might have put their honesty by giving and taking what was just."

"But such has not been their conduct either toward others or toward us. The attitude of our colony toward us has always been one of estrangement, and is now one of hostility; for, say they, 'We were not sent out to be ill-treated.' [2] We rejoin that we did not found the colony to be insulted by them, but to be their head, and to be regarded with a proper respect. [3] At any rate, our other colonies honor us, and we are very much beloved by our colonists; [4] and clearly, if the majority are satisfied with us, these can have no good reason for a dissatisfaction in which they stand alone, and we are not acting improperly in making war against them, nor are we making war against them without having received severe provocation. [5] Besides, if we were in the wrong, it would be honorable in them to give way to our wishes, and disgraceful for us to trample on their moderation; but in the pride and license of wealth they have sinned again and again against us, and never more deeply than when Epidamnus, our dependency, which they took no steps to claim in its distress, upon our coming to relieve it, was by them seized, and is now held by force of arms."

"As to their allegation that they wished the question to be first submitted to arbitration, it is obvious that a challenge coming from the party who is safe in a commanding position cannot gain the

1.38
433
ATHENS
The Corinthians claim that Corcyra has always treated them with inappropriate disdain that now at Epidamnus has become open hostility.

1.39
433
ATHENS
The Corinthians argue that Corcyra offered arbitration only after she began to fear Corinthian retaliation, and that her fear also motivates her request for an Athenian alliance.

credit due only to him who, before appealing to arms, in deeds as well as words, places himself on a level with his adversary. [2] In their case, it was not before they laid siege to the place, but after they at length understood that we would not tamely suffer it, that they thought of the specious word arbitration. And not satisfied with their own misconduct there, they appear here now requiring you to join with them not in alliance, but in crime, and to receive them in spite of their being at enmity with us. [3] But it was when they stood firmest that they should have made overtures to you, and not at a time when we have been wronged and they are in peril; nor yet at a time when you will be admitting to a share in your protection those who never admitted you to a share in their power, and will be incurring an equal amount of blame from us with those in whose offenses you had no hand. No, they should have shared their power with you before they asked you to share your fortunes with them."

"So then the reality of the grievances we come to complain of and the violence and rapacity of our opponents have both been proved. But that you cannot equitably receive them, this you have still to learn. [2] It may be true that one of the provisions of the treaty is that it shall be competent for any state, whose name was not down on the list, to join whichever side it pleases. But this agreement is not meant for those whose object in joining is the injury of other powers, but for those whose need of support does not arise from the fact of defection, and whose adhesion will not bring to the power that is mad enough to receive them war instead of peace; which will be the case with you, if you refuse to listen to us. [3] For you cannot become their auxiliary and remain our friend; if you join in their attack, you must share the punishment which the defenders inflict on them. [4] And yet you have the best possible right to be neutral, or failing this, you should on the contrary join us against them. Corinth is at least in treaty with you; with Corcyra you were never even in truce. But do not propose the principle that those defecting from others are to be welcomed. [5] Did we on the defection of the Samians record our vote against you, when the rest of the Peloponnesian powers were equally divided on the question whether they should assist them?[5a] No, we told them to their face that every power has a right to punish its own allies. [6] Why, if you make it your policy to receive and assist all offenders, you will find that just as many of your dependencies will come over to us, and the principle that you establish will press less heavily on us than on yourselves."

1.40
433
ATHENS
The Corinthians threaten enmity and retaliation if Athens should ally with Corcyra, and remind the Athenians of Corinth's past support for them against rebellious Samos.   ·

1.40.5a   If the Peloponnesian League debated the question of helping Samos in 441/0, Sparta probably proposed that such help be given. The revolt of the island of Samos from the Athenians took place in 441/0 and is described by Thucydides in 1.115–17. See Appendix D, The Peloponnesian League, §5. Samos: Map 1.11, BY, and Map 1.115.

"This then is what Hellenic law entitles us to demand as a right. But we have also advice to offer and claims on your gratitude, which, since there is no danger of our injuring you, as we are not enemies, and since our friendship does not amount to very frequent intercourse, we say ought to be liquidated at the present juncture. [2] When you were in want of ships of war for the war against the Aeginetans, before the Persian invasion, Corinth supplied you with twenty vessels. That good turn, and the line we took on the Samian question, when we were the cause of the Peloponnesians refusing to assist them, enabled you to conquer Aegina,[2a] and to punish Samos. And we acted thus at crises when, if ever, men are wont in their efforts against their enemies to forget everything for the sake of victory, [3] regarding him who assists them then as a friend, even if thus far he has been a foe, and him who opposes them then as a foe, even if he has thus far been a friend; indeed they allow their real interests to suffer from their absorbing preoccupation in the struggle."

"Weigh well these considerations, and let your youth learn what they are from their elders, and let them determine to do unto us as we have done unto you. And let them not acknowledge the justice of what we say, but dispute its wisdom in the contingency of war. [2] Not only is the straightest path generally speaking the wisest; but the coming of the war which the Corcyraeans have used as a specter to persuade you to do wrong, is still uncertain, and it is not worth while to be carried away by it into gaining the instant and declared enmity of Corinth. It were, rather, wise to try and counteract the unfavorable impression which your conduct to Megara[2a] has created. [3] For kindness opportunely shown has a greater power of removing old grievances than the facts of the case may warrant. And do not be seduced by the prospect of a great naval alliance. Abstinence from all injustice to other first-rate powers is a greater tower of strength than anything that can be gained by the sacrifice of permanent tranquillity for an apparent temporary advantage."

"It is now our turn to benefit by the principle that we laid down at Sparta, that every power has a right to punish her own allies. We now claim to receive the same from you, and protest against your rewarding us for benefitting you by our vote by injuring us by yours. [2] On the contrary, return us like for like, remembering that this is that very crisis in which he who lends aid is most a friend, and he who opposes is most a foe. [3] And for these Corcyraeans—neither receive them into alliance in our despite, nor be their abettors in

1.41
433
ATHENS
The Corinthians demand gratitude for their help in Athens' war with Aegina and the revolt of Samos.

1.42
433
ATHENS
The Corinthians call upon the Athenians to return past favors and not incur Corinth's enmity to secure a naval alliance.

1.43
433
ATHENS
The Corinthians conclude by telling the Athenians that their best interests lie in rejecting Corcyra.

1.41.2a The war between Athens and Aegina of 491 B.C. (see Herodotus, Book 6, 87–93). Aegina: Map 1.46, BY.
1.42.2a Megara: Map 1.46, BY. Although some believe Thucydides here refers to the Megara Decree (cf. 1.67.4, 1.139.1,

1.140.3–4, and 1.144.2), and therefore date it prior to mid-433, most take it as a reference to Corinth's hatred for Athens caused by the defection of Megara to the Athenian alliance in about 460; cf. 1.103.4.

crime. [4] So do, and you will act as we have a right to expect of you, and at the same time best consult your own interest."

Such were the words of the Corinthians.

When the Athenians had heard both out, two assemblies were held. In the first there was a manifest disposition to listen to the representations of Corinth; in the second, public feeling had changed, and an alliance with Corcyra was decided on, with certain reservations. It was to be a defensive, not an offensive, alliance. It did not involve a breach of the treaty with the Peloponnesus: Athens could not be required to join Corcyra in any attack upon Corinth. But each of the contracting parties had a right to the other's assistance against invasion, whether of his own territory, or that of an ally. [2] For it began now to be felt that the coming of the Peloponnesian War was only a question of time, and no one was willing to see a naval power of such magnitude as Corcyra sacrificed to Corinth; though if they could let them weaken each other by mutual conflict, it would be no bad preparation for the struggle which Athens might one day have to wage with Corinth and the other naval powers. [3] At the same time the island seemed to lie conveniently on the coasting passage to Italy and Sicily.[3a]

With these views, Athens received Corcyra into alliance, and on the departure of the Corinthians not long afterwards, sent ten ships to their assistance. [2] They were commanded by Lacedaemonius son of Cimon, Diotimus son of Strombichus, and Porteas son of Epicles. [3] Their instructions were to avoid collision with the Corinthian fleet except under certain circumstances. If it sailed to Corcyra and threatened a landing on her coast, or in any of her possessions, they were to do their utmost to prevent it. These instructions were prompted by an anxiety to avoid a breach of the treaty.

Meanwhile the Corinthians completed their preparations, and sailed for Corcyra with a hundred and fifty ships. Of these Elis[1a] furnished ten, Megara[1b] twelve, Leucas[1c] ten, Ambracia[1d] twenty-seven, Anactorium[1e] one, and Corinth herself ninety. [2] Each of these contingents had its own admiral, the Corinthian being under the command of Xenocleides son of Euthycles, with four colleagues. [3] Sailing from Leucas, they made land at the part of the continent opposite Corcyra. [4] They anchored in the harbor of Chimerium, in the territory of Thesprotis,[4a] above which, at some distance from the sea, lies the city of Ephyre,[4b] in the Elean district. By this city the Acherusian lake pours its waters into the sea. It gets its name from the river

1.44
433
ATHENS
The Athenians vote with a view toward a Peloponnesian war, noting Corcyra's large fleet and her position on the route to Italy and Sicily.

1.45
433
ATHENS
Athens enters a defensive alliance with Corcyra and sends ten triremes to assist her.

1.46
433
CORCYRA
A Corinthian fleet sails to Chimerium, near Corcyra.

1.44.3a The geographical relation between Corcyra and Italy–Sicily is displayed in Map 1.14.
1.46.1a Elis: Map 1.46, BX.
1.46.1b Megara: Map 1.46, BY.
1.46.1c Leucas: Map 1.46, BX.
1.46.1d Ambracia: Map 1.46, AX.
1.46.1e Anactorium: Map 1.46, AX.
1.46.4a Chimerium: Map 1.46, inset. Thesprotis: Map 1.46, AX and inset (according to N.G.L. Hammond; see note 1.30.3b).
1.46.4b Ephyre: Map 1.46, inset.

MAP 1.46 THE BATTLE OFF SYBOTA

Acheron[4c] which flows through Thesprotis and falls into the lake. There
also the river Thyamis[4d] flows, forming the boundary between Thesprotis
and Kestrine;[4e] and between these rivers rises the point of Chimerium. [5]
In this part of the continent the Corinthians now came to anchor, and
formed an encampment.

1.46.4c   Acherusian Lake, River Acheron: Map
      1.46, inset.

1.46.4d   Thyamis river, possible location: Map
      1.46, AY.
1.46.4e   Kestrine: Map 1.46, AX.

When the Corcyraeans saw them coming, they manned a hundred and ten ships, commanded by Meikiades, Aisimides, and Eurybatus, and stationed themselves at one of the Sybota isles[1a]; the ten Athenian ships being present. [2] On point Leukimme[2a] they posted their land forces, and a thousand hoplites who had come from Zacynthus[2b] to their assistance. Nor were the Corinthians on the mainland without their allies. [3] The barbarians flocked in large numbers to their assistance, the inhabitants of this part of the continent being old allies of theirs.

When the Corinthian preparations were completed they took three days' provisions, and put out from Chimerium by night, ready for action. [2] Sailing with the dawn, they sighted the Corcyraean fleet out at sea, and coming toward them. [3] When they perceived each other, both sides formed in order of battle. On the Corcyraean right wing lay the Athenian ships, the rest of the line being occupied by their own vessels formed in three squadrons, each of which was commanded by one of the three admirals. [4] Such was the Corcyraean formation. The Corinthian was as follows: on the right wing lay the Megarian and Ambraciot ships, in the center the rest of the allies in order. But the left was composed of the best sailors in the Corinthian navy, to encounter the Athenians and the right wing of the Corcyraeans.[4a]

As soon as the signals were raised on either side, they joined battle. Both sides had a large number of hoplites on their decks, and a large number of archers and javelin throwers, the old imperfect armament still prevailing. [2] The sea fight was an obstinate one, though not remarkable for its science; indeed it was more like a battle by land. [3] Whenever they charged each other, the multitude and crush of the triremes made it by no means easy to get loose; besides, their hopes of victory lay principally in the hoplites on the decks, who stood and fought in order, the ships remaining stationary. The maneuver of passing through the line was not tried: in short, strength and pluck had more share in the fight than science.[3a] [4] Everywhere tumult reigned, the battle being one scene of confusion; meanwhile the Athenian triremes, by coming up to the Corcyraeans whenever they were pressed, served to alarm the enemy, though their commanders could not join in the battle from fear of their instructions. [5] The right wing of the Corinthians suffered most. The Corcyraeans routed it, and chased them in disorder to the continent with twenty ships, sailed up to their camp and burnt the tents which they found empty, and plundered the stuff.[5a] [6] So in this quarter the Corinthians and their allies were defeated, and the Corcyraeans were victorious. But where the Corinthians themselves were, on the left, they gained a decided success; the scanty forces of the

1.47.1a   Sybota isles: Map 1.46, inset.
1.47.2a   Cape Leukimme, Corcyra: Map 1.46, inset.
1.47.2b   Zacynthus: Map 1.46, BX.
1.48.4a   Map 1.46, inset, shows a reconstruction of the battle location and formations from J. S. Morrison and J. R. Coates, *The Athenian Trireme* (Cambridge: Cambridge University Press, 1986), 63. They

follow N.G.L. Hammond, "Naval Operations in the South Channel of Corcyra, 435–433," *Journal of Hellenic Studies*, 65: 26–37.
1.49.3a   For these maneuvers, see the Athenian commander Phormio's speech in 2.89.8, and Appendix G, Trireme Warfare, §5.
1.49.5a   For naval "stuff" at shore bases, see Appendix G, Trireme Warfare, §8.

Corcyraeans being further weakened by the want of the twenty triremes absent on the pursuit. [7] Seeing the Corcyraeans hard pressed, the Athenians began at length to assist them more unequivocally. At first, it is true, they refrained from charging any ships; but when the rout was becoming obvious, and the Corinthians were pressing on, the time at last came when every one set to, and all distinction was laid aside, and it came to this point, that the Corinthians and Athenians raised their hands against each other.

After the rout, the Corinthians, instead of employing themselves in lashing fast and hauling after them the hulls of the triremes which they had disabled, turned their attention to the men, whom they butchered as they sailed through, not caring so much to make prisoners. Some even of their own friends were slain by them, by mistake, in their ignorance of the defeat of the right wing. [2] For the number of the triremes on both sides, and the distance to which they covered the sea, made it difficult after they had once joined, to distinguish between the conquering and the conquered; this battle proving far greater than any before it, any at least between Hellenes, for the number of vessels engaged. [3] After the Corinthians had chased the Corcyraeans to the land, they turned to the wrecks and their dead, most of whom they succeeded in getting hold of and conveying to Sybota,[3a] the rendezvous of the land forces furnished by their barbarian allies. Sybota, it must be known, is a desert harbor of Thesprotis. This task over, they mustered anew, and sailed against the Corcyraeans, [4] who on their part advanced to meet them with all their ships that were fit for service and remaining to them, accompanied by the Athenian vessels, fearing that they might attempt a landing in their territory. [5] It was by this time getting late, and the *paean*[5a] had been sung for the attack, when the Corinthians suddenly began to back water. They had observed twenty Athenian ships sailing up, which had been sent out afterwards to reinforce the ten triremes by the Athenians, who feared, as it turned out justly, the defeat of the Corcyraeans and the inability of their handful of ships to protect them. [1.51.1] These ships were thus seen by the Corinthians first. They suspected that they were from Athens, and that those which they saw were not all, but that there were more behind; they accordingly began to retire. [2] The Corcyraeans meanwhile had not sighted them, as they were advancing from a point which they could not so well see, and were wondering why the Corinthians were backing water, when some caught sight of them, and cried out that there were ships in sight ahead. Upon this they also retired; for it was now getting dark, and the retreat of the Corinthians had suspended hostilities. [3] Thus they parted from each other, and the

1.50
433
CORCYRA
The victorious Corinthians massacre survivors, gather up the dead, and tow off hulks. Returning to battle, they sight approaching Athenian reinforcements and retire.

1.51
433
CORCYRA
Twenty additional Athenian triremes join the Corcyraeans at Leukimme.

1.50.3a Sybota: Map 1.46, inset.
1.50.5a The *paean* was a ritual chant that classical
         Greek soldiers and sailors sang as they
         advanced into battle, rallied, or celebrated
         victory.

battle ceased with night. [4] The Corcyraeans were in their camp at Leukimme,[4a] when these twenty triremes from Athens, under the command of Glaucon son of Leagrus and Andocides son of Leogoras bore on through the corpses and the wrecks, and sailed up to the camp, not long after they were sighted. [5] It was now night, and the Corcyraeans feared that they might be hostile vessels; but they soon recognized them, and the ships came to anchor.

The next day the thirty Athenian vessels put out to sea, accompanied by all the Corcyraean ships that were seaworthy, and sailed to the harbor at Sybota, where the Corinthians lay, to see if they would engage. [2] The Corinthians put out from the land, and formed a line in the open sea, but beyond this made no further movement, having no intention of assuming the offensive. For they saw reinforcements arrived fresh from Athens, and themselves confronted by numerous difficulties, such as the necessity of guarding the prisoners whom they had on board, and the want of all means of refitting their ships in a desert place. [3] What they were thinking more about was how their voyage home was to be effected; they feared that the Athenians might consider that the treaty was dissolved by the fighting which had occurred, and forbid their departure. [1.53.1] Accordingly they resolved to put some men on board a boat, and send them without a herald's wand to the Athenians, as an experiment.[1a] Having done so, they spoke as follows: [2] "You do wrong, Athenians, to begin war and break the treaty. Engaged in chastising our enemies, we find you placing yourselves in our path in arms against us. Now if your intentions are to prevent us sailing to Corcyra, or anywhere else that we may wish, and if you are for breaking the treaty, first take us that are here, and treat us as enemies." [3] Such was what they said, and all the Corcyraean armament that were within hearing immediately called out to take them and kill them. But the Athenians answered as follows: "Neither are we beginning war, Peloponnesians, nor are we breaking the treaty; but these Corcyraeans are our allies, and we are come to help them. So if you want to sail anywhere else, we place no obstacle in your way; but if you are going to sail against Corcyra, or any of her possessions, we shall do our best to stop you."

Receiving this answer from the Athenians, the Corinthians commenced preparations for their voyage home, and set up a trophy in Sybota, on the mainland; while the Corcyraeans took up the wrecks and dead that had been carried out to them by the current, and by a wind which rose in the night and scattered them in all directions, and set up their trophy in Sybota, on the island, as victors. [2] The reasons each side had for claiming

1.52
433
CORCYRA
The Corinthians fear that the Athenians will try to prevent their departure.

1.53
433
CORCYRA
The Athenians tell the Corinthians that the treaty is still valid, that they may not attack Corcyra, but that they may otherwise sail where they wish.

1.54
433
CORCYRA
Both sides erect trophies claiming victory.

1.51.4a　Leukimme, at the northern end of Cape
　　　　　Leukimme on Corcyra: Map 1.46, inset.
1.53.1a　For the significance of the "herald's
　　　　　wand" here, see note 1.29.1a.

the victory were these. The Corinthians had been victorious in the sea fight until night; and having thus been enabled to carry off most wrecks and dead, they were in possession of no fewer than a thousand prisoners of war, and had destroyed nearly seventy vessels. The Corcyraeans had destroyed about thirty ships, and after the arrival of the Athenians had taken up the wrecks and dead on their side; they had besides seen the Corinthians retire before them, backing water on sight of the Athenian vessels, and upon the arrival of the Athenians refuse to sail out against them from Sybota.

The Corinthians on the voyage home took Anactorium, which stands at the mouth of the Ambracian gulf.[1a] The place was taken by treachery, being common ground to the Corcyraeans and Corinthians. After establishing Corinthian settlers there, they retired home. Eight hundred of the Corcyraeans were slaves;[1b] these they sold; two hundred and fifty they retained in captivity, and treated with great attention, in the hope that they might bring over their country to Corinth on their return; most of them being, as it happened, men of very high position in Corcyra. [2] In this way Corcyra maintained her political existence in the war with Corinth, and the Athenian vessels left the island. This was the first cause of the war that Corinth had against the Athenians, namely, that they had fought against them with the Corcyraeans in time of treaty.[2a]

Almost immediately after this, fresh differences arose between the Athenians and Peloponnesians, and contributed their share to the war. [2] Corinth was forming schemes for retaliation, and Athens suspected her hostility. The Potidaeans, who inhabit the isthmus of Pallene,[2a] being a Corinthian colony, but tributary allies of Athens, were ordered to raze the wall on the Pallene side of the city, to give hostages, to dismiss the Corinthian magistrates, and in future not to receive the persons sent from Corinth annually to succeed them.[2b] It was feared that they might be persuaded by Perdiccas[2c] and the Corinthians to revolt, and might draw the rest of the allies in the area of Thrace[2d] to revolt with them.

These precautions against the Potidaeans were taken by the Athenians immediately after the battle at Corcyra. [2] Not only was Corinth at length openly hostile, but Perdiccas son of Alexander, king of the Macedonians, had from an old friend and ally been made an enemy. [3] He had been made an enemy by the Athenians entering into alliance with Philip his brother, and Derdas, who were allied in opposition to him.[3a] [4] In his alarm he had sent to Sparta to try and involve the Athenians in a war with the Peloponnesians, and was endeavoring to win over Corinth in order to bring about the revolt of Potidaea. [5] He also made overtures to the Chal-

1.55
433
CORCYRA
The Athenian role at Sybota was the first Corinthian complaint against Athens.

1.56
433
CHALCIDICE
Athens takes measures against Corinthian influence at Potidaea.

1.57
433
CHALCIDICE
As Perdiccas plots with the Spartans, Chalcidians, and Bottiaeans, Athens sends a fleet to Macedonia.

1.55.1a Anactorium, Ambracian Gulf: Map 1.46, AX.
1.55.1b The Corcyraeans employed slaves in their navy, which was quite unusual; see 7.13.2, 8.15.2, and Appendix G, Trireme Warfare, §12.
1.55.2a Thucydides' narrative returns next to Corcyra in 3.70.
1.56.2a Potidaea, at the isthmus of the Pallene Peninsula in Chalcidice: Map 1.60, BX.
1.56.2b That Potidaea received annual magistrates from Corinth as late as 432 is a notable

comment on the nature of the Athenian Empire at that date.
1.56.2c Perdiccas was the king of Macedonia (Map 1.60, AX).
1.56.2d Thrace: Map 1.60, AY. The Athenians referred to the member states of their empire to the north of the Aegean as "the places in Thrace," though Thrace itself lay largely where Bulgaria is today.
1.57.3a Derdas is thought to have possibly been king of Elymiotis, in upper Macedonia.

cidians[5a] in Thrace, and to the Bottiaeans,[5b] to persuade them to join in the revolt; for he thought that if these places on the border could be made his allies, it would be easier to carry on the war with their cooperation. [6] Alive to all this, and wishing to anticipate the revolt of the cities, the Athenians acted as follows. They were just then sending off thirty ships and a thousand hoplites to Perdiccas' territory under the command of Archestratus son of Lycomedes, with four colleagues. They instructed those in command of the ships to take hostages of the Potidaeans, to raze the wall, and to be on their guard against the revolt of the neighboring cities.

1.58
433/2
CHALCIDICE
When Potidaea fails to placate Athens, and Sparta promises to invade Attica, Potidaea revolts. The Chalcidians move from their coastal cities to Olynthus.

Meanwhile the Potidaeans sent envoys to Athens on the chance of persuading them to take no new steps in regard to them; they also went to Sparta with the Corinthians to secure support in case of need. Failing after prolonged negotiation to obtain anything satisfactory from the Athenians; being unable, for all they could say, to prevent the vessels that were destined for Macedonia from also sailing against them; and receiving from the Spartan authorities a promise to invade Attica if the Athenians should attack Potidaea, the Potidaeans, thus favored by the moment, at last entered into league with the Chalcidians and Bottiaeans, and revolted. [2] And Perdiccas induced the Chalcidians[2a] to abandon and demolish their cities on the seaboard, and settling inland at Olynthus,[2b] to make that one city a strong place: meanwhile to those who followed his advice he gave a part of his territory in Mygdonia[2c] round Lake Bolbe[2d] as a place of abode while the war against the Athenians should last. They accordingly demolished their cities, moved inland, and prepared for war.

1.59
432
CHALCIDICE
The Athenian fleet attacks Macedon.

The thirty ships of the Athenians, arriving in the Thracian[1a] area, found Potidaea and the rest in revolt. [2] Their commanders considering it to be quite impossible with their present force to carry on war with Perdiccas, and with the confederate cities as well, turned to Macedonia, their original destination, and having established themselves there, carried on war in cooperation with Philip, and the brothers of Derdas, who had invaded the country from the interior.

1.60
432
CHALCIDICE
Corinth sends volunteers and mercenaries to Potidaea.

Meanwhile the Corinthians, with Potidaea in revolt and the Athenian ships on the coast of Macedonia, alarmed for the safety of the place, and thinking its danger theirs, sent volunteers from Corinth, and mercenaries from the rest of the Peloponnesus, to the number of sixteen hundred hoplites in all, and four hundred light troops. [2] Aristeus son of Adimantus, who was always a steady friend to the Potidaeans, took command of the expedition, and it was principally for love of him that most of the men from Corinth volunteered. They arrived in Thrace forty days after the revolt of Potidaea.

1.57.5a   Chalcidice: Map 1.60, BY.
1.57.5b   The Bottiaeans are believed to have then inhabited Bottica (Bottike) in central Chalcidice, as shown on Map 1.60, AX (Simon Hornblower, *A Commentary on Thucydides* [Oxford: Clarendon Press, 1991], 1:101).
1.58.2a   The title of the Chalcidian League was "the Chalcidians," a term that Thucy-

dides always employs save for one moment, after the Peace of Nicias, in which Athens sought the dissolution of the league (5.39.1).
1.58.2b   Olynthus: Map 1.60, BX.
1.58.2c   Mygdonia: Map 1.60, AX.
1.58.2d   Lake Bolbe: Map 1.60, AY.
1.59.1a   Thracian area: see note 1.56.2d.

MAP 1.60 POTIDAEA

The Athenians also immediately received the news of the revolt of the cities. On being informed that Aristeus and his reinforcements were on their way, they sent two thousand hoplites of their own citizens and forty ships against the places in revolt, under the command of Callias son of Calliades, and four colleagues. [2] They arrived in Macedonia first, and found the force of a thousand men[2a] that had been first sent out just become masters of Therme[2b] and besieging Pydna.[2c] [3] Accordingly they also joined in the investment, and besieged Pydna for a while. Subsequently they came to terms and concluded a forced alliance with Perdiccas, hastened by the calls of Potidaea, and by the arrival of Aristeus at that place. They withdrew from Macedonia, [4] going to Beroea[4a] and thence to Strepsa,[4b] and, after a futile attempt on the latter place, they pursued by land their march to Potidaea with three thousand hoplites of their own citizens, besides a number of their allies, and six hundred Macedonian horsemen, the followers of Philip and Pausanias. With these sailed seventy ships along the coast. Advancing by short marches, on the third day they arrived at Gigonus,[4c] where they encamped.

1.61
432
CHALCIDICE
The Athenians force Perdiccas to return to his alliance with them, and then march against Potidaea.

1.61.2a These are the thousand men who were
         sent off in 1.57.6.
1.61.2b Therme: Map 1.60, AX.
1.61.2c Pydna: Map 1.60, BX.
1.61.4a Beroea: Map 1.60, AX.
1.61.4b Strepsa, possible location: Map 1.60, AX.
         "Strepsa" is an emendation of this text
         that is not universally accepted.
1.61.4c Gigonus: Map 1.60, BX.

1.62
432
CHALCIDICE
An indecisive battle occurs near Potidaea. Most Potidaeans retire inside their walls.

Meanwhile the Potidaeans and the Peloponnesians with Aristeus were encamped on the Olynthian[1a] side of the city on the isthmus, in expectation of the Athenians, and had established a market outside the city.[1b] [2] The allies had chosen Aristeus general of all the infantry; while the command of the cavalry was given to Perdiccas, who had now left the alliance of the Athenians and gone back to that of the Potidaeans, having deputed Iolaus as his general. [3] The plan of Aristeus was to keep his own force on the isthmus, and await the attack of the Athenians; leaving the Chalcidians and the allies outside the isthmus, and the two hundred cavalry from Perdiccas in Olynthus to act upon the Athenian rear, on the occasion of their advancing against him; and thus to place the enemy between two fires. [4] While Callias the Athenian general and his colleagues despatched the Macedonian horse and a few of the allies to Olynthus, to prevent any movement being made from that quarter, the Athenians themselves broke up their camp and marched against Potidaea. [5] After they had arrived at the isthmus, and saw the enemy preparing for battle, they formed against him, and soon afterwards engaged. [6] The wing of Aristeus, with the Corinthians and other picked troops round him, routed the wing opposed to it, and followed for a considerable distance in pursuit. But the rest of the army of the Potidaeans and of the Peloponnesians was defeated by the Athenians, and took refuge within the fortifications.

1.63
432
CHALCIDICE
Potidaean troops break through the Athenian lines and enter their city. Olynthian forces retire. Losses are enumerated.

Returning from the pursuit, Aristeus perceived the defeat of the rest of the army. Being at a loss which of the two risks to choose, whether to go to Olynthus or to Potidaea, he at last determined to draw his men into as small a space as possible, and force his way with a run into Potidaea. Not without difficulty, through a storm of missiles, he passed along by the breakwater through the sea, and brought off most of his men safe, though a few were lost. [2] Meanwhile the auxiliaries of the Potidaeans from Olynthus, which is about seven miles off, and in sight of Potidaea, when the battle began and the signals were raised, advanced a little way to render assistance; and the Macedonian horse formed against them to prevent it. But on victory speedily declaring for the Athenians and the signals being taken down, they retired back within the wall; and the Macedonians returned to the Athenians. Thus there were no cavalry present on either side. [3] After the battle the Athenians set up a trophy, and gave back their dead to the Potidaeans under truce.[3a] The Potidaeans and their allies had close upon three hundred killed; the Athenians a hundred and fifty of their own citizens, and Callias their general.

1.62.1a   The northern side, toward Olynthus: Map 1.60, BX.
1.62.1b   Greek soldiers and sailors at this time were expected to purchase their food from local markets with their own money, which made prompt disbursement of adequate military pay quite important. For a city to offer a special market at a convenient location for foreign military personnel was a polite and presumably profitable amenity, and it also helped to keep such "visitors" out of the city.

1.63.3a   After a battle in ancient Greece, the victors would gather up their own dead, strip those of the enemy, and raise a trophy. The defeated would collect the bodies of their fallen during a truce that they explicitly requested and were granted for that purpose. In this way, appropriate reverence was shown and proper burial was accorded to all war dead. See Appendix F, Land Warfare, §6.

The wall on the side of the isthmus now had works at once raised against it, and manned by the Athenians. That on the side of Pallene[1a] had no works raised against it. They did not think themselves strong enough at once to keep a garrison in the isthmus, and to cross over to Pallene and raise works there; they were afraid that the Potidaeans and their allies might take advantage of their division to attack them. [2] Meanwhile the Athenians at home learning that there were no works at Pallene, sometime afterwards sent off sixteen hundred hoplites of their own citizens under the command of Phormio son of Asopius. Arrived at Pallene, he fixed his headquarters at Aphytis,[2a] and led his army against Potidaea by short marches, ravaging the country as he advanced. No one venturing to meet him in the field, he raised works against the wall on the side of Pallene. [3] So at length Potidaea was strongly invested on either side, and from the sea by the ships cooperating in the blockade.

Aristeus, seeing its investment complete, and having no hope of its salvation, except in the event of some movement from the Peloponnesus, or of some other improbable contingency, advised all except five hundred to watch for a wind, and sail out of the place, in order that their provisions might last the longer. He was willing to be himself one of those who remained. Unable to persuade them, and desirous of acting on the next alternative, and of having things outside in the best posture possible, he eluded the guard ships of the Athenians and sailed out. [2] Remaining among the Chalcidians, he continued to carry on the war; in particular he set up an ambush near the city of the Sermylians,[2a] and cut off many of them; he also communicated with the Peloponnesus, and tried to contrive some method by which help might be brought. Meanwhile, after the completion of the investment of Potidaea, Phormio next employed his sixteen hundred men in ravaging Chalcidice and Bottica;[2b] some of the cities also were taken by him.

The Athenians and Peloponnesians had these antecedent grounds of complaint against each other: the complaint of Corinth was that her colony of Potidaea, and Corinthian and Peloponnesian citizens within it, was being besieged; that of Athens against the Peloponnesians that they had incited one of the cities in their alliance and liable for tribute, to revolt, and that they had come and were openly fighting against her on the side of the Potidaeans. For all this, war had not yet broken out: there was still truce for a while; for this was a private enterprise on the part of Corinth.

1.64.1a   Potidaea's "Pallene side" would be the
           southern side; see Pallene Peninsula, Map
           1.60, BY.
1.64.2a   Aphytis: Map 1.60, BY.
1.65.2a   Sermylium: Map 1.60, BY.
1.65.2b   Bottica (Bottike): Map 1.60, BX.

1.67
432/1[1a]
SPARTA
Many cities denounce Athens to the allies assembled at Sparta. The Corinthians speak last.

But the siege of Potidaea put an end to her inaction; she had men inside it: besides, she feared for the place. Immediately summoning the allies to Sparta, she came and loudly accused Athens of breach of the treaty and aggression on the rights of the Peloponnesus. [2] With her, the Aeginetans, formally unrepresented from fear of Athens, in secret proved not the least urgent of the advocates for war, asserting that they had not the independence guaranteed to them by the treaty. [3] After extending the summons to any of their allies and others who might have complaints to make of Athenian aggression, the Spartans held their ordinary assembly,[3a] and invited them to speak. [4] There were many who came forward and made their several accusations; among them the Megarians, in a long list of grievances, called special attention to the fact of their exclusion from the ports of the Athenian empire and the market of Athens, in defiance of the treaty.[4a] [5] Last of all the Corinthians came forward, and having let those who preceded them inflame the Spartans, now followed with a speech to this effect:

1.68
432/1
SPARTA
The Corinthians complain of Athenian aggression against them at Corcyra and Potidaea, and also of Spartan inaction, which both injures Sparta's allies and strengthens Sparta's rival.

"Spartans! the confidence which you feel in your constitution and social order inclines you to receive any reflections of ours on other powers with a certain skepticism. Hence springs your moderation, but hence also the rather limited knowledge which you betray in dealing with foreign politics. [2] Time after time was our voice raised to warn you of the blows about to be dealt us by Athens, and time after time, instead of taking the trouble to ascertain the worth of our warnings, you contented yourselves with suspecting the speakers of being inspired by private interest. And so, instead of calling these allies together before the blow fell, you have delayed to do so till we are smarting under it; and of the allies it is not unfitting that we make this speech for we have very great complaints of high-handed treatment by the Athenians and of neglect by you. [3] Now if these assaults on the rights of Hellas had been made in the dark you might be unacquainted with the facts, and it would be our duty to enlighten you. As it is, long speeches are not needed where you see servitude accomplished for some of us, meditated for others—in particular for our allies—and prolonged preparations by the aggressor for the hour of war. [4] Or what, pray, is the meaning of their reception of Corcyra by fraud, and their holding it against us by force? What of the siege of Potidaea?—places one of which lies most conveniently for any action against the Thracian cities; while the other would have contributed a very large navy to the Peloponnesians?"

1.67.1a   The Hellenic year began in the middle of our calendar year, and so "432/1," for example, is used to cover the winter period comprising the latter part of the year 432 and the initial part of the year 431.

1.67.3a   Assembly: see Appendix C, Spartan Institutions, §6.

1.67.4a   The precise date of the Megara Decree is uncertain (see note at 1.42.2a), as also is the way in which it was thought to infringe the Thirty Years' Peace. See also Appendix B, The Athenian Empire, §10.

"For all this you are responsible. You it was who first allowed them to fortify their city after the Persian war,[1a] and afterwards to erect the long walls—you who, then and now, are always depriving of freedom not only those whom they have enslaved, but also those who have as yet been your allies. For the true author of the subjugation of a people is not so much the immediate agent, as the power which permits it having the means to prevent it; particularly if that power aspires to the glory of being the liberator of Hellas. We are at last assembled. [2] It has not been easy to assemble, nor even now are our objects defined. We ought not to be still inquiring into the facts of our wrongs, but into the means for our defense. For the aggressors with matured plans to oppose to our indecision have cast threats aside and betaken themselves to action. [3] And we know what are the paths by which Athenian aggression travels, and how insidious is its progress. A degree of confidence she may feel from the idea that your bluntness of perception prevents your noticing her; but it is nothing to the impulse which her advance will receive from the knowledge that you see, but do not care to interfere. [4] You, Spartans, of all the Hellenes are alone inactive, and defend yourselves not by doing anything but by looking as if you would do something; you alone wait till the power of an enemy is becoming twice its original size, instead of crushing it in its infancy. [5] And yet the world used to say that you were to be depended upon; but in your case, we fear, it said more than the truth. The Mede,[5a] we ourselves know, had time to come from the ends of the earth to the Peloponnesus, without any force of yours worthy of the name advancing to meet him. But this was a distant enemy. Well, Athens at all events is a near neighbor, and yet Athens you utterly disregard; against Athens you prefer to act on the defensive instead of on the offensive, and to make it an affair of chances by deferring the struggle till she has grown far stronger than at first. And yet you know that on the whole the rock on which the barbarian was wrecked was himself, and that if our present enemy Athens has not again and again annihilated us, we owe it more to her blunders than to your protection. [6] Indeed, expectations from you have before now been the ruin of some, whose faith induced them to omit preparation."

"We hope that none of you will consider these words of remonstrance to be rather words of hostility; men remonstrate with friends who are in error, accusations they reserve for enemies who have wronged them."

1.69
432/1
SPARTA
The Corinthians assert that Spartan inaction has permitted Athens to grow at the expense of the Hellenes, and that Athens' perception of Sparta's acquiescence encourages her to commit further aggression. Once the Spartans could have stopped her easily, but Athens has now become such a formidable adversary that Hellenic confidence in Sparta is shaken.

1.69.1a   Thucydides describes how Sparta "let" the Athenians fortify their city after the Persian War in 1.89–92.

1.69.5a   The Greeks regularly referred to the Persians as "the Mede"; see note 1.18.1c.

1.70
432/1
SPARTA
The Corinthians characterize the Athenians and the Spartans as opposites: where the Athenians are active, innovative, daring, quick, enterprising, acquisitive, and opportunistic, the Spartans are passive, cautious, conservative, timid, and slow. The Athenians take no rest and allow none to others.

"Besides, we consider that we have as good a right as anyone to point out a neighbor's faults, particularly when we contemplate the great contrast between the two national characters; a contrast of which, as far as we can see, you have little perception, having never yet considered what sort of antagonists you will encounter in the Athenians, how widely, how absolutely different from yourselves. [2] The Athenians are addicted to innovation, and their designs are characterized by swiftness alike in conception and execution; you have a genius for keeping what you have got, accompanied by a total want of invention, and when forced to act you never go far enough. [3] Again, they are adventurous beyond their power, and daring beyond their judgment, and in danger they are sanguine; your wont is to attempt less than is justified by your power, to mistrust even what is sanctioned by your judgment, and to fancy that from danger there is no release. [4] Further, there is promptitude on their side against procrastination on yours; they are never at home, you are most disinclined to leave it, for they hope by their absence to extend their acquisitions, you fear by your advance to endanger what you have left behind. [5] They are swift to follow up a success, and slow to recoil from a reverse. [6] Their bodies they spend ungrudgingly in their country's cause; their intellect they jealously husband to be employed in her service. [7] A scheme unexecuted is with them a positive loss, a successful enterprise a comparative failure. The deficiency created by the miscarriage of an undertaking is soon filled up by fresh hopes; for they alone are enabled to call a thing hoped for a thing got, by the speed with which they act upon their resolutions. [8] Thus they toil on in trouble and danger all the days of their life, with little opportunity for enjoying, being ever engaged in getting: their only idea of a holiday is to do what the occasion demands, and to them laborious occupation is less of a misfortune than the peace of a quiet life. [9] To describe their character in a word, one might truly say that they were born into the world to take no rest themselves and to give none to others."

1.71
432/1
SPARTA
The Corinthians conclude by blaming Sparta's old-fashioned ways for her failure to perceive the effectiveness of Athenian innovation. They beg Sparta "to assist Potidaea now as she had promised." They threaten to seek another alliance if the Spartans continue to fail them.

"Such is Athens, your antagonist. And yet, Spartans, you still delay, and fail to see that peace stays longest with those who are not more careful to use their power justly than to show their determination not to submit to injustice. On the contrary, your ideal of fair dealing is based on the principle that if you do not injure others, you need not risk your own fortunes in preventing others from injuring you. [2] Now you could scarcely have succeeded in such a policy even with a neighbor like yourselves; but in the present instance, as we have just shown, your habits are old-fashioned as compared with theirs. [3] It is the law, as in the arts so in politics, that improvements ever prevail; and though fixed usages may be best for undisturbed communities, constant necessities of action must be accompanied by the constant improvement of methods. Thus it happens that the vast experience of Athens has carried her further than you on the path of innovation."

[4] "Here, at least, let your procrastination end. For the present, assist your allies and Potidaea in particular, as you promised, by a speedy invasion of Attica, and do not sacrifice friends and kindred to their bitterest enemies, and drive the rest of us in despair to some other alliance. [5] Such a step would not be condemned either by the gods who received our oaths, or by the men who witnessed them. The blame for a breach of a treaty cannot be laid on the people whom desertion compels to seek new relations, but on the power that fails to assist its confederate. [6] But if only you will act, we will stand by you; it would be unnatural for us to change, and never should we meet with such a congenial ally. [7] For these reasons choose the right course, and endeavor not to let the Peloponnesus under your supremacy degenerate from the prestige that it enjoyed under that of your ancestors."

Such were the words of the Corinthians. There happened to be Athenian envoys present at Sparta on other business. On hearing the speeches they thought themselves called upon to come before the Spartans. Their intention was not to offer a defense on any of the charges which the cities brought against them, but to show on a comprehensive view that it was not a matter to be hastily decided on, but one that demanded further consideration. There was also a wish to call attention to the great power of Athens, and to refresh the memory of the old and enlighten the ignorance of the young, from a notion that their words might have the effect of inducing them to prefer tranquillity to war. [2] So they came to the Spartans and said that they too, if there was no objection, wished to speak to their assembly. They replied by inviting them to come forward. The Athenians advanced, and spoke as follows:

1.72
432/1
SPARTA
Some Athenian envoys at Sparta ask for permission to address the assembly; it is granted.

"The object of our mission here was not to argue with your allies, but to attend to the matters on which our state despatched us. However, the vehemence of the outcry that we hear against us has prevailed on us to come forward. It is not to combat the accusations of the cities (indeed you are not the judges before whom either we or they can plead), but to prevent your taking the wrong course on matters of great importance by yielding too readily to the persuasions of your allies. We also wish to show on a review of the whole indictment that we have a fair title to our possessions, and that our country has claims to consideration. [2] We need not refer to remote antiquity: there we could appeal to the voice of tradition, but not to the experience of our audience. But to the Persian wars and contem-

1.73
432/1
SPARTA
The Athenians hope to show that their country merits consideration for its achievements, particularly in the Persian wars in which all Hellenes benefited from extraordinary and courageous Athenian efforts.

porary history we must refer, although we are rather tired of continually bringing this subject forward. In our action during that war we ran great risk to obtain certain advantages: you had your share in the solid results, do not try to rob us of all share in the good that the glory may do us. [3] However, the story shall be told not so much to seek to be spared hostility as to testify against it, and to show, if you are so ill-advised as to enter into a struggle with Athens, what sort of an antagonist she is likely to prove. [4] We assert that at Marathon[4a] we were in the forefront of danger and faced the barbarian by ourselves. That when he came the second time, unable to cope with him by land we went on board our ships with all our people, and joined in the action at Salamis.[4b] This prevented his taking the Peloponnesians city by city, and ravaging them with his fleet; when the multitude of his vessels would have made any combination for self-defense impossible. [5] The best proof of this was furnished by the invader himself. Defeated at sea, he considered his power to be no longer what it had been, and retired as speedily as possible with the greater part of his army."

"Such, then, was the result of the matter, and it was clearly proved that it was on the fleet of Hellas that her cause depended. Well, to this result we contributed three very useful elements, namely, the largest number of ships, the ablest commander, and the most unhesitating patriotism. Our contingent of ships was little less than two-thirds of the whole four hundred; the commander was Themistocles, through whom chiefly it was that the battle took place in the straits,[1a] the acknowledged salvation of our cause. Indeed, this was the reason for your receiving him with honors such as had never been accorded to any foreign visitor. [2] While for daring patriotism we had no competitors. Receiving no reinforcements from behind, seeing everything in front of us already subjugated, we had the spirit, after abandoning our city, after sacrificing our property (instead of deserting the remainder of the league or depriving them of our services by dispersing), to throw ourselves into our ships and meet the danger, without a thought of resenting your having neglected to assist us. [3] We assert, therefore, that we conferred on you quite as much as we received. For you had a stake to fight for; the cities which you had left were still filled with your homes, and you had the prospect of enjoying them again; and your coming was prompted quite as much by fear for yourselves as for us; at all events, you never appeared till we had nothing left to lose. But we left behind us a city that was a city no longer, and staked our lives for a city that had an existence

1.74
432/1
SPARTA
The Athenians claim to have provided the most powerful and essential contributions to the Hellenic success at Salamis, which proved to be the decisive blow to the Persian advance. They remind the Spartans that they courageously abandoned their homes and fought on even before the Peloponnesians arrived to help.

1.73.4a   The battle of Marathon in 490: Map 1.11, BX.
1.73.4b   Salamis, site of the decisive naval battle between Greeks and Persians in 480: Map 1.11, BX.

1.74.1a   The Straits of Salamis where the fighting took place: Map 1.11, BX. For more about Themistocles, see 1.90.3–1.93 and 1.135.2–1.138.6.

only in desperate hope, and so bore our full share in your deliverance and in ours. [4] But if we had copied others, and allowed fears for our territory to make us go over to the Mede before you came, or if we had allowed our ruin to break our spirit and prevent us embarking in our ships, your naval inferiority would have made a sea fight unnecessary, and his objects would have been peaceably attained."

"Surely, Spartans, neither by the patriotism that we displayed at that crisis, nor by the wisdom of our counsels, do we merit our extreme unpopularity with the Hellenes, not at least unpopularity for our empire. [2] That empire we acquired not by violence, but because you were unwilling to prosecute to its conclusion the war against the barbarian, and because the allies attached themselves to us and spontaneously asked us to assume the command. [3] And the nature of the case first compelled us to advance our empire to its present height; fear being our principal motive, though honor and interest afterwards came in. [4] And at last, when almost all hated us, when some had already revolted and had been subdued, when you had ceased to be the friends that you once were, and had become objects of suspicion and dislike, it appeared no longer safe to give up our empire; especially as all who left us would fall to you. [5] And no one can quarrel with a people for making, in matters of tremendous risk, the best provision that it can for its interest."

"You, at all events, Spartans, have used your supremacy to settle the states in the Peloponnesus as is agreeable to you. And if at the period of which we were speaking you had persevered to the end of the matter, and had incurred hatred in your command, we are sure that you would have made yourselves just as galling to the allies, and would have been forced to choose between a strong government and danger to yourselves. [2] It follows that it was not a very remarkable action, or contrary to the common practice of mankind, if we did accept an empire that was offered to us, and refused to give it up under the pressure of three of the strongest motives, fear, honor, and interest. And it was not we who set the example, for it has always been the law that the weaker should be subject to the stronger. Besides, we believed ourselves to be worthy of our position, and so you thought us till now, when calculations of interest have made you take up the cry of justice—a consideration which no one ever yet brought forward to hinder his ambition when he had a chance of gaining anything by might. [3] And praise is due to all who, if not so superior to human nature as to refuse dominion, yet respect justice more than their position compels them to do."

1.75
432/1
SPARTA
The Athenians claim that Athens acquired her empire peacefully, honorably, and by the default of Sparta; now it cannot be given up without risk. No state can be faulted for pursuing its own interest.

1.76
432/1
SPARTA
The Athenians argue that Athens acted normally within the common practices of mankind to maintain her empire; fear, honor, and interest motivate her as they would any others in her place. Indeed, she deserves praise for acting with greater justice and moderation than her power would require.

[4] "We imagine that our moderation would be best demonstrated by the conduct of who should be placed in our position; but even our equity has very unreasonably subjected us to condemnation instead of approval."

The Athenians speculate that Sparta would be equally hated were she to take Athens' place, and perhaps more so, because her peculiar institutions render her people unfit to rule other Hellenes.

"Our abatement of our rights in the contract trials with our allies, and our causing them to be decided by impartial laws at Athens, have gained us the character of being litigious. [2] And none care to inquire why this reproach is not brought against other imperial powers, who treat their subjects with less moderation than we do; the secret being that where force can be used, law is not needed. [3] But our subjects are so habituated to associate with us as equals, that any defeat whatever that clashes with their notions of justice, whether it proceeds from a legal judgment or from the power which our empire gives us, makes them forget to be grateful for being allowed to retain most of their possessions, and more vexed at a part being taken, than if we had from the first cast law aside and openly gratified our covetousness. If we had done so, they would not have disputed that the weaker must give way to the stronger. [4] Men's indignation, it seems, is more excited by legal wrong than by violent wrong; the first looks like being cheated by an equal, the second like being compelled by a superior. [5] At all events they contrived to put up with much worse treatment than this from the Persians, yet they think our rule severe, and this is to be expected, for the present always weighs heavy on the conquered. This at least is certain. [6] If you were to succeed in overthrowing us and in taking our place, you would speedily lose the popularity with which fear of us has invested you, if your policy now were to be at all like the sample you gave during the brief period of your command against the Mede. Not only is your life at home regulated by rules and institutions incompatible with those of others, but your citizens abroad act neither on these rules nor on those which are recognized by the rest of Hellas."

In conclusion, the Athenians advise the Spartans to decide carefully, reminding them of the chances of war and noting that the treaty calls for disputes to be submitted to arbitration.

"Take time then in forming your resolution, as the matter is of great importance; and do not be persuaded by the opinions and complaints of others and so bring trouble on yourselves, but consider the vast influence of accident in war, before you are engaged in it. [2] As it continues, it generally becomes an affair of chances, chances from which neither of us is exempt, and whose event we must risk in the dark. [3] It is a common mistake in going to war to begin at the wrong end, to act first, and wait for disaster to discuss the matter. [4] But we are not yet by any means so misguided, nor, so far as we can see, are you; accordingly, while it is still open to us both to choose aright, we bid you not to dissolve the treaty, or to break your oaths, but to have our differences settled by arbitration according to our agreement. Or else we take the gods who heard the oaths to witness, and if you begin hostilities, whatever line of action you choose, we will endeavor to defend ourselves against you."

Such were the words of the Athenians. After the Spartans had heard the complaints of the allies against the Athenians, and the observations of the latter, they made all withdraw, and consulted by themselves on the question before them. [2] The opinions of the majority all led to the same conclusion; the Athenians were open aggressors, and war must be declared at once. But Archidamus, the Spartan king, who had the reputation of being at once a wise and a moderate man, came forward and made the following speech:

> 1.79
> 432/1
> SPARTA
> The Spartans declare the Athenians to be aggressors.

"I have not lived so long, Spartans, without having had the experience of many wars, and I see those among you of the same age as myself, who will not fall into the common misfortune of longing for war from inexperience or from a belief in its advantage and its safety. [2] This, the war on which you are now debating, would be one of the greatest magnitude, on a sober consideration of the matter. [3] In a struggle with Peloponnesians and neighbors our strength is of the same character, and it is possible to move swiftly on the different points. But a struggle with a people who live in a distant land, who have also an extraordinary familiarity with the sea, and who are in the highest state of preparation in every other department; with wealth private and public, with ships, and horses, and hoplites, and a population such as no one other Hellenic place can equal, and lastly a large number of tributary allies—what can justify us in rashly beginning such a struggle? Wherein is our trust that we should rush on it unprepared? [4] Is it in our ships? There we are inferior; while if we are to practice and become a match for them, time must intervene. Is it in our money? There we have a far greater deficiency. We neither have it in our treasury, nor are we ready to contribute it from our private funds."

> 1.80
> 432/1
> SPARTA
> The Spartan king, Archidamus, warns the Spartans that Athens is a powerful adversary with many advantages in war. He advises them to prepare carefully for such a struggle and not to act rashly.

"Confidence might possibly be felt in our superiority in hoplites and population, which will enable us to invade and devastate their lands. [2] But the Athenians have plenty of other land in their empire, and can import what they want by sea. [3] Again, if we are to attempt an insurrection of their allies, these will have to be supported with a fleet, most of them being islanders. [4] What then is to be our war? For unless we can either beat them at sea, or deprive them of the revenues which feed their navy, we shall meet with little but disaster. [5] Meanwhile our honor will be pledged to keeping on, particularly if it be the opinion that we began the quarrel. [6]

> 1.81
> 432/1
> SPARTA
> Archidamus points out that Sparta can only devastate Attica, which will not harm Athens materially. He warns that the war will not be short, and wonders aloud how Sparta can win.

For let us never be elated by the fatal hope of the war being quickly ended by the devastation of their lands. I fear rather that we may leave it as a legacy to our children; so improbable is it that the Athenian spirit will be the slave of their land, or Athenian experience be cowed by war."

"Not that I would bid you be so unfeeling as to suffer them to injure your allies, and to refrain from unmasking their intrigues; but I do bid you not to take up arms at once, but to send and remonstrate with them in a tone not too suggestive of war, nor again too suggestive of submission, and to employ the interval in perfecting our own preparations. The means will be, first, the acquisition of allies, Hellenic or barbarian it matters not, so long as they are an accession to our strength naval or financial—I say Hellenic or barbarian, because the odium of such an accession to all who like us are the objects of the designs of the Athenians is taken away by the law of self-preservation[1a]—and secondly the development of our home resources. [2] If they listen to our embassy, so much the better; but if not, after the lapse of two or three years our position will have become materially strengthened, and we can then attack them if we think proper. [3] Perhaps by that time the sight of our preparations, backed by language equally significant, will have disposed them to submission, while their land is still untouched, and while their counsels may be directed to the retention of advantages as yet undestroyed. [4] For the only light in which you can view their land is that of a hostage in your hands, a hostage the more valuable the better it is cultivated. This you ought to spare as long as possible, and not make them desperate, and so increase the difficulty of dealing with them. [5] For if while still unprepared, hurried on by the complaints of our allies, we are induced to lay it waste, have a care that we do not bring deep disgrace and deep perplexity upon the Peloponnesus. [6] Complaints, whether of communities or individuals, it is possible to adjust; but war undertaken by a coalition for sectional interests, whose progress there is no means of foreseeing, may not be easily or creditably settled."

"And none need think it cowardice for a large number of confederates to pause before they attack a single city. [2] The Athenians have allies as numerous as our own, and allies that pay tribute, and war is a matter not so much of arms as of money, which makes arms of use. And this is more than ever true in a struggle between a continental and a maritime power. [3] First, then, let us provide money, and not allow ourselves to be carried away by the talk of our allies before we have done so: as we shall have the largest share of respon-

1.82
432/1
SPARTA
Archidamus advises Sparta to continue discussions with Athens and to use the time thus gained to gather allies and to develop its resources for war. Such preparations might induce the Athenians to submit, but if not, Sparta will enter the war much strengthened.

1.83
432/1
SPARTA
Archidamus asserts that Sparta must accumulate money for a war with Athens.

1.82.1a Archidamus here proposes an approach to Persia for aid against Athens. For more on early diplomatic contacts between   Sparta and Persia, see 2.7.1, 2.67.1, and 4.50.2.

sibility for the consequences be they good or bad, we have also a right to a tranquil inquiry respecting them."

"And the slowness and procrastination, the parts of our character that are most assailed by their criticism, need not make you blush. If we undertake the war without preparation, we should by hastening its commencement only delay its conclusion: further, a free and a famous city has through all time been ours. [2] The quality which they condemn is really nothing but a wise moderation; thanks to its possession, we alone do not become insolent in success and give way less than others in misfortune; we are not carried away by the pleasure of hearing ourselves cheered on to risks which our judgment condemns; nor, if annoyed, are we any the more convinced by attempts to exasperate us by accusation. [3] We are both warlike and wise, and it is our sense of order that makes us so. We are warlike, because self-control contains honor as a chief constituent, and honor bravery. And we are wise, because we are educated with too little learning to despise the laws, and with too severe a self-control to disobey them, and are brought up not to be too knowing in useless matters—such as the knowledge which can give a specious criticism of an enemy's plans in theory, but fails to assail them with equal success in practice—but are taught to consider that the schemes of our enemies are not dissimilar to our own, and that the freaks of chance are not determinable by calculation. [4] In practice we always base our preparations against an enemy on the assumption that his plans are good; indeed, it is right to rest our hopes not on a belief in his blunders, but on the soundness of our provisions. Nor ought we to believe that there is much difference between man and man, but to think that the superiority lies with him who is reared in the severest school."

"These practices, then, which our ancestors have delivered to us, and by whose maintenance we have always profited, must not be given up. And we must not be hurried into deciding in a day's brief space a question which concerns many lives and fortunes and many cities, and in which honor is deeply involved—but we must decide calmly. This our strength peculiarly enables us to do. [2] As for the Athenians, send to them on the matter of Potidaea, send on the matter of the alleged wrongs of the allies, particularly as they are prepared to submit matters to arbitration, for one should not proceed against a party who offers arbitration as one would against a wrongdoer. Meanwhile do not omit preparation for war. This decision will be the best for yourselves and the most terrible to your opponents."

1.84
432/1
SPARTA
Archidamus tells Sparta to ignore her allies' impatient calls for action and to move slowly and moderately. He praises Spartan character, a product of practical, limited education, and adds that Sparta traditionally assumes that her adversaries will plan wisely and not blunder.

1.85
432/1
SPARTA
Archidamus concludes that the Spartans must decide calmly. He reminds them that Athens offers arbitration, but asks them to continue to prepare for war.

[3] Such were the words of Archidamus. Last came forward Sthenelaidas, one of the *ephors*[3a] for that year, and spoke to the Spartans as follows:

1.86
432/1
SPARTA
The Spartan ephor
Sthenelaidas demands a dec-
laration of war against
Athens.

"The long speech of the Athenians I do not pretend to understand. They said a good deal in praise of themselves, but nowhere denied that they are injuring our allies and the Peloponnesus. And yet if they behaved well against the Persians in the past, but ill toward us now, they deserve double punishment for having ceased to be good and for having become bad. [2] We meanwhile are the same then and now, and shall not, if we are wise, disregard the wrongs of our allies, or put off till tomorrow the duty of assisting those who must suffer today. [3] Others have much money and ships and horses, but we have good allies whom we must not give up to the Athenians, nor by lawsuits and words decide the matter, as it is anything but in word that we are harmed, but render instant and powerful help. [4] And let us not be told that it is fitting for us to deliberate under injustice; long deliberation is rather fitting for those who have injustice in contemplation. [5] Vote therefore, Spartans, for war, as the honor of Sparta demands, and neither allow the further aggrandizement of Athens, nor betray our allies to ruin, but with the gods let us advance against the aggressors."

1.87
432/1
SPARTA
The Spartans vote by acclamation to declare war and to
convene a decisive meeting
of all their allies.

With these words he, as ephor, himself put the question to the assembly of the Spartans. [2] He said that he could not determine which was the loudest acclamation (their mode of decision is by acclamation, not by voting); the fact being that he wished to make them declare their opinion openly and thus to increase their ardor for war. Accordingly he said, "All Spartans who are of opinion that the treaty has been broken, and that Athens is guilty, leave your seats and go there," pointing out a certain place; "all who are of the opposite opinion, there." [3] They accordingly stood up and divided; and those who held that the treaty had been broken were in a decided majority. [4] Summoning the allies, they told them that their opinion was that Athens had been guilty of injustice, but that they wished to convoke all the allies and put it to the vote; in order that they might make war, if they decided to do so, on a common resolution.[4a] [5] Having thus gained their point, the delegates returned home at once; the Athenian envoys a little later, when they had dispatched the objects of their mission. [6] This decision of the assembly[6a] judging that the treaty had been broken, was made in the fourteenth year of the Thirty Years' Peace,[6b] which was entered into after the affair of Euboea.[6c]

1.85.3a   Spartan *ephors* were powerful government officials; see Appendix C, Sparta, §5–6.
1.87.4a   See Appendix D, The Peloponnesian League, §5, for the League congress.
1.87.6a   See Appendix C, Spartan Institutions, §6.
1.87.6b   The Thirty Years' Peace was sworn in 446/5, which dates this assembly to 432/1.
1.87.6c   The "affair" of Euboea refers to its revolt from Athens, described by Thucydides in 1.114.1. See Appendix K, Calendars and Dating Systems, §2–3.

The Spartans voted that the treaty had been broken, and that war must be declared, not so much because they were persuaded by the arguments of the allies, as because they feared the growth of the power of the Athenians, seeing most of Hellas already subject to them.

The way in which Athens came to be placed in the circumstances under which her power grew was this. [2] After the Persians had returned from Europe, defeated by sea and land by the Hellenes, and after those of them who had fled with their ships to Mycale[2a] had been destroyed, Leotychides, king of the Spartans, the commander of the Hellenes at Mycale, departed home with the allies from the Peloponnesus. But the Athenians and the allies from Ionia[2b] and Hellespont,[2c] who had now revolted from the King, remained and laid siege to Sestos,[2d] which was still held by the Persians. After wintering before it, they became masters of the place on its evacuation by the barbarians; and after this they sailed away from Hellespont to their respective cities. [3] Meanwhile the Athenian people, after the departure of the barbarian from their country, at once proceeded to bring over their children and wives, and such property as they had left, from the places where they had deposited them, and prepared to rebuild their city and their walls. For only isolated portions of the circumference had been left standing, and most of the houses were in ruins; though a few remained, in which the Persian grandees had taken up their quarters.

Perceiving what they were going to do, the Spartans sent an embassy to Athens. They would have themselves preferred to see neither her nor any other city in possession of a wall; though here they acted principally at the instigation of their allies, who were alarmed at the strength of her newly acquired navy, and the valor which she had displayed in the war with the Persians. [2] They begged her not only to abstain from building walls for herself, but also to join them in throwing down the remaining walls of the cities outside the Peloponnesus. They did not express openly the suspicious intention with regard to the Athenians that lay behind this proposal but urged that by these means the barbarians, in the case of a third invasion, would not have any strong place, such as in this invasion he had in Thebes,[2a] for his base of operation; and that the Peloponnesus would suffice for all as a base both for retreat and offense. [3] After the Spartans had thus spoken, they were, on the advice of Themistocles, immediately dismissed by the Athenians, with the answer that ambassadors should be sent to Sparta to discuss the question. Themistocles told the Athenians to send him off with all speed to Lacedaemon, but not to despatch his colleagues as soon as they had selected them, but to wait until they had raised their wall to the height from which defense was possible. Meanwhile the whole popu-

1.88
431
SPARTA
Fearing Athen's growing power, Sparta votes for war.

1.89
479/8
PENTECONTAETIA[1a]
HELLESPONT
Thucydides tells how Athens grew powerful after Persia's defeat.

1.90
479/8
ATHENS
Sparta asks Athens not to rebuild its city wall. Themistocles goes to Sparta to discuss the matter and to delay a Spartan response while the Athenians hastily build a new city wall.

1.89.1a Book 1, chapters 89 to 117, are commonly referred to as the "Pentecontaetia," the latinized version of "Pentekontaetea," which is Greek for "The Fifty Years" covering the period between the withdrawal of the Persians from Greece in 479 and the commencement of the Peloponnesian War in 431.

1.89.2a The Greek victory at Mycale (near Mt. Mycale, Map 1.99, BY) took place in 479.
1.89.2b Ionia: Map 1.99, BY.
1.89.2c Hellespont: Map 1.99, AY.
1.89.2d Sestos: Map 1.99, AY.
1.90.2a Thebes: Map 1.99, BX.

lation in the city was to labor at the wall, the Athenians, their wives, and their children, sparing no edifice, private or public, which might be of any use to the work, but throwing all down. [4] After giving these instructions, and adding that he would be responsible for all other matters there, he departed. [5] Arrived at Sparta he did not seek an audience with the magistrates, but tried to gain time and made excuses. When any of the authorities asked him why he did not appear in the assembly, he would say that he was waiting for his colleagues, who had been detained in Athens by some engagement; however, that he expected their speedy arrival, and wondered that they were yet there.

At first the Spartans trusted the words of Themistocles, through their friendship for him; but when others arrived, all distinctly declaring that the work was going on and already attaining some elevation, they could not fail to believe them. [2] Aware of this, he told them that rumors are deceptive, and should not be trusted; they should send some reputable persons from Sparta to inspect, whose report might be trusted. [3] They despatched them accordingly. Concerning these Themistocles secretly sent word to the Athenians to detain them as far as possible without putting them under open constraint, and not to let them go until they had themselves returned. For his colleagues had now joined him, Abronichus son of Lysicles, and Aristides son of Lysimachus, with the news that the wall was sufficiently advanced; and he feared that when the Spartans heard the facts, they might refuse to let them go. [4] So the Athenians detained the envoys according to his message, and Themistocles had an audience with the Spartans and at last openly told them that Athens was now fortified sufficiently to protect its inhabitants; that any embassy which the Spartans or their allies might wish to send to them should in future proceed on the assumption that the people to whom they were going was able to distinguish both its own and the general interests; [5] that when the Athenians thought fit to abandon their city and to embark in their ships, they ventured on that perilous step without consulting them, and that on the other hand, wherever they had deliberated with the Spartans, they had proved themselves to be in judgment second to none; [6] and that they now thought it fit that their city should have a wall, and that this would be more for the advantage of both the citizens of Athens and the Hellenic confederacy, [7] for without equal military strength it was impossible to contribute equal or fair counsel to the common interest. It followed, he observed, either that all the members of the confederacy should be without walls, or that the present step should be considered a right one.[7a]

1.91
479/8
SPARTA
Themistocles' stratagem succeeds. After the wall is completed, Themistocles tells Sparta that Athens will look after her own interests.

ILLUSTRATION 1.90
BUST OF THEMISTOCLES
(A ROMAN COPY, POSSIBLY
OF A GREEK ORIGINAL)

1.91.7a　It might be noted here that Sparta, alone
　　　　 among important Greek cities, had no
　　　　 defensive wall in 479.

The Spartans did not betray any open signs of anger against the Athenians at what they heard. The embassy, it seems, was prompted not by a desire to obstruct, but to guide the counsels of their government: besides, Spartan feeling was at that time very friendly toward Athens on account of the patriotism which she had displayed in the struggle with the Mede. Still the defeat of their wishes could not but cause them secret annoyance. The envoys of each state departed home without complaint.

In this way the Athenians walled their city in a short space of time. [2] To this day the building shows signs of the haste of its execution; the foundations are laid of stones of all kinds, and in some places not wrought or fitted, but placed just in the order in which they were brought by the different hands; and many columns, too, from tombs and sculptured stones were put in with the rest.[2a] For the bounds of the city were extended at every point of the circumference; and so they laid hands on everything without exception in their haste. [3] Themistocles also persuaded them to finish the walls of the Piraeus,[3a] which had been begun before, in his year of office as *archon*;[3b] being influenced alike by the fineness of a locality that has three natural harbors, and by the great start which the Athenians would gain in the acquisition of power by becoming a naval people. [4] For he first ventured to tell them to stick to the sea and forthwith began to lay the foundations of the empire. [5] It was by his advice, too, that they built the walls of that thickness which can still be discerned round the Piraeus, the stones being brought up by two wagons meeting each other. Between the walls thus formed there was neither rubble nor mortar, but great stones hewn square and fitted together, cramped to each other on the outside with iron and lead. About half the height that he intended was finished. [6] His idea was by their size and thickness to keep off the attacks of an enemy; he thought that they might be adequately defended by a small garrison of invalids, and the rest be freed for service in the fleet. [7] For the fleet claimed most of his attention. He saw, as I think, that the approach by sea was easier for the King's army than that by land: he also thought the Piraeus more valuable than the upper city; indeed, he was always advising the Athenians, if a day should come when they were hard pressed by land, to go down into the Piraeus, and defy the world with their fleet. In this way, therefore, the Athenians completed their wall, and commenced their other buildings immediately after the retreat of the Persians.[7a]

Meanwhile Pausanias son of Cleombrotus was sent out from Sparta as commander-in-chief of the Hellenes, with twenty ships from the Peloponnesus. With him sailed the Athenians with thirty ships, and a number of the other allies. [2] They made an expedition against Cyprus[2a] and sub-

1.92
478
SPARTA
Sparta accepts the Athenian wall with outward grace but secret annoyance.

1.93
478
ATHENS
Themistocles fortifies the Piraeus, foreseeing that Athens would grow great through naval power.

1.94
478
HELLESPONT
Pausanias leads a fleet against Cyprus and Byzantium.

1.93.2a Sections of this "Themistoclean" wall that clearly display the signs of hasty construction mentioned here by Thucydides have been found by archeologists.

1.93.3a For the location of the Piraeus in relation to Athens, see Map 1.107, inset.

1.93.3b For *archon*, see Glossary and Appendix A, The Athenian Government, §6.

1.93.7a Thucydides recounts the end of Themistocles' career in 1.135.2–38.6.

1.94.2a Cyprus: Map 1.99, locator.

Pausanias grows arrogant and unpopular. Spartan leadership at sea is rejected by the allies in favor of Athens. Sparta accepts this decision.

dued most of the island, and afterwards against Byzantium,[2b] which was in the hands of the Persians, and compelled it to surrender. This event took place while the Spartans were still supreme. [1.95.1] But the violence of Pausanias had already begun to be disagreeable to the Hellenes, particularly to the Ionians and the newly liberated populations. These resorted to the Athenians and requested them as their kinsmen to become their leaders, and to stop any attempt at violence on the part of Pausanias. [2] The Athenians accepted their overtures, and determined to put down any attempt of the kind and to settle everything else as their interests might seem to demand. [3] In the meantime the Spartans recalled Pausanias for an investigation of the reports which had reached them. Manifold and grave accusations had been brought against him by Hellenes arriving in Sparta; and, to all appearance, his conduct seemed more like that of a despot than of a general. [4] As it happened, his recall came just at the time when the hatred which he had inspired had induced the allies to desert him, the soldiers from the Peloponnesus excepted, and to range themselves by the side of the Athenians. [5] On his arrival at Lacedaemon, he was censured for his private acts of oppression, but was acquitted on the heaviest counts and pronounced not guilty; it must be known that the charge of Medism formed one of the principal, and to all appearance one of the best-founded, articles against him.[5a] [6] The Spartans did not, however, restore him to his command, but sent out Dorkis and certain others with a small force; who found the allies no longer inclined to concede to them the command. [7] Perceiving this they departed, and the Spartans did not send out any to succeed them. They feared for those who went out a deterioration similar to that observable in Pausanias; besides, they desired to be rid of the war against the Persians, and were satisfied of the competency of the Athenians for the position, and of their friendship at the time toward themselves.

Athens forms a new anti-Persian alliance.

The Athenians having thus succeeded to the supremacy by the voluntary act of the allies through their hatred of Pausanias, determined which cities were to contribute money against the barbarian, and which ships; their professed object being to retaliate for their sufferings by ravaging the King's country. [2] Now was the time that the office of "Treasurers for Hellas" was first instituted by the Athenians. These officers received the tribute, as the money contributed was called. The tribute was first fixed at four hundred and sixty talents.[2a] The common treasury was at

1.94.2b Byzantium: Map 1.99, locator.
1.95.5a Greeks who submitted to the Persians, or who otherwise joined or assisted them, were accused of "Medism." Thucydides describes the end of Pausanias' career in 1.128–34.
1.96.2a Treasurers for Hellas, *Hellenotamiai;* see Appendix B, The Athenian Empire, §10. For the initial tribute, see Appendix B, §2. A talent is a unit of weight and money; see Appendix J, Classical Greek Currency, §5.

Delos,[2b] and the congresses were held in the temple.

Initially, the Athenians commanded autonomous allies and made their decisions in general congresses. Their supremacy grew during the interval between the present war and the Persian wars, through their military and political actions recounted below against the barbarians, against their own allies in revolt, and against the Peloponnesians whom they encountered on various occasions. [2] My reason for relating these events, and for venturing on this digression, is that this passage of history has been omitted by all my predecessors, who have confined themselves either to Hellenic history before the Persian wars, or to the Persian wars itself. Hellanicus, it is true, did touch on these events in his Athenian history;[2a] but he is somewhat concise and not accurate in his dates. Besides, the history of these events contains an explanation of the growth of the Athenian empire.

First, under the command of Cimon son of Miltiades, the Athenians besieged and captured Eion[1b] on the Strymon[1c] from the Persians, and made slaves of the inhabitants. [2] Next they enslaved Scyros[2a] the island in the Aegean, containing a Dolopian population, and colonized it themselves. [3] This was followed by a war against Carystus,[3a] in which the rest of Euboea[3b] remained neutral, and which was ended by surrender on conditions. [4] After this Naxos[4a] left the confederacy, and a war ensued, and she had to return after a siege; this was the first instance of the confederation being forced to subjugate an allied city,[4b] a precedent which was followed by that of the rest in the order which circumstances prescribed.

Of all the causes of defection, that connected with arrears of tribute and vessels, and with failure of service, was the chief; for the Athenians were very severe and exacting, and made themselves offensive by applying the screw of necessity to men who were not used to and in fact not disposed for any continuous labor. [2] In some other respects the Athenians were not the old popular rulers they had been at first; and if they had more than their fair share of service, it was correspondingly easy for them to reduce any that tried to leave the confederacy. [3] For this the allies had themselves to blame; the wish to get off service making most of them arrange to pay their share of the expense in money instead of in ships, and so to avoid having to leave their homes. Thus while Athens was increasing her navy with the funds which they contributed, a revolt always found them without resources or experience for war.

1.97
477–31
HELLAS
Thucydides describes the growth of Athenian power, noting that no other historian has covered this topic adequately.

1.98
476–67[1a]
AEGEAN AREA
Athens' new alliance attacks Eion, Scyros, and Carystus, and defeats a revolt by Naxos.

1.99
AEGEAN AREA
Athens grows less popular as it strictly requires military and monetary contributions to the alliance.

1.96.2b Delos: Map 1.99, BY.
1.97.2a Hellanicus published his *Atthis* after 406, and this allusion has generally been seen as an indication that these chapters on the growth of the Athenian empire from 480 to 431 (the Pentecontaetia) were written after Thucydides' return from exile in 404.
1.98.1a The chronology of the Pentecontaetia is much debated; the dates here aim to cover possibilities rather than record agreed facts.
1.98.1b Eion: Map 1.99, AX.
1.98.1c Strymon River: Map 1.99, AX.
1.98.2a Scyros: Map 1.99, AY.
1.98.3a Carystus: Map 1.99, BY.
1.98.3b Euboea: Map 1.99, AX.
1.98.4a Naxos: Map 1.99, BY.
1.98.4b Dates here are very difficult to establish, but one would not be far wrong to place the capture of Eion in 476; the campaign against Carystus in 474 (?); and the revolt of Naxos and its suppression in 471–70 (though some have assigned it to 468–67).

MAP 1.99 DELIAN LEAGUE OPERATIONS

1.100
467?
ASIA
The Persians are defeated on the Eurymedon River.
465?
THRACE
Thasos revolts. The Athenians are defeated at Amphipolis.

Next we come to the actions by land and by sea at the river Eurymedon,[1a] between the Athenians with their allies, and the Persians, when the Athenians won both battles on the same day under the leadership of Cimon son of Miltiades, and captured and destroyed the whole Phoenician fleet, consisting of two hundred vessels. [2] Some time afterwards occurred the defection of the Thasians, caused by disagreements about the markets on the opposite coast of Thrace, and about the mine in their possession. Sailing with a fleet to Thasos,[2a] the Athenians defeated them at sea and effected a landing on the island. [3] About the same time they sent ten thousand settlers of their own citizens and the allies to settle the place then called Ennea Hodoi (or Nine Ways), now Amphipolis.[3a] They succeeded in gaining possession of Ennea Hodoi from the Edonians, but on advancing

1.100.1a The battles on the Eurymedon River (Map 1.99, locator), can be dated no closer than the years 469–66.
1.100.2a The secession of Thasos (Map 1.99, AY) is estimated to have taken place in 466–5 and to have ended three years later in 463–2.
1.100.3a Ennea Hodoi: Amphipolis on Map 1.99, AX. This failure to establish a colony at

Ennea Hodoi probably occurred in 465–64.

into the interior of Thrace were cut off in Drabescus,[3b] a city of the Edonians, by the assembled Thracians, who regarded the settlement of the place Ennea Hodoi as an act of hostility.

Meanwhile the Thasians being defeated in the field and suffering siege, appealed to Sparta, and desired her to assist them by an invasion of Attica. [2] Unknown to the Athenians, she promised and intended to do so, but was prevented by the occurrence of the earthquake, accompanied by the secession of the Helots[2a] and the Thuriats[2b] and Aethaeans[2c] of the *perioikoi* to Ithome.[2d] Most of the Helots were the descendants of the old Messenians that were enslaved in the famous war;[2e] and so all of them came to be called Messenians. [3] The Spartans thus being engaged in a war with the rebels in Ithome, the Thasians in the third year of the siege obtained terms from the Athenians by razing their walls, delivering up their ships, and arranging to pay the moneys demanded at once, and tribute in future; giving up their possessions on the mainland together with the mine.

The Spartans meanwhile finding the war against the rebels in Ithome was likely to be a long one, invoked the aid of their allies, and especially of the Athenians, who came in some force under the command of Cimon. [2] The reason for this pressing summons lay in their reputed skill in siege operations; a long siege had taught the Spartans their own deficiency in this art, else they would have taken the place by assault. [3] The first open quarrel between the Spartans and Athenians arose out of this expedition. The Spartans, when an assault failed to take the place, apprehensive of the enterprising and revolutionary character of the Athenians, and further looking upon them as of alien extraction, began to fear that if they remained, they might be persuaded by the besieged in Ithome to attempt some political changes. They accordingly dismissed them alone of the allies, without declaring their suspicions, but merely saying that they had now no need of them. [4] But the Athenians, aware that their dismissal did not proceed from the more honorable reason of the two, but from suspicions which had been conceived, went away deeply offended, and conscious of having done nothing to merit such treatment from the Spartans; and the instant that they returned home they broke off the alliance[4a] which had been made against the Mede, and allied themselves with Sparta's enemy Argos;[4b] each of the contracting parties taking the same oaths and making the same alliance with the Thessalians.[4c]

1.101
466–62?
SPARTA
Promised Spartan aid to Thasos is prevented by earthquake and Helot revolt. Thasos surrenders on terms.

1.102
462–61?
MESSENE
Athens sends troops to help the Spartans fight the Helots. When they are rudely dismissed, Athens renounces her alliance with Sparta.

1.100.3b Drabescus and the general location of Edonia: Map 1.99, AX.
1.101.2a The earthquake and the simultaneous revolt of the Helots occurred in 465–64. For information regarding the Spartan Helots and *perioikoi*, see Appendix C, Spartan Institutions, §3, 9.
1.101.2b Thuria in Messenia: Map 1.107, BX.
1.101.2c Aethaea: site unknown, but presumably not far from Thuria.

1.101.2d Mount Ithome, site of the ancient capital of Messenia: Map 1.107, BX.
1.101.2e The Messenian war, about 720 B.C.? See Appendix C, Spartan Institutions §3.
1.102.4a The "alliance" in this case is the Hellenic Alliance against Persia, not the Peloponnesian League.
1.102.4b Argos: Map 1.107, BY.
1.102.4c Thessaly: Map 1.99, AX.

1.103
457–56
MESSENE
Given permission to leave Laconia, the Helots surrender and are settled in Naupactus by the Athenians.
MEGARA
A dispute with Corinth leads Megara to ally herself with Athens.

Meanwhile the rebels in Ithome, unable to prolong further a ten[1a] years' resistance, surrendered to Sparta; the conditions being that they should depart from the Peloponnesus under safe conduct, and should never set foot in it again: [2] anyone who might hereafter be found there was to be the slave of his captor. It must be known that the Spartans had an old oracle from Delphi,[2a] to the effect that they should let go the suppliant of Zeus at Ithome.[2b] [3] So they went forth with their children and their wives, and being received by Athens because of the hatred that she now felt for the Spartans, were located at Naupactus,[3a] which she had lately taken from the Ozolian Locrians.[3b] [4] The Athenians received another addition to their confederacy in the Megarians;[4a] who left the Spartan alliance, annoyed by a war about boundaries forced on them by Corinth.[4b] The Athenians occupied Megara and Pegae,[4c] and built for the Megarians their long walls from the city to Nisaea,[4d] in which they placed an Athenian garrison. This was the principal cause of the Corinthians conceiving such a deadly hatred against Athens.

1.104
460?
EGYPT
An Athenian fleet sails to Egypt to assist a revolt there against the Persians.

Meanwhile Inaros son of Psammetichus, a Libyan king of the Libyans on the Egyptian border, having his headquarters at Marea,[1a] the city above Pharos, caused a revolt of almost the whole of Egypt[1b] from King Artaxerxes, and placing himself at its head, invited the Athenians to his assistance. [2] Abandoning a Cyprian[2a] expedition upon which they happened to be engaged with two hundred ships of their own and their allies, the Athenians arrived in Egypt and sailed from the sea into the Nile,[2b] made themselves masters of the river and two-thirds of Memphis,[2c] and addressed themselves to the attack of the remaining third, which is called White Castle. Within it were Persians and Medes who had taken refuge there, and Egyptians who had not joined the rebellion.

1.105
459?
TROEZEN
An Athenian attack on Halieis is repelled, but the Peloponnesian fleet is defeated off Cecryphalia.
458?
AEGINA
Athens defeats the Aeginetans at sea and besieges their city.
MEGARID
A Corinthian attack on Megara is stopped by a reserve Athenian army.

At this time, other Athenians, making a descent from their fleet upon Halieis,[1a] were engaged by a force of Corinthians and Epidaurians;[1b] and the Corinthians were victorious. Afterwards the Athenians engaged the Peloponnesian fleet off Cecryphalia;[1c] and the Athenians were victorious. [2] Subsequently, war broke out between Aegina[2a] and Athens, and there was a great battle at sea off Aegina between the Athenians and Aeginetans, each being aided by their allies; in which victory remained with the Athenians, who took seventy of the enemy's ships, and landed in the country and commenced a siege under the command of Leocrates son of Stroebus. [3] Upon this the Peloponnesians,[3a] desirous of aiding the Aeginetans, threw

1.103.1a Thucydides is thought by many to have written here "four" instead of "ten."
1.103.2a Delphi: Map 1.107, AY.
1.103.2b Mt. Ithome: Map 1.107, BX.
1.103.3a Naupactus: Map 1.107, AX.
1.103.3b Ozolian Locris: Map 1.107, AX.
1.103.4a Megara: Map 1.107, AY.
1.103.4b Corinth: Map 1.107, AY.
1.103.4c Pegae: Map 1.107, AY.
1.103.4d Nisaea: Map 1.107, AY.
1.104.1a Marea, Egypt: Map 1.110.
1.104.1b Egypt: Map 1.110.
1.104.2a Cyprus: Map 1.110.

1.104.2b Nile River: Map 1.110.
1.104.2c Memphis on the Nile: Map 1.110.
1.105.1a Halieis: Map 1.107, BY.
1.105.1b Epidaurus: Map 1.107, BY.
1.105.1c Cecryphalia: Map 1.107, AY. This action (in 459?) was apparently the initial hostility of what is now called the "First Peloponnesian War" between Sparta and Athens.
1.105.2a Aegina: Map 1.107, AY.
1.105.3a The "Peloponnesians" in this case is probably the Peloponnesian League. See Appendix D, The Peloponnesian League.

into Aegina a force of three hundred hoplites, who had before been serving with the Corinthians and Epidaurians. Meanwhile the Corinthians and their allies occupied the heights of Geraneia,[3b] and marched down into the Megarid, in the belief that with a large force absent in Aegina and Egypt, Athens would be unable to help the Megarians without raising the siege of Aegina. [4] But the Athenians, instead of moving the army at Aegina, raised a force of the old and young men that had been left in the city, and marched into the Megarid under the command of Myronides. [5] After a drawn battle with the Corinthians, the rival hosts parted, each with the impression that they had gained the victory. [6] The Athenians, however, if anything, had rather the advantage, and on the departure of the Corinthians set up a trophy. Urged by the taunts of the elders in their city, the Corinthians made their preparations, and about twelve days afterwards came and set up their trophy as victors. Sallying out from Megara, the Athenians destroyed the party that was employed in erecting the trophy, and engaged and defeated the rest.

In the retreat of the vanquished army, a considerable division, pressed by the pursuers and mistaking the road, dashed into a field on some private property, with a deep trench all round it and no way out. [2] Being acquainted with the place, the Athenians hemmed their front with hoplites, and placing the light troops round in a circle, stoned all who had gone in. Corinth here suffered a severe blow. The bulk of her army continued its retreat home.

About this time the Athenians began to build the long walls to the sea, that toward Phalerum and that toward the Piraeus.[1a] [2] Meanwhile the Phocians[2a] made an expedition against Doris,[2b] the old home of the Spartans, containing the cities of Boeum,[2c] Cytinium,[2d] and Erineum.[2e] They had taken one of these cities, when the Spartans under Nicomedes son of Cleombrotus, commanding for King Pleistoanax son of Pausanias, who was still a minor, came to the aid of the Dorians with fifteen hundred hoplites of their own, and ten thousand of their allies. After compelling the Phocians to restore the city on conditions, they began their retreat. [3] The route by sea across the Crisaean gulf[3a] exposed them to the risk of being stopped by the Athenian fleet; that by land across Geraneia[3b] seemed scarcely safe with the Athenians holding Megara and Pegae,[3c] for the pass was a difficult one, and was always guarded by the Athenians; and in the present instance, the Spartans had information that they meant to dispute

1.106
458?
MEGARID
A division of Corinthians is destroyed.

1.107
457
ATHENS
Athens begins work on the Long Walls.
PHOCIS
A Spartan army rescues Doris from Phocis but retires to Boeotia when the routes home are blocked.
BOEOTIA
The Athenian army advances to engage the Peloponnesians; Thessalian cavalry joins them but defects during the battle.

1.105.3b Mount Geraneia: Map 1.107, AY.
1.107.1a Athenian "Long Walls" to Piraeus, and "Phaleric Wall" to Phalerum: Map 1.107, Athens inset.
1.107.2a Phocis: Map 1.107, AY.
1.107.2b Doris: Map 1.107, AY.
1.107.2c Boeum, possible location: Map 1.107, AX.
1.107.2d Cytinium: Map 1.107, AY.
1.107.2e Erineum, possible location: Map 1.107, AX.
1.107.3a Crisaean Gulf: Map 1.107, AY.

1.107.3b Mount Geraneia: Map 1.107, AY.
1.107.3c Pegae: Map 1.107, AY.

MAP 1.107 THE "FIRST PELOPONNESIAN WAR"

their passage. [4] So they resolved to remain in Boeotia,[4a] and to consider which would be the safest line of march. They had also another reason for this resolve. Secret encouragement had been given them by a party in Athens, who hoped to put an end to the reign of democracy[4b] and the building of the long walls. [5] Meanwhile the Athenians marched against them with their whole levy and a thousand Argives and the respective contingents of the rest of their allies. Altogether they were fourteen thousand strong. [6] The march was prompted by the notion that the Spartans were at a loss how to effect their passage, and also by suspicions of an attempt to overthrow the democracy. [7] Some cavalry also joined the Athenians from their Thessalian allies; but these went over to the Spartans during the battle.

The battle was fought at Tanagra[1a] in Boeotia. After heavy loss on both sides victory declared for the Spartans and their allies. [2] After entering the Megarid and cutting down the fruit trees, the Spartans returned home across Geraneia and the isthmus. Sixty-two days after the battle the Athenians marched into Boeotia under the command of Myronides, [3] defeated the Boeotians in battle at Oenophyta,[3a] and became masters of Boeotia and Phocis.[3b] They dismantled the walls of the Tanagraeans, took a hundred of the richest men of the Opuntian Locrians[3c] as hostages, and finished their own long walls. [4] This was followed by the surrender of the Aeginetans[4a] to Athens on conditions; they pulled down their walls, gave up their ships, and agreed to pay tribute in future. [5] The Athenians sailed round the Peloponnesus under Tolmides son of Tolmaeus, burnt the arsenal of Sparta,[5a] took Chalcis,[5b] a city of the Corinthians, and in a descent upon Sicyon[5c] defeated the Sicyonians in battle.

Meanwhile the Athenians in Egypt and their allies stayed on and encountered all the vicissitudes of war. [2] First the Athenians were masters of Egypt, and the King sent Megabazus, a Persian, to Sparta with money to bribe the Peloponnesians to invade Attica and so draw off the Athenians from Egypt. [3] Finding that the matter made no progress, and that the money was only being wasted, he recalled Megabazus with the remainder of the money, and sent Megabyzus son of Zopyrus, a Persian, with a large army to Egypt. [4] Arriving by land he defeated the Egyptians and their allies in a battle, and drove the Hellenes out of Memphis,[4a] and at length shut them up in the island of Prosopitis,[4b] where he besieged them for a year and six months. At last, draining the canal of its waters, which he diverted into another channel, he left their ships high and dry and joined

1.108
457
BOEOTIA
The Spartans defeat the Athenians at Tanagra and go home. Later the Athenians defeat the Boeotians at Oenophyta and become masters of Boeotia.
AEGINA
Aegina surrenders. The Athenians raid the Peloponnesus.

1.109
454?
EGYPT
The Persians defeat the Egyptians and their Athenian allies.

1.107.4a Boeotia: Map 1.107, AY.
1.107.4b For plots against Athenian democracy, see
          Appendix A, The Athenian Government,
          §11–12.
1.108.1a Tanagra: Map 1.107, AY.
1.108.3a Oenophyta: Map 1.107, AY.
1.108.3b Phocis: Map 1.107, AY.
1.108.3c Opuntian Locris: Map 1.107, AY.

1.108.4a Aegina: Map 1.107, AY.
1.108.5a Presumably the shipyard at Gythion on
          the coast of Laconia: Map 1.107, BY.
1.108.5b Chalcis of the Corinthians: Map 1.107,
          AX.
1.108.5c Sicyon: Map 1.107, AY.
1.109.4a Memphis, Egypt: Map 1.110.
1.109.4b Prosopitis, Egypt: location unknown.

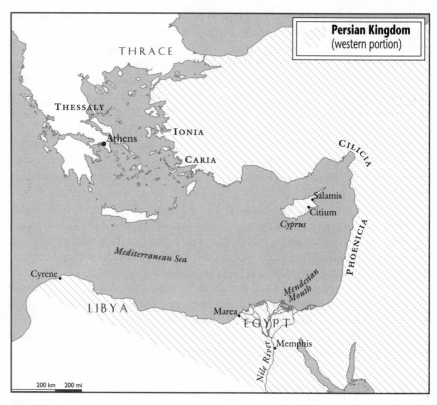

MAP 1.110 THE CAMPAIGN IN EGYPT

most of the island to the mainland, and then marched over on foot and captured it.

    Thus the enterprise of the Hellenes came to ruin after six years of war. Of all that large host a few traveling through Libya[1a] reached Cyrene[1b] in safety, but most of them perished. [2] And thus Egypt returned to its subjection to the King, except Amyrtaeus, the king in the marshes, whom they were unable to capture from the extent of the marsh; the marshmen being also the most warlike of the Egyptians. [3] Inaros, the Libyan king, the sole

1.110
454?
EGYPT
Most of Athens' fleet in Egypt is lost. An Athenian relief fleet, unaware of the defeat, is surprised and destroyed.

1.110.1a Libya: Map 1.110.
1.110.1b Cyrene, Libya: Map 1.110.

author of the Egyptian revolt, was betrayed, taken, and crucified. [4] Meanwhile a relieving squadron of fifty triremes had sailed from Athens and the rest of the confederacy for Egypt. They put in to shore at the Mendesian mouth of the Nile,[4a] in total ignorance of what had occurred. Attacked on the land side by the troops, and from the sea by the Phoenician navy, most of the ships were destroyed; the few remaining being saved by retreat. Such was the end of the great expedition of the Athenians and their allies to Egypt.

Meanwhile Orestes son of the Thessalian king Echecratides, being an exile from Thessaly,[1a] persuaded the Athenians to restore him. Taking with them the Boeotians[1b] and the Phocians[1c] their allies, the Athenians marched to Pharsalus[1d] in Thessaly. They became masters of the country, though only in the immediate vicinity of the camp; beyond which they could not go for fear of the Thessalian cavalry. But they failed to take the city or to attain any of the other objects of their expedition, and returned home with Orestes without having effected anything. [2] Not long after this a thousand of the Athenians embarked in the vessels that were at Pegae[2a] (Pegae, it must be remembered, was now theirs), and sailed along the coast to Sicyon[2b] under the command of Pericles son of Xanthippus. Landing in Sicyon and defeating the Sicyonians who engaged them, [3] they immediately took with them the Achaeans[3a] and sailing across, marched against and laid siege to Oeniadae[3b] in Acarnania.[3c] Failing however to take it, they returned home.

Three years afterwards a truce was made between the Peloponnesians and Athenians for five years. [2] Released from Hellenic war, the Athenians made an expedition to Cyprus[2a] with two hundred vessels of their own and their allies, under the command of Cimon. [3] Sixty of these were detached to Egypt[3a] at the request of Amyrtaeus, the king in the marshes; the rest laid siege to Citium,[3b] from which, however, [4] they were compelled to retire by the death of Cimon and by scarcity of provisions. Sailing off Salamis[4a] in Cyprus, they fought with the Phoenicians,[4b] Cyprians, and Cilicians[4c] by land and sea, and being victorious on both elements departed home, and with them the squadron that had returned from Egypt. [5] After this the Spartans marched out on a sacred war, and becoming masters of the temple at Delphi,[5a] placed it in the hands of the Delphians. Immediately after their retreat, the Athenians marched out, became masters of the temple, and placed it in the hands of the Phocians.[5b]

1.110.4a Mendesian mouth of the Nile River: Map 1.110.
1.111.1a Thessaly: Map 1.110.
1.111.1b Boeotia: Map 1.112, AY.
1.111.1c Phocis: Map 1.112, AY.
1.111.1d Pharsalus in Thessaly: Map 1.112, AY.
1.111.2a Pegae: Map 1.112, BY.
1.111.2b Sicyon: Map 1.112, BY.
1.111.3a Achaea: Map 1.112, BX.
1.111.3b Oeniadae: Map 1.112, AX.

1.111.3c Acarnania: Map 1.112, AX.
1.112.2a Cyprus: Map 1.110.
1.112.3a Egypt: Map 1.110.
1.112.3b Citium, Cyprus: Map 1.110.
1.112.4a Salamis, Cyprus: Map 1.110.
1.112.4b Phoenicia: Map 1.110.
1.112.4c Cilicia: Map 1.110.
1.112.5a Delphi: Map 1.112, AY.
1.112.5b Phocis: Map 1.112, AY.

MAP 1.112 EVENTS OF 451–46

1.113
447
BOEOTIA
Boeotia defeats Athens at
Coronea and regains her
independence.

Some time after this, a thousand Athenians with allied contingents under the command of Tolmides son of Tolmaeus, marched against Orchomenus,[1a] Chaeronea,[1b] and some other places in Boeotia[1c] that were in the hands of the Boeotian exiles. They took Chaeronea, made slaves of the inhabitants, and leaving a garrison, commenced their return. [2] On their way they were attacked at Coronea[2a] by the Boeotian exiles from Orchomenus, with some Locrians[2b] and Euboean[2c] exiles, and others who were of the same way of thinking. The Athenians were defeated in battle

1.113.1a Orchomenus: Map 1.112, AY.
1.113.1b Chaeronea: Map 1.112, AY.
1.113.1c Boeotia: Map 1.112, AY.
1.113.2a Coronea: Map 1.112, AY.
1.113.2b Locris (Opuntian): Map 1.112, AY.
1.113.2c Euboea: Map 1.112, AY.

and some were killed, others taken captive. [3] The Athenians evacuated all
Boeotia by a treaty providing for the recovery of the men; [4] and the
exiled Boeotians returned, and with all the rest regained their independence.

This was soon afterwards followed by the revolt of Euboea from Athens.
Pericles had already crossed over with an army of Athenians to the island,
when news was brought to him that Megara[1a] had revolted, that the Peloponnesians were on the point of invading Attica,[1b] and that the Athenian
garrison had been cut off by the Megarians, with the exception of a few
who had taken refuge in Nisaea.[1c] The Megarians had introduced the
Corinthians,[1d] Sicyonians,[1e] and Epidaurians[1f] into the city before they
revolted. Meanwhile Pericles brought his army back in all haste from
Euboea. [2] After this the Peloponnesians, under the command of King
Pleistoanax son of Pausanias, marched into Attica as far as Eleusis[2a] and
Thria,[2b] ravaging the country and without advancing further returned
home. [3] The Athenians then crossed over again to Euboea under the
command of Pericles, and subdued the whole of the island. While they settled all the rest of the island by means of agreed terms, they expelled the
people of Histiaea[3a] and occupied their territory themselves.

Not long after their return from Euboea, they made a peace treaty with
the Spartans and their allies for thirty years, giving up the posts which they
occupied in the Peloponnesus, Nisaea, Pegae,[1a] Troezen,[1b] and Achaea.[1c]
[2] In the sixth year of the truce, war broke out between the Samians[2a] and
Milesians[2b] about Priene.[2c] Worsted in the war, the Milesians came to
Athens with loud complaints against the Samians. In this they were joined
by certain private persons from Samos itself, who wished to change the
constitution by revolution. [3] Accordingly the Athenians sailed to Samos
with forty ships and set up a democracy;[3a] took hostages from the Samians,
fifty boys and as many men, lodged them in Lemnos,[3b] and after leaving a
garrison in the island returned home. [4] Some of the Samians, however,
had not remained in the island, but had fled to the continent. Making an
agreement with the most powerful of those in the city, and an alliance with
Pissuthnes son of Hystaspes, who at that time controlled Sardis[4a] for the
Persians, they got together a force of seven hundred mercenaries, and
under cover of night crossed over to Samos. [5] Their first step was to rise
against The People, most of whom they secured, their next to steal their
hostages from Lemnos; after which they revolted, gave up the Athenian
garrison left with them and its commanders to Pissuthnes, and instantly

1.114.1a Megara: Map 1.112, BY.
1.114.1b Attica: Map 1.112, BY.
1.114.1c Nisaea: Map 1.112, BY.
1.114.1d Corinth: Map 1.112, BY.
1.114.1e Sicyon: Map 1.112, BY.
1.114.1f Epidaurus: Map 1.112, BY.
1.114.2a Eleusis: Map 1.112, BY.
1.114.2b Thria: Map 1.112, BY.
1.114.3a Histiaea, Euboea: Map 1.112, AY.
1.115.1a Pegae: Map 1.112, BY.

1.115.1b Troezen: Map 1.112, BY.
1.115.1c Achaea: Map 1.112, BX.
1.115.2a Samos: Map 1.115.
1.115.2b Miletus: Map 1.115.
1.115.2c Priene: Map 1.115.
1.115.3a See Appendix B, The Athenian Empire,
    §4.
1.115.3b Lemnos: Map 1.115.
1.115.4a Sardis: Map 1.115. See Appendix E, The
    Persians, §3, 7.

MAP 1.115 REVOLT OF SAMOS

prepared for an expedition against Miletus. The Byzantians[5a] also revolted with them.

1.116
441/0
SAMOS
The Athenians win a battle off Samos and prepare to engage the Phoenician fleet.

As soon as the Athenians heard the news, they sailed with sixty ships against Samos. Sixteen of these went to Caria[1a] to look out for the Phoenician fleet, and to Chios[1b] and Lesbos[1c] carrying round orders for reinforcements, and so never engaged; but forty-four ships under the command of Pericles and nine colleagues gave battle off the island of Tragia[1d] to seventy Samian vessels—of which twenty were transports—as they were sailing from Miletus. Victory remained with the Athenians. [2] Reinforced afterwards by forty ships from Athens, and twenty-five Chian and Lesbian vessels, the Athenians landed, and having the superiority by land besieged the city with three walls and also blockaded it from the sea. [3] Meanwhile Pericles took sixty ships from the blockading squadron and departed in haste for Caunus[3a] and Caria, intelligence having been brought in of the approach of the Phoenician fleet to the aid of the Samians; indeed Stesago-

1.115.5a Byzantium: Map 1.115.
1.116.1a Caria: Map 1.116.
1.116.1b Chios: Map 1.115.
1.116.1c Lesbos: Map 1.115.

1.116.1d Tragia: Map 1.115.1.
1.116.3a Caunus: Map 1.115.

ras and others had left the island with five ships to bring them. [1.117.1] But in the meantime the Samians made a sudden sally, and fell on the camp, which they found unfortified. Destroying the lookout vessels, and engaging and defeating such as were being launched to meet them, they remained masters of their own seas for fourteen days, and carried in and carried out what they pleased. [2] But on the arrival of Pericles, they were once more shut up. Fresh reinforcements afterwards arrived—forty ships from Athens with Thucydides,[2a] Hagnon, and Phormio; twenty with Tlepolemus and Anticles, and thirty vessels from Chios and Lesbos. [3] After a brief attempt at fighting, the Samians, unable to hold out after a nine-month siege, were forced to surrender on terms; they razed their walls, gave hostages, delivered up their ships, and arranged to pay the expenses of the war by installments. The Byzantians also agreed to be subject as before.

After this, though not many years later, we at length come to what has been already related, the affairs of Corcyra and Potidaea and the events that served as a pretext for the present war. [2] All these actions of the Hellenes against each other and the barbarian occurred in the fifty years' interval between the retreat of Xerxes and the beginning of the present war. During this interval the Athenians succeeded in placing their empire on a firmer basis, and themselves advanced their own power to a very great height. The Spartans, though fully aware of it, opposed it only for a little while, but remained inactive during most of the period, being of old slow to go to war except under the pressure of necessity, and in the present instance being hampered by wars at home. Finally, the growth of the Athenian power could no longer be ignored as their own confederacy became the object of its encroachments. They then felt that they could endure it no longer, but that the time had come for them to throw themselves heart and soul upon the hostile power, and break it, if they could, by commencing the present war.[2a] [3] And though the Spartans had made up their own minds on the fact of the breach of the treaty and the guilt of the Athenians, yet they sent to Delphi[3a] and inquired of the god whether it would be well with them if they went to war and, as it is reported, received from him the answer that if they put their whole strength into the war, victory would be theirs, and the promise that he himself would be with them, whether invoked or uninvoked.

Still they wished to summon their allies again, and to take their vote on the propriety of making war.[1a] After the ambassadors from the confederates had arrived and a congress had been convened, they all spoke their minds, most of them denouncing the Athenians and demanding that the war should begin, especially the Corinthians. They had before on their own account canvassed the cities separately to induce them to vote for the war, in

1.117
440
SAMOS
Samos resists for nine months but finally surrenders to Athens.

1.118
432
HELLAS
Thus in the fifty years after the defeat of Persia, the power of Athens grew until Sparta felt compelled to oppose it. This chapter concludes the Pentecontaetia.

1.119
432/1
SPARTA
The Corinthians speak at a meeting of the Spartans and their allies.

1.117.2a This is another Thucydides, not the
          Thucydides son of Olorus who is the
          author of this history.
1.118.2a See 1.88.1.

1.118.3a Delphi: Map 1.115.
1.119.1a See Appendix D, The Peloponnesian
          League, §5.

the fear that it might come too late to save Potidaea; they were present also on this occasion, and came forward the last, and made the following speech:

"Fellow allies, we can no longer accuse the Spartans of having failed in their duty: they have not only voted for war themselves, but have assembled us here for that purpose. We say their duty, for supremacy has its duties. Besides equitably administering private interests, leaders are required to show a special care for the common welfare in return for the special honors accorded to them by all in other ways. [2] All of us who have already had dealings with the Athenians require no warning to be on their guard against them. The states more inland and away from the main routes should understand that if they omit to support the coast powers, the result will be to injure the transit of their produce for exportation and the reception in exchange of their imports from the sea; and they must not be careless judges of what is now said, as if it had nothing to do with them, but must expect that the sacrifice of the powers on the coast will one day be followed by the extension of the danger to the interior, and must recognize that their own interests are deeply involved in this discussion. [3] For these reasons they should not hesitate to exchange peace for war. If wise men remain quiet while they are not injured, brave men abandon peace for war when they are injured, returning to an understanding on a favorable opportunity. In fact, they are neither intoxicated by their success in war nor disposed to take an injury for the sake of the delightful tranquillity of peace. [4] Indeed, to falter for the sake of such delights is, if you remain inactive, the quickest way of losing the sweets of repose to which you cling; while to conceive extravagant pretensions from success in war is to forget how hollow is the confidence by which you are elated. [5] For if many ill-conceived plans have succeeded through the still greater lack of judgment of an opponent, many more, apparently well laid, have on the contrary ended in disgrace. The confidence with which we form our schemes is never completely justified in their execution; speculation is carried on in safety, but, when it comes to action, fear causes failure."

"To apply these rules to ourselves, if we are now kindling war it is under the pressure of injury, and with adequate grounds of complaint; and after we have chastised the Athenians we will in season desist. [2] We have many reasons to expect success—first, superiority in numbers and in military experience, and secondly our general and unvarying obedience in the execution of orders. [3] The naval strength which they possess shall be raised by us from our respective present resources, and from the moneys at Olympia and Delphi.[3a] A loan from these enables us to seduce their foreign sailors by the offer of higher pay. For the power of Athens is more mercenary than national; while ours will not be exposed to the same risk, as its strength lies more in men than in money. [4] A single defeat at sea is in all likelihood their ruin: should they hold out, in that case there will be the more time for us to exercise ourselves in naval matters; and as soon as we have arrived at an equality in science, we need scarcely ask whether we shall be their superiors in courage. For the advantages that we have by nature they cannot acquire by education; while their superiority in science must be removed by our practice. [5] The money required for these objects shall be provided by our contributions: nothing indeed could be more monstrous than the suggestion that, while their allies never tire of contributing for their own servitude, we should refuse to spend for vengeance and self-preservation the treasure which by such refusal we shall forfeit to Athenian rapacity, and see employed for our own ruin."

"We have also other ways of carrying on the war, such as revolt of their allies, the surest method of depriving them of their revenues, which are the source of their strength, and establishment of fortified positions in their country, and various operations which cannot be foreseen at present. For war of all things proceeds least upon definite rules, but draws principally upon itself for contrivances to meet an emergency; and in such cases the party who faces the struggle and keeps his temper best meets with most security, and he who loses his temper about it with correspondent disaster. [2] Let us also reflect that if it was merely a number of disputes of territory between rival neighbors, it might be borne; but here we have in Athens an enemy that is a match for our whole coalition, and more than a match for any of its members; so that unless as a body and as individual nationalities and individual cities we make a unanimous stand against her, she will easily conquer us divided and city by city. That conquest, terrible as it may sound, would, it must be known, have no other end than slavery pure and simple; [3] a word which the Peloponnesus cannot even hear whispered without disgrace, or without disgrace see so many states abused by one. Meanwhile the opinion would be either that we were justly so used, or that we put up with it from cowardice, and were proving degenerate sons in not even securing for ourselves the freedom which our fathers gave to Hellas; and in allowing the establishment in Hellas of a tyrant state, though in indi-

1.122
432/1
SPARTA
The Corinthians add that the Peloponnesians can suborn Athenian allies and establish fortified posts in Attica. They call for unity in the face of Athenian aggression since the alternative is slavery. They assert that the Peloponnesians must prevent Athens from ruling all Hellas as a tyrant state just as they have put down tyrants in individual states.

1.121.3a Olympia, Delphi: Map 1.115. Offerings of silver and gold objects and other valuable material accumulated at major temples and shrines to such a degree that these institutions became unique and tempting repositories of ready capital in ancient Greece. In 2.13.4–5, Pericles lists the vast wealth lying in Athenian temples and shrines that could be called upon—if necessary—to support the war.

vidual states we think it our duty to put down sole rulers. [4] And we do not know how this conduct can be held free from three of the gravest failings, want of sense, of courage, or of vigilance. For we do not suppose that you have taken refuge in that contempt of an enemy which has proved so fatal in so many instances—a feeling which from the numbers that it has ruined has come to be thought not to express contempt but to deserve it."

"There is, however, no advantage in reflections on the past further than may be of service to the present. For the future we must provide by maintaining what the present gives us and redoubling our efforts; it is hereditary to us to win virtue as the fruit of labor, and you must not change the habit, even though you should have a slight advantage in wealth and resources; for it is not right that what was won in want should be lost in plenty. No, we must boldly advance to the war for many reasons; the god has commanded it and promised to be with us, and the rest of Hellas will all join in the struggle, part from fear, part from interest. [2] You will not be the first to break a treaty which the god, in advising us to go to war, judges to be violated already, but rather to support a treaty that has been outraged: indeed, treaties are broken not by resistance but by aggression."

"Your position, therefore, from whatever quarter you may view it, will amply justify you in going to war; and this step we recommend in the interests of all, bearing in mind that identity of interests is the surest of bonds whether between states or individuals. Delay not, therefore, to assist Potidaea,[1a] a Dorian city besieged by Ionians,[1b] which is quite a reversal of the order of things; nor to assert the freedom of the rest. [2] It is impossible for us to wait any longer when waiting can only mean immediate disaster for some of us and, if it comes to be known that we have conferred but do not venture to protect ourselves, likely disaster in the near future for the rest. Delay not, fellow allies, but convinced of the necessity of the crisis and the wisdom of this counsel, vote for the war, undeterred by its immediate terrors, but looking beyond to the lasting peace by which it will be succeeded. Out of war peace gains fresh stability, but to refuse to abandon repose for war is not so sure a method of avoiding danger. [3] We must believe that the tyrant city that has been established in Hellas has been established against

1.124.1a Potidaea: Map 1.129, AX.
1.124.1b For the Dorians and the Ionians, see
           Appendix H, Dialects and Ethnic Groups,
           §7–8.

all alike, with a program of universal empire, part fulfilled, part in contemplation; let us then attack and reduce it, and win future security for ourselves and freedom for the Hellenes who are now enslaved."[3a]

Such were the words of the Corinthians. [1.125.1] The Spartans having now heard all give their opinion, took the vote of all the allied states present in order, great and small alike; and the majority voted for war.[1a] [2] This decided, it was still impossible for them to commence at once, from their want of preparation; but it was resolved that the means requisite were to be procured by the different states, and that there was to be no delay. And indeed, in spite of the time occupied with the necessary arrangements, less than a year elapsed before Attica was invaded, and the war openly begun.

This interval was spent in sending embassies to Athens charged with complaints, in order to obtain as good a pretext for war as possible, in the event of her paying no attention to them. [2] The first Spartan embassy was to order the Athenians to drive out the curse of the goddess;[2a] the history of which is as follows. [3] In former generations there was an Athenian of the name of Cylon, a victor at the Olympic games,[3a] of good birth and powerful position, who had married a daughter of Theagenes, a Megarian, at that time tyrant of Megara.[3b] [4] Now this Cylon was inquiring at Delphi[4a] when he was told by the god to seize the Acropolis of Athens[4b] on the grand festival of Zeus. [5] Accordingly, procuring a force from Theagenes and persuading his friends to join him, he seized the Acropolis when the Olympic festival in the Peloponnesus began with the intention of making himself tyrant, thinking that this was the grand festival of Zeus, and also an occasion appropriate for a victor at the Olympic games. [6] Whether the grand festival that was meant was in Attica or elsewhere was a question which he never thought of, and which the oracle did not offer to solve. For the Athenians also have a festival which is called the grand festival of Zeus Meilichios or Gracious, namely, the Diasia. It is celebrated outside the city, and the whole people sacrifice not real victims but a number of bloodless offerings peculiar to the country. However, fancying he had chosen the right time, he made the attempt. [7] As soon as the Athenians perceived it, they flocked in, one and all, from the country, and sat down, and laid siege to the citadel. [8] But as time went on, weary of the labor of blockade, most of them departed; the responsibility of keeping

1.125
432/1
SPARTA
The Peloponnesians vote for war; less than one year later Attica is invaded.

1.126
432/1
ATHENS
As a pretext for war, Sparta tells Athens to drive out the curse of the goddess. Thucydides describes Cylon's attempted coup, from which the curse derived.

1.124.3a See the Introduction (sec. II.v) for a discussion of speeches in Thucydides.
1.125.1a See Appendix D, The Peloponnesian League, §5.
1.126.2a To "drive out the curse" means to drive away those accursed for pollution (by foul deeds) of the sacred precincts of a god or goddess.
1.126.3a Cylon's name appears in the Olympic-victor lists for the 35th Olympiad of 640 B.C. His attempt to set up a tyranny was therefore made in 636 or 632. See

Appendix K, Classical Greek Calendars and Dating Systems, §4, and Appendix I, Classical Greek Religious Festivals, §5. For the location of Olympia, see Map 1.129, BX.
1.126.3b Megara: Map 1.129, BX.
1.126.4a Delphi: Map 1.129, BX.
1.126.4b The Acropolis of Athens was a steep hill on the top of which stood the city's most ancient religious shrines and temples. At one time it constituted the entire city, as Thucydides notes in 2.15.3–6.

guard being left to the nine archons, with plenary powers to arrange everything according to their good judgment. It must be known that at that time most political functions were discharged by the nine archons.[8a] [9] Meanwhile Cylon and his besieged companions were distressed for want of food and water. [10] Accordingly Cylon and his brother made their escape; but the rest being hard pressed, and some even dying of famine, seated themselves as suppliants at the altar in the Acropolis. [11] The Athenians who were charged with the duty of keeping guard, when they saw them at the point of death in the temple, raised them up on the understanding that no harm should be done to them, led them out, and slew them. Some who as they passed by took refuge at the altars of the awful goddesses were dispatched on the spot. From this deed the men who killed them were called accursed and guilty against the goddess, they and their descendants.[11a] [12] Accordingly these cursed ones were driven out by the Athenians, and driven out again by Cleomenes of Sparta and an Athenian faction; the living were driven out, and the bones of the dead were taken up; thus they were cast out. For all that, they came back afterwards, and their descendants are still in the city.

1.127
432/1
ATHENS
Thucydides reports that the Spartan aim was to discredit Pericles, a powerful Athenian who opposed concessions to Sparta and was one of "the accursed."

This, then, was the curse that the Spartans ordered them to drive out. They were actuated primarily, as they pretended, by care for the honor of the gods; but they also knew that Pericles son of Xanthippus was connected with the curse on his mother's side, and they thought that his banishment would materially advance their designs on Athens. [2] Not that they really hoped to succeed in procuring this; they rather thought to create a prejudice against him in the eyes of his countrymen from the feeling that the war would be partly caused by his misfortune. [3] For being the most powerful man of his time, and the leading Athenian statesman, he opposed the Spartans in everything, and would have no concessions, but ever urged the Athenians on to war.

1.128
432/1
SPARTA
Athens in turn tells Sparta to drive out the curse of Taenarum and the curse of the goddess of the Bronze House, the latter involving Pausanias' attempt to betray the Greeks to Xerxes.

The Athenians retorted by ordering the Spartans to drive out the curse of Taenarum. The Spartans had once raised up some Helot[1a] suppliants from the temple of Poseidon at Taenarum,[1b] led them away, and slain them; for which they believe the great earthquake at Sparta to have been a retribution.[1c] [2] The Athenians also ordered them to drive out the curse of the goddess of the Bronze House; the history of which is as follows. [3] After Pausanias the Spartan had been recalled by the Spartans from his command in the Hellespont[3a] (this is his first recall),[3b] and had been tried by them and acquitted, not being again sent out in a public capacity, he

---

1.126.8a When Thucydides wrote this, the archons at Athens had become officials with no real powers; see Appendix A, The Athenian Government, §6.

1.126.11a Those who sought protection at the altar of a god could not be harmed without risk of sacrilege. See the supplication of the Helots (1.128.1), of the servant of Pausanias (1.133.1), of Themistocles (1.136.1), and of the Mytilenians (3.28.2); also the

excesses of the Corcyraean revolution (3.81.5); and the flights of Thrasyllus (5.60.6) and Astyochus (8.84.3).

1.128.1a For more on the Helots, see Appendix C, Spartan Institutions, §3–4.

1.128.1b Taenarum: Map 1.129, BX.

1.128.1c See note 1.126.11a.

1.128.3a Hellespont: Map 1.129. AY. This picks up the career of Pausanias from 1.95.

1.128.3b For Pausanias' first recall, See 1.95.5.

took a trireme of Hermione[3c] on his own responsibility, without the authority of the Spartans, and arrived as a private person in the Hellespont. He came ostensibly for the Hellenic war, but really to carry on his intrigues with the King, which he had begun before his recall, being ambitious of reigning over Hellas. [4] The circumstance which first enabled him to lay the King under an obligation, and to make a beginning of the whole design was this. [5] Some connections and kinsmen of the King had been taken in Byzantium[5a] on its capture from the Persians, when he was first there after the return from Cyprus.[5b] These captives he sent off to the King without the knowledge of the rest of the allies, the account being that they had escaped from him. [6] He managed this with the help of Gongylus, an Eretrian,[6a] whom he had placed in charge of Byzantium and the prisoners. He also gave Gongylus a letter for the King, the contents of which were as follows, as was afterwards discovered: [7] "Pausanias, the general of Sparta, anxious to do you a favor, sends you these his prisoners of war. I propose also, with your approval, to marry your daughter, and to make Sparta and the rest of Hellas subject to you. I may say that I think I am able to do this, with your cooperation. Accordingly if any of this please you, send a safe man to the sea through whom we may in future conduct our correspondence."

This was all that was revealed in the writing, and Xerxes was pleased with the letter. He sent off Artabazus son of Pharnaces to the sea with orders to supersede Megabates, the previous governor in the province of Dascylium,[1a] and to send over as quickly as possible to Pausanias at Byzantium a letter which he entrusted to him; to show him the royal signet, and to execute any commission which he might receive from Pausanias on the King's business, with all care and fidelity. [2] Artabazus on his arrival carried the King's orders into effect, and sent over the letter, [3] which contained the following answer: "Thus saith King Xerxes to Pausanias. For the men whom you have saved for me from Byzantium across sea,[3a] an obligation is laid up to you in our house, recorded forever; and with your proposals I am well pleased. Let neither night nor day stop you from diligently performing any of your promises to me, neither for cost of gold nor of silver let them be hindered, nor yet for number of troops, wherever it may be that their presence is needed; but with Artabazus, an honorable man whom I send you, boldly advance my objects and yours, as may be most for the honor and interest of us both."

1.129
HELLESPONT
The account of the curse of the goddess of the Bronze House begins with Xerxes' favorable response to Pausanias' letter.

1.128.3c Hermione: Map 1.129, BX.
1.128.5a Byzantium: Map 1.129, AY.
1.128.5b Cyprus: Map 1.110. Pausanias' campaign
          against Cyprus took place in 478.
1.128.6a Eretria, Euboea: Map 1.129, BX.
1.129.1a Dascylium: Map 1.129, AY. See Appen-
          dix E, The Persians, §7.
1.129.3a "Across sea" refers here to the Hellespont
          (Map 1.129, AY), which, although a nar-
          row strait, was still "the sea" to the Per-
          sians.

MAP 1.129 PRETEXTS FOR WAR—THE DEATH OF PAUSANIAS

Previously held in high honor by the Hellenes as the hero of Plataea,[1a] Pausanias, after the receipt of this letter, became prouder than ever, and could no longer live in the usual style, but went out of Byzantium in a Median dress, was attended on his march through Thrace by a bodyguard of Medes and Egyptians, kept a Persian table, and was quite unable to contain his intentions, but he betrayed by his conduct in trifles what his ambition looked one day to enact on a grander scale. [2] He also made himself difficult of access, and displayed so violent a temper to everyone without exception that no one could come near him. Indeed, this was the principal reason why the confederacy went over to the Athenians.

The above-mentioned conduct, coming to the ears of the Spartans, occasioned his first recall. And after his second voyage out in the ship of Hermione,[1a] without their orders, he gave proofs of similar behavior. Besieged and expelled from Byzantium[1b] by the Athenians, he did not return to Sparta; but news came that he had settled at Colonae[1c] in the Troad, and was intriguing with the barbarians, and that his stay there was for no good purpose; and the ephors,[1d] now no longer hesitating, sent him a herald and a *scytale*[1e] with orders to accompany the herald or be declared a public enemy. [2] Anxious above everything to avoid suspicion, and confident that he could quash the charge by means of money, he returned a second time to Sparta.[2a] At first thrown into prison by the ephors (whose powers enable them to do this to the king), he soon compromised the matter and came out again, and offered himself for trial to any who wished to institute an inquiry concerning him.

Now the Spartans had no tangible proof against him—neither his enemies nor the city as a whole—of that indubitable kind required for the punishment of a member of the royal family, and at that moment in high office; he being regent for his first cousin King Pleistarchus, Leonidas' son, who was still a minor. But by his contempt of the laws and imitation of the barbarians, [2] he gave grounds for much suspicion of his being discontented with things established; all the occasions on which he had in any way departed from the regular customs were passed in review, and it was remembered that he had taken upon himself to have inscribed on the tripod at Delphi, which was dedicated by the Hellenes, as the first-fruits of the spoil of the Medes, the following couplet:

> The Mede defeated, great Pausanias raised
> This monument, that Phoebus might be praised.

1.130
HELLESPONT
Pausanias adopts Persian ways and antagonizes the Greeks.

1.131
SPARTA
Suspecting treachery, the ephors recall Pausanias.

1.132
SPARTA
The ephors suspect Pausanias but they lack proof, until one of his servants betrays him.

1.130.1a Plataea: Map 1.129, BX. Pausanias led the Greeks in the great victory over the Persians at Plataea in 479.
1.131.1a Hermione: Map 1.129, BX.
1.131.1b Byzantium: Map 1.129, AY.
1.131.1c Colonae in the Troad: Map 1.129, AY.
1.131.1d The five Spartan ephors had wide-ranging powers; see Appendix C, Spartan Institutions, §5–6.
1.131.1e The *scytale*, a Spartan device for coding secret messages, was a staff around which was rolled a strip of leather so that its edges always met. This surface was then written on crosswise, unrolled, and sent to its destination. It could only be read again when it was wound around an exactly similar staff that was given to an official when going abroad on public service.
1.131.2a Sparta: Map 1.129, BX.

ILLUSTRATION 1.132
SERPENT COLUMN
ERECTED AFTER THE
BATTLE OF PLATAEA AS
IT IS FOUND TODAY IN
THE SITE OF THE HIPPO-
DROME IN ISTANBUL;
AND DETAIL (RIGHT) OF
ITS INSCRIPTION.

[3] At the time the Spartans had at once erased the couplet, and inscribed the names of the cities that had aided in the overthrow of the barbarian and dedicated the offering.[3a] Yet it was considered that Pausanias had here been guilty of a grave offense, which, interpreted by the light of the attitude which he had since assumed, gained a new significance, and seemed to be quite in keeping with his present schemes. [4] Besides, they were informed that he was even intriguing with the Helots;[4a] and such indeed was the fact, for he was promising them freedom and citizenship if they would join him in insurrection, and would help him to carry out his plans to the end. [5] Even now, mistrusting the evidence even of the Helots themselves, the ephors would not consent to take any decided step against him; in accordance with their regular custom toward themselves, namely, to be slow in taking any irrevocable resolve in the matter of a Spartan citizen, without indisputable proof. At last, it is said, the person who was going to carry to Artabazus the last letter for the King, a man of Argilus, once the favorite and most trusty servant of Pausanias, turned

1.132.3a Remains of this tripod, and its inscrip-
          tion, can be seen today in Istanbul; see
          illustration 1.132.

1.132.4a For more on the Helots, see Appendix C,
          Spartan Institutions, §3–4.

informer.[5a] Alarmed by the reflection that none of the previous messengers had ever returned, having counterfeited the seal, in order that, if he found himself mistaken in his surmises, or if Pausanias should ask to make some correction, he might not be discovered, he undid the letter, and found the postscript that he had suspected, namely, an order to put him to death.

On being shown the letter the ephors now felt more certain. Still, they wished with their own ears to hear Pausanias commit himself. Accordingly the man went by appointment to Taenarum as a suppliant,[1a] and there found shelter for himself in a hut divided into two by a partition; within which he concealed some of the ephors and let them hear the whole matter plainly. For Pausanias came to him and asked him the reason of his suppliant position; and the man reproached him with the order that he had written concerning him, and one by one declared all the rest of the circumstances, how he who had never yet brought him into any danger, while employed as agent between him and the King, was yet just like the mass of his servants, to be rewarded with death. Admitting all this, and telling him not to be angry about the matter, Pausanias gave him guarantee of safety in getting him to leave the temple, and begged him to set off as quickly as possible, and not to hinder the business in hand.

The ephors listened carefully, and then departed, taking no action for the moment, but, having at last reached certainty, were preparing to arrest him in the city. It is reported that, as he was about to be arrested in the street, he saw from the face of one of the ephors what he was coming for; another, too, made him a secret signal, and betrayed it to him from kindness. Setting off at a run for the temple of the goddess of the Bronze House, the enclosure of which was near at hand, he succeeded in taking sanctuary before they took him, and entering into a small chamber, which formed part of the temple, to avoid being exposed to the weather, he remained there. [2] The ephors, for the moment distanced in the pursuit, afterwards took off the roof of the chamber, and having made sure that he was inside, shut him in, barricaded the doors, and staying before the place, reduced him by starvation. [3] When they found that he was on the point of expiring, just as he was, in the chamber, they brought him out of the temple, while the breath was still in him, and as soon as he was brought out he died. [4] They were going to throw him into the Kaiadas, where they cast criminals, but finally decided to inter him somewhere near. But the god at Delphi afterwards ordered the Spartans to remove the tomb to the place of his death—where he now lies in the consecrated ground, as an inscription on a monument declares—and, as what had been done was a curse to them, to give back two bodies instead of one to the goddess of the Bronze House. So they had two bronze statues made, and dedicated them

1.133
471?
SPARTA
Posing as a suppliant at Taenarum, the servant tricks Pausanias into disclosing his crimes to the ephors in hiding.

1.134
471?
SPARTA
Pausanias takes sanctuary in the temple of the goddess of the Bronze House. The ephors shut him in there and he starves to death, causing the curse.

1.132.5a Most likely not the Argilus in Chalcidice (Map 1.129, AX) but another unknown site near Sparta.

1.133.1a Taenarum: Map 1.129, BX. Suppliant: see note 1.126.11a.

ILLUSTRATION 1.135 OSTRAKA

1.135
471?
ATHENS
The investigation of
Pausanias implicates
Themistocles, who had been
ostracized from Athens.

as a substitute for Pausanias. [1.135.1] Accordingly the Athenians retorted by telling the Spartans to drive out what the god himself had pronounced to be a curse.

[2] To return to the Medism of Pausanias, matter was found in the course of the inquiry to implicate Themistocles[2a]; and the Spartans accordingly sent envoys to the Athenians and required them to punish him as they had punished Pausanias. The Athenians consented to do so. [3] He had, as it happened, been *ostracized*[3a] and, from a residence at Argos,[3b] was in the habit of visiting other parts of the Peloponnesus. So they sent with the Spartans, who were ready to join in the pursuit, persons with instructions to take him wherever they found him.

1.136
470?
MOLOSSIA
Unable to remain at
Corcyra, Themistocles flees
to Molossia, to whose king,
Admetus, a former adversary,
he now becomes a suppliant.

Themistocles became aware of their intentions, however, and fled from the Peloponnesus to Corcyra,[1a] which was under obligations toward him. But the Corcyraeans alleged that they could not venture to shelter him at the cost of offending Athens and Sparta, and they conveyed him over to the continent opposite. [2] Pursued by the officers who hung on the report of his movements, and at a loss where to turn, he was compelled to stop at the house of Admetus, the Molossian[2a] king, though they were not on friendly terms. [3] Admetus happened not to be indoors, but his wife, to whom he made himself a suppliant, instructed him to take their child in his

1.135.2a Thucydides has already described
Themistocles' role in persuading the
Athenians to build a fleet (1.14.3), in the
victory over the Persians at Salamis,
(1.74.1), and in rebuilding Athens' walls,
(1.89.3–1.93).
1.135.3a Themistocles is thought to have been
ostracized no earlier than 472–1.
Ostracism was a procedure by which an
Athenian citizen could be honorably banished from Athens and her possessions for

ten years without loss of property or citizenship if, after the Athenians had chosen
to hold such a vote, he received the most
votes out of a total of at least six thousand votes cast (votes were noted on
shards of pottery called ostraka). See also
8.74.3; Appendix A, The Athenian Government, §8; and Illustration 1.135.
1.135.3b Argos: Map 1.137, BX.
1.136.1a Corcyra: Map 1.137, AX.
1.136.2a Molossia: Map 1.137, AX.

arms and sit down by the hearth.[3a] [4] Soon afterwards Admetus came in, and Themistocles told him who he was, and begged him not to take revenge on Themistocles in exile for any opposition which his requests might have experienced from Themistocles at Athens. Indeed, he was now far too low for such revenge; retaliation was only honorable between equals. Besides, his opposition to the king had only affected the success of a request, not the safety of his person; if the king were to give him up to the pursuers that he mentioned, and the fate which they intended for him, he would just be consigning him to certain death.

The king listened to him and raised him up with his son, as he was sitting with him in his arms after the most effectual method of supplication, and on the arrival of the Spartans not long afterwards, refused to give him up for anything they could say, but sent him off by land to the other sea to Pydna[1a] in Alexander's dominions, as he wished to go to the Persian King. [2] There he met with a merchant ship on the point of starting for Ionia.[2a] Going on board, he was carried by a storm to the Athenian squadron which was blockading Naxos.[2b] In his alarm—he was luckily unknown to the people in the vessel—he told the master who he was and what he was flying for, and said that, if he refused to save him, he would declare that the captain had been bribed into taking him. Meanwhile their safety consisted in letting no one leave the ship until a favorable time for sailing should arise. If he complied with his wishes, Themistocles promised him a proper recompense. The master acted as he desired, and, after lying at anchor for a day and a night out of the reach of the squadron, at length arrived at Ephesus.[2c]

[3] After having rewarded him with a present of money, as soon as he received some from his friends at Athens and from his secret hoards at Argos, Themistocles started inland with a Persian from the coast, and sent a letter to King Artaxerxes, Xerxes' son, who had just come to the throne.[3a] Its contents were as follows: [4] "I, Themistocles, am come to you, who did your house more harm than any of the Hellenes, when I was compelled to defend myself against your father's invasion—harm, however, far surpassed by the good that I did him during his retreat, which brought no danger for me but much for him. For the past, you owe me a good turn"— here he alluded to the warning sent to Xerxes from Salamis[4a] to retreat, as well as his finding the bridges unbroken, which, as he falsely pretended, was due to him—"for the present, able to do you great service, I am here, pursued by the Hellenes for my friendship for you. However, I desire a year's grace, when I shall be able to declare in person the objects of my coming."

1.137
471/0?
MOLOSSIA
Admetus protects Themistocles and sends him to Pydna.
NAXOS
Sailing to Ionia, his boat is forced to Naxos, a city besieged by Athenians. He avoids discovery and reaches Ephesus.
IONIA
He writes to Xerxes, describing his past services to the Persians and offering future ones.

1.136.3a Suppliant: see note 1.126.11a.
1.137.1a Pydna, Macedonia: Map 1.137, AX. Alexander was then king of Macedonia. By the "other sea"; Thucydides opposes the Ionian Sea (Map 1.137, AX) to the Aegean Sea (Map 1.137, BY).
1.137.2a Ionia: Map 1.137, BY.
1.137.2b Naxos: Map 1.137, BY. Thucydides mentions a siege at Naxos in 1.98.4.
1.137.2c Ephesus: Map 1.137, BY.
1.137.3a The date of the accession of Artaxerxes is 465/4. On any chronology of Themistocles, there is an awkward hiatus between the siege of Naxos (and Themistocles' arrival in Asia) and his meeting with Artaxerxes.
1.137.4a Salamis by Athens: Map 1.137, BX.

MAP 1.137   THE FLIGHT OF THEMISTOCLES

It is said that the King approved his intention, and told him to do as he said. He employed the interval in making what progress he could in the study of the Persian tongue, and of the customs of the country. [2] Arrived at court at the end of the year, he attained to very high consideration there, such as no Hellene has ever possessed before or since; partly from his splendid reputation, partly from the hopes which he held out of effecting the subjugation of Hellas, but principally by the proof which experience daily gave of his intelligence. [3] For Themistocles was a man who exhibited the most indubitable signs of genius; indeed, in this particular he has a claim on our admiration quite extraordinary and unparalleled. By his own native capacity, which was neither shaped by education nor developed by later training, he was at once the best judge in those sudden crises which admit of little or of no deliberation, and the best prophet of the future, even to its most distant possibilities. An able theoretical expositor of all that came within the sphere of his practice, he was not without the power of passing an adequate judgment in matters in which he had no experience. He could also excellently divine the good and evil which lay hidden in the unseen future. To sum up, whether we consider the extent of his natural powers, or the slightness of his application, this extraordinary man must be allowed to have surpassed all others in the faculty of intuitively meeting an emergency. [4] Disease was the real cause of his death; though there is a story of his having ended his life by poison, on finding himself unable to fulfill his promises to the King. [5] However this may be, there is a monument to him in the *agora* of Asiatic Magnesia.[5a] He was governor of the district, the King having given him Magnesia, which brought in fifty talents[5b] a year for bread, Lampsacus,[5c] which was considered to be the richest wine country, for wine, and Myos[5d] for other provisions. [6] His bones, it is said, were conveyed home by his relatives in accordance with his wishes, and interred in Attic ground. This was done without the knowledge of the Athenians; as it is against the law to bury in Attica an outlaw for treason. So ends the history of Pausanias and Themistocles, the Spartan and the Athenian, the most famous men of their time in Hellas.

To return to the Spartans. The history of their first embassy, the injunctions which it conveyed and the rejoinder which it provoked concerning the expulsion of the accursed persons, have been related already. It was followed by a second, which ordered Athens to raise the siege of Potidaea,[1a] and to respect the independence of Aegina.[1b] Above all, it made very clear to the Athenians that war might be prevented if they revoked the Megara

1.138
461?
PERSIAN ASIA
Themistocles is well received by Xerxes. Thucydides applauds Themistocles' extraordinary ability to foresee events and make decisions. Xerxes appoints him a governor.

1.139
432/1
ATHENS
Sparta also demands that Athens raise the siege of Potidaea, restore independence to Aegina, and rescind the Megarian Decree. A final ultimatum orders Athens to let the Hellenes be independent. As the Athenians debate these demands, Pericles rises to speak.

1.138.5a Magnesia on the Meander River: Map 1.137, BY. Thucydides terms it "Asiatic" to distinguish it from the coastal strip of southwest Thessaly also called Magnesia (Map 1.137, BX). The *agora* was a classical city's principal market place—its center for commercial, social, and political activity.

1.138.5b The talent is a unit of weight and money. See Appendix J, Classical Greek Currency, §5.
1.138.5c Lampsacus: Map 1.137, AY.
1.138.5d Myos: Map 1.137, BY.
1.139.1a Potidaea: Map 1.137, AX.
1.139.1b Aegina: Map 1.137, BX.

decree,[1c] excluding the Megarians from the use of Athenian harbors and of the market of Athens. [2] But Athens was not inclined either to revoke the decree, or to entertain their other proposals; she accused the Megarians of pushing their cultivation into the consecrated ground and the unenclosed land on the border, and of harboring her runaway slaves. [3] At last an embassy arrived with the Spartan ultimatum. The ambassadors were Ramphias, Melesippus, and Agesander. Not a word was said on any of the old subjects; there was simply this: "Sparta wishes the peace to continue, and there is no reason why it should not, if you would let the Hellenes be independent." Upon this the Athenians held an assembly,[3a] and laid the matter before their consideration. It was resolved to deliberate once and for all on all their demands, and to give them an answer. [4] There were many speakers who came forward and gave their support to one side or the other, urging the necessity of war, or the revocation of the decree and the folly of allowing it to stand in the way of peace. Among them came forward Pericles son of Xanthippus, the first man of his time at Athens, ablest alike in counsel and in action, and gave the following advice:

1.140
432/1
ATHENS
Pericles demands no concession to Sparta because she has not offered or accepted arbitration, as called for in the treaty, and her demands have grown more dictatorial and threatening. He says the Megarian Decree is not a trifle, but a symbol of Athenian response to Spartan pressure.

"There is one principle, Athenians, which I hold to through everything, and that is the principle of no concession to the Peloponnesians. I know that the spirit which inspires men while they are being persuaded to make war is not always retained in action, that as circumstances change, resolutions change. Yet I see that now as before the same, almost literally the same, counsel is demanded of me; and I put it to those of you who are allowing yourselves to be persuaded, to support the decisions of the assembly even in the case of reverses, or to forfeit all credit for their wisdom in the event of success. For sometimes the course of things is as arbitrary as the plans of man; indeed this is why we usually blame chance for whatever does not happen as we expected. [2] Now it was clear before that Sparta entertained designs against us; it is still more clear now. The treaty provides that we shall mutually submit our differences to arbitration, and that we shall meanwhile each keep what we have. Yet the Spartans never yet made us any such offer, never yet would accept from us any such offer; on the contrary, they wish complaints to be settled by war instead of by negotiation; and in the end we find them here dropping the tone of protest and adopting that of command.[2a] [3] They order us to raise the siege of Potidaea, to let Aegina be independent, to revoke the Megara decree; and they conclude with an ultimatum warning us to leave the Hellenes indepen-

1.139.1c Athens' Megara decree was apparently a powerful sanction. See Appendix B, The Athenian Empire, §10. Megara: Map 1.137, BX.
1.139.3a Assembly: see Appendix A, The Athenian Government, §5, 8.

1.140.2a Failure to offer or to accept Athenian offers of arbitration did have adverse effects upon Spartan morale during the first phase of the Peloponnesian War, as we learn in 7.18.

dent. [4] I hope that you will none of you think that we shall be going to war for a trifle if we refuse to revoke the Megara decree, which appears in front of their complaints, and the revocation of which is to save us from war, or let any feeling of self-reproach linger in your minds, as if you went to war for slight cause. [5] Why, this trifle contains the whole seal and trial of your resolution. If you give way, you will instantly have to meet some greater demand, as having been frightened into obedience in the first instance; while a firm refusal will make them clearly understand that they must treat you as equals."

"Make your decision therefore at once, either to submit before you are harmed, or if we are to go to war, as I for one think we ought, to do so without caring whether the ostensible cause be great or small, resolved against making concessions or consenting to a precarious tenure of our possessions. For all claims from an equal, urged upon a neighbor as commands, before any attempt at arbitration, be they great or be they small, have only one meaning, and that is slavery."

[2] "As to the war and the resources of either party, a detailed comparison will not show you the inferiority of Athens. [3] Personally engaged in the cultivation of their land, without funds either private or public, the Peloponnesians are also without experience in long wars across sea, from the strict limit which poverty imposes on their attacks upon each other. [4] Powers of this description are quite incapable of often manning a fleet or often sending out an army: they cannot afford the absence from their homes, the expenditure from their own funds; and besides, they have not command of the sea. [5] Capital, it must be remembered, maintains a war more than forced contributions. Farmers are a class of men that are always more ready to serve in person than in purse. Confident that the former will survive the dangers, they are by no means so sure that the latter will not be prematurely exhausted, especially if the war last longer than they expect, which it very likely will. [6] In a single battle the Peloponnesians and their allies may be able to defy all Hellas, but they are incapacitated from carrying on a war against a power different in character from their own, by the want of the single council chamber requisite to prompt and vigorous action, and the substitution of a congress composed of various peoples,[6a] in which every state possesses an equal vote, and each presses its own ends—a condition of things which generally results in no action at

1.141
432/1
ATHENS
Pericles says that to heed Sparta's demands can lead only to slavery. He points out that the Peloponnesians lack funds to sustain conflicts and, being farmers, they will not be able to mobilize for long campaigns; that they cannot threaten Athens at sea; and, as a league of states with divergent interests, they will find it hard to act quickly or decisively.

1.141.6a Pericles refers here to the membership of
    the Peloponnesian League.

1.142
432/1
ATHENS
Pericles argues that the enemy's principal handicap will
be lack of money; that
Athenian sea power will be
more effective against them
on land than their land
power against Athens at sea;
and that they will not easily
acquire the skill to challenge
Athens at sea, especially if
Athenian fleets limit their
opportunities to practice.

all. [7] The great wish of some is to avenge themselves on some particular enemy, the great wish of others to save their own pocket.
Slow in assembling, they devote a very small fraction of the time to
the consideration of any matter of common concern, most of it to
the prosecution of their own affairs. Meanwhile each fancies that no
harm will come of his neglect, that it is the business of somebody
else to look after this or that for him; and so, by the same notion
being entertained by all separately, the common cause imperceptibly
decays."

"But the principal point is the hindrance that they will experience from want of money. The slowness with which it comes in will
cause delay; but the opportunities of war wait for no man. [2]
Again, we need not be alarmed either at the possibility of their raising fortifications in Attica, or at their navy.[2a] [3] It would be difficult for any system of fortifications to establish a rival city, even in
time of peace, much more, surely, in an enemy's country, with
Athens just as much fortified against it, as it against Athens; [4]
while a mere post might be able to do some harm to the country by
incursions and by the facilities which it would afford for desertion, it
can never prevent our sailing into their country and raising fortifications there, and making reprisals with our powerful fleet. [5] For
our naval skill is of more use to us for service on land, than their
military skill for service at sea. [6] Familiarity with the sea they will
not find an easy acquisition. [7] If you who have been practicing at
it ever since the Persian invasion have not yet brought it to perfection, is there any chance of anything considerable being effected by
an agricultural, unseafaring population, who will besides be prevented from practicing by the constant presence of strong
squadrons of observation from Athens? [8] With a small squadron
they might hazard an engagement, encouraging their ignorance by
numbers; but the restraint of a strong force will prevent their moving, and through want of practice they will grow more clumsy, and
consequently more timid. [9] It must be kept in mind that seaman-
ship, just like anything else, is a matter requiring skill, and will not
admit of being taken up occasionally as an occupation for times of
leisure; on the contrary, it is so exacting as to leave leisure for nothing else."

1.142.2a Here and in the points below concerning
moneys from Delphi and Olympia, the
suborning of Athens' foreign sailors with
high pay, and the training of a Peloponnesian fleet to match Athens, Thucydides
seems to have Pericles respond directly to
points made by the Corinthians in their
speech to the Spartans and their allies
reported in 1.121–22.

"Even if they were to touch the moneys at Olympia[1a] or Delphi,[1b] and try to seduce our foreign sailors by the temptation of higher pay, that would only be a serious danger if we could not still be a match for them, by embarking our own citizens and the resident aliens.[1c] But in fact by this means we are always a match for them; and, best of all, we have a larger and higher class of native coxswains and sailors among our own citizens than all the rest of Hellas. [2] And to say nothing of the danger of such a step, none of our foreign sailors would consent to become an outlaw from his country, and to take service with them and their hopes, for the sake of a few days' high pay."

[3] "This, I think, is a tolerably fair account of the position of the Peloponnesians; that of Athens is free from the defects that I have criticized in them, and has other advantages of its own, which they can show nothing to equal. [4] If they march against our country we will sail against theirs, and it will then be found that the desolation of the whole of Attica is not the same as that of even a fraction of the Peloponnesus; for they will not be able to supply the deficiency except by a battle, while we have plenty of land both on the islands and the continent. [5] The rule of the sea is indeed a great matter. Consider for a moment. Suppose that we were islanders: can you conceive a more impregnable position? Well, this in future should, as far as possible, be our conception of our position. Dismissing all thought of our land and houses, we must vigilantly guard the sea and the city. No irritation that we may feel for the former must provoke us to a battle with the numerical superiority of the Peloponnesians. A victory would only be succeeded by another battle against the same superiority: a reverse involves the loss of our allies, the source of our strength, who will not remain quiet a day after we become unable to march against them. We must cry not over the loss of houses and land but of men's lives; since houses and land do not gain men, but men them. And if I had thought that I could persuade you, I would have bid you go out and lay them waste with your own hands, and show the Peloponnesians that this at any rate will not make you submit."

"I have many other reasons to hope for a favorable outcome, if you can consent not to combine schemes of fresh conquest with the conduct of the war, and will abstain from willfully involving yourselves in other dangers; indeed, I am more afraid of our own blun-

1.143
432/1
ATHENS
Pericles asserts that Sparta, even if she obtains funds, will never match Athens at sea, for Athens has enough citizen-sailors to match all of Hellas. Athens has lands across the sea that Sparta cannot harm. "Thus we must forgo our properties in Attica and, viewing ourselves as islanders, value most our sea power and its ability to provide us resources from our empire."

1.144
432/1
ATHENS
Pericles concludes his speech by advising the Athenians to accept this war as inevitable, and to avoid any new conquests or unnecessary risks until the war is over. He suggests that they let the Peloponnesians commence hostilities and reminds the Athenians of their glorious past.

1.143.1a Olympia: Map 1.137, BX.
1.143.1b Delphi: Map 1.137, BX.

1.143.1c Athenian resident aliens (*metics*) had both rights and obligations but were not citizens. See Appendix A, The Athenian Government, §2.

ILLUSTRATION 1.144
MARBLE HERM OF
PERICLES; A ROMAN COPY
OF AN ORIGINAL OF
PERHAPS 430 B.C.

ders than of the enemy's devices. [2] But these matters shall be
explained in another speech, as events require; for the present dismiss
these men with the answer that we will allow Megara the use of our
market and harbors when the Spartans suspend their alien acts
against us and our allies, there being nothing in the treaty to prevent
either one or the other; that we will leave the cities independent, if
independent we found them when we made the treaty, and when the
Spartans grant to their cities an independence not involving subservience to Spartan interest, but such as each severally may desire;

that we are willing to give the legal satisfaction which our agreements specify; and that we shall not commence hostilities, but shall resist those who do commence them. This is an answer agreeable at once to the rights and the dignity of Athens. [3] It must be thoroughly understood that war is a necessity, and that the more readily we accept it, the less will be the ardor of our opponents, and that out of the greatest dangers communities and individuals acquire the greatest glory. Did not our fathers resist the Persians not only with resources far different from ours, but even when those resources had been abandoned; and more by wisdom than by fortune, more by daring than by strength, did not they beat off the barbarian and advance their affairs to their present height? We must not fall behind them, but must resist our enemies in any way and in every way, and attempt to hand down our power to our posterity unimpaired."

Such were the words of Pericles. The Athenians, persuaded of the wisdom of his advice, voted as he desired, and answered the Spartans as he recommended, both on the separate points and in general: they would not respond to commands, but were ready to have the complaints settled in a fair and impartial manner by arbitration, which the terms of the truce prescribe. So the envoys departed home, and did not return again.

These were the charges and differences existing between the rival powers before the war, arising immediately from the affair at Epidamnus[1a] and Corcyra.[1b] Still intercourse continued in spite of them, and mutual communication. It was carried on without heralds, but not without suspicion, as events were occurring which were equivalent to a breach of the treaty and matter for war.

1.145
432/1
ATHENS
The Athenians vote as Pericles advises and the Spartan envoys return home.

1.146
432/1
HELLAS
Thus the stage was set for war, though it did not yet begin.

1.146.1a Epidamnus: Map 1.137, AX.
1.146.1b Corcyra: Map 1.137. AX.

BOOK TWO

The war between the Athenians and Peloponnesians and the allies on either side now really begins. For now all intercourse except through the medium of heralds[1a] ceased, and hostilities were commenced and prosecuted without intermission. The history follows the chronological order of events by summers and winters.

The Thirty Years' Peace which was entered into after the conquest of Euboea lasted fourteen years.[1a] In the fifteenth year, the forty-eighth year of the priestess-ship of Chrysis at Argos,[1b] during the ephorate[1c] of Aenesias at Sparta and in the last month but two of the archonship[1d] of Pythodorus at Athens, six months after the battle of Potidaea[1e] and just at the beginning of spring, a Theban[1f] force a little over three hundred strong, under the command of their *boeotarchs*,[1g] Pythangelus son of Phyleides, and Diemporus son of Onetorides, about the first watch of the night, made an armed entry into Plataea,[1h] a city of Boeotia in alliance with Athens.[1i] [2] The gates were opened to them by a Plataean called Naucleides, who, with his party, had invited them in, meaning to put to death the citizens of the opposite party, bring over the city to Thebes, and thus obtain power for themselves. [3] This had been arranged through Eurymachus son of Leontiades, a person of great influence at Thebes. For Plataea had always been at variance with Thebes; and the latter, foreseeing that war was at hand, wished to surprise her old enemy in time of peace, before hostilities had ac-

2.1
431
1st Year/Summer
HELLAS
The war begins.

2.2
431
1st Year/Summer
PLATAEA
In the fifteenth year of the Thirty Years' Peace, Thebes attacks Plataea.

2.1.1a   Heralds, already a venerable Greek institution in Thucydides' day, operated under the protection of the god Hermes, and were easily identified by the staff they carried. They alone could travel unmolested between states or armies during wartime in order to deliver messages, take back replies, and make perfunctory arrangements.

2.2.1a   From 446/5 to 431. This treaty is reported by Thucydides in 1.115.1.

2.2.1b   In the fifteenth year of the treaty, and the forty-eighth year of Chrysis' priestess-ship. She is the same Chrysis, presumably, whose carelessness led to the burning of the temple of Hera at Argos, an incident

described in 4.133.

2.2.1c   For the Spartan ephorate, see Appendix C, Spartan Institutions, §5–6.

2.2.1d   For a discussion of the Athenian eponymous archon, see Appendix A, The Athenian Government, §6; and for the problem of dating events in classical times, see Appendix K, Calendars and Dating Systems, §2–3.

2.2.1e   This battle is described in 1.62–63.

2.2.1f   Thebes: Map 2.5.

2.2.1g   *Boeotarchs* were chief magistrates of the Boeotian federal government.

2.2.1h   Plataea: Map 2.5.

2.2.1i   Athens, in relation to Plataea and Thebes: Map 2.5.

tually broken out. Indeed this was how they got in so easily without being observed, as no guard had been posted. [4] After the soldiers had taken up positions in the *agora*[4a] those who had invited them in wished them to set to work at once and go to their enemies' houses. This, however, the Thebans refused to do, but determined to make a conciliatory proclamation, and if possible to come to a friendly understanding with the citizens. Their herald accordingly invited any who wished to resume their old place in the federation of all the Boeotians[4b] to take up positions beside them, for they thought that in this way the city would readily join them.

2.3
431
1st Year/Summer
PLATAEA
After perceiving the weakness of the occupying enemy force, the Plataeans counterattack.

On becoming aware of the presence of the Thebans within their gates, and of the sudden occupation of the city, the Plataeans concluded in their alarm that more had entered than was really the case, the night preventing their seeing them. They accordingly came to terms, and accepting the proposal, made no movement; especially as the Thebans offered none of them any violence. [2] But somehow or other, during the negotiations, they discovered the scanty numbers of the Thebans, and decided that they could easily attack and overpower them; the mass of the Plataeans being averse to revolting from Athens. [3] At all events they resolved to attempt it. Digging through the common walls of the houses, they thus managed to join each other without being seen going through the streets, in which they placed wagons without the beasts in them, to serve as a barricade, and arranged everything else as seemed suitable for the occasion. [4] When everything had been done that circumstances permitted, they watched their opportunity and went out of their houses against the enemy. It was still night, though daybreak was at hand: in daylight it was thought that their attack would be met by men full of courage and on equal terms with their assailants, while in darkness it would fall upon panic-stricken troops, who would also be at a disadvantage from their enemy's knowledge of the locality. So they made their assault at once, and came to close quarters as quickly as they could.

2.4
431
1st Year/Summer
PLATAEA
The Thebans are defeated; many surrender.

The Thebans, finding themselves outwitted, immediately closed up to repel all attacks made upon them. [2] Twice or thrice they beat back their assailants. But the men shouted and charged them, the women and slaves screamed and yelled from the houses and pelted them with stones and tiles; besides, it had been raining hard all night; and so at last their courage gave way, and they turned and fled through the city. Most of the fugitives were quite ignorant of the right ways out, and this, with the mud, and the darkness caused by the moon being in her last quarter, and the fact that their pursuers knew their way about and could easily stop their escape, proved

2.2.4a   *Agora:* the marketplace and the social
center of a classical Greek city.

2.2.4b   For more on the constitution of the
Boeotian Federation, see note 5.38.2a.

fatal to many. [3] The only gate open was the one by which they had entered, and this was shut by one of the Plataeans driving the spike of a javelin into the bar instead of the bolt; so that even here there was no longer any means of exit. [4] They were now chased all over the city. Some got on the wall and threw themselves over, in most cases with a fatal result. One party managed to find a deserted gate, and obtaining an axe from a woman, cut through the bar;[4a] but as they were soon observed only a few succeeded in getting out. Others, scattered about in different parts of the city, were destroyed. [5] The most numerous and compact body rushed into a large building next to the city wall: the doors on the side of the street happened to be open, and the Thebans fancied that they were the gates of the city, and that there was a passage right through to the outside. [6] The Plataeans, seeing their enemies in a trap, now consulted whether they should set fire to the building and burn them just as they were, or whether there was anything else that they could do with them; [7] until at length these and the rest of the Theban survivors found wandering about the city agreed to an unconditional surrender of themselves and their arms to the Plataeans. [8] While such was the fate of the party in Plataea, [2.5.1] the rest of the Thebans who were to have joined them with all their forces before daybreak, in case of anything miscarrying with the body that had entered, received the news of the affair while on the road, and pressed forward to their assistance. [2] Now Plataea is nearly eight miles from Thebes, and their march was delayed by the rain that had fallen in the night, for the river Asopus[2a] had risen and was not easy of passage; [3] and so, having to march in the rain, and being hindered in crossing the river, they arrived too late, and found the whole party either slain or captive. [4] When they learned what had happened, they at once formed a design against the Plataeans outside the city. As the attack had been made in time of peace, and was perfectly unexpected, there were of course men and stock in the fields; and the Thebans wished if possible to have some prisoners to exchange against their countrymen in the city, should any chance to have been taken alive. [5] Such was their plan. But the Plataeans suspected their intention almost before it was formed, and becoming alarmed for their fellow citizens outside the city, sent a herald to the Thebans, reproaching them for their unscrupulous attempt to seize their city in time of peace, and warning them against any outrage on those outside. Should the warning be disregarded, they threatened to put to death the men they had in their hands, but added that, on the Thebans retiring from their territory, they would surrender the prisoners to their friends. [6] This is the Theban ac-

2.5
431
1st Year/Summer
PLATAEA
Theban reinforcements arrive too late. When the Plataeans threaten to harm the prisoners, the Thebans retire without taking hostages; but the Plataeans execute the prisoners anyway.

2.4.4a   City gates were secured by large wooden bars locked into place with special bolts. Like keys, only these bolts could release the bar and permit the gate to open. Lacking the proper bolt, one could only open the gate by cutting through the bar, a noisy and lengthy process. See also 4.111.2.

2.5.2a   Asopus river: Map 2.5.

count of the matter, and they say that they had an oath given them. The Plataeans, on the other hand, do not admit any promise of an immediate surrender, but make it contingent upon subsequent negotiation: the oath they deny altogether. [7] Be this as it may, upon the Thebans retiring from their territory without committing any injury, the Plataeans hastily got in whatever they had in the country and immediately put the men to death. The prisoners were a hundred and eighty in number; Eurymachus, the person with whom the traitors had negotiated, being one.

MAP 2.5 PLATAEA AND THEBES

2.6
431
1st Year/Summer
PLATAEA
Athenian instructions to preserve the prisoners arrive too late. Athens sends supplies and a garrison, and gives refuge to Plataean noncombatants.

This done, the Plataeans sent a messenger to Athens, gave back the dead to the Thebans under a truce,[1a] and arranged things in the city as seemed best to meet the present emergency. [2] The Athenians meanwhile, having had word of the affair sent them immediately after its occurrence, had instantly seized all the Boeotians in Attica, and sent a herald to the Plataeans to forbid their proceeding to extremities with their Theban prisoners without instructions from Athens. The news of the men's death had of course

2.6.1a   This truce is granted according to the accepted ritual of hoplite warfare. See Appendix F, Land Warfare, §6.

not arrived; [3] the first messenger having left Plataea just when the Thebans entered it, the second just after their defeat and capture; so there was no later news. Thus the Athenians sent their orders in ignorance of the facts; and the herald on his arrival found the men slain. After this the Athenians marched to Plataea and brought in provisions, and left a garrison in the place, also taking away the women and children and such of the men as were least able-bodied.[3a]

With the affair at Plataea the treaty had been broken by an overt act,[1a] and Athens at once prepared for war, as did also Sparta and her allies. They resolved to send embassies to the King and to such other of the barbarian powers as either party could look to for assistance, and tried to ally themselves with the uncommitted states at home.[1b] [2] Sparta, in addition to the existing naval forces, gave orders to the states that had declared for her in Italy and Sicily to build vessels up to a grand total of five hundred, the quota of each city being determined by its size, and also to provide a specified sum of money. Till these were ready they were to remain neutral and to admit single Athenian ships into their harbors. [3] Athens on her part reviewed her existing confederacy, and sent embassies to the places more immediately round the Peloponnesus, Corcyra, Cephallenia, Acarnania, and Zacynthus;[3a] perceiving that if these could be relied upon she could carry the war all round the Peloponnesus.

And if both sides nourished the boldest hopes and put forth their utmost strength for the war, this was only natural. Zeal is always at its height at the commencement of an undertaking; and on this particular occasion the Peloponnesus and Athens were both full of young men whose inexperience made them eager to take up arms, while the rest of Hellas stood straining with excitement at the conflict of its leading cities. [2] Everywhere predictions were being recited and oracles being chanted by such persons as collect them, and this not only in the contending cities. [3] Further, some time before this there was an earthquake at Delos,[3a] for the first time in the memory of the Hellenes.[3b] This was said and thought to be ominous of the events impending; indeed, nothing of the kind that happened was allowed to pass without remark. [4] Men's feelings inclined much more to the Spartans, especially as they proclaimed themselves the liberators of Hellas. No private or public effort that could help them in speech or action was omitted; each thinking that the cause suffered wherever he could not himself see to it. [5] So general was the indignation felt against Athens, whether by those who wished to escape from her empire,

2.7
431
1st Year/Summer
HELLAS
Both sides prepare for war. Sparta sends embassies to neutrals and barbarians, and asks her Italian and Sicilian allies to build triremes.

2.8
431
1st Year/Summer
HELLAS
Enthusiasm for war among young men runs high. Most Hellenes hope for Sparta to win, fearing absorption in Athens' empire or desiring liberation from it.

2.6.3a	The narrative of events at Plataea is continued in 2.71–78.	2.7.3a	Corcyra, Cephallenia, Acarnania, Zacynthus, in relation to the Peloponnesus: Map 2.9, AX, BX.
2.7.1a	That the Thebans opened hostilities with a surprise attack in peacetime had some adverse effect upon Spartan morale, as we learn in 7.18.	2.8.3a	Delos: Map 2.9, BY.
2.7.1b	The "King" is the king of Persia; this is the policy recommended by Archidamus earlier in 1.82.1.	2.8.3b	Since Herodotus (Book 6.98) mentions an earthquake on Delos in 490, this remark has caused some amazement.

MAP 2.8 PELOPONNESIAN LEAGUE AND OTHER SPARTAN ALLIES

2.9
431
1st Year/Summer
HELLAS
The allies of the two
belligerents are listed.

or were apprehensive of being absorbed by it. [2.9.1] Such were the preparations and such the feelings with which the contest opened. The allies of the two belligerents were the following. [2] These were the allies of Sparta: all the Peloponnesians within the Isthmus[2a] except the Argives[2b] and Achaeans,[2c] who were neutral; Pellene[2d] being the only Achaean city that first joined in the war, though her example was afterwards followed by the rest. Outside the Peloponnesus the Megarians,[2e] Locrians,[2f] Boeotians,[2g]

2.9.2a	The Isthmus of Corinth, Corinth: Map 2.8, AY.	
2.9.2b	Argos: Map 2.8, BY.	
2.9.2c	Achaea: Map 2.8, AX.	
2.9.2d	Pellene in Achaea: Map 2.8, AY.	
2.9.2e	Megara, Map 2.8: AY	

2.9.2f	Presumably he means the Opuntian Locrians (Map 2.8, AY), not the Ozolian Locrians who were allied to Athens (see 3.95.3), or the Italian (Epizephyrian) Locrians.
2.9.2g	Boeotia: Map 2.8, AY.

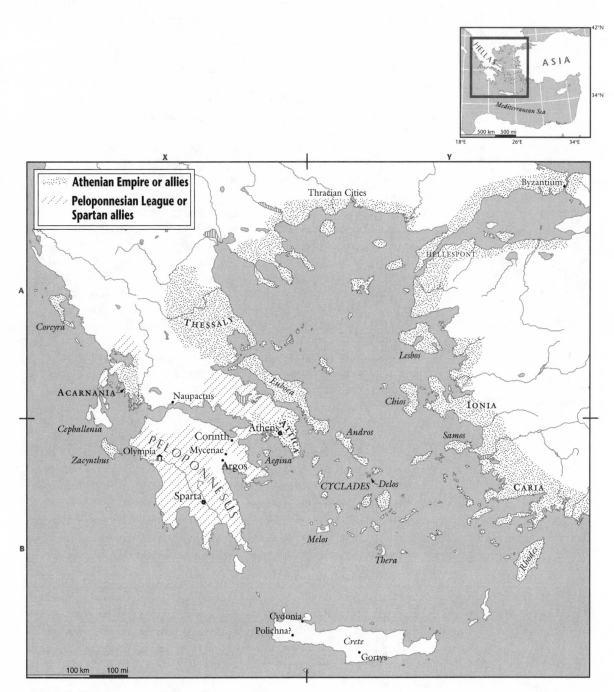

MAP 2.9 THE ATHENIAN SUBJECT STATES AND ALLIES

Phocians,[2h] Ambraciots,[2i] Leucadians,[2j] and Anactorians.[2k] [3] Of these, ships were furnished by the Corinthians, Megarians, Sicyonians,[3a] Pellenians, Eleans,[3b] Ambraciots, and Leucadians; and cavalry by the Boeotians, Phocians, and Locrians. The other states sent infantry. This was the Spartan confederacy.[3c] [4] That of Athens comprised the Chians,[4a] Lesbians,[4b] Plataeans, the Messenians in Naupactus,[4c] most of the Acarnanians,[4d] the Corcyraeans,[4e] Zacynthians,[4f] and some tributary cities in the following countries, namely, the seaboard part of Caria[4g] with its Dorian neighbors, Ionia,[4h] the Hellespont,[4i] the Thracian cities,[4j] the islands lying between the Peloponnesus and Crete[4k] toward the east, and all the Cyclades[4l] except Melos[4m] and Thera.[4n] [5] Of these, ships were furnished by Chios, Lesbos, and Corcyra, infantry and money by the rest. Such were the allies of either party and their resources for the war.

Immediately after the affair at Plataea, Sparta sent round orders to the cities in the Peloponnesus and the rest of her confederacy to prepare troops and the provisions requisite for a foreign campaign, in order to invade Attica. [2] The several states were ready at the time appointed and assembled at the Isthmus; the contingent of each city being two-thirds of its whole force. [3] After the whole army had mustered, the Spartan king, Archidamus, the leader of the expedition, called together the generals of all the states and the principal persons and officers, and exhorted them as follows:

"Peloponnesians and allies, our fathers made many campaigns both within and without the Peloponnesus, and the elder men among us here are not without experience in war. Yet we have never set out with a larger force than the present; and if our numbers and efficiency are remarkable, so also is the power of the state against which we march. [2] We ought not then to show ourselves inferior to our ancestors, or unequal to our own reputation. For the hopes and attention of all Hellas are bent upon the present effort, and its sympathy is with the enemy of the hated Athens. [3] Therefore, numerous as the invading army may appear to be, and certain as some may think it that our adversary will not meet us in the field, this is no

2.9.2h	Phocis: Map 2.8, AY.	2.9.4d	Acarnania: Map 2.9, AX.
2.9.2i	Ambracia: Map 2.8, AX.	2.9.4e	Corcyra: Map 2.9, AX.
2.9.2j	Leucas: Map 2.8, AX.	2.9.4f	Zacynthus: Map 2.9, BX.
2.9.2k	Anactorium: Map 2.8, AX.	2.9.4g	Caria: Map 2.9, BY.
2.9.3a	Sicyon: Map 2.8, AY.	2.9.4h	Ionia: Map 2.9, AY. See Appendix H, Dialects and Ethnic Groups, §7–8, for the Ionians and the Dorians.
2.9.3b	Elis: Map 2.8, BX.		
2.9.3c	The "confederacy" here includes both the Peloponnesian League and the wider Spartan alliance; see Appendix D, The Peloponnesian League, §3.	2.9.4i	Hellespont: Map 2.9, AY.
		2.9.4j	The region here called the Thracian cities: Map 2.9, AY.
2.9.4a	Chios: Map 2.9, AY.	2.9.4k	Peloponnesus: Map 2.9, BX. Crete: Map 2.9, BY.
2.9.4b	Lesbos: Map 2.9, AY.		
2.9.4c	These "Messenians" lived now at Naupactus (Map 2.9, AX), where Athens settled them after they surrendered to Sparta from Ithome and were forced to leave the Peloponnesus; see 1.103.1–3.	2.9.4l	The Cyclades, islands in the Aegean Sea southeast of Attica: Map 2.9, BY.
		2.9.4m	Melos: Map 2.9, BY.
		2.9.4n	Thera: Map 2.9, BY.

sort of justification for the least negligence upon the march; but the officers and men of each particular city should always be prepared for the advent of danger in their own area. [4] The course of war cannot be foreseen, and its attacks are generally dictated by the impulse of the moment; and where overweening self-confidence has despised preparation, a wise apprehension has often been able to make head against superior numbers. [5] Not that confidence is out of place in an army of invasion, but in an enemy's country it should also be accompanied by the precautions of apprehension: troops will by this combination be best inspired for dealing a blow, and best secured against receiving one. [6] In the present instance, the city against which we are going, far from being powerless to defend itself, is on the contrary most excellently equipped at all points; so that we have every reason to expect that they will take the field against us, and that if they have not set out already before we are there, they will certainly do so when they see us in their territory wasting and destroying their property. [7] For men are always exasperated at suffering injuries to which they are not accustomed, and on seeing them inflicted before their very eyes; and where least inclined for reflection, rush with the greatest heat to action. [8] The Athenians are the very people of all others to do this, as they aspire to rule the rest of the world, and are more in the habit of invading and ravaging their neighbors' territory, than of seeing their own treated in the like fashion. [9] Considering, therefore, the power of the state against which we are marching, and the greatness of the reputation which, according to the event, we shall win or lose for our ancestors and ourselves, remember as you follow where you may be led to regard discipline and vigilance as of the first importance, and to obey with alacrity the orders transmitted to you; as nothing contributes so much to the credit and safety of an army as when its soldiers, although numerous, quickly act on the orders transmitted to them."

Dismissing the assembly after this brief speech, Archidamus first sent off Melesippus son of Diacritus, a Spartan, to Athens, in case she should be more inclined to submit on seeing the Peloponnesians actually on the march. [2] But the Athenians did not admit him into the city or to their assembly; Pericles having already carried a motion against admitting either herald or embassy from the Spartans after they had once marched out. The herald was accordingly sent away without an audience, and ordered to be beyond the frontier that same day; in future, if those who sent him had a proposition to make they must retire to their own territory before they dispatched embassies to Athens. An escort was sent with Melesippus to prevent his holding communication with anyone. [3] When he reached the frontier and was just going to be dismissed, he departed with these words: "This day will be the beginning of great misfortunes to the Hellenes." [4]

2.12
431
1st Year/Summer
ATTICA
After the final herald sent by Archidamus to the Athenians is rebuffed, the Peloponnesians invade Attica.

2.13
431
1st Year/Summer
ATHENS
Pericles donates his country estate to the city and describes Athens' best war strategy to the assembly, listing the city's financial and military resources.

As soon as he arrived at the camp, and Archidamus learnt that the Athenians had still no thoughts of submitting, he at length began his march, and advanced with his army into their territory. [5] Meanwhile the Boeotians, sending their contingent and cavalry to join the Peloponnesian expedition, went to Plataea with the remainder and laid waste the country.

While the Peloponnesians were still mustering at the Isthmus, or on the march before they invaded Attica, Pericles son of Xanthippus, one of the ten generals of the Athenians, finding that the invasion was to take place, conceived the idea that Archidamus, who happened to be his guest-friend,[1a] might possibly pass by his estate without ravaging it. This he might do, either from a personal wish to oblige him, or acting under instructions from Sparta for the purpose of creating a prejudice against him, as had been before attempted in the demand for the expulsion of the accursed family. He accordingly took the precaution of announcing to the Athenians in the assembly[1b] that, although Archidamus was his guest-friend, yet this friendship should not extend to the detriment of the state, and that in case the enemy should make his houses and lands an exception to the rest and not pillage them, he at once gave them up to be public property, so that they should not bring him into suspicion. [2] He also gave the citizens some advice on their present affairs in the same strain as before.[2a] They were to prepare for the war, and to carry in their property from the country. They were not to go out to battle, but to come into the city and guard it, and get ready their fleet, in which their real strength lay. They were also to keep a tight rein on their allies—the strength of Athens being derived from the money brought in by their payments, and success in war depending principally upon conduct and capital. [3] Here they had no reason to be despondent. Apart from other sources of income, an average revenue of six hundred *talents*[3a] of silver was drawn from the tribute of the allies; and there were still six thousand talents of coined silver in the Acropolis, out of nine thousand seven hundred that had once been there, from which the money had been taken for the Propylaea,[3b] the other public buildings, and for Potidaea.[3c] [4] This did not include the uncoined gold and silver in public and private offerings, the sacred vessels for the processions and games,[4a] the Median spoils,[4b] and

2.13.1a   Such a relation of "guest-friendship" (*xenia*) was common between eminent citizens of different states; sometimes it was between an individual and a whole state (in which case the term *proxenia*, denoting a formalized relationship, was used; see 2.29.1, 2.85.5, 4.78.1, etc.). Such relationships were often hereditary (see 5.43.2, 6, and 6.89 for Alcibiades and Sparta).

2.13.1b   The Athenian assembly; see Appendix A, The Athenian Government, §5, §7–9.

2.13.2a   Pericles' strategy is set out in his reply to the Spartan envoys (1.144.1); see 2.65.7.

2.13.3a   The *talent* was a large unit of weight and money. See Appendix J, Classical Greek Currency, §5.

2.13.3b   The Propylaea, through the remains of which one still enters the Acropolis at Athens, was the costly and special pride of Pericles' building program. For financial reasons, the work on it was halted when the Peloponnesian War began and was never thereafter resumed.

2.13.3c   For the campaign at Potidaea, which began in 432, see 1.56–65. For the costs of the siege there, see 2.70.2 and 3.17.4.

2.13.4a   See Appendix I, Greek Religious Festivals, which notes that religious festivals often included athletic and cultural contests.

2.13.4b   Booty taken from the Persians, whom the Greeks regularly referred to as "the Mede" or "the Medes," although the Medes and Persians were two distinct peoples.

similar resources to the amount of five hundred talents. [5] To this he added the treasures of the other temples. These were by no means inconsiderable, and might fairly be used. Nay, if they were ever absolutely driven to it, they might take even the gold ornaments of Athena herself; for the statue contained forty talents of pure gold and it was all removable.[5a] This might be used for self-preservation, and must every penny of it be restored. [6] Such was their financial position—surely a satisfactory one. Then they had an army of thirteen thousand *hoplites*,[6a] besides sixteen thousand more in the garrisons and on the battlements at Athens. [7] This was the number of men on guard at the time of the first invasion: it was composed of the oldest and youngest levies and the resident aliens[7a] who had heavy armor. The Phaleric Wall[7b] ran for four miles before it joined the wall that ran round the city; and of this last nearly five miles had a guard, although part of it was left without one, namely, that between the Long Wall and the Phaleric. Then there were the Long Walls to the Piraeus,[7c] a distance of some four miles and a half, the outer of which was manned. Lastly, the circumference of the Piraeus with Munychia[7d] was nearly seven miles and a half; only half of this, however, was guarded. [8] Pericles also showed them that they had twelve hundred horse including mounted archers, with sixteen hundred archers unmounted, and three hundred *triremes*[8a] fit for service. Such were the resources of Athens in the different departments when the Peloponnesian invasion was impending and hostilities were being commenced. Pericles also urged his usual arguments to show that they would survive in the war.

The Athenians listened to his advice, and began to bring in their wives and children from the country, and all their household furniture, even to the woodwork of their houses[1a] which they removed. Their sheep and cattle they sent over to Euboea[1b] and the adjacent islands. But they found it hard to move, as most of them had always been used to living in the country.

From very early times this had been more the case with the Athenians than with others. Under Cecrops and the first kings, down to the reign of Theseus, Attica had always consisted of a number of independent cities,

2.14
431
1st Year/Summer
ATTICA
The Athenians move inside the city walls.

2.15
431
1st Year/Summer
ATTICA
Thucydides tells how the cities of Attica became politically united.

2.13.5a The temples and shrines on the Acropolis, like major shrines elsewhere, accumulated offerings of precious metals and treasure, some of which were used for the ornamentation of the statue of Athena. See note 1.121.3a.

2.13.6a *Hoplite* is the Greek word for a heavily armed infantryman. See Glossary and Appendix F, Land Warfare, §2.

2.13.7a Athenian resident aliens (*metics*) had both rights and obligations but were not citizens. See Appendix A, The Athenian Government, §2, 4.

2.13.7b Phaleric Wall: Map 2.19, inset.

2.13.7c Long Walls between Athens and the Piraeus: Map 2.19, inset.

2.13.7d The city of the Piraeus, the hill of Munychia: Map 2.19, inset.

2.13.8a *Triremes* were the standard warship of this period; see Appendix G, Trireme Warfare, §4–7.

2.14.1a Wooden doors, sills, window frames, shutters, and the like were valuable and so were built to be easily removed. See in 3.68.3 how the Thebans salvaged such items from Plataea when they destroyed that city.

2.14.1b Euboea: Map 2.9, AX, and Map 2.19.

each with its own town hall and magistrates. Except in times of danger the king of Athens was not consulted; in ordinary seasons they carried on their government and settled their affairs without his interference; sometimes they even waged war against him, as in the case of the Eleusinians with Eumolpus against Erechtheus. [2] In Theseus, however, they had a king whose intelligence matched his power; and one of the chief features in his organization of the country was to abolish the council chambers and magistrates of the petty cities, and to merge them in the single council chamber and town hall of the present capital. Individuals might still enjoy their private property just as before, but they were henceforth compelled to have only one political center, namely, Athens; which thus counted all the inhabitants of Attica among her citizens, so that when Theseus died he left a great state behind him. Indeed, from him dates the Synoecia, or Feast of Union,[2a] which is paid for by the state, and which the Athenians still keep in honor of the goddess. [3] Before this the city consisted of the present Acropolis and the district beneath it looking rather toward the south. [4] This is shown by the fact that the temples of the other deities, besides that of Athene, are in the Acropolis; and even those that are outside it are mostly situated in this quarter of the city, as that of the Olympian Zeus, of the Pythian Apollo, of Earth, and of Dionysus in the Marshes, the same in whose honor the older Dionysia are to this day celebrated in the month of Anthesterion not only by the Athenians but also by their Ionian[4a] descendants. [5] There are also other ancient temples in this quarter. The fountain too, which, since the alteration made by the tyrants,[5a] has been called Enneacrounos, or Nine Pipes, but which, when the spring was open, went by the name of Callirhoe, or Fairwater, was in those days, from being so near, used for the most important offices. Indeed, the old fashion of using the water before marriage and for other sacred purposes is still kept up. [6] Again, from their old residence in that quarter, the Acropolis is still known among Athenians as the *city*.

2.16
431
1st Year/Summer
ATTICA
The Athenians are greatly distressed at having to abandon their country homes.

The Athenians thus long lived scattered over Attica in independent cities. Even after the centralization of Theseus, old habit still prevailed; and from the early times down to the present war most Athenians still lived in the country with their families and households, and were consequently not at all inclined to move now, especially as they had only just restored their establishments after the Persian invasion.[1a] [2] Deep was their trouble and discontent at abandoning their houses and the hereditary temples of the ancient state, and at having to change their habits of life and to bid farewell to what each regarded as his native city.

2.15.2a   See Appendix I, Greek Religious Festivals, §8.
2.15.4a   See Appendix H, Dialects and Ethnic Groups, §3–4, 7–8, for more on the Ionians.
2.15.5a   Thucydides refers here to the tyrant Pisistratus and his son Hippias, whose rule

ended at Athens in 510. They are mentioned above in 1.20.2, and below in 3.104.1 and 6.53.3–59.4.
2.16.1a   The Persian invasion of 480–79, when Athens and Attica were pillaged by the Persians. See Appendix E, The Persians, §4.

When they arrived at Athens, though a few had houses of their own to go to, or could find an asylum with friends or relatives, by far the greater number had to take up their dwelling in the parts of the city that were not built over and in the temples and chapels of the heroes, except the Acropolis and the temple of the Eleusinian Demeter and such other places as were always kept closed. The occupation of the plot of ground lying below the Acropolis called the Pelasgian had been forbidden by a curse; and there was also an ominous fragment of a Pythian oracle which said—

2.17
431
1st Year/Summer
ATHENS
Rural Athenians settle wherever they can within the city walls. Athens prepares a fleet of one hundred triremes to raid the Peloponnesus.

> Better it will be to leave the Pelasgian unworked

[2] Yet this too was now built over in the necessity of the moment. And in my opinion, if the oracle proved true, it was in the opposite sense to what was expected. For the misfortunes of the state did not arise from the unlawful occupation, but the necessity of the occupation from the war; and though the god did not mention this, he foresaw that it would be an evil day for Athens in which the plot came to be inhabited. [3] Many also took up their quarters in the towers of the walls or wherever else they could. For when they were all come in, the city proved too small to hold them; though afterwards they divided the long walls and a great part of the Piraeus into lots and settled there. [4] All this took place while great attention was being given to the war; the allies were being mustered, and an armament of a hundred ships equipped for the Peloponnesus. [5] Such was the state of preparation at Athens.

Meanwhile the army of the Peloponnesians was advancing. The first city they came to in Attica[1a] was Oenoe,[1b] where they were to enter the country. Halting before it, they prepared to assault the wall with siege engines and other means. Oenoe, standing upon the Athenian and Boeotian border, was of course a walled city, and was used as a fortress by the Athenians in time of war. So the Peloponnesians prepared for their assault, and wasted some valuable time before the place. This delay brought the gravest censure upon Archidamus. Even during the levying of the war he had gained credit for weakness and Athenian sympathies by the half measures he had advocated; and after the army had assembled he had further injured himself in public estimation by his loitering at the Isthmus and the slowness with which the rest of the march had been conducted. But all this was as nothing to the delay at Oenoe. During this interval the Athenians were carrying in their property; and it was the belief of the Peloponnesians that a quick advance would have found everything still out, had it not been for his pro-

2.18
431
1st Year/Summer
ATTICA
The Peloponnesians besiege Oenoe. Archidamus' slow pace is criticized, but he hopes the Athenians will give in before their property is ravaged.

2.18.1a   Attica and its borders, in relation to
            Boeotia and Megara: Map 2.5 and Map
            2.8, AY.
2.18.1b   Oenoe: Map 2.5 and Map 2.19.

MAP 2.19 ATHENS AND ITS DEFENSES

crastination. Such was the feeling of the army toward Archidamus during the siege. But he, it is said, expected that the Athenians would shrink from letting their land be wasted, and would make their submission while it was still uninjured; and this was why he waited.

But after he had assaulted Oenoe, and every possible attempt to take it had failed, as no herald came from Athens, he at last broke up his camp and invaded Attica. This was about eighty days after the Theban attempt upon Plataea, just in the middle of summer, when the corn was ripe, and Archidamus son of Zeuxis, king of Sparta, was in command. Encamping in Eleusis[1a] and the Thriasian plain,[1b] they began their ravages, and putting to flight some Athenian horse at a place called Rheiti, or the Brooks,[1c] they then advanced, keeping Mount Aegaleus on their right, through Cropia,[1d] until they reached Acharnae,[1e] the largest of the Athenian *demes,* or townships. Sitting down before it, they formed a camp there, and continued their ravages for a long while.

2.19
431
1st Year/Summer
ATTICA
Failing to take Oenoe, Archidamus marches into Attica to Acharnae. It is midsummer and the corn is ripe.

2.19.1a Eleusis: Map 2.19.
2.19.1b Thria in the Thriasian plain: Map 2.19.
2.19.1c Rheiti is thought to be at the southeast corner of the Thriasian plain, at the foot of Mount Aegaleus; see Map 2.19 (A. W.

Gomme, *A Historical Commentary on Thucydides,* ii [Oxford, 1956], 71).
2.19.1d Cropia, possible location: Map 2.19, BY.
2.19.1e Acharnae: Map 2.19.

The reason why Archidamus remained in order of battle at Acharnae during this incursion, instead of descending into the plain, is said to have been this. [2] He hoped that the Athenians might possibly be tempted by the multitude of their youth and by their unprecedented preparedness for war to come out to battle and attempt to stop the devastation of their lands. [3] Accordingly, as they had not met him at Eleusis or the Thriasian plain, he tried to see if they could be provoked to a sally by the spectacle of a camp at Acharnae. [4] He thought the place itself a good position for encamping; and it seemed likely that such an important part of the state as the three thousand hoplites of the Acharnians would refuse to submit to the ruin of their property, and would force a battle on the rest of the citizens. On the other hand, should the Athenians not take the field during this incursion, he could then fearlessly ravage the plain in future invasions, and extend his advance up to the very walls of Athens. After the Acharnians had lost their own property they would be less willing to risk themselves for that of their neighbors; and so there would be division in the Athenian counsels. [5] These were the motives of Archidamus for remaining at Acharnae.

In the meanwhile, as long as the army was at Eleusis[1a] and the Thriasian plain,[1b] hopes were still entertained of its not advancing any nearer. It was remembered that Pleistoanax son of Pausanias, king of Sparta, had invaded Attica with a Peloponnesian army fourteen years before, but had retreated without advancing farther than Eleusis and Thria, which indeed proved the cause of his exile from Sparta, as it was thought he had been bribed to retreat. [2] But when they saw the army at Acharnae,[2a] barely seven miles from Athens, they lost all patience. The territory of Athens was being ravaged before the very eyes of the Athenians, a sight which the young men had never seen before and the old only in the Persian wars;[2b] and it was naturally thought a grievous insult, and the determination was universal, especially among the young men, to sally forth and stop it. [3] Knots were formed in the streets and engaged in hot discussion; for if the proposed sally was warmly recommended, it was also in some cases opposed. Oracles of the most various import were recited by the collectors, and found eager listeners in one or other of the disputants. Foremost in pressing for the sally were the Acharnians, as constituting no small part of the army of the state, and as it was their land that was being ravaged. In short, the whole city was in a most excited state; Pericles was the object of general indignation; his previous counsels were totally forgotten; he was abused for not leading out the army which he commanded, and was made responsible for the whole of the public suffering.

2.20
431
1st Year/Summer
ATTICA
Archidamus hopes that Athens will now give battle, since the Acharnaean hoplites might not fight for the property of others after their own had been destroyed.

2.21
431
1st Year/Summer
ATTICA
Outraged by the sight of the enemy ravaging their land, the Athenians wish to sally out to attack. They turn against Pericles, whose past advice they now forget.

2.21.1a   Eleusis: Map 2.19.
2.21.1b   Thria in the Thriasian plain: Map 2.19.
2.21.2a   Acharnae: Map 2.19.
2.21.2b   Attica had been occupied and despoiled
         by the Persians in 480 and 479.

2.22
431
1st Year/Summer
ATTICA
Pericles, certain that the
Athenians should avoid a
land battle, refuses to call an
assembly or a meeting of the
people. A cavalry skirmish
takes place between
Athenians and Thessalians
against the Boeotians.

He, meanwhile, seeing anger and poor judgment just now in the ascendant, and confident of his wisdom in refusing a sally, would not call either an assembly or a meeting of the people,[1a] fearing the fatal results of a debate inspired by passion and not by prudence. Accordingly, he attended to the defense of the city, and kept it as quiet as possible, [2] though he constantly sent out cavalry to prevent raids on the lands near the city from flying parties of the enemy. There was a trifling affair at Phrygia[2a] between a squadron of the Athenian horse with the Thessalians against the Boeotian cavalry; in which the former had rather the best of it, until the hoplites advanced to the support of the Boeotians, when the Thessalians and Athenians were routed and lost a few men, whose bodies, however, were recovered the same day without a truce. The next day the Peloponnesians set up a trophy.[2b] [3] Ancient alliance brought the Thessalians to the aid of Athens; those who came being the Larissaeans, Pharsalians, Cranaeans, Pyrasians, Gyrtonians, and Pheraeans.[3a] The Larissaean commanders were Polymedes and Aristonus, two party leaders in Larissa; the Pharsalian general was Menon; each of the other cities had also its own commander.

2.23
431
1st Year/Summer
ATTICA
After Athens sends a fleet to
raid Peloponnesus, the
Peloponnesian army returns
home.

In the meantime the Peloponnesians, as the Athenians did not come out to engage them, broke up from Acharnae and ravaged some of the *demes*[1a] between Mounts Parnes[1b] and Brilessus.[1c] [2] While they were in Attica, the Athenians sent off the hundred ships which they had been preparing round the Peloponnesus, with a thousand hoplites and four hundred archers on board,[2a] under the command of Carcinus son of Xenotimus, Proteas son of Epicles, and Socrates son of Antigenes. [3] This armament weighed anchor and started on its cruise, and the Peloponnesians, after remaining in Attica as long as their provisions lasted, retired through Boeotia by a different road to that by which they had entered. As they passed Oropus[3a] they ravaged the territory of Graea which is held by the Oropians from Athens, and reaching the Peloponnesus broke up to their respective cities.

2.24
431
1st Year/Summer
ATTICA
Athens sets aside a reserve of
one thousand talents and
one hundred triremes for
defense against a naval attack.

After they had retired the Athenians set guards by land and sea at the points at which they intended to have regular stations during the war. They also resolved to set apart a special fund of a thousand talents[1a] from the moneys in the Acropolis. This was not to be spent, but the current expenses of the war were to be otherwise provided for. If anyone should

2.22.1a As a general, Pericles was expected to convene an extraordinary assembly, but it is unclear how he was able to prevent an assembly from being held. See Appendix A, The Athenian Government, §7.
2.22.2a Phrygia: the location of Phrygia in Attica is unknown.
2.22.2b After a battle in ancient Greece, the victorious side raised a trophy, usually a set of captured armor arranged on a pole, at or near the battlefield; see Appendix F, Land Warfare, §6.
2.22.3a Ancient alliance, yes, but some Thessalian cavalry betrayed the Athenians and went over to the enemy at the battle of Tanagra, in 457 (see 1.107.7). For the loca-

tions of Thessalian Larissa, Pharsalus, Cranon, Pyrasus, Gyrtone, and Pherae, see Map 2.24, inset.
2.23.1a For an explanation of Athenian *demes,* see Appendix A, The Athenian Government, §4.
2.23.1b Mount Parnes: Map, 2.19.
2.23.1c Mount Brilessus, more generally known as Mount Pentelikos: Map 2.19.
2.23.2a That is, manned with ten hoplites and four archers per trireme, a standard Athenian complement at this time; see Appendix G, Trireme Warfare, §5.
2.23.3a Oropus: Map 2.24.
2.24.1a See Appendix J, Classical Greek Currency, §5.

Illustration 2.22 Athenian cavalry recruits on parade, as represented in the Parthenon frieze

MAP 2.24
ATHENIAN NAVAL RAIDS
IN 431; THESSALIANS
WHO ASSISTED ATHENS IN
431

move or put to the vote a proposition for using the money for any purpose whatever except that of defending the city in the event of the enemy bringing a fleet to make an attack by sea, it should be a capital offense. [2] With this sum of money they also set aside a special fleet of one hundred triremes, the best ships of each year,[2a] with their captains. None of these was to be used except with the money and against the same peril, should such peril arise.

Meanwhile the Athenians in the hundred ships round the Peloponnesus, reinforced by a Corcyraean squadron of fifty vessels and some others of the allies in those parts, cruised about the coasts and ravaged the country. Among other places they landed in Laconia[1a] and made an assault upon Methone;[1b] there being no garrison in the place, and the wall being weak. [2] But it so happened that Brasidas son of Tellis, a *Spartiate*,[2a] was in command of a guard for the defense of the district. Hearing of the attack, he

2.25
431
1st Year/Summer
PELOPONNESUS
The Athenian fleet, reinforced by allies, raids the coast of the Peloponnesus.

2.24.2a New triremes were built every year to replace those that had been lost, worn out, or retired. Although the trireme design was standardized, some were judged to be better built, or proved to be better or faster sailers, than others. These were "the best ships of each year."
2.25.1a Laconia: Map 2.24.
2.25.1b Methone, Messenia: Map 2.24. Methone was a city of the Messenian *perioikoi;* see Appendix C, Spartan Institutions, §9.

2.25.2a A *Spartiate* was a full citizen of Sparta and a member of the highest Spartan military caste.

hurried with a hundred hoplites to the assistance of the besieged, and dashing through the army of the Athenians, which was scattered over the country and had its attention turned to the wall, threw himself into Methone. He lost a few men in making good his entrance, but saved the place and won the thanks of Sparta by his exploit, being thus the first officer who obtained this notice during the war.[2b] [3] The Athenians at once weighed anchor and continued their cruise. Touching at Pheia in Elis,[3a] they ravaged the country for two days and defeated a picked force of three hundred men that had come from the vale of Elis and the immediate neighborhood to the rescue. [4] But a stiff squall came down upon them, and not liking to face it in a place where there was no harbor, most of them got on board their ships, and doubling Cape Ichthys[4a] sailed into the port of Pheia. In the meantime the Messenians,[4b] and some others who could not get on board, marched over by land and took Pheia. [5] The fleet afterwards sailed round and picked them up and then put to sea; Pheia being evacuated, as the main army of the Eleans had now come up. The Athenians continued their cruise, and ravaged other places on the coast.

About the same time the Athenians sent thirty ships to cruise round Locris[1a] and also to guard Euboea;[1b] Cleopompus son of Clinias being in command. [2] Making descents with the fleet he ravaged certain places on the seacoast, captured Thronium,[2a] and took hostages from it. He also defeated at Alope[2b] the Locrians that had assembled to resist him.

During the summer the Athenians also expelled the Aeginetans with their wives and children from Aegina,[1a] on the ground of their having been the chief agents in bringing the war upon them. Besides, Aegina lies so near the Peloponnesus that it seemed safer to send colonists of their own to hold it, and shortly afterwards the settlers were sent out. [2] The banished Aeginetans found an asylum in Thyrea,[2a] which was given to them by Sparta, not only on account of her quarrel with Athens, but also because the Aeginetans had laid her under obligations at the time of the earthquake and the revolt of the Helots.[2b] The territory of Thyrea is on the frontier of Argolis and Laconia, reaching down to the sea. Those of the Aeginetans who did not settle here were scattered over the rest of Hellas.

The same summer, at the beginning of a new lunar month, the only time, by the way, at which it appears possible, the sun was eclipsed after noon. After it had assumed the form of a crescent and some of the stars had come out, it returned to its natural shape.[1a]

2.26
431
1st Year/Summer
LOCRIS
An Athenian fleet attacks Locris.

2.27
431
1st Year/Summer
AEGINA
After Athens expels the Aeginetans Sparta gives them refuge at Thyrea.

2.28
431
1st Year/Summer
HELLAS
An eclipse of the sun.

2.25.2b Brasidas will prove to be a major Spartan figure in Thucydides' history. We next meet him as a commissioner to the Peloponnesian fleet in 2.85.1.	2.27.1a Aegina: Map 2.24.
	2.27.2a Thyrea: Map 2.24. Thucydides describes what happened to the Aeginetans at Thyrea in 4.56.
2.25.3a Pheia in Elis: Map 2.24.	2.27.2b The earthquake in Laconia and the revolt of the Helots (thought to have taken place in 465) is described by Thucydides in 1.101–3. For a discussion of the Spartan Helots, see Appendix C, Spartan Institutions, §3–4, 8.
2.25.4a Cape Ichthys: Map 2.24.	
2.25.4b These were the Messenians from Naupactus; see note 2.9.4c and 1.103.1–3.	
2.26.1a Locris (Opuntian): Map 2.24.	
2.26.1b Euboea: Map 2.24.	
2.26.2a Thronium: Map 2.24, inset.	2.28.1a This partial eclipse took place at Athens on August 3, 431, about 5:22 P.M.
2.26.2b Alope: Map 2.24, inset.	

MAP 2.29 MACEDONIA AND THRACE

2.29
431
1st Year/Summer
THRACE
Athens concludes alliances
with Sitalces, king of Thrace,
and Perdiccas, king of
Macedonia.

During the same summer Nymphodorus son of Pythes, an Abderite[1a] whose sister Sitalces had married, was made their *proxenus*[1b] by the Athenians and sent for to Athens. They had hitherto considered him their enemy; but he had great influence with Sitalces, and they wished this prince to become their ally. Sitalces was the son of Teres and king of the Thracians. [2] Teres, the father of Sitalces, was the first to establish the great kingdom of the Odrysians on a scale quite unknown to the rest of Thrace,[2a] a large portion of the Thracians being independent. [3] This Teres is in no way related to Tereus who married Pandion's daughter Procne from Athens; nor indeed did they belong to the same part of Thrace. Tereus lived in Daulis,[3a] part of what is now called Phocis,[3b] but which at that time was inhabited by Thracians. It was in this land that the women perpetrated the outrage upon Itys;[3c] and many of the poets when they mention the nightingale call it the Daulian bird. Besides, Pandion in contracting an alliance for his daughter, would consider the advantages of mutual assistance, and would naturally prefer a match at the above moderate distance to the journey of many days which separates Athens from the Odrysians. Again the names are different; and this Teres was king of the Odrysians, the first by the way who attained to any real power. [4] Sitalces, his son, was now sought as an ally by the Athenians, who desired his aid in the reduction of the Thracian cities and of Perdiccas.[4a] [5] Coming to Athens, Nymphodorus concluded the alliance with Sitalces, made his son Sadocus an Athenian citizen, and promised to finish the war in Thrace by persuading Sitalces to send the Athenians a force of Thracian horse and *peltasts*.[5a] [6] He also reconciled them with Perdiccas,

2.29.1a Abdera: Map 2.29.
2.29.1b A *proxenus*, although a citizen and resident of his own state, served as a "friend or representative" (much like a modern honorary consul) of a foreign state.
2.29.2a Odrysian Thrace: Map 2.29.
2.29.3a Daulis: Map 2.24.
2.29.3b Phocis: Map 2.24, inset.
2.29.3c When Procne discovered that Tereus had raped and mutilated her sister, Philomela, she took revenge by serving him a meal that included the flesh of their child, Itys. The gods prevented him from punishing

her by turning him into a hoopoe, Philomela into a swallow, and Procne into a nightingale.

2.29.4a Perdiccas was king of Macedonia (Map 2.29). His devious role in the Potidaea affair is described above in 1.56–62.
2.29.5a *Peltasts* were troops armed only with a small light shield, a javelin, and a short sword. Unhindered by body armor, they could move much more quickly than the fully armed hoplite, whose equipment was both far more heavy and far more expensive than theirs.

MAP 2.31 LATER ATHENIAN EXPEDITIONS OF 431

and induced them to restore Therme[6a] to him; upon which Perdiccas at once joined the Athenians and Phormio in an expedition against the Chalcidians.[6b] [7] Thus Sitalces son of Teres, king of the Thracians, and Perdiccas son of Alexander, king of the Macedonians, became allies of Athens.[7a]

Meanwhile the Athenians in the hundred vessels were still cruising round the Peloponnesus. After taking Sollium,[1a] a city belonging to Corinth,[1b] and presenting the city and territory to the Acarnanians of Palaira,[1c] they stormed Astacus,[1d] expelled its tyrant Evarchus, and gained the place for their confederacy. [2] Next they sailed to the island of Cephallenia[2a] and brought it over without using force. Cephallenia lies off Acarnania[2b] and Leucas,[2c] and consists of four states, the Paleans, Cranaeans, Samaeans, and Pronnaeans.[2d] Not long afterwards the fleet returned to Athens.

Toward the autumn of this year the Athenians invaded the Megarid[1a] with their whole levy, resident aliens[1b] included, under the command of Per-

2.30
431
1st Year/Summer
ACARNANIA
The Athenian fleet conducts operations in Acarnania.
CEPHALLENIA
Cephallenia joins the Athenians.

2.31
431
1st Year/Summer
MEGARA
An army under Pericles ravages Megara.

2.29.6a Therme: Map 2.29.
2.29.6b Chalcidice: Map 2.29.
2.29.7a We next hear of Sitalces in 2.67, and of Perdiccas in 2.80.
2.30.1a Sollium: Map 2.31, AX.
2.30.1b Corinth: Map 2.31, AY.
2.30.1c Palaira, Acarnania: Map 2.31, AX.
2.30.1d Astacus: Map 2.31, AX. Evarchus returns to Astacus with Corinthian support in 2.33.
2.30.2a Cephallenia: Map 2.31, AX.

2.30.2b Acarnania: Map 2.31, AX. Events in Acarnania will appear next in 2.33.
2.30.2c Leucas: Map 2.31, AX.
2.30.2d Pale, Cranae, Same, Proni, of Cephallenia: Map 2.31, AX.
2.31.1a Megara: Map 2.31, AY.
2.31.1b Athenian resident aliens (*metics*) had both rights and obligations but were not citizens. See Appendix A, The Athenian Government, §2, 4.

109

icles son of Xanthippus. The Athenians in the hundred ships round the Peloponnesus on their journey home had just reached Aegina, and hearing that the citizens at home were in full force at Megara, now sailed over and joined them. [2] This was without doubt the largest army of Athenians ever assembled, the state being still in the flower of her strength and yet unvisited by the plague. Full ten thousand hoplites were in the field, all Athenian citizens, besides the three thousand before Potidaea. Then the resident aliens who joined in the incursion were at least three thousand strong; besides which there was a multitude of light troops. They ravaged the greater part of the territory, and then retired. [3] Other incursions into the Megarid were afterwards made by the Athenians annually during the war, sometimes only with cavalry, sometimes with all their forces. This went on until the capture of Nisaea.[2b]

2.32
431
1st Year/Summer
OPUNTIAN LOCRIS
The Athenians fortify a base on Atalanta.

Atalanta[1a] also, the deserted island off the Opuntian coast, was toward the end of this summer converted into a fortified post by the Athenians, in order to prevent privateers issuing from Opus[1b] and the rest of Locris[1c] and plundering Euboea.[1d] Such were the events of this summer after the return of the Peloponnesians from Attica.

2.33
431/0
1st Year/Winter
ACARNANIA
A Corinthian fleet retakes Astacus, raids Acarnania, and is repulsed at Cephallenia.

In the ensuing winter the Acarnanian[1a] Evarchus wishing to return to Astacus,[1b] persuaded the Corinthians to sail over with forty ships and fifteen hundred hoplites and restore him; himself also hiring some mercenaries. In command of the force were Euphamidas son of Aristonymus, Timoxenus son of Timocrates, and Eumachus son of Chrysis, [2] who sailed over and restored him, and after failing in an attempt on some places on the Acarnanian coast which they were desirous of gaining, began their voyage home. [3] Coasting along shore they touched at Cephallenia[3a] and made a descent on the Cranian[3b] territory, and losing some men in a surprise attack by the Cranians, put to sea somewhat hurriedly and returned home.

2.34
431/0
1st Year/Winter
ATHENS
The Athenian procedure for burying their war dead is described. Pericles is chosen to deliver this war's first funeral oration.

In the same winter the Athenians gave a funeral at the public cost to those who had first fallen in this war. It was a custom of their ancestors, and the manner of it is as follows. [2] Three days before the ceremony, the bones of the dead[2a] are laid out in a tent which has been erected; and their friends bring to their relatives such offerings as they please. [3] In the funeral procession cypress coffins are borne in carts, one for each tribe; the bones of the deceased being placed in the coffin of their tribe.[3a] Among these is carried one empty bier decked for the missing, that is, for those whose bodies could not be recovered. [4] Any citizen or stranger who pleases joins in the procession: and the female relatives are there to wail at the burial. [5] The dead are laid in the public sepulcher in the most beautiful suburb of the city, in which those who fall in war are always buried; with

2.31.2b Nisaea: Map 2.31, AY. The capture of Nisaea by the Athenians in 424 is described in 4.69.
2.32.1a Atalanta: Map 2.31, AY.
2.32.1b Opus: Map 2.31, AY.
2.32.1c Locris (Opuntian): Map 2.31, AY.
2.32.1d Euboea: Map 2.31, AY.
2.33.1a Acarnania: Map 2.31, AX.
2.33.1b Astacus: Map 2.31, AX.

2.33.3a Cephallenia: Map 2.31, AX.
2.33.3b Cranae on Cephallenia: Map 2.31, AX.
2.34.2a The Greek custom at this time was to burn the bodies of the dead and then to gather up the bones and bury them.
2.34.3a For more on Athenian "tribes," see Appendix A, The Athenian Government, §3–5.

the exception of those slain at Marathon,[5a] who for their singular and extra-ordinary valor were interred on the spot where they fell. [6] After the bodies have been laid in the earth, a man chosen by the state, of approved wisdom and eminent reputation, pronounces over them an appropriate eulogy; after which all retire. [7] Such is the manner of the burying; and throughout the whole of the war, whenever the occasion arose, the established custom was observed. [8] Meanwhile these were the first that had fallen, and Pericles son of Xanthippus was chosen to pronounce their eulogy. When the proper time arrived, he advanced from the sepulcher to an elevated platform in order to be heard by as many of the crowd as possible, and spoke as follows:

"Most of my predecessors in this place have commended him who made this speech part of the law, telling us that it is well that it should be delivered at the burial of those who fall in battle. For myself, I should have thought that the worth which had displayed itself in deeds would be sufficiently rewarded by honors also shown by deeds; such as you now see in this funeral prepared at the people's cost. And I could have wished that the reputations of many brave men were not to be imperiled in the mouth of a single individual, to stand or fall according as he spoke well or ill. [2] For it is hard to speak properly upon a subject where it is even difficult to convince your hearers that you are speaking the truth. On the one hand, the friend who is familiar with every fact of the story may think that some point has not been set forth with that fullness which he wishes and knows it to deserve; on the other, he who is a stranger to the matter may be led by envy to suspect exaggeration if he hears anything above his own nature. For men can endure to hear others praised only so long as they can severally persuade themselves of their own ability to equal the actions recounted: when this point is passed, envy comes in and with it incredulity. [3] However, since our ancestors have stamped this custom with their approval, it becomes my duty to obey the law and to try to satisfy your several wishes and opinions as best I may."

"I shall begin with our ancestors: it is both just and proper that they should have the honor of the first mention on an occasion like the present. They dwelt in the country without break in the succession from generation to generation, and handed it down free to the present time by their valor. [2] And if our more remote ancestors deserve praise, much more do our own fathers, who added to their in-

2.35
431/0
1st Year/Winter
ATHENS
Pericles begins his Funeral Oration by noting how difficult it is to properly praise the dead, but, since it is the law, offers to do his duty and make the attempt.

2.36
431/0
1st Year/Winter
ATHENS
After Pericles praises all those who contributed to Athens' acquisition of its empire he describes the form of government under which the city grew great.

2.34.5a   Marathon (Map 2.31, AY) is where the
          Athenians defeated an invading force of
          Persians in 490.

heritance the empire which we now possess, and spared no pains to be able to leave their acquisitions to us of the present generation. [3] Lastly, there are few parts of our dominions that have not been augmented by those of us here, who are still more or less in the vigor of life; while the mother country has been furnished by us with everything that can enable her to depend on her own resources whether for war or for peace. [4] That part of our history which tells of the military achievements which gave us our several possessions, or of the ready valor with which either we or our fathers stemmed the tide of Hellenic or foreign aggression, is a theme too familiar to my hearers for me to dwell upon, and I shall therefore pass it by. But what was the road by which we reached our position, what the form of government under which our greatness grew, what the national habits out of which it sprang; these are questions which I may try to solve before I proceed to my eulogy upon these men; since I think this to be a subject upon which on the present occasion a speaker may properly dwell, and to which the whole assemblage, whether citizens or foreigners, may listen with advantage."

2.37
431/0
1st Year/Winter
ATHENS
Praising Athens' unique democratic institutions, Pericles says equality before the law leads to rewards based on merit and creates a society both free and law-abiding.

"Our constitution does not copy the laws of neighboring states; we are rather a pattern to others than imitators ourselves. Its administration favors the many instead of the few; this is why it is called a democracy. If we look to the laws, they afford equal justice to all in their private differences; if to social standing, advancement in public life falls to reputation for capacity, class considerations not being allowed to interfere with merit; nor again does poverty bar the way, if a man is able to serve the state, he is not hindered by the obscurity of his condition. [2] The freedom which we enjoy in our government extends also to our ordinary life. There, far from exercising a jealous surveillance over each other, we do not feel called upon to be angry with our neighbor for doing what he likes, or even to indulge in those injurious looks which cannot fail to be offensive, although they inflict no real harm. [3] But all this ease in our private relations does not make us lawless as citizens. Against this fear is our chief safeguard, teaching us to obey the magistrates and the laws, particularly such as regard the protection of the injured, whether they are actually on the statute book, or belong to that code which, although unwritten, yet cannot be broken without acknowledged disgrace."

2.38
431/0
1st Year/Winter
ATHENS
Pericles notes that Athens provides means for pleasure and recreation.

"Further, we provide plenty of means for the mind to refresh itself from business. We celebrate games and sacrifices all the year round, and the elegance of our private establishments forms a daily source of pleasure and helps to distract us from what causes us distress; [2] while the magnitude of our city draws the produce of the world into our harbor, so that to the Athenian the fruits of other countries are as familiar a luxury as those of his own."

"If we turn to our military policy, there also we differ from our antagonists. We throw open our city to the world, and never by alien acts exclude foreigners from any opportunity of learning or observing,[1a] although the eyes of an enemy may occasionally profit by our liberality; trusting less in system and policy than to the native spirit of our citizens; while in education, where our rivals from their very cradles by a painful discipline seek after manliness, at Athens we live exactly as we please, and yet are just as ready to encounter every legitimate danger. [2] In proof of this it may be noticed that the Spartans do not invade our country alone, but bring with them all their confederates; while we Athenians advance unsupported into the territory of a neighbor, and fighting upon a foreign soil usually vanquish with ease men who are defending their homes. [3] Our united force was never yet encountered by any enemy, because we have at once to attend to our marine and to despatch our citizens by land upon a hundred different services; so that, wherever they engage with some such fraction of our strength, a success against a detachment is magnified into a victory over the nation, and a defeat into a reverse suffered at the hands of our entire people. [4] And yet if with habits not of labor but of ease, and courage not of art but of nature, we are still willing to encounter danger, we have the double advantage of not suffering hardships before we need to, and of facing them in the hour of need as fearlessly as those who are never free from them."

"Nor are these the only points in which our city is worthy of admiration."

"We cultivate refinement without extravagance and knowledge without effeminacy; wealth we employ more for use than for show, and place the real disgrace of poverty not in owning to the fact but in declining the struggle against it. [2] Our public men have, besides politics, their private affairs to attend to, and our ordinary citizens, though occupied with the pursuits of industry, are still fair judges of public matters; for, unlike any other nation, we regard the citizen who takes no part in these duties not as unambitious but as useless, and we are able to judge proposals even if we cannot originate them; instead of looking on discussion as a stumbling-block in the way of action, we think it an indispensable preliminary to any wise action at all. [3] Again, in our enterprises we present the singular spectacle of daring and deliberation, each carried to its highest point, and both united in the same persons; although with the rest of mankind deci-

2.39
431/0
1st Year/Winter
ATHENS
Pericles says that Athens is open to the world, relying upon its citizens' natural capacity, not special training, to meet any challenge.

2.40
431/0
1st Year/Winter
ATHENS
Pericles applauds Athens' concern for culture, her sensible use of wealth, her inclusion of all citizens in politics, her combination of daring and deliberation in action, and her liberal generosity.

2.39.1a   As was done regularly by Sparta; see 1.144.2, and Appendix C, Spartan Institutions, §1.

sion is the fruit of ignorance, hesitation of reflection. But the prize for courage will surely be awarded most justly to those who best know the difference between hardship and pleasure and yet are never tempted to shrink from danger. [4] In generosity we are equally singular, acquiring our friends by conferring not by receiving favors. Yet, of course, the doer of the favor is the firmer friend of the two, in order by continued kindness to keep the recipient in his debt; while the debtor feels less keenly from the very consciousness that the return he makes will be a payment, not a free gift. [5] And it is only the Athenians who, fearless of consequences, confer their benefits not from calculations of expediency, but in the confidence of liberality."

2.41
431/0
1st Year/Winter
ATHENS
Pericles says Athens is a model for Hellas, a city worthy to rule others, and worthy of the devotion of the men who died in her cause.

"In short, I say that as a city we are the school of Hellas; while I doubt if the world can produce a man, who where he has only himself to depend upon, is equal to so many emergencies, and graced by so happy a versatility as the Athenian. [2] And that this is no mere boast thrown out for the occasion, but plain matter of fact, is proved by the power of the state acquired by these habits. [3] For Athens alone of her contemporaries is found when tested to be greater than her reputation, and alone gives no occasion to her assailants to blush at the antagonist by whom they have been worsted, or to her subjects to question her title to rule by merit. [4] Rather, the admiration of the present and succeeding ages will be ours, since we have not left our power without witness, but have shown it by mighty proofs; and far from needing a Homer for our eulogist, or other of his craft whose verses might charm for the moment only for the impression which they gave to melt at the touch of fact, we have forced every sea and land to be the highway of our daring, and everywhere, whether for evil or for good, have left imperishable monuments behind us. [5] Such is the Athens for which these men, in the assertion of their resolve not to lose her, nobly fought and died; and well may every one of their survivors be ready to suffer in her cause."

2.42
431/0
1st Year/Winter
ATHENS
Pericles asserts that these men died gloriously, preferring death to submission or dishonor.

"Indeed if I have dwelt at some length upon the character of our country, it has been to show that our stake in the struggle is not the same as theirs who have no such blessings to lose, and also that the eulogy of the men over whom I am now speaking might be by definite proofs established. [2] That eulogy is now in a great measure complete; for the Athens that I have celebrated is only what the heroism of these and their like have made her, men whose fame, unlike that of most Hellenes, will be found to be no greater than what they deserve. And if a test of worth be wanted, it is to be found in their closing scene, and this not only in the cases in which it set the final seal upon their merit, but also in those in which it gave the first intimation of their having any. [3] For there is justice in the claim that steadfastness in his country's battles should be as a cloak to cover a man's other imperfections; since the good action has blotted out the bad, and his merit as a citizen more than outweighed his demerits as an individual. [4] But none of these allowed either wealth with its prospect of future enjoyment to unnerve his spirit, or poverty with its hope of a day of freedom and riches to tempt him to shrink from danger. No, holding that vengeance upon their enemies was more to be desired than any personal blessings, and reckoning this to be the most glorious of hazards, they joyfully determined to accept the risk, to make sure of their vengeance and to let their wishes wait; and while committing to hope the uncertainty of final success, in the business before them they thought fit to act boldly and trust in themselves. Thus choosing to die resisting, rather than to live submitting, they fled only from dishonor, but met danger face to face, and after one brief moment, while at the summit of their fortune, left behind them not their fear, but their glory."

"So died these men as became Athenians. You, their survivors, must determine to have as unaltering a resolution in the field, though you may pray that it may have a happier outcome. And not contented with ideas derived only from words of the advantages which are bound up with the defense of your country, though these would furnish a valuable text to a speaker even before an audience so alive to them as the present, you must yourselves realize the power of Athens, and feed your eyes upon her from day to day, till love of her fills your hearts; and then when all her greatness shall break upon you, you must reflect that it was by courage, sense of duty, and a keen feeling of honor in action that men were enabled to win all this, and that no personal failure in an enterprise could make them consent to deprive their country of their valor, but they laid it at her feet as the most glorious contribution that they could offer. [2] For this offering of their lives, made in common by them all, they each of them individually received that renown which never grows old, and for a tomb, not so much that in which their bones have been deposited, but that noblest of shrines wherein their glory is laid up to be eternally remembered upon every occasion on which deed or story shall be commemorated. [3] For heroes have the whole earth for their tomb; and in lands far from their own, where the column with its epitaph declares it, there is enshrined in every breast a record unwritten with no monument to preserve it, except that of the heart. [4] These take as your model, and judging happiness to be the fruit of freedom and freedom of valor, never decline the dangers of war. [5] For it is not the miserable that would most

2.43
431/0
1st Year/Winter
ATHENS
Pericles calls upon those who survive to emulate the war dead's valor and patriotism, saying that they risked all and lost their lives, but the renown of their deeds will last forever.

ILLUSTRATION 2.44 ATTIC MARBLE RELIEF OF C. 430 B.C. COMMEMORATING THE ATHENIANS WHO DIED IN THE FIRST YEAR'S FIGHTING OF THE PELOPONNESIAN WAR

justly be unsparing of their lives; these have nothing to hope for: it is rather they to whom continued life may bring reverses as yet unknown, and to whom a fall, if it came, would be most tremendous in its consequences. [6] And surely, to a man of spirit, the degradation of cowardice must be immeasurably more grievous than the unfelt death which strikes him in the midst of his strength and patriotism!"

"Comfort, therefore, not condolence, is what I have to offer to the parents of the dead who may be here. Numberless are the chances to which, as they know, the life of man is subject; but fortunate indeed are they who draw for their lot a death so glorious as that which has caused your mourning, and to whom life has been so exactly measured as to terminate in the happiness in which it has been passed. [2] Still I know that this is a hard saying, especially when you will constantly be reminded by seeing in the homes of others blessings of which once you also enjoyed; for grief is felt not so much for the want of what we have never known, as for the loss of that to which we have been long accustomed. [3] Yet you who are still of an age to beget children must bear up in the hope of having others in their stead; not only will they help you to forget those whom you have lost, but will be to the state at once a reinforcement and a security; for never can a fair or just policy be expected of the citizen who does not, like his fellows, bring to the decision the interests and apprehensions of a father. [4] While those of you who have passed your prime must congratulate yourselves with the thought that the best part of your life was fortunate, and that the brief span that remains will be cheered by the fame of the departed. For it is only the love of honor that never grows old; and honor it is, not gain, as some would have it, that rejoices the heart of age and helplessness."

"Turning to the sons or brothers of the dead, I see an arduous struggle before you. When a man is gone, all are wont to praise him, and should your merit be ever so transcendent, you will still find it difficult not merely to overtake, but even to approach their renown. The living have envy to contend with, while those who are no longer in our path are honored with a goodwill into which rivalry does not enter. [2] On the other hand if I must say anything on the subject of female excellence to those of you who will now be in widowhood, it will be all comprised in this brief exhortation. Great will be your glory in not falling short of your natural character; and greatest will be hers who is least talked of among the men whether for good or for bad."

2.44
431/0
1st Year/Winter
ATHENS
Pericles comforts the parents of the war dead while acknowledging their grief. He advises those who can to have more children and those past child-bearing age to ease their years with the knowledge that their sons died with honor.

2.45
431/0
1st Year/Winter
ATHENS
He says that the sons and brothers of the dead may seek to equal their renown, but that their widows should best seek to avoid notice of any sort.

2.46
431/0
1st Year/Winter
ATHENS
Pericles concludes by reminding those present that Athens will pay for the upbringing of the children of the dead.

"My task is now finished. I have performed it to the best of my ability, and in words, at least, the requirements of the law are now satisfied. If deeds be in question, those who are here interred have received part of their honors already, and for the rest, their children will be brought up till manhood at the public expense: the state thus offers a valuable prize, as the garland of victory in this race of valor, for the reward both of those who have fallen and their survivors. And where the rewards for merit are greatest, there are found the best citizens."

[2] "And now that you have brought to a close your lamentations for your relatives, you may depart."[2a]

2.47
430
2nd Year/Summer
ATHENS
The Spartans invade Attica again. Plague appears in Athens.

Such was the funeral that took place during this winter, with which the first year of the war came to an end. [2] In the first days of summer the Spartans and their allies, with two-thirds of their forces as before, invaded Attica, under the command of Archidamus son of Zeuxidamus, king of Sparta, and established themselves and laid waste the country. [3] Not many days after their arrival in Attica the plague first began to show itself among the Athenians. It was said that it had broken out in many places previously in the neighborhood of Lemnos[3a] and elsewhere; but a pestilence of such extent and mortality was nowhere remembered. [4] Neither were the physicians at first of any service, ignorant as they were of the proper way to treat it, but they died themselves the most thickly, as they visited the sick most often; nor did any human art succeed any better. Supplications in the temples, divinations, and so forth were found equally futile, till the overwhelming nature of the disaster at last put a stop to them altogether.

2.48
430
2nd Year/Summer
ATHENS
Thucydides describes the origin and progress of the plague. He himself was stricken by it.

It first began, it is said, in the parts of Ethiopia above Egypt, and thence descended into Egypt and Libya[1a] and into most of the King's country. [2] Suddenly falling upon Athens, it first attacked the population in the Piraeus, which was the occasion of their saying that the Peloponnesians had poisoned the reservoirs, there being as yet no wells there, and afterwards appeared in the upper city, when the deaths became much more frequent. [3] All speculation as to its origin and its causes, if causes can be found adequate to produce so great a disturbance, I leave to other writers, whether lay or professional; for myself, I shall simply set down its nature, and explain the symptoms by which perhaps it may be recognized by the student, if it should ever break out again. This I can the better do, as I had the disease myself, and watched its operation in the case of others.[3a]

2.49
430
2nd Year/Summer
ATHENS
Symptoms of the plague and its progression through the body are described.

That year then is agreed to have been otherwise unprecedentedly free from sickness; and such few cases as occurred, all turned into this. [2] As a

2.46.2a   See the Introduction (sec. II.v) for a discussion of speeches in Thucydides.
2.47.3a   Lemnos: Map 2.29.
2.48.1a   Ethiopia is "above" Egypt—up the Nile River and further away from the sea—from a point of view centered in the

Mediterranean Sea; see Map 2.56, locator.
2.48.3a   See the Introduction (sec. I) for a discussion of what is known about Thucydides' life.

rule, however, there was no ostensible cause; but people in good health were all of a sudden attacked by violent heats in the head, and redness and inflammation in the eyes, the inward parts, such as the throat or tongue, becoming bloody and emitting an unnatural and fetid breath. [3] These symptoms were followed by sneezing and hoarseness, after which the pain soon reached the chest, and produced a hard cough. When it fixed in the stomach, it upset it; and discharges of bile of every kind named by physicians ensued, accompanied by very great distress. [4] In most cases also an ineffectual retching followed, producing violent spasms, which in some cases ceased soon after, in others much later. [5] Externally the body was not very hot to the touch, nor pale in its appearance, but reddish, livid, and breaking out into small pustules and ulcers. But internally it burned so that the patient could not bear to have on him clothing or linen even of the very lightest description; or indeed to be otherwise than stark naked. What they would have liked best would have been to throw themselves into cold water; as indeed was done by some of the neglected sick, who plunged into the rain tanks in their agonies of unquenchable thirst; though it made no difference whether they drank little or much. [6] Besides this, the miserable feeling of not being able to rest or sleep never ceased to torment them. The body meanwhile did not waste away so long as the distemper was at its height, but held out to a marvel against its ravages; so that when they succumbed, as in most cases, on the seventh or eighth day, to the internal inflammation, they had still some strength in them. But if they passed this stage, and the disease descended further into the bowels, inducing a violent ulceration there accompanied by severe diarrhea, this brought on a weakness which was generally fatal. [7] For the disorder first settled in the head, ran its course from thence through the whole of the body, and even where it did not prove mortal, it still left its mark on the extremities; [8] for it settled in the privy parts, the fingers and the toes, and many escaped with the loss of these, some too with that of their eyes. Others again were seized with an entire loss of memory on their first recovery, and did not know either themselves or their friends.[8a]

But while the nature of the distemper was such as to baffle all description, and its attacks almost too grievous for human nature to endure, it was still in the following circumstance that its difference from all ordinary disorders was most clearly shown. All the birds and beasts that prey upon human bodies either abstained from touching them (though there were many lying unburied), or died after tasting them. [2] In proof of this, it was noticed that birds of this kind actually disappeared; they were not about the bodies, or indeed to be seen at all. But of course the effects which I have mentioned could best be studied in a domestic animal like the dog.

2.50
430
2nd Year/Summer
ATHENS
Birds of prey abstained from eating plague victims or were poisoned. Such birds actually vanished from the area.

2.49.8a   Modern medical authorities do not agree
          on the identification of this pestilence.

2.51
430
2nd Year/Summer
ATHENS
Strong and weak alike
succumbed to the illness.
Despair robbed the afflicted
of resistance. Those who
nursed the sick were stricken
in turn. Only people who
had survived the plague
could show compassion with
impunity.

Such then, if we pass over the varieties of particular cases, which were many and peculiar, were the general features of the distemper. Meanwhile the city enjoyed an immunity from all the ordinary disorders; or if any case occurred, it ended in this. [2] Some died in neglect, others in the midst of every attention. No remedy was found that could be used as a specific; for what did good in one case, did harm in another. [3] Strong and weak constitutions proved equally incapable of resistance, all alike being swept away, although dieted with the utmost precaution. [4] By far the most terrible feature in the malady was the dejection which ensued when anyone felt himself sickening, for the despair into which they instantly fell took away their power of resistance, and left them a much easier prey to the disorder; besides which, there was the awful spectacle of men dying like sheep, through having caught the infection in nursing each other. This caused the greatest mortality. [5] On the one hand, if they were afraid to visit each other, they perished from neglect; indeed many houses were emptied of their inmates for want of a nurse: on the other, if they ventured to do so, death was the consequence. This was especially the case with such as made any pretensions to goodness: honor made them unsparing of themselves in their attendance in their friends' houses, where even the members of the family were at last worn out by the moans of the dying, and succumbed to the force of the disaster. [6] Yet it was with those who had recovered from the disease that the sick and the dying found most compassion. These knew what it was from experience, and had now no fear for themselves; for the same man was never attacked twice—never at least fatally. And such persons not only received the congratulations of others, but themselves also, in the elation of the moment, half entertained the vain hope that they were for the future safe from any disease whatsoever.

2.52
430
2nd Year/Summer
ATHENS
The crowded and poor
housing of the refugees
aggravated the calamity.
Burial and cremation rites
were upset due to the large
number of victims.

An aggravation of the existing calamity was the influx from the country into the city, and this was especially felt by the new arrivals. [2] As there were no houses to receive them, they had to be lodged at the hot season of the year in stifling cabins, where the mortality raged without restraint. The bodies of dying men lay one upon another, and half-dead creatures reeled about the streets and gathered round all the fountains in their longing for water. [3] The sacred places also in which they had quartered themselves were full of corpses of persons that had died there, just as they were; for as the disaster passed all bounds, men, not knowing what was to become of them, became utterly careless of everything, whether sacred or profane. [4] All the burial rites before in use were entirely upset, and they buried the bodies as best they could. Many from want of the proper appliances through so many of their friends having died already, had recourse to the most shameless modes of burial: sometimes getting in first before those who had raised a pile, they threw their own dead body upon the stranger's pyre and ignited it; sometimes they tossed the corpse which they were carrying on the top of another that was burning, and so went off.

Nor was this the only form of lawless extravagance which owed its origin to the plague. Men now did just what they pleased, cooly venturing on what they had formerly done only in a corner, seeing the rapid transitions produced by persons in prosperity suddenly dying and those who before had nothing succeeding to their property. [2] So they resolved to spend quickly and enjoy themselves, regarding their lives and riches as alike things of a day. [3] Perseverance in what men called honor was popular with none, it was so uncertain whether they would be spared to attain the object; but it was settled that present enjoyment, and all that contributed to it, was both honorable and useful. [4] Fear of gods or law of man there was none to restrain them. As for the first, they judged it to be just the same whether they worshipped them or not, as they saw all alike perishing; and for the last, no one expected to live to be brought to trial for his offenses, but each felt that a far severer sentence had been already passed upon them all and hung ever over their heads, and before this fell it was only reasonable to enjoy life a little.

2.53
430
2nd Year/Summer
ATHENS
Obsessed by death, men sought pleasure with no respect for honor, law, or the gods.

Such was the nature of the calamity, and heavily did it weigh on the Athenians; death raging within the city and devastation without. [2] Among other things which they remembered in their distress was, very naturally, the following verse which the old men said had long ago been uttered:

A Dorian war shall come and with it pestilence.

2.54
430
2nd Year/Summer
ATHENS
The Athenians argued about ancient prophecies and oracles. The plague struck Athens most severely and never entered the Peloponnesus.

[3] So a dispute arose as to whether dearth and not death[3a] had not been the word in the verse; but at the present juncture, it was of course decided in favor of the latter; for the people made their recollection fit in with their sufferings. I suppose, however, that if another Dorian war should ever afterwards come upon us, and a famine should happen to accompany it, the verse will probably be read accordingly. [4] The oracle also which had been given to the Spartans was now remembered by those who knew of it. When the god was asked whether they should go to war, he answered that if they put their might into it, victory would be theirs, and that he would himself be with them. [5] With this oracle events were supposed to tally.[5a] For the plague broke out so soon as the Peloponnesians invaded Attica, and never entering the Peloponnesus (not at least to an extent worth noticing), committed its worst ravages at Athens, and next to Athens, at the most populous of the other cities. Such was the history of the plague.

2.54.3a The Greek words are *limos,* "famine," and *loimos,* "pestilence."

2.54.5a For Thucydides' attitude toward oracles, see the Introduction (sec. IV.i).

MAP 2.56 ORIGINS OF THE PLAGUE; ATHENIAN RAIDS IN THE PELOPONNESUS, 430

2.55
430
2nd Year/Summer
ATTICA
Attica is ravaged, but Pericles again restrains the Athenians.

2.56
430
2nd Year/Summer
PELOPONNESUS
Pericles leads an expedition to raid Epidaurus and nearby cities.

After ravaging the plain the Peloponnesians advanced into the Paralian region as far as Laurium,[1a] where the Athenian silver mines are, and first laid waste the side looking toward the Peloponnesus, next that which faces Euboea and Andros.[1b] [2] But Pericles, who was still general, held the same opinion as in the former invasion, and would not let the Athenians march out against them.

However while they were still in the plain, and had not yet entered the Paralian land, he had prepared an armament of a hundred ships for the Peloponnesus, and when all was ready put out to sea. [2] On board the ships he took four thousand Athenian heavy infantry, and three hundred cavalry in horse transports, then for the first time made out of old triremes; fifty Chian and Lesbian vessels also joining in the expedition. [3] When this Athenian armament put out to sea, they left the Peloponnesians in Attica in the Paralian region. [4] Arriving at Epidaurus[3a] in the Peloponnesus they ravaged most of the territory, and even had hopes of taking the city by an assault: in this however they were not successful. [5] Putting out from Epidaurus, they laid waste the territory of Troezen, Halieis, and Hermione,[5a] all cities on the coast of the Peloponnesus, and thence sailing to Prasiae,[5b] a maritime city in Laconia, ravaged part of its territory, and took and sacked the place itself; after which they returned home, but

2.55.1a   Paralia, Laurium: Map 2.56.
2.55.1b   Euboea, Andros: Map 2.56.
2.56.3a   Epidaurus: Map 2.56. The unusually large size of this expedition under Pericles is mentioned in 6.31.2.
2.56.5a   Troezen, Halieis, Hermione: Map 2.56.

2.56.5b   Prasiae: Map 2.56.

found the Peloponnesians gone and no longer in Attica.

During the whole time that the Peloponnesians were in Attica and the Athenians on the expedition in their ships, men kept dying of the plague both in the armament and in Athens. Indeed it was actually asserted that the departure of the Peloponnesians was hastened by fear of the disorder; as they heard from deserters that it was in the city, and also could see the burials going on. [2] Yet in this invasion they remained longer than in any other, and ravaged the whole country, for they were about forty days in Attica.

2.57
430
2nd Year/Summer
ATTICA
This longest invasion of Attica lasted forty days.

The same summer Hagnon son of Nicias, and Cleopompus son of Clinias, the colleagues of Pericles, took the armament of which he had lately made use, and went off upon an expedition against the Chalcidians in the Thracian region and against Potidaea,[1a] which was still under siege. As soon as they arrived, they brought up their siege engines against Potidaea and tried every means of taking it, [2] but did not succeed either in capturing the city or in doing anything else worthy of their preparations. For the plague attacked them here also, and committed such havoc as to cripple them completely, even the previously healthy soldiers of the former expedition catching the infection from Hagnon's troops; while Phormio and the sixteen hundred men whom he commanded[2a] only escaped by being no longer in the neighborhood of the Chalcidians. [3] The end of it was that Hagnon returned with his ships to Athens, having lost one thousand and fifty out of four thousand hoplites in about forty days; though the soldiers stationed there before remained in the country and carried on the siege of Potidaea.[3a]

2.58
430
2nd Year/Summer
POTIDAEA
Athenian reinforcements accomplish nothing at Potidaea and suffer heavy losses from the plague.

After the second invasion of the Peloponnesians a change came over the spirit of the Athenians. Their land had now been twice laid waste; and war and pestilence at once pressed heavy upon them. [2] They began to find fault with Pericles, as the author of the war and the cause of all their misfortunes, and became eager to come to terms with Sparta, and actually sent ambassadors thither, who did not however succeed in their mission. Their despair was now complete and all vented itself upon Pericles. [3] When he saw them exasperated at the present turn of affairs and acting exactly as he had anticipated, he called an assembly, being (it must be remembered) still general,[3a] with the double object of restoring confidence and of leading them from these angry feelings to a calmer and more hopeful state of mind. He accordingly came forward and spoke as follows:

2.59
430
2nd Year/Summer
ATHENS
Oppressed by invasion and plague, Athens rejects Pericles and sends peace envoys to Sparta; after they fail, Pericles speaks to the Athenian assembly.

"I was not unprepared for the indignation of which I have been the object, as I know its causes; and I have called an assembly for the purpose of reminding you of certain points, and of protesting against your being unreasonably irritated with me, or cowed by your suffer-

2.60
430
2nd Year/Summer
ATHENS
Pericles rebukes the Athenians, calling upon them to hold the good of the state above private concerns; he describes himself as a wise and honest patriot.

2.58.1a This section continues the history of the Potidaean campaign, which was last described in 1.65. For the location of Chalcidice and Potidaea, see Map 2.72, AY. The size of this expedition is mentioned in 6.31.2.

2.58.2a Phormio and his force of 1,600 citizen hoplites was last mentioned in 1.65.

2.58.3a The end of the siege of Potidaea is described in 2.70.

2.59.3a For the office of Athenian general, see Appendix A, The Athenian Government, §7.

ings. [2] I am of the opinion that national greatness is more to the advantage of private citizens than any individual well-being coupled with public humiliation. [3] A man may be personally ever so well off, and yet if his country be ruined he must be ruined with it; whereas a flourishing commonwealth always affords chances of salvation to unfortunate individuals. [4] Since then a state can support the misfortunes of private citizens, while they cannot support hers, it is surely the duty of everyone to be forward in her defense, and not like you to be so confounded with your domestic afflictions as to give up all thoughts of the common safety, and to blame me for having counseled war and yourselves for having voted it. [5] And yet if you are angry with me, it is with one who, as I believe, is second to no man either in knowledge of the proper policy, or in the ability to expound it, and who is moreover not only a patriot but an honest one. [6] A man possessing that knowledge without that faculty of exposition might as well have no idea at all on the matter: if he had both these gifts, but no love for his country, he would be but a cold advocate for her interests; while were his patriotism not proof against bribery, everything would go for a price. [7] So that if you thought that I was even moderately distinguished for these qualities when you took my advice and went to war, there is certainly no reason now why I should be charged with having done wrong."

"For those of course who have a free choice in the matter and whose fortunes are not at stake, war is the greatest of follies. But if the only choice was between submission with loss of independence, and danger with the hope of preserving that independence—in such a case it is he who will not accept the risk that deserves blame, not he who will. [2] I am the same man and do not alter, it is you who change, since in fact you took my advice while unhurt, and waited for misfortune to repent of it; and the apparent error of my policy lies in the infirmity of your resolution, since the suffering that it entails is being felt by everyone among you, while its advantage is still remote and obscure to all, and a great and sudden reverse having befallen you, your mind is too much depressed to persevere in your resolves. [3] For before what is sudden, unexpected, and least within calculation the spirit quails; and putting all else aside, the plague has certainly been an emergency of this kind. [4] Born, however, as you are, citizens of a great state, and brought up, as you have been, with habits equal to your birth, you should be ready to face the greatest disasters and still to keep unimpaired the luster of your name. For the judgment of mankind is as relentless to the weakness that falls short of a recognized renown, as it is jealous of the arrogance that aspires higher than its due. Cease then to grieve for your private afflictions, and address yourselves instead to the safety of the common-wealth."

"If you shrink before the exertions which the war makes neces-sary, and fear that after all they may not have a happy result, you know the reasons by which I have often demonstrated to you the groundlessness of your apprehension. If those are not enough, I will now reveal an advantage arising from the greatness of your domin-ion, which I think has never yet suggested itself to you, which I never mentioned in my previous speeches, and which has so bold a sound that I should scarce adventure it now were it not for the un-natural depression which I see around me. [2] You perhaps think that your empire extends only over your allies; I will declare to you the truth. The visible field of action has two parts, land and sea. In the whole of one of these you are completely supreme, not merely as far as you use it at present, but also to what further extent you may think fit: in fine, your naval resources are such that your vessels may go where they please, without the King[2a] or any other nation on earth being able to stop them. [3] So that although you may think it a great privation to lose the use of your land and houses, still you must see that this power is something widely different; and instead of fretting on their account, you should really regard them in the light of the gardens and other accessories that embellish a great fortune, and as, in comparison, of little moment. You should know too that liberty preserved by your efforts will easily recover for us what we have lost, while, the knee once bowed, even what you have will pass from you. Your fathers receiving these possessions not from others, but from themselves, did not let slip what their labor had acquired, but delivered them safe to you; and in this respect at least you must prove yourselves their equals, remembering that to lose what one has got is more disgraceful than to be thwarted in getting, and you must confront your enemies not merely with spirit but with disdain. [4] Confidence can indeed a blissful ignorance impart, ay, even to a cow-ard's breast, but disdain is the privilege of those who, like us, have been assured by reflection of their superiority to their adversary. [5] And where the chances are the same, knowledge fortifies courage by the contempt which is its consequence, its trust being placed, not in hope, which is the prop of the desperate, but in a judgment grounded upon existing resources, whose anticipations are more to be depended upon."

"Again, your country has a right to your services in sustaining the glories of her position. These are a common source of pride to you all, and you cannot decline the burdens of empire and still expect to share its honors. You should remember also that what you are fight-

2.62.2a   The King of Persia.

2.62
430
2nd Year/Summer
ATHENS
Pericles argues that the Athenians' naval supremacy permits them to go wherever they wish at sea; that the loss of land and houses is trivial; and that they may face the war with confidence based on a true assessment of their resources.

2.63
430
2nd Year/Summer
ATHENS
Pericles points out that the Athenian empire is a tyranny that cannot be given up without risk.

ing against is not merely slavery as an exchange for independence, but also loss of empire and danger from the animosities incurred in its exercise. [2] Besides, to recede is no longer possible, if indeed any of you in the alarm of the moment has become enamored of the honesty of such an unambitious part. For what you hold is, to speak somewhat plainly, a tyranny; to take it perhaps was wrong, but to let it go is unsafe. [3] And men of these retiring views, making converts of others, would quickly ruin a state; indeed the result would be the same if they could live independent by themselves; for the retiring and unambitious are never secure without vigorous protectors at their side; indeed, such qualities are useless to an imperial city, though they may help a dependency to an unmolested servitude."

"But you must not be seduced by citizens like these, nor be angry with me who, if I voted for war, only did as you did yourselves, in spite of the enemy having invaded your country and done what you could be certain that he would do if you refused to comply with his demands; and in addition to what we expected, the plague has come upon us—the only point indeed at which our calculation has been at fault. It is this, I know, that has had a large share in making me more unpopular than I should otherwise have been, quite undeservedly, unless you are also prepared to give me the credit for any success with which chance may present you. [2] Besides, the hand of Heaven must be borne with resignation, that of the enemy with fortitude; this was the old way at Athens, and do not you prevent it being so still. [3] Remember, too, that if your country has the greatest name in all the world, it is because she never bent before disaster; because she has expended more life and effort in war than any other city, and has won for herself a power greater than any hitherto known, the memory of which will descend to the latest posterity; even if now, in obedience to the general law of decay, we should ever be forced to yield, still it will be remembered that we held rule over more Hellenes than any other Hellenic state, that we sustained the greatest wars against their united or separate powers, and inhabited a city unrivaled by any other in resources or magnitude. [4] These glories may incur the censure of the slow and unambitious; but in the breast of the energetic they will awake emulation, and in those who must remain without them an envious regret. [5] Hatred and unpopularity at the moment have fallen to the lot of all who have aspired to rule others; but where hatred must be incurred, true wisdom incurs it for the highest objects. Hatred also is short-lived; but that which makes the splendor of the present and the glory of the future remains forever unforgotten. [6] Make your decision, therefore, for glory then

2.64
430
2nd Year/Summer
ATHENS
Pericles concludes that all has gone according to plan except for the plague. He calls on the Athenians to cease parleying with the Spartans and to redouble their efforts to win the war.

and honor now, and attain both objects by instant and zealous effort: do not send heralds to Sparta, and do not betray any sign of being oppressed by your present sufferings, since they whose minds are least sensitive to calamity, and whose hands are most quick to meet it, are the greatest men and the greatest communities."

Such were the arguments by which Pericles tried to cure the Athenians of their anger against him and to divert their thoughts from their immediate afflictions. [2] As a community he succeeded in convincing them; they not only gave up all idea of sending to Sparta, but applied themselves with increased energy to the war; still as private individuals they could not help smarting under their sufferings, the common people having been deprived of the little that they ever possessed, while the higher orders had lost fine properties with costly establishments and buildings in the country, and, worst of all, had war instead of peace. [3] In fact, the public feeling against him did not subside until he had been fined.[3a] [4] Not long afterwards, however, according to the way of the multitude, they again elected him general and committed all their affairs to his hands, having now become less sensitive to their private and domestic afflictions, and understanding that he was the best man of all for the needs of the state. [5] For as long as he was at the head of the state during the peace, he pursued a moderate and conservative policy; and in his time its greatness was at its height. When the war broke out, here also he seems to have rightly gauged the power of his country. [6] He outlived its commencement two years and six months, and the correctness of his foresight concerning the war became better known after his death. [7] He told them to wait quietly, to pay attention to their marine, to attempt no new conquests, and to expose the city to no hazards during the war, and doing this, promised them a favorable result. What they did was the very contrary, allowing private ambitions and private interests, in matters apparently quite foreign to the war, to lead them into projects unjust both to themselves and to their allies—projects whose success would only conduce to the honor and advantage of private persons, and whose failure entailed certain disaster on the country in the war. [8] The causes of this are not far to seek. Pericles indeed, by his rank, ability, and known integrity, was enabled to exercise an independent control over the multitude—in short, to lead them instead of being led by them; for as he never sought power by improper means, be was never compelled to flatter them, but, on the contrary, enjoyed so high an estimation that he could afford to anger them by contradiction. [9] Whenever he saw them unseasonably and insolently elated, he would with a word reduce them to alarm; on the other hand, if they fell victims to a panic, he could at once restore them to confidence. In short, what was nominally a democ-

2.65
430
2nd Year/Summer
ATHENS
Thucydides gives an account of Pericles' character, accomplishments, and leadership; and then offers an analysis of why Athens, by failing to follow Pericles' advice, ultimately lost the war.

2.65.3a   It was not all that unusual for Athenians to punish statesmen or generals at whom they were angry or disappointed by fines or exile. Note the fate of the generals Pythodorus, Sophocles, and Eurymedon when they returned to Athens from Sicily in 4.65.3, as well as the punishment of Thucydides himself in 5.26.5.

racy was becoming in his hands government by the first citizen.[9a] [10] With his successors it was different. More on a level with one another, and each grasping at supremacy, they ended by committing even the conduct of state affairs to the whims of the multitude. [11] This, as might have been expected in a great and sovereign state, produced a host of blunders, and amongst them the Sicilian expedition;[11a] though this failed not so much through a miscalculation of the power of those against whom it was sent, as through a fault in the senders in not taking the best measures afterwards to assist those who had gone out, but choosing rather to occupy themselves with private squabbles for the leadership of The People, by which they not only paralyzed operations in the field, but also first introduced civil discord at home. [12] Yet after losing most of their fleet besides other forces in Sicily, and with faction already dominant in the city, they could still for three years make head against their original adversaries, joined not only by the Sicilians, but also by their own allies nearly all in revolt, and at last by the King's son, Cyrus,[12a] who furnished the funds for the Peloponnesian navy. Nor did they finally succumb till they fell the victims of their own intestine disorders. [13] So excessively abundant were the resources from which the genius of Pericles foresaw an easy triumph in the war over the unaided forces of the Peloponnesians.

During the same summer the Spartans and their allies made an expedition with a hundred ships against Zacynthus,[1a] an island lying off the coast of Elis, peopled by a colony of Achaeans from the Peloponnesus, and in alliance with Athens. [2] There were a thousand Spartan hoplites on board, and Cnemus, a Spartiate, as admiral. They made a descent from their ships, and ravaged most of the country; but as the inhabitants would not submit, they sailed back home.

At the end of the same summer the Corinthian Aristeus, with the envoys from Sparta Aneristus, Nicolaus, and Protodamus, and Timagoras from Tegea, and a private individual named Pollis from Argos, came to Sitalces son of Teres, king of Thrace,[1a] on their way to Asia to persuade the King to supply funds and join in the war.[1b] They hoped to induce Teres, if possible, to forsake the alliance of Athens and to march on Potidaea[1c] which was then besieged by an Athenian force. They also hoped to persuade Teres to

2.66
430
2nd Year/Summer
ZACYNTHUS
The Peloponnesians send a fleet to Zacynthus.

2.67
430
2nd Year/Summer
THRACE
With the help of Sadocus, Sitalces' son, Athenians in Thrace capture Spartan envoys to the Persian king. Sent to Athens, the envoys are executed without trial.

2.65.9a   Pericles was an elected general who could be deposed at any time by popular vote, as he was in 430 (see above, 2.65.3). The only passage where he seems to act, as it were, above the constitution is in 2.22.1, when he is said to have refused to call an assembly or a meeting, and this has caused comment. But whatever is said of that, it is clear that Pericles was at all times fully subject to the will of the assembly. See Appendix A, The Athenian Government, §7.

2.65.11a   This Athenian expedition to Sicily is described in Books 6 and 7, below. This chapter was clearly written after the end of the war (see section 12 of the chapter) and scholars have debated whether this statement represents a major change of

mind about the Sicilian Expedition or only a shift of emphasis.

2.65.12a   The intervention of Cyrus is described in Xenophon's account of the end of the Peloponnesian war. Xenophon joined Cyrus' army of mercenaries for the expedition that became the subject of his book *Anabasis*. This passage is one of many that must have been written late by Thucydides. See the Introduction (sec. II.ii) on the composition of Thucydides' text.

2.66.1a   Zacynthus: Map 2.72, BX.

2.67.1a   Sitalces was last mentioned in 2.29, and will appear next in 2.95.

2.67.1b   Spartan contacts with Persia recall Archidamus' speech; see note 1.82.1a.

2.67.1c   Potidaea: Map 2.72, AY.

convey them across the Hellespont[1d] to Pharnabazus,[1e] who was to send them up country to the King. [2] But there chanced to be with Sitalces some Athenian ambassadors, Learchus son of Callimachus, and Ameiniades son of Philemon, who persuaded Sitalces' son, Sadocus, the new Athenian citizen, to put the men into their hands and thus prevent their crossing over to the King and doing their part to injure his city. [3] He accordingly had them seized, as they were traveling through Thrace to the vessel in which they were to cross the Hellespont, by a party whom he had sent on with Learchus and Ameiniades, and gave orders for their delivery to the Athenian ambassadors, by whom they were brought to Athens. [4] On their arrival, the Athenians, afraid that Aristeus,[4a] who had been notably the prime mover in the previous affairs of Potidaea and their Thracian possessions, might live to do them still more mischief if he escaped, slew them all the same day, without giving them a trial or hearing the defense which they wished to offer, and cast their bodies into a pit; thinking themselves justified in using in retaliation the same mode of warfare which the Spartans had begun, when they slew and cast into pits all the Athenian and allied traders whom they caught on board the merchantmen round the Peloponnesus. Indeed, at the outset of the war, the Spartans butchered as enemies all whom they took on the sea, whether allies of Athens or neutrals.

About the same time, toward the close of the summer, the Ambraciot[1a] forces, with a number of barbarians that they had raised, marched against the Amphilochian Argos[1b] and the rest of that country. [2] The origin of their enmity against the Argives was this. [3] This Argos and the rest of Amphilochia were colonized by Amphilochus son of Amphiaraus. Dissatisfied with the state of affairs at home on his return after the Trojan war, he built this city in the Ambracian gulf,[3a] and named it Argos after his own country. [4] This was the largest city in Amphilochia, and its inhabitants the most powerful. [5] Under the pressure of misfortune many generations afterwards, they called in the Ambraciots, their neighbors on the Amphilochian border, to join their colony; and it was by this union with the Ambraciots that they learnt their present Hellenic speech, the rest of the Amphilochians being barbarians. [6] After a time the Ambraciots expelled the Argives and held the city themselves. [7] Upon this the Amphilochians gave themselves over to the Acarnanians;[7a] and the two together called the Athenians, who sent them Phormio as general and thirty ships. Upon his arrival they took Argos by storm, and made slaves of the Ambraciots; and the Amphilochian Argives and Acarnanians inhabited the city in common.

The Ambraciots and their allies attack Amphilochian Argos, but fail to take the city. The history of enmity between these two peoples is described.

2.67.1d   Hellespont: Map 2.72, locator.
2.67.1e   Pharnabazus was the Persian governor (satrap) of the Hellespont region (Map 2.72, locator). See Appendix E, The Persians, §2.
2.67.4a   Aristeus son of Adimantus had led the Corinthians at Potidaea; see 1.60.2–1.65.
2.68.1a   Ambracia: Map 2.72, BX.
2.68.1b   Amphilochian Argos, probable location: Map 2.72, BX.

2.68.3a   Ambracian gulf: Map 2.72, BX.
2.68.7a   Acarnania was last mentioned in 2.33. Acarnania: Map 2.72, BX.

[8] After this began the alliance between the Athenians and Acarnanians. [9] The enmity of the Ambraciots against the Argives thus commenced with the enslavement of their citizens; and afterwards during the war, the Ambraciots collected this armament among themselves and the Chaonians,[9a] and other of the neighboring barbarians. Arrived before Argos, they became masters of the country; but not being successful in their attacks upon the city, returned home and dispersed among their different peoples.[9b]

Such were the events of the summer. The ensuing winter the Athenians sent twenty ships round the Peloponnesus, under the command of Phormio, who stationed himself at Naupactus[1a] and kept watch against anyone sailing in or out of Corinth[1b] and the Crisaean gulf.[1c] Six others went to Caria and Lycia[1d] under Melesander, to collect tribute[1e] in those parts, and also to prevent the Peloponnesian privateers[1f] from taking up their station in those waters and molesting the passage of the merchantmen from Phaselis and Phoenicia[1g] and the adjoining continent. [2] However, Melesander, going up the country into Lycia with a force of Athenians from the ships and the allies, was defeated and killed in battle, with the loss of a number of his troops.

The same winter the Potidaeans[1a] at length found themselves no longer able to hold out against their besiegers. The inroads of the Peloponnesians into Attica had not had the desired effect of making the Athenians raise the siege. There were no provisions left; and so far had distress for food gone in Potidaea that, besides a number of other horrors, instances had even occurred of the people having eaten one another. So in this extremity they at last made proposals for capitulating to the Athenian generals in command against them, Xenophon son of Euripides, Hestiodorus son of Aristocleides, and Phanomachus son of Callimachus. [2] The generals accepted their proposals, seeing the sufferings of the army in so exposed a position; besides which the state had already spent two thousand talents[2a] upon the siege. [3] The terms of the capitulation were as follows: a free passage out for themselves, their children, wives, and auxiliaries, with one garment apiece, the women with two, and a fixed sum of money for their journey. [4] Under this treaty they went out to Chalcidice[4a] and other places, according as was in their power. The Athenians, however, blamed the gener-

2.69
430/29
2nd Year/Winter
NAUPACTUS
Phormio's ships are at Naupactus.
CARIA, LYCIA
Athens' squadron to collect tribute and put down privateers in Caria and Lycia suffers a defeat.

2.70
430/29
2nd Year/Winter
POTIDAEA
Potidaea surrenders on terms. Athens criticizes its generals for granting terms and sends settlers to colonize the site.

2.68.9a Chaonia: Map 2.72, AX.
2.68.9b The history of the conflict between Amphilochian Argos and the Acarnanians on one side, and the Ambraciots on the other, is resumed in 2.80.
2.69.1a Naupactus: Map 2.72, BY.
2.69.1b Corinth: Map 2.72, BY.
2.69.1c Crisaean gulf, now called the Corinthian Gulf: Map 2.72, BY.
2.69.1d Caria and Lycia: Map 2.72, locator.
2.69.1e It is generally believed that when Thucydides reports such collections of money, it is a sign that the tribute has been increased in the course of the preceding summer. See note 4.75.1b; Appendix B, The Athenian Empire, §2, 10; and Illustration 2.69.
2.69.1f Privateers were privately owned boats licensed by the belligerents to attack enemy shipping.
2.69.1g Phaselis and Phoenicia: Map 2.72, locator. Some scholars believe that the region of Phoenicia is not meant here, but some port like Phaselis on the Lycian coast that was called Phoenike.
2.70.1a This picks up the Potidaean narrative from 2.58. For Potidaea, see Map 2.72, AY.
2.70.2a Talent: see Appendix J, Classical Greek Currency, §5.
2.70.4a Chalcidice: Map 2.72, AY. Events in Chalcidice are next mentioned in 2.79.

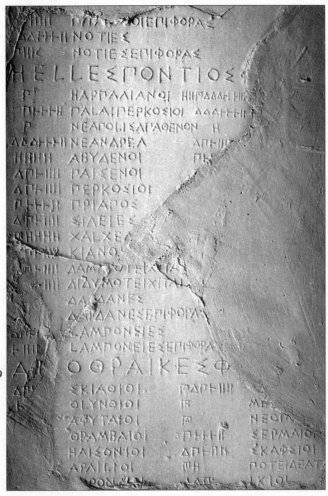

ILLUSTRATION 2.69
FRAGMENT OF
TRIBUTE LIST[4b]
FROM 440/39

als for granting terms without instructions from home, being of opinion that they could have gained control of the city without granting terms. They afterwards sent settlers of their own to Potidaea, and colonized it. Such were the events of the winter, and so ended the second year of this war of which Thucydides was the historian.

The next summer the Peloponnesians and their allies, instead of invading Attica, marched against Plataea,[1a] under the command of Archidamus son of Zeuxidamus, king of the Spartans. He had encamped his army and was about to lay waste the country, when the Plataeans hastened to send envoys to him, and spoke as follows: [2] "Archidamus and Spartans, in invading the Plataean territory you do what is wrong in itself, and worthy neither of yourselves nor of the fathers who begot you. Pausanias son of

2.71
429
3rd Year/Summer
PLATAEA
The Peloponnesians attack Plataea instead of Attica this year, despite Plataean appeals and protests.

2.70.4b For a brief explanation of .tribute lists, see Appendix B, The Athenian Empire in Thucydides, §11.

2.71.1a This picks up the narrative about Plataea (Map 2.72, BY) from 2.6.

Map 2.72 Operations in Asia, Plataea, and Chalcidice

Cleombrotus,[2a] your countryman, after freeing Hellas from the Medes with the help of those Hellenes who were willing to undertake the risk of the battle fought near our city, offered sacrifice to Zeus the Liberator in the agora[2b] of Plataea, and calling all the allies together restored to the Plataeans their city and territory, and declared it independent and inviolate against aggression or conquest. Should any such be attempted, the allies present were to help according to their power. [3] Your fathers rewarded us thus for the courage and patriotism that we displayed at that perilous epoch; but you do just the contrary, coming with our bitterest enemies, the Thebans,[3a] to enslave us. [4] We appeal, therefore, to the gods to whom the oaths were then made, to the gods of your ancestors, and lastly to those of our country, and call upon you to refrain from violating our territory or transgressing the oaths, and to let us live independent, as Pausanias decreed."

The Plataeans had got thus far when they were cut short by Archidamus saying, "There is justice, Plataeans, in what you say, if you act up to your words. According to the grant of Pausanias, continue to be independent yourselves, and join in freeing those of your fellow countrymen who, after sharing in the perils of that period, joined in the oaths to you, and are now subject to the Athenians; for it is to free them and the rest that all this provision and war has been made. I could wish that you would share our labors and abide by the oaths yourselves; if this is impossible, do what we have already required of you—remain neutral, enjoying your own; join neither side, but receive both as friends and neither as allies for the war. With this we shall be satisfied." [2] Such were the words of Archidamus. The Plataeans, after hearing what he had to say, went into the city and acquainted the people with what had passed, and presently returned for answer that it was impossible for them to do what he proposed without consulting the Athenians, with whom their children and wives now were; besides which they had their fears for the city. After his departure, what was to prevent the Athenians from coming and taking it out of their hands, or the Thebans, who would be included in the oaths, from taking advantage of the proposed neutrality to make a second attempt to seize the city? [3] Upon these points he tried to reassure them by saying: "You have only to deliver over the city and houses to us Spartans, to point out the boundaries of your land, the number of your fruit trees, and whatever else can be numerically stated, and yourselves to withdraw wherever you like as long as the war shall last. When it is over we will restore to you whatever we received, and in the interim hold it in trust and keep it in cultivation, paying you a sufficient allowance."

When they had heard what he had to say, they reentered the city, and after consulting with the people said that they wished first to acquaint the

2.72
429
3rd Year/Summer
PLATAEA
Archidamus offers neutrality to Plataea, with guarantees of protection and restitution after the war.

2.73
429
3rd Year/Summer
PLATAEA
Plataea consults Athens, which asks her to honor their alliance.

2.71.2a This Pausanias led the Greek forces to victory over the Persians at the battle of Plataea in 479. His later disgrace and death are described by Thucydides in 1.94–96 and 1.128–34.

2.71.2b Agora: the marketplace and social center of a classical Greek city.

2.71.3a Thebes, in relation to Plataea: Map 2.72, BY.

Athenians with this proposal, and in the event of their approving to accede to it; in the meantime they asked him to grant them a truce and not to lay waste their territory. He accordingly granted a truce for the number of days requisite for the journey, and meanwhile abstained from ravaging their territory. [2] The Plataean envoys went to Athens,[2a] and consulted with the Athenians, and returned with the following message to those in the city: [3] "The Athenians say, Plataeans, that they have never, since we became their allies, on any occasion abandoned you to an enemy, nor will they now neglect you, but will help you according to their ability; and they solemnly call upon you by the oaths which your fathers swore, to keep the alliance unaltered."

2.74
429
3rd Year/Summer
PLATAEA
Plataea decides to remain with Athens. Archidamus offers prayers to justify an assault on Plataea.

On the delivery of this message by the envoys, the Plataeans resolved not to be unfaithful to the Athenians but to endure, if it must be, seeing their lands laid waste and any other trials that might come to them, and not to send out again, but to answer from the wall that it was impossible for them to do as the Spartans proposed. [2] As soon as be had received this answer, King Archidamus proceeded first to make a solemn appeal to the gods and heroes of the country in the following words: "Ye gods and heroes of the Plataean territory, be my witnesses that not as aggressors originally, nor until these had first departed from the common oath, did we invade this land, in which our fathers offered you their prayers before defeating the Medes, and which you made favorable to the Hellenic arms; nor shall we be aggressors in the measures to which we may now resort, since we have made many fair proposals but have not been successful. Graciously accord that those who were the first to offend may be punished for it, and that vengeance may be attained by those who would righteously inflict it."

2.75
429
3rd Year/Summer
PLATAEA
Thucydides describes the Peloponnesian siege operations and the Plataean counterworks.

After this appeal to the gods Archidamus put his army in motion. First he enclosed the city with a palisade formed of the fruit trees which they cut down, to prevent further exit from Plataea; next day they threw up a mound against the city, hoping that the largeness of the force employed would insure the speedy reduction of the place. [2] They accordingly cut down timber from Cithaeron,[2a] and built it up on either side, laying it like latticework to serve as a wall to keep the mound from spreading abroad, and carried to it wood and stones and earth and whatever other material might help to complete it. [3] They continued to work at the mound for seventy days and nights without intermission, being divided into relief parties to allow some to be employed in carrying while others took sleep and refreshment; the Spartan officer attached to each contingent keeping the men to the work. [4] But the Plataeans, observing the progress of the mound, constructed a wall of wood and fixed it upon that part of the city wall against which the mound was being erected, and built up bricks inside it which they took from the neighboring houses. [5] The timbers served to bind the building together, and to prevent its becoming weak as it ad-

2.73.2a   Athens, in relation to Plataea: Map 2.72, BY.
2.75.2a   Mount Cithaeron: Map 2.72, BY.

vanced in height; it had also a covering of skins and hides, which protected the woodwork against the attacks of burning missiles and allowed the men to work in safety. [6] Thus the wall was raised to a great height, and the mound opposite made no less rapid progress. The Plataeans also thought of another expedient; they pulled out part of the wall upon which the mound abutted, and carried the earth into the city.

Discovering this, the Peloponnesians twisted up clay in wattles of reed and threw it into the breach formed in the mound, in order to give it consistency and prevent its being carried away like the soil. [2] Stopped in this way the Plataeans changed their mode of operation, and digging a mine from the city calculated their way under the mound, and began to carry off its material as before. This went on for a long while without the enemy outside finding it out, so that for all they threw on the top their mound made no progress in proportion, being carried away from beneath and constantly settling down in the vacuum. [3] But the Plataeans fearing that even thus they might not be able to hold out against the superior numbers of the enemy, had yet another invention. They stopped working at the large building in front of the mound, and starting at either end of it inside from the old low wall, built a new one in the form of a crescent running in toward the city in order that in the event of the great wall being taken this might remain, and the enemy have to throw up a fresh mound against it, and as they advanced within might not only have their trouble over again, but also be exposed to missiles on their flanks. [4] While raising the mound the Peloponnesians also brought up siege engines against the city, one of which was brought up upon the mound against the great building and shook down a good piece of it, to the no small alarm of the Plataeans. Others were advanced against different parts of the wall but were lassoed and broken by the Plataeans; who also hung up great beams by long iron chains from either extremity of two poles laid on the wall and projecting over it, and drew them up at an angle whenever any point was threatened by the engine, and loosing their hold let the beam go with its chains slack, so that it fell freely and snapped off the nose of the battering ram.

After this the Peloponnesians, finding that their siege engines effected nothing, and that their mound was met by the counterwork, concluded that their present means of offense were unequal to the taking of the city, and prepared for its circumvallation.[1a] [2] First, however, they determined to try the effects of fire and see whether they could not, with the help of a wind, burn the city, as it was not a large one; indeed they thought of every possible expedient by which the place might be reduced without the expense of a siege. [3] They accordingly brought bundles of brushwood and threw them from the mound, first into the space between it and the wall; and this soon becoming full from the number of hands at work, they next heaped the faggots up as far into the city as they could reach from the top,

2.76
429
3rd Year/Summer
PLATAEA
A siege warfare of moves and countermoves is described.

2.77
429
3rd Year/Summer
PLATAEA
Unable to take the city by assault, the Peloponnesians plan to besiege it. A last attempt to burn out the defenders fails.

2.77.1a Circumvallation: the building of a wall to
        surround or isolate a city by land.

and then lighted the wood by setting fire to it with sulfur and pitch. [4] The consequence was a fire greater than anyone had ever yet seen produced by human agency, though it could not of course be compared to the spontaneous conflagrations known to occur sometimes through the wind rubbing the branches of a mountain forest together. [5] And this fire was not only remarkable for its magnitude, but was also, at the end of so many perils, within an ace of proving fatal to the Plataeans; a great part of the city became entirely inaccessible, and had a wind blown upon it, in accordance with the hopes of the enemy, nothing could have saved them. [6] As it was, there is also a story of heavy rain and thunder having come on by which the fire was put out and the danger averted.[6a]

2.78
429
3rd Year/Summer
PLATAEA
The Peloponnesians build a siege wall around Plataea. The defenders are described.

Failing in this last attempt the Peloponnesians left a portion of their forces on the spot, dismissing the rest, and built a wall of circumvallation round the city, dividing the ground among the various cities present; a ditch being made within and without the lines, from which they got their bricks. [2] All being finished by about the rising of Arcturus,[2a] they left men enough to man half the wall, the rest being manned by the Boeotians, and drawing off their army dispersed to their several cities. [3] The Plataeans had before sent off their wives and children and oldest men and the mass of the noncombatants to Athens; so that the number of the besieged left in the place comprised four hundred of their own citizens, eighty Athenians, and a hundred and ten women to bake their bread. [4] This was the sum total at the commencement of the siege, and there was no one else within the walls, bond or free.[4a] Such were the arrangements made for the blockade of Plataea.[4b]

2.79
429
3rd Year/Summer
CHALCIDICE
Athenian forces win an initial success at Spartolus but then suffer heavy losses when defeated by peltasts and cavalry.

The same summer and simultaneously with the expedition against Plataea, the Athenians marched with two thousand hoplites and two hundred horse against the Chalcidians[1a] in the Thracian region and the Bottiaeans,[1b] just as the corn was getting ripe, under the command of Xenophon son of Euripides,[1c] with two colleagues. [2] Arriving before Spartolus[2a] in Bottiaea, they destroyed the corn and had some hopes of the city coming over through the intrigues of a faction within. But those of a different way of thinking had sent to Olynthus;[2b] and a garrison of hoplites and other troops arrived accordingly. These issuing from Spartolus were engaged by the Athenians in front of the city: [3] the Chalcidian hoplites, and some auxiliaries with them, were beaten and retreated into Spartolus; but the Chalcidian horse and light troops defeated the horse and light troops of the

---

2.77.6a   Is Thucydides being skeptical about stories of divine intervention? See the Introduction (sec. IV.ii) for a discussion of Thucydides' attitude toward religion.

2.78.2a   The reference is to the Heliacal rising of Arcturus when it first becomes visible after the forty days of invisibility owing to the fact that it rises after the sun; this occurs on approximately September 20.

2.78.4a   This is one of the few occasions on which Thucydides mentions women, who in this case might have been slaves. See Appendix A, The Athenian Government, §2.

2.78.4b   The narrative of the siege of Plataea is continued in 3.20.

2.79.1a   This picks up the narrative of Chalcidice from 2.70.4, which Thucydides continues next in 2.95. Chalcidice: Map 2.72, AY.

2.79.1b   Bottica (Bottike), the "current" location of the Bottiaeans: Map 2.72, AY.

2.79.1c   Xenephon son of Euripides was one of the Athenian commanders at Potidaea; see 2.70.1.

2.79.2a   Spartolus, approximate location: Map 2.72, AY.

2.79.2b   Olynthus: Map 2.72, AY.

Athenians. [4] The Chalcidians already had a few peltasts from Crusis,[4a] and presently after the battle were joined by some others from Olynthus; [5] upon seeing them the light troops from Spartolus, emboldened by this extra force and by their previous success, with the help of the Chalcidian horse and the reinforcement just arrived again attacked the Athenians, who retired upon the two divisions which they had left with their baggage. [6] Whenever the Athenians advanced, their adversary gave way, pressing them with missiles the instant they began to retire. The Chalcidian horse also, riding up and charging them just as they pleased, at last caused a panic amongst them and routed and pursued them to a great distance. [7] The Athenians took refuge in Potidaea, and afterwards recovered their dead under truce, and returned to Athens with the remnant of their army; four hundred and thirty men and all the generals having fallen. The Chalcidians and Bottiaeans set up a trophy, took up their dead, and dispersed to their several cities.

The same summer, not long after this, the Ambraciots[1a] and Chaonians,[1b] being desirous of reducing the whole of Acarnania[1c] and detaching it from Athens, persuaded the Spartans to equip a fleet from their confederacy and send a thousand hoplites to Acarnania, arguing that if a combined movement were made by land and sea, the coastal Acarnanians would be unable to march, and the conquest of Zacynthus[1d] and Cephallenia[1e] would follow easily upon the possession of Acarnania. Thus, the cruise round the Peloponnesus would no longer be so convenient for the Athenians. Besides which there was a hope of taking Naupactus.[1f] [2] The Spartans accordingly at once sent off a few vessels with Cnemus,[2a] who was still admiral, and the hoplites on board; and sent round orders for the fleet to equip as quickly as possible and sail to Leucas. [3] The Corinthians were the most forward in the business; the Ambraciots being a colony of theirs. While the ships from Corinth,[3a] Sicyon,[3b] and the neighborhood were getting ready, and those from Leucas,[3c] Anactorium,[3d] and Ambracia, which had arrived before, were waiting for them at Leucas, [4] Cnemus and his thousand hoplites had run into the gulf,[4a] giving the slip to Phormio, the commander of the Athenian squadron stationed off Naupactus, and began at once to prepare for the land expedition. [5] The Hellenic troops with him consisted of the Ambraciots, Leucadians, and Anactorians, and the thousand Peloponnesians with whom he came; the thousand barbarian Chaonians, who, belonging to a nation that has no king, were led by Photys and Nicanor, the two mem-

2.80
429
3rd Year/Summer
ACARNANIA
At Ambraciot invitation, a Peloponnesian expedition sails to the Ambracian Gulf and launches an attack on Acarnania.

2.79.4a   Crusis: Map 2.72, AY. Peltasts were troops armed only with a small, light shield, a javelin, and a short sword. Unhindered by body armor, a peltast could move much more quickly than the fully armed hoplite, whose equipment was both far more heavy and far more expensive than theirs.

2.80.1a   This continues the narrative of events in Ambracia and Acarnania from 2.68. Ambracia: Map 2.80, AX.
2.80.1b   Chaonia: Map 2.80, AX.
2.80.1c   Acarnania: Map 2.80, AX.

2.80.1d   Zacynthus: Map 2.80, BX.
2.80.1e   Cephallenia: Map 2.80, BX.
2.80.1f   Naupactus: Map 2.80, BY.
2.80.2a   Cnemus was the Spartiate commander of the Peloponnesian fleet that attacked Zacynthus in 2.66.
2.80.3a   Corinth: Map 2.80, BY.
2.80.3b   Sicyon: Map 2.80, BY.
2.80.3c   Leucas: Map 2.80, AX.
2.80.3d   Anactorium: Map 2.80, AX.
2.80.4a   Crisaean gulf, now called the Corinthian Gulf: Map 2.80, BY.

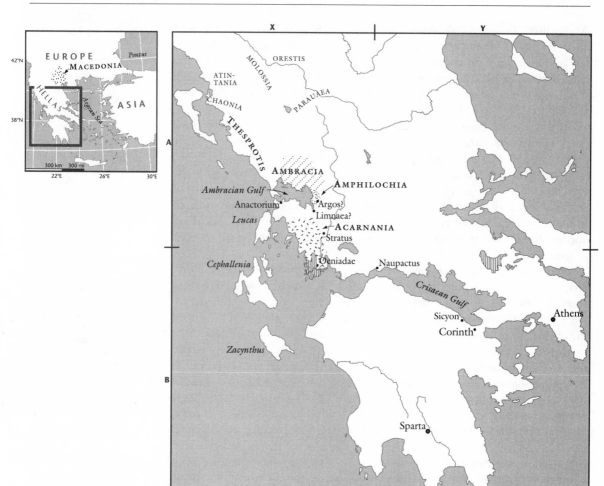

MAP 2.80 AMBRACIAN-PELOPONNESIAN OPERATIONS IN ACARNANIA[5a]

bers of the royal family to whom the chieftainship for that year had
been assigned. With the Chaonians came also some Thesprotians,[5b] like
them without a king, [6] some Molossians[6a] and Atintanians[6b] led by
Sabylinthus, the guardian of King Tharyps who was still a minor, and some
Parauaeans[6c] under their king Oroedus, accompanied by a thousand Ores-
tians,[6d] subjects of king Antiochus and placed by him under the command
of Oroedus. [7] There were also a thousand Macedonians[7a] sent by Perdic-

2.80.5a The source for the possible sites of Am-
         philochian Argos and Limnaea, shown in
         Map 2.80, is N.G.L. Hammond, "The
         Campaign in Amphilochia during the
         Archidamian War," *The Annual of the
         British School at Athens*, 1937, 128–40.
2.80.5b Thesprotis: Map 2.80, AX.

2.80.6a Molossia: Map 2.80, AX.
2.80.6b Atintania: Map 2.80, AX.
2.80.6c Parauaea: Map 2.80, AX.
2.80.6d Orestis: Map 2.80, AX.
2.80.7a The Macedonian king Perdiccas was last
         mentioned in 2.29.6 and will next appear
         in 2.95. Macedonia: Map 2.80, locator.

cas without the knowledge of the Athenians, but they arrived too late. With this force Cnemus set out, without waiting for the fleet from Corinth. Passing through the territory of Amphilochian Argos,[7b] and sacking the open village of Limnaea,[7c] they advanced to Stratus[7d] the Acarnanian capital; convinced that once this was taken, the rest of the country would speedily come over.

The Acarnanians, finding themselves invaded by a large army by land, and from the sea threatened by a hostile fleet, made no combined attempt at resistance, but remained to defend their homes, and sent for help to Phormio, who replied that when a fleet was on the point of sailing from Corinth, it was impossible for him to leave Naupactus unprotected. [2] The Peloponnesians meanwhile and their allies advanced upon Stratus in three divisions, with the intention of encamping near it and attempting the wall by force if they failed to succeed by negotiation. [3] The order of march was as follows: the center was occupied by the Chaonians and the rest of the barbarians, with the Leucadians and Anactorians and their followers on the right, and Cnemus with the Peloponnesians and Ambraciots on the left; each division being a long way off from, and sometimes even out of sight of, the others. [4] The Hellenes advanced in good order, keeping a lookout till they encamped in a good position; but the Chaonians, filled with self-confidence, and having the highest reputation for courage among the tribes of that part of the continent, without waiting to occupy their camp, rushed on with the rest of the barbarians, with the idea that they should take the city by assault and obtain the sole glory of the enterprise. [5] While they were coming on, the Stratians becoming aware how things stood, and thinking that the defeat of this division would considerably dishearten the Hellenes behind it, occupied the environs of the city with ambuscades, and as soon as they approached engaged them at close quarters from the city and the ambuscades. [6] A panic seizing the Chaonians, great numbers of them were slain; and as soon as they were seen to give way the rest of the barbarians turned and fled. [7] Owing to the distance by which their allies had preceded them, neither of the Hellenic divisions knew anything of the battle, but fancied they were hastening on to encamp. [8] However, when the flying barbarians broke in upon them, they opened their ranks to receive them, brought their divisions together, and stopped quiet where they were for the day; the Stratians not offering to engage them, as the rest of the Acarnanians had not yet arrived, but contenting themselves with slinging at them from a distance, which distressed them greatly as they could not move without their armor. The Acarnanians are thought to excel in this mode of warfare.

2.80.7b Amphilochian Argos, possible location: Map 2.80, AX.
2.80.7c Limnaea, possible location: Map 2.80, AX.
2.80.7d Stratus: Map 2.80, AX.

2.82
429
3rd Year/Summer
ACARNANIA
Cnemus withdraws through Oeniadae.

As soon as night fell, Cnemus hastily drew off his army to the river Anapus,[1a] about nine miles from Stratus, recovering his dead next day under truce, and being there joined by the friendly Oeniadae,[1b] fell back upon their city before the enemy's reinforcements came up. From hence each returned home; and the Stratians set up a trophy for the battle with the barbarians.[1c]

2.83
429
3rd Year/Summer
OFF PATRAE
A Peloponnesian fleet carrying troops is attacked in open water by Phormio's triremes. The Peloponnesians form a defensive circle.

Meanwhile the fleet from Corinth and the rest of the confederates in the Crisaean gulf,[1a] which was to have cooperated with Cnemus and prevented the coastal Acarnanians from joining their countrymen in the interior, was stopped from doing so by being compelled about the same time as the battle at Stratus to fight with Phormio and the twenty Athenian vessels stationed at Naupactus. [2] For they were watched, as they coasted along out of the gulf, by Phormio, who wished to attack in the open sea. [3] But the Corinthians and allies had started for Acarnania without any idea of fighting at sea, and with vessels more like transports for carrying soldiers; besides which, they never dreamed of the twenty Athenian ships venturing to engage their forty-seven. However, while they were coasting along their own shore, there were the Athenians sailing along in line with them; and when they tried to cross over from Patrae[3a] in Achaea to the mainland on the other side, on their way to Acarnania, they saw them again coming out from Chalcis[3b] and the river Evenus[3c] to meet them. They slipped from their moorings in the night, but were observed, and were at length compelled to fight in midpassage. [4] Each state that contributed to the armament had its own general; the Corinthian commanders were Machaon, Isocrates, and Agatharchidas. [5] The Peloponnesians ranged their vessels in as large a circle as possible without leaving an opening, with the prows outside and the sterns in; and placed within all the small craft in company and their five best sailers[5a] to move out at a moment's notice and strengthen any point threatened by the enemy.

2.84
429
3rd Year/Summer
OFF PATRAE
Phormio skillfully waits for dawn winds to disturb the enemy formation and then attacks, routing the enemy and capturing twelve triremes.

The Athenians, formed in line, sailed round and round them, and forced them to contract their circle, by continually brushing past and making as though they would attack at once, having been previously cautioned by Phormio not to do so till he gave the signal. [2] His hope was that the Peloponnesians would not retain their order like a force on shore, but that the ships would fall foul of one another and the small craft cause confusion; and if the wind which usually rose toward morning should blow from the gulf (in expectation of which he kept sailing round them), he felt sure they would not remain steady an instant. He also thought that it rested with him to attack when he pleased, as his ships were better sailers, and that an attack

---

2.82.1a　Anapus river, possible location: Map 2.86, AX.
2.82.1b　Oeniadae: Map 2.80, BX. Pericles had failed to capture this city in 1.111.2–3.
2.82.1c　The narrative of events in Acarnania is continued in 2.102.
2.83.1a　Crisaean gulf, today called the Corinthian Gulf: Map 2.86, BY.
2.83.3a　Patrae: Map 2.86, BX.

2.83.3b　For the location of this Chalcis, see Map 2.86, BX.
2.83.3c　Evenus river: Map 2.86, AX.
2.83.5a　The trireme's design was standardized, but evidently some ships excelled in speed due to superior construction, age, condition, the training and vigor of crews, or some combination of these factors.

ILLUSTRATION 2.84
THE MODERN TRIREME *OLYMPIAS* AT
SEA, ROWING (TOP) AND UNDER SAIL

timed by the coming of the wind would tell best. [3] When the wind came up, the enemy's ships were now in a narrow space, and what with the wind and the small craft dashing against them, at once fell into confusion: ship fell foul of ship, while the crews were pushing them off with poles, and by their shouting, swearing, and struggling with one another, made captains' orders and boatswains' cries alike inaudible, and through being unable for want of practice to clear their oars in the rough water, prevented the vessels from obeying their helmsmen properly. At this moment Phormio gave the signal, and the Athenians attacked. Sinking first one of the commanders' ships, they then disabled all they came across, so that no one thought of resistance for the confusion, but all fled for Patrae and Dyme[3a] in Achaea. [4] The Athenians gave chase and captured twelve ships, and taking most of the men out of them[4a] sailed to Molycrium,[4b] and after setting up a trophy on the promontory of Rhium and dedicating a ship to Poseidon, returned to Naupactus. [5] As for the Peloponnesians, they at once sailed with their remaining ships along the coast from Dyme and Patrae to Cyllene,[5a] the Eleian arsenal where Cnemus and the ships from Leucas[5b] that were to have joined them also arrived after the battle of Stratus.[5c]

The Spartans now sent to the fleet of Cnemus three commissioners, Timocrates, Brasidas,[1a] and Lycophron, with orders to prepare to engage again with better fortune, and not to be driven from the sea by a few vessels. [2] For they could not at all explain their defeat, the less so as it was their first attempt at sea; and they fancied that it was not that their navy was so inferior, but that there had been misconduct somewhere, not considering the long experience of the Athenians as compared with the little practice which they had had themselves. The commissioners were accordingly sent in anger. [3] As soon as they arrived they set to work with Cnemus to order ships from the different states, and to put those which they already had in fighting order. [4] Meanwhile Phormio sent word to Athens of their preparations and his own victory, and desired as many ships as possible to be speedily sent to him, as he stood in daily expectation of a battle. [5] Twenty were accordingly sent, but instructions were given to their commander to go first to Crete.[5a] For Nicias, a Cretan of Gortys,[5b] who was proxenus[5c] of the Athenians, had persuaded them to sail against Cydonia,[5d] promising to procure the reduction of that hostile city; his real wish being to oblige the Polichnitans,[5e] neighbors of the Cydonians. [6] He accordingly went with the ships to Crete, and, accompanied by the Polichnitans, laid waste the lands of the Cydonians; and, what with adverse winds and stress of weather, wasted no little time there.

2.84.3a Dyme: Map 2.86, BX.
2.84.4a That is, "taking most of them prisoner."
2.84.4b Molycrium, possible location: Map 2.86, BX.
2.84.5a Cyllene: Map 2.86, BX.
2.84.5b Leucas: Map 2.86, AX.
2.84.5c Stratus: Map 2.86, AX. The battle of Stratus was described in 2.81. 5–8.
2.85.1a This is the same Brasidas who distinguished himself at Methone in 2.25.2.

We shall next hear of him as an adviser to the Spartan admiral Alcidas, in 3.69.1.
2.85.5a Crete: Map 2.86, locator, and Map 2.9, BY.
2.85.5b Gortys, Crete: Map 2.9, BY.
2.85.5c *Proxenus:* see note 2.29.1b.
2.85.5d Cydonia, Crete: Map 2.9, BX.
2.85.5e Polichna, Crete, probable location: Map 2.9, BX.

MAP 2.86 Phormio's Operations off Naupactus; the Peloponnesian Raid on the Piraeus[6a]

2.86
429
3rd Year/Summer
ACHAEAN RHIUM
Both fleets maneuver to gain advantage. The Peloponnesian commanders decide to encourage their men with a speech.

While the Athenians were thus detained in Crete, the Peloponnesians in Cyllene[1a] got ready for battle, and coasted along to Panormus[1b] in Achaea, where their land army had come to support them. [2] Phormio also coasted along to Molycrian Rhium,[2a] and anchored outside it with twenty ships, the same as he had fought with before. [3] This Rhium was friendly to the Athenians. The other, in the Peloponnesus, lies opposite to it; the sea between them is about three-quarters of a mile broad, and forms the mouth of the Crisaean gulf. [4] At this, the Achaean Rhium,[4a] not far off Panormus, where their army lay, the Peloponnesians now cast anchor with seventy-seven ships, when they saw the Athenians do so. [5] For six or seven days they remained opposite each other, practicing and preparing for the battle; the one resolved not to sail out of the Rhia into the open sea, for fear of the disaster which had already happened to them, the other not to sail into the straits, thinking it advantageous to the enemy to fight in the narrows. [6] At last Cnemus and Brasidas and the rest of the Peloponnesian commanders, being desirous of bringing on a battle as soon as possible, before reinforcements should arrive from Athens, and noticing that the men were most of them cowed by the previous defeat and out of heart for the business, first called them together and encouraged them as follows:

2.87
429
3rd Year/Summer
ACHAEAN RHIUM
The Peloponnesian commanders call on their men to be brave despite their inexperience.

"Peloponnesians, the late engagement which may have made some of you afraid of the one now in prospect really gives no just ground for apprehension. [2] Preparation for it, as you know, was little enough; and the object of our voyage was not so much to fight at sea as an expedition by land. Besides this, the chances of war were largely against us; and perhaps also inexperience had something to do with our failure in our first naval action. [3] It was not, therefore, cowardice that produced our defeat, nor ought the determination which force has not quelled, but which still has a word to say with its adversary, to lose its edge from the result of an accident; but admitting the possibility of a chance miscarriage, we should know that brave hearts must be always brave, and while they remain so can never put forward inexperience as an excuse for misconduct. [4] Nor are you so behind the enemy in experience as you are ahead of him in courage; and although the science of your opponents would, if valor accompanied it, have also the presence of mind to carry out in an emergency the lesson it has learnt, yet a faint heart will make all art powerless in the face of danger. For fear takes away presence of mind, and without valor art is useless. [5] Against their superior experience set your superior daring, and against the fear induced by defeat the fact of your having been then unprepared; [6] remember,

2.86.1a   Cyllene: Map 2.86, BX.
2.86.1b   Panormus: Map 2.86, BX.

2.86.2a   Molycrian Rhium: Map 2.86, BX.
2.86.4a   Achaean Rhium: Map 2.86, BX.

too, that you have always the advantage of superior numbers, and of engaging off your own coast, supported by your hoplites; and as a rule, numbers and equipment give victory. [7] At no point, therefore, is defeat likely; and as for our previous mistakes, the very fact of their occurrence will teach us better for the future. [8] Steersmen and sailors may, therefore, confidently attend to their several duties, none quitting the station assigned to them; [9] as for ourselves, we promise to prepare for the engagement at least as well as your previous commanders, and to give no excuse for anyone misconducting himself. Should any insist on doing so, he shall meet with the punishment he deserves, while the brave shall be honored with the appropriate rewards of valor."

The Peloponnesian commanders encouraged their men after this fashion. Phormio, meanwhile, being himself not without fears for the courage of his men, and noticing that they were forming in groups among themselves and were alarmed at the odds against them, desired to call them together and give them confidence and counsel in the present emergency. [2] He had before continually told them, and had accustomed their minds to the idea, that there was no numerical superiority that they could not face; and the men themselves had long been persuaded that Athenians need never retire before any number of Peloponnesian vessels. [3] At the moment, however, he saw that they were dispirited by the sight before them, and wishing to refresh their confidence, called them together and spoke as follows:

2.88
429
3rd Year/Summer
MOLYCRIAN RHIUM
Phormio also encourages his men, seeing that they are frightened by the numerical odds they face.

"I see, my men, that you are frightened by the number of the enemy, and I have accordingly called you together, not liking you to be afraid of what is not really terrible. [2] In the first place, the Peloponnesians, already defeated, and not even themselves thinking that they are a match for us, have not ventured to meet us on equal terms, but have equipped this multitude of ships against us. Next, as to that upon which they most rely, the courage which they suppose constitutional to them, their confidence here only arises from the success which their experience in land service usually gives them, and which they fancy will do the same for them at sea. [3] But this advantage will in all justice belong to us on this element, if to them on that; as they are not superior to us in courage, but we are each of us more confident, according to our experience in our particular department. [4] Besides, as the Spartans use their supremacy over the allies to promote their own glory, they are most of them being

2.89
429
3rd Year/Summer
MOLYCRIAN RHIUM
Phormio explains why his fleet, despite the odds, should face the coming battle with confidence.

brought into danger against their will, or they would never, after such a decided defeat, have ventured upon a fresh engagement. [5] You need not, therefore, be afraid of their dash. You, on the contrary, inspire a much greater and better founded alarm, both because of your late victory and also of their belief that we should not face them unless about to do something worthy of such an outstanding success. [6] An adversary numerically superior, like the one before us, comes into action trusting more to strength than to resolution; while he who voluntarily confronts tremendous odds must have very great internal resources to draw upon. For these reasons the Peloponnesians fear our irrational audacity more than they would ever have done a more commensurate preparation. [7] Besides, many armaments have before now succumbed to an inferior through want of skill or sometimes of courage; neither of which defects certainly are ours. [8] As to the battle, it shall not be, if I can help it, in the strait, nor will I sail in there at all; seeing that in a contest between a number of clumsily managed vessels and a small, fast, well-handled squadron, want of sea room is an undoubted disadvantage. One cannot run down an enemy properly without having a sight of him a good way off, nor can one retire at need when pressed; one can neither break the line nor return upon his rear, the proper tactics for a fast sailer; but the naval action necessarily becomes a land one, in which numbers must decide the matter.[8a] [9] For all this I will provide as far as can be. Do you stay at your posts by your ships, and be sharp at catching the word of command, the more so as we are observing one another from so short a distance; and in action think order and silence all important—qualities useful in war generally, and in naval engagements in particular[9a]—and behave before the enemy in a manner worthy of your past exploits. [10] The issues you will fight for are great—either you will destroy the naval hopes of the Peloponnesians or you will bring nearer to reality the Athenians' fear of losing control of the sea. [11] And I may once more remind you that you have defeated most of them already; and beaten men do not face a danger twice with the same determination."

Such was the exhortation of Phormio. The Peloponnesians finding that the Athenians did not sail into the gulf and the narrows, in order to lead them in whether they wished it or not, put out at dawn, and forming four

2.90
429
3rd Year/Summer
NAUPACTUS
By sailing toward Naupactus, the Peloponnesians lure Phormio into following them into the straits where they successfully attack him, capturing nine triremes.

2.89.8a   See 7.36.4 and Appendix G, Trireme Warfare, §11.
2.89.9a   Silence was particularly vital on warships so that rowers could hear the cadence, which was played on a shrill pipe, and the commands issued by the *keleustes*, the chief rowing officers. See also 2.84.3 and 7.70.6.

abreast, sailed inside the gulf in the direction of their own country, the right wing leading as they had lain at anchor. [2] In this wing were placed twenty of their fastest ships so that in the event of Phormio thinking that their object was Naupactus,[2a] and coasting along thither to save the place, the Athenians might not be able to escape their onset by getting outside their wing, but might be cut off by the vessels in question. [3] As they expected, Phormio, in alarm for the place at that moment emptied of its garrison, as soon as he saw them put out, reluctantly and hurriedly embarked and sailed along shore; the Messenian[3a] land forces moving along also to support him. [4] The Peloponnesians seeing him coasting along with his ships in single file, and already inside the gulf and close in shore as they so much wished, at one signal turned suddenly and bore down in line at their best speed on the Athenians, hoping to cut off the whole squadron. [5] The eleven leading vessels, however, escaped the Peloponnesian wing and its sudden movement, and reached the more open water; but the rest were overtaken as they tried to run through, driven ashore and disabled; such of the crews being slain as had not swum out of them. [6] Some of the ships the Peloponnesians lashed to their own, and towed off empty; one they took with the men in it; others were just being towed off, when they were saved by the Messenians dashing into the sea with their armor and fighting from the decks that they had boarded.

Thus far victory was with the Peloponnesians and the Athenian fleet destroyed; the twenty ships in the right wing being meanwhile in chase of the eleven Athenian vessels that had escaped their sudden movement and reached the more open water. These, with the exception of one ship, all out-sailed them and got safe into Naupactus, and forming close in shore opposite the temple of Apollo, with their prows facing the enemy, prepared to defend themselves in case the Peloponnesians should sail in shore against them. [2] After a while the Peloponnesians came up, chanting the *paean*[2a] for their victory as they sailed on; the single Athenian ship remaining being chased by a Leucadian far ahead of the rest. [3] But there happened to be a merchantman lying at anchor in the roadstead, which the Athenian ship found time to sail round, and struck the Leucadian in chase amidships and sank[3a] her. [4] An exploit so sudden and unexpected produced a panic among the Peloponnesians; and having fallen out of order in the excitement of victory, some of them dropped their oars and stopped their way in order to let the main body come up—an unsafe thing to do considering how near they were to the enemy's prows; while others ran

2.91
429
3rd Year/Summer
NAUPACTUS
The fleeing Athenian ships reach Naupactus. One of them turns and sinks a pursuer, which causes the Peloponnesian vessels to halt. Some Peloponnesian ships run aground.

2.90.2a   Naupactus: Map 2.86, BX.
2.90.3a   These were the Messenians from Naupactus; see note 2.9.4c and 1.103.1–3.
2.91.2a   The *paean* was a ritual chant that the men of classical Greek armies sang as they advanced into battle, rallied, or celebrated victory.
2.91.3a   Triremes, built entirely of wood and carrying no cargo, were so buoyant that they would not have actually sunk to the sea bottom when their seams or planks were

split by ramming. Instead, they filled with water—becoming unmaneuverable—and remained floating just at or below the surface of the sea, whence they were collected and towed back as booty to the victor's camp after battle. When Thucydides uses the word *kataduei* here (and at 3.78.1 and passim), which literally means "sink down," he must be referring to the partial sinking of the hulls as they filled with water.

aground in the shallows, in their ignorance of the localities.

Elated at this incident, the Athenians at one word gave a cheer, and dashed at the enemy, who, embarrassed by his mistakes and the disorder in which he found himself, only stood for an instant, and then fled for Panormus,[1a] from which he had put out. [2] The Athenians following on his heels took the six vessels nearest them, and recovered those of their own which had been disabled close in shore and taken in tow at the beginning of the action; they killed some of the crews and took some prisoners. [3] On board the Leucadian which went down off the merchantman, was the Spartan Timocrates, who killed himself when the ship was sunk, and was cast up in the harbor of Naupactus. [4] The Athenians on their return set up a trophy on the spot from which they had put out and turned the day, and picking up the wrecks and dead that were on their shore, gave back to the enemy their dead under truce. [5] The Peloponnesians also set up a trophy as victors for the defeat inflicted upon the ships they had disabled in shore, and dedicated the vessel which they had taken at Achaean Rhium, side by side with the trophy. [6] After this, apprehensive of the reinforcement expected from Athens, all except the Leucadians sailed into the Crisaean gulf for Corinth. [7] Not long after their retreat, the twenty Athenian ships, which were to have joined Phormio before the battle,[7a] arrived at Naupactus.

Thus the summer ended. Winter was now at hand; but before dispersing the fleet, which had retired to Corinth and the Crisaean gulf, Cnemus, Brasidas, and the other Peloponnesian captains allowed themselves to be persuaded by the Megarians[1a] to make an attempt upon the Piraeus,[1b] the port of Athens, which from her decided superiority at sea had been naturally left unguarded and open. [2] Their plan was as follows: the men were each to take their oar, cushion, and rowlock thong, and going overland from Corinth to the sea on the Athenian side, to get to Megara as quickly as they could, and launching forty vessels, which happened to be in the docks at Nisaea,[2a] to sail at once to the Piraeus. [3] There was no fleet on the lookout in the harbor, and no one had the least idea of the enemy attempting a surprise; while an open attack would, it was thought, never be deliberately ventured or if contemplated, would speedily be known at Athens. Their plan formed, the next step was to put it in execution. [4] Arriving by night, they launched the vessels from Nisaea but sailed not to the Piraeus as they had originally intended, being afraid of the risk (besides which there was some talk of a wind having stopped them), but to the point of Salamis[4a] that looks toward Megara. There the Athenians had

2.92
429
3rd Year/Summer
NAUPACTUS
The Athenian ships counterattack, pursuing the Peloponnessans who flee in turn. The Athenians capture six of them and retake their own vessels lost earlier.

2.93
429/8
3rd Year/Winter
MEGARA-PIRAEUS
The Peloponnesians plan to raid the Piraeus. They march their sailors by night to triremes at Megara. But instead of sailing to the Piraeus, they stop to pillage Salamis.

2.92.1a   Panormus: Map 2.86, BX.
2.92.7a   And which had sailed to Crete; 2.85.4–6.
2.93.1a   Megara: Map 2.86, BY.
2.93.1b   Piraeus: Map 2.86, BY.
2.93.2a   Nisaea: Map 2.86, BY.
2.93.4a   Salamis in relation to Nisaea: Map 2.86, BY, and Map 3.51, inset.

a fort and a squadron of three triremes to prevent any vessels from sailing in or out of Megara. They assaulted this fort, towed off the triremes empty, and surprising the inhabitants began to lay waste the rest of the island.

Meanwhile fire signals were raised to alarm Athens, and a panic ensued there as serious as any that occurred during the war. The idea in the city was that the enemy had already sailed into the Piraeus; in the Piraeus it was thought that they had taken Salamis and might at any moment arrive in the port; as indeed might easily have been done if their hearts had been a little firmer; certainly no wind would have prevented them. [2] As soon as day broke the Athenians assembled in full force, launched their ships, and embarking in haste and uproar went with the fleet to Salamis, while their soldiery mounted guard in the Piraeus. [3] The Peloponnesians, on becoming aware of the coming relief, after they had overrun most of Salamis, hastily sailed off with their plunder and captives and the three ships from Fort Budorum[3a] to Nisaea; the state of their ships also causing them some anxiety, as it was a long while since they had been launched, and they were not watertight.[3b] Arrived at Megara, they returned back on foot to Corinth. [4] The Athenians finding them no longer at Salamis, sailed back themselves; and after this made arrangements for guarding the Piraeus more diligently in future, by closing the harbors, and by other suitable precautions.

About the same time, at the beginning of this winter, Sitalces son of Teres, the Odrysian king of Thrace,[1a] made an expedition against Perdiccas son of Alexander, king of Macedonia,[1b] and the Chalcidians[1c] in the neighborhood of Thrace; his object being to enforce one promise and fullfil another. [2] On the one hand, Perdiccas had made him a promise, when hard pressed at the commencement of the war, upon condition that Sitalces should reconcile the Athenians to him and not attempt to restore his brother and enemy, the pretender Philip, but had not offered to fullfil his engagement; on the other, he, Sitalces, on entering into alliance with the Athenians, had agreed to put an end to the Chalcidian war in Thrace. [3] These were the two objects of his invasion. With him he brought Amyntas the son of Philip, whom he destined for the throne of Macedonia, and some Athenian envoys then at his court on this business, and Hagnon as general; for the Athenians were to join him against the Chalcidians with a fleet and as many soldiers as they could get together.

Beginning with the Odrysians, he first called out the Thracian tribes subject to him between Mounts Haemus[1a] and Rhodope[1b] and the Euxine[1c] and

2.94
429/8
3rd Year/Winter
PIRAEUS
The Athenians, alarmed by fire signals from Salamis, rush to defend the Piraeus. The Peloponnesians hastily depart. Guards are set at the Piraeus to prevent future surprises.

2.95
429/8
3rd Year/Winter
THRACE
Thucydides explains the reasons for the campaign of Sitalces of Thrace against Perdiccas of Macedon.

2.96
429/8
3rd Year/Winter
THRACE
The peoples of Sitalces' empire and the forces available to him for this expedition are described.

2.94.3a   Budorum, possible location: Map 2.86, BY; see also Map 3.51, inset.
2.94.3b   Although it was important to regularly dry out trireme hulls to maintain their speed and performance (see Appendix G, Trireme Warfare, §7), an excessively dry hull would leak until the planks had absorbed enough water to swell and close the joints between them.

2.95.1a   Sitalces was last mentioned in 2.67. Odrysian Thrace: Map 2.97, BY.
2.95.1b   Perdiccas was last mentioned in 2.80. Macedonia: Map 2.97, CX.
2.95.1c   Chalcidean affairs were last mentioned in 2.79. Chalcidice: Map 2.97, CX.
2.96.1a   Haemus mountains: Map 2.97, AY.
2.96.1b   Rhodope mountains: Map 2.97, BY.
2.96.1c   Euxine (Black Sea): Map 2.97, BZ.

MAP 2.97 SITALCES' KINGDOM—ODRYSIAN THRACE

Hellespont;[1d] next the Getae[1e] beyond Haemus, and the other hordes settled south of the Danube[1f] in the neighborhood of the Euxine, who, like the Getae, border on the Scythians[1g] and are armed in the same manner, being all mounted archers. [2] Besides these he summoned many of the independent Thracian hill tribes, swordsmen called Dii,[2a] mostly inhabiting Mount Rhodope, some of whom came as mercenaries, others as volunteers; [3] also the Agrianes and Leaeans, and the rest of the Paeonian[3a] tribes in his empire, at the confines of which these lay, extending up to the Laeaean Paeonians and the river Strymon[3b] which flows from Mount Scombrus[3c] through the country of the Agrianes and Leaeans; there the empire of Sitalces ends and the territory of the independent Paeonians begins. [4] Bordering on the Triballi,[4a] also independent, were the Treres and Tilataeans, who dwell to the north of Mount Scombrus and extend toward the setting sun as far as the river Oskius.[4b] This river rises in the same mountains as the Nestus[4c] and Hebrus,[4d] a wild and extensive range connected with Rhodope.

The empire of the Odrysians extended along the seaboard from Abdera[1a] to the mouth of the Danube[1b] in the Euxine. The navigation of this coast by the shortest route takes a merchantman four days and four nights with a wind astern the whole way: by land an active man, traveling by the shortest road, can get from Abdera to the Danube in eleven days. [2] Such was the length of its coastline. Inland from Byzantium[2a] to the Leaeans and the Strymon, the farthest limit of its extension into the interior, it is a journey of thirteen days for an active man. [3] The tribute from all the barbarian districts and the Hellenic cities, taking what they brought in under Seuthes, the successor of Sitalces, who raised it to its greatest height, amounted to about four hundred talents in gold and silver.[3a] There were also presents in gold and silver to a no less amount, besides cloth, plain and embroidered, and other articles, made not only for the king, but also for the Odrysian lords and nobles. [4] For there was here established a custom opposite to that prevailing in the Persian kingdom, namely, of taking rather than giving; more disgrace being attached to not giving when asked than to asking and being refused; and although this prevailed elsewhere in Thrace, it was practiced most extensively among the powerful Odrysians, it being impossible to get anything done without a present. [5] It was thus a very powerful kingdom; in revenue and general prosperity surpassing all in Europe between the Ionian gulf[5a] and the Euxine, and in numbers and mili-

2.97
429/8
3rd Year/Winter
THRACE
A description of the immense size of Sitalces' empire, as well as its wealth and a few of its customs, illustrates its power.

2.96.1d   Hellespont: Map 2.97, CZ.
2.96.1e   Getae, approximate location of their territory: Map 2.97, AZ.
2.96.1f   Danube river: Map 2.97, AY; and locator.
2.96.1g   Scythians, location of their territory: Map 2.97, locator.
2.96.2a   Dii, approximate location of their territory: Map 2.97, BY. The Dii reappear in Thucydides' account of the tragic fate of Mycallessus in 7.29.
2.96.3a   Paeonian tribes, approximate location of their territory: Map 2.97, BX.
2.96.3b   Strymon river: Map 2.97, BX.
2.96.3c   Mount Scombrus: Map 2.97, BX.
2.96.4a   Triballi, approximate location of their territory: Map 2.97, BX.
2.96.4b   Oskius river: Map 2.97, AY.
2.96.4c   Nestus river: Map 2.97, BX.
2.96.4d   Hebrus river: Map 2.97, BY.
2.97.1a   Abdera: Map 2.97, CY.
2.97.1b   Danube river mouth in the Euxine (Black Sea): Map 2.97, AY, and locator.
2.97.2a   Byzantium: Map 2.97, BZ.
2.97.3a   Talents: see Appendix J, Classical Greek Currency, §5.
2.97.5a   Ionian gulf (Adriatic Sea): Map 2.72, locator.

tary resources coming decidedly next to the Scythians, [6] with whom indeed no people in Europe can bear comparison, there not being even in Asia any nation singly a match for them if unanimous, though of course they are not on a level with other peoples in general intelligence and the arts of civilized life.

2.98
429/8
3rd Year/Winter
THRACE
Sitalces sets out for Macedon, his army increasing until it numbers perhaps 150,000, of which one-third is cavalry.

It was the master of this empire that now prepared to take the field. When everything was ready, he set out on his march for Macedonia, first through his own dominions, next over the desolate range of Cercine[1a] that divides the Sintians[1b] and Paeonians,[1c] crossing by a road which he had made by felling the timber on a former campaign against the latter people. [2] Passing over these mountains, with the Paeonians on his right and the Sintians and Maedians on the left, he finally arrived at Doberus,[2a] in Paeonia, [3] losing none of his army on the march except perhaps by sickness, but receiving some additional troops from many of the independent Thracians volunteering to join him in the hope of plunder; so that the whole is said to have formed a grand total of a hundred and fifty thousand. [4] Most of this was infantry, though there was about a third cavalry, furnished principally by the Odrysians[4a] themselves and next to them by the Getae.[4b] The most warlike of the infantry were the independent swordsmen who came down from Rhodope; the rest of the mixed multitude that followed him being chiefly formidable by their numbers.

2.99
429/8
3rd Year/Winter
THRACE
Thucydides offers a history of Macedon's foundation and growth.

Assembling in Doberus, they prepared to descend from the heights upon Lower Macedonia, where the dominions of Perdiccas lay; [2] for the Lyncestae,[2a] Elimiots,[2b] and other tribes more inland, though Macedonians by blood and allies and dependents of their kindred, still have their own separate governments. [3] The country on the seacoast, now called Macedonia,[3a] was first acquired by Alexander, the father of Perdiccas, and his ancestors, originally Temenids from Argos.[3b] This was effected by the expulsion from Pieria[3c] of the Pierians, who afterwards inhabited Phagres[3d] and other places under Mount Pangaeus[3e] along the sea beyond the Strymon[3f] (indeed the country between Pangaeus and the sea is still called the Pierian gulf), and also by the expulsion of the Bottiaeans, at present neighbors of the Chalcidians[3g] from Bottiaea.[3h] [4] They also acquired in Paeonia a narrow strip along the river Axius[4a] extending to Pella[4b] and the sea; and

2.98.1a Mount Cercine: Map 2.97, BX.
2.98.1b Sintians, approximate location of their territory: Map 2.97, BX.
2.98.1c Paeonians, approximate location of their territory: Map 2.97, BX.
2.98.2a Doberus, approximate location somewhere a little to the west of Mount Cercine: Map 2.97, BX.
2.98.4a Odrysian Thrace: Map 2.97, BY.
2.98.4b Getae, approximate location of their territory: Map 2.97, AZ.
2.99.2a Lyncestis: Map 2.97, CX.
2.99.2b Elimia, territory of the Elimiots: Map 2.97, CX.
2.99.3a Macedonia: Map 2.97, CX.

2.99.3b Fifth-century Greeks believed that the ruling house of Macedon originated in Argos in the Peloponnesus.
2.99.3c Pieria: Map 2.97, CX.
2.99.3d Phagres: Map 2.97, CY.
2.99.3e Mount Pangaeus: Map 2.97, CY.
2.99.3f Strymon river: Map 2.97, BX.
2.99.3g Chalcidice: Map 2.97, CX.
2.99.3h Bottiaea: Map 2.97, CX.
2.99.4a Axius river: Map 2.97, BX.
2.99.4b Pella: Map 2.97, CX.

having expelled the Edonians,[4c] they occupied Mygdonia[4d] between the Axius and the Strymon. [5] From Eordia[5a] also were driven the Eordians, most of whom perished—though a few of them still live round Physca[5b]— and the Almopians from Almopia.[5c] [6] These Macedonians also conquered places belonging to the other tribes, which are still theirs—Anthemus,[6a] Crestonia,[6b] Bisaltia,[6c] and much of Macedonia proper. The whole is now called Macedonia, and at the time of the invasion of Sitalces, Perdiccas, Alexander's son, was the reigning king.

The Macedonians, unable to take the field against so numerous an invader, shut themselves up in such strong places and fortresses as the country possessed. [2] Of these there was no great number, most of those now found in the country having been erected subsequently by Archelaus son of Perdiccas on his accession, who also cut straight roads, and otherwise put the kingdom on a better footing as regards horses, heavy infantry, and other war material than had been done by all the eight kings that preceded him.[2a] [3] Advancing from Doberus,[3a] the Thracian host first invaded what had been once Philip's government, and took Idomene[3b] by assault, Gortynia,[3c] Atalante,[3d] and some other places by negotiation, these last coming over for love of Philip's son, Amyntas, then with Sitalces. Laying siege to Europus,[3e] and failing to take it, [4] he next advanced into the rest of Macedonia to the left of Pella[4a] and Cyrrhus,[4b] not proceeding beyond this into Bottiaea[4c] and Pieria,[4d] but staying to lay waste Mygdonia, Crestonia, and Anthemus. [5] The Macedonians never even thought of meeting him with infantry; but the Thracian host was, as opportunity offered, attacked by handfuls of their horse, which had been reinforced from their allies in the interior. Armed with breastplates, and excellent horsemen, wherever these charged they overthrew all before them, but ran considerable risk in entangling themselves in the masses of the enemy, and so finally desisted from these efforts, deciding that they were not strong enough to venture against numbers so superior.

Meanwhile Sitacles opened negotiations with Perdiccas on the objects of his expedition; and finding that the Athenians, not believing that he would come, did not appear with their fleet, though they sent presents and envoys, despatched a large part of his army against the Chalcidians[1a] and Bot-

2.100
429/8
3rd Year/Winter
MACEDONIA
The Macedonians, unable to oppose directly such large forces, withdraw to forts and occasionally harass the enemy with cavalry.

2.101
429/8
3rd Year/Winter
MACEDONIA
Sitalces fails to reach his goals, runs out of provisions, and is persuaded by his nephew (who had been suborned by Perdiccas) to return to Thrace.

2.99.4c   Edonians, approximate location of their territory after their expulsion by the Macedonians: Map 2.97, CY.
2.99.4d   Mygdonia: Map 2.97, CX.
2.99.5a   Eordia, approximate location: Map 2.97, CX.
2.99.5b   Physca: location unknown.
2.99.5c   Almopia, approximate location: Map 2.97, CX.
2.99.6a   Anthemus: Map 2.97, CX.
2.99.6b   Crestonia, approximate location: Map 2.97, CX.
2.99.6c   Bisaltia, approximate location: Map 2.97, CX.
2.100.2a   Thucydides writes here as if the reign of Archelaus (413–399) was ended, but

some scholars have found it hard to accept that he was still writing after 399; see the Introduction (sec. II.ii) for the date of composition of Thucydides' work.
2.100.3a   Doberus, approximate location a little to the west of Mount Cercine: Map 2.97, BX.
2.100.3b   Idomene: Map 2.97, BX.
2.100.3c   Gortynia: Map 2.97, BX.
2.100.3d   Atalante: Map 2.97, CX.
2.100.3e   Europus: Map 2.97, CX.
2.100.4a   Pella: Map 2.97, CX.
2.100.4b   Cyrrhus: Map 2.97, CX.
2.100.4c   Bottiaea: Map 2.97, CX.
2.100.4d   Pieria: Map 2.97, CX.
2.101.1a   Chalcidice: Map 2.97, CX.

tiaeans,[1b] and shutting them up inside their walls laid waste their country. [2] While he remained in these parts, the people farther south, such as the Thessalians,[2a] and the Hellenes as far as Thermopylae,[2b] all feared that the army might advance against them, and prepared accordingly. [3] These fears were shared by the Thracians beyond the Strymon to the north, who inhabited the plains, such as the Panaeans, the Odomanti,[3a] the Droi, and the Dersaeans, all of whom are independent. [4] It was even matter of conversation among the Hellenes who were enemies of Athens whether Sitalces might not be invited by his ally to advance against them also. [5] Meanwhile he held Chalcidice and Bottica[5a] and Macedonia, and was ravaging them all; but finding that he was not succeeding in any of the objects of his invasion, and that his army was without provisions and was suffering from the severity of the season, he listened to the advice of Seuthes son of Sparadocus, his nephew and highest officer, and decided to retreat without delay. This Seuthes had been secretly won over by Perdiccas by the promise of his sister in marriage with a rich dowry. [6] In accordance with this advice, and after a stay of thirty days in all, eight of which were spent in Chalcidice, he retired home as quickly as he could; and Perdiccas[6a] afterwards gave his sister Stratonice to Seuthes as he had promised. Such was the history of the expedition of Sitalces.[6b]

2.102
429/8
3rd Year/Winter
ACARNANIA
Phormio leads an army into Acarnania to ensure its political loyalty. He decides not to attack Oeniadae in winter. Thucydides describes the Achelous River, the Echinades Islands at its mouth, and the myth of Alcmaeon.

In the course of this winter, after the dispersion of the Peloponnesian fleet, the Athenians in Naupactus[1a] under Phormio coasted along to Astacus,[1b] disembarked, and marched into the interior of Acarnania[1c] with four hundred Athenian hoplites and four hundred Messenians.[1d] After expelling some suspected persons from Stratus,[1e] Coronta,[1f] and other places, and restoring Cynes son of Theolytus to Coronta, they returned to their ships, [2] deciding that it was impossible in the winter season to march against Oeniadae,[2a] a place which, unlike the rest of Acarnania, had been always hostile to them; for the river Achelous[2b] flowing from Mount Pindus[2c] through Dolopia[2d] and the country of the Agraeans[2e] and Amphilochians[2f] and the plain of Acarnania, past the city of Stratus in the upper part of its course, forms lakes where it falls into the sea round Oeniadae, and thus makes it impracticable for an army in winter by reason of the water.[2g] [3] Opposite to Oeniadae lie most of the islands called Echinades,[3a] so close to

2.101.1b They were now settled in Bottica: Map 2.97, CX.
2.101.2a Thessaly: Map 2.97, CX.
2.101.2b Thermopylae, the strategic pass where the Greeks fought the Persians in 480: Map 3.7, BX.
2.101.3a Odomanti, approximate location of their territory: Map 2.97, BY.
2.101.5a Bottica: Map 2.97, CX.
2.101.6a Perdiccas next appears in 4.79.
2.101.6b Sitalces, his nephew Seuthes, and events in Thrace are picked up again in 4.7.
2.102.1a Naupactus: Map 2.102.
2.102.1b Astacus: Map 2.102.
2.102.1c This picks up events in Acarnania from

2.82. Acarnania: Map 2.102.
2.102.1d These were the Messenians from Naupactus; see 1.103.1–3, and note 2.9.4a.
2.102.1e Stratus: Map 2.102.
2.102.1f Coronta: location unknown.
2.102.2a Oeniadae: Map 2.102.
2.102.2b Achelous river: Map 2.102.
2.102.2c Pindus mountain range: Map 2.102.
2.102.2d Dolopia: Map 2.102.
2.102.2e Agraea: Map 2.102.
2.102.2f Amphilochia: Map 2.102.
2.102.2g Thucydides returns to events in Acarnania in 3.7.
2.102.3a Echinades islands: Map 2.102.

MAP 2.102
PHORMIO'S EXPEDITION
TO ACARNANIA IN 429

the mouths of the Achelous that that powerful stream is constantly forming deposits against them, and has already joined some of the islands to the continent, and seems likely in no long while to do the same with the rest. [4] For the current is strong, deep, and turbid, and the islands are so thick together that they serve to imprison the alluvial deposit and prevent its dispersing, lying, as they do, not in one line but irregularly, so as to leave no direct passage for the water into the open sea. [5] The islands in question are uninhabited and of no great size. There is also a story that Alcmaeon son of Amphiaraus, during his wanderings after the murder of his mother, was bidden by Apollo to inhabit this spot, through an oracle which intimated that he would have no release from his terrors until he should find a country to dwell in which had not been seen by the sun; or existed as land at the time he slew his mother; all else being to him polluted ground. [6] Perplexed at this, the story goes on to say, he at last observed this deposit of the Achelous, and considered that a place sufficient to support life might have been thrown up during the long interval that had elapsed since the death of his mother and the beginning of his wanderings. Settling, therefore, in the district around Oeniadae, he founded a dominion and left the country its name from his son Acarnan. Such is the story we have received concerning Alcmaeon.

2.103
429/8
3rd Year/Winter
ATHENS
Phormio returns to
Naupactus and Athens. His
prisoners are exchanged.

The Athenians and Phormio putting back from Acarnania and arriving at Naupactus, sailed home to Athens in the spring, taking with them the ships that they had captured, and such of the prisoners made in the late actions as were freemen; who were exchanged, man for man. And so ended this winter, and the third year of this war, of which Thucydides was the historian.

BOOK THREE

The next summer, just as the corn was getting ripe, the Peloponnesians and their allies invaded Attica[1a] under the command of Archidamus son of Zeuxidamus, king of Sparta, [2] and ravaged the land; the Athenian horse as usual attacking them wherever it was practicable and preventing the mass of the light troops from advancing from their camp and wasting the parts near the city. [3] After staying the time for which they had taken provisions, the invaders retired and dispersed to their several cities.

Immediately after the invasion of the Peloponnesians all Lesbos,[1a] except Methymna,[1b] revolted from the Athenians. The Lesbians had wished to revolt even before the war, but the Spartans would not receive them; and yet now when they did revolt, they were compelled to do so sooner than they had intended. [2] While they were waiting until the moles for their harbors and the ships and walls that they were building should be finished, and for the arrival of archers and grain and other things that they were engaged in bringing from the Pontus,[2a] [3] the Tenedians,[3a] with whom they were at enmity, and the Methymnians, and some dissident persons in Mytilene[3b] itself, who were *proxeni*[3c] of Athens, informed the Athenians that the Mytilenians were forcibly uniting the island under their sovereignty, and that the preparations about which they were so active were all concerted with their kindred the Boeotians,[3d] and with the Spartans, with a view to a revolt, and that unless they were immediately prevented, Athens would lose Lesbos.

However, the Athenians, distressed by the plague, and by the war that had recently broken out and was now raging, thought it a serious matter to add Lesbos with its fleet and untouched resources to the list of their enemies; and at first would not believe the charge, giving too much weight to

3.1
428
4th Year/Summer
ATTICA
The Peloponnesians invade Attica again.

3.2
428
4th Year/Summer
LESBOS
Lesbos revolts from Athens.

3.3
428
4th Year/Summer
MYTILENE
When negotiations fail, Athens sends a fleet to Mytilene.

3.1.1a   Attica: Map 3.7, BX.
3.2.1a   Lesbos: Map 3.7, AY.
3.2.1b   Methymna: Map 3.7, AY.
3.2.2a   The Grain Route from the Pontus (Euxine sea, Map 3.7, locator) region was serviced by cargo ships that passed through the Bosporus (Map 3.7, AY) and the Hellespont (Map 3.7, AY).
3.2.3a   Tenedos: Map 3.7, AY.

3.2.3b   Mytilene, Lesbos: Map 3.7, AY.
3.2.3c   A *proxenus,* although a citizen and resident of his own state, served as a "friend or representative" (much like a modern honorary consul) of a foreign state.
3.2.3d   Boeotia: Map 3.7, BX. The Lesbians were Aeolians, like their founders, the Boeotians; see 7.57.5.

their wish that it might not be true. But when an embassy which they sent had failed to persuade the Mytilenians to give up the union and the preparations complained of, they became alarmed, and resolved to strike the first blow. [2] Accordingly, they suddenly sent off forty ships that had been made ready to sail round the Peloponnesus, under the command of Cleippides son of Deinias, and two others; [3] word having been brought to them of a festival in honor of the Malean Apollo outside the city,[3a] which is celebrated by the whole people of Mytilene, and at which, if haste were made, they might hope to take them by surprise. If this plan succeeded, well and good; if not, they were to order the Mytilenians to deliver up their ships and to pull down their walls, and if they did not obey, to declare war. [4] The ships accordingly set out; the ten Mytilenian *triremes*[4a] present with the fleet according to the terms of the alliance, were detained by the Athenians and their crews placed in custody. [5] However, the Mytilenians were informed of the expedition by a man who crossed from Athens to Euboea, and going overland to Geraestus,[5a] sailed from thence by a merchant vessel which he found on the point of putting to sea, and so arrived at Mytilene the third day after leaving Athens. The Mytilenians accordingly refrained from going out to the temple at Malea, and moreover barricaded and kept guard round the half-finished parts of their walls and harbors.

3.4
428
4th Year/Summer
MYTILENE
During an armistice Mytilene
sends a secret embassy to
Sparta.

When the Athenians sailed in not long after and saw how things stood, the generals delivered their orders, and upon the Mytilenians refusing to obey, commenced hostilities. [2] The Mytilenians, thus compelled to go to war without notice and unprepared, at first sailed out with their fleet and made some show of fighting a little in front of the harbor; but being driven back by the Athenian ships, immediately offered to parley with the commanders, wishing, if possible, to get the ships away for the present upon any tolerable terms. [3] The Athenian commanders accepted their offers, being themselves fearful that they might not be able to cope with the whole of Lesbos; [4] and an armistice having been concluded, the Mytilenians sent to Athens one of the informers, already repentant of his conduct, and others with him, to try to persuade the Athenians of the innocence of their intentions and to get the fleet recalled. [5] In the meantime, having no great hope of a favorable answer from Athens, they also sent off a trireme with envoys to Sparta, unobserved by the Athenian fleet which was anchored at Malea to the north of the city.[5a]

[6] While these envoys, having reached Sparta after a difficult journey across the open sea, were negotiating for assistance to be sent them,

3.3.3a   Cape Malea, Lesbos, probable location of
           the festival: Map 3.7, AY.
3.3.4a   *Triremes* were the standard warship of
           this period; see Appendix G, Trireme
           Warfare, §4–7.
3.3.5a   Cape Geraestus, Euboea: Map 3.7, BX.
3.4.5a   The location of this Malea is unknown.

[3.5.1] the ambassadors from Athens returned without having effected anything; and hostilities were at once renewed by the Mytilenians and the rest of Lesbos, with the exception of the Methymnians, who came to the aid of the Athenians with the Imbrians and Lemnians[1a] and some few of the other allies. [2] The Mytilenians made a sortie with all their forces against the Athenian camp; and a battle ensued, in which they gained some slight advantage, but retired notwithstanding, not feeling sufficient confidence in themselves to spend the night upon the field. After this they kept quiet, wishing to wait for the chance of reinforcements arriving from the Peloponnesus before making a second venture; being encouraged by the arrival of Meleas, a Laconian, and Hermaeondas, a Theban, who had been sent off before the insurrection but had been unable to reach Lesbos before the Athenian expedition, and who now stole in in a trireme after the battle, and advised them to send another trireme and envoys back with them, which the Mytilenians accordingly did.[2a]

Meanwhile the Athenians, greatly encouraged by the inaction of the Mytilenians, summoned allies to their aid, who came in all the quicker from seeing so little vigor displayed by the Lesbians, and bringing round their ships to a new station to the south of the city, fortified two camps, one on each side of the city, and instituted a blockade of both the harbors. [2] The sea was thus closed against the Mytilenians, who however commanded the whole country, with the rest of the Lesbians who had now joined them; the Athenians only holding a limited area round their camps, and using Malea more as the station for their ships and their market.[2a]

While the war went on in this way at Mytilene, the Athenians, about the same time in this summer, also sent thirty ships to the Peloponnesus under Asopius son of Phormio; the Acarnanians insisting that the commander sent should be some son or relative of Phormio. [2] As the ships coasted along shore they ravaged the seaboard of Laconia;[2a] [3] after which Asopius sent most of the fleet home and himself went on with twelve vessels to Naupactus.[3a] Later, raising the whole Acarnanian[3b] population, he made an expedition against Oeniadae,[3c] the fleet sailing along the Achelous,[3d] while the army laid waste the country. [4] When the inhabitants, however, showed no signs of submitting, he dismissed the land forces and himself sailed to Leucas[4a] where, making a descent upon Nericus,[4b] he was cut off during his retreat, and most of his troops with him, by the people in those parts aided by some coast guards; [5] after which the Athenians sailed away, recovering their dead from the Leucadians under truce.[5a]

3.5
428
4th Year/Summer
MYTILENE
Hostilities resume. Mytilene sends more envoys to Sparta.

3.6
428
4th Year/Summer
MYTILENE
Athens blockades Mytilene by sea.

3.7
428
4th Year/Summer
PELOPONNESUS
Asopius leads an Athenian fleet around Peloponnesus.

3.5.1a   Imbros, Lemnos: Map 3.7, AY.
3.5.2a   These Mytilenean envoys to Sparta are mentioned next in 3.8.
3.6.2a   Military market: Greek soldiers and sailors were expected to purchase their food from local markets with their own money. Athenian military efforts at Mytilene are next mentioned in 3.18.
3.7.2a   Laconia: Map 3.7, BX.
3.7.3a   Naupactus: Map 3.7, BX.
3.7.3b   Acarnania: Map 3.7, AX. Thucydides

here picks up the narrative of events in Acarnania from 2.102 and continues it next in 3.94.
3.7.3c   Oeniadae: Map 3.7, BX.
3.7.3d   Achelous river: Map 3.7, AX.
3.7.4a   Leucas: Map 3.7, AX.
3.7.4b   Nericus, Leucas: Map 3.7, AX.
3.7.5a   This truce was granted according to the ritual of hoplite battle; see Appendix F, Land Warfare, §6.

MAP 3.7 MYTILENIAN REVOLT; EXPEDITION OF ASOPIUS

Meanwhile the envoys of the Mytilenians sent out in the first ship were told by the Spartans to come to Olympia,[1a] in order that the rest of the allies[1b] might hear them and decide upon their matter, and so they journeyed thither. It was the Olympiad[1c] in which the Rhodian Dorieus gained his second victory, [2] and the envoys having been introduced to make their speech after the festival, spoke as follows:

"Spartans and allies, the rule established among the Hellenes is not unknown to us. Those who revolt during a war and forsake their former confederacy are favorably regarded by those who receive them, insofar as they are of use to them, but otherwise are thought less well of, through being considered traitors to their former friends. [2] Nor is this an unfair way of judging, where the rebels and the power from whom they secede are at one in policy and sympathy, and a match for each other in resources and power, and where no reasonable ground exists for the rebellion. But with us and the Athenians this was not the case; [3] and no one need think the worse of us for revolting from them in danger, after having been honored by them in time of peace."

"Justice and honesty will be the first topics of our speech, especially as we are asking for alliance; because we know that there can never be any solid friendship between individuals, or union between communities that is worth the name, unless the parties be persuaded of each other's honesty, and be generally congenial the one to the other; since from difference in feeling springs also difference in conduct. [2] The alliance between ourselves and the Athenians began when you withdrew from the war against the Persians[2a] and they remained to finish the business. [3] But we did not become allies of the Athenians for the subjugation of the Hellenes, but allies of the Hellenes for their liberation from the Mede; [4] and as long as the Athenians led us fairly we followed them loyally; but when we saw them relax their hostility to the Mede, and try to make the allies their subjects, then our apprehensions began. [5] Unable, however, to unite and defend themselves, on account of the number of confederates that had votes,[5a] all the allies were enslaved, except ourselves and the Chians,[5b] who continued to send our contingents as independent and nominally free. [6] Given these examples, we could no longer trust Athens as a leader, however, as it seemed unlikely that she

3.8
428
4th Year/Summer
OLYMPIA
Mytilenian envoys travel to Olympia.

3.9
428
4th Year/Summer
OLYMPIA
The Mytilenians argue that their revolt is not dishonorable.

3.10
428
4th Year/Summer
OLYMPIA
The Mytilenians say they ceased to trust Athens when her allies were enslaved.

3.8.1a Olympia: Map 3.7, BX. These are the envoys whose despatch was mentioned in 3.5.
3.8.1b The "rest of the allies" here refers to the Peloponnesian League (See Appendix D, The Peloponnesian League, §3–4).
3.8.1c An "Olympiad" in this case was one of the quadrennial Olympic festivals which were celebrated with athletic contests and games. See Appendix I, Religious Festivals, §5, and Appendix K, Calendars and Dating Systems, §4.
3.10.2a Thucydides describes this withdrawal in 1.95.7. See Appendix E, The Persians, §4.
3.10.5a The Mytilenians here allude to votes of the council of the Delian League (see 1.96.2–1.97.1). See also Appendix B, The Athenian Empire, §2.
3.10.5b Chios: Map 3.7, BY. The Chians and the Lesbians were the only members of Athens' empire still contributing ships and men rather than money to the alliance.

would subject our fellow confederates and not do the same to us who were left, if ever she had the power."

"Had we all been still independent, we could have had more faith in their not attempting any change; but the greater number being their subjects, while they were treating us as equals, they would naturally chafe under this solitary instance of independence as contrasted with the submission of the majority; particularly as they daily grew more powerful, and we more destitute. [2] Now the only sure basis of an alliance is for each party to be equally afraid of the other: he who would like to encroach is then deterred by the reflection that he will not have odds in his favor. [3] Again, if we were left independent, it was only because they thought they saw their way to empire more clearly by specious language and by the paths of policy than by those of force. [4] Not only were we useful as evidence that powers who had votes like themselves would not, surely, join them in their expeditions, against their will, without the party attacked being in the wrong; but the same system also enabled them to lead the stronger states against the weaker first, and so to leave the former to the last, stripped of their natural allies, and less capable of resistance. [5] But if they had begun with us, while all the states still had their resources under their own control and there was a center to rally round, the work of subjugation would have been found less easy. [6] Besides this, our navy gave them some apprehension: it was always possible that it might unite with you or with some other power, and become dangerous to Athens. [7] The respect which we paid to their community and its leaders for the time being also helped us to maintain our independence. [8] However, we did not expect to be able to do so much longer, if this war had not broken out, from the examples that we had of their conduct to the rest."

"How then could we put our trust in such friendship or freedom as we had here? We accepted each other against our inclination; fear made them court us in war, and us them in peace; sympathy, the ordinary basis of confidence, had its place supplied by terror, fear having more share than friendship in detaining us in the alliance; and the first party that should be encouraged by the hope of impunity was certain to break faith with the other. [2] So to condemn us for being the first to break off, because they delay the blow that we dread, instead of ourselves delaying to know for certain whether it will be dealt or not, is to take a false view of the case. [3] For if we were equally able with them to meet their plots and imitate their delay, we should be their equals and should be under no necessity of being their subjects; but the liberty of offense being always theirs, that of defense ought clearly to be ours."

"Such, Spartans and allies, are the grounds and the reasons of our revolt; clear enough to convince our hearers of the fairness of our conduct, and sufficient to alarm ourselves and to make us turn to some means of safety. This we wished to do long ago, when we sent to you on the subject while the peace yet lasted, but were prevented by your refusing to receive us; and now, upon the Boeotians inviting us, we at once responded to the call, and decided upon a twofold revolt, from the Hellenes and from the Athenians, not to aid the latter in harming the former, but to join in their liberation, and not to allow the Athenians in the end to destroy us, but to act in time against them. [2] Our revolt, however has taken place prematurely and without preparation—a fact which makes it all the more incumbent on you to receive us into alliance and to send us speedy relief, in order to show that you support your friends, and at the same time do harm to your enemies. [3] You have an opportunity such as you never had before. Disease and expenditure have wasted the Athenians: their ships are either cruising round your coasts, or engaged in blockading us; [4] and it is not probable that they will have any to spare, if you invade them a second time this summer by sea and land. Either they will offer no resistance to your vessels, or withdraw from both our shores. [5] Nor must it be thought that this is a case of putting yourselves into danger for a country which is not yours. Lesbos may appear far off, but when help is wanted she will be found near enough. It is not in Attica that the war will be decided, as some imagine, but in the countries by which Attica is supported; [6] and the Athenian revenue is drawn from the allies, and will become still larger if they reduce us; as not only will no other state revolt, but our resources will be added to theirs, and we shall be treated worse than those that were enslaved before. [7] But if you will frankly support us, you will add to your side a state that has a large navy, which is your great want; you will smooth the way to the overthrow of the Athenians by depriving them of their allies, who will be greatly encouraged to come over; and you will free yourselves from the accusation made against you of not supporting insurrection. In short, only show yourselves as liberators, and you may count upon having the advantage in the war."

"Respect, therefore, both the hopes placed in you by the Hellenes, and Olympian Zeus in whose temple we stand virtually as suppliants; become the allies and defenders of the Mytilenians, and do not sacrifice us, who put our lives in jeopardy for a cause in which general good will result to all from our success, and still more general harm if we fail through your refusing to help us. [2] Be the men that the Hellenes think you, and that our fears desire."

3.13
428
4th Year/Summer
OLYMPIA
The Mytilenians ask Sparta to receive them as allies, to exploit Athenian weaknesses, and to show themselves as true liberators.

3.14
428
4th Year/Summer
OLYMPIA
The Mytilenians conclude with an appeal for help.

3.15
428
4th Year/Summer
PELOPONNESUS
Sparta accepts Lesbos as an ally and prepares to invade Attica.

Such were the words of the Mytilenians.[1a] After hearing them out, the Spartans and their allies granted what they urged, took the Lesbians into alliance, and deciding in favor of the invasion of Attica, told the allies present to march as quickly as possible to the Isthmus with two-thirds of their forces. Arriving there first themselves, they prepared hauling machines to carry their ships across from Corinth to the sea on the side of Athens,[1b] in order to make their attack by sea and land at once. [2] However, the zeal which they displayed was not imitated by the rest of the allies, who came in but slowly, being both engaged in harvesting their grain and sick of making expeditions.

3.16
428
4th Year/Summer
ATHENS
Athens deploys one hundred triremes to counter the Spartan forty.

Meanwhile the Athenians, who were aware that the preparations of the enemy were due to his conviction of their weakness, wished to show him that he was mistaken, and that they were able, without moving their fleet off Lesbos, to repel with ease the one with which they were menaced from the Peloponnesus. They therefore manned a hundred ships by embarking the citizens of Athens, except the knights and *pentecosiomedimni,* and the resident aliens;[1a] and putting out to the Isthmus, displayed their power and made descents upon the Peloponnesus wherever they pleased. [2] So unexpected was this response that it made the Spartans think that the Lesbians had not spoken the truth; and embarrassed by the nonappearance of the allies, coupled with the news that the thirty ships round the Peloponnesus were ravaging the lands near Sparta, they went back home. [3] Afterwards, however, they prepared a fleet to send to Lesbos, and ordering a total of forty ships from the different cities in the League, appointed Alcidas to command the expedition in his capacity of admiral.[3a] [4] Meanwhile the Athenians in the hundred ships, upon seeing the Spartans go home, went home likewise.

3.17
428
4th Year/Summer
ATHENS
Athens has 250 triremes at sea, her largest naval deployment during the entire war.

If at the time that this fleet was at sea Athens had almost the largest number of first-rate ships in commission that she ever possessed at any one moment, she had as many or even more when the war began. [2] At that time one hundred guarded Attica, Euboea, and Salamis; a hundred more were cruising round the Peloponnesus, besides those employed at Potidaea and in other places; making a grand total of two hundred and fifty vessels employed on active service in a single summer. [3] It was this, with Potidaea, that most exhausted her revenues—[4] Potidaea being blockaded by a force of *hoplites*[4a] (each drawing two *drachmas*[4b] a day,

3.15.1a   See the Introduction (see. II.v) for a discussion of the speeches in Thucydides.
3.15.1b   At the Isthmus of Corinth (Map 3.7, BX) remains of an ancient trackway on which specially made carts hauled ships across the Isthmus to avoid the long and sometimes difficult voyage around the Peloponnesus can still be seen today; see Illustration 8.8.
3.16.1a   The knights and *pentecosiomedimni* were the two richest property classes at Athens and were most likely to serve as heavy infantry or cavalry. Resident aliens (*metics*)

had rights and obligations but were not citizens. See Appendix A, The Athenian Government, §2.
3.16.3a   Alcidas and his fleet are next mentioned in 3.26.
3.17.4a   A *hoplite* is a heavily armed infantry man; see the Glossary or Appendix F, Land Warfare, §2.
3.17.4b   *Drachmas:* see Appendix J, Classical Greek Currency, §3.

one for himself and another for his servant), which amounted to three thousand at first, and was kept at this number down to the end of the siege; besides sixteen hundred with Phormio who went away before it was over; and the ships being all paid at the same rate. In this way her money was wasted at first; and this was the largest number of ships ever manned by her.[4c]

About the same time that the Spartans were at the Isthmus, the Mytilenians marched by land with their mercenaries against Methymna,[1a] which they thought to gain by treachery. After assaulting the city, and not meeting with the success that they anticipated, they withdrew to Antissa, Pyrrha, and Eresus;[1b] and taking measures for the better security of these cities and strengthening their walls, hastily returned home. [2] After their departure the Methymnians marched against Antissa, but were defeated in a sortie by the Antissans and their mercenaries, and retreated in haste after losing many of their number. [3] When word of this reached Athens, and the Athenians learned that the Mytilenians were masters of the country and that their own soldiers were unable to hold them in check, they sent out, at about the beginning of autumn, Paches son of Epicurus, to take command, with a thousand Athenian hoplites [4] who worked their own passage[4a] and who, upon arriving at Mytilene, built a single wall around it with forts at some of the strongest points. [5] Mytilene was thus blockaded strictly on both sides, by land and by sea; and winter now drew near.[5a]

Although they had for the first time raised a war tax of two hundred *talents*[1a] from their own citizens, the Athenians still needed money for the siege, and sent out twelve ships, under the command of Lysicles and four others, to collect money from their allies.[1b] [2] After cruising to different places and laying them under contribution, Lysicles went up the country from Myos,[2a] in Caria,[2b] across the plain of the Meander[2c] as far as the hill of Sandius,[2d] and being attacked by the Carians and the people of Anaia,[2e] was slain with many of his soldiers.

3.18
428
4th Year/Summer
LESBOS
The Athenians blockade Mytilene by land.

3.19
428/7
4th Year/Winter
ATHENS-CARIA
Athens raises money for the siege.

3.17.4c   Some scholars regard this chapter as not genuine, others as misplaced. But from it we may calculate some of the military expenditures draining the Athenian treasury. The three thousand hoplites and their servants at Potidaea would cost six thousand drachmas or one talent per day. Since the two hundred men of a trireme's crew received at this period one drachma a day each, it cost one talent a month to keep a trireme at sea, or one talent per day to keep a fleet of thirty triremes at sea. Thus, if Athens really deployed some 250 triremes at this time, these ships and her siege of Potidaea would have cost her treasury more than nine talents per day.

3.18.1a   Mytilene, Methymna, on Lesbos: Map 3.29, AY. Thucydides here returns to military events on Lesbos from 3.6.

3.18.1b   Antissa, Pyrrha, Eresus, on Lesbos: Map 3.29, AY.

3.18.4a   "Worked their own passage": the hoplites served as rowers in the triremes that carried them to Lesbos.

3.18.5a   The narrative of Mytilene and Lesbos is continued in 3.25.

3.19.1a   *Talent*: a unit of weight and money. See Appendix J, Classical Greek Currency, §5.

3.19.1b   It is generally believed that when Thucydides reports such collections of money, it is a sign that the tribute has been increased in the course of the preceding summer. See Appendix B, The Athenian Empire, §2, 10, and note 4.75.1b.

3.19.2a   Myos: Map 3.29, BY.

3.19.2b   Caria: Map 3.29, BY.

3.19.2c   Meander river: Map 3.29, BY.

3.19.2d   Hill of Sandius, approximate location: Map 3.29, BY.

3.19.2e   Anaia: Map 3.29, BY. Anaia was the base of Samian exiles hostile to Athens; see 3.32.2, 4.75.1.

3.20
428/7
4th Year/Winter
PLATAEA
The Plataeans decide to
break out.

The same winter the Plataeans, who were still being besieged by the Peloponnesians and Boeotians, distressed by the failure of their provisions, and seeing no hope of relief from Athens, nor any other means of safety, formed a scheme with the Athenians besieged with them for escaping, if possible, by forcing their way over the enemy's walls. This attempt was suggested by Theaenetus son of Tolmides, a soothsayer, and Eupompides son of Daimachus, one of their generals. At first all were to join; [2] afterwards, half hung back, thinking the risk too great. About two hundred and twenty, however, voluntarily persevered in the attempt, which was carried out in the following way. [3] Ladders were made to match the height of the enemy's wall, which they measured by the layers of bricks, the side turned toward them not being thoroughly whitewashed. These were counted by many persons at once; and though some might miss the right calculation, most would hit upon it, particularly as they counted over and over again, and were no great way from the wall, but could see it easily enough for their purpose. [4] The length required for the ladders was thus obtained, being calculated from the breadth of the brick.

3.21
428/7
4th Year/Winter
PLATAEA
The Peloponnesian
circumvallation works are
described.

Now the wall of the Peloponnesians was constructed as follows: it consisted of two lines drawn round the place about sixteen feet apart, one against the Plataeans, the other against any attack on the outside from Athens. [2] The intermediate space was occupied by huts portioned out among the soldiers on guard, and built in one block, so as to give the appearance of a single thick wall with battlements on either side. [3] At intervals of every ten battlements were towers of considerable size, and the same breadth as the wall, reaching right across from its inner to its outer face, with no means of passing except through the middle. [4] Accordingly on stormy and wet nights the battlements were deserted and guard was kept from the towers, which were not far apart and roofed in above.

Such was the structure of the wall by which the Plataeans were blockaded.

When their preparations were completed, they waited for a stormy night of wind and rain without any moon and then set out, guided by the authors of the enterprise. Crossing first the ditch that ran round the city, they next reached the wall of the enemy unperceived by the sentinels, who did not see them in the darkness, or hear them, as the wind drowned with its roar the noise of their approach; [2] besides, they kept a good way off from each other so that they might not be betrayed by the clash of their weapons. They were also lightly equipped, and had only the left foot shod to preserve them from slipping in the mire. [3] They came up to the battlements at one of the intermediate spaces which they knew to be unguarded. Those who carried the ladders went first and planted them; next twelve light-armed soldiers with only a dagger and a breastplate mounted, led by

Ammias son of Coroebus (who was the first on the wall), his followers getting up after him and going six to each of the towers. After these came another party of light troops armed with spears whose shields, that they might advance the easier, were carried by men behind, who were to hand them to them when they found themselves in presence of the enemy. [4] After a good many had mounted they were discovered by the sentinels in the towers, by the noise made by a tile knocked down by one of the Plataeans as he was laying hold of the battlements. [5] The alarm was instantly given, and the troops rushed to the wall, not knowing the nature of the danger, owing to the dark night and stormy weather. The Plataeans in the city also chose that moment to make a sortie against the wall of the Peloponnesians upon the side opposite to that on which their men were getting over, in order to divert the attention of the besiegers. [6] Accordingly they remained distracted at their several posts, without any venturing to stir to give help from his own station, and at a loss to guess what was going on. [7] Meanwhile the three hundred set aside for service on emergencies went outside the wall in the direction of the alarm. Fire-signals of an attack were also raised toward Thebes;[7a] [8] but the Plataeans in the city at once displayed a number of others, prepared beforehand for this very purpose, in order to render the enemy's signals unintelligible, and to prevent his friends from getting a true idea of what was happening and coming to his aid before their comrades who had gone out should have made good their escape and be in safety.

Meanwhile the first of the scaling-party that had got up, after carrying both the towers and putting the sentinels to the sword, posted themselves inside to prevent anyone coming through against them; and rearing ladders from the wall, sent several men up on the towers, and from their summit and base kept in check all of the enemy that came up, with their missiles, while their main body planted a number of ladders against the wall, and knocking down the battlements, passed over between the towers. [2] Each as soon as he had got over took up his station at the edge of the ditch, shooting arrows and throwing darts at any who came along the wall to stop the passage of his comrades. [3] When all were over, the party on the towers came down, the last of them not without difficulty, and proceeded to the ditch, just as the three hundred came up carrying torches. [4] The Plataeans, standing on the edge of the ditch in the dark, had a good view of their opponents and discharged their arrows and darts upon the unarmed parts of their bodies, while they themselves could not be so well seen in the obscurity for the torches; and thus even the last of them got over the ditch, though not without effort and difficulty; [5] as ice had formed in it, not strong enough to walk upon, but of that watery kind which generally comes with a wind more east than north, and the snow which this wind

3.23
428/7
4th Year/Winter
PLATAEA
The Plataeans cross over the wall and ditch.

3.22.7a Thebes: Map 3.24.

MAP 3.24 PLATAEAN ESCAPE

3.24
428/7
4th Year/Winter
PLATAEA
The Plataeans evade pursuit and escape to Athens.

had caused to fall during the night, had made the water in the ditch rise, so that they could scarcely breast it as they crossed. However, it was mainly the violence of the storm that enabled them to escape at all.

Starting from the ditch, the Plataeans went all together along the road leading to Thebes,[1a] keeping the chapel of the hero Androcrates upon their right, considering that the last road which the Peloponnesians would suspect them of having taken would be that toward their enemies' country. Indeed they could see them pursuing with torches upon the Athens road toward Cithaeron and Druoskephalai, or Oakheads. [2] After going for rather more than half a mile upon the road to Thebes, the Plataeans turned off and took that leading to the mountain, to Erythrae and Hysiae,[2a] and reaching the hills, made good their escape to Athens,[2b] two hundred and twelve men in all; some of their number having turned back into the outer ditch. [3] Meanwhile the Peloponnesians gave up the pursuit and returned to their posts; and the Plataeans in the city, knowing nothing of what had passed, and informed by those who had turned back that not a man had escaped, sent out a herald[3a] as soon as it was day to make a truce for the recovery of the dead bodies. Then, learning the truth, they desisted. In this way the Plataean party broke out and were saved.[3b]

3.24.1a   For the roads from Plataea, see Map 3.24. This map is based in part on one in J. B. Bury, *A History of Greece* (New York: 1913), Map 51, p. 279.
3.24.2a   Erythrae, Hisiae: Map 3.24.
3.24.2b   Athens: Map 3.24
3.24.3a   Heralds, already a venerable Greek institution in Thucydides' day, operated under the protection of the god Hermes,

and were easily identified by the staff they carried. They alone could travel unmolested between states or armies at war in order to deliver messages, take back replies, and make perfunctory arrangements.
3.24.3b   Events at Plataea are taken up again in 3.52.

Toward the close of the same winter, Salaethus, a Spartan, was sent out in a trireme from Sparta to Mytilene.[1a] Going by sea to Pyrrha,[1b] and from thence overland, he passed along the bed of a torrent, where the line of circumvallation[1c] was penetrable, and thus entered unperceived into Mytilene. He told the magistrates that Attica would certainly be invaded, that the forty ships destined to relieve them would arrive, and that he had been sent on to announce this and to superintend matters generally. [2] The Mytilenians upon this took courage, and laid aside the idea of negotiating with the Athenians; and now this winter ended, and with it ended the fourth year of the war of which Thucydides was the historian.

The next summer the Peloponnesians sent off the forty-two ships for Mytilene, under Alcidas,[1a] the admiral, and themselves and their allies invaded Attica, their object being to distract the Athenians by a double movement, and thus to make it less easy for them to act against the fleet sailing to Mytilene. [2] The commander in this invasion was Cleomenes, in the place of King Pausanias son of Pleistoanax, his nephew, who was still a minor. [3] Not content with laying waste whatever had grown up in the parts which they had before devastated, the invaders now extended their ravages to lands passed over in their previous incursions; so that this invasion was more severely felt by the Athenians than any except the second. [4] The enemy stayed on until they had overrun most of the country, in the expectation of hearing from Lesbos of something having been achieved by their fleet, which they thought must by now have got over. However, as none of their expectations were realized, and their provisions began to run short, they retreated and dispersed to their different cities.

In the meantime the Mytilenians, finding their provisions failing, while the fleet from the Peloponnesus was loitering on the way instead of appearing at Mytilene, were compelled to come to terms with the Athenians in the following manner. [2] Salaethus, having himself ceased to expect the fleet to arrive, now armed The People with heavy armor, which they had not before possessed, with the intention of making a sortie against the Athenians. [3] The People, however, no sooner found themselves in possession of arms than they refused any longer to obey their officers and, meeting in groups, told the authorities to bring the grain reserve out in public and divide it amongst them all, or they would themselves come to terms with the Athenians and deliver up the city.

Those in power, aware of their inability to prevent this, and of the danger they would be in if left out of the capitulation, publicly agreed

3.25
428/7
4th Year/Winter
MYTILENE
The Spartan Salaethus arrives in Mytilene.

3.26
427
5th Year/Summer
ATTICA-AEGEAN
The Peloponnesians invade Attica and send a fleet to Mytilene.

3.27
427
5th Year/Summer
MYTILENE
After Salaethus arms the Mytilenean commoners, they revolt.

3.28
427
5th Year/Summer
MYTILENE
Mytilene surrenders to Athens.

3.25.1a   This chapter continues the narrative of
          Mytilene and Lesbos (Map 3.29, AX.)
          from 3.18.
3.25.1b   Pyrrha: Map 3.29, AX.
3.25.1c   Circumvallation: the building of a wall to
          surround or isolate a city by land.
3.26.1a   This is the fleet described in 3.16.3; it
          will be mentioned next in 3.29.

with Paches[1a] and the army to surrender Mytilene unconditionally and to admit the troops into the city upon the understanding that the Mytilenians should be allowed to send an embassy to Athens to plead their cause, and that Paches should not imprison, make slaves of, or put to death any of the citizens until its return. [2] Such were the terms of the capitulation; in spite of which the chief authors of the negotiation with Sparta were so completely overcome by terror when the army entered, that they went and seated themselves by the altars,[2a] from which they were raised up by Paches under promise that he would do them no wrong, and lodged by him in Tenedos,[2b] until he should learn the pleasure of the Athenians concerning them. [3] Paches also sent some triremes and seized Antissa,[3a] and took such other military measures as he thought advisable.

Meanwhile, the Peloponnesians in the forty ships,[1a] who ought to have made all haste to relieve Mytilene, lost time in coming round the Peloponnesus itself, and proceeding leisurely on the remainder of the voyage, made Delos[1b] without having been seen by the Athenians at Athens, and from thence arriving at Icarus and Myconus,[1c] there first heard of the fall of Mytilene. [2] Wishing to know the truth, they put into Embatum, in the territory of Erythrae,[2a] about seven days after the capture of the city. Here they learned the truth, and began to consider what they were to do; and Teutiaplus, an Elean, addressed them as follows:

"Alcidas and Peloponnesians who share with me the command of this armament, my advice is to sail just as we are to Mytilene, before we have been heard of. [2] We may expect to find the Athenians as much on their guard as men generally are who have just taken a city: this will certainly be so by sea, where they have no idea of any enemy attacking them, and where our strength, as it happens, mainly lies; while even their land forces are probably scattered about the houses in the carelessness of victory. [3] If therefore we were to fall upon them suddenly and in the night, I have hopes, with the help of the well-wishers that we may have left inside the city, that we shall become masters of the place. [4] Let us not shrink from the risk, but let us remember that this is just the occasion for one of the baseless panics common in war; and that to be able to guard against these in one's own case, and to detect the moment when an attack will find an enemy at this disadvantage, is what makes a successful general."

3.29
427
5th Year/Summer
ERYTHRAE
The Spartan fleet crosses the Aegean to Asia.

3.30
427
5th Year/Summer
ERYTHRAE
Alcidas rejects a proposal to surprise the Athenians at Mytilene.

3.28.1a   Paches was sent to take command of the Athenian forces at Mytilene in 3.18.3.
3.28.2a   It would have been sacrilege, an insult to the gods, to harm someone who had taken refuge at an altar; see note 1.126.11a.
3.28.2b   Tenedos: Map 3.29, AX.
3.28.3a   Antissa: Map 3.29 AX.

3.29.1a   These are Alcidas and his forty (or forty-two) ships mentioned in 3.26.
3.29.1b   Delos: Map 3.29, BX.
3.29.1c   Myconus, Icarus: Map 3.29, BX.
3.29.2a   The exact location of Embatum is not known, but it must have been near Erythrae; see Map 3.29, BY.

MAP 3.29
ALCIDAS IN IONIA

These words of Teutiaplus failing to move Alcidas, some of the Ionian exiles and the Lesbians with the expedition began to urge him, since this seemed too dangerous, to seize one of the Ionian cities or the Aeolic city of Cyme, to use as a base for effecting the revolt of Ionia.[1a] This was by no means a hopeless enterprise, as their coming was welcome everywhere; their object would be by this move to deprive Athens of her chief source of revenue, and at the same time to saddle her with expense, if she chose to blockade them; and they would probably induce Pissuthnes[1b] to join them in the war. [2] However, Alcidas gave this proposal as bad a reception as

3.31
427/6
5th Year/Summer
ERYTHRAE
Alcidas also rejects a proposal to foment revolt against Athens in Ionia.

3.31.1a   Cyme, Aeolis: Map 3.29, AY; Ionia: Map
              3.29, BY. See Appendix H, Dialects and
              Ethnic Groups, §6–8, for information on
              the Ionians and the Aeolians.
3.31.1b   Pissuthnes son of Hystaspes was the Per-
              sian governor of Sardis (Map 3.29, AY);
              see 1.115.4.

the other, being eager, since he had come too late for Mytilene, to find himself back in the Peloponnesus as soon as possible.

Accordingly he put out from Embatum and proceeded along shore; and touching at the Teian city, Myonnesus,[1a] there butchered most of the prisoners that he had taken on his passage. [2] Upon his coming to anchor at Ephesus,[2a] envoys came to him from the Samians at Anaia,[2b] and told him that he was not going the right way to free Hellas in massacring men who had never raised a hand against him, and who were not enemies of his, but allies of Athens against their will, and that if he did not stop he would turn many more friends into enemies than enemies into friends. [3] Alcidas agreed to this, and let go all the Chians still in his hands and some of the others that he had taken, since the inhabitants, rather than fleeing, came up to him because they assumed his vessels were Athenian, and had no sort of expectation that Peloponnesian ships would venture over to Ionia while the Athenians commanded the sea.

From Ephesus Alcidas set sail in haste and fled. He had been seen while still at anchor off Clarus[1a] by the Athenian triremes the *Salaminia* and the *Paralus*,[1b] which happened to be sailing from Athens, and fearing pursuit he now made across the open sea, fully determined to touch nowhere, if he could help it, until he got to the Peloponnesus.[1c] [2] Meanwhile news of him had come in to Paches from the territory of Erythrae and indeed from all quarters. As Ionia was unfortified,[2a] great fears were felt that the Peloponnesians coasting along shore, even if they did not intend to stay, might make descents in passing and plunder the cities; and now the triremes *Salaminia* and the *Paralus,* having seen him at Clarus, themselves brought intelligence of the fact. [3] Paches accordingly gave hot chase, and continued the pursuit as far as the isle of Patmos,[3a] and then finding that Alcidas had got on too far to be overtaken, came back again. Meanwhile he thought it fortunate that, as he had not fallen in with them out at sea, he had not overtaken them anywhere where they would have been forced to encamp, and so give him the trouble of blockading them.

On his return along shore Paches touched, among other places, at Notium, the port of Colophon,[1a] where the Colophonians had settled after the capture of the upper city by Itamenes and the barbarians,[1b] who had been called in by certain individuals in a party quarrel. The capture of the

3.32
427
5th Year/Summer
AEGEAN
Before fleeing, Alcidas executes many prisoners. He is finally persuaded to release the rest.

3.33
427
5th Year/Summer
AEGEAN
Paches pursues Alcidas' fleet but fails to catch it.

3.34
427
5th Year/Summer
NOTIUM
Paches tricks Hippias and captures Notium.

3.32.1a　Teos and the Teian town Myonnesus: Map 3.29, BY.
3.32.2a　Ephesus: Map 3.29, BY.
3.32.2b　These were the Samian exiles hostile to Athens; see 3.19.2 and 4.75.1. Anaia, Samos: Map 3.29, BY.
3.33.1a　Clarus: Map 3.29, BY.
3.33.1b　The *Salaminia* and the *Paralus* were special state triremes used on sacred embassies and official business; see 3.77.3 in Corcyra, 6.53.1, and 6.61.4–7 in Sicily to fetch Alcibiades; 8.73.5–6 at Samos, and 8.74.1–2 in the revolution at Athens; and 8.86.9 at Argos and Samos.
3.33.1c　The narrative of Alcidas' fleet continues at 3.69.

3.33.2a　Some scholars hold that the cities of Ionia had been obliged by Athens to pull down their walls for the sake of imperial security. Others think that the measure was required by the terms of the "Peace of Callias," a treaty between the Athenians and the Persians; see Appendix E, The Persians, §5–6.
3.33.3a　Patmos: Map 3.29, BX.
3.34.1a　Notium, Colophon: Map 3.29, BY.
3.34.1b　These barbarians are Persians. Itamenes is otherwise unknown, nor is it known whether he was acting under the orders of Pissuthnes, the Persian governor [satrap] at Sardis.

city took place about the time of the second Peloponnesian invasion of Attica. [2] However, the refugees, after settling at Notium, again split up into factions, one of which called in Arcadian and barbarian mercenaries from Pissuthnes, and entrenching these in a quarter apart, formed a new community with the Median party of the Colophonians who joined them from the upper city. Their opponents had retired into exile, and now called in Paches, [3] who invited Hippias, the commander of the Arcadians in the fortified quarter, to a parley, upon condition that, if they could not agree, he was to be put back safe and sound in the fortification. However, upon his coming out to him, Paches put him into custody, though not in chains, and attacked suddenly and took by surprise the fortification, and putting the Arcadians and the barbarians found in it to the sword, afterwards took Hippias into it as he had promised, and, as soon as he was inside, seized him and slaughtered him. [4] Paches then gave up Notium to the Colophonians not of the Medizing party;[4a] and settlers were afterwards sent out from Athens, and the place colonized according to Athenian laws, after collecting all the Colophonians found in any of the cities.

Arrived at Mytilene, Paches reduced Pyrrha and Eresus;[1a] and finding the Spartan, Salaethus, in hiding in the city, sent him off to Athens, together with the Mytilenians that he had placed in Tenedos,[1b] and any other persons that he thought concerned in the revolt. [2] He also sent back the greater part of his forces, remaining with the rest to settle Mytilene and the rest of Lesbos as he thought best.

Upon the arrival of the prisoners with Salaethus, the Athenians at once put the latter to death, although he offered, among other things, to procure the withdrawal of the Peloponnesians from Plataea, which was still under siege; [2] and after deliberating as to what they should do with the former, in the fury of the moment determined to put to death not only the prisoners at Athens, but the whole adult male population of Mytilene, and to make slaves of the women and children. It was noted that Mytilene had revolted without being, in the same way as the rest, subjected to the empire;[2a] and what above all swelled the wrath of the Athenians was the fact of the Peloponnesian fleet having ventured over to Ionia to her support, a fact which was held to argue a long-meditated rebellion. [3] They accordingly sent a trireme to communicate the decree to Paches, commanding him to

3.35
427
5th Year/Summer
MYTILENE
Paches reconquers Lesbos.

3.36
427
5th Year/Summer
ATHENS
After first condemning the Mytilenians to death, the Athenians decide to vote again.

3.34.4a Greeks who took the Persian side in any conflict were said to have "Medized."
3.35.1a Pyrrha, Eresus: Map 3.29, AX.
3.35.1b Tenedos (Map 3.29, AX), where Paches had sent the authors of the revolt in 3.28.2. Their fate is described in 3.50.1.
3.36.2a As a ship-contributing ally, Mytilene was different from those who paid money tribute; see 7.57.4.

lose no time in despatching the Mytilenians. [4] The morrow brought repentance with it and reflection on the horrid cruelty of a decree which condemned a whole city to the fate merited only by the guilty. [5] This was no
sooner perceived by the Mytilenian ambassadors at Athens and their Athenian supporters than they moved the authorities to put the question again to
the vote;[5a] which they the more easily consented to do, as they themselves
plainly saw that most of the citizens wished someone to give them an opportunity for reconsidering the matter. [6] An assembly was therefore at
once called, and after much expression of opinion upon both sides, Cleon
son of Cleaenetus, the same who had carried the former motion of putting
the Mytilenians to death, the most violent man at Athens, and at that time
by far the most powerful with The People, came forward again and spoke
as follows:

3.37
427
5th Year/Summer
ATHENS
Cleon calls the Athenians
inconstant and argues for the
original decision to execute
the Mytilenians.

"I have often before now been convinced that a democracy is incapable of empire, and never more so than by your present change of
mind in the matter of Mytilene. [2] Fears or plots being unknown to
you in your daily relations with each other, you feel just the same
with regard to your allies, and never reflect that the mistakes into
which you may be led by listening to their appeals, or by giving way
to your own compassion, are full of danger to yourselves, and bring
you no thanks for your weakness from your allies; entirely forgetting
that your empire is a despotism and your subjects disaffected conspirators, whose obedience is insured not by your suicidal concessions,
but by the superiority given you by your own strength and not their
loyalty. [3] The most alarming feature in the case is the constant
change of measures with which we appear to be threatened, and our
seeming ignorance of the fact that bad laws which are never changed
are better for a city than good ones that have no authority; that un-
learned loyalty is more serviceable than quick-witted insubordination; and that ordinary men usually manage public affairs better than
their more gifted fellows. [4] The latter are always wanting to appear
wiser than the laws, and to overrule every proposition brought forward, thinking that they cannot show their wit in more important
matters, and by such behavior too often ruin their country; while
those who mistrust their own cleverness are content to be less
learned than the laws, and less able to pick holes in the speech of a
good speaker; and being fair judges rather than rival athletes, generally conduct affairs successfully. [5] These we ought to imitate, instead of being led on by cleverness and intellectual rivalry to advise
the people against our real opinions."

3.36.5a   To put an issue to the vote a second time
          in the Athenian assembly was not an easy
          or a trivial matter. See 6.14.1 and note
          6.14.1a.

"For myself, I adhere to my former opinion, and wonder at those who have proposed to reopen the case of the Mytilenians, and who are thus causing a delay which is all in favor of the guilty, by making the sufferer proceed against the offender with the edge of his anger blunted; although where vengeance follows most closely upon the wrong, it best equals it and most amply requites it. I wonder also who will be the man who will maintain the contrary, and will pretend to show that the crimes of the Mytilenians are of service to us, and our misfortunes injurious to the allies. [2] Such a man must plainly either have such confidence in his rhetoric as to attempt to prove that what has been once for all decided is still undetermined, or be bribed to try to delude us by elaborate sophistic arguments. [3] In such contests the state gives the rewards to others, and takes the dangers for herself. [4] The persons to blame are you who are so foolish as to institute these contests; who go to see an oration as you would to see a sight, take your facts on hearsay, judge of the practicability of a project by the wit of its advocates, and trust for the truth as to past events, not to the fact which you saw more than to the clever strictures which you heard; [5] the easy victims of newfangled arguments, unwilling to follow received conclusions; slaves to every new paradox, despisers of the commonplace; [6] the first wish of every man being that he could speak himself, the next to rival those who can speak by seeming to keep up with their ideas by applauding every hit almost before it is made, and by being as quick in catching an argument as you are slow in foreseeing its consequences; [7] asking, if I may so say, for something different from the conditions under which we live, and yet comprehending inadequately those very conditions; very slaves to the pleasure of the ear, and more like the audience of a rhetorician than the council of a city."

"In order to keep you from this, I proceed to show that no one state has ever injured you as much as Mytilene. [2] I can make allowance for those who revolt because they cannot bear our empire, or who have been forced to do so by the enemy. But for those who possessed an island with fortifications; who could fear our enemies only by sea, and there had their own force of triremes to protect them; who were independent and held in the highest honor by you—to act as these have done, this is not revolt—revolt implies oppression; it is deliberate and wanton aggression; an attempt to ruin us by siding with our bitterest enemies; a worse offense than a war undertaken on their own account in the acquisition of power. [3] The fate of those of their neighbors who had already rebelled and had been subdued, was no lesson to them; their own prosperity could not dissuade them from affronting danger; but blindly confident in the future, and full of hopes beyond their power though not beyond their ambition, they declared war and made their decision to prefer might to right, their attack being determined not by provocation but by the moment which seemed propitious. [4] The truth is that great good fortune coming suddenly and unexpectedly tends to make a people insolent: in most cases it is safer for mankind to have success in reason than out of reason; and it is easier for them, one may say, to stave off adversity than to preserve prosperity. [5] Our mistake has been to distinguish the Mytilenians as we have done: had they been long ago treated like the rest, they never would have so far forgotten themselves, human nature being as surely made arrogant by consideration, as it is awed by firmness. [6] Let them now therefore be punished as their crime requires, and do not, while you condemn the aristocracy, absolve the people. This is certain, that all attacked you without distinction, although they might have come over to us, and been now again in possession of their city. But no, they thought it safer to throw in their lot with the aristocracy and so joined their rebellion! [7] Consider therefore! if you subject to the same punishment the ally who is forced to rebel by the enemy, and him who does so by his own free choice, which of them, think you, is there that will not rebel upon the slightest pretext; when the reward of success is freedom, and the penalty of failure nothing so very terrible? [8] We meanwhile shall have to risk our money and our lives against one state after another; and if successful, shall receive a ruined city from which we can no longer draw the revenue upon which our strength depends; while if unsuccessful, we shall have an enemy the more upon our hands, and shall spend the time that might be employed in combating our existing foes in warring with our own allies."

"No hope, therefore, must be held out to the Mytilenians, that their rhetoric may inspire or money purchase the mercy due to human infirmity. Their offense was not involuntary, but of malice and deliberate; and mercy is only for unwilling offenders. [2] I therefore now as before persist against your reversing your first decision, or giving way to the three failings most fatal to empire—pity, sentiment, and indulgence. [3] Compassion is due to those who can reciprocate the feeling, not to those who will never pity us in return, but are our natural and necessary foes: the orators who charm us with sentiment may find other less important arenas for their talents, in the place of one where the city pays a heavy penalty for a momentary pleasure, themselves receiving fine acknowledgments for their fine phrases; while indulgence should be shown toward those who will be our friends in future, instead of toward men who will remain just what they were, and as much our enemies as before. [4] To sum up

3.40
427
5th Year/Summer
ATHENS
Cleon concludes that compassion is inappropriate for national foes, and that severe punishment is a necessary example.

shortly, I say that if you follow my advice you will do what is just toward the Mytilenians, and at the same time expedient; while by a different decision you will not oblige them so much as pass sentence upon yourselves. For if they were right in rebelling, you must be wrong in ruling. However, if, right or wrong, you determine to rule, you must carry out your principle and punish the Mytilenians as your interest requires; or else you must give up your empire and cultivate honesty without danger. [5] Make up your minds, therefore, to give them like for like; and do not let the victims who escaped the plot be more insensible than the conspirators who hatched it; but reflect what they would have done if victorious over you, especially as they were the aggressors. [6] It is they who wrong their neighbor without a cause, that pursue their victim to the death, on account of the danger which they foresee in letting their enemy survive; since the object of a wanton wrong is more dangerous, if he escape, than an enemy who has not this to complain of. [7] Do not, therefore, be traitors to yourselves, but recall as nearly as possible the moment of suffering and the supreme importance which you then attached to their reduction; and now pay them back in their turn, without yielding to present weakness or forgetting the peril that once hung over you. Punish them as they deserve, and teach your other allies by a striking example that the penalty of rebellion is death. Let them once understand this and you will not have so often to neglect your enemies while you are fighting with your own confederates."

Such were the words of Cleon. After him Diodotus son of Eucrates, who had also in the previous assembly spoken most strongly against putting the Mytilenians to death, came forward and spoke as follows:

3.41
Diodotus speaks next.

"I do not blame the persons who have reopened the case of the Mytilenians, nor do I approve the protests which we have heard against important questions being frequently debated. I think the two things most opposed to good counsel are haste and passion; haste usually goes hand in hand with folly, passion with coarseness and narrowness of mind. [2] As for the argument that speech ought not to be the exponent of action, the man who uses it must be either senseless or personally interested: senseless if he believes it possible to deal with the uncertain future through any other medium; interested if wishing to carry a disgraceful measure and doubting his ability to speak well in a bad cause, he thinks to frighten opponents and hearers by well-aimed calumny. [3] What is still more intolerable is to accuse a speaker of making a display in order to be paid for it. If ignorance only were imputed, an unsuccessful speaker might retire with a reputation for honesty, if not for wisdom; while the charge of dishonesty makes him suspected, if successful, and thought, if de-

3.42
427
5th Year/Summer
ATHENS
Diodotus argues for calm deliberation without haste or passion.

feated, not only a fool but a rogue. [4] The city is no gainer by such a system, since fear deprives it of its advisers; although in truth, if our speakers are to make such assertions, it would be better for the country if they could not speak at all, as we should then make fewer blunders. [5] The good citizen ought to triumph not by frightening his opponents but by beating them fairly in argument; and a wise city, without overdistinguishing its best advisers, will nevertheless not deprive them of their due, and far from punishing an unlucky counselor will not even regard him as disgraced. [6] In this way successful orators would be least tempted to sacrifice their convictions for popularity, in the hope of still higher honors, and unsuccessful speakers to resort to the same popular arts in order to win over the multitude."

3.43
427
5th Year/Summer
ATHENS
Diodotus declares that
orators deserve respect and
should be heeded.

"This is not our way; and, besides, the moment that a man is suspected of giving advice, however good, from corrupt motives, we feel such a grudge against him for the gain which after all we are not certain he will receive, that we deprive the city of its certain benefit. [2] Plain good advice has thus come to be no less suspected than bad; and the advocate of the most monstrous measures is not more obliged to use deceit to gain the people, than the best counselor is to lie in order to be believed. [3] The city and the city only, owing to these refinements, can never be served openly and without disguise; he who does serve it openly being always suspected of serving himself in some secret way in return. Still, considering the magnitude of the interests involved, and the position of affairs, we orators must make it our business to look a little further than you who judge offhand; especially as we, your advisers, are responsible, while you, our audience, are not so. [5] For if those who gave the advice, and those who took it, suffered equally, you would judge more calmly; as it is, you visit the disasters into which the whim of the moment may have led you, upon the single person of your adviser, not upon yourselves, his numerous companions in error."[5a]

3.44
427
5th Year/Summer
ATHENS
Diodotus argues that
Athens' best interest, not
justice, is the proper
objective of the assembly.

"However, I have not come forward either to oppose or to accuse in the matter of Mytilene; indeed, the question before us as sensible men is not their guilt, but our interests. [2] Though I prove them ever so guilty, I shall not, therefore, advise their death, unless it be expedient; nor though they should have claims to indulgence, shall I recommend it, unless it be clearly for the good of the country. [3] I consider that we are deliberating for the future more than for the present; and where Cleon is so positive as to the useful deterrent effects that will follow from making rebellion a capital offense, I who consider the interests of the future quite as much as he, as positively maintain the contrary. [4] And I require you not to reject my useful considerations for his specious ones: his speech may have the attrac-

3.43.5a   As they did to Pericles in 2.65.3.

tion of seeming the more just in your present temper against Mytilene; but we are not in a court of justice, but in a political assembly;
and the question is not justice, but how to make the Mytilenians useful to Athens."

"Now of course communities have enacted the penalty of death
for many offenses far lighter than this: still hope leads men to venture; and no one ever yet put himself in peril without the inward
conviction that he would succeed in his design. [2] Again, was there
ever city rebelling that did not believe that it possessed either in itself
or in its alliances resources adequate to the enterprise? [3] All, states
and individuals, are alike prone to err, and there is no law that will
prevent them; or why should men have exhausted the list of punishments in search of enactments to protect them from evildoers? It is
probable that in early times the penalties for the greatest offenses
were less severe, and that, as these were disregarded, the penalty of
death has been by degrees in most cases arrived at, which is itself disregarded in like manner. [4] Either then some means of terror more
terrible than this must be discovered, or it must be admitted that this
restraint is useless; and that as long as poverty gives men the courage
of necessity, or plenty fills them with the ambition which belongs to
insolence and pride, and each of the other conditions of life remains
subjugated to some fatal and master passion, so long will the impulse
never be wanting to drive men into danger. [5] Hope also and greed,
the one leading and the other following, the one conceiving the
attempt, the other suggesting the facility of succeeding, cause the
widest ruin, and, although invisible agents, are far stronger than the
dangers that are seen. [6] Fortune, too, powerfully helps the delu-
sion, and by the unexpected aid that she sometimes lends, tempts
men to venture with inferior means; and this is especially the case
with communities, because the stakes played for are the highest, freedom or empire, and, when all are acting together, each man irra-
tionally magnifies his own capacity. [7] In short, it is impossible to
prevent, and only great simplicity can hope to prevent, human nature
doing what it has once set its mind upon, by force of law or by any
other deterrent force whatsoever."

"We must not, therefore, commit ourselves to a false policy
through a belief in the efficacy of the punishment of death, or exclude rebels from the hope of repentance and an early atonement of
their error. [2] Consider a moment! At present, if a city that has already revolted perceive that it cannot succeed, it will come to terms
while it is still able to refund expenses, and pay tribute afterwards. In
the other case, what city think you would not prepare better than is
now done, and hold out to the last against its besiegers, if it is all one

3.45
427
5th Year/Summer
ATHENS
Diodotus points out that
some people will transgress
regardless of the severity of
punishments.

3.46
427
5th Year/Summer
ATHENS
Diodotus says that Athens'
advantage here requires
moderation.

whether it surrender late or soon? [3] And how can it be otherwise than hurtful to us to be put to the expense of a siege, because surrender is out of the question; and if we take the city, to receive a ruined city from which we can no longer draw the revenue which forms our real strength against the enemy? [4] We must not, therefore, sit as strict judges of the offenders to our own prejudice, but rather see how by moderate chastisements we may be enabled to benefit in future by the revenue-producing powers of our dependencies; and we must make up our minds to look for our protection not to legal terrors but to careful administration. [5] At present we do exactly the opposite. When a free community, held in subjection by force, rises, as is only natural, and asserts its independence, it is no sooner reduced than we fancy ourselves obliged to punish it severely; [6] although the right course with freemen is not to chastise them rigorously when they do rise, but rigorously to watch them before they rise, and to prevent their ever entertaining the idea, and, the insurrection suppressed, to make as few responsible for it as possible."

"Only consider what a blunder you would commit in doing as Cleon recommends. [2] As things are at present, in all the cities The People is your friend, and either does not revolt with the oligarchy, or, if forced to do so, becomes at once the enemy of the insurgents; so that in the war with the hostile city you have the masses on your side. [3] But if you butcher The People of Mytilene, who had nothing to do with the revolt, and who, as soon as they got arms, of their own motion surrendered the city, first you will commit the crime of killing your benefactors; and next you will play directly into the hands of the higher classes, who when they induce their cities to rise, will immediately have The People on their side, through your having announced in advance the same punishment for those who are guilty and for those who are not. [4] On the contrary, even if they were guilty, you ought to seem not to notice it, in order to avoid alienating the only class still friendly to us. [5] In short, I consider it far more useful for the preservation of our empire to put up with injustice voluntarily, than to put to death, however justly, those whom it is our interest to keep alive. As for Cleon's idea that in punishment the claims of justice and expediency can both be satisfied, facts do not confirm the possibility of such a combination."

"Confess, therefore, that this is the wisest course, and without conceding too much either to pity or to indulgence, by neither of which motives do I any more than Cleon wish you to be influenced, upon the plain merits of the case before you, be persuaded by me to try calmly those of the Mytilenians whom Paches sent off as guilty, and to leave the rest undisturbed. [2] This is at once best for the future, and most terrible to your enemies at the present moment; inas-

3.47
427
5th Year/Summer
ATHENS
Diodotus argues that since the commons are friendly to Athens and delivered the city when they could, it would be a blunder to execute them.

3.48
427
5th Year/Summer
ATHENS
Diodotus concludes with a plea for calm consideration.

0   5
Centimeters

Illustration 3.48 Four sides of a bronze spear butt found at Athens showing traces of letters saying that it was taken from Lesbians and dedicated to the Dioscuri, undoubtedly when the Athenians put down the revolt of their Lesbian allies in 427

much as good policy against an adversary is superior to the blind attacks of brute force."

Such were the words of Diodotus. The two opinions thus expressed were the ones that most directly contradicted each other; and the Athenians, notwithstanding their change of feeling, now proceeded to a vote in which the show of hands was almost equal, although the motion of Diodotus carried the day. [2] Another trireme was at once sent off in haste, for fear that the first might reach Lesbos in the interval, and the city be found destroyed; the first ship having about a day and a night's start. [3] Wine and barley-cakes were provided for the vessel by the Mytilenian ambassadors, and great promises made if they arrived in time; which caused the men to use such diligence upon the voyage that they took their meals of barley-cakes kneaded with oil and wine as they rowed, and only slept by turns while the others were at the oar. [4] Luckily they met with no contrary wind, and the first ship making no haste upon so horrid an errand, while the second pressed on in the manner described, the first arrived so little before them that Paches had only just had time to read the decree, and to prepare to execute the sentence, when the second put into port and prevented the massacre. The danger of Mytilene had indeed been great.

3.49
427
5th Year/Summer
ATHENS
Athens votes to spare Mytilene.
MITYLENE
The news arrives just in time to save the Mytilenians.

MAP 3.51 MEGARA, NISAEA, MINOA

3.50
427
5th Year/Summer
LESBOS
Mytilene is punished.

The other party whom Paches had sent off as the prime movers in the rebellion were, upon Cleon's motion, put to death by the Athenians, the number being rather more than a thousand. The Athenians also demolished the walls of the Mytilenians, and took possession of their ships. [2] Afterwards tribute was not imposed upon the Lesbians; but all their land, except that of the Methymnians, was divided into three thousand allotments, three hundred of which were reserved as sacred for the gods, and the rest assigned by lot to Athenian shareholders, who were sent out to the island. With these the Lesbians agreed to pay a rent of two *minae*[2a] a year for each allotment, and cultivated the land themselves. [3] The Athenians also took possession of the cities on the continent belonging to the Mytilenians, which thus became for the future subject to Athens. Such were the events that took place at Lesbos.[3a]

3.51
427
5th Year/Summer
MEGARA-MINOS
Nicias fortifies Minoa
opposite Megara.

During the same summer, after the reduction of Lesbos, the Athenians under Nicias son of Niceratus made an expedition against the island of Minoa,[1a] which lies off Megara[1b] and was used as a fortified post by the Megarians, who had built a tower upon it. [2] Nicias wished to enable the Athenians to maintain their blockade from this nearer station instead of from Budorum and Salamis;[2a] to stop the Peloponnesian triremes and privateers sailing out unobserved from the island, as they had been in the habit of doing; and at the same time prevent anything from coming into

3.50.2a A *mina* was a unit of currency equal to one sixtieth of a *talent,* or one hundred *drachmae.* The 2,700 allotments renting for two minae each produced an annual rental of 5,400 minae or ninety talents. See Appendix J, Classical Greek Currency, §5. See also Appendix B, The Athenian Empire, §9, on Athenian *clerouchs.*

3.50.3a The story of Mytilene is resumed in 4.52.

3.51.1a Minoa: Map 3.51, inset, shows a possible location of the ancient island, which is no longer an island today. The map above is based in part on one in A.W. Gomme, *A Historical Commentary on Thucydides,* ii (Oxford, 1956), 334–36.

3.51.1b Megara: Map 3.51.

3.51.2a Budorum, possible location: Map 3.51, inset; Salamis: Map 3.51, and inset.

Megara. [3] Accordingly, after taking two towers projecting on the side of Nisaea[3a] by siege engines from the sea, and clearing the entrance into the channel between the island and the shore, he next proceeded to cut off all communication by building a wall on the mainland at the point where a bridge across a morass enabled reinforcements to be thrown into the island, which was not far off from the continent. [4] A few days sufficing to accomplish this, he afterwards raised a fort on the island also, and leaving a garrison there, departed with his forces.

About the same time in this summer, the Plataeans[1a] being now without provisions, and unable to support the siege, surrendered to the Peloponnesians in the following manner. [2] An assault had been made upon the wall, which the Plataeans were unable to repel. The Spartan commander, perceiving their weakness, wished to avoid taking the place by storm; his instructions from Sparta having been so conceived, in order that if at any future time peace should be made with Athens, and they should agree each to restore the places that they had taken in the war, Plataea might be held to have come over voluntarily, and not be included in the list. He accordingly sent a herald to them to ask if they were willing voluntarily to surrender the city to the Spartans, and accept them as their judges, upon the understanding that the guilty should be punished, but no one without form of law. [3] The Plataeans were now in the last state of weakness, and the herald had no sooner delivered his message than they surrendered the city. The Peloponnesians fed them for some days until the judges from Sparta, who were five in number, arrived. [4] Upon their arrival no charge was preferred; they simply called up the Plataeans, and asked them whether they had done the Spartans and allies any service in the war then raging. The Plataeans asked leave to speak at greater length, and deputed two of their number to represent them, Astymachus son of Asopolaus, and Lacon son of Aeimnestus, *proxenus* of the Spartans,[4a] who came forward and spoke as follows:

> "Spartans, when we surrendered our city we trusted in you, and looked forward to a trial more agreeable to the forms of law than the present, to which we had no idea of being subjected; the judges also in whose hands we consented to place ourselves were you, and you only (from whom we thought we were most likely to obtain justice), and not other persons, as is now the case. [2] As matters stand, we are afraid that we have been doubly deceived. We have good reason to suspect, not only that the issue to be tried is the most terrible of all, but that you will not prove impartial; if we may argue from the

3.52
427
5th Year/Summer
PLATAEA
Plataea surrenders.

3.53
427
5th Year/Summer
PLATAEA
The Plataeans complain of the unusual and summary form of their trial.

3.51.3a   Nisaea: Map 3.51.
3.52.1a   This picks up the Plataean narrative from 3.24.
3.52.4a   *Proxenus:* see note 3.2.3c.

fact that no accusation was first brought forward for us to answer, but we had ourselves to ask leave to speak, and from the question being put so shortly, that a true answer to it tells against us, while a false one can be contradicted. [3] In this dilemma, our safest, and indeed our only course, seems to be to say something at all risks: placed as we are, we could scarcely be silent without being tormented by the damning thought that speaking might have saved us. [4] Another difficulty that we have to encounter is the difficulty of convincing you. Were we unknown to each other we might profit by bringing forward new matter with which you were unacquainted: as it is, we can tell you nothing that you do not know already, and we fear, not that you have condemned us in your own minds of having failed in our duty toward you, and make this our crime, but that to please a third party we have to submit to a trial the result of which is already decided."

"Nevertheless, we will place before you what we can justly urge, not only on the question of the quarrel which the Thebans have against us, but also as addressing you and the rest of the Hellenes; and we will remind you of our good services, and endeavor to prevail with you. [2] To your short question, whether we have done the Spartans and allies any service in this war, we say, if you ask us as enemies, that to refrain from serving you was not to do you injury; if as friends, that you are more in fault for having marched against us. [3] During the peace, and against the Mede, we acted well: we have not now been the first to break the peace, and we were the only Boeotians who then joined in defending the liberty of Hellas against the Persian. [4] Although an inland people, we were present at the action at Artemisium;[4a] in the battle that took place in our territory we fought by the side of yourselves and Pausanias; and in all the other Hellenic exploits of the time we took a part quite out of proportion to our strength. [5] Besides, you, as Spartans, ought not to forget that at the time of the great panic at Sparta, after the earthquake, caused by the secession of the Helots to Ithome,[5a] we sent the third part of our citizens to assist you."

"On these great occasions in the past such was the part that we chose, although afterwards we became your enemies. For this you were to blame. When we asked for your alliance against our Theban oppressors, you rejected our petition, and told us to go to the Athenians who were our neighbors, as you lived too far off. [2] In the war we never have done to you, and never would have done to you, anything unreasonable. [3] If we refused to desert the Athenians when you asked us, we did no wrong; they had helped us against the Thebans when you drew back, and we could no longer give them up

3.54
427
5th Year/Summer
PLATAEA
The Plataeans claim to have helped Sparta against both the Persians and the Messenian Helots.

3.55
427
5th Year/Summer
PLATAEA
The Plataeans argue that since Sparta sent Plataea to Athens for alliance, Sparta must now accept Plataean loyalty to Athens.

3.54.4a Artemisium: Map 3.93, AY; site of a naval battle between Persians and Greeks in 480.

3.54.5a For this earthquake and the revolt of the Helots, see 1.101 and 2.27.2.

with honor; especially as we had obtained their alliance and had been admitted to their citizenship at our own request, and after receiving benefits at their hands; but it was plainly our duty loyally to obey their orders. [4] Besides, the faults that either of you may commit in your supremacy must be laid, not upon the followers, but on the chiefs that lead them astray."

"With regard to the Thebans, they have wronged us repeatedly, and their last aggression, which has been the means of bringing us into our present position, is within your own knowledge. [2] In seizing our city in time of peace, and what is more at a holy time in the month, they justly encountered our vengeance, in accordance with the universal law which sanctions resistance to an invader; and it cannot now be right that we should suffer on their account.[1a] [3] By taking your own immediate interest and their animosity as the test of justice, you will prove yourselves to be servants of expediency rather than judges of right; [4] although if they seem useful to you now, we and the rest of the Hellenes gave you much more valuable help at a time of greater need. Now you are the assailants, and others fear you; but at the crisis to which we allude, when the barbarian threatened all with slavery, the Thebans were on his side. [5] It is just, therefore, to put our patriotism then against our error now, if error there has been; and you will find the merit outweighing the fault, and displayed at a juncture when there were few Hellenes who would set their valor against the strength of Xerxes,[5a] and when greater praise was theirs who preferred the dangerous path of honor to the safe course of consulting their own interest with respect to the invasion. [6] To these few we belonged, and highly were we honored for it; and yet we now fear to perish by having again acted on the same principles, and chosen to act well with Athens sooner than wisely with Sparta. [7] Yet in justice the same cases should be decided in the same way, and policy should not mean anything else than lasting gratitude for the service of a good ally combined with a proper attention to one's own immediate interest."

"Consider also that at present the Hellenes generally regard you as a model of worth and honor; and if you pass an unjust sentence upon us in this which is no obscure cause—but one in which you, the judges, are as illustrious as we, the prisoners, are blameless—take care that displeasure be not felt at an unworthy decision in the matter of honorable men made by men yet more honorable than they, and at the consecration in the national temples of spoils taken from the Plataeans, the benefactors of Hellas. [2] Shocking indeed will it seem for Spartans to destroy Plataea, and for the city whose name

3.56
427
5th Year/Summer
PLATAEA
The Plataeans call on Sparta to deny Theban wrath and to reward past Plataean help.

3.57
427
5th Year/Summer
PLATAEA
The Plataeans say that Sparta's reputation will suffer if she permits Thebes to destroy Plataea.

3.56.1a   The Plataeans refer here to the Theban attack of 431 described in 2.2–2.6.

3.56.5a   Xerxes was the Persian King who led the invasion of Greece in 480.

your fathers inscribed upon the tripod at Delphi[2a] for its good service, to be by you blotted out from the map of Hellas to please the Thebans. [3] To such a depth of misfortune have we fallen, that while the Medes' success had been our ruin, Thebans now supplant us in your once fond regards; and we have been subjected to two dangers, the greatest of any—that of dying of starvation then, if we had not surrendered our city, and now of being tried for our lives. [4] So that we Plataeans, after exertions beyond our power in the cause of the Hellenes, are rejected by all, forsaken and unassisted; helped by none of our allies, and reduced to doubt the stability of our only hope, yourselves."

"Still, in the name of the gods who once presided over our confederacy, and of our own good service in the Hellenic cause, we appeal to you to relent; to rescind the decision which we fear that the Thebans may have obtained from you; to ask back the gift that you have given them, that they disgrace not you by slaying us; to gain a pure instead of a guilty gratitude, and not to gratify others to be yourselves rewarded with shame. [2] Our lives may be quickly taken, but it will be a heavy task to wipe away the infamy of the deed; as we are no enemies whom you might justly punish, but friends forced into taking arms against you. [3] To grant us our lives would be, therefore, a righteous judgment; if you consider also that we are prisoners who surrendered of their own accord, stretching out our hands for quarter, whose slaughter Hellenic law forbids, and who besides were always your benefactors. [4] Look at the tombs of your fathers, slain by the Persians and buried in our country, whom year by year we honored with garments and all other dues, and the first fruits of all that our land produced in their season, as friends from a friendly country and allies to our old companions in arms! Should you not decide aright, your conduct would be the very opposite to ours. Consider only: [5] Pausanias buried them thinking that he was laying them in friendly ground and among men as friendly; but you, if you kill us and make the Plataean territory Theban, will leave your fathers and kinsmen in a hostile soil and among their murderers, deprived of the honors which they now enjoy. What is more, you will enslave the land in which the freedom of the Hellenes was won, make desolate the temples of the gods to whom they prayed before they overcame the Persians, and take away your ancestral sacrifices from those who founded and instituted them."

"It were not to your glory, Spartans, either to offend in this way against the common law of the Hellenes and against your own ancestors, or to kill us, your benefactors, to gratify another's hatred without

3.58
427
5th Year/Summer
PLATAEA
The Plataeans contrast themselves, who care for the graves of Spartans who fell beside them fighting the Persians, with the Thebans, who fought against the Spartans with the Persians.

3.59
427
5th Year/Summer
PLATAEA
The Plataeans conclude that they surrendered their city to Sparta, not to Thebes.

3.57.2a   The Plataeans refer here to the tripod dedicated at Delphi in celebration of the victory over the Persians at Plataea

(1.132.2–3.) Much of this tripod still exists in Istanbul and its inscription can still be read today. See Illustration 1.132.

having been wronged yourselves: it would be more to your glory to spare us and to yield to the impressions of a reasonable compassion; reflecting not merely on the awful fate in store for us, but also on the character of the sufferers, and on the impossibility of predicting how soon misfortune may fall even upon those who deserve it not. [2] We, as we have a right to do and as our need impels us, entreat you, calling aloud upon the gods at whose common altar all the Hellenes worship, to hear our request, to be not unmindful of the oaths which your fathers swore, and which we now plead. We supplicate you by the tombs of your fathers and appeal to those that are gone to save us from falling into the hands of the Thebans and prevent the dearest friends of the Hellenes from being given up to their most detested foes. We also remind you of that day on which we did the most glorious deeds by your fathers' sides, we who now on this day are likely to suffer the most dreadful fate. [3] Finally, to do what is necessary and yet most difficult for men in our situation—that is, to make an end of speaking, since with that ending the peril of our lives draws near—[4] we say in conclusion that we did not surrender our city to the Thebans (to that we would have preferred inglorious starvation), but trusted in and capitulated to you; and it would be just, if we fail to persuade you, to put us back in the same position and let us take the chance that falls to us. And at the same time we Plataeans, foremost among the Hellenic patriots, and suppliants to you, beseech you not to give us up out of your hands and faith to our most hated enemies, the Thebans, but to be our saviors. Do not, while you free the rest of the Hellenes, bring us to destruction."

Such were the words of the Plataeans. The Thebans, afraid that the Spartans might be moved by what they had heard, came forward and said that they too desired to address them, since the Plataeans had, against their wish, been allowed to speak at length instead of being confined to a simple answer to the question. Leave being granted, the Thebans spoke as follows:

3.60
427
5th Year/Summer
PLATAEA
The Thebans ask to speak.

"We should never have asked to make this speech if the Plataeans on their side had contented themselves with briefly answering the question, and had not turned round and made charges against us, coupled with a long defense of themselves upon matters outside the present inquiry and not even the subject of accusation, and with praise of what no one finds fault with. However, since they have done so, we must answer their charges and refute their self-praise, in order that neither our bad name nor their good may help them, but that you may hear the real truth on both points, and so decide. [2] The

3.61
427
5th Year/Summer
PLATAEA
The Thebans describe the origin of their quarrel with the Plataeans.

origin of our quarrel was this. We settled Plataea some time after the rest of Boeotia, together with other places out of which we had driven the mixed population. The Plataeans not choosing to recognize our supremacy, as had been first arranged, but separating themselves from the rest of the Boeotians, and proving traitors to their nationality, we used compulsion; upon which they went over to the Athenians, and with them did us much harm, for which we retaliated."

"Next, when the barbarian invaded Hellas, they say that they were the only Boeotians who did not Medize; and this is where they most glorify themselves and abuse us.[1a] We say that if they did not Medize, it was because the Athenians did not do so either; just as afterwards when the Athenians attacked the Hellenes they, the Plataeans, were again the only Boeotians who Atticized. [2] And yet consider the forms of our respective governments when we so acted. Our city at that juncture had neither an oligarchic constitution in which all the nobles enjoyed equal rights nor a democracy, but that which is most opposed to law and good government and nearest a tyranny—the rule of a close cabal. [3] These, hoping to strengthen their individual power by the success of the Persians, kept the people down by force, and brought them into the city. The city as a whole was not its own mistress when it so acted, and ought not to be reproached for the errors that it committed while deprived of its constitution. [4] Examine only how we acted after the departure of the Persians and the recovery of the constitution; when the Athenians attacked the rest of Hellas and endeavored to subjugate our country, of the greater part of which faction had already made them masters. Did we not fight and conquer at Coronea[4a] and liberate Boeotia, and do we not now actively contribute to the liberation of the rest, providing horses to the cause and a force unequaled by that of any other state in the confederacy?"

"Let this suffice to excuse us for our Medism. We will now endeavor to show that you have injured the Hellenes more than we, and are more deserving of condign punishment. [2] It was in defense against us, say you, that you became allies and citizens of Athens. If so, you ought only to have called in the Athenians against us, instead of joining them in attacking others: it was open to you to do this if you ever felt that they were leading you where you did not wish to follow, as Sparta was already your ally against the Mede, as you so much insist; and this was surely sufficient to keep us off, and above all to allow you to deliberate in security. Nevertheless, of your own choice and without compulsion you chose to throw your lot in with Athens. [3] And you say that it had been base for you to betray your

3.62
427
5th Year/Summer
PLATAEA
The Thebans say their government was a tyranny when it Medized, acting against the desires of the people. Now that they have recovered their constitution, Thebes is foremost in the fight against Athenian hegemony.

3.63
427
5th Year/Summer
PLATAEA
The Thebans criticize the Plataeans for helping the Athenians to subjugate other Hellenes.

3.62.1a   See Appendix E, The Persians, §4.

3.62.4a   Thucydides mentions the battle of Coronea in 1.113.2; for its location, see Map 4.5, BY.

benefactors; but it was surely far baser and more iniquitous to sacrifice the whole body of the Hellenes, your fellow confederates, who were liberating Hellas, than the Athenians only, who were enslaving it. [4] The return that you made them was therefore neither equal nor honorable, since you called them in, as you say, because you were being oppressed yourselves, and then became their accomplices in oppressing others; one should indeed return like for like, but it is base to do so when such repayment unjustly harms others."

"Meanwhile, after thus plainly showing that it was not for the sake of the Hellenes that you alone then did not Medize, but because the Athenians did not do so either, and you wished to side with them and to be against the rest; [2] you now claim the benefit of good deeds done to please your neighbors. This cannot be admitted: you chose the Athenians, and with them you must stand or fall. Nor can you plead the league then made and claim that it should now protect you. [3] You abandoned that league, and offended against it by helping instead of hindering the subjugation of the Aeginetans and others of its members, and that not under compulsion, but while in enjoyment of the same institutions that you enjoy to the present hour, and no one forcing you as in our case. Lastly, an invitation was addressed to you before you were besieged to be neutral and join neither party: this you did not accept. [4] Who then merit the detestation of the Hellenes more justly than you, you who sought their ruin under the mask of honor? The former virtues that you allege you now show not to be proper to your character; the real bent of your nature has been at length damningly proved: when the Athenians took the path of injustice you followed them."

[5] "Of our unwilling Medism and your willful Atticizing this, then, is our explanation."

"The last wrong of which you complain consists in our having, as you say, lawlessly invaded your city in time of peace and festival. Here again we cannot think that we were more in fault than yourselves. [2] If of our own proper motion we made an armed attack upon your city and ravaged your territory, we are guilty; but if the first men among you in estate and family, wishing to put an end to the foreign connection and to restore you to the common Boeotian country, of their own free will invited us, wherein is our crime? Where wrong is done, those who lead, as you say, are more to blame than those who follow. [3] Not that, in our judgment, wrong was done either by them or by us. Citizens like yourselves, and with more at stake than you, they opened their own walls and introduced us into their own city, not as foes but as friends, to prevent the bad

3.64
427
5th Year/Summer
PLATAEA
The Thebans emphasize the willingness of the Plataeans to serve Athens, pointing out that they rejected an offer to remain neutral in the current struggle.

3.65
427
5th Year/Summer
PLATAEA
Though Theban Medizing was unwilling, Plataean Atticizing was willful. Some Plataean citizens acted honorably to help Thebes in the attack on their city to save it from its worst elements.

among you from becoming worse; to give honest men their due; to reform principles without attacking persons, since you were not to be banished from your city, but brought home to your kindred, nor to be made enemies to any, but friends alike to all."

3.66
427
5th Year/Summer
PLATAEA
The Thebans say their intentions were not hostile, but that the Plataeans criminally violated their own agreement when they slew their prisoners.

"That our intention was not hostile is proved by our behavior. We did no harm to anyone, but publicly invited those who wished to live under a national, Boeotian government to come over to us; [2] which at first you gladly did, and made an agreement with us and remained tranquil, until you became aware of the smallness of our numbers. Now it is possible that there may have been something not quite fair in our entering without the consent of your People. At any rate you did not repay us in kind. Instead of refraining, as we had done, from violence, and inducing us to retire by negotiation, you fell upon us in violation of your agreement, and slew some of us in fight, of which we do not so much complain, for in that there was a certain justice; but others who held out their hands and received quarter, and whose lives you subsequently promised us, you lawlessly butchered. If this was not abominable, what is? [3] And after these three crimes committed one after the other—the violation of your agreement, the murder of the men afterwards, and the lying breach of your promise not to kill them, if we refrained from injuring your property in the country—you still affirm that we are the criminals and yourselves pretend to escape justice. Not so, if these your judges decide aright, but you will be punished for all together."

3.67
427
5th Year/Summer
PLATAEA
The Thebans conclude that the Plataeans are unworthy of pity, for they bear full responsibility for their plight after rejecting the Hellenes.

"Such, Spartans, are the facts. We have gone into them at some length both on your account and on our own, that you may feel that you will justly condemn the prisoners, and we, that we have given an additional sanction to our vengeance. [2] We would also prevent you from being melted by hearing of their past virtues, if any such they had: these may be fairly appealed to by the victims of injustice, but only aggravate the guilt of criminals, since they offend against their better nature. Nor let them gain anything by crying and wailing, by calling upon your fathers' tombs and their own desolate condition. [3] Against this we point to the far more dreadful fate of our youth, butchered at their hands; the fathers of whom either fell at Coronea,[3a] bringing Boeotia over to you, or seated, forlorn old men by desolate hearths, who with far more reason implore your justice upon the prisoners. [4] The pity which they appeal to is due rather to men who suffer unworthily; those who suffer justly, as they do, are on the contrary subjects for triumph. [5] For their present desolate condition they have themselves to blame, since they willfully rejected the better alliance. Their lawless act was not provoked by any

---

3.67.3a Thucydides mentions the battle of Coronea in 1.113.2; for its location, see Map 4.7, BY.

action of ours; hate, not justice, inspired their decision; and even now the satisfaction which they afford us is not adequate; they will suffer by a legal sentence not, as they pretend, as suppliants asking for quarter in battle, but as prisoners who have surrendered upon agreement to take their trial. [6] Vindicate, therefore, the Hellenic law which they have broken, Spartans, and grant to us, the victims of its violation, the reward merited by our zeal. Nor let us be supplanted in your favor by their harangues, but offer an example to the Hellenes that the contests to which you invite them are of deeds, not words: good deeds can be shortly stated, but where wrong is done a wealth of language is needed to veil its deformity. [7] However, if leading powers were to do what you are now doing, and putting one short question to all alike, were to decide accordingly, men would be less tempted to seek fine phrases to cover bad actions."

Such were the words of the Thebans. The Spartan judges decided that the question, whether they had received any service from the Plataeans in the war, was a fair one for them to put; as they had always invited them to be neutral, agreeably to the original covenant of Pausanias after the defeat of the Persians, and had again definitely offered them the same conditions before the blockade. This offer having been refused, they were now, they conceived, by the loyalty of their intention released from their covenant; and having, as they considered, suffered evil at the hands of the Plataeans, they brought them in again one by one and asked each of them the same question, that is to say, whether they had done the Spartans and allies any service in the war; and upon their saying that they had not, took them out and slew them all without exception. [2] The number of Plataeans thus massacred was not less than two hundred, with twenty-five Athenians who had shared in the siege. The women were taken as slaves. [3] The city the Thebans[3a] gave for about a year to some political emigrants from Megara, and to the surviving Plataeans of their own party to inhabit, and afterwards razed it to the ground from the very foundations, and built on to the precinct of Hera an inn two hundred feet square, with rooms all round above and below, making use for this purpose of the roofs and doors of the Plataeans:[3b] of the rest of the materials in the wall, the brass and the iron, they made couches which they dedicated to Hera, for whom they also built a stone chapel of a hundred feet square. The land they confiscated and let out on a ten-years' lease to Theban occupiers. [4] The adverse attitude of the Spartans in the whole Plataean affair was mainly adopted to please the Thebans, who were thought to be useful in the war at that moment raging. Such was the end of Plataea in the ninety-third year after she became the ally of Athens.[4a]

3.68
427
5th Year/Summer
PLATAEA
The Plataeans are executed
and their city razed.

3.68.3a Some scholars do not accept that Thucydides wrote "the Thebans" here, and suppose that it was the Spartans, their allies, that carried out these acts.

3.68.3b This is another instance of the salvage of woodwork; see note at 2.14.1a.

3.68.4a Plataea was restored in 386 B.C. under the "King's Peace"; see Epilogue, §4, and Appendix E, The Persians, §11.

3.69
427
5th Year/Summer
PELOPONNESUS
The Peloponnesian fleet
returns to Cyllene.

Meanwhile, the forty ships of the Peloponnesians[1a] that had gone to the relief of the Lesbians, and which we left flying across the open sea, pursued by the Athenians, were caught in a storm off Crete, and scattering from thence made their way to the Peloponnesus, where they found at Cyllene[1b] thirteen Leucadian and Ambraciot triremes, with Brasidas son of Tellis lately arrived as counselor to Alcidas; [2] the Spartans, upon the failure of the Lesbian expedition, resolved to strengthen their fleet and sail to Corcyra, where a revolution had broken out, and to arrive there before the twelve Athenian ships at Naupactus could be reinforced from Athens. Brasidas and Alcidas began to prepare accordingly.

3.70
427
5th Year/Summer
CORCYRA
The Corcyraean oligarchs
revolt.

The Corcyraean revolution began with the return of the prisoners taken in the sea fights off Epidamnus.[1a] These the Corinthians had released, nominally upon the security of eight hundred talents[1b] given by their *proxeni*[1c] but in reality upon their engagement to bring over Corcyra to Corinth. These men proceeded to canvass each of the citizens, and to intrigue with the aim of detaching the city from Athens. [2] Upon the arrival of an Athenian and a Corinthian vessel, with envoys on board, a conference was held in which the Corcyraeans voted to remain allies of the Athenians according to their agreement, but to be friends of the Peloponnesians as they had been formerly. [3] Meanwhile, the returned prisoners brought Peithias, a volunteer proxenus of the Athenians and leader of the commons, to trial, upon the charge of enslaving Corcyra to Athens. [4] He, being acquitted, retorted by accusing five of the richest of their number of cutting stakes in the ground sacred to Zeus and Alcinous; the legal penalty being a *stater*[4a] for each stake. [5] Upon their conviction, the amount of the penalty being very large, they seated themselves as suppliants in the temples, to be allowed to pay it by installments; but Peithias, who was one of the council, prevailed upon that body to enforce the law; [6] upon which the accused, rendered desperate by the law, and also learning that Peithias had the intention, while still a member of the council, to persuade the people to conclude a defensive and offensive alliance with Athens, banded together armed with daggers, and suddenly bursting into the Council killed Peithias and sixty others, council members and private persons; some few only of the party of Peithias taking refuge in the Athenian trireme, which had not yet departed.

3.69.1a This picks up the narrative of Alcidas'
 fleet from 3.33.
3.69.1b Cyllene: Map 3.76.
3.70.1a These sea battles were fought near Sybota,
 a long way from Epidamnus. They are
 described in 1.49–50. Thucydides last
 described events on Corcyra in 1.55.
3.70.1b Eight hundred talents was an enormous
 sum, more than Athens' annual tribute at
 that time. See A. W. Gomme, *A Historical Commentary on Thucydides*, iii (Oxford, 1956), 359, and Appendix J,
 Classical Greek Currency, §5.
3.70.1c *Proxeni*: see note 3.2.3c.

3.70.4a The *stater* was a unit of currency; probably in this case the Corinthian stater, almost equal to two Attic *drachmas;* see
 Appendix J, Classical Greek Currency, §4.
 According to A. W. Gomme, *A Historical
 Commentary on Thucydides*, iii (Oxford,
 1956), 360, this fine seems too small to
 distress rich men, unless they had cut
 thousands of the stakes over many years.
 It was of course criminal sacrilege to
 touch land dedicated to a god. Athens
 based her Megarian Decree publicly on
 the grounds that the Megarians had cultivated consecrated ground (1.139.2).

After this outrage, the conspirators summoned the Corcyraeans to an assembly, and said that this would turn out for the best and would save them from being enslaved by Athens: for the future, they moved to receive neither party unless they came peacefully in a single ship, treating any larger number as enemies. This motion made, they compelled it to be adopted, [2] and instantly sent off envoys to Athens to justify what had been done and to dissuade the refugees there from any hostile proceedings which might lead to a reaction.

Upon the arrival of the embassy, the Athenians arrested the envoys and all who listened to them as revolutionists, and lodged them in Aegina.[1a] [2] Meanwhile a Corinthian trireme arriving in the island with Spartan envoys, those in control of Corcyra attacked The People and defeated them in battle. [3] Night coming on, The People took refuge in the Acropolis and the higher parts of the city,[3a] and concentrated themselves there, having also possession of the Hyllaic harbor, their adversaries occupying the *agora*,[3b] where most of them lived, and the harbor adjoining, looking toward the mainland.

The next day passed in skirmishes of little importance, each party sending into the country to offer freedom to the slaves and to invite them to join them. The mass of the slaves answered the appeal of The People; their antagonists being reinforced by eight hundred mercenaries from the mainland.

After a day's interval hostilities recommenced, victory remaining with The People, who had the advantage in numbers and position, the women also valiantly assisting them, pelting with tiles from the houses, and supporting the mêlée with a fortitude beyond their sex. [2] Toward dusk, the oligarchs in full rout, fearing that the victorious commons might assault and carry the arsenal and put them to the sword, set fire to the houses round the agora and the lodging-houses, in order to bar their advance; sparing neither their own, nor those of their neighbors; by which much stuff of the merchants was consumed and the city risked total destruction if a wind had come to help the flame by blowing on it. [3] Hostilities now ceased, and while both sides kept quiet, passing the night on guard, the Corinthian ship stole out to sea upon the victory of The People, and most of the mercenaries passed over secretly to the continent.

3.71
427
5th Year/Summer
CORCYRA
The oligarchs declare Corcyra's neutrality.

3.72
427
5th Year/Summer
CORCYRA
Corcyraean oligarchs attack The People.

3.73
427
5th Year/Summer
CORCYRA
Both sides seek support from the slaves.

3.74
427
5th Year/Summer
CORCYRA
The oligarchs are defeated.

3.72.1a Aegina: Map 3.93, BY.
3.72.3a For possible locations of the Acropolis and other "high parts" of the city of Corcyra, see Map 3.76, inset. This inset of the city of Corcyra follows the map and discussion of A. W. Gomme, *A Historical Commentary on Thucydides,* ii (Oxford, 1956), 370–72.
3.72.3b *Agora:* the marketplace and the social center of a classical Greek city.

3.75
427
5th Year/Summer
CORCYRA
The Athenian Nicostratus
attempts to arrange a truce.

The next day the Athenian general, Nicostratus son of Diitrephes, came up from Naupactus with twelve ships and five hundred Messenian hoplites.[1a] He at once endeavored to bring about a settlement, and persuaded the two parties to agree together to bring to trial ten of the ringleaders, who were no longer in the city, while the rest were to live in peace, making terms with each other, and entering into an alliance with the Athenians. [2] This arranged, he was about to sail away, when the leaders of The People induced him to leave them five of his ships to make their adversaries less disposed to make trouble, while they manned and sent with him an equal number of their own. [3] He had no sooner consented, than they began to enroll their enemies for the ships; and these fearing that they might be sent off to Athens seated themselves as suppliants in the temple of the Dioscuri.[3a] [4] When an attempt by Nicostratus to reassure them and to persuade them to rise proved unsuccessful, The People armed upon this pretext, alleging the refusal of their adversaries to sail with them as a proof of the hollowness of their intentions, and took their arms out of their houses, and would even have killed some whom they fell in with if Nicostratus had not prevented it. [5] The rest of the party, being not less than four hundred in number, seeing what was going on, seated themselves as suppliants in the temple of Hera until The People, fearing that they might adopt some desperate resolution, induced them to rise, and conveyed them over to the island in front of the temple[5a] where provisions were sent across to them.

3.76
427
5th Year/Summer
CORCYRA
The Peloponnesian fleet
arrives at Corcyra.

At this stage in the revolution, on the fourth or fifth day after the removal of the men to the island, the Peloponnesian ships arrived from Cyllene[1a] where they had been stationed since their return from Ionia, fifty-three in number, still under the command of Alcidas, but with Brasidas also on board as his adviser; and dropping anchor at Sybota,[1b] a harbor on the mainland, at daybreak made sail for Corcyra.

3.77
427
5th Year/Summer
CORCYRA
The Corcyraeans launch a
disorganized naval attack.

The Corcyraeans in great confusion and alarm at the state of things in the city and at the approach of the invader, at once proceeded to equip sixty vessels, which they sent out, as fast as they were manned, against the enemy, in spite of the Athenians recommending them to let them sail out first, and to follow themselves afterwards with all their ships together. [2] Upon their vessels coming up to the enemy in this straggling fashion, two immediately deserted: in others the crews were fighting among themselves, and there was no order in anything that was done; [3] so that the Peloponnesians, seeing their confusion, placed twenty ships to oppose the Corcyraeans, and ranged the rest against the twelve Athenian ships, amongst which were the two vessels *Salaminia* and *Paralus*.[3a]

3.75.1a   These "Messenians" now lived at Naupactus (Map 3.76), where Athens had settled them after they surrendered to Sparta at Ithome and were forced to leave the Peloponnesus (see 1.103.1–3).
3.75.3a   No suppliant could be molested without insult to the gods, particularly that god or gods in whose temple or at whose altar the suppliant had taken refuge.
3.75.5a   The temple of Hera and the island in front of it, possible location: Map 3.76, inset.
3.76.1a   Cyllene: Map 3.76.
3.76.1b   Sybota: Map 3.76.
3.77.3a   The *Salaminia* and the *Paralus* were special state triremes used for official business.

MAP 3.76 CORCYRA AND VICINITY: CITY OF CORCYRA

3.78
427
5th Year/Summer
CORCYRA
The Peloponnesians defeat
the Corcyraeans at sea.

While the Corcyraeans, attacking without judgment and in small detachments, were already crippled by their own misconduct, the Athenians, afraid of the numbers of the enemy and of being surrounded, did not venture to attack the main body or even the center of the division opposed to them, but fell upon its wing and sank one vessel;[1a] after which the Peloponnesians formed in a circle, and the Athenians rowed round them and tried to throw them into disorder. [2] Perceiving this, the Peloponnesian division opposed to the Corcyraeans, fearing a repetition of the disaster of Naupactus,[2a] came to support their friends, and the whole fleet, now united, bore down upon the Athenians, [3] who retired before it, backing water, withdrawing as leisurely as possible in order to give the Corcyraeans time to escape while the enemy was thus kept occupied. [4] Such was the character of this sea fight, which lasted until sunset.

3.79
427
5th Year/Summer
CORCYRA
The Peloponnesians fail to
exploit their victory.

The Corcyraeans now feared that the enemy would follow up their victory and sail against the city and rescue the men in the island, or strike some other equally decisive blow, and accordingly carried the men over again to the temple of Hera, and kept guard over the city. [2] The Peloponnesians, however, although victorious in the sea fight, did not venture to attack the city, but took the thirteen Corcyraean vessels which they had captured, and with them sailed back to the continent from whence they had put out. [3] The next day they again refrained from attacking the city, although the disorder and panic were at their height, and though Brasidas, it is said, urged Alcidas, his superior officer, to do so, but they landed upon the promontory of Leukimme and laid waste the country.[3a]

3.80
427
5th Year/Summer
CORCYRA
The Peloponnesians learn of
the approach of a large
Athenian fleet.

Meanwhile The People in Corcyra, being still in great fear of the fleet attacking them, came to a parley with the suppliants and their friends, in order to save the city; and prevailed upon some of them to go on board the ships, of which they still manned thirty, against the expected attack. [2] But the Peloponnesians after ravaging the country until midday sailed away, and toward nightfall were informed by beacon signals of the approach of sixty Athenian vessels from Leucas,[2a] under the command of Eurymedon son of Thucles; which had been sent off by the Athenians upon the news of the revolution and of the fleet with Alcidas being about to sail for Corcyra.

3.81
427
5th Year/Summer
CORCYRA
As the Peloponnesians flee,
the Corcyraean popular
faction massacres its
domestic foes.

The Peloponnesians accordingly at once set off in haste by night for home, coasting along shore; and hauling their ships across the Isthmus of Leucas,[1a] in order not to be seen doubling it, so departed. [2] The Corcyraeans, made aware of the approach of the Athenian fleet and of the departure of the enemy, brought the Messenians[2a] from outside the walls into the city, and ordered the fleet which they had manned to sail round into the Hyllaic harbor;[2b] and while it was so doing, slew such of their enemies

---

3.78.1a On the "sinking" of triremes, see note 2.91.3a and Appendix G, Trireme Warfare, §9.

3.78.2a Thucydides refers here to the naval battle in 429 that took place in the sea off Patrae, and which he described in 2.83–84.

3.79.3a Cape Leukimme: Map 3.76.

3.80.2a Leucas: Map 3.76.

3.81.1a Isthmus of Leucas: Map 3.76.

3.81.2a These are the five hundred Messenian hoplites who had arrived with Nicostratus in 3.75.1.

3.81.2b Hyllaic harbor at Corcyra, probable location: Map 3.76, inset.

as they laid hands on, killing afterwards as they landed them, those whom they had persuaded to go on board the ships. Next they went to the sanctuary of Hera[2b] and persuaded about fifty men to take their trial, and condemned them all to death. [3] The mass of the suppliants who had refused to do so, on seeing what was taking place, slew each other there in the consecrated ground; while some hanged themselves upon the trees, and others destroyed themselves as they were severally able. [4] During seven days that Eurymedon stayed with his sixty ships, the Corcyraeans were engaged in butchering those of their fellow-citizens whom they regarded as their enemies: and although the crime imputed was that of attempting to put down the democracy, some were slain also for private hatred, others by their debtors because of the moneys owed to them. [5] Death thus raged in every shape; and, as usually happens at such times, there was no length to which violence did not go; sons were killed by their fathers, and suppliants dragged from the altar or slain upon it;[5a] while some were even walled up in the temple of Dionysus and died there.

So bloody was the march of the revolution, and the impression which it made was the greater as it was one of the first to occur. Later on, one may say, the whole Hellenic world was convulsed; struggles being everywhere made by the popular leaders to bring in the Athenians, and by the oligarchs to introduce the Spartans. In peace there would have been neither the pretext nor the wish to make such an invitation; but in war, with an alliance always at the command of either faction for the hurt of their adversaries and their own corresponding advantage, opportunities for bringing in the foreigner were never wanting to the revolutionary parties. [2] The sufferings which revolution entailed upon the cities were many and terrible, such as have occurred and always will occur as long as the nature of mankind remains the same; though in a severer or milder form, and varying in their symptoms, according to the variety of the particular cases. In peace and prosperity states and individuals have better sentiments, because they do not find themselves suddenly confronted with imperious necessities; but war takes away the easy supply of daily wants and so proves a rough master that brings most men's characters to a level with their fortunes. [3] Revolution thus ran its course from city to city, and the places which it arrived at last, from having heard what had been done before, carried to a still greater excess the refinement of their inventions, as manifested in the cunning of their enterprises and the atrocity of their reprisals. [4] Words had to change their ordinary meaning and to take that which was now given them. Reckless audacity came to be considered the courage of a loyal supporter; prudent hesitation, specious cowardice; moderation was held to be a cloak for

3.82
427
5th Year/Summer
CORCYRA
Thucydides describes the evils of revolution.

3.81.2b Temple of Hera, Corcyra, approximate
          location: Map 3.76, inset.
3.81.5a To harm someone who had taken refuge
          at an altar was a sacrilegious crime.

unmanliness; ability to see all sides of a question incapacity to act on any. Frantic violence became the attribute of manliness; cautious plotting a justifiable means of self-defense. [5] The advocate of extreme measures was always trustworthy; his opponent a man to be suspected. To succeed in a plot was to have a shrewd head, to divine a plot a still shrewder; but to try to provide against having to do either was to break up your party and to be afraid of your adversaries. In short, to forestall an intending criminal, or to suggest the idea of a crime where it was lacking was equally commended, [6] until even blood became a weaker tie than party, from the superior readiness of those united by the latter to dare everything without reserve; for such associations sought not the blessings derivable from established institutions but were formed by ambition to overthrow them; and the confidence of their members in each other rested less on any religious sanction than upon complicity in crime. [7] The fair proposals of an adversary were met with jealous precautions by the stronger of the two, and not with a generous confidence. Revenge also was held of more account than self-preservation. Oaths of reconciliation, being only offered on either side to meet an immediate difficulty, only held good so long as no other weapon was at hand; but when opportunity arose, he who first ventured to seize it and to take his enemy off his guard, thought this perfidious vengeance sweeter than an open one since, considerations of safety apart, success by treachery won him the prize for superior intelligence. Indeed it is generally the case that men are readier to call rogues clever than simpletons honest, and are as ashamed of being the second as they are proud of being the first. [8] The cause of all these evils was the lust for power arising from greed and ambition; and from these passions proceeded the violence of parties once engaged in contention. The leaders in the cities made the fairest professions: on the one side with the cry of political equality of The People, on the other of a moderate aristocracy; but they sought prizes for themselves in those public interests which they pretended to cherish and, stopping at nothing in their struggles for ascendancy, engaged in direct excesses. In their acts of vengeance they went to even greater lengths, not limiting them to what justice or the good of the state demanded, but making the party caprice of the moment their only standard, and invoking with equal readiness the condemnation of an unjust verdict or the authority of the strong arm to glut the animosities of the hour. Thus religion was in honor with neither party; but the use of fair phrases to arrive at guilty ends was in high reputation. Meanwhile the moderate part of the citizens perished between the two, either for not joining in the quarrel, or because envy would not suffer them to escape.

Thus every form of iniquity took root in the Hellenic countries by reason of the troubles. The ancient simplicity into which honor so largely entered was laughed down and disappeared; and society became divided into camps in which no man trusted his fellow. [2] To put an end to this, there was neither promise to be depended upon, nor oath that could command respect; but all parties dwelling rather in their calculation upon the hopelessness of a permanent state of things, were more intent upon self-defense than capable of confidence. [3] In this contest the blunter wits were most successful. Apprehensive of their own deficiencies and of the cleverness of their antagonists, they feared to be worsted in debate and to be surprised by the combinations of their more versatile opponents, and so at once boldly had recourse to action: while their adversaries, arrogantly thinking that they should know in time, and that it was unnecessary to secure by action what policy could provide, often fell victims to their lack of precaution.

Meanwhile Corcyra gave the first example of most of the crimes alluded to; of the reprisals exacted by the governed who had never experienced equitable treatment or indeed anything but insolence from their rulers—when their hour came; of the iniquitous resolves of those who desired to get rid of their accustomed poverty and ardently coveted their neighbors' goods; and lastly, of the savage and pitiless excesses into which men who had begun the struggle not in a class but in a party spirit, were hurried by their ungovernable passions. [2] In the confusion into which life was now thrown in the cities, human nature, always rebelling against the law and now its master, gladly showed itself ungoverned in passion, above respect for justice, and the enemy of all superiority; since revenge would not have been set above religion, and gain above justice, had it not been for the fatal power of envy. [3] Indeed men too often take upon themselves in the prosecution of their revenge to set the example of doing away with those general laws to which all alike can look for salvation in adversity, instead of allowing them to subsist against the day of danger when their aid may be required.

While the revolutionary passions thus for the first time displayed themselves in the factions of Corcyra, Eurymedon and the Athenian fleet sailed away; [2] after which some five hundred Corcyraean exiles who had succeeded in escaping took some forts on the mainland and, becoming masters of the Corcyraean territory on the mainland, made this their base to plunder their countrymen in the island, and did so much damage as to cause a severe famine in the city. [3] They also sent envoys to Sparta and Corinth to negotiate their restoration; but meeting with no success, afterwards got together boats and mercenaries and crossed over to the island, being about six hundred in all; and burning their boats so as to have no hope except in becoming masters of the country, went up to Mount Istone[3a] and fortifying themselves there, began to harm those in the city and obtain command of the country.

At the close of the same summer the Athenians sent twenty ships under the command of Laches son of Melanopus, and Charoeades son of Euphiletus, to Sicily,[1a] [2] where the Syracusans[2a] and Leontines[2b] were at war.

3.85.3a Mount Istone, Corcyra: Map 3.76.
         Thucydides' narrative returns to Corcyra
         in 4.46.
3.86.1a Sicily: Map 3.86.
3.86.2a Syracuse: Map 3.86.
3.86.2b Leontini: Map 3.86.

MAP 3.86 SICILIAN OPERATIONS IN 427

The Syracusans had for allies all the Dorian cities except Camarina[2c]—these had all been included in the Lacedaemonian confederacy from the commencement of the war, though they had not taken any active part in it—the Leontines had Camarina and the Chalcidian cities.[2d] In Italy the Locrians[2e] were for the Syracusans, the Rhegians[2f] for their Leontine kinsmen. [3] The allies of the Leontines now sent to Athens and appealed to their ancient alliance and to their Ionian origin, to persuade the Athenians to send them a fleet, as the Syracusans were blockading them by land and sea. [4] The Athenians sent it upon the plea of their common descent, but in reality to prevent the exportation of Sicilian corn to the Peloponnesus and to test the possibility of bringing Sicily into subjection. Accordingly they established themselves at Rhegium in Italy, and from thence carried on the war in concert with their allies.[4a]

Summer was now over. The winter following, the plague a second time attacked the Athenians; for although it had never entirely left them, still there had been a notable abatement in its ravages.[1a] [2] The second visit lasted no less than a year, the first having lasted two; and nothing distressed the Athenians and reduced their power more than this. [3] No less than four thousand four hundred hoplites in the ranks died of it and three hundred cavalry, besides a number of the multitude that was never ascertained. [4] At the same time took place the numerous earthquakes in Athens, Euboea, and Boeotia, particularly at Orchomenus[4a] in the last-named country.

3.87
427/6
5th Year/Winter
ATHENS
The plague returns to
Athens.

3.86.2c Camarina: Map 3.86. For the Dorian cities, see Appendix H, Dialects and Ethnic Groups, §4–8.
3.86.2d Leontini, Naxos, and Rhegium (Map 3.86) were all founded by Chalcis of Euboea (Map 4.7, BY).
3.86.2e Locri (Epizephyrian, in Italy): Map 3.86.
3.86.2f Rhegium: Map 3.86.
3.86.4a Events in Sicily are continued at 3.88.
3.87.1a The first outbreak of plague in Athens was extensively described in 2.47–55.
3.87.4a Orchomenus, Boeotia, and Euboea: Map 3.93, AY.

ILLUSTRATION 3.86 FRAGMENT OF A TREATY BETWEEN ATHENS AND
RHEGIUM FROM 433 B.C.

The same winter the Athenians in Sicily and the Rhegians, with thirty ships, made an expedition against the islands of Aeolus:[1a] it being impossible to invade them in summer, owing to the want of water. [2] These islands are occupied by the Liparians, a Cnidian[2a] colony, who live in one of them of no great size called Lipara; and from this as their headquarters cultivate the rest, Didyme, Strongyle, and Hiera.[2b] [3] In Hiera the people in those parts believe that Hephaestus has his forge, from the quantity

3.88
427/6
5th Year/Winter
SICILY
The Athenians raid the Aeolian islands.

3.88.1a Aeolian islands: Map 3.86. This continues
the narrative from 3.86.
3.88.2a Cnidus: Map 4.44, locator.
3.88.2b Lipara, Didyme, Strongyle, Hiera, Aeolian islands: Map 3.86.

of flame which they see it send out by night, and of smoke by day. These islands lie off the coast of the Sicels and Messanians, and were allies of the Syracusans. [4] The Athenians laid waste their land, and as the inhabitants did not submit, sailed back to Rhegium. Thus the winter ended, and with it ended the fifth year of this war, of which Thucydides was the historian.[4a]

3.89
426
6th Year/Summer
ATTICA-EUBOEA
The Peloponnesian invasion of Attica turns back due to earthquakes.

The next summer the Peloponnesians and their allies set out to invade Attica under the command of Agis son of Archidamus, and went as far as the Isthmus,[1a] but numerous earthquakes occurring, turned back again without the invasion taking place. [2] About the same time that these earthquakes were so common, the sea at Orobiae, in Euboea,[2a] retiring from the then line of coast, returned in a huge wave and invaded a great part of the city, and retreated leaving some of it still under water; so that what was once land is now sea; such of the inhabitants perishing as could not run up to the higher ground in time. [3] A similar inundation also occurred at Atalanta,[2b] the island off the Opuntian-Locrian[3a] coast, carrying away part of the Athenian fort and wrecking one of two ships which were drawn up on the beach. [4] At Peparethus[4a] also the sea retreated a little, without however any inundation following; and an earthquake threw down part of the wall, the city hall, and a few other buildings. [5] The cause, in my opinion, of this phenomenon must be sought in the earthquake. At the point where its shock has been the most violent the sea is driven back, and suddenly recoiling with redoubled force, causes the inundation. Without an earthquake I do not see how such an accident could happen.

3.90
426
6th Year/Summer
SICILY
Messana submits to the Athenians.

During the same summer different operations were carried on by the different belligerents in Sicily; by the Sicelians themselves against each other, and by the Athenians and their allies: I shall however confine myself to the actions in which the Athenians took part, choosing the most important. [2] The death of the Athenian general Charoeades, killed by the Syracusans in battle, left Laches in sole command of the fleet, which he now directed in concert with the allies against Mylae, a place belonging to the Messanians. Two Messanian battalions in garrison at Mylae[2a] laid an ambush for the party landing from the ships, [3] but were routed with great slaughter by the Athenians and their allies, who thereupon assaulted the fortification and compelled them to surrender the Acropolis and to march with them upon Messana.[3a] [4] This city afterwards also submitted upon the approach of the Athenians and their allies, and gave hostages and all other securities required.[4a]

3.91
426
6th Year/Summer
MELOS-BOEOTIA
Nicias' expedition to Melos and Tanagra is described.

The same summer the Athenians sent thirty ships round the Peloponnesus under Demosthenes son of Alcisthenes, and Procles son of Theodorus,[1a] and sixty others, with two thousand hoplites, against Melos,[1b] under Nicias son

3.88.4a   Events in Sicily are continued at 3.90.
3.89.1a   The Isthmus of Corinth: Map 3.93, BY.
3.89.2a   Orobiae, in Euboea: Map 3.93, AY.
3.89.2b   Atalanta: Map 3.93, AY; see 2.32.
3.89.3a   Locris (Opuntian): Map 3.93, AY.
3.89.4a   Peparethus: Map 3.93, AY.
3.90.2a   Mylae: Map 3.86. This continues the narrative from 3.88.

3.90.3a   Messana: Map 3.86.
3.90.4a   Events in Sicily continue at 3.99.
3.91.1a   The voyage of this fleet is described in 3.94ff.
3.91.1b   Melos: Map 3.93, BY. A second Athenian assault on Melos is described in 5.84.

of Niceratus. [2] They wished to reduce the Melians, who, although islanders, refused to be subjects of Athens or even to join her confederacy.
[3] When the devastation of their land failed to make the Melians submit,
the fleet left Melos and sailed to Oropus[3a] in the territory of Graea where,
landing at nightfall, the hoplites started at once from the ships by land for
Tanagra[3b] in Boeotia. [4] There they were met by the whole levy from
Athens, according to their prearranged signal, under the command of
Hipponicus son of Callias, and Eurymedon son of Thucles. [5] They encamped and, passing that day in ravaging the Tanagran territory, remained
there for the night. The next day, after defeating those Tanagrans who sallied out against them and some Thebans who had come up to help the
Tanagrans, they took some arms, set up a trophy,[4a] and retired—one
group to the city and the other to the ships. [6] Nicias with his sixty ships
coasted along shore and ravaged the Locrian seaboard, and so returned
home.

About this time the Spartans founded their colony of Heraclea in Trachis,[1a] their object being the following: [2] the Malians are divided into
three tribes—the Paralians, the Hiereans, and the Trachinians. The last of
these, having suffered severely in a war with their neighbors the Oetaeans,[2a]
at first intended to give themselves up to Athens; but afterwards, fearing
not to find in her the security that they sought, sent Tisamenus, whom they
chose as ambassador, to Sparta. [3] The Dorians from the mother country
of the Spartans also joined in this embassy with the same request, as they
themselves also suffered from the same enemy. [4] After hearing them, the
Spartans determined to send out the colony, wishing to assist the Trachinians and Dorians, and also because they thought that the proposed city
would be effectively located for the purposes of the war against the Athenians. A fleet might be made ready there against Euboea,[4a] with the advantage of a short passage to the island; and the city would also be useful as a
station on the road to Thrace.[4b] In short, everything made the Spartans
eager to found the place. [5] After first consulting the god at Delphi and
receiving a favorable answer, they sent off the colonists, Spartans and *Perioikoi*,[5a] inviting also any of the rest of the Hellenes who might wish to accompany them, except Ionians, Achaeans, and certain other nationalities;
three Spartans leading as founders of the colony, Leon, Alcidas, and Dam-
agon. [6] They established and fortified the city, now called Heraclea, on a
new site, about four miles and a half from Thermopylae[6a] and two miles
and a quarter from the sea; and commenced building docks, closing the
side toward Thermopylae just by the pass itself, in order that they might be
easily defended.

3.92
426
6th Year/Summer
HERACLEA IN TRACHIS
Sparta establishes the new
polis of Heraclea in Trachis.

3.91.3a   Oropus: Map 3.93, AY.
3.91.3b   Tanagra: Map 3.93, AY.
3.91.4a   A trophy was a set of captured armor
            arranged on a pole and raised at or near
            the battlefield by the victors. See Appen-
            dix F, Land Warfare, §6.
3.92.1a   Heraclea in Trachis: Map 3.93, AX. The
            city next appears in Thucydides at 3.100.

3.92.2a   Territory of the Malians: Map 3.93, AY.
            Territory of the Oetae: Map 3.93, AX.
3.92.4a   Euboea: Map 3.93, AY.
3.92.4b   Thrace: Map 3.93, locator.
3.92.5a   For a description of the *perioikoi*, see the
            Glossary and Appendix C, Spartan Insti-
            tutions, §9.
3.92.6a   Thermopylae: Map 3.93, AY. See note
            4.36.3a.

3.93
426
6th Year/Summer
HERACLEA IN TRACHIS
Heraclea does not thrive.

The foundation of this city, evidently meant to annoy Euboea (the passage across to Cenaeum in that island being a short one),[1a] at first caused some alarm at Athens, but in fact the city never caused them any trouble. [2] The reason for this was as follows: the Thessalians,[2a] who were sovereign in those parts and whose territory was menaced by its foundation, were afraid that it might prove a very powerful neighbor, and so they harassed and made war upon the new settlers continually until they at last wore them out in spite of their originally considerable numbers—people had flocked there from all quarters, believing that any place founded by the Spartans was sure to prosper. On the other hand the Spartans themselves, in the persons of their governors, did their full share toward ruining its prosperity and reducing its population, as they frightened away the greater part of the inhabitants by governing harshly and in some cases not fairly, and thus made it easier for their neighbors to prevail against them.

3.94
426
6th Year/Summer
LEUCAS
Demosthenes attacks Leucas.

The same summer, about the same time that the Athenians were detained at Melos, their fellow citizens in the thirty ships cruising round the Peloponnesus,[1a] after cutting off some guards in an ambush at Ellomenus[1b] in the territory of Leucas, subsequently went against Leucas[1c] itself with a large armament, having been reinforced by the whole levy of the Acarnanians[1d] except Oeniadae,[1e] and by the Zacynthians[1f] and Cephallenians[1g] and fifteen ships from Corcyra.[1h] [2] While the Leucadians witnessed the devastation of their land, without and within the isthmus upon which the city of Leucas and the temple of Apollo stand, without making any movement on account of the overwhelming numbers of the enemy, the Acarnanians urged Demosthenes, the Athenian general, to build a wall so as to cut off the city from the continent, a measure which they were convinced would secure its capture and rid them once and for all of a most troublesome enemy.

[3] Demosthenes however had in the meanwhile been persuaded by the Messenians[3a] that it was a fine opportunity for him, having so large an army assembled, to attack the Aetolians,[3b] who were not only the enemies of Naupactus,[3c] but whose reduction would further make it easy to gain the rest of that part of the mainland region for the Athenians. [4] The Aetolians, although numerous and warlike, dwelt in unwalled villages scattered far apart, had nothing but light armor, and might, according to the Messenians, be subdued without much difficulty before help could arrive. [5]

3.93.1a Cenaeum, western cape of Euboea: Map 3.93, AY.
3.93.2a Thessaly: Map 3.93, AY.
3.94.1a Operations at Melos were described in 3.91. These thirty ships were the fleet under Demosthenes and Procles mentioned in 3.91.1.
3.94.1b Ellomenus on Leucas: precise location unknown.
3.94.1c Leucas: Map 3.93, AX.
3.94.1d Acarnania: Map 3.93, AX. This briefly picks up the narrative of Acarnanian events

3.94.1e Oeniadae: Map 3.93, AX.
3.94.1f Zacynthus: Map 3.93, BX.
3.94.1g Cephallenia: Map 3.93, AX.
3.94.1h Corcyra: Map 3.93, AX
3.94.3a These were Messenians from Naupactus where Athens settled them; see 1.103.1–3 and note 3.75.1a.
3.94.3b Aetolia: Map 3.93, BX.
3.94.3c Naupactus: Map 3.93, AX, and Map 3.98, AX.

from 3.7; it continues next in 3.102.

MAP 3.93 EXPEDITIONS OF NICIAS AND DEMOSTHENES, EARLY 426

The plan which they recommended was to attack first the Apodotians, next the Ophionians, and after these the Eurytanians.[5a] These last are the largest tribe in Aetolia. They speak, as is said, a language exceedingly difficult to understand and eat their flesh raw. Once these tribes were subdued, the rest would readily come over.

To this plan Demosthenes consented, not only to please the Messenians, but also in the belief that by adding the Aetolians to his other mainland allies he would be able, without aid from home, to march against the Boeotians[1a] by way of Ozolian Locris[1b] to Cytinium in Doris,[1c] keeping Parnassus[1d] on his right until he descended to the Phocians,[1e] whom he could force to join him if their ancient friendship for Athens did not, as he anticipated, at once persuade them to do so. Once in Phocis he would be upon the frontier of Boeotia. Accordingly, he sailed from Leucas against the wish of the Acarnanians, and with his whole armament cruised along the coast to Sollium[1f] [2] where he communicated to them his intention. When they refused to agree to his plan because he would not build the wall against Leucas, Demosthenes sailed against the Aetolians with the rest of the forces: the Cephallenians, the Messenians, the Zacynthians, and the three hundred Athenian marines from his own ships (the fifteen Corcyraean vessels having departed). [3] He established his base at Oeneon[3a] in Locris, as the Ozolian Locrians were allies of Athens and were to meet him with all their forces in the interior. Being neighbors of the Aetolians and armed in the same way, it was thought that they would be of great service upon the expedition, from their acquaintance with the localities and the warfare of the inhabitants.

After bivouacking with the army in the precinct of Nemean Zeus—in which the poet Hesiod is said to have been killed by the people of the country, according to an oracle which had foretold that he should die in Nemea,[1a] Demosthenes set out at daybreak to invade Aetolia. [2] The first day he took Potidania, the next Krokyle, and the third Tichium,[2a] where he halted and sent back the booty to Eupalium[2b] in Locris, having determined to pursue his conquests as far as the Ophionians, and in the event of their refusing to submit, to return to Naupactus and make them the objects of a second expedition. [3] However, the Aetolians had been aware of his design from the moment of its formation, and as soon as the army invaded their country, had come up in great force with all their tribes; even the most remote Ophionians, the Bomiensians, and the Calliensians, whose

---

3.94.5a The boundaries of the territories of these peoples are unclear, but the territory of the Apodotians bordered Ozolian Locris (Map 3.93, AX) to the east, and the Ophionions and Eurytanions each lived successively further north.
3.95.1a Boeotia: Map 3.98, BY.
3.95.1b Locris (Ozolian): Map 3.93, AX.
3.95.1c Cytinium in Doris: Map 3.98, AY.
3.95.1d Mount Parnassus: Map 3.98, AY.
3.95.1e Phocis: Map 3.98, AY.
3.95.1f Sollium: Map 3.93, AX.

3.95.3a Oeneon in Ozolian Locris: Map 3.98, AX.
3.96.1a This religious precinct of Nemean Zeus must have been in Ozolian Locris (Map 3.98, AY), whereas the famous sanctuary of Nemea was situated in the Peloponnesus between Argos and Corinth. See Map 5.58, AY.
3.96.2a The locations of Potidania, Krokyle, and Tichium, all small unwalled places, have not been established.
3.96.2b Eupalium: Map 3.98, AX.

territory extends toward the Malian gulf,[3a] being among the number.

The Messenians, adhering to their original advice, assured Demosthenes that the Aetolians were an easy conquest. They urged him to push on as rapidly as possible to try to take the villages as fast as he came up to them, without waiting until the whole nation should be in arms against him. [2] Led on by his advisers and trusting in his fortune—as he had met with no opposition—and without waiting for his Locrian reinforcements who were to have supplied him with the light-armed darters in which he was most deficient, he advanced and stormed Aegitium,[2a] whose inhabitants fled before him and posted themselves upon the hills above the city, which stood on high ground about nine miles from the sea. [3] Meanwhile the Aetolians had gathered to the rescue, and now attacked the Athenians and their allies, running down from the hills on every side and darting their javelins, falling back when the Athenian army advanced, and coming on as it retired; and for a long while the battle was of this character, alternate advance and retreat, in both of which operations the Athenians had the worst.

Still, as long as their archers had arrows left and were able to use them, they held out, the light-armed Aetolians retiring before the arrows; but after the captain of the archers had been killed and his men scattered, the soldiers, worn out with the constant repetition of the same exertions and hard pressed by the Aetolians with their javelins, at last turned and fled, and falling into pathless gullies and places that they were unacquainted with, thus perished, the Messenian Chromon, their guide, having also unfortunately been killed. [2] A great many were overtaken in the pursuit by the swift-footed and light-armed Aetolians, and fell beneath their javelins; the greater number however missed their road and rushed into the wood, which had no ways out, and which was soon ignited and burnt round them by the enemy. [3] Indeed the Athenian army fell victims to death in every form, and suffered all the vicissitudes of flight; the survivors escaped with difficulty to the sea and Oeneon in Locris, whence they had set out. [4] Many of the allies were killed, and about one hundred and twenty Athenian hoplites, not a man less, and all in the prime of life. These were by far the best men in the city of Athens that fell during this war. Among the slain was also Procles, the colleague of Demosthenes. [5] Meanwhile the Athenians took up their dead under truce[5a] from the Aetolians, and retired to Naupactus, and from thence went in their ships to Athens; Demosthenes staying behind in Naupactus and in the neighborhood, being afraid to face the Athenians after the disaster.

3.97
426
6th Year/Summer
AETOLIA
The Aetolians counterattack at Aegitium.

3.98
426
6th Year/Summer
AETOLIA
The Athenians are routed with heavy losses.

3.96.3a   Malian gulf: Map 3.98, AY.
3.97.2a   Aegitium, possible location: Map 3.98, AX.
3.98.5a   Even the relatively uncivilized Aetolians respect this traditional truce for the return of the dead that must be granted according to the ritual of the hoplite battle; see Appendix F, Land Warfare, §6.

MAP 3.98 DEMOSTHENES IN AETOLIA; EURYLOCHUS' ATTACK AGAINST NAUPACTUS

3.99
SICILY
The Athenians attack Locris.

3.100
426
6th Year/Summer
SPARTA
The Aetolians persuade the Spartans to attack Naupactus.

3.101
426
6th Year/Summer
DELPHI
The Spartan general Eurylochus prepares to attack Naupactus.

About the same time the Athenians on the coast of Sicily sailed to Locris, and in a descent which they made from the ships defeated the Locrians who came against them, and took a fort upon the river Halex.[1a]

The same summer the Aetolians, who before the Athenian expedition had sent an embassy to Corinth and Sparta, composed of Tolophus, an Ophionian, Boriades, an Eurytanian, and Tisander, an Apodotian, persuaded them that an army should be sent to join them in an attack on Naupactus,[1a] which had prompted the Athenian invasion. [2] Accordingly, toward autumn, the Spartans sent out, under the command of the *Spartiates*[2a] Eurylochos, Macarius, and Menedaius, a force of three thousand hoplites of the allies, five hundred of whom came from the recently founded city of Heraclea[2b] in Trachis.

The army having assembled at Delphi,[1a] Eurylochus sent a herald to the Ozolian Locrians,[1b] as the road to Naupactus ran through their territory, and he had also conceived the idea of detaching them from Athens. [2] His chief abettors in Locris were the Amphissians,[2a] who were alarmed at the hostility of the Phocians.[2b] These first gave hostages themselves, and induced the rest to do the same for fear of the invading army; first, their

3.99.1a This chapter continues the Sicilian narrative from 3.90; it will be continued further at 3.103. The location of the fort on the river Halex is unknown (it is probably the same as the one mentioned in 3.116). For the Halex river and (Epizephyrian) Locri in Italy, see Map 3.86 or Map 3.115.
3.100.1a Naupactus: Map 3.98, AX.
3.100.2a A *Spartiate* is a full citizen of Sparta and a

member of the highest Spartan military caste.
3.100.2b Heraclea in Trachis: Map 3.98, AY. The city's foundation is described in 3.92. It next appears in the narrative in 4.78.
3.101.1a Delphi: Map 3.98, AY.
3.101.1b Locris (Ozolian): Map 3.98, AY.
3.101.2a Amphissa: Map 3.98, AY.
3.101.2b Phocis: Map 3.98, AY.

neighbors the Myonians, who held the most difficult of the passes, and after them the Ipnians, Messapians, Tritaeans, Chalaeans, Tolophonians, Hessians, and Oeanthians, all of whom joined in the expedition; the Olpaeans contenting themselves with giving hostages, without accompanying the invasion; and the Hyaeans[2c] refusing to do either, until the capture of Polis, one of their villages.

His preparations completed, Eurylochus lodged the hostages in Cytinium, in Doris,[1a] and advanced upon Naupactus through the country of the Locrians, taking upon his way Oeneon and Eupalium,[1b] two of their cities that refused to join him. [2] Having arrived in the Naupactian territory, and having been now joined by the Aetolians,[2a] the army laid waste the land and took the suburb of the city, which was unfortified; and after this Molycrium[2b] also, a Corinthian colony subject to Athens.

[3] Meanwhile the Athenian Demosthenes, who since the affair in Aetolia had remained near Naupactus, having had intelligence of the army's approach, and fearing for the city, went and persuaded the Acarnanians,[3a] although not without difficulty because of his departure from Leucas,[3b] to go to the relief of Naupactus. [4] They accordingly sent with him on board his ships a thousand hoplites, who threw themselves into the place and saved it; the extent of its wall and the small number of its defenders otherwise placing it in the greatest danger.

[5] Meanwhile Eurylochus and his companions, finding that this force had entered and that it was impossible to storm the city, withdrew, not to the Peloponnesus, but to the country once called Aeolis and now Calydon[5a] and Pleuron,[5b] and to the places in that neighborhood and Proschium[5c] in Aetolia; [6] because the Ambraciots[6a] had come and urged them to combine with them in attacking Amphilochian Argos[6b] and the rest of Amphilochia and Acarnania; affirming that the conquest of these countries would bring all the continent into alliance with Sparta. [7] To this Eurylochus consented, and dismissing the Aetolians, now remained quiet with his army in those parts, until the time should come for the Ambraciots to take the field, and for him to join them before Argos.[7a]

Summer was now over. The winter ensuing, the Athenians in Sicily with their Hellenic allies, and such of the Sicel subjects or allies of Syracuse as had revolted from her and joined their army, marched against the Sicel city

3.102
426
6th Year/Summer
NAUPACTUS
Eurylochus' attack on Naupactus is thwarted by the arrival of Acarnanian hoplites.

3.103
426/5
6th Year/Winter
SICILY
The Athenians attack Inessa and Locri.

3.101.2c The Myonians, Messapians, Tritaeans, Chalaeans, Tolophonians, Hessians, Oeanthians, Olpaeans and Hyaeans are peoples of Ozolian Locris, all but the last two apparently listed in order of their locations from east to west (according to Simon Hornblower, *A Commentary on Thucydides*, i (Oxford, 1991), 515.
3.102.1a Cytinium in Doris: Map 3.98, AY.
3.102.1b Oeneon, Eupalium: Map 3.98, AX.
3.102.2a Aetolia: Map 3.98, AX.
3.102.2b Molycrium, possible location: Map 3.98, AX.
3.102.3a Acarnania: Map 3.106, AX. This briefly

picks up the Acarnanian narrative from 3.94; it will be continued next in 3.105.
3.102.3b For Demosthenes' departure from Leucas (Map 3.106, AX), see 3.94–95.
3.102.5a Calydon: Map 3.106, BY.
3.102.5b Pleuron: Map 3.106, BY.
3.102.5c Proschium: Map 3.106, BY.
3.102.6a Ambracia: Map 3.106, AX.
3.102.6b Amphilochia: Map 3.106, AY, and inset; Amphilochian Argos, possible location: Map 3.106, inset.
3.102.7a The narrative of events in the west of Hellas is continued at 3.105.

Inessa,[1a] the Acropolis of which was held by the Syracusans,[1b] and after attacking it without being able to take it, retired. [2] In the retreat, the allies marching behind the Athenians were attacked by the Syracusans from the fort, and a large part of their army was routed with great slaughter. [3] After this, Laches and the Athenians from the ships made some descents in Locri[3a] and, defeating the Locrians who came against them with Proxenus son of Capaton, upon the river Caicinus, took some arms and departed.[3b]

The same winter the Athenians purified Delos[1a] in compliance, it appears, with a certain oracle. It had been purified before by Pisistratus the tyrant; not indeed the whole island, but as much of it as could be seen from the temple. All of it was, however, now purified in the following way. [2] All the remains of those that had died in Delos were removed, and for the future it was commanded that no one should be allowed either to die or to give birth to a child in the island; but that they should be carried over to Rhenea,[2a] which is so near to Delos that Polycrates, tyrant of Samos, having added Rhenea to his other island conquests during his period of naval ascendancy, dedicated it to the Delian Apollo by binding it to Delos with a chain.

After the purification, the Athenians celebrated, for the first time, the quinquennial festival of the Delian games.[2b] [3] Once upon a time, indeed, there was a great assemblage of the Ionians and the neighboring islanders at Delos, who used to come to the festival, as the Ionians now do to that of Ephesus,[3a] and athletic and poetical contests took place there, and the cities brought choirs of dancers. [4] Nothing can be clearer on this point than the following verses of Homer, taken from a hymn to Apollo:—

Phoebus, where'er thou strayest, far or near,
Delos was still of all thy haunts most dear.
Thither the robed Ionians take their way
With wife and child to keep thy holiday,
Invoke thy favor on each manly game,
And dance and sing in honor of thy name.

[5] That there was also a poetical contest in which the Ionians went to contend is shown again by the following, taken from the same hymn. After celebrating the Delian dance of the women, he ends his song of praise with these verses, in which he also alludes to himself:—

3.104
426/5
6th Year/Winter
DELOS
The Athenians purify Delos and celebrate the first Delian Games.

3.103.1a Inessa: Map 3.115. This follows the last narrative concerning Sicily at 3.99.
3.103.1b Syracuse: Map 3.115.
3.103.3a Locri (Epizephyrian, in Italy): Map 3.115.
3.103.3b Caicinus river, probable course: Map 3.115. Events in Sicily are picked up again in 3.115.
3.104.1a Delos: Map 3.93, BY. This purification, and the Carian artifacts discovered when the graves were dug up, is mentioned in

1.8. Further purification steps are described in 5.1.
3.104.2a Rhenea: Map 3.93, BY.
3.104.2b See Appendix I, Classical Greek Religious Festivals, §5 and 8. These festivals often included athletic and cultural contests like those held every five years at Delos.
3.104.3a Ephesus: Map 4.44, AY.

Well, may Apollo keep you all! and so,
Dear hearts, goodbye—yet tell me not I go
Out from your hearts; and if in after hours
Some other wanderer in this world of ours
Touch at your shores, and ask your maidens here
Who sings the songs the sweetest to your ear,
Think of me then, and answer with a smile,
A blind old man of Scio's rocky isle.

[6] Homer thus attests that there was a great assembly and festival at Delos in ancient times. Later, although the islanders and the Athenians continued to send the choirs of dancers with sacrifices, the contests and most of the ceremonies were abolished, probably through adversity, until the Athenians celebrated the games upon this occasion with the novelty of horse races.

The same winter the Ambraciots, as they had promised Eurylochus when they retained his army,[1a] marched out against Amphilochian Argos[1b] with three thousand hoplites, and invading the Argive territory occupied Olpae,[1c] a stronghold on a hill near the sea, which had been formerly fortified by the Acarnanians[1d] and used as the court of justice for their nation, and which lies about two miles and three-quarters from the city of Argos upon the seacoast. [2] Meanwhile the Acarnanians went with a part of their forces to the relief of Argos, and with the rest encamped in Amphilochia[2a] at the place called Crenae,[2b] or the Wells, to watch for Eurylochus and his Peloponnesians, and to prevent their passing through and joining up with the Ambraciots. [3] They also sent for Demosthenes, the commander of the Aetolian expedition,[3a] to be their leader, and for the twenty Athenian ships that were cruising off the Peloponnesus under the command of Aristotle son of Timocrates, and Hierophon son of Antimnestus. [4] For their part, the Ambraciots at Olpae sent a messenger to their own city[4a] to beg them to come with their whole levy to their assistance, fearing that the army of Eurylochus might not be able to pass through the Acarnanians, and that they might themselves be obliged to fight on their own, or be unable to retreat if they wished, without danger.

Meanwhile Eurylochus and his Peloponnesians, learning that the Ambraciots at Olpae had arrived, set out from Proschium[1a] with all haste to join them, and crossing the Achelous[1b] advanced through Acarnania (which they

3.105
426/5
6th Year/Winter
AMPHILOCHIA
Ambracia attacks Amphilochia; allies of both sides march to help.

3.106
426/5
6th Year/Winter
AMPHILOCHIA
Eurylochus joins the Ambraciots at Olpae.

3.105.1a This continues the narrative that ended at 3.102.
3.105.1b Amphilochian Argos, possible location: Map 3.106, inset.
3.105.1c Olpae, possible location: Map 3.106, inset.
3.105.1d Acarnania: Map 3.106, AX.
3.105.2a Amphilochia: Map 3.106, AY and inset.
3.105.2b Crenae, possible location: Map 3.106, inset.

3.105.3a For Demosthenes' Aetolian expedition, see 3.95–98.
3.105.4a Ambracia: Map 3.106, AX.
3.106.1a Proschium: Map 3.106, BY.
3.106.1b Achelous river: Map 3.106, BY.

MAP 3.106 EURYLOCHUS' AND DEMOSTHENES'
CAMPAIGN IN AMPHILOCHIA[1c]

found deserted by its population, who had gone to the relief of Amphilochian Argos);[1c] keeping on their right the city of Stratus[1d] and its garrison, and on their left the rest of Acarnania. [2] Traversing the territory of the Stratians, they advanced through Phytia, next, skirting Medeon, through Limnaea:[2a] after which they left Acarnania behind them and entered a friendly country, that of the Agraeans.[2b] [3] From thence they reached and crossed Mount Thyamus,[3a] which belongs to the Agraeans, and descended into the Argive territory after nightfall, and passing between the city of Argos and the Acarnanian posts at Crenae, joined the Ambraciots at Olpae.

Uniting here at daybreak, they halted at the place called Metropolis,[1a] and encamped. Not long afterwards the Athenians in the twenty ships came into the Ambracian gulf[1b] to support the Argives, with Demosthenes and two hundred Messenian hoplites, and sixty Athenian archers. [2] While the

3.107
426/5
6th Year/Winter
AMPHILOCHIA
Demosthenes plans an
ambush.

3.106.1c The source of the possible sites of Amphilochian Argos, Limnaea, Crenae, Olpae, Metropolis, and Idomene is N.G.L. Hammond, "The Campaign in Amphilochia during the Archidamian War," *The Annual of the British School at Athens*, 1937, 128–40.
3.106.1d Stratus: Map 3.106, AX.

3.106.2a Phytia, Medeon, and Limnaea cannot be definitely located; possible sites for them are shown on Map 3.106, AX, and inset.
3.106.2b Agraea: Map 3.106, AY, and inset.
3.106.3a Mount Thyamus: Map 3.106, inset.
3.107.1a "Metropolis," possible location: Map 3.106, inset.
3.107.1b Ambracian gulf: Map 3.106, AX.

fleet off Olpae blockaded the hill from the sea, the Acarnanians and a few of the Amphilochians (for most of them were perforce detained by the Ambraciots) had already arrived at Argos, and were preparing to give battle to the enemy, having chosen Demosthenes to command the whole of the allied army in concert with their own generals. [3] Demosthenes led them near to Olpae and encamped, a great ravine separating the two armies. During five days they remained inactive; on the sixth both sides formed in order of battle. The army of the Peloponnesians was the largest and outflanked their opponents; and Demosthenes, fearing that his right might be surrounded, placed some four hundred hoplites and light troops in ambush in a sunken road overgrown with bushes. These were to rise up at the onset of battle behind the projecting left wing of the enemy, and to take them in the rear. [4] When both sides were ready they joined battle; Demosthenes being on the right wing with the Messenians and a few Athenians, while the rest of the line was made up of the different divisions of the Acarnanians, and of the Amphilochian dart throwers. The Peloponnesians and Ambraciots were drawn up mixed together, except for the Mantineans, who were massed on the left, without however reaching to the extremity of the wing where Eurylochus and his men confronted the Messenians and Demosthenes.

The Peloponnesians were now well engaged and with their outflanking wing were upon the point of turning their enemy's right when the Acarnanians from the ambuscade set upon them from behind, and broke them at the first attack, without their staying to resist; while the panic into which they fell caused the flight of most of their army, terrified beyond measure at seeing the division of Eurylochus and their best troops cut to pieces. Most of the work was done by Demosthenes and his Messenians, who were posted in this part of the field. [2] Meanwhile the Ambraciots (who are the best soldiers in those parts), and the troops upon the right wing, defeated the division opposed to them and pursued it to Argos. [3] Returning from the pursuit, they found their main body defeated and hard pressed by the Acarnanians; they made good their passage to Olpae with difficulty, suffering heavy loss on the way, as they dashed on without discipline or order, except for the Mantineans, who kept their ranks better than any in the army during the retreat. The battle did not end until the evening.

The next day Menedaïus, who on the death of Eurylochus and Macarius had succeeded to the sole command, being at a loss after so severe a defeat how to stay and sustain a siege, cut off as he was by land and by the Athenian fleet by sea, and equally unable to retreat in safety, opened a parley with Demosthenes and the Acarnanian generals for a truce and permission to re-

3.108
426/5
6th Year/Winter
AMPHILOCHIA
The Peloponnesians and Ambraciots are defeated.

3.109
426/5
6th Year/Winter
AMPHILOCHIA
The Peloponnesians secretly request and receive permission to withdraw.

treat, and at the same time for the recovery of the dead. [2] The dead they gave back to him, and setting up a trophy[2a] took up their own also to the number of about three hundred. The requested retreat they refused publicly to the army; but permission to depart without delay was secretly granted to the Mantineans and to Menedaïus and the other commanders and principal men of the Peloponnesians by Demosthenes and his Acarnanian colleagues. They desired thus to strip the Ambraciots and their foreign mercenaries of their Peloponnesian supporters; and, above all, to discredit the Spartans and Peloponnesians with the Hellenes in those parts, as traitors and self-seekers. [3] While the enemy was taking up his dead and hastily burying them as he could, [and] those who obtained permission were secretly planning their retreat, [3.110.1] word was brought to Demosthenes and the Acarnanians that the Ambraciots from the city, in compliance with the first message from Olpae,[1a] were on the march with their whole levy through Amphilochia to join their countrymen at Olpae, knowing nothing of what had occurred. [2] Demosthenes prepared to march with his army against them, and meanwhile sent on at once a strong division to set ambushes on the roads and occupy the strong positions.

In the meantime the Mantineans and others included in the agreement went out under the pretense of gathering herbs and firewood, and stole off by twos and threes, picking on the way the things which they professed to have come out for, until they had gone some distance from Olpae, when they quickened their pace. [2] The Ambraciots and such of the rest as had accompanied them in larger parties, seeing them going on, pushed on in their turn, and began running in order to catch up to them. [3] The Acarnanians at first thought that all alike were departing without permission, and began to pursue the Peloponnesians; and believing that they were being betrayed, even threw a dart or two at some of their own generals who tried to stop them and told them that leave had been given. Eventually, however, they let pass the Mantineans and Peloponnesians, and slew only the Ambraciots, [4] there being much dispute and difficulty in distinguishing whether a man was an Ambraciot or a Peloponnesian. The number thus slain was about two hundred; the rest escaped into the bordering territory of Agraea,[4a] and found refuge with Salynthius, the friendly king of the Agraeans.

Meanwhile the Ambraciots from the city arrived at Idomene.[1a] Idomene consists of two lofty hills, the highest of which the troops sent on by Demosthenes succeeded in occupying after nightfall, unobserved by the Ambraciots, who had previously ascended the smaller and bivouacked upon it. [2] After supper Demosthenes set out with the rest of the army, as soon as it was evening; himself with half his force making for the pass, and the remainder going by the Amphilochian hills. [3] At dawn he fell upon the

3.109.2a Truce, return of the dead, and trophy, all according to the ritual of hoplite warfare; see Appendix F, Land Warfare, §6.
3.110.1a The message referred to can be found in 3.105.4.
3.111.4a Agraea: Map 3.106, AX, and inset.
3.112.1a Idomene, possible location: Map 3.106, inset.

3.110
426/5
6th Year/Winter
AMPHILOCHIA
Demosthenes learns of the approach of another Ambraciot army.

3.111
426/5
6th Year/Winter
AMPHILOCHIA
The Peloponnesians attempt to leave their Ambraciot allies and escape.

3.112
426/5
6th Year/Winter
AMPHILOCHIA
Demosthenes routs the Ambraciot reinforcements in a dawn attack.

Ambraciots while they were still abed, ignorant of what had passed, and fully thinking that it was their own countrymen—[4] Demosthenes having purposely put the Messenians[4a] in front with orders to address them in the Doric dialect, and thus to inspire confidence in the sentinels who would not be able to see them, as it was still night. [5] In this way he routed their army as soon as he attacked it, slaying most of them where they were, the rest breaking away in flight over the hills, [6] hindered by the fact that they wore heavy armor against a light-armed foe. The roads, however, were already occupied, and while the Amphilochians knew their own country, the Ambraciots were ignorant of it and could not tell which way to turn, and so fell into ravines and into the ambushes which had been set for them, and perished there. [7] In their manifold efforts to escape some even turned to the sea, which was not far off, and seeing the Athenian ships coasting along shore just while the action was going on, swam off to them, thinking it better in the panic they were in, to perish, if perish they must, by the hands of the Athenians, than by those of the barbarous and detested Amphilochians. [8] Of the large Ambraciot force destroyed in this manner, only a few reached the city in safety; while the Acarnanians, after stripping the dead and setting up a trophy, returned to Argos.

The next day a herald arrived from the Ambraciots who had fled from Olpae to the Agraeans, to ask leave to take up the dead that had fallen after the first engagement, when they left the camp with the Mantineans and their companions, without, like them, having had permission to do so. [2] At the sight of the arms of the Ambraciots from the city, the herald was astonished at their number, knowing nothing of the disaster and fancying that they were those of their own party. [3] Someone asked him what he was so astonished at, and how many of them had been killed, fancying in his turn that this was the herald from the troops at Idomene. He replied, "About two hundred"; upon which his interrogator took him up, saying, [4] "Why, the arms you see here are of more than a thousand." The herald replied, "Then they are not the arms of those who fought with us?" The other answered, "Yes, they are, if at least you fought at Idomene yesterday." "But we fought with no one yesterday; but the day before in the retreat." "However that may be, we fought yesterday with those who came to reinforce you from the city of the Ambraciots." [5] When the herald heard this and knew that the reinforcement from the city had been destroyed, he broke into wailing, and stunned at the magnitude of the present evils, went away at once without having performed his errand, or again asking for the dead bodies.[5a] [6] Indeed, this was by far the greatest disaster that befell any one Hellenic city in an equal number of days during this war; and I have not set down the number of the dead, because the amount stated seems so out of proportion to the size of the city as to be incredible.

3.112.4a These Messenians, although settled now in Naupactus (see note 3.75.1a), were Dorians from Messenia in the Peloponnesus (Map 4.5, BX), and spoke the contemporary Doric dialect of Greek. See

Appendix H, Ancient Greek Dialects and Ethnic Groups, §9.
3.113.5a The herald's errand: see Appendix F, Land Warfare, §6.

In any case I know that if the Acarnanians and Amphilochians had wished to take Ambracia as the Athenians and Demosthenes advised, they would have done so without striking a blow; as it was, they feared that if the Athenians had it they would be worse neighbors to them than the present.

3.114
426/5
6th Year/Winter
AMPHILOCHIA
Demosthenes returns to Athens. The Amphilochians and Ambraciots make peace.

After this the Acarnanians allotted a third of the spoils to the Athenians, and divided the rest among their own different cities. The share of the Athenians was captured on the voyage home; the arms now deposited in the Attic temples are three hundred panoplies, which the Acarnanians set apart for Demosthenes, and which he brought to Athens in person, his return to his country after the Aetolian disaster being rendered less hazardous by this exploit. [2] The Athenians in the twenty ships also went off to Naupactus. The Acarnanians and Amphilochians, after the departure of Demosthenes and the Athenians, granted the Ambraciots and Peloponnesians who had taken refuge with Salynthius and the Agraeans a free retreat from Oeniadae,[2a] to which place they had removed from the country of Salynthius, [3] and for the future concluded with the Ambraciots a treaty and alliance for one hundred years, upon the terms following. It was to be a defensive, not an offensive, alliance; the Ambraciots could not be required to march with the Acarnanians against the Peloponnesians, nor the Acarnanians with the Ambraciots against the Athenians; for the rest the Ambraciots were to give up the places and hostages that they held of the Amphilochians, and not to give help to Anactorium,[3a] which was at enmity with the Acarnanians. [4] With this arrangement they put an end to the war. After this the Corinthians sent a garrison of their own citizens to Ambracia, composed of three hundred hoplites, under the command of Xenocleides son of Euthycles, who reached their destination after a difficult journey across the continent. Such was the history of the affair of Ambracia.

3.115
426/5
6th Year/Winter
SICILY
The Athenians send reinforcements to Sicily.

The same winter the Athenians in Sicily[1a] made a descent from their ships upon the territory of Himera,[1b] in concert with the Sicels, who had invaded its borders from the interior, and also sailed to the islands of Aeolus.[1c] [2] Upon their return to Rhegium they found the Athenian general, Pythodorus son of Isolochus, come to supersede Laches in the command of the fleet. [3] The allies in Sicily had sailed to Athens and induced the Athenians to send out more vessels to their assistance, pointing out that the Syracusans who already commanded their land were making efforts to get together a navy, to avoid being any longer excluded from the sea by a few vessels. [4] The Athenians proceeded to man forty ships to send to them, thinking that the war in Sicily would thus be the sooner ended, and also

3.114.2a Oeniadae: Map 3.106, BX.
3.114.3a Anactorium: Map 3.106, AX.
3.115.1a This picks up the Sicilian narrative from 3.103.
3.115.1b Himera: Map 3.115.

3.115.1c Aeolian (Lipari) islands: Map 3.115.

MAP 3.115
SICILIAN OPERATION,
426/5

wishing to exercise their navy.[4a] [5] One of the generals, Pythodorus, was accordingly sent out with a few ships; Sophocles son of Sostratides, and Eurymedon son of Thucles, being destined to follow with the main body. [6] Meanwhile Pythodorus had taken the command of Laches' ships, and toward the end of winter sailed against the Locrian fort, which Laches had formerly taken, and returned after being defeated in battle by the Locrians.[6a]

In the first days of this spring, the stream of fire issued from Etna,[1a] as on former occasions, and destroyed some land of the Catanians,[1b] who live upon Mount Etna, which is the largest mountain in Sicily. [2] Fifty years, it is said, had elapsed since the last eruption, there having been three in all since the Hellenes have inhabited Sicily. [3] Such were the events of this winter; and with it ended the sixth year of this war, of which Thucydides was the historian.

3.116
426/5
6th Year/Winter
SICILY
Mount Etna erupts.

3.115.4a The story of these forty ships is contin-
    ued at 4.2.
3.115.6a The location of this fort is unknown. It
    was probably the fort on the River Halex,
    captured by Laches in 3.99 and undoubt-

edly retaken by the Locrians. Locri
    (Epizephyrian): Map 3.115.
3.116.1a Mount Etna: Map 3.115.
3.116.1b Catana: Map 3.115.

BOOK FOUR

Next summer, about the time of the grain's coming into ear, ten Syracusan[1a] and as many Locrian[1b] vessels sailed to Messana,[1c] in Sicily, and occupied the city upon the invitation of the inhabitants; and Messana revolted from the Athenians. [2] The Syracusans contrived this chiefly because they saw that the place afforded an approach to Sicily, and feared that the Athenians might hereafter use it as a base for attacking them with a larger force; the Locrians because they wished to carry on hostilities from both sides of the Strait[2a] and to reduce their enemies, the people of Rhegium.[2b] [3] Meanwhile, the Locrians had invaded the Rhegian territory with all their forces, to prevent their assisting Messana, and also at the request of some exiles from Rhegium who were with them. Moreover, the long-standing factions by which that city had been torn rendered it for the moment incapable of resistance, and thus furnished an additional temptation to the invaders. [4] After devastating the country the Locrian land forces retired, their ships remaining to guard Messana, while others were being manned for the same destination to carry on the war from there.[4a]

About the same time in the spring, before the corn was ripe, the Peloponnesians and their allies invaded Attica under Agis son of Archidamus, king of the Spartans, and established themselves there and laid waste the country. [2] Meanwhile the Athenians sent off to Sicily the forty ships which they had been preparing, with the remaining generals Eurymedon and Sophocles; [3] their colleague Pythodorus having already preceded them there.[3a] These had also instructions as they sailed by to assist the Corcyraeans[3b] in the city, who were being plundered by the exiles in the mountain.[3c] To support these exiles sixty Peloponnesian vessels had recently

4.1.1a	Syracuse: Map 3.115.
4.1.1b	Locri (Epizephyrian), in Italy: Map 3.115.
4.1.1c	Messana: Map 3.115.
4.1.2a	The "Strait" referred to here is the Strait of Messana, between Rhegium on the toe of Italy and the island of Sicily near the Sicilian city of Messana; see Map 3.115.
4.1.2b	Rhegium: Map 3.115.

4.1.4a	The narrative of Sicilian events will be continued in 4.24.
4.2.3a	These preparations were mentioned in 3.115.
4.2.3b	Corcyra: Map 4.5, AX.
4.2.3c	Mount Istone: Map 4.5, AX. These oligarchic partisans were last mentioned in 3.85.

sailed, it being thought that the famine raging in the city would make it easy for them to reduce it. [4] Demosthenes also, who had remained without employment since his return from Acarnania,[4a] applied for and obtained permission to use the fleet, if he wished, upon the coast of the Peloponnesus.

4.3
425
7th year/Summer
PYLOS
A storm forces the Athenian fleet to put into Pylos. Demosthenes wants to fortify the place but the generals refuse.

Off Laconia they heard that the Peloponnesian ships were already at Corcyra, upon which Eurymedon and Sophocles wished to hasten to the island, but Demosthenes required them first to touch at Pylos and do what was wanted there, before continuing their voyage. While they were making objections, a squall chanced to come on and carried the fleet into Pylos.[1a] [2] Demosthenes at once urged them to fortify the place, as this was the reason why he had come on the voyage. He made them observe that there was plenty of stone and timber on the spot and that the place was strong by nature, and together with much of the country round unoccupied; Pylos, or Coryphasium, as the Spartans call it, lies about forty-five miles distant from Sparta in the former country of the Messenians. [3] The commanders told him that there was no lack of desert headlands in the Peloponnesus if he wished to put the city to expense by occupying them. He, however, thought that this place was distinguished from others of the kind by having a harbor close by; while the Messenians, the old natives of the country, speaking the same dialect as the Spartans,[3a] could do them the greatest harm by their incursions from it, and would at the same time be a trusty garrison.

4.4
425
7th year/Summer
PYLOS
The bored Athenian soldiers suddenly and impulsively decide to build a fort.

After speaking to the captains of companies on the subject, and failing to persuade either the generals or the soldiers, he remained inactive with the rest from stress of weather; until the soldiers themselves wanting occupation were seized with a sudden impulse to go round and fortify the place. [2] Accordingly they set to work in earnest, and having no iron tools,[2a] picked up stones, and put them together as they happened to fit, and where mortar was needed, carried it on their backs for want of hods, stooping down to make it stay on, and clasping their hands together behind to prevent it falling off; [3] sparing no effort to complete the most vulnerable points before the arrival of the Spartans, most of the place being sufficiently strong by nature without further fortification.

4.5
425
7th year/Summer
SPARTA
The Spartans make light of the news about Pylos and permit the Athenians to complete their fort.

Meanwhile the Spartans were celebrating a festival, and also at first made light of the news, thinking that whenever they chose to take the field the place would be immediately evacuated by the enemy or easily taken by force. The absence of their army before Athens also had something to do with their delay. [2] The Athenians fortified the place on the land side and where it most required it in six days, and leaving Demosthenes with five

4.2.4a	Acarnania: Map 4.5, BX.
4.3.1a	Pylos: Map 4.5, BX.
4.3.3a	Originally Messenians, but now settled in Naupactus. For the Spartan (Dorian)

dialect, see Appendix H, Dialects and Ethnic Groups, §7–9.

4.4.2a Literally, having no masonry tools (*lithourga*) for cutting and shaping stone.

MAP 4.5   THE OPENING OF THE PYLOS CAMPAIGN

ships to garrison it, hastened with the main body of the fleet on their voyage to Corcyra and Sicily.

As soon as the Peloponnesians in Attica[1a] heard of the occupation of Pylos, they hurried back home, the Spartans and their king Agis thinking that the matter touched them nearly. Besides having made their invasion early in the season while the grain was still green, most of their troops were short of provisions: the weather also was unusually bad for the time of year, and greatly distressed their army. [2] Many reasons thus combined to hasten their departure and to make this invasion a very short one; indeed they stayed only fifteen days in Attica.

About the same time[1a] the Athenian general Simonides getting together a few Athenians from the garrisons, and a number of the allies in those parts, took by treachery the Mendaean[1b] colony of Eion[1c] in Thrace, which was hostile to Athens, but he had no sooner done so than the Chalcidians[1d] and Bottiaeans[1e] came up and beat him out of it, with the loss of many of his soldiers.[1f]

On the return of the Peloponnesians from Attica the Spartans themselves and the nearest of the *perioikoi* at once set out for Pylos,[1a] the other Spartans following more slowly as they had just come in from another campaign. [2] Word was also sent round the Peloponnesus to come as quickly as possible to Pylos; while the sixty Peloponnesian ships were sent for from Corcyra,[2a] and being dragged by their crews across the isthmus of Leucas,[2b] passed unperceived by the Athenian squadron at Zacynthus,[2c] and reached Pylos, where the land forces had arrived before them. [3] Before the Peloponnesian fleet sailed in, Demosthenes found time to send out unobserved two ships to inform Eurymedon and the Athenians on board the fleet at Zacynthus of the danger to Pylos and to summon them to his assistance. [4] While the ships hastened on their voyage in obedience to the orders of Demosthenes, the Spartans prepared to assault the fort by land and sea, hoping to capture with ease a work constructed in haste, and held by a feeble garrison. [5] Meanwhile, as they expected the Athenian ships to arrive from Zacynthus, they intended, if they failed to take the place before, to block the entrances of the harbor to prevent their being able to anchor inside it. [6] For the island of Sphacteria[6a] stretches along in a line close in front of the harbor and at once makes it safe and narrows its entrances, leaving a passage for two ships on the side nearest

---

4.6.1a	Attica: Map 4.5, BY.	4.7.1f	The narrative of events in Thrace is
4.7.1a	This chapter deals with events in Thrace,		picked up again in 4.78.
	which was last mentioned in 2.101.	4.8.1a	Pylos: Map 4.5, BX. For information
4.7.1b	Mende, on the Chalcidian peninsula of		about the Spartan class of *perioikoi*, see
	Pallene: Map 4.5, AX.		the Glossary and Appendix C, Spartan
4.7.1c	This Eion in Thrace, whose location is		Institutions, §9.
	unknown, cannot be the more familiar	4.8.2a	Corcyra: Map 4.5, AX.
	Eion on the Strymon River (Map 4.5,	4.8.2b	Isthmus of Leucas: Map 4.5, AX.
	AY), which had for some time now been	4.8.2c	Zacynthus: Map 4.5, BX.
	subject to the Athenians.	4.8.6a	Island of Sphacteria: Map 4.8.
4.7.1d	Chalcidice: Map 4.5, AX.		
4.7.1e	Bottiaeans, living at that time in Bottica:		
	Map 4.5, AX.		

MAP 4.8 POSSIBLE LOCATIONS FOR
THE "HARBOR" AT PYLOS

Pylos and the Athenian fortifications, and for eight or nine ships on that
next the mainland on the other side: for the rest, the island was entirely
covered with wood, and without paths through not being inhabited, and
about fifteen *stades* in length.[6b] [7] The Spartans meant to close the
entrances with a line of ships placed close together with their prows
turned toward the sea and, meanwhile, fearing that the enemy might make
use of the island to operate against them, carried over some *hoplites*[7a] to it,
stationing others along the coast. [8] By this means both the island and
the continent would be hostile to the Athenians, as they would be unable
to land on either; and since the shore of Pylos itself outside the inlet
toward the open sea had no harbor, there would be no point that the
Athenians could use as a base from which to relieve their countrymen.
Thus the Spartans would in all probability become masters of the place
without a sea fight or risk, as there had been little preparation for the

4.8.6b Thucydides erroneously writes that
Sphacteria's length is about 15 *stades* (1.6
miles), but its true length is closer to 24
or 25 stades (3 miles); the Attic stade was
607 feet, the Olympic stade 630.8 feet.
All of Thucydides' distance measurements
are given in stades and were rounded off
to miles or furlongs by Crawley and to
just miles in this edition.
4.8.7a *Hoplite* is the Greek word for a heavily
armed infantryman. See Glossary and
Appendix F, §2.

227

occupation and there was no food there.[8a] [9] This being decided, they carried the hoplites over to the island, drafting them by lot from all the companies. Some others had crossed over before in relief parties, but these last who were left there were four hundred and twenty in number, with their *Helot*[9a] attendants, and were commanded by Epitadas son of Molobrus.

Meanwhile Demosthenes, seeing that the Spartans were about to attack him by sea and land simultaneously, was himself not idle. He drew up under the fortification the *triremes*[1a] remaining to him of those which had been left him and enclosed them in a stockade, arming the sailors taken out of them with poor shields, most of them made of osier,[1b] it being impossible to procure arms in such a desert place. Indeed, even these were obtained from a thirty-oared Messenian privateer and a boat belonging to some Messenians who happened to have come to them. Among these Messenians were forty hoplites, whom he made use of with the rest. [2] Posting most of his men, unarmed and armed, upon the best fortified and strong points of the place facing the interior, with orders to repel any attack of the land forces, he picked sixty hoplites and a few archers from his whole force, and with these went outside the wall down to the sea, where he thought that the enemy would most likely attempt to land. Although the ground was difficult and rocky, looking toward the open sea, the fact that this was the weakest part of the wall would, he thought, encourage their ardor, [3] as the Athenians, confident in their naval superiority, had here paid little attention to their defenses, and the enemy, if he could force a landing, might feel sure of taking the place. [4] At this point, accordingly, going down to the water's edge, he posted his hoplites to prevent, if possible, a landing, and encouraged them in the following terms:

> "Soldiers and comrades in this adventure, I hope that none of you in our present strait will think to show his wit by exactly calculating

4.9
425
7th year/Summer
PYLOS
Demosthenes, joined by some Messenians, prepares to defend Pylos and personally leads the defense against an anticipated Spartan amphibious attack.

4.10
425
7th year/Summer
PYLOS
Demosthenes addresses his troops, advising them to offer firm resistance at the water's edge to repulse the enemy's amphibious assault.

4.8.8a Thucydides' description of the Pylos campaign continues to be the subject of much debate; indeed, scholars have not yet reached a consensus even on such basic elements as the location of the harbor at the site. Most have identified Thucydides' harbor as the entire Bay of Navarino (Map 4.8), despite general recognition that it is much too large for an ancient "harbor," and that its wide and deep southern entrance could not have been blocked by Peloponnesian triremes. The Bay Harbor does, however, accord with important parts of the text, and would explain why the Spartans seem not to have carried out their blockade. I have argued that the harbor may best be located in a cove at the south end of Pylos itself, near the east end of the Sikia Channel (Map 4.8). The main virtue of the Cove Harbor is that it has narrow entrances that *could* be blocked (Thucydides says three times that this was the Spartan plan), and that the feasibility of this

Spartan plan may provide an explanation for why the Spartans exposed their fleet at all here after avoiding naval battle for four years, why they placed troops on Sphacteria, and why the Athenian fleet went to Prote (Map 4.5, BX) and not to Pylos on the night before the naval battle (4.13.3). But while the Cove Harbor fits some parts of Thucydides' description of the site, and explains some parts of his story, it conflicts with others, and seems to be too small, in the opinion of many, for the action described to have taken place there. See A.W. Gomme, *A Historical Commentary on Thucydides,* iii (Oxford, 1956), 438–63, 466–89. See also R. B. Strassler, "The Harbor at Pylos: 425 B.C.," Note, *Journal of Hellenic Studies,* cviii (1988), 198.

4.8.9a For information on *Helots,* see Appendix C, Spartan Institutions, §3–4.

4.9.1a *Triremes* were the standard warship of the period; see Appendix G, Trireme Warfare, §4–7.

all the perils that encompass us, but that you will rather hasten to close with the enemy, without staying to weigh the odds, seeing in this your best chance of safety. In emergencies like ours calculation is out of place; the sooner the danger is faced the better. [2] To my mind also most of the chances are for us, if we will only stand fast and not throw away our advantages, overawed by the numbers of the enemy. [3] One of the points in our favor is the awkwardness of the landing. This, however, only helps us if we stand our ground. If we give way it will, without a defender, prove practicable enough, in spite of its natural difficulty, without a defender; and the enemy will instantly become more formidable from the difficulty he will have in retreating, supposing that we succeed in repulsing him. Surely we shall find it easier to repel him while he is on board his ships, than after he has landed and meets us on equal terms. [4] As to his numbers, these need not too much alarm you. Large as they may be he can only engage in small detachments, from the difficulty of landing. Besides, the numerical superiority that we have to meet is not that of an army on land with everything else equal, but of troops on board ship, upon an element where many favorable accidents are required to act effectively. [5] I therefore consider that his difficulties may be fairly set against our numerical deficiencies, and at the same time I charge you as Athenians who know by experience what landing from ships on a hostile territory means, and how impossible it is to drive back an enemy determined enough to stand his ground and not to be frightened away by the surf and the terrors of the ships sailing in, to stand fast in the present emergency, beat back the enemy at the water's edge, and save yourselves and the place."

Thus encouraged by Demosthenes, the Athenians felt more confident, and went down to meet the enemy, posting themselves along the edge of the sea. [2] The Spartans now put themselves in motion and simultaneously assaulted the fortification with their land forces and with their ships, forty-three in number, under their admiral, Thrasymelidas son of Cratesicles, a *Spartiate*,[2a] who made his attack just where Demosthenes expected. [3] The Athenians had thus to defend themselves on both sides, from the land and from the sea; the enemy rowing up in small detachments, the one relieving the other—it being impossible for many to engage at once—and showing great ardor and cheering each other on, in the endeavor to force a landing and to take the fortification. [4] He who most distinguished himself was Brasidas, captain of a trireme.[4a] Seeing that the captains and steersmen, impressed by the difficulty of the position, hung back even where a landing might have seemed possible, for fear of wrecking their vessels, he

4.11
425
7th year/Summer
PYLOS
The Spartans attack both by land and sea. Brasidas displays unusual zeal and bravery.

4.11.2a   A *Spartiate* is a full citizen of Sparta and a member of the highest Spartan military caste.

4.11.4a   This is Brasidas son of Tellis, now a ship captain, whom we have met previously as

a local commander at Methone (2.25.2), as a fleet commissioner (2.85.1), and then as adviser to the admiral (3.69.1).

shouted out to them that they must never allow the enemy to fortify himself in their country for the sake of saving timber, but must shiver their vessels and force a landing. He bade the allies, instead of hesitating in such a moment, to sacrifice their ships for Sparta in return for her many benefits, to run them boldly aground, land in one way or another, and make themselves masters of the place and its garrison.

Not content with this exhortation, he forced his own steersman to run his ship ashore, and stepping onto the gangway, was endeavoring to land when he was beaten back by the Athenians and after receiving many wounds fainted away. Falling into the bow, his shield slipped off his arm into the sea, and being thrown ashore was picked up by the Athenians and afterwards used for the trophy[1a] which they set up for this attack. [2] The rest also did their best, but were not able to land, owing to the difficulty of the ground and the unflinching tenacity of the Athenians. [3] It was a strange reversal of the order of things for Athenians to be fighting from the land and from Laconian land too, against Spartans coming from the sea; while Spartans were trying to land from shipboard in their own country, now become hostile, to attack Athenians, although the former were chiefly famous at the time as an inland people and superior by land, the latter as a maritime people with a navy that had no equal.[3a]

After continuing their attacks during that day and most of the next, the Peloponnesians desisted, and the day after sent some of their ships to Asine[1a] for timber to make siege engines with which they hoped to take, in spite of its height, the wall opposite the harbor where the landing was easiest. [2] At this moment the Athenian fleet from Zacynthus[2a] arrived, now numbering fifty sail, having been reinforced by some of the ships on guard at Naupactus[2b] and by four Chian[2c] vessels. [3] Seeing both the coast and the island crowded with hoplites, and the hostile ships in the harbor showing no signs of sailing out, and at a loss where to anchor, they sailed for the moment to the desert island of Prote,[3a] not far off, where they passed the night. The next day they got under weigh in readiness to engage in the open sea if the enemy chose to put out to meet them, being determined in the event of his not doing so to sail in and attack him. [4] The Spartans did not put out to sea, and having omitted to close the entrances as they had intended, remained quiet on shore, engaged in manning their ships and getting ready, in the case of any one sailing in, to fight in the harbor, which is a fairly large one.

Perceiving this, the Athenians advanced against them through both entrances and falling on the enemy's fleet, most of which was by this time

Margin notes

4.12
425
7th year/Summer
PYLOS
Brasidas is wounded and faints. The Athenians recover his shield and use it for their victory trophy. Thucydides notes the irony of Athenians defending Spartan land against Spartans attacking from the sea.

4.13
425
7th year/Summer
PYLOS
The Spartans attack Pylos for two days without success. The Athenian fleet from Zacynthus arrives and, unable to land at Pylos, camps for the night at Prote. The next morning it attacks the Spartans, who are taken by surprise.

4.14
425
7th year/Summer
PYLOS
The Peloponnesian fleet is routed, but Spartan troops prevent the Athenians from dragging off their beached triremes. The Athenians cruise around Sphacteria to cut off the island's garrison.

Footnotes

4.12.1a   After a battle in ancient Greece, the victorious side raised a trophy, usually a set of captured armor on a pole at or near the battlefield, in thanks to the god who had defeated the enemy. Brasidas reappears next in 4.70.

4.12.3a   This text must have been written a good deal after the battle, as no readers in 425 B.C. would need to be reminded of Athenian supremacy on the sea or Spartan superiority on the land.

4.13.1a   Asine: Map 4.5, BX.
4.13.2a   Zacynthus: Map 4.5, BX.
4.13.2b   Naupactus: Map 4.5, BX.
4.13.2c   Chios: Map 4.5, BY.
4.13.3a   Prote, an island about eight miles north of Pylos up the coast: Map 4.5, BX.

afloat and in line, they at once put it to flight, and giving chase as far as the short distance allowed, disabled a good many vessels and took five, one with its crew on board. Then, dashing in at the rest that had taken refuge on shore, they rammed some that were still being manned before they could put out, and lashed on to their own ships and towed off empty others whose crews had fled. [2] At this sight the Spartans, maddened by a disaster which cut off their men on the island, rushed to the rescue, and going into the sea with their heavy armor, laid hold of the ships and tried to drag them back, each man thinking that success depended on his individual exertions. [3] Great was the mêlée, and quite in contradiction to the naval tactics usual to the two combatants; the Spartans in their excitement and dismay being actually engaged in a sea fight on land, while the victorious Athenians, in their eagerness to push their success as far as possible, were carrying on a land fight from their ships. [4] After great exertions and numerous wounds on both sides they separated, the Spartans saving their empty ships, except those first taken; [5] and both parties returning to their camp, the Athenians set up a trophy, gave back the dead,[5a] secured the wrecks, and at once began to cruise round and carefully watch the island, with its intercepted garrison, while the Peloponnesians on the mainland, whose contingents had now all come up, stayed where they were before Pylos.

When the news of what had happened at Pylos reached Sparta, the disaster was thought so serious that the Spartans resolved that the authorities should go down to the camp and decide on the spot what was best to be done. [2] There, seeing that it was impossible to help their men and not wishing to risk their being reduced by hunger or overpowered by numbers, they determined, with the consent of the Athenian generals, to conclude an armistice at Pylos, to send envoys to Athens to obtain a convention, and to endeavor to get back their men as quickly as possible.

The generals accepting their offers, an armistice was concluded upon the following terms:

That the Spartans should bring to Pylos and deliver to the Athenians the ships that had fought in the late engagement, and all in Laconia[1a] that were vessels of war, and should make no attack on the fortification either by land or by sea. That the Athenians should allow the Spartans on the mainland to send to the men in the island a certain fixed quantity of already kneaded grain, that is to say, two quarts of barley meal, one pint of wine, and a piece of meat for each man, and half the same quantity for a servant. That this allowance should be sent in under the eyes of the Athenians, and that no

4.15
425
7th year/Summer
PYLOS
Worried Spartan authorities arrive at Pylos and quickly conclude an armistice.

4.16
425
7th year/Summer
PYLOS
Thucydides lists the terms of the armistice.

4.14.5a   The setting up of a trophy and the return
           of the bodies of the dead were in accord
           with post-battle ritual of hoplite warfare.
           See Appendix F, Land Warfare, §6.
4.16.1a   Laconia: Map 4.5, BX.

boat should sail to the island except openly. That the Athenians should continue to guard the island the same as before, without however landing upon it, and should refrain from attacking the Peloponnesian troops either by land or by sea. [2] That if either party should infringe any of these terms in the slightest particular, the armistice should be at once void. That the armistice should hold good until the return of the Spartan envoys from Athens—the Athenians sending them thither in a trireme and bringing them back again—and upon the arrival of the envoys should be at an end, and the ships be restored by the Athenians in the same state as they received them. [3] Such were the terms of the armistice, and the ships were delivered over to the number of sixty, and the envoys sent off accordingly.[3a] When they arrived at Athens they spoke as follows:

4.17
425
7th year/Summer
ATHENS
Addressing the Athenian Assembly, Spartan envoys convey their wish to settle the war in a manner consistent with Athenian interests and Spartan dignity in its time of misfortune.

"Athenians, the Spartans sent us to try to find some way of settling the affair of our men on the island, that shall be at once satisfactory to your interests, and as consistent with our dignity in our misfortune as circumstances permit. [2] We can venture to speak at some length without any departure from the habit of our country. Men of few words where many are not wanted, we can be less brief when there is a matter of importance to be discussed and an end to be served by its illustration.[2a] [3] Meanwhile we beg you to take what we may say, not in a hostile spirit, nor as if we thought you ignorant and wished to lecture you, but rather as a suggestion on the best course to be taken, addressed to intelligent judges. [4] You can now, if you choose, employ your present success to advantage, so as to keep what you have got and gain honor and reputation besides, and you can avoid the mistake of those who meet with an extraordinary piece of good fortune, and are led on by hope to grasp continually at something further, through having already succeeded without expecting it. [5] While those who have known most vicissitudes of good and bad, have also and rightly, least confidence in their prosperity; and experience has not been wanting to teach your city and ours this lesson."

4.18
425
7th year/Summer
ATHENS
The Spartan envoys blame Sparta's current troubles on errors of judgment, not loss of power, and urge the Athenians to use their success wisely and moderately.

"To be convinced of this you have only to look at our present misfortune. What power in Hellas stood higher than we did? And yet we have come to you, although we formerly thought ourselves more able to grant what we are now here to ask. [2] Nevertheless, we have not been brought to this by any decay in our power, or through having our heads turned by aggrandizement; no, our resources are what they have always been, and our error has been an error of judgment, to which all are equally liable. [3] Accordingly the prosperity which your city now enjoys, and the accessions that it has lately received,

---

4.16.3a   The narrative of events at Pylos will be taken up again in 4.23.
4.17.2a   The Spartans here acknowledge their reputation for speaking "laconically"—that

is, bluntly, ungraciously, and with as few words as possible. See Appendix C, Spartan Institutions, §2, and Appendix H, Dialects and Ethnic Groups, §8.

must not make you suppose that fortune will be always with you. [4] Indeed sensible men are prudent enough to treat their gains as precarious, just as they would also keep a clear head in adversity, and think that war, so far from staying within the limit to which a combatant may wish to confine it, will run the course that its chances prescribe; and thus, not being puffed up by confidence in military success, they are less likely to come to grief and most ready to make peace, if they can, while their fortune lasts. [5] This, Athenians, you have a good opportunity to do now with us, and thus to escape the possible disasters which may follow upon your refusal, and the consequent imputation of having owed to accident even your present advantages when you might have left behind you a reputation for power and wisdom which nothing could endanger."

"The Spartans accordingly invite you to make a treaty and to end the war, and offer peace and alliance and the most friendly and intimate relations in every way and on every occasion between us; and in return ask for the men on the island, thinking it better for both parties not to hold out to the end, hoping that some favorable accident will enable the men to force their way out, or of their being compelled to succumb under the pressure of blockade. [2] Indeed if great enmities are ever to be really settled, we think it will be, not by the system of revenge and military success, and by forcing an opponent to swear to a treaty to his disadvantage; but when the more fortunate combatant waives his privileges and, guided by gentler feelings, conquers his rival in generosity and accords peace on more moderate conditions than expected. [3] From that moment, instead of the debt of revenge which violence must entail, his adversary owes a debt of generosity to be paid in kind, and is inclined by honor to stand by his agreement. [4] And men more often act in this manner toward their greatest enemies than where the quarrel is of less importance; they are also by nature as glad to give way to those who first yield to them, as they are apt to be provoked by arrogance to risks condemned by their own judgment."

"To apply this to ourselves: if peace was ever desirable for both parties, it is surely so at the present moment, before anything irremediable befall us and force us to hate you eternally, personally as well as politically, and you to miss the advantages that we now offer you. [2] While the issue is still in doubt, and you have reputation and our friendship in prospect, and we the compromise of our misfortune before anything fatal occur, let us be reconciled, and for ourselves choose peace instead of war, and grant to the rest of the Hellenes a remission from their sufferings, for which be sure they will think they

4.19
425
7th year/Summer
ATHENS
The Spartan envoys offer Athens a treaty of peace and alliance, pointing out that real peace must arise through generosity, not through military success that spawns a desire for revenge.

4.20
425
7th year/Summer
ATHENS
The Spartan envoys conclude by saying that Athens will receive credit for the ensuing peace, which will endure, since no one in Hellas could challenge the combined hegemony of Athens and Sparta.

have chiefly you to thank. They know not who began this war, but their gratitude for concluding it, as it depends on your decision, will surely be laid at your door. [3] By such a decision you can become firm friends with the Spartans at their own invitation, which you do not force from them, but oblige them by accepting. [4] And from this friendship consider the advantages that are likely to follow: when Attica and Sparta are in concord, the rest of Hellas, you may be sure, will remain in respectful inferiority before its heads."

Such were the words of the Spartans, their idea being that the Athenians, already desirous of a truce and only kept back by their opposition, would joyfully accept a peace freely offered, and give back the men.[1a] [2] The Athenians, however, having the men on the island, thought that the treaty would be ready for them whenever they chose to make it, and grasped at something further. [3] Foremost to encourage them in this policy was Cleon son of Cleaenetus, a popular leader of the time and very powerful with the multitude, who persuaded them to answer as follows: First, the men in the island must surrender themselves and their arms and be brought to Athens. Next, the Spartans must restore Nisaea,[3a] Pegae,[3b] Troezen,[3c] and Achaea,[3d] all places acquired not by arms, but by the previous convention, under which they had been ceded by Athens herself at a moment of disaster, when a truce was more necessary to her than at present.[3e] This done they might take back their men, and make a truce for as long as both parties might agree.

To this answer the envoys made no reply, but asked that commissioners might be chosen with whom they might confer on each point, and quietly talk the matter over and try to come to some agreement. [2] Hereupon Cleon violently assailed them, saying that he knew from the first that they had no right intentions, and that it was clear enough now by their refusing to speak before the people, and wanting to confer in secret with a committee of two or three. No! if they meant anything honest let them say it out before all. [3] The Spartans, however, seeing that whatever concessions they might be prepared to make in their misfortune, it was impossible to express them before the multitude and lose credit with their allies for a negotiation which might after all miscarry, and on the other hand, that the Athenians would never grant what they asked upon moderate terms, returned from Athens without having effected anything.

Their arrival at once put an end to the armistice at Pylos, and the Spartans asked for the return of their ships according to the truce.[1a] The Athenians, however, alleged an attack on the fort in violation of the truce, and other grievances seemingly not worth mentioning, and refused to give

4.21.1a   Spartan confidence that Athens would welcome peace derived probably from the fact that Athens had sent ambassadors to Sparta to obtain peace in 430 (2.59.2).
4.21.3a   Nisaea: Map 4.21.
4.21.3b   Pegae: Map 4.21.
4.21.3c   Troezen: Map 4.21.
4.21.3d   Achaea: Map 4.21.
4.21.3e   Thucydides refers here to the Thirty Years' Peace Treaty of 446, mentioned in 1.115.
4.23.1a   This continues the narrative of events at Pylos from 4.16.

MAP 4.21
LOCATIONS IN ATHENIAN
PEACE DEMANDS

them back, insisting upon the clause by which the slightest infringement made the armistice void. The Spartans, after denying the violation and protesting against their bad faith in the matter of the ships, went away and earnestly addressed themselves to the war. [2] Hostilities were now carried on at Pylos by both sides with vigor. The Athenians cruised round the island all day with two ships going different ways; and by night, except on the seaward side in windy weather, anchored round it with their whole fleet, which having been reinforced by twenty ships from Athens come to aid in the blockade, now numbered seventy sail; while the Peloponnesians remained encamped on the mainland, making attacks on the fort, and on the lookout for any opportunity which might offer itself for the deliverance of their men.[2a]

Meanwhile the Syracusans[1a] and their allies in Sicily had brought up to the squadron guarding Messana[1b] the reinforcement which they had been preparing,[1c] and carried on the war from there, [2] incited chiefly by the Locrians[2a] from their hatred of the Rhegians,[2b] whose territory they had invaded with all their forces. [3] The Syracusans also wished to try their fortune at sea, seeing that the Athenians had only a few ships actually at Rhegium, and hearing that the main fleet destined to join them was engaged in blockading the island. [4] A naval victory, they thought, would enable them to blockade Rhegium by sea and land, and to reduce it easily; a success which would at once place their affairs upon a solid basis, as the promontory of Rhegium in Italy and Messana in Sicily are so near each

4.24
425
7th Year/Summer
SICILY
The Syracusans reinforce their fleet at Messana and prepare to attack the Athenians at Rhegium to take control of the strait between the two cities.

4.23.2a   The narration of events at Pylos is
            resumed at 4.26.
4.24.1a   Syracuse: Map 4.25. This continues the
            narrative of events in Sicily from 4.1.
4.24.1b   Messana: Map 4.25.

4.24.1c   For these preparations, see 4.1.4.
4.24.2a   Locri (Epizephyrian): Map 4.25.
4.24.2b   Rhegium: Map 4.25.

other that it would be impossible for the Athenians to cruise against them and command the strait. [5] The strait in question consists of the sea between Rhegium and Messana, at the point where Sicily approaches nearest to the continent, and is the Charybdis through which the story makes Odysseus sail;[5a] and the narrowness of the passage, and the strength of the current that pours in from the vast Tyrrhenian and Sicilian mains,[5b] have rightly given it a bad reputation.

In this strait the Syracusans and their allies were compelled to engage, late in the day, about a merchant ship sailing through, putting out with rather more than thirty ships against sixteen Athenian and eight Rhegian vessels. [2] Defeated by the Athenians they hastily set off, each for himself, to their own stations at Messana and Rhegium, with the loss of one ship; night coming on before the battle was finished. [3] After this the Locrians retired from the Rhegian territory, and the ships of the Syracusans and their allies united and came to anchor at Cape Pelorus,[3a] in the territory of Messana, where their land forces joined them. [4] Here the Athenians and Rhegians sailed up, and seeing the ships unmanned made an attack, in which they in their turn lost one vessel, which was caught by a grappling iron,[4a] the crew saving themselves by swimming. [5] After this the Syracusans got on board their ships, and while they were being towed along shore to Messana, were again attacked by the Athenians, but suddenly headed out to sea and became the assailants, and caused the Athenians to lose another vessel. [6] After thus holding their own in the voyage along shore and in the engagement as above described, the Syracusans sailed on into the harbor of Messana.

[7] Meanwhile the Athenians, having received warning that Camarina[7a] was about to be betrayed to the Syracusans by Archias and his party, sailed to that place; and the Messanians took this opportunity to attack their Chalcidian neighbor, Naxos[7b] by sea and land with all their forces. [8] The first day they forced the Naxians to stay within their walls, and laid waste their country; the next they sailed round with their ships, and laid waste their land on the river Akesines,[8a] while their land forces menaced the city. [9] Meanwhile the Sicels came down from the high country in great numbers to aid against the Messanians; and the Naxians, elated at the sight, and animated by a belief that the Leontines[9a] and their other Hellenic allies were coming to their support, suddenly sallied out from the city, and attacked and routed the Messanians killing more than a thousand of them; while the remainder suffered severely in their retreat home, being attacked

4.25
425
7th Year/Summer
SICILY
Fighting on land and sea between Athenians, Naxians, Rhegians, Sicels, and Leontines, on one side, and Syracusans, Locrians, and Messanians, on the other, is inconclusive.

4.24.5a Thucydides refers to the monster whirlpool Charybdis of Homer's *Odyssey*, Book 12.
4.24.5b Tyrrhenian Sea, Sicilian Sea: Map 4.25.
4.25.3a Cape Pelorus: Map 4.25.
4.25.4a Grappling irons were large metal hooks with attached lines that were designed to be thrown so as to catch at the bulwarks (railings) of enemy ships; the lines were then used to pull the hostile ships alongside one another so that crews could engage in hand-to-hand combat. See 7.62.3a and Appendix G, Trireme Warfare, §11.
4.25.7a Camarina: Map 4.25.
4.25.7b Naxos: Map 4.25.
4.25.8a Akesines river: Map 4.25.
4.25.9a Leontini: Map 4.25.

MAP 4.25
EVENTS IN SICILY AND
ITALY, 425

by the barbarians on the road, and most of them cut down. [10] The ships put in to Messana, and afterwards dispersed to their different homes. The Leontines and their allies, with the Athenians, upon this at once turned their arms against the now weakened Messana, and attacked, the Athenians with their ships on the side of the harbor, and the land forces on that of the city. [11] The Messanians, however, sallying out with Demoteles and some Locrians who had been left to garrison the city after the disaster, suddenly attacked and routed most of the Leontine army, killing a great number; upon seeing which the Athenians landed from their ships, and falling on the disordered Messanians, chased them back into the city, and setting up a trophy retired to Rhegium. [12] After this the Hellenes in Sicily continued to make war on each other by land, without the Athenians.[12a]

Meanwhile the Athenians at Pylos[1a] were still besieging the Spartans in the island, the Peloponnesian forces on the continent remaining where they were. [2] The blockade was very laborious for the Athenians from want of food and water; there was no spring except one in the citadel of Pylos itself, and that not a large one, and most of them were obliged to scrape away the gravel on the sea beach and drink such water as they could find. [3] They also suffered from want of room, being encamped in a narrow space; and as there was no anchorage for the ships, some took their meals on shore in their turn, while the others were anchored out at sea.[3a] [4] But their greatest discouragement arose from the unexpectedly long time which it took to reduce a body of men shut up in a desert island, with only brackish water

4.26
425
7th year/Summer
PYLOS
The hardships of the blockading Athenians are described. Spartan Helots risk their lives to bring food to the Sphacteria garrison, and thus win their freedom.

4.25.12a The narrative of events in Sicily is con-
          tinued in 4.58.
4.26.1a   This chapter continues the narrative of
          events at Pylos from 4.23.
4.26.3a   Since a trireme had no space for the
          preparation of food, the crew had to be
          fed ashore; see Appendix G, Trireme
          Warfare, §7.

to drink, a matter which they had imagined would take them only a few days. [5] The fact was, that the Spartans had made advertisement for volunteers to carry into the island flour, wine, cheese, and any other food useful in a siege; high prices being offered, and freedom promised to any of the Helots[5a] who should succeed in doing so. [6] The Helots accordingly were most forward to engage in this risky traffic, putting off from this or that part of the Peloponnesus, and running in by night on the seaward side of the island. [7] They were best pleased, however, when they could catch a wind to carry them in. It was more easy to elude the triremes on guard, when it blew from the seaward, as it then became impossible for them to anchor round the island; while the Helots had their boats valued at their worth in money, and ran them ashore without caring how they landed, being sure to find the soldiers waiting for them at the landing places. But all who risked it in fair weather were taken. [8] Divers also swam in under water from the harbor, dragging by a cord in skins poppyseed mixed with honey, and bruised linseed; these at first escaped notice, but afterwards a lookout was kept for them. [9] In short, both sides tried every possible contrivance, the one to throw in provisions, and the other to prevent their introduction.[9a]

At Athens, meanwhile, the news that the army was in great distress and that grain found its way in to the men in the island caused no small perplexity; and the Athenians began to fear that winter might come on and find them still engaged in the blockade. They saw that the convoying of provisions round the Peloponnesus would be then impossible. The country offered no resources in itself, and even in summer they could not send round enough. The blockade of a place without harbors could then no longer be kept up; and the men would either escape by the siege being abandoned, or would watch for bad weather and sail out in the boats that brought in their grain. [2] What caused still more alarm was the attitude of the Spartans, who must, it was thought by the Athenians, feel themselves on strong ground not to send them any more envoys; and they began to repent having rejected the treaty. [3] Cleon, perceiving the disfavor with which he was regarded for having stood in the way of the convention, now said that their informants did not speak the truth; and upon the messengers recommending that, if they did not believe them, they send some commissioners to see, Cleon himself and Theagenes were chosen by the Athenians as commissioners. [4] Aware that he would now be obliged either to say what had been already said by the men whom he was slandering, or be proved a liar if he said the contrary, he told the Athenians, whom he saw to be not altogether disinclined for a fresh expedition, that instead of sending commissioners and wasting their time and opportunities, if they believed what was told them, they ought to sail against the men. [5] And pointing

4.26.5a   Spartan Helots; see Appendix C, Spartan   4.26.9a   The narrative of events at Pylos is
Institutions, §3–4.   resumed in 4.30.

at Nicias son of Niceratus, then general, whom he hated, he tauntingly said that it would be easy, if they had men for generals, to sail with a force and take those in the island, and that if he had himself been in command, he would have done it.

Nicias, seeing the Athenians murmuring against Cleon for not sailing now if it seemed to him so easy, and further seeing himself the object of attack, told him that for all that the generals cared, he might take what force he chose and make the attempt. [2] At first Cleon fancied that this resignation was merely a figure of speech, and was ready to go, but finding that it was seriously meant, he drew back, and said that Nicias, not he, was general, being now frightened, and having never supposed that Nicias would go so far as to retire in his favor. [3] Nicias, however, repeated his offer and resigned the command against Pylos, calling upon the Athenians to witness that he did so. And as the multitude is wont to do, the more Cleon shrank from the expedition and tried to back out of what he had said, the more they encouraged Nicias to hand over his command, and clamored at Cleon to go. [4] At last, not knowing how to get out of his words, he undertook the expedition, and came forward and said that he was not afraid of the Spartans, but would sail without taking anyone from the city with him except the Lemnians and Imbrians[4a] that were at Athens, with some *peltasts* that had come up from Aenus,[4b] and four hundred archers from elsewhere. With these and the soldiers at Pylos, he would within twenty days either bring the Spartans alive, or kill them on the spot. [5] The Athenians could not help laughing at his empty words, while sensible men comforted themselves with the reflection that they must gain in either circumstance; either they would be rid of Cleon, which they rather hoped, or if disappointed in this expectation, would reduce the Spartans.

After he had settled everything in the assembly, and the Athenians had voted him the command of the expedition, he chose as his colleague Demosthenes, one of the generals at Pylos, and pushed forward the preparations for his voyage. [2] His choice fell upon Demosthenes because he heard that he was contemplating a descent on the island and because the soldiers, distressed by the difficulties of the position and feeling more like besieged than besiegers, were eager to fight it out. Moreover, the firing of the island had increased the confidence of the general. [3] At first he had been afraid that the uninhabited island's pathless woods would favor the enemy, as he might land a large force and yet suffer losses from an attack from an unseen position. He thought the woods would in great measure conceal from him the mistakes and forces of the enemy, while the blunders of his own troops would be quickly detected by the enemy who, retaining always the ability to attack, would fall upon his troops unexpectedly wherever they pleased. [4] If, on the other hand, he should force them to

4.28
425
7th Year/Summer
ATHENS
Nicias withdraws from the command. The Athenian People now insist that Cleon take it and he does so, asking only for peltasts and archers, and promising to return victorious in twenty days.

4.29
425
7th Year/Summer
ATHENS-PYLOS
Cleon chooses Demosthenes as his partner in command and prepares to depart. Thucydides lists the reasons why Demosthenes feared the Spartans on the island, although his forces far outnumbered them.

4.28.4a Lemnos, Imbros: Map 4.5, AY.
4.28.4b *Peltasts* were troops armed only with a small, light shield, a javelin, and a short

sword. Unhindered by body armor, they could move much more quickly than the fully armed hoplite. Aenus: Map 4.5, AY.

engage in the thicket, the smaller number who knew the country would, he thought, have the advantage over the larger who were ignorant of it, and thus his own army might be imperceptibly destroyed in spite of its numbers, as his men would not be able to see where to support each other.

The Aetolian disaster,[1a] which had been mainly caused by the wood, had not a little to do with these reflections. [2] Meanwhile, one of the soldiers who were compelled by want of room to land on the extremities of the island and take their dinners, with outposts fixed to prevent a surprise, set fire to a little of the wood without meaning to do so; and as it came on to blow soon afterwards, almost the whole was consumed before they were aware of it. [3] Demosthenes was now able for the first time to see how numerous the Spartans really were, having up to this moment been under the impression that they took in provisions for a smaller number; he also saw that the Athenians thought success important and were anxious about it, and that it was now easier to land on the island, and accordingly got ready for the attempt, sending for troops from the allies in the neighborhood, and pushing forward his other preparations. [4] At this moment Cleon arrived at Pylos with the troops which he had asked for, having sent on word to say that he was coming. The first step taken by the two generals after their meeting was to send a herald[4a] to the camp on the mainland, to ask if they were disposed to avoid all risk and to order the men on the island to surrender themselves and their arms, to be kept in gentle custody until some general settlement should be concluded.

On the rejection of this proposition the generals let one day pass, and the next embarking all their hoplites on board a few ships, put out by night, and a little before dawn landed on both sides of the island from the open sea and from the harbor, being about eight hundred strong, and advanced with a run against the first post in the island. [2] The enemy had distributed his force as follows: In this first post there were about thirty hoplites; the center and most level part, where the water was, was held by the main body, and by Epitadas their commander; while a small party guarded the very end of the island, toward Pylos, which was precipitous on the sea side and very difficult to attack from the land, and where there was also a sort of old fort of stones rudely put together, which they thought might be useful to them, in case they should be forced to retreat. Such was their disposition.[2a]

The advanced post thus attacked by the Athenians was at once put to the sword, the men being scarcely out of bed and still arming, the landing having taken them by surprise, as they fancied the ships were only sailing as usual to their stations for the night. [2] As soon as day broke, the rest of

4.30.1a For the Aetolian disaster, see 3.94–98.
4.30.4a Heralds, already a venerable Greek institution in Thucydides' day, operated under the protection of the god Hermes, and were easily identified by the staff they carried. They alone could travel unmo-

lested between states or armies during wartime in order to deliver messages, take back replies, and make perfunctory arrangements.
4.31.2a Sphacteria and its features are described in Map 4.35.

4.30
425
7th Year/Summer
PYLOS
A fire burns off the brush cover on the island, permitting Demosthenes to see the enemy and better plan his attack. Cleon arrives with his force. A herald is sent to demand the Spartans' surrender.

4.31
425
7th Year/Summer
PYLOS
The Athenians embark at night and land on Sphacteria just before dawn. Spartan troops are divided into three unequal forces.

4.32
425
7th Year/Summer
PYLOS
The Spartan advance post is taken by surprise, and the rest of the Athenians land. Demosthenes' plan to refuse close combat and to attack the Spartans from all sides with missiles is described.

the army landed,[2a] that is to say, all the crews of rather more than seventy ships, except the lowest rank of oars,[2b] with the arms they carried, eight hundred archers, and as many peltasts, the Messenian reinforcements, and all the other troops on duty round Pylos, except the garrison in the fort. [3] The tactics of Demosthenes had divided them into companies of two hundred, more or less, and made them occupy the highest points in order to paralyze the enemy by surrounding him on every side. By refusing to engage closely, the Athenians would leave him without any tangible adversary and expose him to the cross-fire of their host; plied by those in his rear if he attacked in front, and by those on one flank if he moved against those on the other. [4] In short, wherever he went he would have assailants behind him, and these light-armed attackers would prove the most difficult to deal with; their arrows, darts, stones, and slings making them formidable at a distance, and there being no means of getting at them at close quarters, as they could flee if pursued, and the moment their pursuer turned they would be upon him. Such was the idea that Demosthenes had in the first place when he was planning the landing and so he arranged its execution.

Meanwhile the main body of the troops in the island (that under Epitadas), seeing their outpost cut off and an army advancing against them, serried their ranks and pressed forward to close with the Athenian hoplites in front of them, the light troops being upon their flanks and rear. [2] However, they were not able to engage or to profit by their superior skill, the light troops keeping them in check on either side with their missiles, and the hoplites remaining stationary instead of advancing to meet them; and although they routed the light troops wherever they ran up and approached too closely, yet they retreated fighting, being lightly equipped, and easily getting away in their flight, from the difficult and rugged nature of the ground, in an island hitherto uninhabited, over which the Spartans could not pursue them in their heavy armor.

After this skirmishing had lasted some little while, the Spartans became unable to dash out with the same rapidity as before upon the points attacked, and the light troops, finding that they now fought with less vigor, became more confident. They could see with their own eyes that they were many times more numerous than the enemy; they were now more familiar with his aspect and found him less terrible, the event not having justified the apprehensions which they had suffered when they first landed in slavish dismay at the idea of attacking Spartans; and accordingly their fear changing to disdain, they now rushed upon them all together with loud shouts, and pelted them with stones, darts, and arrows, whichever came first to

4.33
425
7th Year/Summer
PYLOS
The main Spartan force advances but is thwarted by Demosthenes' tactics.

4.34
425
7th Year/Summer
PYLOS
As the Spartans tire, the Athenians grow more confident. Blinded by dust and deafened by the noise of battle, the Spartans find it impossible either to attack or to defend themselves effectively.

4.32.2a   Probable landing sites on Sphacteria:
          Map 4.35, BX.
4.32.2b   For the "lowest rank of oars," see Appendix G, Trireme Warfare, §5, 12.

hand. [2] The shouting accompanying their onset confounded the Spartans, unaccustomed to this mode of fighting; dust rose from the newly burnt wood, and it was impossible to see in front of one with the arrows and stones flying through clouds of dust from the hands of numerous assailants. [3] The Spartans had now to sustain a difficult conflict; their caps would not keep out the arrows, and darts had broken off in the bodies of the wounded. They themselves were unable to retaliate, being prevented from using their eyes to see what was before them, and unable to hear the words of command for the hubbub raised by the enemy; danger encompassed them on every side, and there was no hope of any means of defense or safety.

At last, after many had been already wounded in the confined space in which they were fighting, they formed in close order and retired to the fort at the end of the island, which was not far off, and to their friends who held it.[1a] [2] The moment they gave way, the light troops became bolder and pressed upon them, shouting louder than ever, and killed as many as they caught up with in their retreat, but most of the Spartans made good their escape to the fort, and with the garrison in it ranged themselves all along its whole extent to repulse the enemy wherever it was assailable. [3] The Athenians pursuing, unable to surround and hem them in, owing to the strength of the ground, attacked them in front and tried to storm the position. [4] For a long time, indeed for most of the day, both sides held out against all the torments of the battle, thirst, and sun, the one endeavoring to drive the enemy from the high ground, the other to maintain himself upon it, it being now more easy for the Spartans to defend themselves than before, as they could not be surrounded upon the flanks.

The struggle began to seem endless, when the commander of the Messenians came to Cleon and Demosthenes, and told them that they were wasting their efforts but that if they would give him some archers and light troops to go round on the enemy's rear by a way he would undertake to find, he thought he could force the approach. [2] Upon receiving what he asked for, he started from a point out of sight in order not to be seen by the enemy, and creeping on wherever the precipices of the island permitted, and where the Spartans, trusting to the strength of the ground, kept no guard, succeeded after the greatest difficulty in getting round without their seeing him, and suddenly appeared on the high ground in their rear, to the dismay of the surprised enemy and the still greater joy of his expectant friends. [3] The Spartans thus placed between two fires, and in the same dilemma, to compare small things with great, as at Thermopylae,[3a] where the defenders were cut off through the Persians getting round by the path, being now attacked in front and behind, began to give way, and overcome

4.35
425
7th Year/Summer
PYLOS
After many Spartans are wounded, they retire to an old fort at the end of the island, and the Athenians pursue them. There the ground favors defense and prevents encirclement. Both sides endure the torments of sun and thirst.

4.36
425
7th Year/Summer
PYLOS
The Messenian commander leads a force by a hidden route to a position above and behind the Spartans, surprising them and forcing them to give way.

4.35.1a Fort at the north end of Sphacteria. Map 4.35.
4.36.3a Thermopylae (Map 4.52, AX) was the site of a heroic battle in 480 B.C. A small Spartan-led force of Greeks occupied a

narrow pass and held off a huge Persian army for several days until they were outflanked and surrounded. Even then the Greeks fought to the last man. See Appendix E, The Persians, §4.

MAP 4.35
THE ATHENIAN ASSAULT
ON SPHACTERIA

by the odds against them and exhausted from want of food, retreated.

The Athenians were already masters of the approaches [4.37.1] when Cleon and Demosthenes, perceiving that the enemy, should he give way a single step further, would be destroyed by their soldiery, put a stop to the battle and held their men back. They wished to take the Spartans alive to Athens and hoped that their stubbornness might relax on hearing the offer of terms, and that they might surrender and yield to the present overwhelming danger. [2] Proclamation was accordingly made, to determine whether they would surrender themselves and their arms to the Athenians to be dealt with at their discretion.

When the Spartans heard this offer, most of them lowered their shields and waved their hands to show that they accepted it. Hostilities now ceased, and a parley was held between Cleon and Demosthenes, and Styphon son of Pharax, for the other side; since Epitadas, the first of the previous commanders, had been killed, and Hippagretas, the next in command, left for dead among the slain, though still alive; and thus the command had devolved upon Styphon according to the law in case of anything happening

4.37
425
7th Year/Summer
PYLOS
Demosthenes and Cleon halt the advance and ask the Spartans if they will now surrender.

4.38
425
7th Year/Summer
PYLOS
The Spartans surrender after consulting their forces on the mainland. The Spartans have lost about 130 men. Athenian losses are small, as there was no fighting at close quarters.

to his superiors. [2] Styphon and his companions said they wished to send a herald to the Spartans on the mainland, to know what they were to do. [3] The Athenians would not let any of them go, but themselves called for heralds from the mainland, and after questions had been carried backwards and forwards two or three times, the last man that passed over from the Spartans on the continent brought this message: "The Spartans bid you to decide for yourselves so long as you do nothing dishonorable"; upon which after consulting together they surrendered themselves and their arms. [4] The Athenians, after guarding them that day and night, the next morning set up a trophy in the island, and got ready to sail, giving their prisoners in batches to be guarded by the captains of the triremes; and the Spartans sent a herald and took up their dead. [5] The number of the killed and prisoners taken in the island was as follows: of the four hundred and twenty hoplites who had passed over originally, two hundred and ninety-two were taken alive to Athens; the rest were killed. About a hundred and twenty of the prisoners were Spartiates. The Athenian loss was small, the battle not having been fought at close quarters.

The blockade lasted seventy-two days in all, counting from the naval fight to the battle on the island. [2] For twenty of these, during the absence of the envoys sent to negotiate for peace, the men had provisions given them; for the rest they were fed by the smugglers. Grain and other victuals were found in the island, the commander Epitadas having kept the men upon half rations. [3] The Athenians and Peloponnesians now each withdrew their forces from Pylos, and went home, and mad as Cleon's promise was, he fulfilled it, by bringing the men to Athens within the twenty days as he had pledged himself to do.

Nothing that happened in the war surprised the Hellenes so much as this. It was the general opinion that no force or famine could make the Spartans give up their arms, but that they would fight on as they could, and die with them in their hands: [2] indeed people could scarcely believe that those who had surrendered were of the same stuff as the fallen; and an Athenian ally, who some time after insultingly asked one of the prisoners from the island if those that had fallen were noble and good men, received for answer that the *atraktos*—that is, the arrow—would be worth a great deal if it could pick out noble and good men from the rest; in allusion to the fact that the killed were those whom the stones and the arrow happened to hit.

Upon the arrival of the men the Athenians determined to keep them in prison until the peace, and if the Peloponnesians invaded their country in the interval, to bring them out and put them to death. [2] Meanwhile the defense of Pylos was not forgotten; the Messenians from Naupactus[2a] sent to their old country, to which Pylos formerly belonged, some of the most suitable of their number, and began a series of incursions into Laconia, which their common dialect[2b] rendered most destructive. [3] The Spartans,

4.41.2a Naupactus: Map 4.44, locator.
4.41.2b For the Dorian dialect see Appendix H, Dialects and Ethnic Groups, §9.

4.39
425
7th Year/Summer
PYLOS
The blockade lasted seventy-two days. Cleon returns to Athens with the prisoners, his promise fulfilled

4.40
425
7th Year/Summer
PYLOS
All Greece is amazed that the Spartans at Sphacteria surrendered. Thucydides' recounts the anecdote of the clever arrows.

4.41
425
7th Year/Summer
PYLOS-ATHENS
The captured Spartans are imprisoned at Athens. The Messenians launch effective raids on Laconia. The Spartans send envoys to Athens to negotiate a peace, but the Athenians reject their proposals, "always grasping for more."

ILLUSTRATION 4.41
SHIELD FOUND AT ATHENS: THE INSCRIPTION READS THAT IT WAS TAKEN BY THE
ATHENIANS FROM THE SPARTANS (LACEDAIMONIANS) AT PYLOS

hitherto without experience of incursions or a warfare of the kind, finding the Helots deserting, and fearing the march of revolution in their country, began to be seriously uneasy, and in spite of their unwillingness to betray this to the Athenians began to send envoys to Athens, and tried to recover Pylos and the prisoners. [4] The Athenians, however, kept grasping at more, and dismissed envoy after envoy without their having effected anything. Such was the history of the affair of Pylos.

The same summer, directly after these events, the Athenians made an expedition against the territory of Corinth[1a] with eighty ships and two thousand Athenian hoplites and two hundred cavalry on board horse transports, accompanied by the Milesians,[1b] Andrians,[1c] and Carystians[1d] from the allies; under the command of Nicias son of Niceratus, with two colleagues. [2] Putting out to sea they made land at daybreak between Chersonese and Rheitus,[2a] at the beach of the country underneath the Solygian hill, upon which the Dorians in old times established themselves and carried on war against the Aeolian inhabitants of Corinth, and where a village now stands called Solygia.[2b] The beach where the fleet put in is about a mile and a half from the village, seven miles from Corinth, and two and a quarter from the Isthmus.[2c] [3] The Corinthians had heard from Argos[3a] of the coming of the Athenian armament, and had all come up to the Isthmus long before, with the exception of those who lived beyond it, and also of five hundred who were away in garrison in Ambracia and Leucas;[3b] and they were there in full force watching for the Athenians to land. [4] These last, however, gave them the slip by coming in the dark; and being informed by signals of the fact, the Corinthians left half their number at Cenchreae,[4a] in case the Athenians should go against Crommyon,[4b] and marched in all haste to the rescue.

Battus, one of the two generals present at the action, went with a company to defend the village of Solygia, which was unfortified; Lycophron remaining to give battle with the rest. [2] The Corinthians first attacked the right wing of the Athenians, which had just landed in front of Chersonese, and afterwards the rest of the army. The battle was an obstinate one, and fought throughout hand to hand. [3] The right wing of the Athenians and Carystians, who had been placed at the end of the line, received and with some difficulty repulsed the Corinthians, who thereupon retreated to a wall upon the rising ground behind, and throwing down the stones upon them, came on again singing the *paean*[2a] and being received by the Atheni-

4.42
425
7th Year/Summer
CORINTH
An Athenian expedition under Nicias attacks Corinthian territory near the Isthmus. Warned from Argos, Corinth prepares to meet the invaders.

4.43
425
7th Year/Summer
CORINTH
The Corinthians attack the Athenians just after they land and a hard-fought battle at close quarters takes place.

4.42.1a	Corinth: Map 4.44, AX.	4.42.3b	Three hundred of these Corinthians are
4.42.1b	Miletus: Map 4.44, locator.		mentioned in 3.114 as being sent to
4.42.1c	Andros: Map 4.44, locator.		Ambracia. For the locations of Ambracia
4.42.1d	Carystus, Map 4.44, locator.		and Leucas, see Map 4.52, AX.
4.42.2a	Chersonese, Rheitus in Corinthian terri-	4.42.4a	Cenchreae: Map 4.44, AX.
	tory, possible locations: Map 4.44, AX.	4.42.4b	Crommyon: Map 4.44, AX.
4.42.2b	Solygia, possible location: Map 4.44, AX.	4.43.2a	The *paean* was a ritual chant that the
	For the Dorians and Aeolians, see Appen-		men of classical Greek armies sang as they
	dix H, Dialects and Ethnic Groups, §6–8.		advanced into battle, rallied, or celebrated
4.42.2c	Isthmus of Corinth: Map 4.44, AX.		victory.
4.42.3a	Argos: Map 4.44, BX.		

MAP 4.44 ATHENIAN ATTACKS ON CORINTH
AND THE ARGOLID

ans, were again engaged at close quarters. [4] At this moment a Corinthian
company having come to the relief of the left wing, routed and pursued the
Athenian right to the sea, whence they were in their turn driven back by
the Athenians and Carystians from the ships. [5] Meanwhile the rest of the
army on either side fought on tenaciously, especially the right wing of the
Corinthians, where Lycophron sustained the attack of the Athenian left,
which it was feared might attempt the village of Solygia.

After holding on for a long while without either giving way, the Athenians aided by their horse, of which the enemy had none, at length routed
the Corinthians, who retired to the hill and halting remained quiet there,
without coming down again. [2] It was in this rout of the right wing that
they had the most killed, Lycophron their general being among the number. The rest of the army, broken and put to flight in this way without
being seriously pursued or hurried, retired to the high ground and there
took up its position. [3] The Athenians, finding that the enemy no longer
offered to engage them, stripped his dead and took up their own and

4.44
425
7th Year/Summer
CORINTH
The Corinthians are finally
routed, but the Athenians,
seeing other enemy forces
approaching, withdraw by
ship to nearby islands.

immediately set up a trophy. [4] Meanwhile, the half of the Corinthians left at Cenchreae to guard against the Athenians sailing on Crommyon, although unable to see the battle for Mount Oneion,[4a] found out what was going on by the dust, and hurried up to the rescue; as did also the older Corinthians from the city, upon discovering what had occurred. [5] The Athenians seeing them all coming against them, and thinking that they were reinforcements from the neighboring Peloponnesians, withdrew in haste to their ships with their spoils and their own dead, except two that they left behind, not being able to find them, [6] and going on board crossed over to the islands opposite and from thence sent a herald, and took up under truce the bodies which they had left behind. Two hundred and twelve Corinthians fell in the battle, and rather less than fifty Athenians.

4.45
425
7th Year/Summer
CORINTH
The Athenians ravage Crommyon and fortify Methana as a base for future raids

Weighing from the islands, the Athenians sailed the same day to Crommyon in the Corinthian territory, about thirteen miles from the city, and coming to anchor laid waste the country, and passed the night there. [2] The next day, after first coasting along to the territory of Epidaurus[2a] and making a descent there, they came to Methana[2b] between Epidaurus and Troezen,[2c] and drew a wall across and fortified the isthmus of the peninsula, and left a post there from which incursions were henceforth made upon the country of Troezen, Halieis,[2d] and Epidaurus. After walling off this spot the fleet sailed off home.

4.46
425
7th Year/Summer
CORCYRA
The Athenian fleet from Pylos sails to Corcyra; attacks and secures the surrender of the Corcyraeans from Mount Istone; and imprisons them on the island of Ptychia. The Corcyraean People plot to kill the prisoners.

While these events were going on, Eurymedon and Sophocles had put to sea with the Athenian fleet from Pylos on their way to Sicily, and arriving at Corcyra, joined the townsmen in an expedition against the party established on Mount Istone[1a] who, as I have mentioned, had crossed over after the revolution, and become masters of the country, to the great hurt of the inhabitants. [2] Their stronghold having been taken by an attack, the garrison took refuge in a body upon some high ground and there capitulated, agreeing to give up their mercenary auxiliaries, lay down their arms, and commit themselves to the discretion of the Athenian people. [3] The generals carried them across under truce to the island of Ptychia,[3a] to be kept in custody until they could be sent to Athens, upon the understanding that if any were caught running away, all would lose the benefit of the treaty. [4] Meanwhile the leaders of the Corcyraean commons, afraid that the Athenians might spare the lives of the prisoners, had recourse to the following stratagem. [5] They gained over some few men on the island by secretly sending friends with instructions to provide them with a boat, and to tell them, as if for their own sakes, that they had best escape as quickly as

---

4.44.4a　Mount Oneion, possible location: Map
　　　　 4.44, AX.
4.45.2a　Epidaurus: Map 4.44, BX.
4.45.2b　Methana: Map 4.44, BY.
4.45.2c　Troezen: Map 4.44, BY.

4.45.2d　Halieis: Map 4.44, BX.
4.46.1a　These partisans were mentioned in 3.85
　　　　 and 4.2. Mount Istone: Map 4.47.
4.46.3a　Ptychia: Map 4.47.

MAP 4.47 ATHENIANS IN CORCYRA

possible, as the Athenian generals were going to give them up to the Corcyraean people.

These representations succeeding, it was so arranged that the men were
caught sailing out in the boat that was provided, and the treaty became
void accordingly, and the whole were given up to the Corcyraeans. [2] For
this result the Athenian generals were in a great measure responsible; their
evident disinclination to sail for Sicily, and thus to leave to others the honor

4.47
425
7th Year/Summer
CORCYRA
Caught trying to escape, the
prisoners are executed by the
Corcyraean People. The
Athenian generals bear much
responsibility for this massacre.

of conducting the men to Athens, encouraged the intriguers in their design and seemed to affirm the truth of their representations. [3] The prisoners thus handed over were shut up by the Corcyraeans in a large building, and afterwards taken out by twenties and led past two lines of hoplites, one on each side, being bound together, and beaten and stabbed by the men in the lines whenever any saw pass a personal enemy; while men carrying whips went by their side and hastened on the road those that walked too slowly.

As many as sixty men were taken out and killed in this way without the knowledge of their friends in the building, who fancied they were merely being moved from one prison to another. At last, however, someone opened their eyes to the truth, upon which they called upon the Athenians to kill them themselves, if such was their pleasure, and refused any longer to go out of the building, and said they would do all they could to prevent anyone coming in. [2] The Corcyraeans, not wishing themselves to force a passage through the doors, got up on the top of the building, and breaking through the roof, threw down the tiles and let fly arrows at them, from which the prisoners sheltered themselves as well as they could. [3] Most of their number, meanwhile, were engaged in killing themselves by thrusting into their throats the arrows shot by the enemy, and hanging themselves with the cords taken from some beds that happened to be there, and with strips made from their clothing; adopting, in short, every possible means of self-destruction, and also falling victims to the missiles of their enemies on the roof. Night came on while these horrors were taking place, and most of it had passed before they were concluded. [4] When it was day the Corcyraeans threw them in layers upon wagons and carried them out of the city. All the women taken in the stronghold were sold as slaves. [5] In this way the Corcyraeans from the mountain were destroyed by the People; and so after terrible excesses the party strife came to an end, at least as far as the period of this war is concerned, for of one party there was practically nothing left. Meanwhile the Athenians sailed off to Sicily, their primary destination, and carried on the war with their allies there.

At the close of the summer, the Athenians at Naupactus[1a] and the Acarnanians[1b] made an expedition against Anactorium,[1c] the Corinthian city lying at the mouth of the Ambracian gulf, and took it by treachery; and the Acarnanians themselves sending settlers from all parts of Acarnania occupied the place.

Summer was now over. [4.50.1] During the following winter Aristides son of Archippus, one of the commanders of the Athenian ships sent to collect money from the allies,[1a] arrested at Eion on the Strymon[1b] Arta-

4.49.1a Naupactus: Map 4.52, AX.
4.49.1b The enmity between Anactorium and Acarnania was mentioned in 3.114. Acarnania: Map 4.52, AX.
4.49.1c Anactorium: Map 4.52, AX.
4.50.1a For Athenian collections of tribute, see

note 4.75.1b; also Appendix B, The Athenian Empire, §2, 10.
4.50.1b Eion, on the Strymon River in Thrace: Map 4.52, AX. Thucydides describes an Athenian siege of the Persians in this city in 1.98.

phernes, a Persian,[1c] on his way from the King to Sparta. [2] He was conducted to Athens, where the Athenians had his dispatches translated from the Assyrian characters[2a] and read them. With numerous references to other subjects, they in substance told the Spartans that the King did not know what they wanted, as of the many ambassadors they had sent him no two ever told the same story; if however they were prepared to speak plainly they might send him some envoys with this Persian. [3] The Athenians afterwards sent back Artaphernes in a trireme to Ephesus,[3a] and ambassadors with him, who heard there of the death of King Artaxerxes son of Xerxes,[3b] which took place about that time, and so returned home.

The same winter the Chians[1a] pulled down their new wall at the command of the Athenians, who suspected them of meditating an insurrection, after first however obtaining pledges from the Athenians, and security as far as this was possible for their continuing to treat them as before. Thus the winter ended, and with it ended the seventh year of this war of which Thucydides is the historian.

In the first days of the next summer there was an eclipse of the sun[1a] at the time of the new moon, and in the early part of the same month an earthquake. [2] Meanwhile, the Mytilenian[2a] and other Lesbian exiles set out, for the most part from the continent, with mercenaries hired in the Peloponnesus, and others levied on the spot, and took Rhoeteum,[2b] but restored it without injury on the receipt of two thousand Phocaean *staters*.[2c] [3] After this they marched against Antandrus[3a] and took the city by treachery, their plan being to free Antandrus and the rest of the Actaean cities, formerly owned by Mytilene but now held by the Athenians. Once fortified there, they would have every facility for shipbuilding from the vicinity of Mount Ida[3b] and the consequent abundance of timber, and plenty of other supplies, and might from this base easily ravage Lesbos, which was not far off, and make themselves masters of the Aeolian cities on the continent.[3c]

4.51
425/4
7th Year/Winter
CHIOS
The Chians dismantle their new wall.

4.52
424
8th Year/Summer
LESBOS
Thucydides notes an eclipse of the sun, and describes the maneuvers and plans of the Mytilenian exiles.

4.50.1c Persian envoy Atarphernes: see Appendix E, The Persians, §6.
4.50.2a Assyrian characters: possibly the message was written in Old Persian cuneiform, but more likely it was in Aramaic.
4.50.3a Ephesus: Map 4.52, BY.
4.50.3b This chapter has played a large part in discussions of Athenian relations with Persia: was there a treaty between the two powers in the fifth century? See Appendix E, The Persians, §5–6. The dating of the reigns of Persian kings depends largely on the exact dates to be found on Babylonian cuneiform tablets. With one curious exception (which is perhaps an error), all the Babylonian evidence shows that Darius, who succeeded Artaxerxes, did not become king until 424/3, at least fourteen months after the date Thucydides gives (or appears to give by his mention of a precisely datable eclipse in 4.52.1) for the capture of Artaphernes. Can Thucydides have erred and assigned the

incident to the wrong winter? Or does his use of the word "afterwards" cover quite a long delay before Artaphernes was escorted to Ephesus? Both alternatives have caused scholars discomfort.

4.51.1a Chios: Map 4.52, AY.
4.52.1a This eclipse took place on March 21, 424 B.C.; see A. W. Gomme, *A Historical Commentary on Thucydides,* iii (Oxford, 1956), 505.
4.52.2a This picks up the story of Mytilene from 3.50. Mytilene, Lesbos: Map 4.52, AY.
4.52.2b Rhoeteum: Map 4.52, AY.
4.52.2c Phocaean *staters* were a unit of currency thought to be worth twenty-four Attic drachmas, which would make the above sum equal to eight talents. See Appendix J, Classical Greek Currency, §4.
4.52.3a Antandrus: Map 4.52, AY.
4.52.3b Mount Ida: Map 4.52, AY.
4.52.3c We next hear of these Mytilenian exiles in 4.75.1.

MAP 4.52 EVENTS IN LESBOS AND CHIOS; NICIAS' CYTHERAN CAMPAIGN

While these were the schemes of the exiles, [4.53.1] the Athenians in the same summer made an expedition with sixty ships, two thousand hoplites, a few cavalry, and some allied troops from Miletus[1a] and other parts, against Cythera, under the command of Nicias son of Niceratus, Nicostratus son of Diotrephes, and Autocles son of Tolmaeus. [2] Cythera is an island lying off Laconia, opposite Malea;[2a] the inhabitants are Spartans of the class of the *perioikoi*;[2b] and an officer called the Judge of Cythera went over to the place annually from Sparta. A garrison of hoplites was also regularly sent there, and great attention paid to the island, [3] as it was the landing place for the merchant ships from Egypt and Libya,[3a] and at the same time secured Laconia from the attacks of privateers[3b] from the sea, at the only point where it is assailable, as the whole coast rises abruptly toward the Sicilian and Cretan seas.[3c]

Coming to land here with their armament, the Athenians with ten ships and two thousand Milesian hoplites took the city of Scandea,[1a] on the sea; and with the rest of their forces landing on the side of the island looking toward Malea, went against the lower city of Cythera,[1b] where they found all the inhabitants encamped. [2] A battle ensuing, the Cytherans held their ground for some little while, and then turned and fled into the upper city, where they soon afterwards capitulated to Nicias and his colleagues, agreeing to leave their fate to the decision of the Athenians, their lives only being safe. [3] A correspondence had previously been going on between Nicias and certain of the inhabitants, which caused the surrender to be effected more speedily, and upon terms more advantageous, present and future, for the Cytherans; who would otherwise have been expelled by the Athenians on account of their being Spartans and their island being so near to Laconia.[3a] [4] After the capitulation, the Athenians occupied the city of Scandea near the harbor, and appointing a garrison for Cythera, sailed to Asine,[4a] Helus,[4b] and most of the places on the sea, and making descents and passing the night on shore at such spots as were convenient, continued ravaging the country for about seven days.

The Spartans seeing the Athenians masters of Cythera, and expecting descents of the kind upon their coasts, nowhere opposed them in force, but sent garrisons here and there through the country, consisting of as many hoplites as the points menaced seemed to require, and generally stood very

4.53
424
8th Year/Summer
CYTHERA
Athens sends an expedition against Cythera. Thucydides describes the island, its inhabitants, and its importance to Sparta.

4.54
424
8th Year/Summer
CYTHERA
The Athenians under Nicias defeat the Cytherans who surrender on terms.

4.55
424
8th Year/Summer
LACONIA
Unnerved by its losses at Pylos and Cythera, Sparta organizes cavalry and archers and disperses hoplites to provide a mobile coast defense.

4.53.1a   Miletus: Map 4.52, BY.
4.53.2a   Island of Cythera, in relation to Laconia and Cape Malea: Map 4.52, BX.
4.53.2b   *Perioikoi*: See Appendix C, Spartan Institutions, §9.
4.53.3a   Egypt and Libya, in relation to Cythera: Map 4.52, locator.
4.53.3b   Privateers were privately owned boats licensed by the belligerents to attack enemy shipping.
4.53.3c   For the location of the Sicilian and Cretan Seas in relation to Cythera, see Map 4.52, BX.

4.54.1a   Scandea, on the island of Cythera: Map 4.52, BX.
4.54.1b   City of Cythera, on the island of Cythera: Map 4.52, BX.
4.54.3a   The terms of this agreement are described in 4.57.4.
4.54.4a   Asine in Messenia: Map 4.52, BX. This Asine seems too far away from Cythera to be raided from there, so Thucydides may have been referring here to another Asine located near Gythion: Map 4.52, BX.
4.54.4b   Helus: Map 4.52, BX.

much upon the defensive. After the severe and unexpected blow that had befallen them in the island, the occupation of Pylos and Cythera, and the apparition on every side of a war whose rapidity defied precaution, they lived in constant fear of internal revolution, [2] and now took the unusual step of raising four hundred horse and a force of archers, and became more timid than ever in military matters, finding themselves involved in a maritime struggle, which their organization had never contemplated, and that against Athenians, with whom an enterprise unattempted was always looked upon as a success sacrificed. [3] Besides this, their late numerous reverses of fortune, coming close one upon another without any reason, had thoroughly unnerved them, and they were always afraid of a second disaster like that on the island, [4] and thus scarsely dared to take the field, but fancied that they could not stir without a blunder, for being new to the experience of adversity they had lost all confidence in themselves.

4.56
424
8th Year/Summer
LACONIA
Sparta cannot defend its coasts from naval raids like the one against Thyrea, a district occupied by Aeginetan exiles.

Accordingly they now allowed the Athenians to ravage their seaboard, without making any movement, the garrisons in whose neighborhood the descents were made always thinking their numbers insufficient, and sharing the general feeling. A single garrison which ventured to resist, near Cotyrta and Aphrodisia,[1a] struck terror by its charge into the scattered mob of light troops, but retreated, upon being received by the hoplites, with the loss of a few men and some arms, for which the Athenians set up a trophy, and then sailed off to Cythera. [2] From thence they sailed round to Epidaurus Limera,[2a] ravaged part of the country, and so came to Thyrea[2b] in the Cynurian territory, upon the Argive and Laconian border. This district had been given by its Spartan owners to the expelled Aeginetans[2c] to inhabit, in return for their good offices at the time of the earthquake and the rising of the Helots;[2d] and also because, although subjects of Athens, they had always sided with Sparta.

4.57
424
8th Year/Summer
LACONIA
The Athenians capture Thyrea. Aeginetan prisoners are executed. A few Cytherans are sent to Athens as hostages.

While the Athenians were still at sea, the Aeginetans evacuated a fort which they were building upon the coast, and retreated into the upper city where they lived, rather more than a mile from the sea. [2] One of the Spartan district garrisons which was helping them in the work refused to enter here with them at their entreaty, thinking it dangerous to shut themselves up within the wall, and retiring to the high ground remained quiet, not considering themselves a match for the enemy. [3] Meanwhile the Athenians landed, and instantly advanced with all their forces and took Thyrea. The city they burnt, pillaging what was in it; the Aeginetans who were not slain in action they took with them to Athens, with Tantalus son of Patrocles, their Spartan commander, who had been wounded and taken

---

4.56.1a Cotyrta, Aphrodisia: locations unknown.
4.56.2a Epidaurus Limera: Map 4.52, BX.
4.56.2b Thyrea: Map 4.52, BX.
4.56.2c Aegina: Map 4.52, BX. Thucydides mentions the expulsion of the Aeginetans from their island by the Athenians in 2.27.

4.56.2d The earthquake and the Helot revolt that followed it are described in 1.101–3.

prisoner. [4] They also took with them a few men from Cythera whom they thought it safest to remove. These the Athenians decided to lodge in the islands: the rest of the Cytherans were to retain their lands and pay four *talents*[4a] as tribute; the Aeginetans captured were all to be put to death on account of the old and inveterate feud between Athens and Aegina; and Tantalus was to share the imprisonment of the Spartans taken on the island.

The same summer,[1a] the inhabitants of Camarina[1b] and Gela[1c] in Sicily first made an armistice with each other, after which embassies from all the other Sicilian cities assembled at Gela to try to bring about a pacification. After many expressions of opinion on one side and the other, according to the griefs and pretensions of the different parties complaining, Hermocrates son of Hermon, a Syracusan,[1d] the most influential man among them, addressed the following words to the assembly:

> "If I now address you, Sicilians, it is not because my city is the least in Sicily or the greatest sufferer by the war, but in order to state publicly what appears to me to be the best policy for the whole island. [2] That war is an evil is a proposition so familiar to everyone that it would be tedious to develop it. No one is forced to engage in it by ignorance, or kept out of it by fear, if he fancies there is anything to be gained by it. To the former the gain appears greater than the danger, while the latter would rather stand the risk than put up with any immediate sacrifice. [3] But if both should happen to have chosen the wrong moment for acting in this way, advice to make peace would be useful; and this, if we did but see it, is just what we stand most in need of at the present juncture."

> "I suppose that no one will dispute that we went to war at first in order to serve our own individual interests, and that we are now, in view of these same interests, debating how we can make peace; and that if we separate without having reached a fair agreement, we shall go to war again."

> "And yet, as men of sense, we ought to see that our separate interests are not alone at stake in the present congress: there is also the question whether we have still time to save Sicily, the whole of which in my opinion is menaced by Athenian ambition; and we ought to find in the name of that people more imperious arguments for peace than any which I can advance, when we see the first power in Hellas watching our mistakes with the few ships[1a] that she has at present in our waters, and under the fair name of alliance speciously

4.58
424
8th Year/Summer
SICILY
Hermocrates addresses the Sicilians at Gela.

4.59
424
8th Year/Summer
SICILY
Hermocrates begins his speech by declaring Sicily's need for peace.

4.60
424
8th Year/Summer
SICILY
Hermocrates argues that war among Sicilians will only weaken them all and render them vulnerable to subjugation by Athens.

4.57.4a   A *talent* is a unit of weight and/or money; see Appendix J, Classical Greek Currency, §5.
4.58.1a   This picks up the narrative of events in Sicily from 4.25.
4.58.1b   Camarina: Map 4.25.

4.58.1c   Gela: Map 4.25.
4.58.1d   Syracuse: Map 4.25.
4.60.1a   "Few ships"? At that time Athens had sixty triremes in Sicilian waters, no mean fleet. Was this written after the Sicilian expedition of 415?

seeking to exploit the natural hostility that exists between us. [2] If we go to war, and call in to help us a people that are ready enough to carry their arms even where they are not invited; and if we injure ourselves at our own expense, and at the same time serve as the pioneers of their dominion, we may expect when they see us worn out, that they will one day come with a larger armament, and seek to bring all of us into subjection."

4.61
424
8th Year/Summer
SICILY
Hermocrates claims that
Athens is the common
enemy of all Sicilians.

"And yet as sensible men, if we call in allies and court danger, it should be in order to enrich our different countries with new acquisitions, and not to ruin what they possess already; and we should understand that the internal discords which are so fatal to communities generally will be equally so to Sicily if we, its inhabitants, absorbed in our local quarrels, neglect the common enemy. [2] These considerations should reconcile individual with individual, and city with city, and unite us in a common effort to save the whole of Sicily. Nor should anyone imagine that the Dorians only are enemies of Athens, while the Chalcidian race is secured by its Ionian blood; [3] the attack in question is not inspired by hatred of one of two nationalities, but by a desire for the good things in Sicily, the common property of us all. [4] This is proved by the Athenian reception of the Chalcidian invitation: an ally who has never given them any assistance whatever, at once receives from them almost more than the treaty entitles him to. [5] That the Athenians should cherish this ambition and practice this policy is very excusable; and I do not blame those who wish to rule, but those who are too ready to serve. It is just as much in men's nature to rule those who submit to them, as it is to resist those who molest them. [6] Meanwhile all who see these dangers and refuse to provide for them properly, or who have come here without having made up their minds that our first duty is to unite to get rid of the common peril, are mistaken. [7] The quickest way to be rid of it is to make peace with each other; since the Athenians menace us not from their own country, but from that of those who invited them here. In this way instead of war resulting in war, peace quietly ends our quarrels; and the guests who come hither under fair pretenses for bad ends, will have good reason for going away without having attained them."

4.62
424
8th Year/Summer
SICILY
Hermocrates argues that
regardless of the Athenian
menace, peace itself is a
blessing well worth seeking.

"So far as regards the Athenians such are the great advantages proved inherent in a wise policy. [2] Independently of this, in the face of the universal consent that peace is the first of blessings, how can we refuse to make it amongst ourselves; or do you not think that the good which you have, and the ills that you complain of, would be better preserved and cured by quiet than by war; that peace has its honors and splendors of a less perilous kind, not to mention the numerous other blessings that one might expand on, with the not less numerous miseries of war? These considerations should teach you not to disregard my words, but rather for everyone to look into them for his own safety. [3] If there be any here who feels certain either by right or might to effect his object, let not this surprise be too severe a disappointment to him. Let him remember that many before now have tried to chastise a wrongdoer, and failing to punish their enemy have not even saved themselves; while many who have trusted in force to gain an advantage, instead of gaining anything more, have been doomed to lose what they had. [4] Vengeance is not necessarily successful because wrong has been done, or strength sure because it is confident; but the incalculable element in the future exercises the widest influence, and is the most treacherous, and yet in fact the most useful of all things, as it frightens us all equally, and thus makes us consider before attacking each other."

"Let us therefore now allow the undefined fear of this unknown future, and the immediate terror of the Athenians' presence to produce their natural impression, and let us consider any failure to carry out the programs that we may each have sketched out for ourselves as sufficiently accounted for by these obstacles, and send away the intruder from the country; and if everlasting peace be impossible between us, let us at all events make a treaty for as long a term as possible, and put off our private differences to another day. [2] In short, let us recognize that the adoption of my advice will leave us each citizens of a free state, and as such arbiters of our own destiny, able to return good or bad deeds with equal effect; while its rejection will make us dependent on others, and thus not only impotent to repel an insult, but on the most favorable supposition, friends to our direst enemies, and at feud with our natural friends."

"For myself, though, as I said at first, the representative of a great city able to think less of defending myself than of attacking others, I am prepared to concede something in anticipation of these dangers. I am not inclined to ruin myself for the sake of hurting my enemies, or so blinded by animosity as to think myself equally master of my own plans and of fortune which I cannot command; but I am ready to give up anything in reason. [2] I call upon the rest of you to imitate my conduct of your own free will, without being forced to do so by the enemy. [3] There is no disgrace in connections giving way to one another, a Dorian to a Dorian, or a Chalcidian to his brethren; above and beyond this we are neighbors, live in the same country, are girt by the same sea, and go by the same name of Sicilians. We shall go to war again, I suppose, when the time comes, and again make peace among ourselves by means of future congresses; [4] but the foreign

4.63
424
8th Year/Summer
SICILY
Hermocrates asserts that peace will leave Sicilians free, while continued war will lead to dependence on others.

4.64
424
8th Year/Summer
SICILY
Hermocrates concludes by arguing that Sicilians should always unite against any foreign invader.

invader, if we are wise, will always find us united against him, since the hurt of one is the danger of all; and we should never, in future, invite into the island either allies or mediators. [5] By so acting we shall at the present moment do for Sicily a double service, ridding her at once of the Athenians, and of civil war, and in future shall live in freedom at home, and be less menaced from abroad."

4.65
424
8th Year/Summer
SICILY-ATHENS
The Sicilians make peace among themselves. The Athenians return home, where their generals are prosecuted for bribery.

Such were the words of Hermocrates. The Sicilians took his advice, and came to an understanding among themselves to end the war, each keeping what they had—the Camarinaeans taking Morgantina[1a] at a fixed price to be paid to the Syracusans—[2] and the allies of the Athenians called the officers in command, and told them that they were going to make peace and that they would be included in the treaty. The generals assenting, the peace was concluded, and the Athenian fleet afterwards sailed away from Sicily.[2a] [3] Upon their arrival at Athens, the Athenians banished Pythodorus and Sophocles, and fined Eurymedon for having taken bribes to depart when they might have subdued Sicily.[3a] [4] So thoroughly had the present prosperity persuaded the Athenians that nothing could withstand them, and that they could achieve what was possible and what was impracticable alike, with means ample or inadequate it mattered not. The reason for this was their general extraordinary success, which made them confuse their strength with their hopes.

4.66
424
8th Year/Summer
MEGARA
The Megarian popular party plots with Athens to open their gates to a surprise attack against Nisaea and Megara.

The same summer the Megarians[1a] in the city, pressed by the hostilities of the Athenians, who invaded their country twice every year with all their forces, and harassed by the incursions of their own exiles at Pegae,[1b] who had been expelled in a revolution by the popular party, began to ask each other whether it would not be better to receive back their exiles, and free the city from one of its two scourges. [2] The friends of the exiles perceiving the agitation, now more openly than before demanded the adoption of this proposition; [3] and the leaders of The People, seeing that the sufferings of the times had worn down the determination of their supporters, entered in their alarm into correspondence with the Athenian generals, Hippocrates son of Ariphron, and Demosthenes son of Alcisthenes, and resolved to betray the city, thinking this less dangerous to themselves than the return of the party which they had banished. It was accordingly arranged that the Athenians should first take the long walls extending for nearly a mile from the city to the port of Nisaea[3a] to prevent the Peloponnesians coming to the rescue from that place, where they formed the sole garrison to secure the fidelity of Megara; and that after this the attempt

---

4.65.1a   Morgantina: Map 4.25.
4.65.2a   The story of Athenian activity in Sicily is continued in 5.5.
4.65.3a   It was not all that unusual for Athenians to punish statesmen or generals with whom they were angry or disappointed

by fines or exile. Note also the fining of Pericles (2.65.3), as well as the banishment of Thucydides himself (5.26.5).
4.66.1a   Megara: Map 4.69.
4.66.1b   Pegae: Map 4.69.
4.66.3a   Nisaea: Map 4.69.

should be made to gain control of the upper city which, it was thought, would then come over with less difficulty.

The Athenians, after plans had been arranged between themselves and their correspondents both as to words and actions, sailed by night to Minoa[1a] the island off Megara, with six hundred hoplites under the command of Hippocrates, and took a position in a ditch not far off, out of which bricks[1b] used to be taken for the walls; while [2] Demosthenes, the other commander, with a detachment of Plataean light troops and another of *peripoli,*[2a] placed himself in ambush in the precinct of Enyalius,[2b] which was still nearer. No one knew of it, except those whose business it was to know that night. [3] A little before daybreak, the traitors in Megara began to act. Every night for a long time back, under pretense of marauding, and in order to have a means of opening the gates, they had been used, with the consent of the officer in command, to carry by night a rowboat upon a cart along the ditch to the sea and to sail out, bringing it back again before day upon the cart and taking it within the wall through the gates in order, as they pretended, to baffle the Athenian blockade from Minoa, there being no boat to be seen in the harbor. [4] On the present occasion the cart was already at the gates, which had been opened in the usual way for the boat, when the Athenians, with whom this had been arranged, saw it, and ran at top speed from the ambush in order to reach the gates before they were shut again, and while the cart was still there to prevent their being closed. At the same moment their Megarian accomplices killed the guard at the gates. [5] The first to run in was Demosthenes with his Plataeans and *peripoli,* just where the trophy now stands; and he was no sooner within the gates than the Plataeans engaged and defeated the nearest party of Peloponnesians who had taken the alarm and come to the rescue, and secured the gates for the approaching Athenian hoplites.

After this, each of the Athenians as fast as they entered went against the wall. [2] A few of the Peloponnesian garrison stood their ground at first, and tried to repel the assault, and some of them were killed, but the main body took fright and fled; the night attack and the sight of the Megarian traitors in arms against them making them think that all Megara had gone over to the enemy. [3] It so happened also that the Athenian herald of his own idea called out and invited any of the Megarians to join the Athenian ranks, and this was no sooner heard by the garrison than they gave way and, convinced that they were the victims of a prearranged attack, took refuge in Nisaea. [4] By daybreak, the walls being now taken and the Megarians in the city in great agitation, the persons who had negotiated

4.67
424
8th Year/Summer
MEGARA
The Athenians attack from ambush and gain entrance by a gate that has been opened by a stratagem of their Megarian confederates.

4.68
424
8th Year/Summer
MEGARA
The Athenians capture the long walls but the popular party's plot to open the city gates is betrayed to their Megarian opponents, who prevent its execution.

4.67.1a   Minoa: Map 4.69. For this island's capture by Nicias in 427, see 3.51, and Map 3.51.
4.67.1b   Mud bricks, commonly used for buildings and city walls.
4.67.2a   Little is known about the *peripoli.* They may have been a special mobile force of young recruits serving as a frontier guard; see A.W. Gomme, *A Historical Commentary on Thucydides,* iii (Oxford, 1956), 529.
4.67.2b   The location of this sanctuary or shrine of Enyalius has not been identified.

with the Athenians, supported by the rest of the popular party which was privy to the plot, said that they ought to open the gates and march out to battle. [5] It had been agreed between them that the Athenians should rush in the moment that the gates were opened, and that the conspirators were to be distinguished from the rest by being anointed with oil, and so avoid being hurt. They could open the gates with more security, as four thousand Athenian hoplites from Eleusis,[5a] and six hundred horse, had marched all night according to plan and were now close at hand. [6] The conspirators were all anointed and at their posts by the gates when one of their accomplices denounced the plot to the opposite party, who gathered together and came in a body, and roundly said that they must not march out—a thing they had never yet ventured on even when they were in greater force than at present—or wantonly compromise the safety of the city; and that if what they said was not heeded the battle would have to be fought in Megara. For the rest, they gave no sign of their knowledge of the intrigue, but stoutly maintained that their advice was the best, and meanwhile kept close by and watched the gates, making it impossible for the conspirators to effect their purpose.

The Athenian generals seeing that some obstacle had arisen, and that the capture of the city by force was no longer practicable, at once proceeded to invest Nisaea, thinking that if they could take it before relief arrived, the surrender of Megara would soon follow. [2] Iron, stonemasons, and everything else required quickly coming up from Athens, the Athenians started from the wall which they occupied, and from this point built a cross wall looking toward Megara down to the sea on either side of Nisaea;[2a] the ditch and the walls being divided among the army, stones and bricks taken from the suburb, and the fruit trees and timber cut down to make a palisade wherever this seemed necessary; the houses also in the suburb with the addition of battlements sometimes became part of the fortification. The whole of this day the work continued, [3] and by the afternoon of the next the wall was all but completed, when the garrison in Nisaea, alarmed by the absolute want of provisions, which they used to take in for the day from the upper city, not anticipating any speedy relief from the Peloponnesians, and supposing Megara to be hostile, capitulated to the Athenians on condition that they should give up their arms, and should each be ransomed for a stipulated sum; their Spartan commander, and any others of his countrymen in the place, being left to the discretion of the Athenians. [4] On these conditions they surrendered and came out, and the Athenians broke down the long walls at their point of junction with Megara, took possession of Nisaea, and went on with their other preparations.

4.68.5a Eleusis: Map 4.69.
4.69.2a Presumably "looking toward Megara" from Nisaea. See the scheme of the Athenian siege walls of Nisaea in Map 4.69.

MAP 4.69 THE ATHENIAN ATTACK ON MEGARA

Just at this time the Spartan Brasidas son of Tellis happened to be in the neighborhood of Sicyon and Corinth,[1a] getting ready an army for Thrace.[1b] As soon as he heard of the capture of the walls, fearing for the Peloponnesians in Nisaea and the safety of Megara, he sent to the Boeotians to meet him as quickly as possible at Tripodiscus,[1c] a village of the Megarid on the slopes of Mount Geraneia.[1d] He then went himself, with two thousand seven hundred Corinthian hoplites, four hundred Phliasians,[1e] six hundred Sicyonians, and such troops of his own as he had already levied, expecting to find Nisaea not yet taken. [2] Hearing of its fall (he had marched out by night to Tripodiscus), he took three hundred picked men from the army, without waiting till his coming should be known, and came up to Megara unobserved by the Athenians, who were down by the sea, ostensibly, and really if possible, to attempt Nisaea, but above all to get into Megara and secure the city. He accordingly invited the townspeople to admit his party, saying that he had hopes of recovering Nisaea.

However, one of the Megarian factions feared that he might expel them and restore the exiles, and the other that the popular party, apprehensive of

4.70
424
8th Year/Summer
MEGARA
The Spartan Brasidas, calling for Boeotian help, marches with local allied forces to Megara, hoping to rescue Nisaea and at the least to occupy Megara before it falls.

4.71
424
8th Year/Summer
MEGARA
The Megarians decide to see which side will win before admitting anyone into their city.

4.70.1a   Sicyon, Corinth: Map 4.69. Brasidas last appeared in 4.12.1, dropping his shield and falling wounded into his ship at Pylos.
4.70.1b   Thucydides describes the march of Brasi-
das and his army to Thrace (Map 4.78, AY) in 4.78.
4.70.1c   Tripodiscus: Map 4.69.
4.70.1d   Mount Geraneia: Map 4.69.
4.70.1e   Phlius: Map 4.69.

this very danger, might set upon them, and that the city would be thus destroyed by a battle within its gates under the eyes of the Athenians lying in ambush. He was accordingly refused admittance, both parties electing to remain quiet and await the event; [2] each expecting a battle between the Athenians and the relieving army, and thinking it safer to see their friends victorious before declaring in their favor.

Unable to get his way, Brasidas went back to the rest of the army. [4.72.1] At daybreak the Boeotians joined him. Having determined to relieve Megara, whose danger they considered their own, even before hearing from Brasidas, they were already in full force at Plataea[1a] when his messenger arrived to add spurs to their resolution; and they at once sent on to him two thousand two hundred hoplites, and six hundred horse, returning home with the main body. [2] The whole army thus assembled numbered six thousand hoplites. The Athenian hoplites were drawn up by Nisaea and the sea; but the light troops being scattered over the plain were attacked by the Boeotian horse and driven to the sea, being taken entirely by surprise, as on previous occasions no relief had ever come to the Megarians from any quarter. [3] Here the Boeotians were in their turn charged and engaged by the Athenian horse, and a cavalry action ensued which lasted a long time, and in which both parties claimed the victory. [4] The Athenians killed and stripped the leader of the Boeotian horse and some few of his comrades who had charged right up to Nisaea, and remaining masters of the bodies gave them back under truce, and set up a trophy; but regarding the action as a whole the forces separated without either side having gained a decisive advantage, the Boeotians returning to their army and the Athenians to Nisaea.

After this Brasidas and the army came nearer to the sea and to Megara, and taking up a convenient position, remained quiet in order of battle, expecting to be attacked by the Athenians and knowing that the Megarians were waiting to see which would be the victor. [2] This attitude seemed to present two advantages. Without taking the offensive or willingly provoking the hazards of a battle, they openly showed their readiness to fight, and thus without bearing the burden of the day would fairly reap its honors; while at the same time they effectually served their interests at Megara. [3] For if they had failed to show themselves, they would not have had a chance, but would have certainly been considered vanquished, and have lost the city. As it was, the Athenians might possibly not be inclined to accept their challenge, and their object would be attained without fighting. [4] And so it turned out. The Athenians formed outside the long walls, and the enemy not attacking, there remained motionless; their generals having decided that the risk was too unequal. In fact most of their objects had been already attained; and they would have to begin a battle against supe-

---

4.72
424
8th Year/Summer
MEGARA
The Boeotians arrive; their cavalry attacks the Athenian light troops and are countered by the Athenian cavalry.

4.73
424
8th Year Summer
MEGARA
The Peloponnesians offer battle but do not attack. The Athenians also hold back, unwilling to risk defeat. The Megarians view the failure to fight as a Spartan victory and open their gates to Brasidas.

4.72.1a   Thebes and Plataea, in relation to Megara: Map 4.69. The occupation of Megara by the Athenians would have cut

Boeotian land communications with the Peloponnesus.

rior numbers,[3a] and if victorious could only gain Megara, while a defeat would destroy the flower of their hoplite forces. For the enemy it was different; as even the states actually represented in his army risked each only a part of its entire force, he might well be more audacious. Accordingly after waiting for some time without either side attacking, the Athenians withdrew to Nisaea, and the Peloponnesians after them to the point from which they had set out. The friends of the Megarian exiles now threw aside their hesitation, and opened the gates to Brasidas and the commanders from the different states—looking upon him as the victor and upon the Athenians as having declined the battle—and receiving them into the city proceeded to discuss matters with them; the party in correspondence with the Athenians being paralyzed by the turn things had taken.

Afterwards Brasidas let the allies go home, and himself went back to Corinth, to prepare for his expedition to Thrace, his original destination. [2] The Athenians also returning home, the Megarians in the city most implicated in the Athenian negotiation, knowing that they had been detected, presently disappeared; while the rest conferred with the friends of the exiles, and restored the party at Pegae, after binding them under solemn oaths to take no vengeance for the past, and only to consult the real interests of the city. [3] However, as soon as they were in office, they held a review of the hoplites, and separating the battalions, picked out about a hundred of their enemies, and of those who were thought to be most involved in the correspondence with the Athenians, brought them before the people, and compelling the vote to be given openly, had them condemned and executed, and established a close oligarchy in the city—[4] a revolution which lasted a very long while, although effected by a very few partisans.

The same summer the Mytilenians were about to fortify Antandrus[1a] as they had intended, when Demodocus and Aristides, the commanders of the Athenian squadron engaged in collecting tribute,[1b] heard on the Hellespont[1c] of what was being done to the place (Lamachus their colleague having sailed with ten ships into the Pontus[1d]) and conceived fears of its becoming a second Anaia,[1e] the place in which the Samian exiles had established themselves to annoy Samos,[1f] helping the Peloponnesians by sending pilots to their navy, and keeping the city in agitation and receiving

4.74
424
8th Year/Summer
MEGARA
Both sides return home, leaving Megara firmly in the hands of the oligarchs, who then execute one hundred of their foes.

4.75
424
8th Year/Summer
LESBOS-PONTUS
Athenians prevent the Mytilenian exiles from fortifying Antandrus. Lamachus loses his ships in Pontus and marches home by land.

4.73.3a Brasidas had six thousand hoplites and six hundred Boeotian horse (4.72). The Athenians had four thousand hoplites who had marched in from Eleusis (4.68), six hundred hoplites who had arrived with Hippocrates, and Demosthenes' detachments of light troops (4.67).

4.75.1a These were the Mytilenian exiles hostile to Athens (see 4.52.2–3). Mytilene, Antandrus: Map 4.75.

4.75.1b Thucydides mentions specific missions of Athenian generals to collect tribute in 2.69 (Winter 430/29), 3.19 (Winter 428/7), 4.50 (Winter 425/4), and here

in Summer 424. For various reasons these notices have been thought to signify reassessments of tribute in 430, 428, and 425, for which last a large inscription survives indicating great increases all around and including cities in the Pontus (Map 4.75), to which Lamachus had now gone, as described in 4.75.2. See Appendix B, The Athenian Empire, §2, 10.

4.75.1c Hellespont: Map 4.75.

4.75.1d Pontus (the Euxine or Black Sea): Map 4.75.

4.75.1e Anaia: Map 4.75.

4.75.1f Samos: Map 4.75.

MAP 4.75 THE NORTH AEGEAN THEATER, 424

all its outlaws. They accordingly got together a force from the allies and set sail, defeated in battle the troops that met them from Antandrus, and retook the place. [2] Not long after, Lamachus, who had sailed into the Pontus, lost his ships at anchor in the river Calex, in the territory of Heraclea, rain having fallen in the interior and the flood coming suddenly down upon them; and himself and his troops passed by land through the Bithynian Thracians on the Asiatic side, and arrived at Chalcedon,[2a] the Megarian colony at the mouth of the Pontus.

4.76
424
8th Year/Summer
BOEOTIA
Athens plans a series of simultaneous attacks in Boeotia.

The same summer immediately after his return from the Megarid, the Athenian general Demosthenes arrived at Naupactus[1a] with forty ships. [2] He and Hippocrates had had overtures made to them by certain men in the cities in Boeotia[2a] who wished to change the constitution and introduce a democracy as at Athens.[2b] Ptoeodorus, a Theban exile, was the chief mover in this intrigue. [3] The seaport city of Siphae,[3a] on the bay of Crisae[3b] in the territory of Thespiae,[3c] was to be betrayed to them by one party; and Chaeronea[3d] (a dependency of what was formerly called the Minyan, but now the Boeotian, Orchomenus[3e]) was to be put into their hands by

4.75.2a Heraclea, Bithynia, Chalcedon: Map 4.75.
4.76.1a Naupactus: Map 4.77, AX.
4.76.2a Boeotia: Map 4.77, BY.
4.76.2b For the Boeotian constitution, see 5.38 and note 5.38.2a.

4.76.3a Siphae: Map 4.77, BY.
4.76.3b Bay of Crisae: Map 4.77, BY.
4.76.3c Thespiae: Map 4.77, BY.
4.76.3d Chaeronea: Map 4.77, AY.
4.76.3e Orchomenus: Map 4.77, AY.

MAP 4.77 THE ATHENIAN PLAN TO ATTACK BOEOTIA

another from that city, whose exiles were very active in the business, hiring men in the Peloponnesus. Some Phocians also were in the plot, Chaeronea being the frontier city of Boeotia and close to Phanotis in Phocis.[3f] [4] At the same time the Athenians were to seize the sanctuary of Apollo at Delium, in the territory of Tanagra[4a] looking toward Euboea;[4b] and all these events were to take place simultaneously upon an appointed day in order that the Boeotians might be unable to unite to oppose them at Delium, being everywhere detained by disturbances at home. [5] Should the enterprise succeed, and Delium be fortified, its authors confidently expected that even if no revolution should immediately follow in Boeotia, yet with these places in their hands, and the country being harassed by incursions, and a refuge in each instance nearby for the partisans engaged in them, things would not remain as they were, but that the rebels being supported by the Athenians, and the forces of the oligarchs divided, it would be possible after a while to settle matters according to their wishes.

Such was the plot in preparation. Hippocrates, with a force raised at home, awaited the proper moment to take the field against the Boeotians,

4.76.3f Phanotis (Panopeus) in Phocis: Map 4.77, AY.
4.76.4a Delium, Tanagra: Map 4.77, BY.
4.76.4b Euboea: Map 4.77, AY.

4.77
424
8th Year/Summer
ACARNANIA
The Acarnanians compel Oeniadae to join the Athenians; Demosthenes enlists allies and conquers Salynthius of Agrae.

while he sent on Demosthenes with the forty ships above mentioned to Naupactus to raise in those parts an army of Acarnanians and other allies, and sail for Siphae, expecting that it would be betrayed; a day having been agreed on for the simultaneous execution of both these operations. [2] Demosthenes on his arrival found Oeniadae[2a] already compelled by the united Acarnanians to join the Athenian confederacy, and himself raising all the allies in those countries, marched against and subdued Salynthius and the Agraeans;[2b] after which he devoted himself to the preparations necessary to enable him to be at Siphae on the appointed day.[2c]

About the same time in the summer, Brasidas set out on his march for the Thracian region with seventeen hundred hoplites, and arriving at Heraclea in Trachis,[1a] sent on from there a messenger to his friends at Pharsalus[1b] to ask them to conduct himself and his army through the country. Accordingly there came to Melitia in Achaea[1c] Panaerus, Dorus, Hippolochidas, Torylaus, and Strophacus, the Chalcidian *proxenus*,[1d] under whose escort he resumed his march. [2] He was also accompanied by other Thessalians, among whom was Niconidas from Larissa,[2a] a friend of Perdiccas. It was never very easy to traverse Thessaly[2b] without an escort; and throughout all Hellas for an armed force to pass without leave through a neighbor's country was a delicate step to take. Besides this the Thessalian people had always sympathized with the Athenians. [3] Indeed if instead of the customary close oligarchy there had been a constitutional government in Thessaly, he would never have been able to proceed; since even as it was, he was met on his march at the river Enipeus[3a] by certain of the opposite party who forbade his further progress, and complained of his making the attempt without the consent of the nation. [4] To this his escort answered that they had no intention of taking him through against their will; they were only friends in attendance on an unexpected visitor. Brasidas himself added that he came as a friend to Thessaly and its inhabitants; his arms not being directed against them but against the Athenians, with whom he was at war, and that although he knew of no quarrel between the Thessalians and Spartans to prevent the two nations having access to each other's territory, he neither would nor could proceed against their wishes; he could only beg them not to stop him. [5] With this answer they went away, and he took the advice of his escort, and pushed on without halting, before a greater force might gather to prevent him. Thus in the day that he set out from Melitia he performed the whole distance to Pharsalus, and encamped

---

4.77.2a Oeniadae: Map 4.77, AX.
4.77.2b Agraea, a pro-Peloponnesian state in 425
　　　　　(see 3.106.2): Map 4.77. AX.
4.77.2c The narrative of this planned attack on
　　　　　Boeotia is continued in 4.89.
4.78.1a Heraclea in Trachis: Map 4.78, BX. This
　　　　　city was last mentioned in 3.100 and
　　　　　appears again in 5.12.
4.78.1b Pharsalus: Map 4.78, BX.
4.79.1c Melitia in Achaea: Map 4.78, BX.

4.78.1d A *proxenus,* though a citizen and resident
　　　　　of his own state, served as a "friend or
　　　　　representative" (much like a modern
　　　　　honorary consul) of a foreign state.
4.78.2a Larissa: Map 4.78, BX.
4.78.2b Thessaly: Map 4.78, BX.
4.78.3a The Enipeus river runs near to Melitia:
　　　　　Map 4.78, BX.

MAP 4.78
BRASIDAS' MARCH
THROUGH THESSALY

on the river Apidanus;[5a] and so to Phacium,[5b] and from there to Perrhaebia.[5c] [6] Here his Thessalian escort went back and the Perrhaebians, who are subjects of Thessaly, brought him to Dium,[6a] a Macedonian city on the slopes of Mount Olympus,[6b] looking toward Thessaly in the dominions of Perdiccas.

In this way Brasidas hurried through Thessaly and reached Perdiccas and Chalcidice[1a] before any armed force could be assembled to stop him. [2] The departure of the army from the Peloponnesus had been obtained by the Thracian cities that were in revolt against Athens and by Perdiccas, who was alarmed at the successes of the Athenians. The Chalcidians thought that they would be the first objects of an Athenian expedition (not that the neighboring cities which had not yet revolted did not also secretly join in the invitation), and Perdiccas, although not openly at war with the

4.79
424
8th Year/Summer
THRACE
Brasidas had been invited by Perdiccas of Macedonia and by Chalcidian and Thracian cities who had revolted, or wished to revolt, from Athens.

4.78.5a   The Apidanus river runs by Pharsalus:
          Map 4.78, BX.
4.78.5b   Phacium: Map 4.78, BX.
4.78.5c   Perrhaebia: Map 4.78, BX.
4.78.6a   Dium: Map 4.78, AX.
4.78.6b   Mount Olympus: Map 4.78, AX.
4.79.1a   Chalcidice: Map 4.78, AY.

Athenians, also had his apprehensions on account of his old quarrels with them, and above all wished to subdue Arrhabaeus king of the Lyncestians.[2a] [3] It had been less difficult for them to get an army to leave the Peloponnesus, because of the ill fortune of the Spartans at the present moment.

The attacks of the Athenians upon the Peloponnesus, and in particular upon Laconia, might, it was hoped, be diverted most effectively by annoying them in return, and by sending an army to their allies, especially as they were willing to maintain it and asked for it to aid them in revolting. [2] The Spartans were also glad to have an excuse for sending some of the Helots[2a] out of the country, for fear that the present aspect of affairs and the occupation of Pylos might encourage them to revolt. [3] Indeed fear of their numbers and obstinacy even persuaded the Spartans to the action which I shall now relate, their policy at all times having been governed by the necessity of taking precautions against them.[3a] The Helots were invited by a proclamation to pick out those of their number who claimed to have most distinguished themselves in the wars, in order that they might receive their freedom; the object being to test them, as it was thought that the first to claim their freedom would be the most high-spirited and the most apt to rebel. [4] As many as two thousand were selected accordingly, who crowned themselves and went round the temples, rejoicing in their new freedom. [5] The Spartans, however, soon afterwards did away with them, and no one ever knew how each of them perished. The Spartans now therefore gladly sent seven hundred Helots as hoplites with Brasidas,[5a] who recruited the rest of his force by means of money in the Peloponnesus.

Brasidas himself was sent out by the Spartans mainly at his own desire, although the Chalcidians also were eager to have a man so energetic as he had shown himself whenever there was anything to be done at Sparta, and whose later service abroad proved of the utmost use to his country. [2] At the present moment his just and moderate conduct toward the cities generally succeeded in persuading many to revolt, besides the places which he managed to take by treachery; and thus when the Spartans desired to negotiate, as they ultimately did, they had places to offer in exchange, and the burden of war meanwhile shifted from the Peloponnesus. Later on in the war, after the events in Sicily,[2a] the present valor and conduct of Brasidas, which was known by experience to some, by hearsay to others, was what mainly created an esteem for the Spartans among the allies of Athens. [3] He was the first who went out and showed himself so good a man at all points as to leave behind him the conviction that the rest were like him.

Meanwhile his arrival in the Thracian region no sooner became known

4.79.2a   Two campaigns against Arrhabaeus in Lyncestis (Map 4.78, AX) are described in 4.83 and 4.124–28.
4.80.2a   Helots of Sparta: See Appendix C, Spartan Institutions, §3–4.
4.80.3a   This famous comment by Thucydides has also been taken in a more restricted sense, to wit, "their policy with regard to the

Helots has been governed by the necessity of taking precautions."
4.80.5a   The return, emancipation, and settlement of these Helots is described in 5.34; see Appendix C, Spartan Institutions, §9.
4.81.2a   This remark sheds light on the date of the composition of this section of the history; see the Introduction (sect. II.ii).

to the Athenians than they declared war against Perdiccas, whom they regarded as the author of the expedition, and kept a closer watch on their allies in that quarter.

Upon the arrival of Brasidas and his army, Perdiccas immediately set out with them and with his own forces against his neighbor Arrhabaeus son of Bromerus, king of the Lyncestian Macedonians, with whom he had a quarrel and whom he wished to subdue. [2] However, when he arrived with his army and Brasidas at the pass leading into Lyncestis,[2a] Brasidas told him that before commencing hostilities he wished to try to persuade Arrhabaeus to become the ally of Sparta, [3] as Arrhabaeus had already made overtures indicating his willingness to let Brasidas arbitrate between them, and the Chalcidian envoys who accompanied Brasidas had warned him not to remove all the apprehensions of Perdiccas, in order to insure his greater zeal in their cause. [4] Besides, the envoys of Perdiccas had talked at Sparta about his bringing many of the places round him into alliance with them; and thus Brasidas thought he might take a larger view of the question of Arrhabaeus. [5] Perdiccas however retorted that he had not brought Brasidas with him to arbitrate in their quarrel but to subdue the enemies whom he might point out to him; and that while he, Perdiccas, was paying for half of his army it was a breach of faith for Brasidas to parley with Arrhabaeus. [6] Nevertheless, Brasidas disregarded the wishes of Perdiccas and held the parley in spite of him, and allowed himself to be persuaded to lead off the army without invading the country of Arrhabaeus; after which Perdiccas, holding that Brasidas had not kept faith with him, contributed only a third instead of half of the support of the army.

The same summer, without delay, Brasidas marched with the Chalcidians against Acanthus, a colony of the Andrians,[1a] and arrived just before the grape harvest. [2] The inhabitants were divided into two parties on the question of receiving him; those who had joined the Chalcidians in inviting him, and the popular party. However, fear for their grapes, which were still on the vines, enabled Brasidas to persuade the multitude to admit him alone to hear what he had to say before making a decision; and he was admitted accordingly and appeared before the people and, not being a bad speaker for a Spartan,[2a] addressed them as follows:

"Acanthians, the Spartans have sent me out with an army to make good the reason that we gave for the war when we began it, namely, that we were going to war with the Athenians in order to free Hellas. [2] Our delay in coming has been caused by mistaken expectations

---

4.83
424
8th Year/Summer
LYNCESTIS
Perdiccas and Brasidas march against Arrhabaeus, king of Lyncestis. Brasidas insists on parleying first, and agrees to withdraw without invading Lyncestis. Perdiccas is furious and thereafter reduces his subsidy to Brasidas.

4.84
424
8th Year/Summer
ACANTHUS
Brasidas threatens Acanthus just before the grape harvest. He enters the city alone to address the citizens.

4.85
424
8th Year/Summer
ACANTHUS
Brasidas speaks to the Acanthians, asking them to aid Sparta against Athens.

4.83.2a   Lyncestis: Map 4.78, AX.
4.84.1a   Acanthus: Map 4.78, AY; Andros, Map
          4.75, or Map 4.128.
4.84.2a   Spartans were notorious for speaking
          "laconically," that is, bluntly, ungra-
          ciously, and with few words. See Appen-
          dix H, Dialects and Ethnic Groups, §8,
          which mentions Greek stereotypes con-
          nected with regional dialects.

about the war in Greece which led us to hope that by our own unassisted efforts, and without your risking anything, we could effect the speedy downfall of the Athenians; and you must not blame us for this, as we have now come at the first moment we could, prepared with your aid to do our best to defeat them. [3] I am therefore astonished at finding your gates shut against me, and at not meeting with a better welcome. [4] We Spartans thought of you as allies eager to have us, to whom we should come in spirit even before we were with you in body; and in this expectation undertook all the risks of a march of many days through a strange country, so far did our zeal carry us. [5] It will be a terrible thing if after this you have other intentions, and mean to stand in the way of your own and Hellenic freedom. [6] It is not merely that you oppose me yourselves; but wherever I may go people will be less inclined to join me, on the score that you, to whom I first came—an important city like Acanthus, and prudent men like the Acanthians—refused to admit me. I shall have nothing to prove that the reason which I advance is the true one; it will be said either that there is something unfair in the freedom which I offer, or that I am here in insufficient force and unable to protect you against an attack from Athens. [7] Yet when I went with the army which I now have to the relief of Nisaea, the Athenians did not venture to engage me although in greater force than I;[7a] and it is not likely they will ever send by sea against you an army as numerous as they had at Nisaea."

"And for myself, I have come here not to hurt but to free the Hellenes: witness the solemn oaths by which I have bound my government that the allies that I may bring over shall be independent; and besides my object in coming is not to obtain your alliance by force or fraud, but to offer you mine to help you against your Athenian masters. [2] I protest, therefore, against any suspicions of my intentions after the guarantees which I offer, and equally so against doubts of my ability to protect you, and I invite you to join me without hesitation."

[3] "Some of you may hang back because they have private enemies, and fear that I may put the city into the hands of a party: none need be more tranquil than they. [4] I am not come here to help this party or that; and I do not consider that I should be bringing you freedom in any real sense, if I should disregard your constitution, and enslave the many to the few or the few to the many. [5] This would be heavier than a foreign yoke; and we Spartans instead of being thanked for our pains, should get neither honor nor glory but,

4.86
424
8th Year/Summer
ACANTHUS
Brasidas guarantees that Sparta will respect Acanthus' independence and will not interfere in her affairs.

4.85.7a   As Thucydides comments in 4.108.5, Brasidas is lying, or at best stretching the truth, here. His forces at Nisaea, combined with the Boeotians present (4.70–72), were certainly more numerous than the Athenians on that occasion, at least according to Thucydides' account (4.67–68); see note 4.73.3a.

on the contrary, reproaches. The charges which strengthen our hands in the war against the Athenians would on our own showing be merited by ourselves, and more hateful in us than in those who make no pretensions to honesty; [6] as it is more disgraceful for persons of character to take what they covet by fair-seeming fraud than by open force; the one aggression having for its justification the might which fortune gives, the other being simply a piece of clever roguery."

"As this matter concerns us greatly, we attend to it with great care. Above and beyond the oaths that I have mentioned, what stronger assurance can you have that it is indeed in our interests to do what we say here, than when you compare our words with our actual past deeds and find that they are consistent."

"[2] If to these considerations of mine you put in the plea of inability, and claim that your friendly feeling should save you from being hurt by your refusal; if you say that freedom, in your opinion, is not without its dangers, and that it is right to offer it to those who can accept it, but not to force it on any against their will, then I shall take the gods and heroes of your country to witness that I came for your good and was rejected, and shall do my best to compel you by laying waste your land. [3] I shall do so without scruple, being justified by the necessity which constrains me; first, to prevent the Spartans from being damaged by you, their friends, in the event of your nonadhesion, through the moneys that you pay to the Athenians; and secondly, to prevent the Hellenes from being hindered by you in shaking off their servitude. [4] Otherwise indeed we should have no right to act as we propose; except in the name of some public interest, what call should we Spartans have to free those who do not wish it? [5] Empire we do not aspire to: it is what we are laboring to put down; and we should wrong the greater number if we allowed you to stand in the way of the independence that we offer to all. [6] Endeavor, therefore, to decide wisely, and strive to begin the work of liberation for the Hellenes, and gain for yourselves endless renown, while you escape private loss, and cover your commonwealth with glory."[6a]

Such were the words of Brasidas. The Acanthians, after much had been said on both sides of the question, gave their votes in secret, and the majority, influenced by the seductive arguments of Brasidas and by fear for their vintage, decided to revolt from Athens; not however admitting the army until they had taken his personal security for the oaths sworn by his govern-

4.87
424
8th Year/Summer
ACANTHUS
Brasidas concludes by threatening to ravage Acanthian territory if Acanthus refuses to join his "Hellenic liberation."

4.88
424
8th Year/Summer
ACANTHUS
The Acanthians decide to revolt from Athens.

4.87.6a   See the Introduction (sect. II.ii) for a discussion of speeches in Thucydides.

ment before they sent him out, assuring the independence of the allies whom he might bring over. [2] Not long after, Stagirus,[2a] a colony of the Andrians, followed their example and revolted. Such were the events of this summer.[2b]

It was in the first days of the winter following that the places in Boeotia were to be put into the hands of the Athenian generals, Hippocrates and Demosthenes, the latter of whom was to go with his ships to Siphae, the former to Delium.[1a] A mistake, however, was made in the days on which they were each to start; and Demosthenes sailing first to Siphae, with the Acarnanians and many of the allies from those parts on board, failed to effect anything because the plot had been betrayed by Nicomachus, a Phocian from Phanotis,[1b] who informed the Spartans and they the Boeotians. [2] Help accordingly flocked in from all parts of Boeotia, and since Hippocrates had not yet entered the country to make his diversion, Siphae and Chaeronea[2a] were promptly secured and the conspirators, informed of the mistake, did not cause any trouble in the cities.

Meanwhile Hippocrates called out the Athenians in full force, citizens and resident aliens, and the foreigners in Athens,[1a] and arrived at his destination after the Boeotians had already come back from Siphae, and encamping his army began to fortify the sanctuary of Apollo at Delium,[1b] in the following manner. [2] A trench was dug all round the temple and the consecrated ground, and the earth thrown up from the excavation was made to do duty as a wall, in which stakes were also planted, the vines round the sanctuary being cut down and thrown in, together with stones and bricks pulled down from the houses near, using, in short, every means to build the rampart. Wooden towers were also erected where they were wanted, and where there was no part of the temple buildings left standing, as on the side where the gallery once existing had fallen in. [3] The work was begun on the third day after leaving home, and continued during the fourth till dinnertime on the fifth, [4] when most of it being now finished, the army marched about a mile and a quarter from Delium on its way home. From this point, most of the light troops went straight on, while the hoplites halted and remained where they were; Hippocrates stayed behind at Delium to arrange the posts and to give directions for the completion of such part of the outworks as had been left unfinished.

During the days thus employed the Boeotians were mustering at Tanagra,[1a] and by the time that they had come in from all the cities, they found the Athenians already on their way home. The rest of the eleven *boeotarchs*[1b] were against giving battle, as the enemy was no longer in

4.88.2a   Stagirus: Map 4.78, AY.
4.88.2b   Thucydides' narrative returns to Thrace in 4.101.5.
4.89.1a   Thucydides returns here to the Athenian plan to attack Boeotia described in 4.77. Siphae: Map 4.96, BY; Delium: Map 4.96, AY.
4.89.1b   Phanotis (Panopeus) in Phocis: Map 4.96, AX.

4.89.2a   Chaeronea: Map 4.96, AX.
4.90.1a   Athens, in relation to Delium: Map 4.96, BY. For resident aliens (*metics*), see Appendix A, The Athenian Government, §2, 4.
4.90.1b   Delium: Map 4.96, AY.
4.91.1a   Tanagra: Map 4.96, AY.
4.91.1b   *Boeotarchs* were chief magistrates of the Boeotian federal government; see note 5.38.2a.

Boeotia, the Athenians having just crossed over the Oropian[1c] border when they halted; but Pagondas son of Aeolidas, one of the boeotarchs of Thebes[1d] (Arianthides son of Lysimachidas, being the other), and then commander-in-chief, thought it best to fight a battle. He accordingly called the men to him, company after company, to prevent their all leaving their arms at once, and urged them to attack the Athenians, and face the hazards of a battle, speaking as follows:

"Boeotians, the idea that we ought not to give battle to the Athenians unless we come upon them in Boeotia is one which should never have entered into the head of any of us, your generals. It was to damage Boeotia that they crossed the frontier and built a fort in our country; and they are therefore, I imagine, our enemies wherever we may come upon them, wherever they may have come to act as enemies do. [2] And if anyone has taken up with the idea in question for reasons of safety, it is high time for him to change his mind. The party attacked, whose own country is in danger, can scarcely discuss what is prudent with the calmness of men who are in full enjoyment of what they have, and are thinking of attacking a neighbor in order to get more. [3] It is your national habit to resist a foreign invader, regardless of whether he is in your country or not; and when that invader is Athenian, and lives upon your frontier as well, it is doubly imperative to do so. [4] As between neighbors generally, freedom means simply a determination to hold one's own; and with neighbors like these, who are trying to enslave near and far alike, there is nothing for it but to fight it out to the last. Look at the condition of the Euboeans[4a] and of most of the rest of Hellas and you will be convinced that while others have to fight with their neighbors for this frontier or that, for us being conquered means one frontier for the whole country, about which there will be no dispute, for they will simply come and take by force what we have. [5] So much more have we to fear from this neighbor than from another. Besides, people who, like the Athenians in the present instance, are tempted by pride of strength to attack their neighbors, usually march most confidently against those who keep still, and only defend themselves in their own country, but think twice before they grapple with those who meet them outside their frontier and strike the first blow if opportunity offers. [6] The Athenians have shown us this themselves; the defeat which we inflicted upon them at Coronea,[6a] at the

4.92
424/3
8th Year/Winter
DELIUM
Pagondas speaks to the Boeotian army to encourage it to attack the Athenians; he calls the fortification of Delium an assault that must be repulsed.

4.91.1c Oropus (Map 4.96, AY) lay on the border between Boeotia and Attica.
4.91.1d Thebes: Map 4.96, AY. For the Boeotian Federal Constitution, see note 5.38.2a
4.92.4a Euboea (Map 4.96, AY) is very near to Boeotia.
4.92.6a Pagondas refers to the battle at Coronea (Map 4.96, AX), in 447; see 1.113.

time when our quarrels had allowed them to occupy the country, has given great security to Boeotia until the present day. [7] Remembering this, the old must equal their ancient exploits, and the young, the sons of the heroes of that time, must endeavor not to disgrace their native valor; and trusting in the help of the god whose temple has been sacrilegiously fortified, and in the victims which, when we sacrificed, appeared propitious, we must march against the enemy and teach him that he must go and get what he wants by attacking someone who will not resist him, but that men whose glory it is to be always ready to give battle for the liberty of their own country and never unjustly to enslave that of others, will not let him go without a struggle."

4.93
424/3
8th Year/Winter
DELIUM
Persuaded to attack, the Boeotians advance late in the day; their numbers, types, and disposition are described.

By these arguments Pagondas persuaded the Boeotians to attack the Athenians, and quickly breaking up his camp led his army forward, it being now late in the day. On nearing the enemy, he halted in a position where a hill intervening prevented the two armies from seeing each other, and then formed and prepared for action. [2] Meanwhile Hippocrates at Delium, informed of the approach of the Boeotians, sent orders to his troops to throw themselves into line, and himself joined them not long afterwards, leaving about three hundred horse behind him at Delium to guard the place in case of attack, and at the same time to watch their opportunity and fall upon the Boeotians during the battle. [3] The Boeotians placed a detachment to deal with these, and when everything was arranged to their satisfaction appeared over the hill, and halted in the order which they had decided on, to the number of seven thousand hoplites, more than ten thousand light troops, one thousand horse, and five hundred peltasts.[3a] [4] On their right were the Thebans and those of their division,[4a] in the center the Haliartians, Coronaeans, Copaeans,[4b] and the other people around the lake, and on the left the Thespians, Tanagrans, and Orchomenians,[4c] the cavalry and the light troops being at the extremity of each wing. The Thebans formed twenty-five shields deep, the rest as they pleased.[4d] [5] Such was the strength and disposition of the Boeotian army.

4.94
424/3
8th Year/Winter
DELIUM
The Athenians form their battle line.

On the side of the Athenians, the hoplites throughout the whole army formed eight deep, being in numbers equal to the enemy, with the cavalry upon the two wings. Light troops regularly armed there were none in the army, nor had there ever been any at Athens. Those who had joined in the invasion, though many times more numerous than those of the enemy, had mostly followed unarmed, as part of the citizens and foreigners at Athens, and having started first on their way home were not present in any

---

4.93.3a   Peltasts were troops armed only with a small, light shield, a javelin, and a short sword. Unhindered by body armor, they could move much more quickly than the fully armed hoplite. Aenus: Map 4.5, AY.

4.93.4a   See note 5.38.2a for the "divisions" of the Boeotian Confederacy.

4.93.4b   Haliartus: Map 4.96, AX; Coronea: Map 4.96, AX; Lake Copais: Map 4.96, AY.

4.93.4c   Thespiae, Tanagra: Map 4.96, AY; Orchomenus: Map 4.96, AX.

4.93.4d   This deep formation was peculiarly Theban; see Appendix F, Ancient Greek Land Warfare, §3.

number.[1a] [2] The armies being now in line and upon the point of engaging, Hippocrates, the general, passed along the Athenian ranks, and encouraged them as follows:

"Athenians, I shall only say a few words to you, but brave men require no more, and they are addressed more to your understanding than to your courage. [2] None of you must suppose that we are going out of our way to run this risk in the country of another. Fought in their territory the battle will be for ours: if we conquer, the Peloponnesians will never invade your country without the Boeotian horse, and in one battle you will win Boeotia and in a manner free Attica. [3] Advance to meet them then like citizens of a country in which you all glory as the first in Hellas, and like sons of the fathers who beat them at Oenophyta[3a] with Myronides and thus gained possession of Boeotia."[3b]

Hippocrates had got half through the army with his exhortation, when the Boeotians, after a few more hasty words from Pagondas, struck up the *paean*,[1a] and came against them from the hill; the Athenians advancing to meet them, and closing at a run. [2] The extreme wing of neither army came into action, one like the other being stopped by the water courses in the way; the rest engaged with the utmost obstinacy, shield against shield. [3] The Boeotian left, as far as the center, was worsted by the Athenians. The Thespians in that part of the field suffered most severely. The troops alongside them having given way, they were surrounded in a narrow space and cut down fighting hand to hand; some of the Athenians also fell into confusion in surrounding the enemy and mistook and so killed each other. [4] In this part of the field the Boeotians were beaten, and retreated upon the troops still fighting; but the right, where the Thebans were, got the better of the Athenians and shoved them further and further back, though gradually at first.[4a] [5] It so happened also that Pagondas, seeing the distress of his left, had sent two squadrons of horse, where they could not be seen, round the hill, and their sudden appearance struck a panic into the victorious wing of the Athenians, who thought that it was another army coming against them. [6] At length in both parts of the field, disturbed by this panic, and with their line broken by the advancing Thebans, the whole

4.95
424/3
8th Year/Winter
DELIUM
Hippocrates encourages the Athenian army.

4.96
424/3
8th Year/Winter
DELIUM
After a long struggle, the Athenians give way and retreat, pursued by the Boeotian cavalry. The onset of night limits the pursuit and many Athenians escape.

4.94.1a The departure of the light troops was mentioned in 4.90.4, but Thucydides does say that many Athenian light troops were among the battle casualties in 4.102.2. See note 4.101.2a. Most poor Athenians, who might have made up a corps of light troops in another state's armed forces, probably served Athens in her navy.
4.95.3a The battle at Oenophyta (Map 4.96, BY) in the year 457 is mentioned in 1.108.
4.95.3b Boeotia: Map 4.96, AX.
4.96.1a The *paean* was a ritual chant that the

men of classical Greek armies sang as they advanced into battle, rallied, or celebrated victory.
4.96.4a See Appendix F, Ancient Greek Land Warfare, for a discussion of such implications of this chapter as that these combatants wore no uniforms or national identifying emblems; that once the phalanx formation was broken, heavy casualties were inflicted; and that the depth of the Theban formation probably permitted them to "shove" the thinner Athenian lines backward.

MAP 4.96 THE DELIUM CAMPAIGN

Athenian army took to flight. [7] Some made for Delium and the sea, some for Oropus, others for Mount Parnes,[7a] or wherever they had hopes of safety, [8] pursued and cut down by the Boeotians, and in particular by the cavalry, composed partly of Boeotians and partly of Locrians,[8a] who had come up just as the rout began. Night however coming on to interrupt the pursuit, the mass of the fugitives escaped more easily than they would otherwise have done. [9] The next day the troops at Oropus and Delium returned home by sea, after leaving a garrison in the latter place, which they continued to hold notwithstanding the defeat.

The Boeotians set up a trophy, took up their own dead, and stripped those of the enemy, and leaving a guard over them retired to Tanagra, there to take measures for attacking Delium. [2] Meanwhile a herald came from the Athenians to ask for the dead, but was met and turned back by a Boeotian herald, who told him that he would effect nothing until the return of himself (the Boeotian herald), and who then went on to the Athenians and told them on behalf of the Boeotians that they had done wrong in transgressing the law of the Hellenes. [3] Of what use was the

4.97
424/3
8th Year/Winter
DELIUM
The Boeotians refuse to return the Athenian dead until Athens evacuates Delium. They call the occupation of this shrine a sacrilegious violation of Hellenic law.

4.96.7a Delium Oropus: Map 4.96, AY; Mount Parnes: Map 4.96, BY.

4.96.8a The horsemen came from Opuntian Locris (Map 4.96, AX), which borders Boeotia on the northwest.

universal custom protecting the temples in an invaded country if the Athenians were to fortify Delium and live there, acting exactly as if they were on unconsecrated ground, and drawing and using for their purposes the water which they, the Boeotians, never touched except for sacred uses? [4] Accordingly for the god as well as for themselves, in the name of the deities concerned and of Apollo, the Boeotians called on them first to evacuate the temple if they wished to take up the dead that belonged to them.

After these words from the herald, the Athenians sent their own herald to the Boeotians to say that they had not done any wrong to the temple, and for the future would do it no more harm than they could help; not having occupied it originally for this purpose, but to defend themselves from it against those who were really wronging them. [2] The law of the Hellenes was that conquest of a country, whether more or less extensive, carried with it possession of the temples in that country, with the obligation to keep up the usual ceremonies, at least as far as possible. [3] The Boeotians and most other people who had turned out the owners of a country, and put themselves in their places by force, now held as of right the temples which they originally entered as usurpers. [4] If the Athenians could have conquered more of Boeotia this would have been the case with them: as things stood, the piece of it which they had got they should treat as their own, and not quit unless obliged. [5] The water they had disturbed out of a necessity which they had not wantonly incurred, having been forced to use it in defending themselves against the Boeotians who had first invaded Attica. [6] Besides, anything done under the pressure of war and danger might reasonably claim indulgence even in the eye of the god; or why, pray, were the altars the asylum for involuntary offenses? Transgression also was a term applied to presumptuous offenders, not to the victims of adverse circumstances. [7] In short, which were most impious—the Boeotians who wished to barter dead bodies for holy places, or the Athenians who refused to give up holy places to obtain what was theirs by right? [8] The condition of evacuating Boeotia must therefore be withdrawn. They were no longer in Boeotia. They stood where they stood by the right of the sword. All that the Boeotians had to do was to tell them to take up their dead under a truce according to the national custom.

The Boeotians replied that if they were in Boeotia, they must evacuate that country before taking up their dead; if they were in their own territory, they could do as they pleased: for they knew that, although the territory of Oropus where the bodies as it chanced were lying (the battle having been fought on the borders) was subject to Athens, yet the Athenians could not get them without their leave. Besides, why should they grant a truce for Athenian ground? And what could be fairer than to tell the Athenians to

4.98
424/3
8th Year/Winter
DELIUM
Justifying their occupation of Delium, the Athenians call the Boeotian refusal to return their dead a greater sacrilege.

4.99
424/3
8th Year/Winter
DELIUM
The Boeotians again refuse to give up the dead until the Athenians vacate Boeotian territory.

evacuate Boeotia if they wished to get what they asked? The Athenian herald accordingly returned with this answer, without having accomplished his object.

Meanwhile the Boeotians at once sent for darters and slingers from the Malian gulf,[1a] and with two thousand Corinthian hoplites who had joined them after the battle, the Peloponnesian garrison which had evacuated Nisaea, and some Megarians[1b] with them, marched against Delium, and attacked the fort, and after divers efforts finally succeeded in taking it by means of a device of the following description. [2] They sawed in two and scooped out a great beam from end to end, and fitting it nicely together again like a flute, hung by chains a cauldron at one extremity, from which there was free passage to an iron tube projecting from the beam, which was itself in great part plated with iron. [3] This they brought up from a distance upon carts to the part of the wall principally composed of vines and timber, and when it was near, inserted huge bellows into their end of the beam and blew with them. [4] The blast passing closely confined into the cauldron, which was filled with lighted coals, sulfur and pitch, made a great blaze, and set fire to the wall, which soon became untenable for its defenders, who left it and fled; and in this way the fort was taken.[4a] [5] Of the garrison some were killed and two hundred made prisoners; most of the rest got on board their ships and returned home.

Soon after the fall of Delium, which took place seventeen days after the battle, the Athenian herald, without knowing what had happened, came again for the dead, which were now restored by the Boeotians, who no longer answered as at first. [2] Not quite five hundred Boeotians fell in the battle, and nearly one thousand Athenians, including Hippocrates the general, besides a great number of light troops and camp followers.[2a]

[3] Soon after this battle Demosthenes, after the failure of his voyage to Siphae and of the plot on the city, availed himself of the Acarnanian and Agraean troops and of the four hundred Athenian hoplites which he had on board, to make a descent on the Sicyonian coast.[3a] [4] Before all his ships had come to shore, however, the Sicyonians came up and routed those that had landed and chased them to their ships, killing some and taking others prisoner; after which they set up a trophy, and gave back the dead under truce.

[5] About the same time as the affair of Delium, Sitalces[5a] king of the Odrysians died, defeated in battle while campaigning against the Triballi; Seuthes son of Sparadocus, his nephew, succeeded to the kingdom of the Odrysians, and of the rest of Thrace ruled by Sitalces.

4.100
424/3
8th Year/Winter
DELIUM
The Boeotians assault Delium and take it, setting fire to its wooden walls with an ingenious "flamethrower."

4.101
424/3
8th Year/Winter
DELIUM
After the fall of Delium the Boeotians give up the Athenian dead. Thucydides recounts both sides' casualties.
SICYON
Demosthenes is repulsed at Sicyon with losses.
THRACE
Sitalces, king of Odrysiann Thrace, dies.

4.100.1a Malian Gulf: Map 4.96, AX.
4.100.1b Nisaea, Megara: Map 4.96, BY.
4.100.4a For the development of siege warfare, see Appendix F, Ancient Greek Land Warfare, §10.
4.101.2a Since few Athenian light troops were at the battle (4.94.1), we can only assume that such casualties were caused later by pursuing Boeotian cavalry, which caught up with these retreating Athenians.
4.101.3a Sicyon: Map 4.96, BX.
4.101.5a Sitalces and his nephew Seuthes were last mentioned in the Thracian campaign of 428, recounted in 2.95–101. Events in Thrace are resumed here from 4.88.

The same winter Brasidas, with his allies in Thrace, marched against Amphipolis, the Athenian colony on the river Strymon.[1a] [2] Aristagoras the Milesian attempted to establish a settlement upon the spot on which the city now stands when he fled from King Darius,[2a] but he was dislodged by the Edonians.[2b] Thirty-two years later the Athenians sent ten thousand of their own citizens (and whoever else chose to go) to settle the region, but these were destroyed at Drabescus[2c] by the Thracians. [3] Twenty-nine years later the Athenians returned—Hagnon, son of Nicias, being sent out as a leader of the colony. He drove out the Edonians and founded a city on the spot, which was formerly called Ennea-hodoi, or Nine Ways. The base from which they started was Eion,[3a] their commercial seaport at the mouth of the river, not more than three miles from the present city, which Hagnon named Amphipolis, because the Strymon flows round it on two sides, and he built it so as to be conspicuous from the sea and land alike, running a long wall across from river to river, to complete the circumference.

Brasidas now marched against this city, starting from Arne in Chalcidice.[1a] Arriving about dusk at Aulon and Bromiscus, where the lake of Bolbe runs into the sea,[1b] he took supper there, and went on during the night. [2] The weather was stormy and it was snowing a little, which encouraged him to hurry on in order, if possible, to take everyone at Amphipolis by surprise (except the party who were to betray it). [3] The plot involved some natives of Argilus,[3a] an Andrian[3b] colony, who resided in Amphipolis, where they had also other accomplices won over by Perdiccas or the Chalcidians. [4] But the most active in the matter were the inhabitants of Argilus itself, which is close by, who had always been suspected by the Athenians, and had designs on the place. These men now saw their opportunity arrive with Brasidas, and having for some time been in correspondence with their countrymen in Amphipolis for the betrayal of the city, at once received him into Argilus, and revolted from the Athenians. That same night they took him on to the bridge over the river, [5] where he found only a small guard to oppose him, the city being at some distance from the passage and the walls not reaching down to it as at present. He easily forced his way through this guard, partly through there being treason in their ranks, partly from the stormy state of the weather and the suddenness of his attack; and so got across the bridge and immediately became master of all the property outside—the Amphipolitans having houses all over the quarter.

The passage of Brasidas was a complete surprise to the people in the city; and the capture of many of those outside, as well as the flight of the

4.102
424/3
8th Year/Winter
AMPHIPOLIS
Brasidas marches against Amphipolis, whose history and geography is described.

4.103
424/3
8th Year/Winter
AMPHIPOLIS
Brasidas, aided by Argilians and conspirators inside Amphipolis, marches quickly on a stormy night to the Strymon bridge and occupies it easily.

4.104
424/3
8th Year/Winter
AMPHIPOLIS
Despite surprise and confusion, the gates of Amphipolis are secured and a message sent to Thucydides, general and author of this history, who after receiving it leaves immediately from Thasos with seven triremes.

4.102.1a Thucydides records the attempt to found Amphipolis in 1.100.3. Amphipolis, Strymon River: Map 4.106, AY.
4.102.2a For the story of Aristagoras and the attempt to found a city there, see Herodotus, Book 5, 124–26. See also Appendix E, The Persians, §2–3.
4.102.2b Edonia: Map 4.106, AY.
4.102.2c Drabescus: Map 4.106, AY; also see 1.100.3.

4.102.3a Eion: Map 4.106, AY.
4.103.1a Arne in Chalcidice: location unknown. For the location of Chalcidice, see Map 4.106, AX.
4.103.1b Aulon: location unknown. Bromiscus: Map 4.106, AY; Lake Bolbe: Map 4.106, AX.
4.103.3a Argilus: Map 4.106, AY.
4.103.3b Andros: Map 4.128, BY.

rest within the wall, combined to produce great confusion among the citizens; especially as they did not trust one another. [2] It is even said that if Brasidas, instead of stopping to pillage, had advanced straight against the city, he would probably have taken it. [3] Instead, however, he established himself where he was, overran the country outside, and for the present remained inactive, vainly awaiting a demonstration on the part of his friends within. [4] Meanwhile the party opposed to the traitors proved numerous enough to prevent the gates being immediately thrown open, and in concert with Eucles, the general, who had come from Athens to defend the place, sent to the other commander in Thrace, Thucydides son of Olorus, the author of this history,[4a] who was at the isle of Thasos,[4b] a Parian colony,[4c] half a day's sail from Amphipolis, to tell him to come to their relief. [5] On receipt of this message he at once set sail with seven ships which he had with him, in order, if possible, to reach Amphipolis in time to prevent its capitulation, or in any case to save Eion.

Meanwhile Brasidas, afraid that help would arrive by sea from Thasos, and learning that Thucydides possessed the right of working the gold mines in that part of Thrace, and had thus great influence with the inhabitants of the mainland, hastened to gain the city, if possible, before the people of Amphipolis should be encouraged by his arrival to hope that he could save them by getting together a force of allies from the sea and from Thrace, and so refuse to surrender. [2] He accordingly offered moderate terms, proclaiming that any of the Amphipolitans and Athenians who so chose, might continue to enjoy their property with full rights of citizenship; while those who did not wish to stay had five days to depart, taking their property with them.

Upon hearing this, the bulk of the inhabitants began to change their minds, especially as only a small number of the citizens were Athenians, the majority having come from various places, and also because many of the prisoners Brasidas had taken outside had relatives within the walls. They found the proclamation a fair one in comparison to what their fears had suggested. The Athenians were glad to get out, as they thought they ran more risk than the rest, and did not expect any speedy relief. The multitude were generally content at being left in possession of their civic rights, and at such an unexpected reprieve from danger. [2] The partisans of Brasidas now openly advocated this course, seeing that the feeling of the people had changed, and that they no longer gave ear to the Athenian general present; and thus the surrender was made and Brasidas was admitted by them on the terms of his proclamation. [3] In this way they gave up the city, and late in the same day, Thucydides and his ships entered the harbor of Eion,[3a]

4.105
424/3
8th Year/Winter
AMPHIPOLIS
Brasidas, anxious to capture the place before Thucydides arrives, offers generous terms to the citizens.

4.106
424/3
8th Year/Winter
AMPHIPOLIS
The Amphipolitans decide to capitulate. Thucydides arrives too late to save Amphipolis, but he does save Eion.

4.104.4a This statement, and that in 4.105.1 just below it, are two of Thucydides' rare and restrained remarks about himself. See the Introduction (sect. I) for what is known of the life of Thucydides.

4.104.4b Thasos: Map 4.106, AY.
4.104.4c Paros: Map 4.128, BY.
4.106.3a Eion: Map 4.106, AY.

MAP 4.106 OPERATIONS OF BRASIDAS AGAINST AMPHIPOLIS, ACTE, AND TORONE

[4] Brasidas having just got hold of Amphipolis, and having been within a night of taking Eion; had the ships been less prompt in relieving it, in the morning it would have been his.

After this Thucydides put all in order at Eion to secure it against any present or future attack of Brasidas, and received such as had elected to come there from the interior according to the agreed-upon terms. [2] Meanwhile Brasidas suddenly sailed with a number of boats down the river to Eion to see if he could not seize the point running out from the wall, and so command the entrance; and at the same time he attacked the city by land, but was beaten off on both sides and had to content himself with arranging matters at Amphipolis and in the neighborhood. [3] Myrcinus,[3a] an Edonian city, also came over to him (the Edonian king Pittacus having been killed by the sons of Goaxis and his own wife Brauro); and Galepsus[3b]

4.107
424/3
8th Year/Winter
AMPHIPOLIS
Brasidas attacks Eion but is beaten off. Other nearby cities now revolt against Athens.

4.107.3a Myrcinus: Map 4.106, AY.
4.107.3b Galepsus: Map 4.106, AY.

and Oesime,[3c] which are Thasian colonies, followed its example not long afterward. Perdiccas too came up immediately after the capture and joined in these arrangements.

4.108
424/3
8th Year/Winter
ATHENS
Athens is alarmed by the fall of Amphipolis because all Thrace is now threatened and more revolts are feared. Indeed, many cities go over to Brasidas, for they believe revolt would be painless and underestimate Athens' power.

The news that Amphipolis was in the hands of the enemy caused great alarm at Athens. Not only was the city valuable for the timber it afforded for shipbuilding and the tribute money that it brought in; but it also was a barrier to movement across Thrace. The escort of the Thessalians had brought the Spartans within reach of the allies of Athens as far as the river Strymon, yet as long as they were not masters of the bridge and were blocked toward the sea by the Athenian triremes at Eion,[1a] and impeded on the inland side by a large and extensive lake formed by the waters of the river,[1b] they could not advance further. Now, however, their way forward seemed open. The Athenians also feared that more allies would revolt, [2] particularly because Brasidas displayed such moderation in all his conduct, and declared everywhere that he had been sent out to free Hellas. [3] The cities subject to the Athenians, hearing of the capture of Amphipolis and of the terms accorded to it, and of the gentleness of Brasidas, felt most strongly encouraged to change their condition, and sent secret messages to him, begging him to come to them; each wishing to be the first to revolt. [4] Indeed, there seemed to be no danger in so doing; their mistake in their estimate of the Athenian power was as great as that power afterwards turned out to be, and their judgment was based more upon blind wishing than upon any sound prediction; for it is a habit of mankind to entrust to careless hope what they long for, and to use sovereign reason to thrust aside what they do not desire. [5] Besides the late severe blow which the Athenians had met with in Boeotia,[5a] joined to the seductive, though untrue, statements of Brasidas, about the Athenians not having ventured to engage his single army at Nisaea,[5b] made the allies confident, and caused them to believe that no Athenian force would be sent against them. [6] Above all the wish to do what was agreeable at the moment, and the likelihood that they would find the Spartans full of zeal from the outset, made them eager to run the risk. Observing this, the Athenians sent garrisons to the different cities, as far as was possible at such short notice and in winter; while Brasidas sent dispatches to Sparta asking for reinforcements, and made preparations for building triremes in the Strymon. [7] The Spartans however did not support him, partly out of envy on the part of their chief

4.107.3c Oesime: Map 4.106, AY.
4.108.1a Eion: Map 4.106, AY.
4.108.1b Thucydides refers here to Lake Cercinitis;
　　　　　see Map 4.106, AX.
4.108.5a Boeotia: Map 4.118.
4.108.5b As Brasidas told the Acanthians in 4.85.7.
　　　　　Nisaea: Map 4.118.

men, partly because they were more bent on recovering the prisoners from the island[7a] and ending the war.

The same winter the Megarians took and razed to the foundations the long walls which had been occupied by the Athenians;[1a] and Brasidas, after the capture of Amphipolis, marched with his allies against Acte,[1b] [2] a promontory running out from the King's canal[2a] with an inward curve and ending in Athos,[2b] a lofty mountain looking toward the Aegean sea. [3] In it are various cities: Sane is an Andrian[3a] colony lying close to the canal, and facing the sea in the direction of Euboea;[3b] the others are Thyssus, Cleone, Acrothoi, Olophyxus, [4] and Dium.[4a] They are inhabited by mixed barbarian peoples speaking the two languages. There is also a small Chalcidian element; but the greater number are Tyrrheno-Pelasgians (formerly settled in Lemnos[4b] and Athens), and Bisaltians, Crestonians, and Edonians.[4c] The cities are all small ones [5] and most of these came over to Brasidas; but Sane and Dium held out and saw their land ravaged by him and his army.

Upon their not submitting, he at once marched against Torone[1a] in Chalcidice, which was held by an Athenian garrison, having been invited by a few persons who were prepared to hand over the city. Arriving in the dark a little before daybreak, he halted with his army near the temple of the Dioscuri, rather more than a quarter of a mile from the city. [2] The rest of the city of Torone and the Athenian garrison did not perceive his approach; but his partisans knowing that he was coming (a few of them had secretly gone out to meet him) were on the watch for his arrival, and were no sooner aware of it than they let in to them seven light armed men with daggers (who alone of twenty men ordered on this service dared to enter), commanded by Lysistratus an Olynthian. These passed through the sea wall and without being seen went up and put to the sword the garrison of the highest post in the city, which stands on a hill, and broke open the postern gate on the side of Canastraeum.[2a]

Brasidas meanwhile came a little nearer and then halted with his main body, sending on one hundred peltasts[1a] to be ready to rush in first, the moment that a gate should be thrown open and the beacon lighted as agreed. [2] After some time passed in waiting and wondering at the delay, the peltasts by degrees got up close to the city. The Toronaeans inside who were working with the party that had entered, had by this time broken

4.109
424/3
8th Year/Winter
MEGARA
The Megarians raze their long walls.
ACTE, THRACE
Brasidas secures most of the small non-Greek-speaking cities in Acte.

4.110
424/3
8th Year/Winter
TORONE
Brasidas sends a small party inside Torone with the help of conspirators. They occupy a high point in the city and open a gate.

4.111
424/3
8th Year/Winter
TORONE
Brasidas sends in peltasts and, the gates finally being opened, ignites a fire-signal to start the main assault.

4.108.7a These were the prisoners taken on the island of Sphacteria at Pylos; see 4.31–39.
4.109.1a These walls were taken by the Athenians in the fighting at Megara described in 4.66–74. Megara: Map 4.118.
4.109.1b Acte Peninsula: Map 4.106, BY.
4.109.2a This canal was dug by the Persians at Xerxes' command in preparation for his invasion of Greece in 490. Its construction is described by Herodotus, Book 7, 22ff. See Appendix E, The Persians, §4.
4.109.2b Mount Athos: Map 4.106, BY.
4.109.3a Sane: Map 4.106, AY; Andros: Map 4.128, BY.

4.109.3b Euboea: Map 4.128, BY; in relation to Chalcidice, Map 4.128, AY.
4.109.4a Thyssus, Cleone, Acrothoi, Olophyxus, and Dium, all on the Acte Peninsula: Map 4.106, BY.
4.109.4b Lemnos: Map 4.128, AY.
4.109.4c Bisaltia, Crestonia: Map 4.106, AX; Edonia: Map 4.106, AY.
4.110.1a Torone: Map 4.106, AY.
4.110.2a The postern faced west, toward Point Canastraeum, the easternmost cape of the Pallene Peninsula: Map 4.106, BY
4.111.1a Peltasts: see note 4.93.3a.

down the postern and opened the gates leading to the marketplace by cutting through the bar.[2a] They first brought some men round and let them in by the postern in order to strike panic into the surprised townsmen by suddenly attacking them from behind and on both sides at once; after which they raised the fire-signal as had been agreed, and took in by the market gates the rest of the peltasts.

Brasidas seeing the signal told the troops to rise, and dashed forward amid the loud hurrahs of his men, which caused dismay among the astonished townspeople. [2] Some burst in straight by the gate, others over some square pieces of timber placed against the wall (which had fallen down and was being rebuilt) to draw up stones; [3] Brasidas and the greater number making straight uphill for the higher part of the city, in order to take it from top to bottom, once and for all, while the rest of the multitude spread in all directions.

The capture of the city was effected before the great body of the Toronaeans had recovered from their surprise and confusion; [2] but the conspirators and the citizens of their party at once joined the invaders. About fifty of the Athenian hoplites happened to be sleeping in the marketplace when the alarm reached them. A few of these were killed fighting; the rest escaped, some by land, others to the two ships on the station, and took refuge in Lecythus, a fort garrisoned by their own men in the corner of the city running out into the sea at the end of a narrow isthmus. [3] There they were joined by the Toronaeans of their party.

Day now arrived, and the city being secured, Brasidas made a proclamation to the Toronaeans who had taken refuge with the Athenians, to come out as many as chose, to their homes, without fearing for their rights or persons, and he sent a herald to invite the Athenians to accept a truce, and to evacuate Lecythus with their property, as being Chalcidian ground. [2] The Athenians refused this offer, but asked for a truce for a day to take up their dead. Brasidas granted it for two days, which he employed in fortifying the houses near the fort and the Athenians in doing the same to their positions. [3] Meanwhile he called a meeting of the Toronaeans, and said very much what he had said at Acanthus, namely, that they must not look upon those who had negotiated with him for the capture of the city as bad men or as traitors, as they had not acted as they had done from corrupt motives or in order to enslave the city, but for the good and freedom of Torone; nor again must those who had not shared in the enterprise suppose that they would not equally reap its fruits, as he had not come to destroy either the city or any individual in it. [4] This was the reason for his proclamation to those that had fled for refuge to the Athenians: he thought none the worse of them for their friendship for the Athenians; he believed that they had only to make trial of the Spartans to like them as well, or even

4.111.2a Cut through the bar of the gate: see note
            2.4.4a.

much better, as acting much more justly: it was for want of such a trial that they were now afraid of them. [5] Meanwhile he warned all of them to prepare to be staunch allies and as such to be held responsible for all faults in future: for the past, they had not wronged the Spartans but had been wronged by others who were too strong for them, and any opposition that they might have offered him could be excused.

Having encouraged them with this address, he made his attack upon Lecythus as soon as the truce expired, and the Athenians defended themselves from a poor wall and from some houses with parapets. [2] For one day they beat him off. On the next the enemy were preparing to bring up a siege engine against them from which they meant to throw fire upon the wooden defenses; and as the troops were already coming up to the point where they supposed they could best bring up the engine, and where the place was most assailable; meanwhile the Athenians put a wooden tower upon a house opposite and carried up a quantity of jars and casks of water and big stones, and a large number of men also climbed up. [3] The house thus laden too heavily suddenly broke down with a loud crash; at which the men who were near and saw it were more vexed than frightened; but those not so near, and still more those furthest off, thought that the place was already taken at that point, and fled in haste to the sea and the ships.

Brasidas, perceiving that they were deserting the parapet, and seeing what was going on, dashed forward with his troops, and immediately took the fort, and put to the sword all whom he found in it. [2] In this way the place was evacuated by the Athenians, who went across in their boats and ships to Pallene.[2a] Now there is a temple of Athena in Lecythus, and Brasidas had proclaimed in the moment of making the assault that he would give thirty silver *minae*[2b] to the man first on the wall. Being now of the opinion that the capture was scarcely due to human agency, he gave the thirty minae to the goddess for her temple, and razed and cleared Lecythus, and made the whole of it consecrated ground. [3] The rest of the winter he spent in settling the places in his hands, and in making designs upon the rest; and with the expiration of the winter the eighth year of this war ended.

In the spring of the summer following, the Spartans and Athenians made an armistice for a year. The Athenians thought that they would thus gain time to take precautions before Brasidas could procure the revolt of any more of their cities, and that they might also, if it suited them, conclude a general peace; the Spartans suspecting the actual fears of the Athenians, and thinking that once they had enjoyed a respite from trouble and misery, they would be more disposed to consent to a reconciliation, to give back the prisoners, and to make a treaty for the longer period. [2] The more important thing for the Spartans was to get back their men while

4.116.2a Pallene Peninsula: Map 4.106, BX.
4.116.2b *Mina* (plural *minae*): a unit of currency equal to one sixtieth of a talent, or one

hundred drachmas; see Appendix J, Classical Greek Currency, §5.

Brasidas' good fortune lasted; further successes might make the struggle a less unequal one in Chalcidice, but would leave them still deprived of their men, and even in Chalcidice not more than a match for the Athenians and by no means certain of victory. [3] An armistice was accordingly concluded by Sparta and her allies upon the terms following:

4.118
423
9th Year/Summer
ATHENS-SPARTA
The terms of the armistice are described.

- As to the temple and oracle of the Pythian Apollo,[1a] we are agreed that whoever so wishes shall have access to it, without fraud or fear, according to the usages of his forefathers. [2] The Spartans and the allies present agree to this, and promise to send heralds to the Boeotians and Phocians, and to do their best to persuade them to agree likewise.

- [3] As to the treasure of the god, we agree to exert ourselves to detect all wrongdoers, truly and honestly following the customs of our forefathers, we and you and all others willing to do so, all following the customs of our forefathers. [4] As to these points the Spartans and the other allies are agreed as has been said.

- As to what follows, the Spartans and the other allies agree, if the Athenians conclude a treaty, to remain, each of us in our own territory, retaining our respective acquisitions; the garrison in Coryphasium keeping within Buphras and Tomeus;[4a] that in Cythera[4b] attempting no communication with the Peloponnesian confederacy, neither we with them, or they with us; that in Nisaea and Minoa[4c] not crossing the road leading from the gates of the temple of Nisus to that of Poseidon and from thence straight to the bridge at Minoa;[4d] the Megarians and the allies being equally bound not to cross this road, and the Athenians retaining the island they have taken, without any communication on either side; as to Troezen,[4e] each side retaining what it has, and as was arranged with the Athenians.

- [5] As to the use of the sea, so far as refers to their own coast and to that of their confederacy, that the Spartans and their allies may voyage upon it in any vessel rowed by oars and of not more than five hundred talents' tonnage,[5a] not a vessel of war.

- [6] That all heralds and embassies, with as many attendants as they please, for concluding the war and adjusting claims, shall have free passage, going and coming, to the Peloponnesus or Athens by land and by sea.

4.118.1a For the temple and oracle of Pythian Apollo at Delphi, see Map 4.118.
4.118.4a "Coryphasium" is the Spartan name for Pylos (Map 4.118); the locations of Buphras and Tomeus are unknown.
4.118.4b Cythera: Map 4.118.
4.118.4c Nisaea, Minoa: Map 4.118.
4.118.4d The locations of the temple of Nisus and Poseidon are not known, but a possible site for the bridge to Minoa, if that is the island meant here, is shown on Map 3.51, BX.
4.118.4e Troezen: Map 4.118. We do not know

the reason why Troezen is included here. It probably concerns territory on Methana which Athens captured in 4.45.2, and presumably still held, or about which she had made some arrangement with Troezen.
4.118.5a The talent is a unit of weight, whose value varied over time and place between sixty and eighty pounds. Hence these vessels would be limited to something between fifteen and twenty tons—quite small even then. The boat in 7.25.5 is twenty times larger.

MAP 4.118
LOCATIONS IN THE
ARMISTICE TERMS

• [7] That during the truce, deserters whether slave or free shall be received neither by you, nor by us.

• [8] Further, that satisfaction shall be given by you to us and by us to you according to the public law of our several countries, [9] all disputes being settled by law without recourse to hostilities.

The Spartans and allies agree to these articles: but if you have anything more fair or just to suggest, come to Sparta and let us know; whatever shall be just will meet with no objection either from the Spartans or from the allies.

• [10] Only let those who come come with full powers, as you bid us to come. The truce shall be for one year.

Approved by the people

• [11] The tribe of Acamantis had the *prytany*,[11a] Phoenippus was secretary, Niciades chairman. Laches moved that in the name of the good fortune of the Athenians, they should conclude the armistice upon the terms agreed upon by the Spartans and the allies.

• [12] It was agreed accordingly in the popular assembly, that the armistice should be for one year, beginning that very day, the fourteenth of the month of Elaphebolion;[12a] [13] during which time ambassadors and heralds should go and come between the two countries to discuss the bases of a peace. [14] That the generals and prytanes

4.118.11a *Prytany, prytanes* (plural); see Appendix
           A, The Athenian Government, §5.
4.118.12a By the Athenian calendar: see Appendix

K, Classical Greek Calendars and Dating
Systems, §1–3.

should call an assembly of the people, in which the Athenians should first consult on the peace, and on the mode in which the embassy for putting an end to the war should be admitted. And that the embassy now present should at once pledge on oath before the people to keep well and truly this truce for one year.

4.119
423
9th Year/Summer
ATHENS-SPARTA
Thucydides lists the signers of the armistice. Discussions on a general peace take place.

On these terms the Spartans concluded a truce with the Athenians and their allies on the twelfth day of the Spartan month Cerastius;[1a] [2] the allies also taking the oaths. Those who concluded and poured the libation[2a] were Taurus son of Echetimides, Athenaeus son of Pericleidas, and Philocharidas son of Eryxilaidas, Spartans; Aeneas son of Aeneas, and Euphamidas son of Aristonymus, Corinthians; Damotimus son of Naucrates, and Onasimus son of Megacles, Sicyonians; Nicasus son of Cecalus, and Menecrates son of Amphidorus, Megarians; and Amphias son of Eupaidas, an Epidaurian; and the Athenian generals Nicostratus son of Diitrephes, Nicias son of Niceratus, and Autocles son of Tolmaeus. [3] Such was the armistice, and during the whole of it conferences were held on the subject of a full peace.

4.120
423
9th Year/Summer
SCIONE
Scione, although isolated like an island, revolts from Athens after the armistice negotiations are concluded, but before that is known in Chalcidice. Brasidas sails there, welcomes the Scionaeans as allies, and praises their courage.

In the days in which they were going backwards and forwards to these conferences, Scione, a city in Pallene,[1a] revolted from Athens, and went over to Brasidas. The Scionaeans say that they are Pallenians from the Peloponnesus, and that their first founders settled the place when they were carried to it by the storm which caught the Achaeans on their return voyage from Troy. [2] The Scionaeans had no sooner revolted than Brasidas crossed over by night to Scione, with a friendly trireme ahead and himself in a small boat some way behind; his idea being that if he fell in with a vessel larger than the boat he would have the trireme to defend him, while a ship that was a match for the trireme would probably neglect the small vessel to attack the large one, and thus leave him time to escape. [3] When he had completed the crossing, he called a meeting of the Scionaeans and spoke to the same effect as at Acanthus[3a] and Torone,[3b] adding that they merited the utmost commendation in that, in spite of their insular position, located as they were on Pallene, an isthmus cut off from the mainland by the Athenian occupation of Potidaea,[3c] they had of their own free will gone forward to gain their liberty instead of timorously waiting until they had been by force compelled to accept their own manifest good. This was a sign that they would valiantly undergo any trial, however great; and if he were to order affairs as he intended, he would count them among the truest and sincerest friends of the Spartans, and would in every other way honor them.

4.119.1a By the Spartan calendar: see Appendix K, Classical Greek Calendars and Dating Systems, §1–3.
4.119.2a The pouring of the libations was ritually necessary to complete the agreement.
4.120.1a Scione, Pallene Peninsula: Map 4.122.

4.120.3a Acanthus: Map 4.122; see 4.84–87.
4.120.3b Torone: Map 4.122; see 4.114.3.
4.120.3c Potidaea: Map 4.122.

MAP 4.122
BRASIDAS' OPERATIONS IN
CHALCIDICE

The Scionaeans were elated by his language, and when even those who had at first disapproved of what was being done caught the general confidence, they decided on a vigorous conduct of the war. They welcomed Brasidas with all possible honors, publicly crowning him with a wreath of gold as the liberator of Hellas; private persons crowded round him and decked him with garlands as though he had been an athlete.[1a] [2] Meanwhile Brasidas left them a small garrison for the present and crossed back again, and not long afterwards sent over a larger force, intending with the help of the Scionaeans to attempt Mende[2a] and Potidaea before the Athenians should arrive. Scione, he felt, was too like an island for them not to attempt to relieve it. Indeed, with regard to these cities, he was actively seeking their betrayal.

In the midst of his designs upon the cities in question, a trireme arrived with the commissioners carrying round the news of the armistice, Aristonymus for the Athenians and Athenaeus for the Spartans. [2] The troops now crossed back to Torone, and the commissioners gave Brasidas notice of the truce. All the Spartan allies in Thrace accepted what had been done; [3] and Aristonymus made no difficulty about the rest, but finding, on counting the days, that the Scionaeans had revolted after the date of the convention, refused to include them in it. To this Brasidas earnestly objected, asserting that the revolt took place before, and would not give up the city. [4] When Aristonymus reported the case to Athens, the people at once pre-

4.121
423
9th Year/Summer
SCIONE
Brasidas hopes to contrive the revolt of Mende and Potidaea to end Scione's isolation.

4.122
423
9th Year/Summer
SCIONE
Commissioners arrive with news of the armistice. Brasidas falsely claims that Scione had revolted before the armistice. Athens prepares to attack Scione.

4.121.1a A victorious athlete; see Appendix I,
        Classical Greek Religious Festivals, §5.
4.121.2a Mende: Map 4.122.

pared to send an expedition to Scione. Upon this, envoys arrived from Sparta, alleging that this would be a breach of the truce, and laid claim to the city, trusting the word of Brasidas, and at the same time offering to submit the question to arbitration. [5] Arbitration, however, was what the Athenians did not choose to risk; they were determined to send troops at once to the place, and furious at the idea of even the islanders now daring to revolt, in a vain reliance upon the power of the Spartans by land. [6] Besides the facts of the revolt were rather as the Athenians contended, the Scionaeans having revolted two days after the convention. Cleon accordingly succeeded in carrying a decree to reduce and put to death the Scionaeans and the Athenians employed the leisure which they now enjoyed in preparing for the expedition.

4.123
423
9th Year/Summer
MENDE-SCIONE
Mende revolts after the armistice, but Brasidas sends troops and prepares both it and Scione for an anticipated Athenian attack.

Meanwhile the city of Mende in Pallene, a colony of the Eretrians,[1a] revolted and was received without scruple by Brasidas, in spite of its having evidently come over during the armistice, on account of certain infringements of the truce alleged by him against the Athenians. [2] This audacity of Mende was partly caused by seeing Brasidas so active in the matter and by the conclusions they drew from his refusal to betray Scione. Besides, the conspirators in Mende were few, and had carried on their practices too long not to fear detection for themselves, and had forced the multitude to go against their own inclination. [3] This news made the Athenians more furious than ever, and they at once prepared an expedition against both cities. [4] Expecting their arrival, Brasidas conveyed the women and children of the Scionaeans and Mendaeans away to Olynthus[4a] in Chalcidice, and sent over to them five hundred Peloponnesian hoplites and three hundred Chalcidian peltasts,[4b] all under the command of Polydamidas.

4.124
423
9th Year/Summer
LYNCESTIS
Brasidas and Perdiccas lead a second expedition against Arrhabaeus and rout the Lyncestians in battle. Perdiccas wants to advance but Brasidas needs to return to Chalcidice.

Leaving these two cities to prepare together against the speedy arrival of the Athenians, [4.124.1] Brasidas and Perdiccas started on a second joint expedition into Lyncestis[1a] against Arrhabaeus; the latter with the forces of his Macedonian subjects, and a corps of hoplites composed of Hellenes dwelling in his country; the former with the Peloponnesians whom he still had with him and the Chalcidians,[1b] Acanthians,[1c] and the rest in such force as they could muster. In all there were about three thousand Hellenic hoplites accompanied by all the Macedonian cavalry together with the Chalcidians, almost one thousand strong, besides an immense crowd of barbarians. [2] On entering the country of Arrhabaeus, they found the Lyncestians encamped and waiting for them, and themselves took up a position opposite. [3] The infantry on either side were upon a hill, with a plain between them, into which the horse of both armies first galloped

---

4.123.1a Eretria, a city on the island of Euboea: Map 4.128, BY.
4.123.4a Olynthus (Map 4.122), where Perdiccas had already (in 433) induced many of the Chalcidians to settle inland, abandoning and demolishing their cities on the seaboard, to make that one city a strong place; see 1.58.2.

4.123.4b Peltasts: see note 4.93.3a.
4.124.1a Lyncestis: Map 4.128, AX. Their previous attack against Lyncestis was described in 4.83.
4.124.1b Chalcidice: Map 4.128, AY.
4.124.1c Acanthus: Map 4.128, AY.

down, and engaged in a cavalry action. After this the Lyncestian hoplites advanced from their hill to join their cavalry and offered battle; upon which Brasidas and Perdiccas also came down to meet them, and engaged and routed them with heavy loss; the survivors taking refuge upon the heights and there remaining inactive. [4] The victors now set up a trophy and waited two or three days for the Illyrian[4a] mercenaries who were to join Perdiccas. Perdiccas then wished to go on and attack the villages of Arrhabaeus, and to sit still no longer; but Brasidas, far from seconding this wish, refused it; he was anxious to return, seeing that the Illyrians did not appear, and feared that the Athenians might sail up during his absence and attack Mende.

While they were thus disputing, the news arrived that the Illyrians had actually betrayed Perdiccas and had joined Arrhabaeus; and the fear inspired by their warlike character made both parties now think it best to withdraw. However, owing to the dispute, nothing had been settled as to when they should start; and when night came on, the Macedonians and the barbarian crowd suddenly took fright in one of those mysterious panics to which great armies are liable,[1a] and persuaded that an army many times more numerous than that which had really arrived was advancing and all but upon them, suddenly broke and fled in the direction of home. This compelled Perdiccas, who at first did not perceive what had occurred, to depart without seeing Brasidas, the two armies being encamped at a considerable distance from each other. [2] At daybreak, Brasidas, seeing that the Macedonians had gone on, and that the Illyrians and Arrhabaeus were on the point of attacking him, formed his hoplites into a square with the light troops in the center, and prepared to retreat. [3] Posting his youngest soldiers to dash out wherever the enemy should attack them, he himself with three hundred picked men in the rear intended to face about during the retreat and beat off the most forward of their assailants. [4] Meanwhile, before the enemy approached, he sought to sustain the courage of his soldiers with the following hasty exhortation:

"Peloponnesians, if I did not suspect you of being dismayed at being left alone to sustain the attack of a numerous and barbarian enemy, I should just have said a few words to you as usual without further explanation. As it is, in the face of the desertion of our friends and the numbers of the enemy, I have some advice and information to offer, which, brief as it must be, will, I hope, suffice for the more important points. [2] The bravery that you habitually dis-

4.125
423
9th Year/Summer
LYNCESTIS
The defection of Illyrian allies to Arrhabaeus forces Perdiccas and Brasidas to retreat. During the night the Macedonians panic and flee; Brasidas arranges his force to repel attacks while retreating.

4.126
423
9th Year/Summer
LYNCESTIS
Brasidas encourages his troops as the Lyncestians prepare to attack; he says that the barbarians, however numerous, cannot defeat a determined defense.

4.124.4a Illyria: Map 4.128, AX.
4.125.1a See Thucydides' account of the Athenians in retreat in Sicily in 7.80.3.

play in war does not depend on your having allies at your side in this or that encounter, but on your native courage; nor have numbers any terrors for citizens of states like yours, in which the many do not rule the few, but rather the few the many, owing their position to nothing else than to superiority in the field. [3] Inexperience now makes you afraid of barbarians; and yet the trial of strength which you had with the Macedonians among them, and my own judgment (confirmed by what I hear from others), should be enough to satisfy you that they will not prove formidable. [4] Where an enemy seems strong but is really weak, a true knowledge of the facts makes his adversary the bolder, just as a serious antagonist is encountered most confidently by those who do not know him. [5] Thus the present enemy might terrify an inexperienced imagination; they are formidable in outward bulk; their loud yelling is unbearable; and the brandishing of their weapons in the air has a threatening appearance. But when it comes to real fighting with an opponent who stands his ground, they are not what they seemed; they have no regular order that they should be ashamed of deserting their positions when hard pressed; flight and attack are equally honorable with them, and afford no test of courage; their independent mode of fighting never leaving anyone who wants to run away without a fair excuse for doing so. In short, they think frightening you at a secure distance a surer game than meeting you hand to hand; otherwise they would have done the one and not the other. [6] You can thus plainly see that the terrors with which they were at first invested are in fact trifling enough, though to the eye and ear very prominent. Stand your ground therefore when they advance, and wait your opportunity to retire in good order, and you will reach a place of safety all the sooner. Thus you will know forever afterwards that rabble such as these, to those who sustain their first attack, do but show off their courage by threats of the terrible things that they are going to do at a distance, but with those who give way to them are quick enough to display their heroism in pursuit when they can do so without danger."

4.127
423
9th Year/Summer
LYNCESTIS
After their attack is resolutely repulsed, the Lyncestian barbarians pursue the Macedonians and block Brasidas' route at a pass.

With this brief address Brasidas began to lead off his army. Seeing this, the barbarians came on with much shouting and hubbub, thinking that he was flying and that they would overtake him and cut him off. [2] But wherever they charged they found the young men ready to dash out against them, while Brasidas with his picked company sustained their onset. Thus the Peloponnesians withstood the first attack, to the surprise of the enemy, and afterwards received and repulsed them as fast as they came on, retiring as soon as their opponents became quiet. The main body of the barbarians ceased therefore to molest the Hellenes with Brasidas in the open country,

MAP 4.128 OPERATIONS DURING THE WINTER OF 423

and leaving behind a certain number to harass their march, the rest went on after the flying Macedonians, slaying those with whom they came up, and so arrived in time to occupy the narrow pass between two hills that leads into the country of Arrhabaeus.[2a] They knew that this was the only way by which Brasidas could retreat, and now proceeded to surround him just as he entered the most difficult part of the road, in order to cut him off.

Brasidas, perceiving their intention, told his three hundred to run on without order, each as quickly as he could, to the hill which seemed easiest to take, and to try to dislodge the barbarians already there, before they should be joined by the main body closing round him. [2] These attacked and overpowered the party upon the hill, and the main army of the Hellenes now advanced with less difficulty toward it; the barbarians being terri-

4.128
423
9th Year/Summer
LYNCESTIS
Brasidas drives the barbarians away. His enraged soldiers pillage the Macedonian baggage train and kill the oxen. From this moment, Perdiccas and Brasidas drift apart.

4.127.2a The location of this pass, also mentioned
above in 4.83.2, is not precisely determined.

fied at seeing their men on that side driven from the height, and no longer following the main body who they considered had gained the frontier and made good their escape. [3] The heights once gained, Brasidas now proceeded more securely, and the same day arrived at Arnisa,[3a] the first city in the dominions of Perdiccas. [4] The soldiers, enraged at the desertion of the Macedonians, vented their rage on all their yokes of oxen which they found on the road, and on any baggage which had tumbled off (as might easily happen in the panic of a night retreat), by unyoking and cutting down the cattle and taking the baggage for themselves. From this moment [5] Perdiccas began to regard Brasidas as an enemy and to feel against the Peloponnesians a hatred which could not suit well the adversary of the Athenians. Indeed, he now departed from his natural interests and made it his endeavor to come to terms with the latter and to get rid of the former.

On his return from Macedonia to Torone,[1a] Brasidas found that the Athenians were already masters of Mende,[1b] and remained quiet where he was, thinking it now out of his power to cross over into Pallene and assist the Mendaeans, but he kept good watch over Torone. [2] For about the same time as the campaign in Lyncestis, the Athenians sailed upon the expedition which we left them preparing against Mende and Scione,[2a] with fifty ships (ten of which were Chians[2b]), one thousand Athenian hoplites and six hundred archers, one hundred Thracian mercenaries and some peltasts drawn from their allies in the neighborhood, under the command of Nicias son of Niceratus, and Nicostratus son of Diitrephes. [3] Departing from Potidaea,[3a] the fleet came to land opposite the temple of Poseidon, and proceeded against Mende; there they found the men of this city, reinforced by three hundred Scionaeans, with their Peloponnesian auxiliaries, seven hundred hoplites in all, under Polydamidas, encamped upon a strong hill outside the city. [4] These Nicias, with one hundred and twenty light-armed Methonaeans,[4a] sixty picked men from the Athenian hoplites, and all the archers, tried to reach by a path running up the hill, but he received a wound and found himself unable to force the position. Nicostratus, meanwhile, with all the rest of the army, advanced upon the hill, which was naturally difficult, by a different approach further off. His troops were thrown into utter disorder and the whole Athenian army narrowly escaped being defeated. [5] For that day, as the Mendaeans and their allies showed no signs of yielding, the Athenians retreated and encamped, and the Mendaeans at nightfall returned into the city.

The next day the Athenians sailed round to the Scione side[1a] and took the suburb there, and all day plundered the country, without anyone coming out against them, partly because of intestine disturbances in the city; and the following night the three hundred Scionaeans returned home. [2]

4.129
423
9th Year/Summer
MENDE
An Athenian attack on Mende is initially repulsed.

4.130
423
9th Year/Summer
MENDE
The gates of Mende are opened after disputes between Mendaean and Peloponnesian troops; the Athenians take and sack the city.

4.128.3a Arnisa: location unknown.
4.129.1a Torone: Map 4.128, AY.
4.129.1b Mende: Map 4.128, AY.
4.129.2a These Athenian preparations were mentioned in 4.122.6. Scione: Map 4.128, AY.
4.129.2b Island of Chios: Map 4.75, and Map 5.3.
4.129.3a Potidaea: Map 4.128, AY.
4.129.4a Methone in Macedonia: Map 4.128, AX.
4.130.1a The south side of Mende: Map 4.128, AY.

On the morrow Nicias advanced with half the army to the frontier of Scione and laid waste the country; while Nicostratus with the remainder stationed themselves before the city near the upper gate on the road to Potidaea. [3] The arms of the Mendaeans and of their Peloponnesian auxiliaries within the wall happened to be piled in that quarter, where Polydamidas accordingly began to draw them up for battle, encouraging the Mendaeans to make a sortie. [4] At this moment one of the popular party answered him rebelliously that they would not go out and did not want a war, and for thus answering was dragged by the arm and knocked about by Polydamidas. Hereupon the popular party at once seized their arms and rushed at the Peloponnesians and at their allies of the opposite faction. [5] The troops thus assaulted were at once routed, partly from the suddenness of the conflict and partly through fear of the gates being opened to the Athenians, with whom they imagined that the attack had been planned. [6] As many as were not killed on the spot took refuge in the citadel, which they had held from the first; and the whole Athenian army, Nicias having by this time returned and being close to the city, now burst into Mende, which had opened its gates without any agreed terms, and sacked it just as if they had taken it by storm, the generals even finding some difficulty in restraining them from also massacring the inhabitants. [7] After this the Athenians told the Mendaeans that they might retain their civil rights, and themselves judge the supposed authors of the revolt; and cut off the party in the citadel by a wall built down to the sea on either side, appointing troops to maintain the blockade. Having thus secured Mende, they proceeded against Scione.

The Scionaeans and Peloponnesians marched out against them, occupying a strong hill in front of the city, which had to be captured by the enemy before they could invest the place. [2] The Athenians stormed the hill, defeated and dislodged its occupants, and having encamped and set up a trophy, prepared for the work of circumvallation.[2a] [3] Not long after they had begun their operations, the auxiliaries besieged in the citadel of Mende forced the guard by the sea side and arrived by night at Scione, into which most of them succeeded in entering, passing through the besieging army.

4.131
423
9th Year/Summer
SCIONE
The Athenians win a victory outside Scione and then besiege the city.

While the investment of Scione was in progress, Perdiccas sent a herald to the Athenian generals and made peace with the Athenians, through spite against Brasidas for the retreat from Lyncestis, from which moment indeed he had begun to negotiate. [2] The Spartan Ischagoras was just then upon the point of starting with an army overland to join Brasidas; and Perdiccas, being now required by Nicias to give some proof of the sincerity of his reconciliation to the Athenians, and being himself no longer disposed to let

4.132
423
9th Year/Summer
THRACE
After making peace with Athens, Perdiccas prevents reinforcements from reaching Brasidas. Spartan commissioners do arrive, and bring young Spartans to take charge of the allied cities.

4.131.2a Circumvallation: the building of a wall to surround or isolate a city by land; see Appendix F, Ancient Greek Land Warfare, §10.

the Peloponnesians into his country, put in motion his friends in Thessaly,[2a] with whose chief men he always took care to have relations, and so effectually stopped the army and its preparation that they did not even try the Thessalians. [3] Ischagoras himself, however, with Amaeinias and Aristeus, succeeded in reaching Brasidas; they had been commissioned by the Spartans to inspect the state of affairs, and in breach of the law brought out from Sparta some of their young men to put in command of the cities, to prevent their being entrusted to the persons upon the spot. Brasidas accordingly placed Clearidas son of Cleonymus in Amphipolis, and Pasitelidas son of Hegesander in Torone.[3a]

4.133
423
9th Year/Summer
BOEOTIA
Thebes dismantles the wall of Thespiae.
ARGOS
The temple of Hera at Argos burns down.
SCIONE
Scione is completely invested by the Athenians.

The same summer the Thebans[1a] dismantled the wall of the Thespians[1b] on the charge of Atticism, having always wished to do so, and now finding it an easy matter, as the flower of the Thespian youth had perished in the battle with the Athenians.[1c] [2] The same summer also the temple of Hera at Argos[2a] was burnt down, through Chrysis, the priestess, placing a lighted torch near the garlands and then falling asleep, so that they all caught fire and were in a blaze before she observed it. [3] Chrysis that very night fled to Phlius[3a] for fear of the Argives, who, following the law in such a case, appointed another priestess named Phaeinis. Chrysis at the time of her flight had been priestess for eight years of the present war and half the ninth.[3b] [4] At the close of the summer the siege works around Scione[4a] were completed and the Athenians, leaving a detachment to maintain the blockade, returned with the rest of their army.[4b]

4.134
423/2
9th Year/Winter
LAODICIUM
Mantinea and Tegea fight an indecisive battle at Laodicium.

During the following winter the Athenians and Spartans were kept quiet by the armistice; but the Mantineans and Tegeans,[1a] and their respective allies, fought a battle at Laodicium,[1b] in the territory of Oresthis. The victory remained doubtful, as each side routed one of the wings opposed to them, and both set up trophies and sent spoils to Delphi. [2] After heavy loss on both sides the battle was undecided, and night interrupted the action; yet the Tegeans passed the night on the field and set up a trophy at once, while the Mantineans withdrew to Bucolion and set up theirs afterwards.

4.132.2a Thessaly: Map 4.128, AX.
4.132.3a Amphipolis, Torone: Map 4.128, AY. Thucydides' meaning is not clear here, but a breach of the law could be found on two possible counts: (1) that it was not Spartan custom to send out young men of military age as governors of allied cities; and (2) that this move violated Brasidas' promise to the Chalcidian cities that the Spartans would not interfere in their governments but would leave them free.
4.133.1a Thebes: Map 4.128, BY.
4.133.1b Thespiae: Map 4.128, BY.

4.133.1c For the losses suffered by the Thespians in the battle of Delium, see 4.96.3.
4.133.2a Argos: Map 4.128, BY.
4.133.3a Phlius: Map 4.128, BY.
4.133.3b Chrysis must have been very old, for she had already served as priestess at the temple of Hera for forty-eight years some eight and one half years earlier when the war began; see 2. 2.1.
4.133.4a Scione: Map 4.128, AY.
4.133.4b For the end of the siege of Scione, see 5.32.1.
4.134.1a Mantinea, Tegea: Map 4.128, BX.
4.134.1b Laodicium: location unknown.

At the close of the same winter, in fact almost in spring, Brasidas made an attempt upon Potidaea.[1a] He arrived by night, and succeeded in placing a ladder against the wall without being discovered, the ladder being planted just in the interval between the passing round of the bell and the return of the man who brought it back. Upon the garrison, however, taking the alarm immediately afterwards, before his men came up, he quickly led off his troops, without waiting until it was day.[1b] So ended the winter and the ninth year of this war of which Thucydides is the historian.

4.135
423/2
9th Year/Winter
POTIDAEA
Brasidas' attempt to take
Potidaea fails.

4.135.1a Potidaea: Map 4.128, AY.
4.135.1b The story of the campaign in Thrace continues in 5.2.

BOOK FIVE

The next summer the truce for a year ended, after lasting until the Pythian games.[1a] During the armistice the Athenians expelled the Delians from Delos,[1b] concluding that they must have been polluted by some old offense at the time of their consecration, and that this had been the omission in the previous purification of the island which, as I have related, had been thought to have been duly accomplished by the removal of the graves of the dead. The Delians had Atramyttium[1c] in Asia given them by Pharnaces,[1d] and settled there when they left Delos.

Meanwhile Cleon prevailed on the Athenians to let him set sail at the expiration of the armistice for the cities in the Thracian[1a] district with twelve hundred *hoplites*[1b] and three hundred horse from Athens, a larger force of the allies, and thirty ships. [2] First touching at the still-besieged Scione,[2a] and taking some hoplites from the army there, he next sailed into Cophosa harbor in the territory of Torone,[2b] which is not far from the city. [3] From thence, having learnt from deserters that Brasidas was not in Torone, and that its garrison was not strong enough to give him battle, he advanced with his army against the city, sending ten ships to sail round into the harbor. [4] He came first to the fortification recently built in front of the city by Brasidas in order to take in the suburb, to do which he had pulled down part of the original wall and made it one city [5.3.1] Pasitelidas, the Spartan commander, with such garrison as there was in the place, hurried to this point to repel the Athenian assault; but finding himself hard

5.1.1a   The Pythian games were athletic and musical contests held at Delphi (Map 4.128, BX) every four years. See Appendix I, Greek Religious Festivals, §5.
5.1.1b   Delos: Map 5.3. The earlier purification of Delos was described in 3.104.
5.1.1c   Atramyttium, in Asia Minor: Map 5.3. In 5.32 Thucydides says that the Delians were allowed to return to Delos, but some of them must have remained in Atramyttium because he mentions them again in 8.108 as residing there.
5.1.1d   This Pharnaces was the Persian governor

of the Hellespontine region (Map 5.3), whom the Peloponnesian envoys to the Persian king were trying to reach in 2.67 when the Thracians detained them and turned them over to the Athenians.
5.2.1a   Thrace: Map 5.3. This continues the narrative of events in Thrace from 4.135.
5.2.1b   *Hoplites* were heavily armed Greek infantrymen. See Appendix F, Land Warfare, §2.
5.2.2a   Scione: Map 5.3. The siege of Scione began in the summer of 423; see 4.131.
5.2.2b   Torone: Map 5.3.

5.1
422
10th Year/Summer
DELOS
The truce ends. The Athenians expel the Delians from Delos; they settle at Atramyttium.

5.2
422
10th Year/Summer
THRACE
Cleon leads an expedition to Thrace, going first to Scione and then to Torone, which he attacks.

5.3
422
10th Year/Summer
THRACE
The Athenians take Torone before Brasidas can come to its support. Torone's women and children are enslaved, and its men and garrison sent to Athens, from which they are later exchanged or freed by the peace.
ATTICA
The Boeotians capture Panactum by treachery.

MAP 5.3 CLEON'S EXPEDITION TO THRACE

pressed, and seeing the ships that had been sent round sailing into the harbor, Pasitelidas began to be afraid that they might get up to the city before its defenders were there, and the fortification being also carried, he might be taken prisoner, and so abandoned the outer fortification and ran into the city. [2] But the Athenians from the ships had already taken Torone, and their land forces following at his heels burst in with him with a rush over the part of the old wall that had been pulled down, killing some of the Peloponnesians and Toronaeans in the mêlée, and making prisoners of the rest, and Pasitelidas their commander amongst them. [3] Brasidas meanwhile had advanced to relieve Torone, and had only about four miles more to go when he heard of its fall on the road and turned back again. [4] Cleon and the Athenians set up two trophies,[4a] one by the harbor, the

5.3.4a   A trophy was set up by the victors after an ancient Greek battle. It usually consisted of a set of captured armor arranged on a pole that was raised on or near the battlefield.

MAP 5.4
TRAVELS OF PHAEAX IN
SICILY AND ITALY

other by the fortification, and making slaves of the wives and children of the Toronaeans, sent the men with the Peloponnesians and any Chalcidians that were there, to the number of seven hundred, to Athens; from which, however, they all came home afterwards, the Peloponnesians on the conclusion of peace, and the rest by being exchanged against other prisoners with the Olynthians.[4b] [5] About the same time Panactum,[5a] a fortress on the Athenian border, was taken by treachery by the Boeotians.[5b] [6] Meanwhile Cleon, after placing a garrison in Torone, weighed anchor and sailed round Athos[6a] on his way to Amphipolis.[6b]

About the same time Phaeax son of Erasistratus set sail with two colleagues as ambassador from Athens to Italy and Sicily.[1a] [2] The Leontines,[2a] upon the departure of the Athenians from Sicily after the peace agreement,[2b] had enrolled many new citizens and The People planned to redistribute the land; but those in power, aware of their intention, called in the Syracusans and expelled The People. [3] These last were scattered in various directions; but the upper classes came to an agreement with the Syracusans, abandoned and laid waste their city, and went to live at Syracuse, where they were made citizens. [4] Afterwards some of them were dissatisfied, and leaving Syracuse occupied Phocaeae, a quarter of the city of Leontini, and Bricinniae,[4a] a fortified place in the Leontine country, and being there joined by most of the exiled People carried on war from the fortifications. [5] The Athenians hearing this, sent Phaeax to see if they could not by some means so convince their allies there and the rest of the Sicilians of the ambitious designs of Syracuse, as to induce them to form a

5.4
422
10th Year/Summer
SICILY
The Athenians send Phaeax to Sicily to form a coalition against Syracuse and to rescue the exiled Leontines. Phaeax returns to Athens unsuccessful.

5.3.4b	Olynthus: Map 5.3.
5.3.5a	Panactum: Map 5.3.
5.3.5b	Boeotia: Map 5.3.
5.3.6a	Mount Athos: Map 5.3.
5.3.6b	Amphipolis: Map 5.3. The narrative of Cleon's voyage will be continued in 5.6.
5.4.1a	This episode resumes the narrative of events in Sicily from 4.65.
5.4.2a	Leontini: Map 5.4.
5.4.2b	Thucydides is referring to the Peace of Gela; see 4.65.
5.4.4a	Bricinniae, possible location: Map 5.4.

general coalition against her, and thus save The People of Leontini. [6] Arrived in Sicily, Phaeax succeeded at Camarina[6a] and Agrigentum,[6b] but meeting with a repulse at Gela[6c] did not go on to the rest, as he saw that he should not succeed with them, but returned through the country of the Sicels to Catana,[6d] and after visiting Bricinniae as he passed, and encouraging its inhabitants, sailed back to Athens.

During his voyage along the coast to and from Sicily, he talked with some cities in Italy on the subject of friendship with Athens, and also encountered some Locrian[1a] settlers exiled from Messana,[1b] who had been sent there when the Locrians were called in by one of the factions that divided Messana after the pacification of Sicily,[1c] and Messana came for a time into the hands of the Locrians. [2] These being met by Phaeax on their return home received no injury at his hands, as the Locrians had agreed with him for a treaty with Athens. [3] They were the only people of the allies of Syracuse who, when the reconciliation between the Sicilians took place, had not made peace with Athens; nor indeed would they have done so now, if they had not been pressed by a war with the Hipponians[3a] and Medmaeans[3b] who lived on their border, and were colonists of theirs. Phaeax meanwhile proceeded on his voyage, and at length arrived at Athens.

Cleon, having sailed round from Torone[1a] to Amphipolis,[1b] made Eion[1c] his base, and after an unsuccessful assault upon the Andrian[1d] colony of Stagirus,[1e] took Galepsus,[1f] a colony of Thasos,[1h] by storm. [2] He now sent envoys to Perdiccas to command his attendance with an army, as provided by the alliance; and others to Thrace, to Polles, king of the Odomantians,[2a] who was to bring as many Thracian mercenaries as possible; and himself remained inactive in Eion, awaiting their arrival. [3] Informed of this, Brasidas on his part took up a position of observation upon Cerdylium,[3a] a place situated in the Argilian[3b] country on high ground across the river, not far from Amphipolis, and commanding a view on all sides, and thus made it impossible for Cleon's army to move without his seeing it; for he fully expected that Cleon, contemptuous of the scanty numbers of his opponent, would march against Amphipolis with the force that he had with him. [4] At the same time Brasidas made his preparations, calling to his standard fifteen hundred Thracian mercenaries, and all the Edonians,[4a] horse and *peltasts*;[4b] he also had a thousand Myrcinian[4c] and Chalcidian peltasts,[4d]

5.5
422
10th Year/Summer
ITALY
Phaeax tries to secure the friendship of some Italian cities for Athens. Epizephyrian Locri, at war with its neighbors, makes peace with Athens.

5.6
422
10th Year/Summer
THRACE
Cleon makes Eion his base and calls upon local allies for additional troops. Brasidas establishes a base at Amphipolis.

5.4.6a	Camarina: Map 5.4.	5.6.1d	Andros: Map 5.3.
5.4.6b	Agrigentum: Map 5.4.	5.6.1e	Stagirus: Map 5.7, AX.
5.4.6c	Gela: Map 5.4.	5.6.1f	Galepsus: Map 5.7, AY.
5.4.6d	Catana: Map 5.4.	5.6.1h	Thasos: Map 5.7, AY.
5.5.1a	Locri (Epizephyrian): Map 5.4.	5.6.2a	Odomantian territory, approximate location: Map 5.7, AY.
5.5.1b	Messana: Map 5.4.		
5.5.1c	The pacification, or "reconciliation between the Sicilians," took place in 424; see 4.65.	5.6.3a	Cerdylium, a hill near Amphipolis: exact location unknown.
		5.6.3b	Argilus: Map 5.7, AX.
5.5.3a	Hipponium: Map 5.4.	5.6.4a	Edonian territory, approximate location: Map 5.7, AX.
5.5.3b	Medma: Map 5.4.		
5.6.1a	Torone, Map 5.7, BX. Cleon's voyage is continued from 5.3.	5.6.4b	*Peltasts* were lightly armed troops; see note 4.111.1a.
5.6.1b	Amphipolis: Map 5.7, AX.	5.6.4c	Myrcinus: Map 5.7, AX.
5.6.1c	Eion: Map 5.7, AX.	5.6.4d	Chalcidice, Map 5.7, AX.

MAP 5.7 BATTLE OF AMPHIPOLIS

besides those in Amphipolis, [5] and a force of hoplites numbering altogether about two thousand, and three hundred Hellenic horse. Fifteen
hundred of these he had with him upon Cerdylium; the rest were stationed
with Clearidas in Amphipolis.

After remaining quiet for some time, Cleon was at length obliged to do
as Brasidas expected. [2] His soldiers, tired of their inactivity, began seriously to reflect on the weakness and incompetence of their commander and
the skill and valor that would be opposed to him, and on their own original
unwillingness to accompany him. These murmurs coming to the ears of
Cleon, he resolved not to disgust the army by keeping it in the same place,
and broke up his camp and advanced. [3] The temper of the general was
what it had been at Pylos,[3a] his success on that occasion having given him
confidence in his capacity. He never dreamed of anyone coming out to
fight him, but said that he was rather going up to view the place; and if he

5.7
422
10th Year/Summer
AMPHIPOLIS
In order to satisfy his
men, Cleon makes a
reconnaissance in force to
Amphipolis. He does not
expect to fight or to be
attacked.

5.7.3a   The Pylos campaign is described in
         4.2–41. Cleon's role in it begins at
         4.21.3.

waited for his reinforcements it was not in order to make victory secure in case he should be compelled to engage, but to be enabled to surround and storm the city. [4] He accordingly came and posted his army upon a strong hill in front of Amphipolis, and proceeded to examine the lake formed by the Strymon,[4a] and how the city lay on the side of Thrace. [5] He thought to retire when he chose without fighting, as there was no one to be seen upon the wall or coming out of the gates, all of which were shut. Indeed, it seemed a mistake not to have brought down siege engines with him; he could then have taken the city, there being no one to defend it.

As soon as Brasidas saw the Athenians in motion he descended himself from Cerdylium and entered Amphipolis. [2] He did not venture to go out in regular order against the Athenians: he mistrusted his strength, and thought it inadequate to the attempt; not in numbers—these were not so unequal—but in quality, the flower of the Athenian army being in the field, with the best of the Lemnians[2a] and Imbrians.[2b] He therefore prepared to assail them by stratagem. [3] For if he let the enemy see both the numbers of his men and the makeshift nature of their armament, he thought he was less likely to win than if the enemy did not have a view of them in advance and thus come rightly to despise them. [4] He accordingly picked out a hundred and fifty hoplites, and putting the rest under Clearidas, determined to attack suddenly before the Athenians retired; thinking that he should not again have such a chance of catching them alone if their reinforcements were once allowed to come up; and so calling all his soldiers together in order to encourage them and explain his intention, spoke as follows:

5.8
422
10th Year/Summer
AMPHIPOLIS
Recognizing Cleon's ineptitude, Brasidas decides that this is an opportune moment to attack, and explains his plan to his troops.

5.9
422
10th Year/Summer
AMPHIPOLIS
Brasidas says that the Athenians are careless and their advance to Amphipolis is a blunder. He divides his force and plans to launch a double surprise attack in order to panic the enemy. He promises to set an example by his own courage.

"Peloponnesians, the character of the country from which we have come, one which has always owed its freedom to valor, and the fact that you are Dorians and the enemy you are about to fight Ionians whom you are accustomed to beat, are things that do not need further comment.[1a] [2] But as for the plan of attack that I propose to pursue, this it is well to explain, in order that the fact of our adventuring with a part instead of with the whole of our forces may not damp your courage by the apparent disadvantage at which it places you. [3] I imagine it is the poor opinion that he has of us, and the fact that he has no idea of anyone coming out to engage him, that has made the enemy march up to the place and carelessly look about him as he is doing, without noticing us. [4] But the most successful soldier will always be the man who most happily detects a blunder like this, and who carefully consulting his own means makes his attack not so much by open and regular approaches, as by seizing the

5.7.4a The Strymon River (Map 5.7, AX) flowed through Lake Cercinitis (Map 5.7, AX).
5.8.2a Lemnos: Map 5.7, BY.
5.8.2b Imbros: Map 5.7, AY.

5.9.1a This is one of several manifestations in Thucydides of Dorian contempt for Ionian valor; see Appendix H, Dialects and Ethnic Groups, §8.

opportunity of the moment; [5] and these stratagems, which do the greatest service to our friends by most completely deceiving our enemies, have the most brilliant name in war. [6] Therefore, while their careless confidence continues, and they are still thinking, as in my judgment they are now doing, more of retreat than of maintaining their position, while their spirit is slack and not high-strung with expectation, I with the men under my command will, if possible, take them by surprise and fall with a run upon their center; [7] and do you, Clearidas, afterwards, when you see me already upon them, and, as is likely, dealing terror among them, take with you the Amphipolitans, and the rest of the allies, and suddenly open the gates and dash at them, and hasten to engage as quickly as you can. [8] That is our best chance of establishing a panic among them, as a fresh assailant has always more terrors for an enemy than the one he is immediately engaged with. [9] Show yourself a brave man, as a *Spartiate*[9a] should; and do you, allies, follow him like men, and remember that zeal, honor, and obedience mark the good soldier, and that this day will make you either free men and allies of Sparta, or slaves of Athens; even if you escape without personal loss of liberty or life, your bondage will be on harsher terms than before, and you will also hinder the liberation of the rest of the Hellenes. [10] Make no show of cowardice then on your part, seeing the greatness of the issues at stake, and I will show that what I preach to others I can practice myself."[10a]

After this brief speech Brasidas himself prepared for the sally, and placed the rest with Clearidas at the Thracian gates to support him as had been agreed. [2] Meanwhile he had been seen coming down from Cerdylium and then in the city (which is overlooked from the outside), sacrificing near the temple of Athena; in short, all his movements had been observed, and word was brought to Cleon, who had at the moment gone on to look about him, that the whole of the enemy's force could be seen in the city, and that the feet of horses and men in great numbers were visible under the gates, as if a sally were intended. [3] Upon hearing this he went up to look, and having done so, being unwilling to venture upon the decisive step of a battle before his reinforcements came up, and thinking that he would have time to retire, bid the retreat be sounded and sent orders to the men to execute it by moving on the left wing in the direction of Eion,[3a] which was indeed the only way practicable. [4] This however not being quick enough for him, he joined the retreat in person and made the right wing wheel round, thus turning its unarmed side to the enemy. [5] It was then that

5.10
422
10th Year/Summer
AMPHIPOLIS
When Brasidas' preparations are observed by the Athenians, Cleon orders his army to return to Eion. Brasidas' sudden attack overwhelms the Athenians. Cleon is killed in the rout. Brasidas, however, is mortally wounded.

5.9.9a   A *Spartiate* is a full citizen of Sparta and a member of the highest Spartan military caste.
5.10.10a See the Introduction (sect. II.v) for a discussion of speeches in Thucydides.

5.10.3a   Eion: Map 5.7, AX.

Brasidas seeing the Athenian force in motion and his opportunity come, said to the men with him and the rest, "Those fellows will never stand before us, one can see that by the way their spears and heads are going. Troops which do as they do seldom stand a charge. Quick, someone, open the gates I spoke of, and let us be out and at them with no fears for the result." [6] Accordingly moving out by the palisade gate and by the first gate in the long wall then existing, he ran at top speed along the straight road, where the trophy now stands as you go by the steepest part of the hill, and fell upon and routed the center of the Athenians, panic-stricken by their own disorder and astounded at his audacity. [7] At the same moment Clearidas in execution of his orders issued out from the Thracian gates to support him, and also attacked the enemy. [8] The result was that the Athenians, suddenly and unexpectedly attacked on both sides, fell into confusion; and their left toward Eion, which had already got on some distance, at once broke and fled. Just as it was in full retreat and Brasidas was passing on to attack the right, he received a wound; but his fall was not perceived by the Athenians, as he was taken up by those near him and carried off the field. [9] The Athenian right made a better stand, and though Cleon, who from the first had no thought of fighting, at once fled and was overtaken and slain by a Myrcinian peltast,[9a] his infantry forming in close order upon the hill twice or thrice repulsed the attacks of Clearidas, and did not finally give way until they were surrounded and routed by the missiles of the Myrcinian and Chalcidian[9b] horse and the peltasts. [10] Thus all the Athenian army was now in flight; and those who escaped being killed in the battle by the Chalcidian horse and the peltasts dispersed among the hills, and with difficulty made their way to Eion. [11] The men who had taken up and rescued Brasidas, brought him into the city with the breath still in him: he lived to hear of the victory of his troops, and not long after expired. [12] The rest of the army returning with Clearidas from the pursuit stripped the dead and set up a trophy.

5.11
422
10th Year/Summer
AMPHIPOLIS
The Amphipolitans bury Brasidas and honor him as if he were their city's founder. The Athenian casualties are very heavy.

After this all the allies attended in arms and buried Brasidas at the public expense in the city, in front of what is now the marketplace, and the Amphipolitans having enclosed his tomb, ever afterwards sacrifice to him as a hero and have given to him the honor of games and annual offerings. They constituted him the founder of their colony, and pulled down the Hagnonic erections and obliterated everything that could be interpreted as a memorial of his [Hagnon] having founded the place; for they considered that Brasidas had been their preserver and courting as they did the alliance of Sparta for fear of Athens, in their present hostile relations with the latter they could no longer with the same advantage or satisfaction pay Hagnon his honors.[1a] [2] They also gave the Athenians back their dead.[2a] About six

5.10.9a Myrcinus: Map 5.7, AX.
5.10.9b Chalcidice: Map 5.7, AX.
5.11.1a For Hagnon's foundation of Amphipolis in 437/6, see 4.102.3.
5.11.2a The return of the vanquished dead was part of the post-battle ritual of hoplite

warfare. See Appendix F, Land Warfare, §6.

hundred of the latter had fallen and only seven of the enemy, owing to there having been no regular engagement, but the affair of accident and panic that I have described. [3] After taking up their dead the Athenians sailed off home, while Clearidas and his troops remained to arrange matters at Amphipolis.

About the same time three Spartans—Ramphias, Autocharidas, and Epicydidas—led a reinforcement of nine hundred hoplites to the cities in the Thracian region, and arriving at Heraclea in Trachis[1a] made changes and reforms there as they thought best. [2] While they delayed there, this battle took place and so the summer ended.

With the beginning of winter Ramphias and his companions penetrated as far as Pierium in Thessaly;[1a] but as the Thessalians opposed their further advance, and Brasidas whom they came to reinforce was dead, they turned back home, thinking that the moment had gone by, the Athenians being defeated and gone, and themselves not equal to the execution of Brasidas' designs. [2] The main cause however of their return was because they knew that when they set out, Spartan opinion was really in favor of peace.

Indeed it so happened that directly after the battle of Amphipolis and the retreat of Ramphias from Thessaly, both sides ceased to prosecute the war and turned their attention to peace. Athens had suffered severely at Delium,[1a] and again shortly afterwards at Amphipolis, and had no longer that confidence in her strength which had made her before refuse to accept the offer of peace, in the belief of ultimate victory which her success at the moment had inspired; [2] besides, she was afraid of her allies being tempted by her reverses to rebel more generally, and repented having let go the splendid opportunity for peace which the affair of Pylos had offered. [3] Sparta, on the other hand, found the actuality of the war falsify her notion that devastating their land for a few years would suffice for the overthrow of the power of the Athenians. She had suffered on the island a disaster hitherto unknown at Sparta; she saw her country plundered from Pylos[3a] and Cythera;[3b] the *Helots*[3c] were deserting, and she was in constant apprehension that those who remained in the Peloponnesus would rely upon those outside and take advantage of the situation to renew their old attempts at revolution. [4] Besides this, as chance would have it, her thirty years' truce with the Argives[4a] was upon the point of expiring; and they refused to renew it unless Cynuria[4b] were restored to them; so that it seemed impossible to fight Argos and Athens at once. She also suspected some of the cities in the Peloponnesus of intending to go over to the enemy, as was indeed the case.

These considerations made both sides disposed for an accommodation; the Spartans being probably the most eager, as they ardently desired to

5.12
422
10th Year/Summer
HERACLEA
Spartan reinforcements for Thrace delay at Heraclea.

5.13
422/1
10th Year/Winter
THESSALY
The Spartan reinforcements halt because of Thessalian opposition and Spartan desire for peace.

5.14
422/1
10th Year/Winter
ATHENS-SPARTA
Both sides now desire peace, and Thucydides explains why this is so.

5.15
422/1
10th Year/Winter
ATHENS-SPARTA
The Spartans are eager for peace in order to liberate the prisoners taken at Pylos, some of whom belonged to the first families of Sparta.

5.12.1a Heraclea in Thracis: Map 5.7, BX. This city was last mentioned in 4.78 and appears once more in 5.52.
5.13.1a Pierium, location unknown, but probably in southern Thessaly: Map 5.7, BX.
5.14.1a The Delium campaign is described in 4.89–101.
5.14.3a Pylos: Map 5.17, BX.
5.14.3b Cythera: Map 5.17, BY.
5.14.3c For information on Spartan *Helots*, see Appendix C, Spartan Institutions, §3–4.
5.14.4a Argos: Map 5.17, BY.
5.14.4b Cynuria: Map 5.17, BY.

recover the men taken on the island,[1a] the Spartiates among whom belonged to the first families and were accordingly related to leading men in Sparta.[1b] [2] Negotiations had been begun directly after their capture, but the Athenians in their hour of triumph would not consent to any reasonable terms; though after their defeat at Delium Sparta, knowing that they would now be more inclined to listen, at once concluded the truce for a year, during which they were to confer together and see if a longer period could not be agreed upon.

5.16
422/1
10th Year/Winter
ATHENS-SPARTA
With Brasidas and Cleon dead, new leaders (king Pleistoanax in Sparta and Nicias in Athens) come to prominence. They are eager for peace. The campaign behind Pleistoanax's return from exile is described.

Now, however, after the Athenian defeat at Amphipolis, and the death of Cleon and Brasidas, who had been the two principal opponents of peace on either side—the latter from the success and honor which war gave him, the former because he thought that, if tranquillity were restored, his crimes would be more open to detection and his slanders less credited—the foremost candidates for power in either city, Pleistoanax son of Pausanias, king of Sparta, and Nicias son of Niceratus, the most fortunate general of his time, each desired peace more ardently than ever. Nicias, while still happy and honored, wished to secure his good fortune, to obtain a present release from trouble for himself and his countrymen, and hand down to posterity a name as an ever-successful statesman, and thought the way to do this was to keep out of danger and commit himself as little as possible to fortune, and that peace alone made this keeping out of danger possible. Pleistoanax, on the other hand, was assailed by his enemies for his restoration, and regularly criticized by them in front of his countrymen for every reverse that befell them, as though his unjust restoration were the cause. [2] They accused him and his brother Aristocles of having bribed the prophetess of Delphi[2a] to tell the Spartan deputations which successively arrived at the temple to bring home the seed of the demigod son of Zeus[2b] from abroad, else they would have to plough with a silver share. [3] They insisted that in time, he had in this way induced the Spartans to restore him with the same dances and sacrifices with which they had instituted their kings upon the first settlement of Sparta. This they did in the nineteenth year of his exile to Lycaeum[3a] where he had gone when banished on suspicion of having accepted a bribe to retreat from Attica, and where he had built half his house within the consecrated precinct of Zeus for fear of the Spartans.

5.17
422/1
10th Year/Winter
ATHENS-SPARTA
As peace negotiations drag on, Sparta threatens to fortify a post in Attica. The final treaty involves compromises and is not approved by certain members of the Peloponnesian League.

The sting of this accusation, and the reflection that in peace no disaster could occur, and that when Sparta had recovered her men there would be nothing for his enemies to seize upon (whereas, while war lasted the highest station must always bear the scandal of everything that went wrong), made him ardently desire a settlement. [2] Accordingly this winter was employed in conferences; and as spring rapidly approached, the Spartans

5.15.1a   Thucydides is referring to the men captured on the island of Sphacteria in the final action at Pylos; see 4.31–38.
5.15.1b   The text of Thucydides is corrupt at this point. (Translators generally seek to reproduce the sense of Plutarch, *Nicias,* 10.8.) See note at 5.34 for the Spartan population problem.
5.16.2a   Delphi: Map 5.17, BX.
5.16.2b   The demigod son of Zeus referred to here is Heracles.
5.16.3a   Lycaeum: Map 5.17, BX. Pleistoanax's withdrawal from Attica is described in 1.114.2.

MAP 5.17 LOCATIONS MENTIONED IN THE FIFTY-YEAR TREATY OF PEACE

sent round orders to the cities to prepare for a fortified occupation of Attica,[2a] and held this as a sword over the heads of the Athenians to induce them to listen to their overtures; and at last, after many claims had been urged on either side at the conferences, a peace was agreed to upon the following basis: each party was to restore its conquests, but Athens was to keep Nisaea;[2b] her demand for Plataea[2c] being countered by the Thebans asserting that they had acquired the place not by force or treachery, but by the voluntary adhesion upon agreement of its citizens; and the same, according to the Athenian account, being the history of her acquisition of Nisaea. This arranged, the Spartans summoned their allies, and all voting for peace except the Boeotians,[2d] Corinthians,[2e] Eleans,[2f] and Megarians,[2g] who did not approve of these proceedings, they concluded the treaty and made peace, each of the contracting parties swearing to the following articles:

5.18
422/1
10th Year/Winter
ATHENS-SPARTA
Thucydides lists the articles of the treaty.

The Athenians and Spartans and their allies made a treaty, and swear to it, city by city, as follows:

• [2] Regarding the national temples, there shall be a free passage by land and by sea to all who wish it, to sacrifice, travel, consult, and attend the oracle or games, according to the customs of their countries.

• The temple and shrine of Apollo at Delphi[2a] and the Delphians shall be governed by their own laws, taxed by their own state, and judged by their own judges, the land and the people, according to the customs of their country.

• [3] The treaty shall be binding for fifty years upon the Athenians and the allies of the Athenians, and upon the Spartans and the allies of the Spartans, without fraud or harm by land or by sea.

• [4] It shall not be lawful to take up arms, with intent to do injury either for the Spartans and their allies against the Athenians and their allies, or for the Athenians and their allies against the Spartans and their allies, in any way or means whatsoever. But should any difference arise between them they are to have recourse to law and oaths, according as may be agreed between the parties.

• [5] The Spartans and their allies shall give back Amphipolis[5a] to the Athenians. Nevertheless, in the case of cities given up by the Spartans to the Athenians, the inhabitants shall be allowed to go where they please and to take their property with them; and the cities shall be independent, paying only the tribute of Aristides.[5b]

5.17.2a   Attica: Map 5.17, BY. The "cities" Sparta
          called on here were the members of the
          Peloponnesian League; see Appendix D,
          The Peloponnesian League, §3–4.
5.17.2b   Nisaea: Map 5.17, BY.
5.17.2c   Plataea: Map 5.17, BY.
5.17.2d   Boeotia: Map 5.17, BY.
5.17.2e   Corinth: Map 5.17, BY.
5.17.2f   Elis: Map 5.17, BX.
5.17.2g   Megara: Map 5.17, BY.
5.18.2a   Delphi: Map 5.17, BX.
5.18.5a   Amphipolis: Map 5.17, AY.
5.18.5b   By this clause the Spartans agree to
          return to Athens not only Amphipolis but
          certain other cities of the Thracian district

of the Athenian Empire that had revolted. This involved not only the dissolution of the Chalcidian League, to which Thucydides refers by the term "Chalcidians," but also the physical return to their own cities of the people who had migrated to Olynthus, Acanthus, or other large cities. For the cities that were to be restored to Athens, Sparta secured a guarantee of autonomy, provided that they paid to Athens the tribute assessed by Aristides in 478/7 at the foundation of the Delian League. The peace proved largely abortive. Thucydides mentions Aristides in 1.91.3.

And it shall not be lawful for the Athenians or their allies to carry on war against them after the treaty has been concluded, so long as the tribute is paid. The cities referred to are Argilus, Stagirus, Acanthus, Scolus, Olynthus, and Spartolus.[5c] These cities shall be neutral, allies neither of the Spartans nor of the Athenians; but if the cities consent, it shall be lawful for the Athenians to make them their allies, provided always that the cities wish it. [6] The Mecybernaeans, Sanaeans, and Singaeans[6a] shall inhabit their own cities, as also the Olynthians and Acanthians; [7] but the Spartans and their allies shall give back Panactum[7a] to the Athenians.

• The Athenians shall give back Coryphasium, Cythera, Methana,[7b] Pteleum,[7c] and Atalanta[7d] to the Spartans, and also all Spartans that are in the prison at Athens or elsewhere in the Athenian dominions, and shall let go the Peloponnesians besieged in Scione[7e] and all others in Scione that are allies of the Spartans, and all whom Brasidas sent in there, and any others of the allies of the Spartans that may be in the prison at Athens or elsewhere in the Athenian dominions.

• The Spartans and their allies shall in like manner give back any of the Athenians or their allies that they may have in their hands.

• [8] In the case of Scione, Torone,[8a] and Sermylium[8b] and any other cities that the Athenians may have, the Athenians may adopt such measures as they please.

• [9] The Athenians shall take an oath to the Spartans and their allies, city by city. Every man shall swear by the most binding oath of his country, seventeen from each city. The oath shall be as follows:— "I will abide by this agreement and treaty honestly and without deceit." In the same way an oath shall be taken by the Spartans and their allies to the Athenians;

• [10] and the oath shall be renewed annually by both parties. Pillars shall be erected at Olympia,[10a] Pythia,[10b] the Isthmus,[10c] at Athens in the Acropolis, and at Sparta in the temple at Amyclae.

• [11] If anything be forgotten, whatever it be, and on whatever point, it shall be consistent with their oath for both parties the Athenians and Spartans to alter it, according to their discretion.

The treaty begins from the ephorate[1a] of Pleistolas in Sparta, on the 27th day of the month of Artemisium, and from the archon-

5.18.5c   Argilus, Stagirus, Acanthus, Scolus, Olynthus, Spartolus: Map 5.17, AY.
5.18.6c   Mecyberna, Sane, Singos: Map 5.17, AY.
5.18.7a   Panactum: Map 5.17, BY.
5.18.7b   Coryphasium (Pylos): Map 5.17, BX; Cythera, Methana: Map 5.17, BY.
5.18.7c   Pteleum, possible location: Map 5.17, AY.
5.18.7d   Atalanta: Map 5.17, BY.
5.18.7e   Scione: Map 5.17, AY.
5.18.8a   Torone: Map 5.17, AY.
5.18.8b   Sermylium: Map 5.17, AY.
5.18.10a Olympia: Map 5.17, BX.
5.18.10b Pythia (Delphi): Map 5.17, BX.
5.18.10c Isthmus of Corinth: Map 5.17, BY.

5.19.1a   An ephor was one of the most powerful officials of the Spartan government; see Appendix C, Spartan Institutions, §5. See also Appendix K, Calendars and Dating Systems, §1–2.

5.19
422/1
10th Year/Winter
ATHENS-SPARTA
Thucydides gives the date of the treaty and names of the oath-takers who acted as the representatives for Sparta and Athens.

ship[1b] of Alcaeus at Athens, on the 25th day of the month of Elaphebolion. [2] Those who took the oath and poured the libations for the Spartans were Pleistoanax, Agis, Pleistolas, Damagetus, Chionis, Metagenes, Acanthus, Daithus, Ischagoras, Philocharidas, Zeuxidas, Antippus, Tellis, Alcinadas, Empedias, Menas, and Laphilus; for the Athenians, Lampon, Isthmionicus, Nicias, Laches, Euthydemus, Procles, Pythodorus, Hagnon, Myrtilus, Thrasycles, Theagenes, Aristocrates, Iolcius, Timocrates, Leon, Lamachus, and Demosthenes.

This treaty was made in the spring, just at the end of winter, directly after the city festival of Dionysus,[1a] just ten years, with the difference of a few days, from the first invasion of Attica and the commencement of this war. [2] This must be calculated by the seasons rather than by trusting to the enumeration of the names of the various magistrates or offices of honor that are used to mark past events. Accuracy is impossible where an event may have occurred in the beginning, or middle, or at any period in their tenure of office.[2a] [3] But by computing by summers and winters, the method adopted in this history, it will be found that, each of these amounting to half a year, there were ten summers and as many winters contained in this first war.

Meanwhile the Spartans, to whose lot it fell to begin the work of restitution, immediately set free all the prisoners of war in their possession, and sent Ischagoras, Menas, and Philocharidas as envoys to the cities in the Thracian region, to order Clearidas to hand over Amphipolis[1a] to the Athenians, and the rest of their allies each to accept the treaty as it affected them. [2] The allies, however, did not like its terms, and refused to accept it; Clearidas also, wishing to oblige the Chalcidians, would not hand over the city, declaring he could not do so against their will. [3] Meanwhile he hastened in person to Sparta with envoys from the place, to defend his disobedience against the possible accusations of Ischagoras and his companions, and also to see whether it was too late for the agreement to be altered; and on finding the Spartans were bound, quickly set out back again with instructions from them to hand over the place, if possible, or at all events to bring out the Peloponnesians that were in it.

The allies happened to be present in person at Sparta, and those who had not accepted the treaty were now asked by the Spartans to adopt it. This, however, they refused to do, for the same reasons as before, unless a fairer one than the present were agreed upon; [2] and remaining firm in their determination were dismissed by the Spartans, who now decided to

5.19.1b Archons were the chief administrative officers of the Athenian government. Alcaeus was the Eponymous archon for that year; see Appendix A, The Athenian Government, §6.

5.20.1a For the Festival of Dionysus, see Appendix I, Greek Religious Festivals, §8.

5.20.2a See Appendix K, Classical Greek Calendars and Dating Systems, §1–3, 8.

5.21.1a Amphipolis: Map 5.17, AY.

form an alliance with the Athenians, thinking that Argos, who had refused the application of Ampelidas and Lichas for a renewal of the treaty, would without Athens no longer be formidable, and that the rest of the Peloponnesus would most likely keep quiet if the desired alliance of Athens were shut against them. [3] Accordingly, after conference with the Athenian ambassadors, an alliance was agreed upon and oaths were exchanged, upon the following terms:

- The Spartans shall be allies of the Athenians for fifty years.
- Should any enemy invade the territory of Sparta and injure the Spartans, the Athenians shall help them in such way as they most effectively can, according to their power. But if the invader is no longer there after plundering the country, that city shall be the enemy of Sparta and Athens, and shall be chastised by both, and one shall not make peace without the other. This to be performed honestly, loyally, and without fraud.
- [2] Should any enemy invade the territory of Athens and injure the Athenians, the Spartans shall help them in such way as they most effectively can, according to their power. But if the invader is no longer there after plundering the country, that city shall be the enemy of Sparta and Athens, and shall be chastised by both, and one shall not make peace without the other. This to be performed honestly, loyally, and without fraud.
- [3] Should the slave population rise,[3a] the Athenians shall help the Spartans with all their might, according to their power.
- [4] This treaty (of alliance) shall be sworn to by the same persons on either side that swore to the other treaty. It shall be renewed annually by the Spartans going to Athens for the Dionysia, and the Athenians to Sparta for the Hyacinthia,[4a] [5] and a pillar shall be set up by either party; at Sparta near the statue of Apollo at Amyclae, and at Athens on the Acropolis near the statue of Athena. [6] Should the Spartans and Athenians see fit to add to or take away from the alliance in any particular, it shall be consistent with their oaths for both parties to do so, according to their discretion.

Those who took the oath for the Spartans were Pleistoanax, Agis, Pleistolas, Damagetus, Chionis, Metagenes, Acanthus, Daithus, Ischagoras, Philocharidas, Zeuxidas, Antippus, Alcinadas, Tellis, Empedias, Menas, and Laphilus; for the Athenians, Lampon, Isthmionicus, Laches, Nicias, Euthydemus, Procles, Pythodorus, Hagnon, Myrtilus, Thrasycles, Theagenes, Aristocrates, Iolcius, Timocrates, Leon, Lamachus, and Demosthenes.

[2] This alliance was made not long after the treaty; and the Athenians gave back the men from the island to the Spartans, and the summer of the

5.23
422/1
10th Year/Winter
ATHENS-SPARTA
Thucydides reports the text of the treaty of alliance between Athens and Sparta.

5.24
422/1
10th Year/Winter
ATHENS-SPARTA
Thucydides lists the names of the oath-takers of the treaty of alliance. The Athenians return their Spartan prisoners. This ends the history of the "first war" that lasted ten years.

5.23.3a   "The slave population" refers to the Spartan Helots (see 4.80.3 and 5.14.3 for Sparta's constant fear of Helot revolt). Athenian slaves did desert later on in the war (see 7.27.5), but there are no indications that Athens at any time feared a revolt of its slaves as Sparta always feared an uprising of the Helots. See 4.80.2–5, 5.14.3, and Appendix C, Spartan Institutions, §3–4.

5.23.4a   The Dionysia at Athens and the Hyacinthia at Sparta were annual religious festivals; see Appendix I, Classical Greek Religious Festivals, §8.

eleventh year began.[2a] This completes the history of the first war, which occupied the whole of the ten previous years.

After the treaty and the alliance between the Spartans and Athenians, concluded after the ten years' war (in the ephorate of Pleistolas at Sparta, and the archonship of Alcaeus at Athens), the states which had accepted these agreements were at peace; but the Corinthians and some of the cities in the Peloponnesus tried to disturb the settlement and immediately agitated against Sparta. [2] Moreover, the Athenians, as time went on, began to suspect the Spartans because they had not performed some of the provisions of the treaty; [3] and though for six years and ten months they abstained from invasion of each other's territory, yet abroad an unstable armistice did not prevent either party doing the other serious injury, until they were finally obliged to break the treaty made after the ten years' war and to have recourse to open hostilities.

The history of this period has also been written by the same Thucydides, an Athenian, in the chronological order of events by summers and winters, up to the time when the Spartans and their allies put an end to the Athenian empire, and took the Long Walls and the Piraeus. The war had then lasted for twenty-seven years in all.[1a] [2] Only a mistaken judgment can object to including the interval of treaty in the war. Looked at in the light of the facts it cannot, it will be found, be rationally considered a state of peace, as neither party either gave or got back all that they had agreed, apart from the violations of it which occurred on both sides in the Mantinean[2a] and Epidaurian[2b] wars and other instances, and the fact that the allies in the region of Thrace were in as open hostility as ever, and that the Boeotians had only a truce renewed every ten days. [3] So that the first ten years' war, the treacherous armistice that followed it, and the subsequent war will, calculating by the seasons, be found to make up the number of years which I have mentioned, with the difference of a few days, and to provide an instance of faith in oracles being for once justified by the event.[3a] [4] I certainly remember that all along from the beginning to the end of the war it was commonly declared that it would last thrice nine years. [5] I lived through the whole of it, being of an age to comprehend events, and giving my attention to them in order to know the exact truth about them. It was also my fate to be an exile from my country for twenty years after my command at Amphipolis;[5a] and being present with both parties, and more especially with the Peloponnesians by reason of my exile, I had leisure to observe affairs more closely. [6] I will accordingly now relate

5.25
421
11th Year/Summer
HELLAS
The peace lasts almost seven years but is not accepted by all parties and proves unstable. Both sides continue to injure each other until they finally resume open hostilities.

5.26
421
11th Year/Summer
HELLAS
Thucydides argues that the peace was not a genuine peace between wars but merely an interval of limited hostility during a single long war.

5.24.2a	Thucydides refers to the men captured on the island of Sphacteria in the final action at Pylos; see 4.31–38.	5.26.3a	See the Introduction (sect. IV. i) for a discussion of Thucydides' attitude to oracles and to religion.
5.26.1a	This comment was certainly written after the end of the war in 404, although Thucydides' narrative breaks off in 411; see the Introduction (sect. II. ii).	5.26.5a	Amphipolis: Map 5.17, AY. Thucydides describes his role in Brasidas' attack on Amphipolis in 4.104.4–4.107.3.
5.26.2a	For the Mantinean War, see 5.64–74. Mantinea: Map 5.29.		
5.26.2b	For the Epidaurian War, see 5.53–80. Epidaurus: Map 5.29.		

the differences that arose after the ten years' war, the breach of the treaty, and the hostilities that followed.[6a]

After the conclusion of the fifty years' peace and of the subsequent alliance, the embassies from the Peloponnesus which had been summoned for this business returned from Sparta. [2] Most of them went straight home, but the Corinthians first turned aside to Argos and opened negotiations with some of the men in office there, pointing out that Sparta could have no good end in view, but only the subjugation of the Peloponnesus, or she would never have entered into treaty and alliance with the once detested Athenians, and that the duty of consulting for the safety of the Peloponnesus had now fallen upon Argos,[2a] who should immediately pass a decree inviting any Hellenic state that chose (such state being independent and accustomed to meet fellow powers upon the fair and equal ground of law and justice), to make a defensive alliance with the Argives and appoint a few individuals with plenipotentiary powers, instead of making the people the medium of negotiation, in order that, in the case of an applicant being rejected, the fact of his overtures might not be made public. They said that many would come over from hatred of the Spartans. [3] After this explanation of their views the Corinthians returned home.

The persons with whom they had communicated reported the proposal to their government and people, and the Argives passed the decree and chose twelve men to negotiate an alliance for any Hellenic state that wished it, except Athens and Sparta, neither of which should be able to join without referring the issue to the Argive people. [2] Argos came in to the plan all the more readily because she saw that war with Sparta was inevitable, her treaty with Sparta being on the point of expiring; and also because she hoped to gain the supremacy of the Peloponnesus. For at this time Sparta had sunk very low in public estimation because of her disasters, while the Argives were in a most flourishing condition, having taken no part in the war against Athens,[2a] but having on the contrary profited largely by their neutrality. [3] The Argives accordingly prepared to receive into alliance any of the Hellenes that desired it.

The Mantineans[1a] and their allies were the first to come over through fear of the Spartans. Having taken advantage of the war against Athens to

5.27
421
11th Year/Summer
ARGOS
Corinthian envoys visit Argos to express their fear that Sparta will use her alliance with Athens to dominate the Peloponnesus. They advise Argos to develop alliances to counter Sparta.

5.28
421
11th Year/Summer
ARGOS
Argos follows the Corinthian envoys' advice, believing war with Sparta to be inevitable and hoping herself to gain Peloponnesian supremacy.

5.29
421
11th Year/Summer
PELOPONNESE
Mantinea allies with Argos to protect her own recent conquests in Arcadia. Other Peloponnesian states, unhappy that Athens and Sparta can alter the treaty without the consent of Sparta's allies, begin to consider an Argive alliance.

5.26.6a This is one of Thucydides' infrequent but informative remarks about himself. See the Introduction (sect. I) for a discussion of what is known about the life of Thucydides.

5.27.2a The claims of Argos to the "leadership" of the Peloponnesus (or the "supremacy" as Crawley translates the word) came to an abrupt halt in 546 B.C. when Sparta defeated the Argives at the battle of the Champions (described by Herodotus at i, 82). The Corinthians now seek to revive their hopes, as they had earlier threatened Sparta that they might (see 1.71.6ff.). The Argives accepted the call (5.28.2 and 5.40.3) and before the battle of Mantinea

their army was urged to fight for their ancient "supremacy" (5.69.1). Some Argives even proposed that the dispute over the border territory of Cynuria (Map 5.29) should be settled by another battle of the Champions (see 5.41.2).

5.28.2a Perhaps Thucydides reflects a Peloponnesian point of view here when he calls the subject of his history the "war against Athens," as the Peloponnesians may well have done, instead of the "Peloponnesian War," as the Athenians called it, and as it has come down to us.

5.29.1a Mantinea: Map 5.29.

MAP 5.29 SUMMER OF 421, PELOPONNESUS

reduce a large part of Arcadia[1b] into subjection, they thought that Sparta would not leave them undisturbed in their conquests now that she had leisure to interfere,[1c] and consequently were glad to turn to a powerful city like Argos, the historical enemy of the Spartans, and a sister democracy. [2] Upon the defection of Mantinea the rest of the Peloponnesus at once began to consider following her example, thinking that the Mantineans would not have changed sides without good reason. Besides, they were angry with Sparta among other reasons for having inserted in the treaty with Athens that it should be consistent with their oaths for both parties, Spartans and Athenians, to add to or take away from it according to their discretion.[2a] [3]

5.29.1b   Arcadia: Map 5.29.
5.29.1c   These Mantinean fears were well
          founded; see 5.33.
5.29.2a   The clause referred to was that of the
          peace treaty described in 5.18.11, not

that of the Athens-Sparta alliance
(5.23.6), which it seems to echo.

It was this clause that was the real origin of the panic in the Peloponnesus, by exciting suspicions of a Spartan and Athenian combination against their liberties: any alteration should properly have been made conditional upon the consent of the whole body of the allies. [4] Because of these apprehensions there was a very general desire in each state to place itself in alliance with Argos.

In the meantime the Spartans, perceiving the agitation going on in the Peloponnesus and that Corinth was the author of it and was herself about to enter into alliance with the Argives, sent ambassadors there in the hope of preventing what was in contemplation. They accused Corinth of having brought it all about, and told her that she could not desert Sparta and become the ally of Argos without adding violation of her oaths to the crime which she had already committed in not accepting the treaty with Athens, when it had been explicitly agreed that the decision of the majority of the allies should be binding upon all, unless the gods or heroes stood in the way.[1a] [2] Corinth in her answer, which she delivered before those of her allies who had like her refused to accept the treaty, and whom she had previously invited to attend, refrained from openly stating the injuries she complained of, such as the the failure to recover Sollium or Anactorium[2a] from the Athenians, or any other point in which she thought she had come off badly. Instead she took shelter under the pretext that she could not give up her Thracian[2c] allies, to whom her separate individual security had been given when they first rebelled with Potidaea,[2d] as well as upon subsequent occasions. [3] She denied, therefore, that she committed any violation of her oaths to the allies by not entering into the treaty with Athens. Since she had sworn upon the faith of the gods to her Thracian friends, she could not honestly give them up. Besides, the clause of the treaty was, "unless the gods or heroes stand in the way," and it appeared to her in this case that the gods stood in the way. [4] This was what she said on the subject of her former oaths. As to the Argive alliance she would confer with her friends, and do whatever was right. [5] The Spartan envoys returning home, some Argive ambassadors who happened to be in Corinth urged her to conclude the alliance without further delay, but were told to attend at the next congress to be held at Corinth.

Immediately afterwards an Elean[1a] embassy arrived, and first making an alliance with Corinth went on from there to Argos, according to their instructions, and became allies of the Argives, their country being just then at enmity with Sparta and Lepreum.[1b] [2] Some time back there had been a war between the Lepreans and some of the Arcadians; and the Eleans being called in by the former with the offer of half their lands, had put an end to the war, and leaving the land in the hands of its Leprean occupiers had imposed upon them the tribute of a *talent*[2a] to the Olympian Zeus. [3] Till

5.30
421
11th Year/Summer
CORINTH
Sparta tells Corinth to stay in the league and abide by the majority's decision to accept the treaty. The Corinthians respond that their oaths prevent acceptance of the treaty and that they would continue to discuss the Argive alliance with their friends.

5.31
421
11th Year/Summer
PELOPONNESUS
Angered by Sparta's support of Lepreum, Elis allies with Corinth and Argos. Corinth and the Thracian Chalcidians also ally with Argos, but Boeotia and Megara remain quiet, finding Argos too democratic.

5.30.1a See Appendix D, The Peloponnesian League, §5, for the "gods and heroes clause" of the treaties of the league.
5.30.2a Sollium, Anactorium: Map 5.29.
5.30.2c Thrace: Map 5.35, AY.
5.30.2d Potidaea: Map 5.35, AY.
5.31.1a Elis: Map 5.29.
5.31.1b Lepreum: Map 5.29.
5.31.2a A *talent* is a unit of weight and money. See Appendix J, Classical Greek Currency, § 5.

the war against Athens[3a] this tribute was paid by the Lepreans, who then took the war as an excuse for no longer doing so, and upon the Eleans using force appealed to Sparta. The case was thus submitted to her arbitration; but the Eleans, suspecting the fairness of the tribunal, abandoned the submission and laid waste the Leprean territory. [4] The Spartans nevertheless decided that the Lepreans were independent[4a] and the Eleans aggressors, and as the latter did not abide by the arbitration, sent a garrison of hoplites into Lepreum. [5] Upon this the Eleans, holding that Sparta had received one of their rebel subjects, put forward the agreement providing that each allied state should come out of the war against Athens in possession of what it had at the beginning, and considering that justice had not been done them, went over to the Argives and now made the alliance through their ambassadors, who had been instructed for that purpose. [6] Immediately after them the Corinthians and the Thracian Chalcidians[6a] became allies of Argos. Meanwhile the Boeotians and Megarians,[6b] who acted together, remained quiet, being left to do as they pleased by Sparta, and thinking that the Argive democracy would not agree so well with their aristocratic forms of government as the Spartan constitution.

About the same time in this summer Athens succeeded in reducing Scione,[1a] put the adult males to death and, making slaves of the women and children, gave the land to the Plataeans to live in. She also brought back the Delians to Delos,[1b] moved by her misfortunes in the field and by the commands of the god at Delphi.[1c] [2] Meanwhile the Phocians[2a] and Locrians[2b] commenced hostilities. [3] The Corinthians and Argives being now in alliance, went to Tegea[3a] to bring about its defection from Sparta, thinking that if so considerable a state could be persuaded to join, all the Peloponnesus would be on their side. [4] But when the Tegeans said that they would do nothing against Sparta, the hitherto zealous Corinthians relaxed their activity, and began to fear that none of the rest would now come over. [5] Still they went to the Boeotians and tried to persuade them to join the alliance and adopt common action generally with Argos and themselves, and also begged them to go with them to Athens and obtain for them[5c] a ten days' truce similar to that made between the Athenians and Boeotians not long after the fifty years' treaty, and in the event of the Athenians refusing, to renounce the armistice, and not make any truce in future without Corinth. These were the requests of the Corinthians. [6] The Boeotians refused them on the subject of the Argive alliance, but went with them to Athens where, however, they failed to obtain the ten days' truce; the Athenian answer being that the Corinthians had truce already, as allies of

5.31.3a   For the "Attic war," see note 5.28.2a.
5.31.4a   Being independent and paying tribute were not incompatible; see 5.18.5.
5.31.6a   Chalcidice: Map 5.35, AY.
5.31.6b   Megara: Map 5.29 and Map 5.35, BY.
5.32.1a   This harsh punishment was carried out in accordance with the decree moved by Cleon in 4.122.6. Scione: Map 5.35, AY.
5.32.1b   Delos: Map 5.35, BY. Some Delians must

have remained in Atramyttium, however, where Thucydides describes them as residing in 8.108.4.
5.32.1c   Delphi: Map 5.35, BX.
5.32.2a   Phocis: Map 5.35, BY.
5.32.2b   Locris (presumably Opuntian Locris): Map 5.35, BY.
5.32.3a   Tegea: Map 5.29 and Map 5.35, BY.
5.32.5c   I.e., for Corinth.

Sparta. [7] Nevertheless the Boeotians did not renounce their ten days' truce, in spite of the prayers and reproaches of the Corinthians for their breach of faith; and these last had to content themselves with a de facto armistice with Athens.

The same summer the Spartans marched into Arcadia[1a] with their whole levy under Pleistoanax son of Pausanias, king of Sparta, against the Parrhasians,[1b] who were subjects of Mantinea, and a faction of whom had invited their aid. They also meant to demolish, if possible, the fort of Cypsela which the Mantineans had built and garrisoned in the Parrhasian territory as a hostile base against the district of Sciritis[1c] in Laconia. [2] The Spartans accordingly laid waste the Parrhasian country, and the Mantineans, placing their city in the hands of an Argive garrison, addressed themselves to the defense of their confederacy, but being unable to save Cypsela or the Parrhasian cities went back to Mantinea.[2a] [3] Meanwhile the Spartans made the Parrhasians independent, razed the fortress, and returned home.

The same summer the soldiers from Thrace who had gone out with Brasidas came back, having been brought from thence after the treaty by Clearidas; and the Spartans decreed that the Helots who had fought with Brasidas should be free and allowed to live where they liked, and not long afterwards settled them with the Neodamodeis[1b] at Lepreum,[1c] which is situated on the Laconian and Elean border; Sparta being at this time at enmity with Elis. [2] Those, however, of the Spartans who had been taken prisoner on the island[2a] and had surrendered their arms might, it was feared, suppose that they were to be subjected to some degradation in consequence of their misfortune, and so make some attempt at revolution, if left in possession of their full rights. These were therefore at once deprived of some of their rights, although some of them were in office at the time, and thus they were barred from taking office, or buying and selling anything. After some time, however, their rights were restored to them.[2b]

5.33
421
11th Year/Summer
ARCADIA
Sparta invades Parrhasia, a district subject to Mantinea, destroys the Mantinaean fort of Cypsela, and makes the Parrhasians independent.

5.34
421
11th Year/Summer
SPARTA
Helots among Spartan troops returning from Thrace are freed and allowed to live where they like. The disgraced Spartans captured at Sphacteria are at first restricted, but later restored to their full rights.

5.33.1a Arcadia: Map 5.29.
5.33.1b Parrhasia: Map 5.29.
5.33.1c Sciritis: Map 5.29.
5.33.2a Mantinea: Map 5.29.
5.34.1b When Brasidas took the seven hundred Helots to fight in Thrace (4.80) he inaugurated the radical policy change at Sparta of using Helots for military purposes rather than keeping them all in bitter subjection. Brasidas' Helots were not liberated until their return, as this chapter shows, but in the meantime Sparta had further developed that policy by creating a special class of *neodamodeis* whose numbers seem to increase steadily in the succeeding half century (see 7.19.3). Their precise status remains unknown, and although the name implies that they were made part of the citizen body, most scholars reject this notion. See Appendix C, Spartan Institutions, §9.
5.34.1c Lepreum: Map 5.35, BX. The settlement of these former Helots and *neodamodeis*

in Lepreum was undoubtedly connected with Sparta's contemporary difficulties with Elis (see 5.31.2ff.).

5.34.2a Thucydides refers to the men captured on the island of Sphacteria in the final action at Pylos; see 4.31–38.
5.34.2b Spartan concern to recover the 120 Spartiates taken prisoner on Sphacteria is evident (4.41.3, 4.108.7, 4.117.1, and 5.15.1). The reason may lie in the serious decline in the number of Spartiates—from eight thousand in 480 (Herodotus, 7.234.2) to about two thousand five hundred in 418, judging from Thucydides' comments in 5.68.3 (see note there), and to less than one thousand by 371 (according to Aristotle's *Politics*, 1270[a] 30ff.). To be taken prisoner of war was a dreadful disgrace at Sparta, and the lenient treatment of the survivors of Sphacteria shows that they were badly needed at home.

5.35
421
11th Year/Summer
THRACE
The Dians take Thyssus.

ATHENS-SPARTA
Athens and Sparta are still at
peace, but Sparta's failure to
fulfill her treaty obligations
arouses Athenian suspicions.
Athens holds onto Pylos and
the other places she had
agreed to give up, but does
withdraw the Messenians and
the Laconian deserters from
Pylos.

The same summer the Dians[2c] took Thyssus,[2d] a city on Acte[2e] near Athos[1d] and in alliance with Athens. [2] During the whole of this summer, intercourse between the Athenians and Peloponnesians continued, although each party began to suspect the other immediately after the treaty, because of the places specified in it not being restored. [3] Sparta, to whose lot it had fallen to begin by restoring Amphipolis[3a] and the other cities, had not done so. She had equally failed to get the treaty accepted by her Thracian allies, or by the Boeotians or the Corinthians; although she was continually promising to unite with Athens in compelling their compliance, if it were longer refused. She also kept fixing a time at which those who still refused to come in were to be declared enemies to both parties, but took care not to bind herself by any written agreement. [4] Meanwhile the Athenians, seeing none of these promises actually fulfilled, began to suspect the honesty of her intentions, and consequently not only refused to comply with her demands for Pylos,[4a] but also repented having given up the prisoners from the island, and kept tight hold of the other places, until Sparta's part of the treaty should be fulfilled. [5] Sparta, on the other hand, said she had done what she could, having given up the Athenian prisoners of war in her possession, evacuated Thrace, and performed everything else in her power. Amphipolis, she said, it was out of her ability to restore; but she would endeavor to bring the Boeotians and Corinthians in to the treaty, to recover Panactum,[5a] and send home all the Athenian prisoners of war in Boeotia. [6] Meanwhile she insisted that Pylos should be restored, or at least that the Messenians and Helots should be withdrawn (as her troops had been from Thrace), and the place garrisoned, if necessary, by the Athenians themselves. [7] After a number of different conferences held during the summer she succeeded in persuading Athens to withdraw the Messenians from Pylos and the rest of the Helots and deserters from Laconia, who were accordingly settled by her at Cranae in Cephallenia.[7a] [8] Thus during this summer there was peace and intercourse between the two peoples.

Next winter, however, the ephors under whom the treaty had been made were no longer in office, and some of their successors were directly opposed to it. Embassies now arrived from the Spartan confederacy, and the Athenians, Boeotians, and Corinthians also presented themselves at Sparta, and after much discussion and no agreement between them, were returning to their homes; when Cleobulus and Xenares, the two ephors who were the most anxious to terminate the treaty, took advantage of this

5.36
421/0
11th Year/Winter
SPARTA
Two of the new Spartan
ephors oppose the treaty
with Athens and plot with
Corinth and Boeotia to
bring Argos into alliance
with Sparta—even if that
should cause a break with
Athens. Sparta asks Boeotia
for Panactum in order to
exchange it for Pylos.

5.34.2c The Dians lived at Dium on the Acte
Peninsula of Chalcidice (Map 5.35, AY).
5.34.2d Thyssus: Map 5.35, AY.
5.34.2e Acte Peninsula: Map 5.35, AY.
5.35.1d Mount Athos, on the Acte Peninsula:
Map 5.35, AY.
5.35.3a Amphipolis: Map 5.35, AY.

5.35.4a Pylos: Map 5.35, BX.
5.35.5a Panactum (Map 5.35, BY) was the
Athenian border fort captured by the
Boeotians in 422; see 5.3.5.
5.35.7a Cranae, on the island of Cephallenia:
Map 5.35, BX.

MAP 5.35 EVENTS IN THRACE, ATTICA, AND PHOCIS, SUMMER 421

opportunity to communicate privately with the Boeotians and Corinthians, and advising them to act as much as possible together, instructed the former first to enter into alliance with Argos, and then to try and bring themselves and the Argives into alliance with Sparta. The Boeotians would thereby feel least compulsion to join the Attic treaty; and the Spartans would prefer to gain the friendship and alliance of Argos even at the price of the hostility of Athens and the rupture of the treaty. The Boeotians knew that an honorable friendship with Argos had long been the desire of Sparta; for the Spartans believed that this would considerably facilitate the conduct of the war outside the Peloponnesus. [2] Meanwhile they begged the Boeotians to place Panactum[2a] in Sparta's hands in order that she might, if possible, obtain Pylos[2b] in exchange for it, and so be in a better position to resume hostilities with Athens.

After receiving these instructions for their governments from Xenares and Cleobulus and their other friends at Sparta, the Boeotians and Corinthians departed. [2] On their way home they were joined by two persons in high office at Argos who had waited for them on the road, and who now explored with them the possibility of the Boeotians joining the Corinthians, Eleans, and Mantineans in becoming the allies of Argos, thinking that if this could be effected they would be able, thus united, to make peace or war as they pleased either against Sparta or any other power. [3] The Boeotian envoys were pleased at thus hearing themselves accidentally asked to do what their friends at Sparta had told them; and the two Argives perceiving that their proposal was agreeable, departed with a promise to send ambassadors to the Boeotians. [4] On their arrival the Boeotians reported to the *boeotarchs*[4a] what had been said to them at Sparta and also by the Argives who had met them, and the boeotarchs, pleased with the idea, embraced it with all the more eagerness from the lucky coincidence of Argos soliciting the very thing wanted by their friends at Sparta. [5] Shortly afterwards ambassadors appeared from Argos with the proposals indicated; and the boeotarchs approved of the terms and dismissed the ambassadors with a promise to send envoys to Argos to negotiate the alliance.

In the meantime it was decided by the boeotarchs, the Corinthians, the Megarians, and the envoys from Thrace[1a] first to exchange oaths together to give help to each other whenever it was required and not to make war or peace except in common; after which the Boeotians and Megarians, who acted together, should make the alliance with Argos. [2] But before the oaths were taken the boeotarchs communicated these proposals to the four councils of the Boeotians, in whom the supreme power resides, and advised them to exchange oaths with all such cities as should be willing to enter into a

5.37
421/0
11th Year/Winter
BOEOTIA
Boeotia happily accepts Argos' invitation to join her alliance, as this is exactly what the Spartan ephors had advised Boeotia to do. Boeotia promises to send delegates to Argos to negotiate alliance terms.

5.38
421/0
11th Year/Winter
BOEOTIA
Boeotia, Corinth, Megara, and Thrace form a pact, and agree to ally with Argos. However, the Boeotian councils, unwilling to offend Sparta and ignorant of the Spartan ephors' wishes, refuse to ally with Argos.

5.36.2a   Panactum: Map 5.35, BY.
5.36.2b   Pylos: Map 5.35, BX.

5.37.4a   *Boeotarchs* were the chief magistrates of the Boeotian Federal government. See note 5.38.2a.
5.38.1a   Thrace: Map 5.35, AY.

defensive league with the Boeotians.[2a] [3] But the members of the Boeotian councils refused their assent to the proposal, being afraid of offending Sparta by entering into a league with the deserter Corinth; the boeotarchs not having acquainted them with what had passed at Sparta and with the advice given by Cleobulus and Xenares and the Boeotian partisans there, namely, that they should become allies of Corinth and Argos as a preliminary to joining up with Sparta; they having supposed that even if they should say nothing about all this, the councils would not vote against what had been decided and recommended by the boeotarchs. [4] When this difficulty arose, the Corinthians and the envoys from Thrace departed without anything having been concluded; and the boeotarchs, who had previously intended (after carrying this point) to try and effect the alliance with Argos, now gave up bringing the Argive question before the councils, or sending to Argos the envoys whom they had promised; and a general coldness and delay ensued in the matter.

In this same winter Mecyberna,[1a] which had an Athenian garrison inside it, was assaulted and taken by the Olynthians.[1b]

[2] All this time negotiations had been going on between the Athenians and Spartans about the conquests still retained by each, and Sparta hoping that if Athens were to get back Panactum[2a] from the Boeotians, she might herself recover Pylos,[2b] now sent an embassy to the Boeotians and begged them to place Panactum and their Athenian prisoners in her hands, in order that she might exchange them for Pylos. [3] This the Boeotians refused to do unless Sparta made a separate alliance with them as she had done with Athens. Sparta knew that this would be a breach of faith with Athens, as it had been agreed that neither of them should make peace or war without the other; yet wishing to obtain Panactum which she hoped to exchange for Pylos, and the party who pressed for the dissolution of the treaty strongly pressing for the Boeotian alliance, she at length concluded the alliance just as winter gave way to spring; and Panactum was instantly razed. And so the eleventh year of the war ended.

In the first days of the following summer, the Argives, seeing that the promised ambassadors from Boeotia did not arrive, and that Panactum was being demolished, and that a separate alliance had been concluded between the Boeotians and Spartans, began to be afraid that Argos might be left iso-

5.39
421/0
11th Year/Winter
THRACE
The Olynthians take Mecyberna from the Athenians.
ATTICA
Sparta allies with Boeotia to gain Panactum (to exchange for Pylos), but the Boeotians raze the fort before delivering it to them.

5.40
420
12th Year/Summer
ARGOS
The Argives misinterpret recent events and, fearful of being left isolated, send envoys to Sparta to negotiate as favorable a treaty as possible with her.

5.38.2a   The federal constitution of Boeotia of 396/5 was described by the Oxyrhynchus Historian (the unknown author of a major history of Greece written by a younger contemporary of Thucydides, of which fragments on papyri were discovered in the sands of Oxyrhynchus, Egypt). According to him, there were eleven "divisions" with a boeotarch for each (see 4.91); Thebes, the real power, constituted four divisions; all divisions contributed hoplites and cavalry to the federal army; every division was divided into four councils, each of which in turn served as the body preparing business for the whole division; and each division sent sixty representatives to a central Boeotian council. The Oxyrhynchus History does not say that this central council was divided into four, and many scholars incline to the view that Thucydides has here erred.

5.39.1a   Mecyberna, in Chalcidice: Map 5.35, AY.
5.39.1b   Olynthus: Map 5.35, AY. Mecyberna was the port city for Olynthus. The Olynthians, by expelling the Athenian garrison from it, signified their rejection of the peace treaty described in 5.18.5.
5.39.2a   Panactum: Map 5.35, BY.
5.39.2b   Pylos: Map 5.35, BX.

lated, and all her allies would go over to Sparta. [2] They supposed that the Boeotians had been persuaded by the Spartans to raze Panactum and to enter into the treaty with the Athenians, and that Athens was privy to this arrangement, so that an alliance with Athens would no longer be open to her. This was a resource which she had always counted upon, by reason of the existing tensions, if her treaty with Sparta were not maintained. [3] In this crisis the Argives, afraid that, as the result of refusing to renew the treaty with Sparta and aspiring to the supremacy of the Peloponnesus,[3a] they would at the same time be at war with the Spartans, Tegeans, Boeotians, and Athenians, now hastily sent off Eustrophus and Aeson, who seemed the persons most likely to be acceptable as envoys to Sparta, with the goal of making as good a treaty as they could with the Spartans, upon such terms as could be obtained, and of being left in peace.

Having reached Sparta, their ambassadors proceeded to negotiate the terms of the proposed treaty. [2] What the Argives first demanded was that they might be allowed to refer to the arbitration of some state or private person the question of the Cynurian land,[2a] a piece of frontier territory about which they have always been disputing, which contains the cities of Thyrea and Anthene,[2b] and which is occupied by the Spartans. The Spartans at first said that they could not allow this point to be discussed, but were ready to conclude upon the old terms. Eventually, however, the Argive ambassadors succeeded in obtaining from them this concession:— For the present there was to be a truce for fifty years, but it should be competent for either party, there being neither plague nor war in Sparta or Argos, to give a formal challenge and decide the question of this territory by battle, as on a former occasion,[2c] when both sides claimed the victory; pursuit not being allowed beyond the frontier of Argos or Sparta. [3] The Spartans at first thought this mere folly; but at last, anxious at any cost to have the friendship of Argos, they agreed to the terms demanded, and committed them to writing. However, before any of this should become binding, the ambassadors were to return to Argos and communicate with their people, and in the event of their approval, to come at the feast of the Hyacinthia and take the oaths. The envoys returned accordingly.

In the meantime, while the Argives were engaged in these negotiations, the Spartan ambassadors, Andromedes, Phaedimus, and Antimenidas, who were to receive the prisoners from the Boeotians and restore them and Panactum[1a] to the Athenians, found that the Boeotians had themselves razed Panactum, upon the plea that oaths had been anciently exchanged between their people and the Athenians, after a dispute on the subject, to the effect

5.41
420
12th Year/Summer
SPARTA
Argos and Sparta agree on the terms for a treaty, including a prospective trial by battle to determine the ownership of Cynuria. The Argive delegates return home to secure the approval of the Argive people.

5.42
420
12th Year/Summer
ATHENS
Sparta returns Athenian prisoners held by Boeotia and the razed fort of Panactum, but Athens responds indignantly to the razing of the fort, to the clauses of the treaty which the Spartans had not fulfilled, and to the alliance that Sparta had made with Boeotia.

5.40.3a For details about Argive aspirations to the supremacy of the Peloponnesus, see note at 5.27.2e.
5.41.2a Cynuria: Map 5.45.
5.41.2b Thyrea and the possible location of Anthene: Map 5.45.

5.41.2c For the battle of the Champions in 546 B.C., see note at 5.27.2a.
5.42.1a Panactum, Boeotia: Map 5.45.

that neither should inhabit the place, but that they should graze it in common. As for the Athenian prisoners of war in the hands of the Boeotians, these were delivered over to Andromedes and his colleagues, and by them conveyed to Athens and given back. The envoys at the same time announced the razing of Panactum, which to them seemed as good as its restitution, as it would no longer lodge an enemy of Athens. [2] This announcement was received with great indignation by the Athenians, who thought that the Spartans had played them false, both in the matter of the demolition of Panactum, which ought to have been restored to them standing, and in having, as they now heard, made a separate alliance with the Boeotians, in spite of their previous promise to join Athens in compelling the adherence of those who refused to accede to the treaty. The Athenians also considered the other points in which Sparta had failed in her compact, and thinking that they had been deceived, gave an angry answer to the ambassadors and sent them away.

The breach between the Spartans and Athenians having gone thus far, the party at Athens who wished to cancel the treaty immediately put themselves in motion. [2] Foremost amongst these was Alcibiades son of Clinias, a man still young in years for any other Hellenic city, but distinguished by the splendor of his ancestry. Alcibiades thought the Argive alliance really preferable, not that personal pique had not also a great deal to do with his opposition; he being offended with the Spartans for having negotiated the treaty through Nicias and Laches, and having overlooked him on account of his youth, and also for not having shown him the respect due to the ancient connection of his family with them as their *proxenii*[2a] which, renounced by his grandfather, he had himself recently attempted to renew by his attentions to their prisoners taken in the island.[2b] [3] Being thus, as he thought, slighted by all, he had in the first instance spoken against the treaty, saying that the Spartans were not to be trusted, but that they only negotiated in order to be enabled by this means to crush Argos, and afterwards to attack Athens alone; and now immediately upon the occurrence of this breach, he sent privately to the Argives, telling them to come as quickly as possible to Athens, accompanied by the Mantineans and Eleans, with proposals of alliance; as the moment was propitious and he himself would do all he could to help them.

Upon receiving this message and discovering that the Athenians, far from being privy to the Boeotian alliance, were involved in a serious quarrel with the Spartans, the Argives paid no further attention to the embassy which they had just sent to Sparta on the subject of the treaty, and began to incline rather toward the Athenians, reflecting that, in the event of war,

5.43
420
12th Year/Summer
ATHENS
Alcibiades, who feels personally slighted by the Spartans, leads the faction opposed to the treaty with Sparta. He sends hastily to Argos advising them to send envoys to Athens, for now conditions are favorable for an anti-Sparta alliance.

5.44
420
12th Year/Summer
ATHENS
Argos drops negotiations with Sparta and moves to conclude an alliance with Athens. Spartan envoys come to Athens to explain their alliance with Boeotia and ask for the return of Pylos.

5.43.2a   A *proxenus*, although a citizen and resident of his own state, served as a "friend or representative" (much like a modern honorary consul) of a foreign state.
5.43.2b   Thucydides refers to the men captured on the island of Sphacteria in the final action at Pylos; see 4.31–38.

they would thus have on their side a city that was not only an ancient ally of Argos, but a sister democracy and very powerful at sea. [2] They accordingly at once sent ambassadors to Athens to negotiate for an alliance, accompanied by others from Elis and Mantinea.

[3] At the same time an embassy consisting of persons reputed to be well disposed toward the Athenians—Philocharidas, Leon, and Endius[3a]—arrived in haste from Sparta, out of fear that the Athenians in their irritation might conclude an alliance with the Argives. They also intended to ask for the return of Pylos in exchange for Panactum, and to defend their alliance with the Boeotians by pleading that it had not been made to hurt the Athenians.

When the envoys spoke in the council upon these points, stating that they had come with full powers to settle all others at issue between them, Alcibiades became afraid that if they were to repeat these statements to the popular assembly,[1a] they might gain the support of the multitude and cause the Argive alliance to be rejected, [2] so he resorted to the following stratagem. He persuaded the Spartans by a solemn assurance that if they would say nothing of their full powers in the assembly, he would give back Pylos[2a] to them (himself, the present opponent of its restitution, engaging to obtain this from the Athenians), and would settle the other points at issue. [3] His plan was to detach them from Nicias and to disgrace them before the people, as being without sincerity in their intentions, or even common consistency in their language, and so to get the Argives, Eleans, and Mantineans taken into alliance. [4] This plan proved successful. When the envoys appeared before the people, and upon the question being put to them, did not say as they had said in the council, that they had come with full powers, the Athenians lost all patience, and carried away by Alcibiades, who thundered more loudly than ever against the Spartans, were ready instantly to introduce the Argives and their companions and to take them into alliance. An earthquake, however, occurring before anything definite had been done, this assembly was adjourned.

In the assembly held the next day, Nicias, in spite of the Spartans having been deceived themselves, and having also allowed him to be deceived in not admitting that they had come with full powers, still maintained that it was best to be friends with the Spartans. He argued that they should postpone action on the Argive proposals and send once more to Sparta and learn her intentions. The postponement of the war could only increase their own prestige and injure that of their rivals; the excellent state of their affairs making it in their interest to preserve this prosperity as long as possible, while the affairs of Sparta were so desperate that the sooner she could try her fortune again the better. [2] He succeeded accordingly in persuading them to send ambassadors, himself being among them, to invite the Spar-

5.45
420
12th Year/Summer
ATHENS
After Alcibiades persuades the Spartan envoys to deny before the Athenian assembly that they were fully empowered to negotiate, he attacks them and urges the assembly to choose alliance with Argos, Mantinea, and Elias.

5.46
420
12th Year/Summer
ATHENS-SPARTA
Nicias persuades the Athenians to delay the Argive alliance while he attempts to obtain Spartan fulfillment of the treaty. When he fails, however, Athens enters into alliances with Argos, Mantinea, and Elis.

5.44.3a   For the relationship between Endius and
            Alcibiades, see 8.6.3.
5.45.1a   For the council and the assembly, see
            Appendix A, The Athenian Government.

5.45.2a   Pylos: Map 5.45.

MAP 5.45 PELOPONNESUS, SUMMER 420

tans, if they were really sincere, to restore Panactum[2a] intact with Amphipolis,[2b] and to abandon their alliance with the Boeotians (unless they consented to accede to the treaty), in agreement with the stipulation which
forbade either party to negotiate without the other. [3] The ambassadors
were also directed to say that the Athenians, had they wished to play false,
might already have made alliance with the Argives, who had indeed come
to Athens for that very purpose, and they went off furnished with instructions as to any other complaints that the Athenians had to make. [4] Having reached Sparta they communicated their instructions, and concluded by
telling the Spartans that unless they gave up their alliance with the Boeotians, should the latter refuse to accept their treaty, the Athenians for their
part would ally themselves with the Argives and their friends. The Spartans,
however, refused to give up the Boeotian alliance—the party of Xenares the
ephor, and others who shared their view, carrying the day upon this
point—but renewed the oaths at the request of Nicias, who feared to
return without having accomplished anything and to be disgraced; as was

5.46.2a Panactum: Map 5.45.
5.46.2b Amphipolis: Map 5.35, AY.

indeed his fate, he being held the author of the treaty with Sparta. [5] When he returned, and the Athenians heard that nothing had been done at Sparta, they flew into a rage, and deciding that faith had not been kept with them, took advantage of the presence of the Argives and their allies, who had been introduced by Alcibiades, and made a treaty and alliance with them upon the terms following:

The Athenians, Argives, Mantineans, and Eleans, acting for themselves and the allies in their respective empires, made a treaty for a hundred years, to be without fraud or injury by land and by sea.[1a]

• [2] It shall not be lawful to carry on war, either for the Argives, Eleans, Mantineans, and their allies, against the Athenians, or the allies in the Athenian empire; or for the Athenians and their allies against the Argives, Eleans, Mantineans, or their allies, in any way or means whatsoever. The Athenians, Argives, Eleans, and Mantineans shall be allies for a hundred years upon the terms following:—

• [3] If an enemy invade the country of the Athenians, the Argives, Eleans, and Mantineans shall go to the relief of Athens, according as the Athenians may require by message, in such way as they most effectively can, to the best of their power. But if the invader be gone after plundering the territory, the offending state shall be the enemy of the Argives, Mantineans, Eleans, and Athenians, and war shall be made against it by all these cities; and no one of the cities shall be able to make peace with that state, except all the above cities agree to do so.

• [4] Likewise the Athenians shall go to the relief of Argos, Mantinea, and Elis, if an enemy invade the country of Elis, Mantinea, or Argos, according as the above cities may require by message, in such way as they most effectively can, to the best of their power. But if the invader be gone after plundering the territory, the state offending shall be the enemy of the Athenians, Argives, Mantineans, and Eleans, and war shall be made against it by all these cities, and peace may not be made with that state except all the above cities agree to it.

• [5] No armed force shall be allowed to pass for hostile purposes through the country of the powers contracting, or of the allies in their respective empires, or to go by sea, except all the cities—that is to say, Athens, Argos, Mantinea, and Elis—vote for such passage.

• [6] The relieving troops shall be maintained by the city sending them for thirty days from their arrival in the city that has required them, and upon their return in the same way; if their services be desired for a longer period the city that sent for them shall maintain them, at the rate of three Aeginetan *obols* per day for a heavy-armed soldier, archer, or light soldier, and an Aeginetan *drachma*[6a] for a cavalryman.

5.47.1a   The members of this alliance, Elis, Mantinea, Argos, and Athens, are shown on Map 5.45.

5.47.6a   For the Aeginetan *obol* and the *drachma*, see Appendix J, Classical Greek Currency, §3.

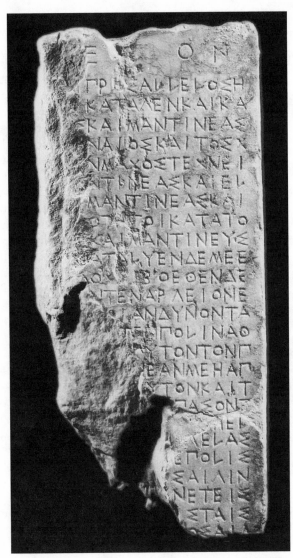

ILLUSTRATION 5.47
INSCRIPTION WITH
PARTIAL TEXT OF THE
TREATY BETWEEN ATHENS,
ELIS, ARGOS, AND
MANTINEA

• [7] The city sending for the troops shall have the command when the war is in its own country; but in case of the cities resolving upon a joint expedition the command shall be equally divided among all the cities.

• [8] The treaty shall be sworn to by the Athenians for themselves and their allies, by the Argives, Mantineans, Eleans, and their allies, by each state individually. Each shall swear the oath most binding in his country over full-grown victims; the oath being as follows:

"I will stand by the alliance and its articles, justly, innocently, and sincerely, and I will not transgress the same in any way or means whatsoever."

• [9] The oath shall be taken at Athens by the council and the magistrates, the *prytaneis* administering it; at Argos by the council, the Eighty, and the artynae, the Eighty administering it; at Mantinea by the demiurgi,[9a] the council, and the other magistrates, the theori and polemarchs administering it; at Elis by the demiurgi, the magistrates, and the Six Hundred, the demiurgi and the thesmophylakes administering it. [10] The oaths shall be renewed by the Athenians going to Elis, Mantinea, and Argos thirty days before the Olympic games; by the Argives, Mantineans, and Eleans going to Athens ten days before the feast of the Great Panathenaea.[10a] [11] The articles of the treaty, the oaths, and the alliance shall be inscribed on a stone pillar by the Athenians in the Acropolis,[11a] by the Argives in the *agora*,[11b] in the temple of Apollo; by the Mantineans in the temple of Zeus, in the agora and a bronze pillar shall be erected jointly by them at the Olympic games now at hand. [12] Should the above cities see fit to make any addition to these articles, whatever all the above cities shall agree upon, after consulting together, shall be binding.

5.48
420
12th Year/Summer
CORINTH
Neither Athens nor Sparta renounce their treaty. Although allied with Argos, Corinth refuses to join the new alliance.

Although the treaty and alliances were thus concluded, still the treaty between the Spartans and Athenians was not renounced by either party. [2] Meanwhile Corinth, although the ally of the Argives, did not accede to the new treaty, any more than she had done to the defensive and offensive alliance formed before this between the Eleans, Argives, and Mantineans, when she declared herself content with the first alliance, which was defensive only, and which bound them to help each other, but not to join in attacking any. [3] The Corinthians thus stood aloof from their allies, and again turned their thoughts toward Sparta.

5.49
420
12th Year/Summer
OLYMPIA
Elis excludes Sparta from the Olympic festival, alleging that Sparta violated the Olympic truce when she invaded Lepreum. Elis offers relief if Sparta restores Lepreum. Sparta protests but to no avail.

At the Olympic games[1a] which were held this summer, and in which the Arcadian Androsthenes was victor the first time in the wrestling and boxing, the Spartans were excluded from the temple by the Eleans, and thus prevented from sacrificing or contending, for having refused to pay the fine specified in the Olympic law imposed upon them by the Eleans, who alleged that they had attacked Fort Phyrcus,[1b] and sent some of their hoplites into Lepreum[1c] during the Olympic truce. The amount of the fine

---

5.47.9a Demiurgi: the title of high officers in a number of states, most of them Dorian.
5.47.10a The Olympic games and the great feast of the Panathenaea were quadrennial religious festivals; see Appendix I, Classical Greek Religious Festivals, §5, 8.
5.47.11a A fragment of the Athenian copy of this treaty was found on the south slope of the Acropolis (IG i² 86 (GHI 72, not in

ML)). There are only minor variations from the text given by Thucydides. See Illustration 5.47.
5.47.11b The *agora* was a city's main square for commercial, social, and political activity.
5.49.1a Olympia: Map 5.45. See Appendix I, Classical Greek Religious Festivals, §5.
5.49.1b Fort Phyrcus: site unknown.
5.49.1c Lepreum: Map 5.45.

was two thousand *minae*,[1d] two for each hoplite, as the law prescribes. [2] The Spartans sent envoys, and pleaded that the penalty was unjust; saying that the truce had not yet been proclaimed at Sparta when the hoplites were sent off.[2a] [3] But the Eleans affirmed that the armistice with them had already begun (they proclaim it first among themselves), and that the aggression of the Spartans had taken them by surprise while they were living quietly as in time of peace, and not expecting anything. [4] The Spartans responded that if the Eleans really believed that Sparta had committed an aggression, they would not have subsequently proclaimed the truce at Sparta; but they had proclaimed it notwithstanding (as if they had believed nothing of the kind), and after the proclamation, the Spartans had made no attack upon their country. [5] Nevertheless the Eleans adhered to what they had said, that nothing would persuade them that an aggression had not been committed; if, however, the Spartans would restore Lepreum to them, they would give up their own share of the money and pay that of the god for them.

As this proposal was not accepted, the Eleans tried a second. Instead of restoring Lepreum, if this was objected to, the Spartans should ascend the altar of the Olympian Zeus, as they were so anxious to have access to the temple, and swear before the Hellenes that they would surely pay the fine at a later day. [2] This also being refused, the Spartans were excluded from the temple, the sacrifice, and the games, and sacrificed at home; the Lepreans being the only other Hellenes who did not attend. [3] Still the Eleans were afraid the Spartans would sacrifice by force, and kept guard with a heavy-armed company of their young men; being also joined by a thousand Argives, the same number of Mantineans, and by some Athenian cavalry who stayed at Harpina[3a] during the feast. [4] Great fears were felt in the assembly of the Spartans coming in arms, especially after Lichas son of Arcesilaus, a Spartan, had been whipped on the course by the umpires because, upon his horses being the winners, and the Boeotian people being proclaimed the victor on account of his having no right to enter, he came forward on the course and crowned the charioteer in order to show that the chariot was his. After this incident all were more afraid than ever, and expected a disturbance: the Spartans, however, kept quiet and let the feast pass by, as we have seen. [5] After the Olympic games, the Argives and the allies repaired to Corinth to invite her to come over to them. There they found some Spartan envoys; and a long discussion ensued, which after all ended in nothing because an earthquake occurred and they all dispersed to their homes.

5.50
420
12th Year/Summer
OLYMPIA
The festival and games are conducted in the presence of Elean and allied armed forces to prevent a Spartan intrusion, which does not take place.
ARGOS
Argos invites Corinth to ally with her, but achieves nothing.

5.49.1d   At sixty *minae* to the *talent*, this sum amounts to more than thirty-three talents. See Appendix J, Classical Greek Currency, §3–4.
5.49.2a   For a discussion of the truces that were regularly declared during certain great religious festivals, see Appendix I, Classical Greek Religious Festivals, §7.
5.50.3a   Harpina: site unknown.

5.51
420/9
12th Year/Winter
HERACLEA
The Heracleots are defeated by their neighbors; their Spartan general is killed.

5.52
419
13th Year/Summer
HERACLEA
The Boeotians occupy Heraclea and offend Sparta.
PELOPONNESUS
Alcibiades leads a small Athenian force through the territories of the Peloponnesian allies.

5.53
419
13th Year/Summer
EPIDAURUS
Argos attacks Epidaurus to neutralize Corinth and shorten her communication route with Athens.

5.54
419
13th Year/Summer
SPARTA
The Spartans under Agis march out on a secret mission but turn back after unfavorable sacrifices.
EPIDAURUS
Argos invades Epidaurus during Carneia.

Summer was now over. During the following winter a battle took place between the Heracleots in Trachinia and the Aenianians, Dolopians, Malians, and certain of the Thessalians,[1a] [2] all tribes bordering on and hostile to the city, which directly menaced their country. Accordingly, after having opposed and harassed it from its very foundation by every means in their power, they now in this battle defeated the Heracleots, Xenares son of Cnidis, their Spartan commander, being among the slain. Thus the winter ended and the twelfth year of this war ended also.

After the battle Heraclea was so terribly reduced that in the first days of the following summer the Boeotians occupied the place and sent away the Spartan Agesippidas for misgovernment, fearing that the city might be taken by the Athenians while the Spartans were distracted with the affairs of the Peloponnesus. The Spartans, nevertheless, were offended with them for what they had done. [2] The same summer Alcibiades son of Clinias, now one of the generals at Athens, in concert with the Argives and the allies, went into the Peloponnesus with a few Athenian hoplites and archers, and some of the allies in those parts whom he gathered up as he passed, and with this army marched here and there through the Peloponnesus, and settled various matters connected with the alliance, and among other things induced the Patrians[2a] to carry their walls down to the sea, intending himself also to build a fort near the Achaean Rhium,[2b] but the Corinthians and Sicyonians,[2c] and all others who would have suffered by its being built, came up and hindered him.

The same summer war broke out between the Epidaurians[1a] and Argives. The pretext was that the Epidaurians did not send an offering for their pasture land to Apollo Pythaeus, as they were bound to do, the Argives having the chief management of the temple; but, apart from this pretext, Alcibiades and the Argives were determined, if possible, to gain possession of Epidaurus, and thus to insure the neutrality of Corinth and give the Athenians a shorter passage for their reinforcement from Aegina[1b] than if they had to sail round Scyllaeum.[1c] The Argives accordingly prepared to invade Epidaurus by themselves, to exact the offering.

About the same time the Spartans marched out with all their people to Leuctra[1a] upon their frontier, opposite to Mount Lycaeum,[1b] under the command of Agis son of Archidamus, without anyone knowing their destination, not even the cities that sent the contingents.[1c] [2] The sacrifices,

5.51.1a Heraclea in Trachis was last mentioned in 5.12. For its location, and that of Aenis of the Aenianians, Malis, and Thessaly: Map 5.54, AY. Dolopia (possible location): Map 5.54, AX.
5.52.2a Patrae: Map 5.54, AX.
5.52.2b Achaean Rhium: Map 5.54, AX.
5.52.2c Sicyon: Map 5.54, AY.
5.53.1a Epidaurus: Map 5.54, BY.
5.53.1b Aegina: Map 5.54, BY.
5.53.1c Point Scyllaeum: Map 5.54, BY; the strategic position of Epidaurus across Athenian lines of communication with

Argos and its other allies can also be seen on Map 5.58.
5.54.1a Leuctra: the site of this Leuctra in the Peloponnesus is unknown. There is another Leuctra in Boeotia which is the site of a famous defeat inflicted upon the Spartans by the Boeotians in 371.
5.54.1b Mount Lycaeum: Map 5.54, BX.
5.54.1c The cities that sent contingents were probably those of the *perioikoi*, not those of the Peloponnesian League; see Appendix C, Spartan Institutions, §9.

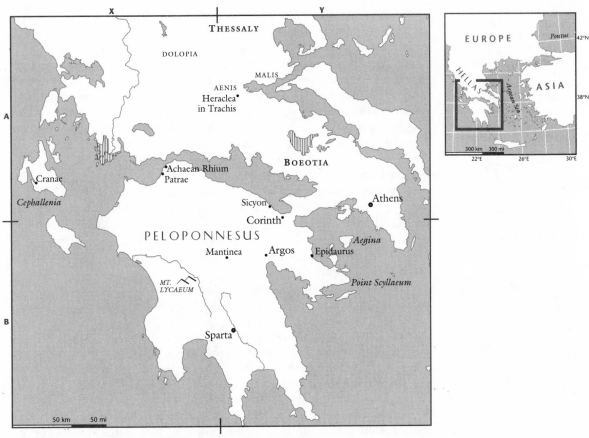

MAP 5.54 LOCATIONS IN THE NARRATIVE FOR THE YEAR 419

however, for crossing the frontier not proving propitious, the Spartans returned home themselves, and sent word to the allies to be ready to march after the month ensuing, which happened to be the month of Carneia, a holy time for the Dorians.[2a] [3] Upon the retreat of the Spartans the Argives marched out on the last day but three of the month before Carneia, and keeping this as the day during the whole time that they were out,[3a] invaded and plundered Epidaurus. [4] The Epidaurians summoned their allies to their aid, some of whom pleaded the month as an excuse; others came as far as the frontier of Epidaurus and there remained inactive.

5.54.2a   Only the Spartans among the Greeks are known to have conducted ritual sacrifices to determine the attitude of the gods to a planned military action.

5.54.3a   Some scholars think that this means that the Argives extended the number of days

before their Carneian truce by adding intercalated days; see Appendix K, Calendars and Dating Systems, §7.

5.55
419
13th Year/Summer
MANTINEA
Corinth commands Argos to leave Epidaurus. The Argives retire but reinvade after no agreements are reached. Athens and Sparta threaten to intervene but the Spartans return home after unfavorable sacrifices.

While the Argives were in Epidaurus embassies from the cities assembled at Mantinea, upon the invitation of the Athenians. The conference having begun, the Corinthian Euphamidas said that their actions did not agree with their words; while they were sitting deliberating about peace, the Epidaurians and their allies and the Argives were arrayed against each other in arms; deputies from each party should first go and separate the armies, and then the talk about peace might be resumed. [2] In compliance with this suggestion they went and made the Argives withdraw from Epidaurus, and afterwards reassembled, but without succeeding any better in coming to a conclusion; and the Argives a second time invaded Epidaurus and plundered the country. [3] The Spartans also marched out to Caryae;[3a] but the frontier sacrifices again proving unfavorable, they went back again, [4] and the Argives, after ravaging about a third of the Epidaurian territory, returned home. Meanwhile a thousand Athenian hoplites had come to their aid under the command of Alcibiades, but finding that the Spartan expedition was at an end, and that they were no longer wanted, went back again. So passed the summer.

5.56
419/8
13th Year/Winter
EPIDAURUS
After Sparta reinforces Epidaurus, Argos persuades Athens to return the Helots to Pylos. An Argive attempt to take Epidaurus fails.

The next winter the Spartans managed to elude the vigilance of the Athenians, and sent in a garrison of three hundred men to Epidaurus, under the command of Agesippidas. [2] Upon this the Argives went to the Athenians and complained of their having allowed an enemy to pass by sea, in spite of the clause in the treaty by which the allies were not to allow an enemy to pass through their country. Unless, therefore, the Athenians now put the Messenians and Helots in Pylos[2a] to harass the Spartans, they, the Argives, would consider that Athens had not kept faith with them. [3] The Athenians were persuaded by Alcibiades to inscribe at the bottom of the Laconian pillar that the Spartans had not kept their oaths, and to convey the Helots at Cranae[3a] to Pylos to plunder the country; but for the rest they remained quiet as before. [4] During this winter hostilities went on between the Argives and Epidaurians, without any pitched battle taking place, but only forays and ambushes, in which the losses were small and fell now on one side and now on the other. [5] At the close of the winter, toward the beginning of spring, the Argives went with scaling ladders to Epidaurus, expecting to find it left unguarded on account of the war and to be able to take it by assault, but returned unsuccessful. And the winter ended, and with it the thirteenth year of the war ended also.

5.57
418
14th Year/Summer
PELOPONNESUS
Sparta and her allies prepare a major effort against the Argive alliance.

In the middle of the next summer the Spartans, seeing the Epidaurians, their allies, in distress, and the rest of the Peloponnesus either in revolt or disaffected, concluded that it was high time for them to interfere if they wished to stop the progress of the evil, and accordingly with their full force, the Helots included, took the field against Argos, under the command of

---

5.55.3a   Caryae: Map 5.58, BY.
5.56.2a   Pylos: Map 5.58, BX. These Helots, of course, were those who had escaped from Spartan rule and had sought refuge with the Messenians at Pylos.

5.56.3a   This Cranae was on the island of Cephallenia (Map 5.54, AX), to which the Helots who had escaped to Pylos had been transferred in 421, at Sparta's request; see 5.35.7.

MAP 5.58 PELOPONNESIAN INVASION OF ARGOS

Agis son of Archidamus, king of the Spartans. [2] The Tegeans[2a] and the other Arcadian[2b] allies of Sparta joined in the expedition. The allies from the rest of the Peloponnesus and from outside mustered at Phlius;[2c] the Boeotians with five thousand hoplites and as many light troops, and five hundred horse and the same number of dismounted troopers; the Corinthians with two thousand hoplites; the rest more or less as might happen; and the Phliasians with all their forces, the army being in their country.

The preparations of the Spartans had from the first been known to the Argives, who did not, however, take the field until the enemy was on his way to join the rest at Phlius. Reinforced by the Mantineans with their allies, and by three thousand Elean hoplites, [2] they advanced and

5.57.2a Tegea: Map 5.58, AX.
5.57.2b Arcadia: Map 5.58, AX.
5.57.2c Phlius: Map 5.58, AX.

5.58
418
14th Year/Summer
ARGOS
The Argives confront the Spartans alone in Arcadia but Agis eludes them and joins his allies at Phlius. He advances by three roads toward Argos.

fell in with the Spartans at Methydrium in Arcadia.[2a] Each party took up its position upon a hill, and the Argives prepared to engage the Spartans while they were alone; but Agis eluded them by breaking up his camp in the night, and proceeded to join the rest of the allies at Phlius. [3] The Argives discovering this at daybreak, marched first to Argos and then up the Nemean road,[3a] down which they expected the Spartans and their allies would come. [4] Agis, however, instead of taking this road as they expected, ordered the Spartans, Arcadians, and Epidaurians to descend into the plain of Argos by a different, difficult road. The Corinthians, Pellenians,[4a] and Phliasians marched by another steep road; while the Boeotians, Megarians, and Sicyonians[4b] had instructions to come down by the Nemean road where the Argives were posted, so that if the enemy advanced into the plain against the troops of Agis, they might fall upon his rear with their cavalry. [5] These dispositions concluded, Agis invaded the plain and began to ravage Saminthus[5a] and other places.

Discovering this, the Argives came down from Nemea,[1a] day having now dawned. On their way they fell in with the troops of the Phliasians and Corinthians, and killed a few of the Phliasians, and had perhaps a few more of their own men killed by the Corinthians. [2] Meanwhile the Boeotians, Megarians, and Sicyonians, advancing upon Nemea according to their instructions, found the Argives no longer there as they had gone down on seeing their property ravaged, and were now forming for battle, the Spartans imitating their example. [3] The Argives were now completely surrounded; from the plain the Spartans and their allies shut them off from their city; above them were the Corinthians, Phliasians, and Pellenians; and on the side of Nemea the Boeotians, Sicyonians, and Megarians. Meanwhile their army was without cavalry, the Athenians alone among the allies not having yet arrived. [4] Now the bulk of the Argives and their allies did not see the danger of their position, but thought that they could not have a fairer field, having intercepted the Spartans in their own country and close to the city. [5] Two men, however, in the Argive army, Thrasylus, one of the five generals, and Alciphron, the Spartan *proxenus*,[5a] just as the armies were upon the point of engaging, went and held a parley with Agis and urged him not to bring on a battle, as the Argives were ready to refer to fair and equal arbitration whatever complaints the Spartans might have against them, and to make a treaty and live in peace in future.

The Argives who made these statements did so upon their own authority, not by order of the people, and Agis on his accepted their proposals, and without himself either consulting the majority, simply communicated the matter to a single individual, one of the high officers accompanying the

5.59
418
14th Year/Summer
ARGOS
The Argives and their allies are surrounded by the Spartans and their allies, but do not recognize their danger. Two Argive leaders offer to submit all problems to arbitration and to make peace with Sparta.

5.60
418
14th Year/Summer
ARGOS
Agis and the two Argives agree to a truce and, without consulting anyone else, Agis leads the Spartan forces away. Both sides attack the authors of this truce, thinking they had lost a favorable opportunity to defeat their opponents.

5.58.2a	Methydrium in Arcadia: Map 5.58, AX.	5.59.1a	Nemea: Map 5.58, AY.
5.58.3a	The road from Argos to Nemea: for Nemea's location, see Map 5.58, AY.	5.59.5a	*Proxenus:* see note 5.43.2a or Glossary.
5.58.4a	Pellene: Map 5.58, AX.		
5.58.4b	Sicyon, Megara: Map 5.58, AY.		
5.58.5a	Saminthus in the Argive plain: exact site unknown.		

expedition, and granted the Argives a truce for four months, in which to fulfill their promises; after which he immediately led off the army without giving any explanation to any of the other allies. [2] The Spartans and allies followed their general out of respect for the law, but amongst themselves loudly blamed Agis for going away from so fair a field (the enemy being hemmed in on every side by infantry and cavalry) without having done anything worthy of their strength. [3] Indeed this was by far the finest Hellenic army ever yet brought together; and it should have been seen while it was still united at Nemea, with the Spartans in full force, the Arcadians, Boeotians, Corinthians, Sicyonians, Pellenians, Phliasians and Megarians,[3a] and all these the flower of their respective populations, thinking themselves a match not merely for the Argive confederacy but for another added to it. [4] The army thus retired blaming Agis, and returned every man to his home. [5] The Argives however blamed still more loudly the persons who had concluded the truce without consulting the people, themselves thinking that they had let escape with the Spartans an opportunity such as they should never see again; as the struggle would have been under the walls of their city, and by the side of many and brave allies. [6] On their return accordingly they began to stone Thrasylus in the bed of the Charadrus,[6a] where they try all military cases before entering the city. Thrasylus fled to the altar, and so saved his life;[6b] his property however they confiscated.

After this arrived a thousand Athenian hoplites and three hundred horse, under the command of Laches and Nicostratus; whom the Argives, being nevertheless reluctant to break the truce with the Spartans, begged to depart, and refused to bring before the people, to whom they had a communication to make, until compelled to do so by the entreaties of the Mantineans and Eleans, who were still at Argos. [2] The Athenians, through Alcibiades their ambassador who was present there, told the Argives and the allies that they had no right to make a truce at all without the consent of their fellow confederates, and now that the Athenians had arrived so opportunely the war ought to be resumed. [3] These arguments proving successful with the allies, they immediately marched upon Orchomenos,[3a] all except the Argives, who, although they had consented like the rest, stayed behind at first, but eventually joined the others. [4] They now all besieged Orchomenos and made assaults upon it; one of their reasons for desiring to gain this place being that hostages from Arcadia[4a] had been lodged there by the Spartans. [5] The Orchomenians, alarmed at the weakness of their wall and the numbers of the enemy, and at the risk they ran of perishing before relief arrived, capitulated upon condition of joining the league, of giving hostages of their own to the Manti-

5.61
418
14th Year/Summer
ARGOS
After Athenian troops arrive, Alcibiades denounces the Argive-Spartan truce and calls for a resumption of the war. The Argives agree and join the allied siege of Orchomenos, which then capitulates and joins the alliance.

5.60.3a Arcadia, Pellene, and Phlius: Map 5.58, AX. Nemea, Boeotia, Corinth, Sicyon, and Megara: Map 5.58, AY.
5.60.6a Thucydides refers here to the bed of a usually dry watercourse—the Charadrus—that ran along the north and east sides of the city of Argos.
5.60.6b It would have been sacrilege, an insult to the gods, to harm someone who had taken refuge at an altar.
5.61.3a Orchomenos: Map 5.58, AX.
5.61.4a Arcadia: Map 5.58, AX.

neans, and giving up those lodged with them by the Spartans.

5.62
418
14th Year/Summer
ORCHOMENOS
Because the allies vote to
attack Tegea instead of
Lepreum, the Eleans leave in
anger.

Orchomenos thus secured, the allies now consulted as to which of the remaining places they should attack next. The Eleans were urgent for Lepreum;[1a] the Mantineans for Tegea; and the Argives and Athenians giving their support to the Mantineans, [2] the Eleans went home in a rage at their not having voted for Lepreum; while the rest of the allies made ready at Mantinea for going against Tegea, which a party inside had arranged to put into their hands.

5.63
418
14th Year/Summer
SPARTA
The loss of Orchomenos
makes the Spartans furious at
Agis; they threaten to punish
him but relent when he
promises to fight well. A new
law attaches counselors to
the king when he leads the
army.

Meanwhile the Spartans, upon their return from Argos after concluding the four months' truce, vehemently blamed Agis for not having subdued Argos, after an opportunity such as they thought they had never had before; for it was no easy matter to bring so many allies, and such good ones, together. [2] But when the news arrived of the capture of Orchomenos,[2a] they became more angry than ever, and, departing from all precedent, in the heat of the moment had almost decided to raze his house, and to fine him ten thousand drachmas. [3] Agis however entreated them to do none of these things, promising to atone for his fault by good service in the field, failing which they might then do to him whatever they pleased; [4] and they accordingly abstained from razing his house or fining him as they had threatened to do, and now made a law, hitherto unknown at Sparta, attaching to him ten Spartiates as counselors, without whose consent he should have no power to lead an army out of the city.

5.64
418
TEGEA
The Spartans receive word of
Tegea's peril and march out,
summoning their allies to
join them at Mantinea. The
allies try to join them, but
some are delayed by having
to cross hostile territory.

At this juncture word arrived from their friends in Tegea that unless they speedily appeared, Tegea would go over from them to the Argives and their allies, if it had not gone over already. [2] Upon this news a force marched out from Sparta of Spartans and Helots and all their people immediately and upon a scale never before witnessed. [3] Advancing toward Orestheum in Maenalia,[3a] they directed the Arcadians[3b] in their league to follow close after them to Tegea, and going on themselves as far as Orestheum, from there sent back the sixth part of the Spartans, consisting of the oldest and youngest men, to guard their homes, and with the rest of their army arrived at Tegea; where their Arcadian allies soon after joined them. [4] Meanwhile they sent to Corinth, to the Boeotians, the Phocians,[4a] and Locrians,[4b] with orders to come up as quickly as possible to Mantinea. These had but short notice; and it was not easy except all together, and after waiting for each other, to pass through the enemy's country, which lay right across and blocked the line of march. Nevertheless they made what haste they could. [5] Meanwhile the Spartans, with the Arcadian allies that had joined them, entered the territory of Mantinea, and encamping near the temple of Heracles began to plunder the country.

5.62.1a　Lepreum: Map 5.58, BX.
5.63.2a　Orchomenos: Map 5.71, BX.
5.64.3a　Maenalia, a district in Arcadia in which
　　　　　Orestheum was located. Orestheum: Map
　　　　　5.58, BX.
5.64.3b　Arcadia: Map 5.58, AX, and Map 5.71,
　　　　　BX.
5.64.4a　Phocis: Map 5.71, AY.
5.64.4b　Locris (Opuntian Locris): Map 5.71, AY.

Here they were seen by the Argives and their allies, who immediately took up a strong position, difficult to approach, and formed up in order of battle. [2] The Spartans at once advanced against them, and came on within a stone's throw or javelin's cast, when one of the older men, seeing the enemy's position to be a strong one, shouted to Agis that he must be thinking to cure one evil with another; meaning that he wished to make amends for his retreat from Argos, for which he had been so much blamed, by his present untimely wish to engage. [3] Meanwhile Agis, whether in consequence of this message or of some sudden new idea of his own, quickly led his army back without engaging, [4] and entering the Tegean territory, began to divert into Mantinean land the water about which the Mantineans and Tegeans are always fighting, on account of the extensive damage it does to whichever of the two countries it flows into. [5] His purpose in this was to make the Argives and their allies come down from the hill to resist the diversion of the water, as they would be sure to do when they knew of it, and thus to fight the battle in the plain. He accordingly stayed that day where he was, engaged in changing the course of the water. The Argives and their allies were at first amazed at the sudden retreat of the enemy after advancing so near, and did not know what to make of it; but when he had gone away and disappeared, without their having stirred to pursue him, they began anew to find fault with their generals, who had not only let the Spartans get off before, when they were so happily intercepted before Argos, but who now again allowed them to run away, without anyone pursuing them, and to escape at their leisure while the Argive army was leisurely betrayed. [6] The generals, half-stunned for the moment, afterwards led them down from the hill, and went forward and encamped in the plain, with the intention of attacking the enemy.

The next day the Argives and their allies formed up in the order in which they meant to fight if they chanced to encounter the enemy; and the Spartans returning from the water to their old encampment by the temple of Heracles, suddenly saw their adversaries close in front of them, all in complete order, and advanced from the hill. [2] A shock like that of the present moment the Spartans do not ever remember to have experienced: there was scant time for preparation, as they instantly and hastily fell into their ranks. Agis, their king, directing everything, according to the law, [3] for when a king is in the field all commands proceed from him: he gives the word to the *polemarchs,* they to the *lochagoi,* these to the *pentecostyes,* these again to the *enomotarchs,* and these last to the *enomoties.*[3a] [4] In short all orders are required to pass in the same way and quickly reach the troops; as almost the whole Spartan army, save for a small part, consists of officers

5.66.3a   Military officers and units of the Spartan
army, see Appendix C, Spartan Institu-
tions, §7–9.

5.65
418
14th Year/Summer
MANTINEA
Agis advances upon the Argive army's strong position but decides at the last minute to withdraw, to flood Mantinean territory, and thus to force the enemy to descend and fight in the plain. The Argives, after criticizing their generals for letting the enemy escape, do descend into the plain.

5.66
418
14th Year/Summer
MANTINEA
Returning to camp, the Spartans discover the enemy close by in battle order. Agis quickly orders the Spartans into proper formation to face the enemy.

under officers, and the care of what is to be done falls upon many.

In this battle the left wing was composed of the *sciritae*,[1a] who in a Spartan army always have that post to themselves alone; next to these were the soldiers of Brasidas from Thrace,[1b] and the *neodamodeis* with them; then came the Spartans themselves, company after company, with the Arcadians of Heraea[1c] at their side. After these were the Maenalians,[1d] and on the right wing the Tegeans with a few of the Spartans at the extremity; their cavalry being posted upon the two wings. [2] Such was the Spartan formation. That of their opponents was as follows: On the right were the Mantineans, the action taking place in their country; next to them the allies from Arcadia; after whom came the thousand picked men of the Argives, to whom the state had given a long course of military training at the public expense;[2a] next to them the rest of the Argives, and after them their allies, the Cleonaeans;[2b] and Orneans;[2c] and lastly the Athenians on the extreme left, and their own cavalry with them.

Such were the order and the forces of the two combatants. The Spartan army looked the largest; [2] though as to putting down the numbers of either host, or of the contingents composing it, I could not do so with any accuracy. Owing to the secrecy of their government the number of the Spartans was not known, and men are so apt to brag about the forces of their country that the estimate of their opponents was not trusted. The following calculation, however, makes it possible to estimate the numbers of the Spartans present upon this occasion. [3] There were seven companies in the field without counting the *sciritae*, who numbered six hundred men: in each company there were four *pentecostyes*, and in the *pentecosty* four *enomoties*. The first rank of the *enomoty* was composed of four soldiers: as to the depth, although they had not been all drawn up alike, but as each captain chose, they were generally ranged eight deep; the first rank along the whole line, exclusive of the *sciritae*, consisted of four hundred and forty-eight men.[3a]

5.67
418
14th Year/Summer
MANTINEA
Thucydides describes both sides' order of battle.

5.68
418
14th Year/Summer
MANTINEA
The Spartan army appears larger than that of its opponent. Thucydides calculates its numbers.

5.67.1a For the *sciritae*, see Appendix C, Spartan Institutions, §9.
5.67.1b The return of these troops, the granting of freedom to these Helots among them, and their settlement with the *neodamodeis* in Lepreum was mentioned in 5.34.
5.67.1c Heraea, in Arcadia: Map 5.71, BX.
5.67.1d Maenalia, in Arcadia: Map 5.71, BX.
5.67.2a For the Argive picked force trained at public expense, see Appendix F, Ancient Greek Land Warfare, §7.
5.67.2b Cleonae: Map 5.71, BY.
5.67.2c Orneae: Map 5.71, BX.
5.68.3a Taking into account the one sixth of the army sent home before the battle (5.64.3), and including the six hundred *sciritae*, one reaches by Thucydides' method of calculation a total Spartan army in 418 of about five thousand. If the numbers of Spartiates and *perioikoi* (see Glossary) in the "companies" (*lochoi*)

were roughly equal, one arrives at a total of no more than two thousand five hundred Spartiates in all. But some have argued that Thucydides has made a serious mistake. His calculations are based on an army of seven "companies," but in Xenophon's *History of Greece*, which covers the period from the end of Thucydides to 362 B.C., one encounters a Spartan army of six "divisions" (*morae*) with two "companies" in each. Was Thucydides unaware that there had been by 418 a great reform of the army? The answer greatly affects both our understanding of the developing Spartan demographic problem (see note 5.34.1b and Appendix G, Spartan Institutions §7–9) and our estimate of Thucydides' credibility. Scholarly opinion is much divided.

The armies being now on the eve of engaging, each contingent received some words of encouragement from its own commander. The Mantineans were reminded that they were going to fight for their country and to avoid returning to the experience of servitude after having tasted that of empire; the Argives, that they would contend for their ancient supremacy, to regain their once equal share of the Peloponnesus of which they had been so long deprived, and to punish an enemy and a neighbor for a thousand wrongs; the Athenians, of the glory of gaining the honors of the day with so many and brave allies in arms, and that a victory over the Spartans in the Peloponnesus would cement and extend their empire, and would besides preserve Attica from all invasions in future. [2] These were the incitements addressed to the Argives and their allies. The Spartans meanwhile, man to man, and with their war songs in the ranks, exhorted each brave comrade to remember what he had learnt before; well aware that the long training of action was of more use for saving lives than any brief verbal exhortation, though ever so well delivered.

After this they joined battle, the Argives and their allies advancing with haste and fury, the Spartans slowly and to the music of many flute players—a standing institution in their army, that has nothing to do with religion, but is meant to make them advance evenly, stepping in time, without breaking their order, as large armies are apt to do in the moment of engaging.

Just before the battle joined, King Agis resolved upon the following maneuver. All armies are alike in this: on going into action they get forced out rather on their right wing, and one and the other overlap with this their adversary's left; because fear makes each man do his best to shelter his unarmed side with the shield of the man next him on the right, thinking that the closer the shields are locked together the better will he be protected. The man primarily responsible for this is the first upon the right wing, who is always striving to withdraw from the enemy his unarmed side; and the same apprehension makes the rest follow him. [2] On the present occasion the Mantineans reached with their wing far beyond the *sciritae*, and the Spartans and Tegeans still farther beyond the Athenians, as their army was the largest. [3] Agis afraid of his left being surrounded, and thinking that the Mantineans outflanked it too far, ordered the sciritae and Brasideans to move out from their place in the ranks and make the line even with the Mantineans, and told the polemarchs Hipponoidas and Aristocles to fill up the gap thus formed, by throwing themselves into it with two companies taken from the right wing; thinking that his right would still be strong enough and to spare, and that the line fronting the Mantineans would gain in solidity.

MAP 5.71 THE BATTLE OF MANTINEA CAMPAIGN

5.72
418
14th Year/Summer
MANTINEA
The polemarchs on the right refuse to move their units, and Agis rescinds his order. The Spartan left is defeated but the Spartan right easily routs its opponents.

However, as he gave these orders in the moment of the onset, and at short notice, Aristocles and Hipponoidas refused to move (for which offense they were afterwards found guilty of cowardice and banished from Sparta); and although Agis, when he saw that the two companies did not move, ordered the sciritae to return to their place in line, they did not have time to fill up the breach in question before the enemy closed. [2] Now it was, however, that the Spartans, utterly worsted in respect of skill, showed themselves as superior in point of courage. [3] As soon as they came to close quarters with the enemy, the Mantinean right broke the sciritae and Brasideans, and bursting in with their allies and the thousand picked Argives into the unclosed breach in their line cut up and surrounded the Spartans, and drove them in full rout to the wagons, slaying some of the older men on guard there. [4] But if the Spartans got the worst of it in this part of the field, it was not so with the rest of their army, and especially the center, where the three hundred knights,[4a] as they are called, fought round King Agis, and fell on the older men of the Argives and the five companies so named, and on the Cleonaeans, the Orneans, and the Athenians next them, and instantly routed them; the greater number not even waiting to strike a blow, but giving way the moment that they came on, some even being trodden under foot, in their fear of being overtaken by their assailants.

The army of the Argives and their allies having given way in this quarter was now completely cut in two, and as the Spartan and Tegean right simultaneously closed round the Athenians with the troops that outflanked them, these last found themselves placed between two fires, being surrounded on one side and already defeated on the other. Indeed they would have suffered more severely than any other part of the army, but for the services of the cavalry which they had with them. [2] Agis also, on perceiving the distress of his left opposed to the Mantineans and the thousand Argives, ordered all the army to advance to the support of the defeated wing; [3] and while this took place, as the enemy moved past and slanted away from them, the Athenians escaped at their leisure, and with them the beaten Argive division. Meanwhile the Mantineans and their allies and the picked body of the Argives ceased to press the enemy and, seeing their friends defeated and the Spartans in full advance upon them, took to flight. [4] Many of the Mantineans perished; but the bulk of the picked body of the Argives made good their escape. The flight and retreat, however, were neither hurried nor long; the Spartans fighting long and stubbornly until the rout of their enemy, but that once accomplished, pursuing for a short time and not far.

Such was the battle, as nearly as possible as I have described it; the greatest that had occurred for a very long while among the Hellenes, and joined by the most considerable states. [2] The Spartans took up a position in front of the enemy's dead, and immediately set up a trophy and stripped the slain; they took up their own dead and carried them back to Tegea,[2a] where they buried them, and restored those of the enemy under truce. [3] The Argives,[3a] Orneans,[3b] and Cleonaeans[3c] had seven hundred killed; the Mantineans two hundred, and the Athenians and Aeginetans[3d] also two hundred, with both their generals. On the side of the Spartans, the allies did not suffer any loss worth speaking of: as to the Spartans themselves it was difficult to learn the truth; it is said, however, that there were slain about three hundred of them.

5.72.4a   The three hundred so-called knights of the Spartan army were the king's bodyguard, who fought on foot around him.
5.74.2a   Tegea: Map 5.71, BX.
5.74.3a   Argos: Map 5.71, BY.
5.74.3b   Orneae: Map 5.71, BX.
5.74.3c   Cleonae: Map 5.71, BY.

5.74.3d   Aegina: Map 5.71, BY. These Aeginitan casualties were Athenian settlers; Thucydides mentions the expulsion of the Aeginetans from their island and its resettlement by Athenians in 2.27 and 7.57.2.

5.75
418
14th Year/Summer
MANTINEA
The Spartans dismiss their
allies and celebrate the
Carneia.
EPIDAURUS
Epidaurians plunder Argive
territory. The Argives return
and begin a circumvallation
of Epidaurus.

While the battle was impending, Pleistoanax, the other king, set out with a reinforcement composed of the oldest and youngest men, and got as far as Tegea, where he heard of the victory and went back again. [2] The Spartans also sent a message to turn back the allies from Corinth and from beyond the Isthmus,[2a] and returning home themselves dismissed their allies, and celebrated the Carneian festival,[2b] which happened to be at that time. [3] The imputations cast upon them by the Hellenes at the time, whether of cowardice on account of the disaster in the island,[3a] or of mismanagement and slowness generally, were all wiped out by this single action: fortune, it was thought, might have humbled them, but the men themselves were the same as ever. [4] The day before this battle, the Epidaurians with all their forces invaded the deserted Argive territory, and killed many of the guards left there in the absence of the Argive army. [5] After the battle three thousand Elean hoplites arrived to aid the Mantineans, as well as a reinforcement of one thousand Athenians; all these allies marched at once against Epidaurus while the Spartans were keeping the Carneia and, dividing the work among themselves, began to build a wall round the city. [6] The rest left off; but the Athenians finished at once the part assigned to them round Cape Heraeum;[6a] and after all joined in leaving a garrison in the fortification in question, they returned to their respective cities. Summer now came to an end.

5.76
418/7
14th Year/Winter
ARGOS
Sparta, relying upon a strengthened antidemocratic party in Argos after the battle, offers to negotiate a peace. After much discussion, Argos accepts the Spartan proposal.

In the first days of the next winter, when the Carneian holidays were over, the Spartans took the field, and arriving at Tegea sent on to Argos proposals for an accommodation. [2] There had before been a party in the city desirous of overthrowing the democracy; and after the battle that had been fought, these were now in a far better position to persuade the people to listen to terms. Their plan was to make a treaty with the Spartans first, follow it with an alliance, and after this to fall upon the popular party. [3] Lichas son of Arcesilaus, the Argive *proxenus*,[3a] accordingly arrived at Argos with two proposals from Sparta, to regulate the conditions of war or peace, according to whichever one they preferred. After much discussion, Alcibiades happening to be in the city, the Spartan party, who now ventured to act openly, persuaded the Argives to accept the proposal for a peace treaty, which ran as follows:

5.77
418/7
14th Year/Winter
ARGOS-SPARTA
Thucydides presents the text of the peace proposal offered by Sparta to Argos.

The assembly of the Spartans agrees to negotiate with the Argives upon the terms following:

• The Argives shall restore to the Orchomenians[1a] their children,

5.75.2a   Isthmus of Corinth: Map 5.71, AY.
5.75.2b   For the Carneian festival, see Appendix I, Religious Festivals, §8, and Appendix H, Dialects and Ethnic Groups, §5.
5.75.3a   The island referred to is Sphacteria at Pylos, where almost three hundred Spartans surrendered to Athenian forces in 425; see 4.31–40.

5.75.6a   Cape Heraeum juts out northward into the sea from Old Epidaurus. Epidaurus: Map 5.71, BY.
5.76.3a   *Proxenus:* see note 5.43.2a or Glossary. This Lichas may be remembered as the owner of victorious racehorces at Olympia; see 5.50.4.
5.77.1a   Orchomenos: Map 5.71, BX.

and to the Maenalians[1b] their men, and shall restore the men they have in Mantinea to the Spartans.

- [2] They shall evacuate Epidaurus, and raze the fortification there. If the Athenians refuse to withdraw from Epidaurus, they shall be declared enemies of the Argives and of the Spartans, and of the allies of the Spartans and the allies of the Argives.
- [3] If the Spartans have any children in their custody, they shall restore them every one to his city.
- [4] As to the offering to the god,[4a] the Argives, if they wish, shall impose an oath upon the Epidaurians, but, if not, they shall swear it themselves.
- [5] All the cities in the Peloponnesus, both small and great, shall be independent according to the customs of their country.
- [6] If any of the powers outside the Peloponnesus invade Peloponnesian territory, the parties contracting shall unite to repel them, on such terms as they may agree upon, as being most fair for the Peloponnesians.
- [7] All allies of the Spartans outside the Peloponnesus shall be on the same footing as the Spartans, and the allies of the Argives shall be on the same footing as the Argives, being left in enjoyment of their own possessions.
- [8] This treaty shall be shown to the allies,[8a] and shall be concluded, if they approve: if the allies think fit, they may send the treaty to be considered at home.

The Argives began by accepting this proposal, and the Spartan army returned home from Tegea. After this, normal intercourse was renewed between them, and not long afterwards the same faction contrived that the Argives should give up the alliance with the Mantineans, Eleans, and Athenians, and should make a treaty of alliance with the Spartans; which was consequently done upon the following terms:

5.78
418/7
14th Year/Winter
ARGOS
Renouncing her pact with Athens, Elis, and Mantinea, Argos allies with Sparta.

The Spartans and Argives agree to a treaty and alliance for fifty years upon the terms following:
- All disputes shall be decided by fair and impartial arbitration, consistent with the customs of the two countries.
- The rest of the cities in the Peloponnesus may be included in this treaty and alliance, as independent and sovereign, in full enjoy-

5.79
418/7
14th Year/Winter
ARGOS-SPARTA
Thucydides offers the text of the treaty of alliance between Argos and Sparta.

5.77.1b Maenalia, in Arcadia: Map 5.71, BX.
5.77.4a The offering to the god refers here to the ostensible cause of the war between Argos and Epidaurus; see 5.53.1.
5.77.8a The "allies" here are probably the states of the Peloponnesian League, a Spartan-

led coalition which Argos would not have been willing to join. See Appendix D, The Peloponnesian League, §3, 5–6.

ment of what they possess; all disputes being decided by fair and impartial arbitration, consistent with the customs of the said cities.

• [2] All allies of the Spartans outside the Peloponnesus shall be upon the same footing as the Spartans themselves, and the allies of the Argives shall be upon the same footing as the Argives themselves, continuing to enjoy what they possess.

• [3] If it shall be anywhere necessary to make an expedition in common, the Spartans and Argives shall consult upon it and decide, as may be most fair for the allies.

• [4] If any of the cities, whether inside or outside the Peloponnesus, have a question of frontiers or of other matters, it must be settled; but if one allied city should have a quarrel with another allied city, it must be referred to some third city thought impartial by both parties. Private citizens shall have their disputes decided according to the laws of their respective countries.

5.80
418/7
14th Year/Winter
ARGOS-SPARTA
Argos and Sparta fulfill the terms of their treaty and extend their alliance to Perdiccas and the Chalcidian cities.
EPIDAURUS
As ordered by Argos, the Athenians leave Epidaurus.

The treaty and above alliance concluded, each party at once released everything whether acquired by war or otherwise, and thereafter acting in common voted to receive neither herald nor embassy from the Athenians unless they evacuated their forts and withdrew from the Peloponnesus, and also to make neither peace nor war with anyone, except jointly. [2] Zeal was not wanting: both parties sent envoys to the Thracian district[2a] and to Perdiccas,[2b] and persuaded the latter to join their league. Still he did not at once break with Athens, although inclined to do so upon seeing the way shown him by Argos, the original home of his family. They also renewed their old oaths with the Chalcidians and took new ones: [3] the Argives, besides, sent ambassadors to the Athenians, bidding them evacuate the fort at Epidaurus. The Athenians, seeing their own men outnumbered by the rest of the garrison, sent Demosthenes to bring them out. This general, under color of a gymnastic contest which he arranged on his arrival, got the rest of the garrison out of the place and shut the gates behind them. Afterwards the Athenians renewed their treaty with the Epidaurians, and by themselves gave up the fortress.

5.81
418/7
14th Year/Winter
MANTINEA-SPARTA
Mantinea and Sparta make peace; a Spartan-Argive army strengthens the oligarchy at Sicyon and establishes an oligarchy at Argos.

After the defection of Argos from the league, the Mantineans, though they held out at first, in the end found themselves powerless without the Argives; they too came to terms with Sparta,[1a] and gave up their rule over the cities. [2] The Spartans and Argives, each a thousand strong, now took the field together, and the former first went by themselves to Sicyon[2a] and made the government there more oligarchic than before, and then both, uniting, put down the democracy at Argos and set up an oligarchy favorable to Sparta. These events occurred at the close of the winter, just before spring; and the fourteenth year of the war ended.

5.80.2a Thracian district, including Chalcidice: Map 5.82, AX, AY.
5.80.2b Perdiccas was the king of Macedonia (Map 5.82, AX).
5.81.1a This special treaty with Mantinea, now a Peloponnesian League ally (see Appendix

D, The Peloponnesian League, §5), is also mentioned in what is probably a near-contemporary treaty between Sparta and Aetolian Erxadieis.
5.81.2a Sicyon: Map 5.82, BX.

MAP 5.82 EVENTS OF THE YEARS 417 AND 416

The next summer the people of Dium, in Athos,[1a] revolted from the Athenians to the Chalcidians,[1b] and the Spartans settled affairs in Achaea[1c] in a way more agreeable to the interests of their country. [2] Meanwhile the popular party at Argos little by little gathering strength and courage, waited for the moment of the Gymnopaedic festival at Sparta and then fell upon the oligarchs. After a fight in the city victory declared for the popular party, who slew some of their opponents and banished others. [3] The Spartans for a long while disregarded the messages of their friends at

5.82
417
15th Year/Summer
ARGOS
Argive democrats revive and overthrow the oligarchs, killing some and banishing others. Sparta resolves to attack Argos, but procrastinates. Argos renews ties with Athens and begins to build long walls to the sea.

5.82.1a   Dium in Mount Athos (on the Acte
          Peninsula): Map 5.82, AX.
5.82.1b   "The Chalcidians" are the Chalcidian
          League referred to in note 5.18.5b; Chal-
          cidice: Map 5.82, AX.
5.82.1c   Achaea: Map 5.82, BX.

Argos; at last they postponed the Gymnopaediae and marched to their assistance, but learning at Tegea of the defeat of the oligarchs, refused to go any further in spite of the entreaties of those who had escaped, and returned home and celebrated the festival. [4] Later on, envoys arrived with messages from the Argives in the city and from the exiles, when the allies were also at Sparta; and after much had been said on both sides, the Spartans decided that the party in the city had done wrong and resolved to march against Argos, but kept delaying and putting off the matter. [5] Meanwhile the popular party at Argos, in fear of the Spartans, began again to court the Athenian alliance, which they were convinced would be of the greatest service to them; and accordingly proceeded to build long walls to the sea, in order that in case of a blockade by land, with the help of the Athenians they might have the advantage of importing what they wanted by sea. [6] Some of the cities in the Peloponnesus were also privy to the building of these walls; and the Argives with all their people, women and slaves not excepted, applied themselves to the work, while carpenters and masons came to them from Athens. Summer was now over.

The following winter the Spartans, hearing of the walls that were being built, marched against Argos with their allies (except for the Corinthians), under the command of their king Agis son of Archidamus. [2] They had intelligence of affairs in the city itself but this intelligence, which they counted upon, came to nothing; however, they took and razed the walls which were being built, and after capturing the Argive city Hysiae[2a] and killing all the freemen that fell into their hands, went back and dispersed every man to his city. [3] After this the Argives marched into Phlius[3a] and plundered it for harboring their exiles, most of whom had settled there, and so returned home. [4] The same winter the Athenians blockaded Macedonia[4a] in retaliation for the alliance entered into by Perdiccas with the Argives and Spartans, and also because of his breach of his engagements on the occasion of the expedition prepared by Athens against the Chalcidians in the Thracian region[4b] and against Amphipolis,[4c] under the command of Nicias son of Niceratus, which had to be abandoned mainly because of his desertion. He was therefore proclaimed an enemy. And thus the winter ended, and the fifteenth year of the war ended with it.

The next summer Alcibiades sailed with twenty ships to Argos and seized the suspected persons still left of the Spartan faction to the number of three hundred, whom the Athenians forthwith lodged in the neighboring islands of their empire.[1a] The Athenians also made an expedition against the isle of Melos[1b] with thirty ships of their own, six Chian,[1c] and two Les-

5.83.2a Hysiae: Map 5.82, BX.
5.83.3a Phlius: Map 5.82, BX.
5.83.4a Macedonia: Map 5.82, AX.
5.83.4b Chalcidice, Thrace: Map 5.82, AX, AY. "The Chalcidians" here are the members of the Chalcidian League; see note 5.18.5b.
5.83.4c Amphipolis: Map 5.82, AX.

5.84.1a For what happened to these unfortunate hostages, see 6.61.3.
5.84.1b Melos: Map 5.82, BY. An earlier Athenian expedition to Melos was described in 3.91, but the background to this invasion is not fully explained by Thucydides.
5.84.1c Chios: Map 5.82, BY.

bian[1d] vessels, sixteen hundred hoplites, three hundred archers, and twenty mounted archers from Athens, and about fifteen hundred hoplites from the allies and the islanders. [2] The Melians are a colony of Sparta that would not submit to the Athenians like the other islanders, and at first remained neutral and took no part in the struggle, but afterwards upon the Athenians using violence and plundering their territory, assumed an attitude of open hostility. [3] Cleomedes son of Lycomedes, and Tisias son of Tisimachus, the generals, encamping in their territory with the above armament, before doing any harm to their land, sent envoys to negotiate. These the Melians did not bring before the people, but bade them state the object of their mission to the magistrates and the few; upon which the Athenian envoys spoke as follows:

Athenians: "Since the negotiations are not to go on before the people, in order that we may not be able to speak straight on without interruption, and deceive the ears of the multitude by seductive arguments which would pass without refutation (for we know that this is the meaning of our being brought before the few), what if you who sit there were to pursue a method more cautious still! Make no set speech yourselves, but take us up at whatever you do not like, and settle that before going any farther. And first tell us if this proposition of ours suits you."

5.85
416
16th Year/Summer
MELOS
Noting that only the Few, not The People, are present, the Athenians offer to debate frankly and spontaneously.

The Melian commissioners answered:

Melians: "To the fairness of quietly instructing each other as you propose there is nothing to object; but your military preparations are too far advanced to agree with what you say, as we see you are come to be judges in your own cause, and that all we can reasonably expect from this negotiation is war, if we prove to have right on our side and refuse to submit, or in the contrary case, slavery."

5.86
416
16th Year/Summer
MELOS
The Melians agree to talk, but feel that their only choices are war or slavery.

Athenians: "If you have met to reason about presentiments of the future, or for anything else than to consult for the safety of your state upon the facts that you see before you, we will cease talking; otherwise we will go on."

5.87
416
16th Year/Summer
MELOS

Melians: "It is natural and excusable for men in our position to turn more ways than one both in thought and utterance. However, the question in this conference is, as you say, the safety of our country; and the discussion, if you please, can proceed in the way which you propose."

5.88
416
16th Year/Summer
MELOS

5.84.1d Lesbos: Map 5.82, AY.

5.89
416
16th Year/Summer
MELOS
The Athenians say that the strong do what they can and the weak suffer what they must.

Athenians: "For ourselves, we shall not trouble you with specious pretenses—either of how we have a right to our empire because we overthrew the Mede, or are now attacking you because of wrong that you have done us—and make a long speech which would not be believed; and in return we hope that you, instead of thinking to influence us by saying that you did not join the Spartans, although their colonists, or that you have done us no wrong, will aim at what is feasible, holding in view the real sentiments of us both; since you know as well as we do that right, as the world goes, is only in question between equals in power, while the strong do what they can and the weak suffer what they must."

5.90
416
16th Year/Summer
MELOS
The Melians point out how useful moral arguments could be to Athens if her empire fell.

Melians: "As we think, at any rate, it is expedient—we speak as we are obliged, since you enjoin us to let right alone and talk only of interest—that you should not destroy what is our common protection, namely, the privilege of being allowed in danger to invoke what is fair and right, and even to profit by arguments not strictly valid if they can be persuasive. And you are as much interested in this as any, as your fall would be a signal for the heaviest vengeance and an example for the world to meditate upon."

5.91
416
16th Year/Summer
MELOS
The Athenians reply that it is in their mutual interests for Melos to peacefully accept Athenian rule.

Athenians: "The end of our empire, if end it should, does not frighten us: a rival empire like Sparta, even if Sparta was our real antagonist, is not so terrible to the vanquished as subjects who by themselves attack and overpower their rulers.[1a] [2] This, however, is a risk that we are content to take. We will now proceed to show you that we have come here in the interest of our empire, and that we shall say what we are now going to say, for the preservation of your country; as we would desire to exercise that empire over you without trouble, and see you preserved for the good of us both."

5.92

Melians: "And how, pray, could it turn out as good for us to serve as for you to rule?"

5.93

Athenians: "Because you would have the advantage of submitting before suffering the worst, and we should gain by not destroying you."

5.94

Melians: "So you would not consent to our being neutral, friends instead of enemies, but allies of neither side."

5.95

Athenians: "No; for your hostility cannot so much hurt us as your friendship will be an argument to our subjects of our weakness, and your enmity of our power."

5.96

Melians: "Is that your subjects' idea of equity, to put those who have nothing to do with you in the same category with peoples that are most of them your own colonists, and some conquered rebels?"

5.97
416
16th Year/Summer
MELOS
The Athenians say that Athens must subdue Melos to keep the respect of its subjects.

Athenians: "As far as right goes they think one has as much of it as the other, and that if any maintain their independence it is because

5.91.1a Scholars have differed as to whether this statement could have been written only after 404, when Athens did get off more lightly than was to be expected. See the Introduction (sect. II.ii).

they are strong, and that if we do not molest them it is because we are afraid; so that besides extending our empire we should gain in security by your subjection; the fact that you are islanders and weaker than others rendering it all the more important that you should not succeed in thwarting the masters of the sea."

Melians: "But do you consider that there is no security in the policy which we indicate? For here again if you debar us from talking about justice and invite us to obey your interest, we also must explain ours, and try to persuade you, if the two happen to coincide. How can you avoid making enemies of all existing neutrals who shall look at our case and conclude from it that one day or another you will attack them? And what is this but to make greater the enemies that you have already, and to force others to become so who would otherwise have never thought of it?"

Athenians: "Why, the fact is that mainlanders generally give us but little alarm; the liberty which they enjoy will long prevent their taking precautions against us; it is rather islanders like yourselves, outside our empire, and subjects smarting under the yoke, who would be the most likely to take a rash step and lead themselves and us into obvious danger."

Melians: "Well then, if you risk so much to retain your empire, and your subjects to get rid of it, it were surely great baseness and cowardice in us who are still free not to try everything that can be tried, before submitting to your yoke."

Athenians: "Not if you are well advised, the contest not being an equal one, with honor as the prize and shame as the penalty, but a question of self-preservation and of not resisting those who are far stronger than you are."

Melians: "But we know that the fortune of war is sometimes more impartial than the disproportion of numbers might lead one to suppose; to submit is to give ourselves over to despair, while action still preserves for us a hope that we may stand erect."

Athenians: "Hope, danger's comforter, may be indulged in by those who have abundant resources, if not without loss, at all events without ruin; but its nature is to be extravagant, and those who go so far as to stake their all upon the venture see it in its true colors only when they are ruined; but so long as the discovery would enable them to guard against it, it is never found wanting. [2] Let not this be the case with you, who are weak and hang on a single turn of the scale; nor be like the vulgar, who, abandoning such security as human means may still afford, when visible hopes fail them in extremity, turn to the invisible, to prophecies and oracles, and other

5.98
416
16th Year/Summer
MELOS
The Melians argue that Athens' policy will only create more enemies for her.

5.99
416
16th Year/Summer
MELOS

5.100
416
16th Year/Summer
MELOS

5.101
416
16th Year/Summer
MELOS

5.102
416
16th Year/Summer
MELOS

5.103
416
16th Year/Summer
MELOS
The Melians are advised to avoid hope, which deludes men and leads them to ruin.

such inventions that delude men with hopes to their destruction."

Melians: "You may be sure that we are as well aware as you of the difficulty of contending against your power and fortune, unless the terms be equal. But we trust that the gods may grant us fortune as good as yours, since we are just men fighting against unjust, and that what we want in power will be made up by the alliance of the Spartans, who are bound, if only for very shame, to come to the aid of their kindred. Our confidence, therefore, after all is not so utterly irrational."

Athenians: "When you speak of the favor of the gods, we may as fairly hope for that as yourselves; neither our pretensions nor our conduct being in any way contrary to what men believe of the gods, or practice among themselves.[1a] [2] Of the gods we believe, and of men we know, that by a necessary law of their nature they rule wherever they can. And it is not as if we were the first to make this law, or to act upon it when made: we found it existing before us, and shall leave it to exist forever after us; all we do is to make use of it, knowing that you and everybody else, having the same power as we have, would do the same as we do. [3] Thus, as far as the gods are concerned, we have no fear and no reason to fear that we shall be at a disadvantage. But when we come to your notion about the Spartans, which leads you to believe that shame will make them help you, here we bless your simplicity but do not envy your folly. [4] The Spartans, when their own interests or their country's laws are in question, are the worthiest men alive; of their conduct toward others much might be said, but no clearer idea of it could be given than by shortly saying that of all the men we know they are most conspicuous in considering what is agreeable honorable, and what is expedient just. Such a way of thinking does not promise much for the safety which you now unreasonably count upon."

Melians: "But it is for this very reason that we now trust to their respect for expediency to prevent them from betraying the Melians, their colonists, and thereby losing the confidence of their friends in Hellas and helping their enemies."

Athenians: "Then you do not adopt the view that expediency goes with security, while justice and honor cannot be followed without danger; and danger the Spartans generally court as little as possible."

Melians: "But we believe that they would be more likely to face even danger for our sake, and with more confidence than for others, as our nearness to the Peloponnesus makes it easier for them to act; and our common blood insures our fidelity."

5.105.1a See the Introduction (sect. IV.i) for a discussion of Thucydides' view of religion.

5.104
416
16th Year/Summer
MELOS

5.105
416
16th Year/Summer
MELOS
The Athenians also hope for the gods' favor, since they only do what is natural to both gods and men: "rule where they can." It is foolish to believe that the Spartans, who are moral hypocrites when the interests of others are concerned, will aid Melos because of sentiment or shame.

5.106
416
16th Year/Summer
MELOS

5.107
416
16th Year/Summer
MELOS

5.108
416
16th Year/Summer
MELOS

Athenians: "Yes, but what an intending ally trusts to is not the goodwill of those who ask his aid, but a decided superiority of power for action; and the Spartans look to this even more than others. At least, such is their distrust of their home resources that it is only with numerous allies that they attack a neighbor; now is it likely that while we are masters of the sea they will cross over to an island?"

Melians: "But they would have others to send. The Cretan sea[1a] is a wide one, and it is more difficult for those who command it to intercept others, than for those who wish to elude them to do so safely. [2] And should the Spartans miscarry in this, they would fall upon your land, and upon those left of your allies whom Brasidas did not reach; and instead of places which are not yours, you will have to fight for your own country and your own confederacy."

Athenians: "Some diversion of the kind you speak of you may one day experience, only to learn, as others have done, that the Athenians never once yet withdrew from a siege for fear of any. [2] But we are struck by the fact, that after saying you would consult for the safety of your country, in all this discussion you have mentioned nothing which men might trust in and think to be saved by. Your strongest arguments depend upon hope and the future, and your actual resources are too scanty, as compared with those arrayed against you, for you to come out victorious. [3] You will therefore show great blindness of judgment, unless, after allowing us to retire, you can find some counsel more prudent than this. You will surely not be caught by that idea of disgrace, which in dangers that are disgraceful, and at the same time too plain to be mistaken, proves so fatal to mankind; since in too many cases the very men that have their eyes perfectly open to what they are rushing into, let the thing called disgrace, by the mere influence of a seductive name, lead them on to a point at which they become so enslaved by the phrase as in fact to fall willfully into hopeless disaster, and incur disgrace more disgraceful as the companion of error, than when it comes as the result of misfortune.[3a] [4] This, if you are well advised, you will guard against; and you will not think it dishonorable to submit to the greatest city in Hellas, when it makes you the moderate offer of becoming its tributary ally, without ceasing to enjoy the country that belongs to you; nor when you have the choice given you between war and security, will you be so blinded as to choose the worse. And it is certain that those who do not yield to their equals, who keep terms with their superiors, and are moderate toward their inferiors, on the whole succeed best. [5] Think over the matter,

5.109
416
16th Year/Summer
MELOS

5.110
416
16th Year/Summer
MELOS

5.111
416
16th Year/Summer
MELOS
The Athenians advise the Melians not to act from fear of dishonor or disgrace, saying that Melos lacks the resources for such concepts and that heeding them now will bring her to ruin.

5.110.1a Cretan sea: Map 5.82, BY.
5.111.3a For another Athenian general's attitude
          toward risk and disgrace, see 8.27.2–3.

therefore, after our withdrawal, and reflect once and again that it is for your country that you are consulting, that you have not more than one, and that upon this one deliberation depends its prosperity or ruin."

The Athenians now withdrew from the conference; and the Melians, left to themselves, came to a decision corresponding to what they had maintained in the discussion, and answered, [2] "Our resolution, Athenians, is the same as it was at first. We will not in a moment deprive of freedom a city that has been inhabited these seven hundred years; but we put our trust in the fortune by which the gods have preserved it until now, and in the help of men, that is, of the Spartans; and so we will try and save ourselves. [3] Meanwhile we invite you to allow us to be friends to you and foes to neither party, and to retire from our country after making such a treaty as shall seem fit to us both."

Such was the answer of the Melians. The Athenians now departing from the conference said, "Well, you alone, as it seems to us, judging from these resolutions, regard what is future as more certain than what is before your eyes, and what is out of sight, in your eagerness, as already coming to pass; and as you have staked most on, and trusted most in, the Spartans, your fortune, and your hopes, so will you be most completely deceived."

The Athenian envoys now returned to the army; and as the Melians showed no signs of yielding, the generals at once commenced hostilities, and built a wall around the Melians, dividing the work among the different states. [2] Subsequently the Athenians returned home with most of their army, leaving behind them a certain number of their own citizens and of the allies to keep guard by land and sea. The force thus left stayed on and besieged the place.

About the same time the Argives invaded the territory of Phlius[1a] and lost eighty men cut off in an ambush by the Phliasians and Argive exiles. [2] Meanwhile the Athenians at Pylos[2a] took so much plunder from the Spartans that the latter, although they still refrained from breaking off the treaty and going to war with Athens, yet proclaimed that any of their people that chose might plunder the Athenians. [3] The Corinthians also commenced hostilities with the Athenians for private quarrels of their own; but the rest of the Peloponnesians stayed quiet. [4] Meanwhile the Melians attacked by night and took the part of the Athenian lines near the market, and killed some of the men, and brought in corn and all else that they could find useful to them, and so returned and kept quiet, while the Athenians took measures to keep better guard in future.[4a] Summer was now over.

5.115.1a Phlius: Map 5.82, BX.
5.115.2a Pylos: Map 5.82, BX.
5.115.4a Melos: Map 5.82, BY.

The next winter the Spartans intended to invade the Argive territory, but arriving at the frontier found the sacrifices for crossing unfavorable, and went back again. This attempt of theirs made the Argives suspicious of certain of their fellow citizens, some of whom they arrested; others, however, escaped them. [2] About the same time the Melians again took another part of the Athenian lines which were but feebly garrisoned. [3] Reinforcements afterwards arriving from Athens in consequence, under the command of Philocrates son of Demeas, the siege was now pressed vigorously, and some treachery taking place inside, the Melians surrendered at discretion to the Athenians, [4] who put to death all the grown men whom they took, and sold the women and children for slaves, and subsequently sent out five hundred colonists and settled the place themselves.

5.116
416/5
16th Year/Winter
ARGOS
Sparta threatens Argos but withdraws.
MELOS
After some treachery, the Melians surrender. The men are executed, the women and children enslaved.

BOOK SIX

The same winter the Athenians resolved to sail again to Sicily,[1a] with a greater armament than that under Laches and Eurymedon,[1b] and, if possible, to conquer the island; most of them being ignorant of its size and of the number of its inhabitants, Hellenic and barbarian, and of the fact that they were undertaking a war not much inferior to that against the Peloponnesians. [2] For the voyage round Sicily in a merchant vessel is not far short of eight days; and yet, large as the island is, there are only two miles of sea to prevent its being mainland.

It was settled originally as follows, and the peoples that occupied it are these. The earliest inhabitants spoken of in any part of the country are the Cyclopes and Laestrygones; but I cannot tell of what race they were, or from where they came or to where they went, and must leave my readers to what the poets have said of them and to what may be generally known concerning them. [2] The Sicanians appear to have been the next settlers, although they pretend to have been the first of all and aborigines; but the facts show that they were Iberians, driven by the Ligurians from the river Sicanus in Iberia.[2a] It was from them that the island, before called Trinacria, took its name of Sicania, and to the present day they inhabit the west of Sicily. [3] On the fall of Ilium,[3a] some of the Trojans escaped from the Achaeans, came in ships to Sicily, and settled next to the Sicanians under the general name of Elymi; their cities being called Eryx[3b] and Egesta.[3c] With them settled some of the Phocians carried on their way from Troy by a storm, first to Libya,[3d] and afterwards from there to Sicily. [4] The Sicels crossed over to Sicily from their first home Italy,[4a] fleeing from the Opicans, as tradition says and as seems not unlikely, upon rafts, having watched till the wind steadied down the strait to make the passage; although perhaps

6.1
416/5
16th Year/Winter
ATHENS
The Athenians vote to attack Sicily, though most are ignorant of the island's size.

6.2
SICILY
Thucydides describes the history of the settlement of barbarian peoples— Sicanians, Trojans, Sicels, and Phoenicians—in Sicily.

6.1.1a Sicily: Map 6.4, Sicily and locator.
6.1.1b For Laches in Sicily, see 3.86.1, 3.90.2, and 3.115.2; for Eurymedon in Sicily, see 3.115.5, 4.2ff., and 4.65.
6.2.2a Iberia: Map 6.4, locator.
6.2.3a Ilium (Troy): Map 6.4, locator.
6.2.3b Eryx: Map 6.4, AX.
6.2.3c Egesta: Map 6.4, AX.
6.2.3d Libya: Map 6.4, locator.
6.2.4a Italy: Map 6.4, AY, locator.

they may have sailed over in some other way. Even at the present day there are still Sicels in Italy; and the country got its name of Italy from a king of the Sicels called Italus. [5] These went with a great host to Sicily, defeated the Sicanians in battle and forced them to withdraw to the south and west of the island, which thus came to be called Sicily instead of Sicania. After they crossed over, they continued to enjoy the richest parts of the country for nearly three hundred years before any Hellenes came to Sicily; indeed they still hold the center and north of the island. [6] There were also Phoenicians[6a] who had occupied promontories upon the sea coasts and nearby islands for the purpose of trading with the Sicels. But when the Hellenes began to arrive in considerable numbers by sea, the Phoenicians abandoned most of their stations, and drawing together took up their abode in Motya,[6b] Soloeis,[6c] and Panormus,[6d] near the Elymi, partly because they trusted in their alliance with them, and also because these are the nearest points for the voyage between Carthage[6e] and Sicily. These were the barbarians in Sicily, settled as I have said.

Of the Hellenes, the first to arrive were Chalcidians from Euboea[1a] with Thoucles, their founder. They founded Naxos[1b] and built the altar to Apollo Archegetes, which now stands outside the city, and upon which the deputies for the games sacrifice before sailing from Sicily. [2] Syracuse[2a] was founded the year afterwards by Archias, one of the Heraclids from Corinth,[2b] who began by driving out the Sicels from the island upon which the inner city now stands, though it is no longer surrounded by water: over time, the outer city also was enclosed within the walls and became populous. [3] Meanwhile Thoucles and the Chalcidians set out from Naxos in the fifth year after the foundation of Syracuse, and drove out the Sicels by arms and founded Leontini[3a] and afterwards Catana;[3b] the Catanians themselves choosing Evarchus as their founder.

About the same time Lamis arrived in Sicily with a colony from Megara.[1a] He founded a place called Trotilus[1b] beyond the river Pantacyas,[1c] and afterwards left it and for a short while joined the Chalcidians at Leontini, but was driven out by them and founded Thapsus.[1d] After his death his companions were driven out of Thapsus, and founded a place called the Hyblaean Megara;[1e] Hyblon, a Sicel king, having given up the place and inviting them there. [2] Here they lived two hundred and forty-five years; after which they were expelled from the city and the country by the Syracusan tyrant Gelon. Before their expulsion, however, a hundred years after they had settled there, they sent out Pamillus and established Selinus;[2a] he

6.3
SICILY
The first Hellenes to settle in Sicily were Euboeans, who founded Naxos, Leontini, and Catana. The Dorians of Corinth settled Syracuse.

6.4
SICILY
Thucydides reports the settlement of other principal Hellenic cities in Sicily: Thapsus, Hyblaean Megara, Selinus, Gela, Agrigentum, and Zancle which became Messana.

6.2.6a	Phoenicia: Map 6.4, locator.
6.2.6b	Motya: Map 6.4, AX.
6.2.6c	Soloeis: Map 6.4, AX.
6.2.6d	Panormus: Map 6.4, AX.
6.2.6e	Carthage: Map 6.4, locator.
6.3.1a	Chalcidians from Chalcis, Euboea: Map 6.4, Hellas.
6.3.1b	Naxos, Sicily: Map 6.4, AY.
6.3.2a	Syracuse: Map 6.4, BY.
6.3.2b	Corinth: Map 6.4, Hellas.

6.3.3a	Leontini: Map 6.4, BY.
6.3.3b	Catana: Map 6.4, BY.
6.4.1a	Megara: Map 6.4, Hellas.
6.4.1b	Trotilus, possible location: Map 6.4, BY.
6.4.1c	Pantacyas River, possible location: Map 6.4, BY.
6.4.1d	Thapsus: Map 6.4, BY.
6.4.1e	Megara Hyblaea: Map 6.4, BY.
6.4.2a	Selinus: Map 6.4, AX.

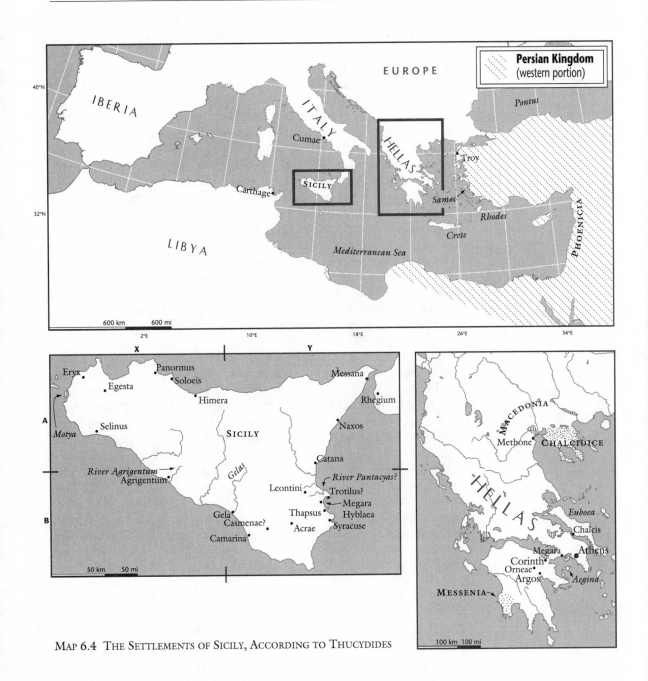

MAP 6.4 THE SETTLEMENTS OF SICILY, ACCORDING TO THUCYDIDES

having come from their mother country Megara to join them in its foundation. [3] Gela[3a] was founded by Antiphemus from Rhodes[3b] and Entimus from Crete,[3c] who joined in leading a colony there, in the forty-fifth year after the foundation of Syracuse. The city took its name from the river Gelas,[3d] and the place which was first fortified, where the citadel now stands, was called Lindii. The institutions which they adopted were Dorian.[3e] [4] Nearly one hundred and eight years after the foundation of Gela, the Geloans founded Acragas[4a] (Agrigentum), so called from the river of that name, and made Aristonous and Pystilus their founders; giving their own institutions to the colony. [5] Zancle[5a] was originally founded by pirates from Cumae,[5b] the Chalcidian city in the country of the Opicans: afterwards, however, large numbers came from Chalcis and the rest of Euboea, and helped to people the place; the founders being Perieres and Crataemenes from Cumae and Chalcis respectively. It first had the name of Zancle given it by the Sicels, because the place is shaped like a sickle, which the Sicels call *zanclon*; but when the original settlers were later expelled by some Samians[5c] and other Ionians who landed in Sicily fleeing from the Persians,[5d] [6] and the Samians driven out in their turn not long afterwards by Anaxilas, tyrant of Rhegium,[6a] the city was by him colonized with a mixed population, and its name changed to Messana, after his old country.[6b]

6.5
SICILY
Thucydides recounts the founding of other Sicilian Greek cities: Himera, Acrae, Casmenae, and Camarina.

Himera[1a] was founded from Zancle by Euclides, Simus, and Sacon. Most of those who went to the colony were Chalcidians; though they were joined by some exiles from Syracuse who had been defeated in a civil war, called the Myletidae. The language was a mixture of Chalcidian and Doric, but the institutions which prevailed were the Chalcidian.[1b] [2] Acrae[2a] and Casmenae[2b] were founded by the Syracusans; Acrae seventy years after Syracuse, Casmenae nearly twenty after Acrae. [3] Camarina[3a] was first founded by the Syracusans, close upon a hundred and thirty-five years after the building of Syracuse; its founders being Dascon and Menecolus. But after the Camarinaeans were expelled by arms by the Syracusans for having revolted, Hippocrates, tyrant of Gela,[3b] who some time later received their land in ransom for some Syracusan prisoners, resettled Camarina, himself acting as its founder. Lastly, it was again depopulated by Gelon and settled once more for the third time by the people of Gela.

6.4.3a	Gela: Map 6.4, BX.		Persia's expansion into Asian Ionia.
6.4.3b	Rhodes: Map 6.4, locator.	6.4.6a	Rhegium: Map 6.4, AY.
6.4.3c	Crete: Map 6.4, locator.	6.4.6b	His "old country" was Messenia in
6.4.3d	Gelas River, Map 6.4, BX.		Peloponnesus (Map 6.4, Hellas).
6.4.3e	See Appendix H, Dialects and Ethnic	6.5.1a	Himera: Map 6.4, AX.
	Groups, for a brief description of the dif-	6.5.1b	See Appendix H, Dialects and Ethnic
	ferent ethnic and dialect groups into		Groups, §3, for a discussion of the
	which the Greeks were divided.		Dorians.
6.4.4a	Acragas (Agrigentum): Map 6.4, BX.	6.5.2a	Acrae: Map 6.4, BY.
6.4.5a	Zancle (Messana): Map 6.4, AY.	6.5.2b	Casmenae, possible location: Map 6.4,
6.4.5b	Cumae: Map 6.4, locator and Map 6.88.		BY.
6.4.5c	Samos: Map 6.4, locator.	6.5.3a	Camarina: Map 6.4, BX.
6.4.5d	Persia, Map 6.4, locator. See Appendix E,	6.5.3b	Gela: Map 6.4, BX.
	The Persians, §3, for a description of		

Such is the list of the peoples, Hellenic and barbarian, inhabiting Sicily, and such the magnitude of the island which the Athenians were now bent upon invading; being ambitious in real truth[1a] of conquering the whole, although they had also the specious design of aiding their kindred and other allies in the island. [2] But they were especially incited by envoys from Egesta,[2a] who had come to Athens and invoked their aid more urgently than ever. The Egestaeans had gone to war with their neighbors the Selinuntines[2b] over questions of marriage and disputed territory, and the Selinuntines had procured the alliance of the Syracusans,[2c] and pressed Egesta hard by land and sea. The Egestaeans now reminded the Athenians of the alliance made in the time of Laches, during the former Leontine war,[2d] and begged them to send a fleet to their aid. Their main argument, among a number of other considerations urged, was that if the Syracusans were allowed to go unpunished for their depopulation of Leontini,[2e] to ruin the allies still left to Athens in Sicily, and to get the whole power of the island into their hands, there would be a danger of their one day coming with a large force as Dorians to the aid of their Dorian brethren,[2f] and as colonists, to the aid of the Peloponnesians who had sent them out, and joining these in pulling down the Athenian empire. The Athenians would, therefore, do well to unite with the allies still left to them, and to make a stand against the Syracusans; especially as they, the Egestaeans, were prepared to furnish money sufficient for the war. [3] The Athenians, hearing these arguments constantly repeated in their assemblies[3a] by the Egestaeans and their supporters, voted first to send envoys to Egesta, to see if there was really the money that they talked of in the treasury and temples,[3b] and at the same time to ascertain the truth about the war with the Selinuntines.

The envoys of the Athenians were accordingly dispatched to Sicily. That same winter the Spartans and their allies (except for the Corinthians), marched into the Argive territory,[1a] ravaged a small part of the land, took some yokes of oxen, and carried off some grain. They also settled the Argive exiles at Orneae[1b] and left them a few soldiers taken from the rest of

6.6
416/5
16th Year/Winter
ATHENS
Egestan envoys seek help at Athens for their war with Selinus. They warn of potential Syracusan domination of Sicily and aid to Sparta, and promise to pay Athens' war expenses in Sicily. The Athenians send envoys to Egesta.

6.7
416/5
16th Year/Winter
ARGOS
The Spartans plunder Argos and settle exiles in Orneae. Reinforced by Athens, Argos demolishes Orneae.
MACEDONIA
The Athenians, joined by Macedonian exiles, ravage Macedonia. Sparta fails to persuade the Chalcidians to join Perdiccas against Athens.

6.6.1a	Crawley here translates as "in real truth" the same phrase in 1.23.6 which he translates as "the real cause."	6.6.2e	Leontini: Map 6.4, BY.
		6.6.2f	Dorian: see Appendix H, Dialects and Ethnic Groups, for a brief description of the groups into which the Greeks were divided.
6.6.2a	Egesta: Map 6.4, AX.		
6.6.2b	Selinus: Map 6.4, AX.		
6.6.2c	Syracuse: Map 6.4, BY.	6.6.3a	Athenian assemblies are briefly discussed in Appendix A, The Athenian Government, §8.
6.6.2d	The Egestaeans are referring to the Athenian operations in Sicily in 427–26 which Thucydides describes in 3.86, 3.88, 3.90, 3.99, 3.103, and 3.115–16. This alliance is mentioned in 3.86. The text actually says "the Egestaeans now reminded the Athenians of the alliance with the people of Leontini during the former war." Whichever is the correct translation, it is incredible that the envoys could talk like this of an alliance that had been made with Egesta in 418/7, as some scholars now claim; see the Introduction (sect. IV.ii).	6.6.3b	Offerings of silver and gold objects and other valuable material accumulated at major temples and shrines to such a degree that these institutions became unique and tempting repositories of ready capital in ancient Greece. In 2.13.4–5, Pericles lists the vast wealth lying in Athenian temples and shrines that could be called upon, if necessary, to support the war.
		6.7.1a	Argos: Map 6.4, Hellas.
		6.7.1b	Orneae: Map 6.4, Hellas.

the army, and after making a truce for a certain period, according to which neither Orneatae nor Argives were to injure each other's territory, returned home with the army. [2] Not long afterwards the Athenians came with thirty ships and six hundred *hoplites*,[2a] and the Argives joining them with all their forces, marched out and besieged the men in Orneae for one day; but the garrison escaped by night, the besiegers having camped some way off. The next day the Argives, discovering this, razed Orneae to the ground, and went back again; after which the Athenians went home in their ships. [3] Meanwhile the Athenians took some cavalry of their own and the Macedonian exiles that were at Athens by sea to Methone[3a] on the Macedonian[3b] border and plundered the country of Perdiccas. [4] Upon this the Spartans sent to the Thracian Chalcidians,[4a] who had a truce with Athens from one ten days to another, urging them to join Perdiccas in the war, which they refused to do. And the winter ended, and with it ended the sixteenth year of this war of which Thucydides is the historian.

Early in the spring of the following summer the Athenian envoys arrived from Sicily, and the Egestaeans[1a] with them, bringing the sixty *talents*[1b] of uncoined silver, as a month's pay for sixty ships, which they were to ask to have sent to them. [2] The Athenians held an assembly, and after hearing from the Egestaeans and their own envoys a report, as attractive as it was untrue, upon the state of affairs generally, and in particular as to the money, of which, it was said, there was abundance in the temples and the treasury, voted to send sixty ships to Sicily, under the command of Alcibiades son of Clinias, Nicias son of Niceratus, and Lamachus son of Xenophanes, who were appointed with full powers;[2a] they were to help the Egestaeans against the Selinuntines,[2b] to restore Leontini[2c] upon gaining any advantage in the war, and to order all other matters in Sicily as they should deem best for the interests of Athens. [3] Five days after this a second assembly was held, to consider the speediest means of equipping the ships, and to vote whatever else might be required by the generals for the expedition. [4] Nicias, who had been chosen to the command against his will, and who thought that the state was not well advised, but upon a slight and specious pretext was aspiring to the conquest of the whole of Sicily, a great matter to achieve, came forward in the hope of diverting the Athenians from the enterprise, and gave them the following counsel:

"Although this assembly was convened to consider the preparations to be made for sailing to Sicily, I think, notwithstanding, that we should still examine whether it be better to send out the ships at

6.8
415
17th Year/Summer
ATHENS
Athenian envoys return from Egesta with favorable (but untrue) reports. Athens votes to send a fleet to Sicily to assist Egesta, restore Leontini, and order Sicilian affairs to suit Athens' interests.

6.9
415
17th Year/Summer
ATHENS
Nicias speaks to Athens' assembly to dissuade the Athenians from the Sicilian expedition.

6.7.2a	*Hoplite* is the Greek word for a heavily armed infantryman. See Appendix F, Land Warfare, §2.		money; see Appendix J, Classical Greek Currency, §5.
6.7.3a	Methone in Macedonia: Map 6.4, Hellas. Perdiccas was the king of Macedonia.	6.8.2a	By "full powers" was meant that the generals could decide matters for themselves without referring back to Athens, but decide only within stated terms of reference. Cf. the situation in 5.45.
6.7.3b	Macedonia: Map 6.4, Hellas.		
6.7.4a	Chalcidice in Thrace: Map 6.4, Hellas.		
6.8.1a	Egesta: Map 6.4, AX.	6.8.2b	Selinus: Map 6.4, AX.
6.8.1b	The *talent* was a unit of weight and of	6.8.2c	Leontini: Map 6.4, BY.

all; that we ought not to give so little consideration to a matter of such import, or let ourselves be persuaded by foreigners into undertaking a war with which we have nothing to do. [2] And yet, individually, I gain in honor by such a course, and fear as little as other men for my person—not that I think a man need be any the worse citizen for taking some thought for his person and estate; on the contrary, such a man would for his own sake desire the prosperity of his country more than others—nevertheless, as I have never spoken against my convictions to gain honor, I shall not begin to do so now, but shall say what I think best. [3] Against your character any words of mine would be weak enough; particularly if I were to advise you to keep what you have and not risk it for advantages which are dubious in themselves, and which you may or may not attain. I will, therefore, content myself with showing that your ardor is untimely, and your ambition not easily accomplished."

"I affirm, then, that you leave many enemies behind you here to go there far away and bring more back with you. [2] You imagine, perhaps, that the treaty[2a] which you have made can be trusted; a treaty that will continue to exist nominally, as long as you keep quiet—for nominal it has become, owing to the practices of certain men here and at Sparta—but which in the event of a serious reverse in any quarter would not delay our enemies a moment in attacking us; first, because the convention was forced upon them by disaster and was less honorable to them than to us; and secondly, because in this very convention there are many points that are still disputed. [3] Again, some of the most powerful states have never yet accepted the arrangement at all. Some of these are at open war with us; others (as the Spartans do not yet move) are restrained by truces renewed every ten days, [4] and it is only too probable that if they found our power divided, as we are hurrying to divide it, they would attack us vigorously with the Siceliots, whose alliance they would have in the past valued as they would that of few others. [5] A man ought, therefore, to consider these points, and not to think of running risks with a country placed so critically, or of grasping at another empire before we have secured the one we have already; for in fact the Thracian Chalcidians have been all these years in revolt from us without being yet subdued, and others on the mainland[5a] yield us but a doubtful obedience. Meanwhile the Egestaeans, our allies, have been wronged, and we run to help them, while the rebels who

6.10
415
17th Year/Summer
ATHENS
Nicias argues that it is imprudent to attack Sicily while affairs nearer home are still precarious. He emphasizes the fragility of the current peace, since many enemies await an opportune moment to attack Athens again, and points out that rebels in Chalcidice have not yet been subdued.

6.10.2a   The "treaty" referred to here is the fifty-
          year alliance between Athens and Sparta
          described in 5.23.
6.10.5a   Mainland: Thucydides must be referring
          to Thrace and Asia Minor.

6.11
415
17th Year/Summer
ATHENS
Nicias says that Sicily is too far away to be permanently subdued, and that the Sicilians, even if united under Syracuse, are most unlikely to attack the Athenian empire. He argues that Athens' reputation is higher in Sicily because it is untested, and will decline immediately after the first reverse. He points out that Sparta is still the main threat to Athens.

have so long wronged us still wait for punishment."

"And yet the latter, if brought under might be kept under; while the Sicilians, even if conquered, are too far off and too numerous to be ruled without difficulty. Now it is folly to go against men who could not be kept under even if conquered, while failure would leave us in a very different position from that which we occupied before the enterprise. [2] The Sicilians, again, to take them as they are at present, in the event of a Syracusan conquest (which the Egestaeans most use to frighten us), would to my thinking be even less dangerous to us than before. [3] At present they might possibly come here as separate states for love of Sparta; in the other case one empire would scarcely attack another; for after joining the Peloponnesians to overthrow ours, they could only expect to see the same hands overthrow their own in the same way. [4] The Hellenes in Sicily would fear us most if we never went there at all, and next to this, if after displaying our power we went away again as soon as possible. We all know that which is farthest off and the reputation of which can least be tested, is the object of admiration; at the least reverse to us they would at once begin to look down upon us, and would join our enemies here against us. [5] You have yourselves experienced this with regard to the Spartans and their allies, whom your unexpected success, as compared with what you feared at first, has made you suddenly despise, tempting you further to aspire to the conquest of Sicily. [6] Instead, however, of being puffed up by the misfortunes of your adversaries, you ought to think of breaking their spirit before giving yourselves up to confidence, and to understand that the one thought awakened in the Spartans by their disgrace is how they may even now, if possible, overthrow us and repair their dishonor; inasmuch as they have for a very long time devoted themselves to the cultivation of military renown above all. [7] Our struggle therefore, if we are wise, will not be for the barbarian Egestaeans[7a] in Sicily, but to defend ourselves most effectively against the oligarchic machinations of Sparta."

6.12
415
17th Year/Summer
ATHENS
Nicias reminds the Athenians that having only recently suffered plague and war, they should use the respite properly and not be swayed by young hotbloods whose leader may be eager for command and desperate to cover the expenses of his private life.

"We should also remember that we are only now enjoying some respite from a great pestilence and from war, to the no small benefit of our estates and persons, and that it is right to employ these at home on our own behalf, instead of using them on behalf of these exiles[1a] whose interest it is to lie as well as they can, who do nothing but talk themselves and leave the danger to others, and who if they

6.11.7a It is only here and at 6.2.3 that it plainly emerges that the Egestaeans are not Greek.
6.12.1a Nicias refers to the Leontines exiled in 422; see 5.4.3 and 6.19.1.

succeed will show no proper gratitude, and if they fail will drag down their friends with them. [2] And if there be any man here, overjoyed at being chosen to command, who urges you to make the expedition, merely for ends of his own—especially if he is still too young to command—who seeks to be admired for his stud of horses, but on account of heavy expenses hopes for some profit from his appointment, do not allow such a one to maintain his private splendor at his country's risk, but remember that such persons injure the public fortune while they squander their own, and that this is a matter of importance, and not for a young man to decide or hastily to take in hand."

"When I see such persons now sitting here at the side of that same individual and summoned by him, alarm seizes me; and I, in my turn, summon any of the older men that may have such a person sitting next him, not to let himself be checked by shame, for fear of being thought a coward if he does not vote for war, but, remembering how rarely success is gained by wishing and how often by forecast, to leave to them the mad dream of conquest, and as a true lover of his country, now threatened by the greatest danger in its history, to hold up his hand on the other side to vote that the Sicilians be left in the limits now existing between us—limits of which no one can complain (the Ionian sea for the coasting voyage[1a] and the Sicilian across the open main)[1b]—to enjoy their own possessions and to settle their own quarrels. [2] Let the Egestaeans, for their part, be told to end by themselves the war with the Selinuntines which they began without consulting the Athenians; and that for the future we do not enter into alliance, as we have been used to do, with people whom we must help in their need, and who can never help us in ours."

"And you, *Prytanis*,[1a] if you think it your duty to care for the commonwealth, and if you wish to show yourself a good citizen, put the question to the vote, and take a second time the opinions of the Athenians. If you are afraid to move the question again, consider that a violation of the law cannot with so many abettors, incur any charge, that you will be the physician of your misguided city, and that the virtue of men in office is briefly this, to do their country as much good as they can, or in any case no harm that they can avoid."

6.13
415
17th Year/Summer
ATHENS
Nicias calls on the older men to curb the enthusiasm of the young, asserting that Athens should not help allies who could not help Athens in turn, and who did not consult Athens when they went to war with their neighbors.

6.14
415
17th Year/Summer
ATHENS
Nicias concludes by asking for a second vote on the Sicilian expedition.

6.13.1a   Ionian sea, for coasting and the narrowest crossing, i.e., for triremes. Map 6.20. See Appendix G, Trireme Warfare, §7, for an explanation of why triremes were forced to follow coastlines and rarely ventured out, like merchant vessels, into the open sea.
6.13.1b   Sicilian sea for sailing due west from the Peloponnesus, i.e., for merchant vessels. Map 6.20; Map 6.38, BX.
6.14.1a   *Prytanis*: a member of the council who served in the assembly as its chairman.

He was normally termed the *Epistates*, not the *Prytanis*. He was a member of the *Prytaneis*, a group that acted as a standing committee for both the council and the assembly during the tenth of the year that it was each tribe's turn to "preside." (See Appendix A, The Athenian Government, §5.) Whether it was illegal for the *Epistates* to put to the vote a matter previously decided, as would seem to be the case here, has been disputed.

6.15
415
17th Year/Summer
ATHENS
How the character and
habits of Alcibiades, who
now comes forward to speak
in favor of the expedition,
caused Athens to distrust
him as a potential tyrant and
contributed to Athens'
eventual ruin.

Such were the words of Nicias.[1a] Most of the Athenians who came forward spoke in favor of the expedition and of not annulling what had been voted, although some spoke on the other side. [2] By far the warmest advocate of the expedition was, however, Alcibiades son of Clinias, who wished to thwart Nicias both as his political opponent and also because of the attack he had made upon him in his speech, and who was, besides, exceedingly ambitious of a command by which he hoped to reduce Sicily[2a] and Carthage,[2b] and personally to gain in wealth and reputation by means of his successes. [3] For the position he held among the citizens led him to indulge his tastes beyond what his real means would bear, both in keeping horses and in the rest of his expenditure; and this later on had not a little to do with the ruin of the Athenian state. [4] Alarmed at the greatness of the license in his own life and habits, and at the ambition which he showed in all things whatsoever that he undertook, the mass of the people marked him as an aspirant to the tyranny and became his enemies; and although in his public life his conduct of the war was as good as could be desired, in his private life his habits gave offense to everyone, and caused them to commit affairs to other hands, and thus before long to ruin the city.[4a] [5] Meanwhile he now came forward and gave the following advice to the Athenians:

6.16
415
17th Year/Summer
ATHENS
Alcibiades speaks to the
assembly, asserting his right
to command the Sicilian
expedition. He argues that
the magnificence of his
private life has added to
Athens' prestige abroad, that
his arrogance should be
accepted as properly based
on excellence, and that he
deserves credit for having
formed the recent coalition
against Sparta.

"Athenians, I have a better right to command than others—I must begin with this as Nicias has attacked me—and at the same time I believe myself to be worthy of it. The things for which I am abused bring fame to my ancestors and to myself, and also profit to my country. [2] The Hellenes, after expecting to see our city ruined by the war, concluded it to be even greater than it really is, by reason of the magnificence with which I represented it at the Olympic games,[2a] when I sent into the lists seven chariots, a number never before entered by any private person, and won the first prize, and was second and fourth, and took care to have everything else in a style worthy of my victory. Custom regards such displays as honorable, and they cannot be made without leaving behind them an impression of power. [3] Again, any splendor that I may have exhibited at home in providing choruses or otherwise, is naturally envied by my fellow citizens, but in the eyes of foreigners has an air of strength as in the other instance. And this is no useless folly, when a man at his own private cost benefits not himself only, but his city: [4] nor is it unfair that he who prides himself on his position should refuse to be upon an equality with the rest. He who is badly off has his misfortunes all to

---

6.15.1a　See the Introduction (sect. II.v) for a discussion of speeches in Thucydides.
6.15.2a　Sicily: Map 6.20.
6.15.2b　Carthage: Map 6.20. Regarding the plan to conquer it, see 6.90.2.
6.15.4a　Since Thucydides seems here to refer

Athens' defeat in the Peloponnesian War, it has been thought that 6.16.3 and 4 were inserted after 404 BC.
6.16.2a　Alcibiades refers to the Olympic Games of 416 B.C. See Appendix I, Religious Festivals, §5, 8.

himself, and as we do not see men courted in adversity, on the like principle a man ought to accept the insolence of prosperity; or else, let him first mete out equal measure to all, and then demand to have it meted out to him. [5] What I know is that persons of this kind and all others that have attained to any distinction, although they may be unpopular in their lifetime in their relations with their fellow men and especially with their equals, leave to posterity the desire of claiming connection with them even without any ground, and are vaunted by the country to which they belonged, not as strangers or evildoers, but as fellow countrymen and heroes. [6] Such are my aspirations, and however I am abused for them in my private life, the question is whether anyone manages public affairs better than I do. Having united the most powerful states of the Peloponnesus, without great danger or expense to you, I compelled the Spartans to stake their all upon the issue of a single day at Mantinea;[6a] and although victorious in the battle, they have never since fully recovered confidence."

"Thus did my youth and so-called monstrous folly find fitting arguments to deal with the power of the Peloponnesians, and by its ardor win their confidence and prevail. And do not be afraid of my youth now, but while I am still in its flower, and Nicias appears fortunate, avail yourselves to the utmost of the services of us both. [2] Nor should you rescind your resolution to sail to Sicily, on the ground that you would be going to attack a great power. The cities in Sicily are peopled by motley rabbles, and easily change their institutions and adopt new ones in their stead; [3] and consequently the inhabitants, being without any feeling of patriotism, are not provided with arms for their persons, and have not regularly established themselves on the land; every man thinks that either by fair words or by party strife he can obtain something at the public expense, and then in the event of a catastrophe settle in some other country, and makes his preparations accordingly. [4] From a mob like this you need not look for either unanimity in counsel or unity in action; but they will probably one by one come in as they get a fair offer, especially if they are torn by civil strife as we are told. [5] Moreover, the Sicilians have not so many hoplites as they boast; just as the Hellenes generally did not prove so numerous as each state reckoned itself, but Hellas greatly overestimated their numbers, and has hardly had an adequate force of hoplites throughout this war. [6] The states in Sicily, therefore, from all that I can hear, will be found as I say, and I have not pointed out all our advantages, for we shall have the help of many

6.17
415
17th Year/Summer
ATHENS
Alcibiades bids the Athenians to make use of his youthful energy and Nicias' good fortune together in command. He argues that the Sicilians are politically weak and will be easily divided; that barbarians will help the Athenians, and that the Spartans, whose navy will remain inferior to the Athenian fleet left at home, will be unable to injure Athens during the Sicilian expedition.

6.16.6a   Alcibiades refers to the battle of Mantinea; see 5.71–74.

barbarians, who from their hatred of the Syracusans will join us in attacking them; nor will the powers at home prove any hindrance, if you judge rightly. [7] Our fathers with these same adversaries, which it is said we shall now leave behind us when we sail, and the Mede[7a] as their enemy as well, were able to win the empire, depending solely on their superiority at sea. [8] The Peloponnesians have never had so little hope against us as at present; and let them be ever so optimistic, although strong enough to invade our country even if we stay at home, they can never hurt us with their navy, as we leave one of our own behind us that is a match for them."

"In this state of affairs what reason can we give to ourselves for holding back, or what excuse can we offer to our allies in Sicily for not helping them? They are our confederates, and we are bound to assist them, without objecting that they have not assisted us. We did not take them into alliance to have them help us in Hellas, but that they might so annoy our enemies in Sicily as to prevent them from coming over here and attacking us. [2] It is thus that empire has been won, both by us and by all others that have held it, by a constant readiness to support all, whether barbarians or Hellenes, that invite assistance; since if all were to keep quiet or to pick and choose whom they ought to assist, we should make but few new conquests, and should imperil those we have already won. Men do not rest content with parrying the attacks of a superior, but often strike the first blow to prevent the attack being made. [3] Moreover, we cannot fix the exact point at which our empire shall stop; we have reached a position in which we must not be content with retaining what we have but must scheme to extend it for, if we cease to rule others, we shall be in danger of being ruled ourselves. Nor can you look at inaction from the same point of view as others, unless you are prepared to change your habits and make them resemble theirs."

[4] "Be convinced then that we shall augment our power at home by this adventure abroad, and let us make the expedition, and so humble the pride of the Peloponnesians by sailing off to Sicily, and letting them see how little we care for the peace that we are now enjoying. At the same time we shall either become masters, as we very easily may, of the whole of Hellas through the accession of the Sicilian Hellenes, or in any case ruin the Syracusans, to the no small advantage of ourselves and our allies. [5] Our ability to stay if successful, or to return if not, will be secured to us by our navy, as we shall be superior at sea to all the Sicilians put together. [6] And do not let the passive policy which Nicias advocates, or his setting of the

6.18
415
17th Year/Summer
ATHENS
Alcibiades argues that Athens must help its allies—if only to extend its empire further. He claims that to sit and enjoy what it has, as Nicias advises, will risk atrophy and the loss of her present empire. He concludes by urging the Athenians to unite in support of the Sicilian expedition which, if it should fail to achieve a permanent conquest, will certainly injure Syracuse, increase Athens' prestige, and incur little risk of loss due to Athens' naval superiority.

6.17.7a By "Mede," Alcibiades means here the Persians; see Appendix E, The Persians, §1.

young against the old, turn you from your purpose, but in the good old fashion by which our fathers, old and young together, by their united counsels brought our affairs to their present height, do you endeavor still to advance them; understanding that neither youth nor old age can do anything the one without the other, but that levity, sobriety, and deliberate judgment are strongest when united, and that, by sinking into inaction, the city, like everything else, will wear itself out, and its skill in everything decay; while each fresh struggle will give it fresh experience, and make it more used to defend itself not in word but in deed. [7] In short, my conviction is that a city not inactive by nature could not choose a quicker way to ruin itself than by suddenly adopting such a policy, and that the safest rule of life is to take one's character and institutions for better and for worse, and to live up to them as closely as one can."

Such were the words of Alcibiades. After hearing him and the Eges-taeans and some Leontine exiles, who came forward reminding them of their oaths and imploring their assistance, the Athenians became more eager for the expedition than before. [2] Nicias, perceiving that it would now be useless to try to deter them by the old line of argument, but thinking that he might perhaps alter their resolution by the extravagance of his estimates, came forward a second time and spoke as follows:

"I see, Athenians, that you are thoroughly bent upon the expedi-tion, and therefore hope that all will turn out as we wish, and I pro-ceed to give you my opinion at the present juncture. [2] From all that I hear we are going against cities that are great and not subject to one another, or in need of change, so as to wish to pass from en-forced servitude to an easier condition, or be in the least likely to ac-cept our rule in exchange for freedom; and, to take only the Hellenic cities, they are very numerous for one island. [3] Besides Naxos and Catana, which I expect to join us from their connection with Leon-tini, there are seven others armed in every way just like our own power, particularly Selinus and Syracuse,[3a] the main objectives of our expedition. [4] These are full of hoplites, archers, and dart throwers, have triremes in abundance and multitudes to man them; they also have money, partly in the hands of private persons, partly in the tem-ples at Selinus, and at Syracuse tribute of first-fruits from some of the barbarians as well. But their chief advantage over us lies in the num-ber of their horses, and in the fact that they grow their grain at home instead of importing it."

6.20.3a Naxos, Catana, Leontini, Selinus, Syra-cuse: Map 6.20.

MAP 6.20 KEY SICILIAN CITIES

6.21
415
17th Year/Summer
ATHENS
Nicias argues that because of
Sicily's strength and its great
distance from Athens, the
Athenian expedition must be
very powerful in order to
obviate the need to send
more forces later or to avoid
a disgraceful withdrawal.

"Against a power of this kind it will not do to have merely a weak
naval armament, but we shall want also a large land army to sail with
us, if we are to do anything worthy of our ambition and are not to
be shut out from the country by a numerous cavalry; especially if the
cities should take alarm and combine, and we should be left without
friends (except the Egestaeans) to furnish us with cavalry with which
to defend ourselves. [2] It would be disgraceful to have to retire
under compulsion, or to send back for reinforcements, owing to
want of reflection at first. We must therefore start from home with a
competent force, seeing that we are going to sail far from our country, and upon an expedition not like any which you may have undertaken in the quality of allies. Among your subject states here in
Hellas, any additional supplies needed are easily drawn from the
friendly territory; but we are cutting ourselves off, and going to a
land entirely strange, from which during four months in winter it is
not even easy for a messenger to get to Athens."

6.22
415
17th Year/Summer
ATHENS
Nicias says the expedition
should be strong in all arms,
recruited from Athens as well
as the empire, and include
mercenary troops too. He
demands that it be well
provisioned and financed.

"I think, therefore, that we ought to take great numbers of
hoplites, both from Athens and from our allies, and not merely from
our subjects,[1a] but also any we may be able to get for love or for
money in the Peloponnesus, and great numbers also of archers and
slingers, to oppose the Sicilian horse. Meanwhile we must have an
overwhelming superiority at sea to enable us the more easily to carry
in what we want; and we must take our own grain in merchant vessels, that is to say, wheat and roasted barley, and bakers from the
mills compelled to serve for pay in the proper proportion; so that if

6.22.1a See 7.57 for a list by status of the allies
         who came with the Athenians to Sicily.
         See 2.7.3.

we become weather-bound the armament may not lack provisions, as it is not every city that will be able to sustain numbers like ours. We must also provide ourselves with everything else as far as we can, so as not to be dependent upon others; and above all we must take with us from home as much money as possible, as the sums talked of as ready at Egesta[1b] are readier, you may be sure, in talk than in any other way."

"Indeed, even if we leave Athens with a force not only equal to that of the enemy except in the number of hoplites in the field, but even at all points superior to him, we shall still find it difficult to conquer Sicily or save ourselves. [2] We must not disguise from ourselves that we go to found a city among strangers and enemies, and that he who undertakes such an enterprise should be prepared to become master of the country the first day he lands, or failing in this to find everything hostile to him. [3] Fearing this, and knowing that we shall have need of much good counsel and more good fortune—a hard matter for mortal men to aspire to—I wish as much as possible to make myself independent of fortune before sailing, and when I do sail, to be as safe as a strong force can make me. This I believe to be surest for the country at large, and safest for us who are to go on the expedition. If any one thinks differently I resign to him my command."

With this Nicias concluded, thinking that he should either put the Athenians off by the magnitude of the undertaking or, if obliged to sail on the expedition, would thus do so in the safest way possible. [2] The Athenians, however, far from having their enthusiasm for the voyage destroyed by the burdensomeness of the preparations, became more eager for it than ever; and just the contrary took place of what Nicias had thought, as it was held that he had given good advice, and that the expedition would be the safest in the world. [3] Everyone fell in love with the enterprise. The older men thought that they would either subdue the places against which they were to sail, or at all events, with so large a force, meet with no disaster; those in the prime of life felt a longing for foreign sights and spectacles, and had no doubt that they should come safe home again; while the idea of the common people and the soldiery was to earn wages at the moment, and make conquests that would supply a never-ending fund of pay for the future. [4] With this enthusiasm of the majority, the few that did not like it feared to appear unpatriotic by holding up their hands against it, and so kept quiet.

At last one of the Athenians came forward and called upon Nicias and told him that he ought not to make excuses or put them off, but say at once before them all what forces the Athenians should vote him. [2] Upon

6.23
415
17th Year/Summer
ATHENS
Nicias reiterates how difficult and dangerous the expedition's mission will be and concludes that it must have overwhelming power in order to succeed.

6.24
415
17th Year/Summer
ATHENS
Although Nicias intended to deter the Athenians from such a huge undertaking, his speech actually fuels enthusiasm for the expedition.

6.25
415
17th Year/Summer
ATHENS
Nicias says Athens must send one hundred triremes, transports, five thousand hoplites, and other arms in proportion.

6.22.1b Egesta: Map 6.20.

this he said, not without reluctance, that he would advise upon that matter more at leisure with his colleagues; as far however as he could see at present, they must sail with at least one hundred triremes—the Athenians providing as many transports as they might determine, and sending for others from the allies—not less than five thousand hoplites in all, Athenian and allied, and if possible more; and the rest of the armament in proportion; archers from home and from Crete, and slingers, and whatever else might seem desirable, being made ready by the generals and taken with them.

Upon hearing this the Athenians at once voted that the generals should have full powers[1a] in the matter of the numbers of the army and of the expedition generally, to do as they judged best for the interests of Athens. [2] After this the preparations began; messages being sent to the allies and the enlistment rolls drawn up at home. And as the city had just recovered from the plague and the long war, and a number of young men had grown up and capital had accumulated by reason of the peace, everything was the more easily provided.

In the midst of these preparations all the stone Hermae in the city of Athens, that is to say the customary square figures so common in the doorways of private houses and temples, had in one night most of them their faces mutilated. [2] No one knew who had done it, but large public rewards were offered to find those responsible; and it was further voted that anyone who knew of any other act of impiety having been committed should come and give information without fear of consequences, whether he were citizen, alien, or slave. [3] The matter was taken up the more seriously, as it was thought to be ominous for the expedition, and part of a conspiracy to bring about a revolution and to upset the democracy.

Information was accordingly given by some resident aliens and body servants, not about the Hermae but of some previous mutilations of other images perpetrated by young men in a drunken frolic, and of mock celebrations of the Mysteries,[1a] alleged to have taken place in private houses. [2] When Alcibiades was implicated in this charge, it was taken up by those who could least endure him, because he stood in the way of their obtaining the undisturbed leadership of The People, and who thought that if he were once removed the first place would be theirs. These accordingly magnified the matter and loudly proclaimed that the affair of the Mysteries and the mutilation of the Hermae were part and parcel of a scheme to overthrow the democracy, and that nothing of all this had been done without Alcibiades; the proofs alleged being the general and undemocratic license of his life and habits.

6.26.1a   For the meaning of "full powers," see note 6.8.2a.
6.28.1a   The Mysteries were religious ceremonies celebrated twice a year at Eleusis in Attica (Map 4.69). Only those who had been solemnly initiated were permitted to share the secret of what happened, and to profane these sacred rites by divulging their content or mocking them was a most grievous offense.

Alcibiades immediately denied the charges in question, and also offered to stand his trial before going on the expedition (for which the preparations were now complete), so that it might be determined whether he was guilty of the acts imputed to him; as he was willing to be punished if found guilty, but ready, if acquitted, to take the command. [2] Meanwhile he protested against their receiving slanders against him in his absence, and begged them rather to put him to death at once if he were guilty, and pointed out the imprudence of sending him out at the head of so large an army, with so serious a charge still undecided. [3] But his enemies feared that he would have the army's support if he were tried immediately, and that the people might relent in favor of the man and protect him as the cause of the Argives and some of the Mantineans joining in the expedition, and did their utmost to have this proposition rejected, putting forward other orators who said that he ought at present to sail and not delay the departure of the army, and be tried on his return within a fixed number of days; their plan being to have him sent for and brought home for trial upon some graver charge, which they would the more easily trump up in his absence. Accordingly it was decreed that he should sail.[3a]

After this the departure for Sicily took place, it being now about midsummer. Most of the allies, with the grain transports and the smaller craft and the rest of the expedition, had already received orders to assemble at Corcyra,[1a] to cross the Ionian sea[1b] from there in a body to the Iapygian promontory.[1c] But the Athenians themselves, and such of their allies as happened to be with them, went down to the Piraeus[1d] upon a day appointed at daybreak, and began to man the ships for putting out to sea. [2] With them also went the whole population, one may say, of the city, both citizens and foreigners; the inhabitants of the country each escorting those that belonged to them, their friends, their relatives, or their sons, with hope and lamentation upon their way, as they thought of the conquests which they hoped to make, or of the friends whom they might never see again, considering the long voyage which they were going to make for their country. [6.31.1] Indeed, at this moment, when they were now upon the point of parting from one another, the danger came home to them more than when they had voted for the expedition; although the strength of the armament, and the profuse provision which they observed in every department, was a sight that could not but comfort them. As for the foreigners and the rest of the crowd, they simply went to see a sight worth looking at and passing all belief. [2] Indeed this armament that first sailed out was by far the most costly and splendid Hellenic force that had ever been sent out by a single city up to that time. In mere number of

6.29
415
17th Year/Summer
Athens
Alcibiades demands a trial on all charges to clear his name before the expedition sails. His foes, fearing the army's support for him, succeed in postponing a trial though they plot to recall him later.

6.30
415
17th Year/Summer
Athens
Their preparations now complete, the Athenian forces go to the Piraeus to man the ships. The citizenry bid farewell to the fleet. Many allies muster at Corcyra.

6.31
415
17th Year/Summer
Athens
The Athenians now become aware of the danger and magnitude of their expedition, but they are comforted by the unprecedented wealth and magnificence of the fleet.

6.29.3a   We next hear of Alcibiades and the affair
          of the Mysteries and the Hermae in 6.53.
6.30.1a   Corcyra: Map 6.38, AX.
6.30.1b   Ionian sea: Map 6.38, AX.

6.30.1c   Iapygian promontory (Cape Iapygium):
          Map 6.38, AX.
6.30.1d   Piraeus: Map 6.38, inset.

ships and hoplites that against Epidaurus[2a] under Pericles, and the same fleet when it was going against Potidaea[2b] under Hagnon, was not inferior; containing as it did four thousand Athenian hoplites, three hundred horse, and one hundred triremes accompanied by fifty Lesbian[2c] and Chian[2d] vessels and many allies besides. [3] But these were sent upon a short voyage and with scanty equipment. The present expedition was formed in contemplation of a long term of service by land and sea alike, and was furnished with ships and troops so as to be ready for either as required. The fleet had been elaborately equipped at great cost to the captains and the state; the treasury giving a *drachma*[3a] a day to each seaman, and providing empty ships, sixty warships and forty transports, and manning these with the best crews obtainable; while the captains gave a bounty in addition to the pay from the treasury to the *thranitae* and crews generally,[3b] besides spending lavishly upon figureheads and equipments, and one and all making the utmost exertions to enable their own ships to excel in beauty and fast sailing. Meanwhile the land forces had been picked from the best enlistment rolls, and vied with each other in attention to their arms and personal accouterments. [4] From this resulted not only a rivalry among themselves in their different departments, but an idea among the rest of the Hellenes that it was more a display of power and resources than an armament against an enemy. [5] For if anyone had counted up the public expenditure of the state, and the private outlay of individuals—that is to say, the sums which the state had already spent upon the expedition and was sending out in the hands of the generals, and those sums which individuals had expended upon their personal outfit, or as captains of triremes had laid out and were still to lay out upon their vessels; and if he had added to this the journey money which each was likely to have provided himself with, independently of the pay from the treasury, for a voyage of such length, and what the soldiers or traders took with them for the purpose of exchange—it would have been found that many talents in all were being taken out of the city. [6] Indeed the expedition became not less famous for its wonderful boldness and for the splendor of its appearance, than for its overwhelming strength as compared with the peoples against whom it was directed, and for the fact that this was the longest passage from home hitherto attempted, and the most ambitious in its objectives considering the resources of those who undertook it.

The ships being now manned, and everything put on board with which they meant to sail, the trumpet commanded silence, and the prayers customary before putting out to sea were offered, not in each ship by itself, but by all together to the voice of a herald; and bowls of wine were mixed

6.32
415
17th Year/Summer
ATHENS
The fleet departs with proper ceremony.
SYRACUSE
At Syracuse, many doubt the Athenian threat. Hermocrates rises to speak to the assembly.

6.31.2a   Epidaurus: Map 6.38, inset. This expedition is mentioned in 2.56.3 and 2.58.3.
6.31.2b   Potidaea: Map 6.38, AY.
6.31.2c   Lesbos: Map 6.38, AY.
6.31.2d   Chios: Map 6.38, AY.
6.31.3a   The *drachma* is a unit of currency. See Appendix J, Classical Greek Currency, §3.

6.31.3b   For the role of the captains and the skilled crewmen in the Athenian navy, and of the different classes of oarsmen, such as *thranitae,* see note 1.31.1a and Appendix G, Trireme Warfare, §5, 12.

through all the armament, and libations made by the soldiers and their officers in gold and silver goblets. [2] They were joined in their prayers by the crowds on shore, by the citizens and all others who wished them well. The hymn sung and the libations finished, they put out to sea, and first sailing out in column then raced each other as far as Aegina,[2a] and so hastened to reach Corcyra[2b] where the rest of the allied forces were also assembling.

[3] Meanwhile at Syracuse news of the expedition came in from many quarters, but for a long while met with no credence whatsoever. Indeed, an assembly was held in which speeches, as will be seen, were delivered by different orators, believing or contradicting the report of the Athenian expedition; among whom Hermocrates son of Hermon came forward, being persuaded that he knew the truth of the matter, and gave the following counsel:

"Although I shall perhaps be no better believed than others have been when I speak about the reality of the expedition, and although I know that those who either make or repeat statements thought not worthy of belief not only gain no converts, but are thought fools for their pains, I shall certainly not be frightened into holding my tongue when the state is in danger, and when I am persuaded that I can speak with more authority on the matter than other persons. [2] Much as you wonder at it, the Athenians nevertheless have set out against us with a large force, naval and military, professedly to help the Egestaeans and to restore Leontini, but really to conquer Sicily, and above all our city, which once gained, the rest, they think, will easily follow. [3] Make up your minds, therefore, to see them speedily here, and see how you can best repel them with the means at hand, and do not be taken off guard through scorning the news, or neglect the common good through disbelieving it. [4] Meanwhile those who believe me need not be dismayed at the force or daring of the enemy. They will not be able to do us more hurt than we shall do them; nor is the greatness of their armament altogether without advantage to us. Indeed, the greater it is the better, with regard to the rest of the Sicilians, whom dismay will make more ready to join us; and if we defeat or drive them away, having failed in their ambition (for I do not fear for a moment that they will get what they want), it will be a most glorious exploit for us, and in my judgment by no means an unlikely one. [5] Few indeed have been the large armaments, either Hellenic or barbarian, that have gone far from home

6.33
415
17th Year/Summer
SYRACUSE
Hermocrates warns that Athens is about to attack Syracuse, but stresses the difficulties they face and the favorable position Syracuse holds. The great size of their expedition, for example, will frighten other Sicilians and induce them to unite with Syracuse. Logistical difficulties alone may defeat them, without Syracusan effort, but to her ultimate renown.

6.32.2a   Aegina: Map 6.38, inset.
6.32.2b   Corcyra: Map 6.38, AX.

and been successful. They cannot be more numerous than the people of the country and their neighbors, whom fear unites; and if they fail for want of supplies in a foreign land, to those against whom their plans were laid they nonetheless leave renown, although they may themselves have been the main cause of their own discomfort. [6] Thus these very Athenians rose by the defeat of the Persians, in a great measure due to accidental causes, from the mere fact that Athens had been the object of his attack; and this may very well be the case with us also."

6.34
415
17th Year/Summer
SYRACUSE
Hermocrates advises the Syracusans to confirm old allies and seek new ones. He calls upon the Sicilians to unite their fleets and meet the Athenians at the Iapygian promontory. He concludes by begging the Syracusans, even if they will not adopt this proposal, to make preparations to defend themselves.

"Let us, therefore, confidently begin preparations here; let us send to and confirm the support of some of the Sicels, and obtain the friendship and alliance of others, and despatch envoys to the rest of Sicily to show that the danger is common to all, and to Italy to get them to become our allies, or at all events to refuse to receive the Athenians. [2] I also think that it would be best to send to Carthage[2a] as well; they are by no means without apprehension there, for it is their constant fear that the Athenians may one day attack their city, and they may perhaps think that they might themselves suffer by letting Sicily be sacrificed, and be willing to help us secretly if not openly, in one way if not in another. They are the best able to do so, if they will, of any of the present day, as they possess most gold and silver, by which war, like everything else, flourishes. [3] Let us also send to Sparta[3a] and Corinth,[3b] and ask them to come here and help us as soon as possible, and to keep alive the war in Hellas. [4] But in my opinion the most important thing to do at the present moment is what you, with your constitutional love of quiet, will be slow to see, and what I must nevertheless mention. If we Sicilians all together, or at least as many as possible besides ourselves, would only launch the whole of our present navy with two months' provisions, and meet the Athenians at Tarentum[4a] and the Iapygian promontory,[4b] and show them that before fighting for Sicily they must first fight for their passage across the Ionian sea,[4c] we would strike dismay into their army, and make them realize that we have a base for our defense—for Tarentum is ready to receive us—while they have a wide sea to cross with all their armament, which could with difficulty keep its order through so long a voyage, and would be easy for us to attack as it came on slowly and in small detachments. [5] On the other hand, if they were to lighten their vessels,[5a] and draw together their fast sailers and attack us with these, we could ei-

---

6.34.2a Carthage: Map 6.20.
6.34.3a Sparta: Map 6.38, BY.
6.34.3b Corinth: Map 6.38, inset.
6.34.4a Tarentum: Map 6.38, AX.
6.34.4b Iapygian promontory (Cape Iapygium): Map 6.38, AX.
6.34.4c Ionian sea: Map 6.38, AX.
6.34.5a Warships were "lightened" by being

stripped of all nonessential equipment (such as masts and sails used for long-distance travel). This gear might be immediately jettisoned in an emergency but more often would be stored at a shore camp before the ships entered into battle. See 7.24.2, 8.28.1, 8.43.1, and Appendix G, Trireme Warfare, §8.

ther fall upon them when they were wearied with rowing or, if we chose not to do so, retire to Tarentum; while they, having crossed with few provisions just to give battle, would have a difficult time in desolate places, and would either have to remain and be blockaded, or to try to sail along the coast, abandoning the rest of their armament, and being further discouraged by not knowing for certain whether the cities would receive them. [6] In my opinion this consideration alone would be sufficient to deter them from putting out from Corcyra;[6a] and what with deliberating and reconnoitering our numbers and whereabouts, they would let the season go on until winter was upon them, or, confounded by so unexpected a circumstance, would break up the expedition, especially as their most experienced general has, as I hear, taken the command against his will, and would grasp at the first excuse offered by any serious demonstration of ours. [7] We should also be reported, I am certain, as more numerous than we really are, and men's minds are affected by what they hear. Besides, the first to attack, or to show that they mean to defend themselves against an attack, inspire greater fear because men see that they are ready for the emergency. [8] This would be precisely the case with the Athenians at present. They are now attacking us in the belief that we shall not resist, having a right to judge us severely because we did not help the Spartans to destroy them; but if they were to see us showing a courage for which they are not prepared, they would be more dismayed by the surprise than they could ever be by our actual power. [9] I could wish to persuade you to show this courage; but if this cannot be, at all events lose not a moment in preparing generally for the war; and remember all of you that contempt for an assailant is best shown by bravery in action, but that for the present the best course is to accept the preparations which fear inspires as giving the surest promise of safety, and to act as if the danger was real. That the Athenians are coming to attack us, and are already upon the voyage, and all but here—this is what I am sure of."

Thus spoke Hermocrates. Meanwhile the people of Syracuse[1a] were at great strife among themselves; some contending that the Athenians had no idea of coming and that there was no truth in what he said; some asking if they did come what harm they could do that would not be repaid them tenfold in return; while others made light of the whole affair and turned it

6.35
415
17th Year/Summer
SYRACUSE
Many Syracusans do not agree with Hermocrates. Athenagoras, a leader of The People, rises to speak.

6.34.6a   Corcyra: Map 6.38, AX.
6.35.1a   Syracuse: Map 6.38, BX.

into ridicule. In short, there were few that believed Hermocrates and feared for the future. [2] Meanwhile Athenagoras, the leader of The People and very powerful at that time with the masses, came forward and spoke as follows:

6.36
415
17th Year/Summer
SYRACUSE
Athenagoras argues that men like Hermocrates spread alarm for their own political purposes. He says that the Athenians are unlikely to come to Sicily while the Peloponnesians so near them at home remain hostile.

"For the Athenians, he who does not wish that they may be as misguided as they are supposed to be, and that they may come here to become our subjects, is either a coward or a traitor to his country; while as for those who carry such tidings and fill you with so much alarm, I wonder less at their audacity than at their folly if they flatter themselves that we do not see through them. [2] The fact is that they have their private reasons to be afraid, and wish to throw the city into consternation to have their own terrors cast into the shade by the public alarm. In short, this is what these reports are worth; they do not arise of themselves, but are concocted by men who are always causing agitation here in Sicily. [3] However, if you are well advised, you will not be guided in your calculation of probabilities by what these persons tell you, but by what shrewd men and of large experience, as I esteem the Athenians to be, would be likely to do. [4] Now it is not likely that they would leave the Peloponnesians behind them, and before they have well ended the war in Hellas wantonly come in quest of a new war quite as arduous, in Sicily; indeed, in my judgment, they are only too glad that we do not go and attack them, being so many and so great cities as we are."

6.37
415
17th Year/Summer
SYRACUSE
Athenagoras argues that even a very large expedition would probably fail in a hostile Sicily, shut up in a camp near their ships by superior Sicilian cavalry. He doubts whether it could escape annihilation.

"However, if they should come as is reported, I consider Sicily better able to go through with the war than the Peloponnesus, being at all points better prepared, and our city by itself far more than a match for this alleged army of invasion, even were it twice as large again. I know that they will not have horses with them, or get any here (except a few perhaps from the Egestaeans) or be able to bring a force of hoplites equal in number to our own, in ships which will already have enough to do to come all this distance, however lightly laden, not to speak of the transport of the other stores required against a city of this magnitude, which will be no slight quantity. [2] In fact, so strong is my opinion upon the subject, that I do not well see how they could avoid annihilation if they brought with them another city as large as Syracuse, and settled down and carried on war from our frontier; much less can they hope to succeed with all Sicily hostile to them, as all Sicily will be, and with only a camp pitched from the ships, and composed of tents and bare necessaries, from which they would not be able to stir far for fear of our cavalry."

MAP 6.38
ALLIES OF THE ATHENIANS LISTED FOR THE EXPEDITION TO SICILY IN 415

"But the Athenians see this as I tell you, and as I have reason to know are looking after their possessions at home, while persons here invent stories that neither are true nor ever will be. [2] Nor is this the first time that I see these persons, when they cannot resort to deeds, trying by such stories and by others even more abominable to frighten The People and themselves take over the government: it is what I see always. And I cannot help fearing that trying so often they may one day succeed, and that we, as long as we do not suffer, may prove too weak for the task of prevention, or, when the offenders are known, of pursuit. [3] The result is that our city is rarely at rest, but

6.38
415
17th Year/Summer
SYRACUSE
Athenagoras argues that the Athenians are too smart to risk such an attempt. He warns against those who spread such rumors in hopes of seizing power from The People. He condemns the conspiracies that threaten Syracuse's government and advises the citizenry to remain vigilant against such plots.

is subject to constant troubles and to conflicts as frequent against herself as against the enemy, not to speak of occasional tyrannies and other infamous forms of government. [4] However, I will try, if you will support me, to let nothing of this happen in our time, by winning over you, the many, and by chastising the authors of such machinations, not merely when they are caught in the act—a difficult feat to accomplish—but also for what they have the wish though not the power to do; as it is necessary to punish an enemy not only for what he does, but also beforehand for what he intends to do, if the first to relax precaution would not also be the first to suffer. I shall also reprove, watch, and on occasion warn The Few—the most effective way, in my opinion, of turning them from their evil courses. [5] And after all, as I have often asked—What would you have, young men? Would you hold office immediately? The law forbids it, a law enacted rather because you are not competent than to disgrace you when competent. Meanwhile you wish not to be on a legal equality with the many! But how can it be right that citizens of the same state should be held unworthy of the same privileges?"

"It will be said, perhaps, that democracy is neither wise nor equitable, but that the holders of property are also the best fitted to rule. I say, on the contrary, first, that the word *demos*, or people, includes the whole state, oligarchy only a part; next, that if the best guardians of property are the rich, and the best counselors the wise, none can hear and decide so well as the many; and that all these talents, individually and collectively, have their just place in a democracy. [2] But an oligarchy gives the many their share of the danger, and not content with the largest part takes and keeps the whole of the profit; and this is what the powerful and young among you aspire to, but in a great city cannot possibly obtain."

"But even now, foolish men, most senseless of all the Hellenes that I know, if you have no sense of the wickedness of your designs, or most criminal if you have that sense and still dare to pursue them, [6.40.1] even now, if it is not a case for repentance, you may still learn wisdom, and thus advance the interest of the country, the common interest of us all. Reflect that in the country's prosperity the men of merit in your ranks will have a share and a larger share than the great mass of your fellow countrymen, but that if you have other designs you run a risk of being deprived of all; and cease to spread reports like these, as The People realize your purpose and will not put up with it. [2] If the Athenians arrive, this city will repulse them in a manner worthy of itself; we have generals who will see to this matter. And if nothing of this be true, as I incline to believe, the city will not be thrown into a panic by your reports, or impose upon itself a voluntary servitude by choosing you for its rulers; the city itself will look into the matter, and will judge your words as if they were acts, and instead of allowing itself to be deprived of its liberty by listening to you, will strive to preserve that liberty, by taking care to have always at hand the means of making itself respected."

Such were the words of Athenagoras. One of the generals now stood up and stopped any other speakers coming forward, adding these words of his own with reference to the matter in hand:

[2] "It is not well for speakers to utter calumnies against one another, or for their hearers to entertain them; we ought rather to look to the information that we have received, and see how each man by himself and the city as a whole may best prepare to repel the invaders. [3] Even if there should be no need, there is no harm in the state being furnished with horses and arms and all other accouterments of war; [4] and we will undertake to see to and order this, and to send round to the cities to reconnoiter and do all else that may appear desirable. Part of this we have seen to already, and whatever we discover shall be laid before you."

After these words from the general, the Syracusans departed from the assembly.

In the meantime the Athenians and all their allies had now arrived at Corcyra.[1a] Here the generals began by again reviewing the armament, and made arrangements as to the order in which they were to anchor and encamp, and dividing the whole fleet into three divisions, allotted one to each of their number, to avoid sailing all together and thus lacking sufficient water, or provisions at the stations where they might land, and at the same time to be generally better ordered and easier to handle, by each squadron having its own commander. [2] Next they sent three ships ahead to Italy[2a] and Sicily[2b] to find out which of the cities would receive them, with instructions to meet them on the way and let them know before they put in to land.

After this the Athenians sailed from Corcyra, and proceeded to cross to Sicily with an armament now consisting of one hundred and thirty-four triremes in all (besides two Rhodian *penteconters*)[1a] of which one hundred were Athenian vessels—sixty men-of-war, and forty troopships—and the remainder from Chios[1b] and the other allies; five thousand and one hundred hoplites in all, of which fifteen hundred were Athenian citizens from the

6.41
415
17th Year/Summer
SYRACUSE
A Syracusan general then speaks, affirming that the city should prepare its defense and scout the enemy's approach. The assembly ends.

6.42
415
17th Year/Summer
CORCYRA
From Corcyra the Athenian expedition sends scouts to Italy and Sicily to test the cities there.

6.43
415
17th Year/Summer
CORCYRA
The forces of the Athenian expedition are described.

6.42.1a Corcyra: Map 6.38, AX.
6.42.2a Italy: Map 6.38, AX.
6.42.2b Sicily: Map 6.38, BX.

6.43.1a Rhodes: Map 6.38, BY. *Penteconters*, 50-oared warships, were smaller than triremes, with 170 oars.
6.43.1b Chios: Map 6.38, AY.

rolls at Athens and seven hundred *Thetes* shipped as marines,[1c] and the rest allied troops, some of them Athenian subjects, and besides these five hundred Argives[1d] and two hundred and fifty Mantineans[1e] serving for hire; four hundred and eighty archers in all, eighty of whom were Cretans,[1f] seven hundred slingers from Rhodes, one hundred and twenty light-armed exiles from Megara,[1g] and one horse-transport carrying thirty horses.

6.44
415
17th Year/Summer
ITALY
Carrying abundant supplies, the Athenians were not distressed that most Italian cities refused to provide markets for them.
RHEGIUM
The Athenians stop at Rhegium, send to Egesta for support, and discuss their next move.

Such was the strength of the first armament that sailed over for the war. The supplies for this force were carried by thirty merchant ships laden with grain, which conveyed the bakers, stonemasons and carpenters, and the tools for raising fortifications, accompanied by one hundred boats, like the former conscripted into the service, besides many other boats and merchant ships which followed the armament voluntarily for purposes of trade; all of which now left Corcyra and struck across the Ionian sea[1a] together. [2] The whole force made land at the Iapygian promontory[2a] and Tarentum,[2b] with more or less good fortune. They then coasted along the shores of Italy,[2c] the cities shutting their markets and gates against them, and according them nothing but water and liberty to anchor (and Tarentum and Locri[2d] not even that), until they arrived at Rhegium,[2e] the extreme point of Italy. [3] Here at length they reunited, and not gaining admission within the walls, pitched a camp outside the city in the precinct of Artemis, where a market was also provided for them,[3a] and drew their ships on shore and kept quiet. Meanwhile they opened negotiations with the Rhegians, and called upon them as Chalcidians to assist their Leontine[3b] kinsmen; to which the Rhegians replied that they would not side with either party, but should await the decision of the rest of the Italians, and do as they did.[3c] [4] Upon this the Athenians now began to consider what would be the best action to take in the affairs of Sicily, and meanwhile waited for the ships sent on to come back from Egesta,[4a] in order to know whether there was really there the money mentioned by the messengers at Athens.

6.45
415
17th Year/Summer
SYRACUSE
Syracuse learns the Athenians are at Rhegium, and rushes to prepare her defense.

In the meantime reliable reports came in from all quarters to the Syracusans, as well as from their own officers sent to reconnoiter, that the fleet was at Rhegium; upon which they laid aside their incredulity and threw

6.43.1c The *thetes* were the poorest of the four property classes at Athens. Since they were unable to afford the cost of hoplite equipment, their principal military employment was to serve in the fleet as rowers. Their role as marines here is quite anomalous. Perhaps they had been equipped and armed at public expense. See Appendix G, Trireme Warfare, §8, 11, 14, and Appendix A, The Athenian Government, §2.
6.43.1d Argos: Map 6.38, inset.
6.43.1e Mantinea: Map 6.38, BY.
6.43.1f Crete: Map 6.38, BY.
6.43.1g Megara: Map 6.38, inset.
6.44.1a Ionian sea: Map 6.38, AX.
6.44.2a Iapygian promontory (Cape Iapygium): Map 6.38, AX.
6.44.2b Tarentum: Map 6.38, AX.

6.44.2c Italy: Map 6.38, AX.
6.44.2d Locri (Epizephyrian Locri, in Italy): Map 6.38, AX.
6.44.2e Rhegium: Map 6.38, AX.
6.44.3a Greek soldiers and sailors at this time were expected to purchase their food from local markets with their own money, which made prompt and adequate military pay quite important. For a city to offer a special market at a convenient and exterior location for foreign troops was a polite and presumably profitable amenity; and it also helped to keep such visitors out of the city.
6.44.3b Leontini: Map 6.38, BX.
6.44.3c See Illustration 3.86, of a fragment of a treaty between Athens and Rhegium dated from 433 B.C.
6.44.4a Egesta: Map 6.49.

themselves ardently into the work of preparation. They sent round guards or envoys, as the case might be, to the Sicels, put garrisons into the posts of the *peripoli*[1a] in the country, reviewed horses and arms in the city to see that nothing was wanting, and took all other steps to prepare for a war which might be upon them at any moment.

Meanwhile the three ships that had been sent ahead returned from Egesta[1a] to the Athenians at Rhegium, with the news that far from there being the sums promised, all that could be produced was thirty talents. [2] The generals were not a little disheartened at being thus disappointed at the outset, and by the refusal of the Rhegians to join in the expedition, they being the first people they had tried to gain and had most reason to count upon, from their relationship to the Leontines and constant friendship for Athens. If Nicias was prepared for the news from Egesta, his two colleagues were taken completely by surprise. [3] The Egestaeans had had recourse to the following stratagem when the first envoys from Athens came to inspect their resources. They took the envoys in question to the temple of Aphrodite at Eryx[3a] and showed them the treasures deposited there; bowls, wine ladles, censers, and a large number of other objects which from being in silver gave an impression of wealth quite out of proportion to their really small value. They also privately entertained the ships' crews, and collected all the cups of gold and silver that they could find in Egesta itself or could borrow in the neighboring Phoenician and Hellenic cities, and each brought them to the banquets as their own; [4] and as all used pretty nearly the same, and everywhere a great quantity of silver was shown, the effect of which was most dazzling upon the Athenian sailors, and made them talk loudly of the riches they had seen when they got back to Athens. [5] The dupes in question—who had in their turn persuaded the rest—were much blamed by the soldiers when the news got abroad that there was not the money supposed at Egesta.

Meanwhile the generals discussed what was to be done. [6.47.1] The opinion of Nicias was to sail with all the armament to Selinus,[1a] the main objective of the expedition, and if the Egestaeans could provide money for the whole force, to make their plans accordingly; but if they could not, to require them to supply provisions for the sixty ships that they had asked for, to stay and settle matters between them and the Selinuntines either by force or by agreement, and then to coast past the other cities and, after displaying the power of Athens and proving their zeal for their friends and allies, to sail home again (unless they should have some sudden and unexpected opportunity of serving the Leontines,[1b] or of bringing over some of the other cities), and not to endanger the state by wasting its home resources.

6.46
415
17th Year/Summer
RHEGIUM
The Athenians are dismayed to discover that Rhegium refuses to join them and that Egesta can provide only thirty talents. The Egestaean ruse that had duped the Athenian envoys is described.

6.47
415
17th Year/Summer
RHEGIUM
Nicias proposes that with so little Egestaean support, they try to settle the war with Selinus, display their power, and then return home.

6.45.1a   It is thought that the *peripoli* in Athens were a force of young men normally employed in patrolling the countryside, though that is not their role on the occasions Thucydides refers to them (4.67.2 and 8.92.2 and 5). There seems to have been a similar institution at Syracuse. See 7.45.5 for these guardposts.
6.46.1a   Egesta: Map 6.49.
6.46.3a   Eryx: Map 6.49.
6.47.1a   Selinus: Map 6.49.
6.47.1b   Leontini: Map 6.49.

6.48
415
17th Year/Summer
RHEGIUM
Alcibiades suggests offering alliance to all Sicilian cities. Once Athens' allies are known, the expedition might then attack Syracuse and Selinus.

6.49
415
17th Year/Summer
RHEGIUM
Lamachus advocates an immediate attack on Syracuse, thus exploiting surprise and the formidable reputation that unfamiliarity still accords them.

6.50
415
17th Year/Summer
CATANA
Failing to secure Messanian alliance, the Athenians sail to Naxos, Catana, and Syracuse; they reconnoiter the harbor and nearby coast before returning to Catana.

Alcibiades said that a great expedition like the present must not disgrace itself by going away without having accomplished anything; heralds must be sent to all the cities except Selinus and Syracuse, and efforts be made to make some of the Sicels revolt from the Syracusans, and to gain the friendship of others, in order to obtain grain and troops; and first of all to win over the Messanians,[1a] who lay right in the passage and entrance to Sicily, and would afford an excellent harbor and base for the army. Thus, after bringing over the cities and knowing who would be their allies in the war, they might then indeed attack Syracuse and Selinus—unless the latter came to terms with Egesta and the former ceased to oppose the restoration of Leontini.

Lamachus, on the other hand, said that they ought to sail straight to Syracuse, and fight their battle at once under the walls of the city while the people were still unprepared, and the panic at its height. [2] Every armament was most terrible at first; if it allowed time to run on without showing itself, men's courage revived, and they saw it appear at last almost with indifference. By attacking suddenly, while Syracuse still trembled at their coming, they would have the best chance of gaining a victory for themselves and of striking a complete panic into the enemy by the aspect of their numbers—which would never appear so considerable as at present—by the anticipation of coming disaster, and above all by the immediate danger of the engagement. [3] They might also count upon surprising many in the fields outside, incredulous of their coming; and at the moment that the enemy was carrying in his property the army would not want for booty if it settled in force before the city. [4] The rest of the Sicilians would thus be immediately less disposed to enter into alliance with the Syracusans, and would join the Athenians, without waiting to see which were the strongest. They must make Megara[4a] their naval station as a place to retreat to and a base from which to attack: it was an uninhabited place at no great distance from Syracuse either by land or by sea.

Having spoken to this effect, Lamachus nevertheless gave his support to the opinion of Alcibiades. After this Alcibiades sailed in his own vessel across to Messana[1a] with proposals of alliance, but met with no success, the inhabitants answering that they could not receive him within their walls, though they would provide him with a market outside.[1b] Upon this he sailed back to Rhegium.[1c] [2] Immediately upon his return the generals manned and provisioned sixty ships out of the whole fleet and coasted along to Naxos,[2a] leaving the rest of the armament behind them at Rhegium with one of their number. [3] Received by the Naxians, they then coasted on to Catana,[3a] and being refused admittance by the inhabitants (there being a pro-Syracusan party in the city), went on to the river

6.48.1a   Messana: Map 6.49.
6.49.4a   Megara (Hyblaea): Map 6.49.
6.50.1a   Messana: Map 6.49.
6.50.1b   Markets for military forces: see note at 6.44.3a.

6.50.1c   Rhegium: Map 6.49.
6.50.2a   Naxos: Map 6.49.
6.50.3a   Catana: Map 6.49.

MAP 6.49
FIRST ATHENIAN PLANS AND
MILITARY OPERATIONS IN
SICILY IN 415

Terias.[3b] [4] Here they bivouacked, and the next day sailed in single file to Syracuse[4a] with all their ships except ten which they sent on in front to sail into the great harbor and see if there was any fleet launched, and to proclaim by herald from shipboard that the Athenians had come to restore the Leontines[4b] to their country, as being their allies and kinsmen, and that such of them, therefore, as were in Syracuse should leave it without fear and join their friends and benefactors the Athenians. [5] After making this proclamation and reconnoitering the city and the harbors, and the features of the country which they would have to make their base of operations in the war, they sailed back to Catana.

An assembly being held here, the inhabitants refused to receive the armament, but invited the generals to come in and say what they desired; and while Alcibiades was speaking and the citizens were intent on the assembly, the soldiers broke down a badly walled-up postern gate without being observed, and getting inside the city, flocked into the marketplace. [2] The Syracusan party in the city no sooner saw the army inside than they became frightened and withdrew, not being at all numerous; while the rest voted for an alliance with the Athenians and invited them to bring the rest of their forces from Rhegium. [3] After this the Athenians sailed to Rhegium and put off, this time with all the armament, for Catana,[3a] where they began to build a camp immediately upon their arrival.

Meanwhile word was brought them from Camarina[1a] that if they went there the city would go over to them, and also that the Syracusans were manning a fleet. The Athenians accordingly sailed along shore with all their

6.51
415
17th Year/Summer
CATANA
The Catanians refuse to receive the Athenians, but when the Athenians gain entrance to the city, they change their minds.

6.52
415
17th Year/Summer
CAMARINA
When Camarina refuses to receive the Athenians, they return to Catana, raiding Syracusan territory on their way.

6.50.3b   Terias River: Map 6.49.
6.50.4a   Syracuse: Map 6.49.
6.50.4b   Leontini: Map 6.49.
6.51.3a   Catana: Map 6.49.
6.52.1a   Camarina: Map 6.49.

armament, first to Syracuse,[1b] where they found no fleet being manned, and then along the coast to Camarina, where they stopped at the beach and sent a herald to the people who, however, refused to receive them, saying that their oaths bound them to receive only a single vessel of the Athenians unless they themselves sent for more. [2] Disappointed here, the Athenians now sailed back again, and after landing on and plundering Syracusan territory and losing some stragglers from their light-armed troops through the coming up of the Syracusan horse, so got back to Catana.

There they found the *Salaminia*[1a] come from Athens for Alcibiades, with orders for him to sail home to answer the charges which the state brought against him, and for certain others of the soldiers who with him were accused of sacrilege in the matter of the Mysteries and of the Hermae.[1b] [2] For the Athenians, after the departure of the expedition, had continued as active as ever in investigating the facts of the Mysteries and of the Hermae, and, instead of testing the informers, in their suspicious temper welcomed all indifferently, arresting and imprisoning the best citizens upon the evidence of rascals, and preferring to sift the matter to the bottom sooner than to let an accused person of good character pass unquestioned, owing to the rascality of the informer. [3] The People had heard how oppressive the tyranny of Pisistratus and his sons had become before it ended, and further that his tyranny had been put down at last, not by themselves and Harmodius, but by the Spartans,[3a] and so were always in fear and took everything suspiciously.

Indeed, the daring action of Aristogiton and Harmodius was undertaken in consequence of a love affair, which I shall relate at some length, to show that the Athenians are no more accurate than the rest of the world in their accounts of their own tyrants and of the facts of their own history. [2] Pisistratus dying at an advanced age in possession of the tyranny, was succeeded by his eldest son, Hippias, and not Hipparchus, as is commonly believed.[2a] Harmodius was then in the flower of youthful beauty, and Aristogiton, a citizen in the middle rank of life, was his lover and possessed him. [3] Solicited without success by Hipparchus son of Pisistratus, Harmodius told Aristogiton, and the enraged lover, afraid that the powerful Hipparchus might take Harmodius by force, immediately formed a design, such as his condition in life permitted, for overthrowing the tyranny. [4] In the meantime Hipparchus, after a second solicitation of Harmodius met with no better success, unwilling to use violence, arranged to insult him in some covert way. [5] Indeed, generally their government was not grievous to the multitude, or in any way odious in practice; and these tyrants culti-

---

6.53
415
17th Year/Summer
CATANA
Alcibiades is summoned home to face trial for his supposed role in the Hermae and the Mysteries affairs. Inquiry into these cases had become rabid as many Athenians feared an attempt to establish a tyranny.

6.54
514
ATHENS
To show that Athenians do not know their own history, Thucydides recounts the story of Aristogiton and Harmodius, and their true role in the fall of the Pisistratidean tyranny nearly one hundred years earlier.

6.52.1b Syracuse: Map 6.49.
6.53.1a The *Salaminia* and her sister ship the *Paralus* were special state triremes used on sacred embassies and official business. Thucydides mentions them several times in his history (3.33.1, 3.77.3, 6.61.4–7, 8.73.5–6, and 8.74.1–2).
6.53.1b For Thucydides' account of the blasphe-

mous affairs of the Mysteries and the Hermae, and their political effects, see 6.27–29 and note 6.28.1a.
6.53.3a Tyrannies overthrown by Sparta: see 1.18.1 and 1.122.3; also 6.59.4.
6.54.2a This common belief was first described by Thucydides in 1.20.

ILLUSTRATION 6.54   THE ALTAR STONE DESCRIBED BY THUCYDIDES IN 6.54 WITH THE
INSCRIPTION DEDICATED BY PISISTRATUS THE SON OF HIPPIAS

vated wisdom and virtue as much as any, and without exacting from the
Athenians more than a twentieth of their income, splendidly adorned their
city, and carried on their wars, and provided sacrifices for the temples. [6]
For the rest, the city was left in full enjoyment of its existing laws, except
that care was always taken to have some one of the family among the *archons*.[6a] Among those relatives that held the yearly archonship at Athens was
Pisistratus, son of the tyrant Hippias, and named after his grandfather, who
when he was archon dedicated the altar to the twelve gods in the marketplace,[6b] and that of Apollo in the Pythian precinct.[6c] [7] The Athenian people afterwards built on to and lengthened the altar in the marketplace, and
obliterated the inscription; but that in the Pythian precinct can still be seen,
though in faded letters, and is to the following effect:

> Pisistratus, the son of Hippias,
> Set up this record of his archonship
> In the precinct of Apollo Pythias.[7a]

That Hippias was the eldest son and succeeded to the government is
what I positively assert as a fact upon which I have had more exact accounts
than others, and may be also ascertained by the following circumstance. He
is the only one of the legitimate brothers that appears to have had children;
as the altar shows, and the pillar placed in the Athenian Acropolis,[1a] com-

6.55
514
ATHENS
Thucydides describes
epigraphic and circumstantial
evidence which proves that
Hippias, not Hipparchus,
became tyrant of Athens
after Pisistratus.

6.54.6a   *Archon*: a political officer of Athens; see
          Appendix A, The Athenian Government,
          §6.
6.54.6b   The site of the altar of the twelve gods
          has been located in the Athenian *agora*;
          see Map 6.56, inset.
6.54.6c   The sanctuary of Apollo in the Pythian
          district is believed to have been in the

          southeast part of the city, between the
          Athenian Olympieum sanctuary and the
          Ilissos river; see Map 6.56, inset.
6.55.1a   Acropolis of Athens: Map 6.56, inset.
6.54.7a   This altar stone exists today and its in-
          scription is still legible. See Illustration
          6.54.

memorating the crime of the tyrants, which mentions no child of Thessalus or of Hipparchus,[1b] but five of Hippias, which he had by Myrrhine, who was the daughter of Callias son of Hyperechides; and naturally the eldest would have married first. [2] Again, his name comes first on the pillar after that of his father, and this too is quite natural, as he was the eldest after him, and the reigning tyrant. [3] Nor can I ever believe that Hippias would have obtained the tyranny so easily, if Hipparchus had been in power when he was killed, and he, Hippias, had had to establish himself upon the same day; but he had no doubt been long accustomed to overawe the citizens, and to be obeyed by his mercenaries, and thus not only conquered, but conquered with ease, without experiencing any of the embarrassment of a younger brother unused to the exercise of authority. [4] It was the sad fate which made Hipparchus famous that got him also the credit with posterity of having been tyrant.

To return to Harmodius: Hipparchus having been repulsed in his solicitations insulted him as he had resolved, by first inviting a sister of Harmodius, a young girl, to come and bear a basket in a certain procession, and then rejecting her, on the grounds that she had never been invited at all owing to her unworthiness. [2] If Harmodius was indignant at this, Aristogiton for his sake now became more exasperated than ever; and having arranged everything with those who were to join them in the enterprise, they only waited for the great feast of the Panathenaea,[2a] the sole day in which the citizens forming part of the procession could meet together in arms without suspicion. Aristogiton and Harmodius were to begin, but were to be supported immediately by their accomplices against the bodyguard. [3] The conspirators were not many, for better security, besides which they hoped that those not in the plot would be carried away by the example of a few daring spirits, and use the arms in their hands to recover their liberty.

At last the festival arrived; and Hippias with his bodyguard was outside the city in the Ceramicus,[1a] arranging how the different parts of the procession were to proceed. Harmodius and Aristogiton had already their daggers and were getting ready to act, [2] when seeing one of their accomplices talking familiarly with Hippias, who was easily accessible to everyone, they took fright and concluded that they had been discovered and were on the point of being arrested; [3] and eager if possible to be revenged first upon the man who had wronged them and for whom they had undertaken all this risk, they rushed, as they were, within the gates, and meeting with Hipparchus by the Leocorium[3a] recklessly fell upon him at once, infuriated, Aristogiton by love, and Harmodius by insult, and struck and killed him. [4] Aristogiton escaped the guards at the moment, through the crowd run-

---

6.55.1b   Thessalus and Hipparchus were, with Hippias, the sons of Pisistratus the tyrant; see 1.20.2.

6.56.2a   For the Feast of the Panathenaea, see Appendix I, Religious Festivals, §8.

6.57.1a   The Ceramicus district of Athens, which lay both inside and outside the walls: Map 6.56, inset.

6.57.3a   Leocorium, possible location: Map 6.56, inset.

MAP 6.56 HIPPARCHUS, HARMODIUS, AND ARISTOGITON

ning up, but was afterwards taken and executed in no merciful way: Harmodius was killed on the spot.

When the news was brought to Hippias in the Ceramicus, he at once proceeded not to the scene of action, but to the armed men in the procession[1a] before they, being some distance away, knew anything of the matter. Composing his features for the occasion so as not to betray himself, he pointed to a certain spot and bade them assemble there without their arms. [2] They withdrew accordingly, supposing that he had something to say; whereupon he told the mercenaries to remove the arms, and then and there picked out the men he thought guilty and all who were found with daggers (the shield and spear being the usual weapons for a procession).

6.58
514
17th Year/Summer
ATHENS
Hippias swiftly disarmed all Athenians in the procession.

6.58.1a   The Panathenaean festival included a ceremonial procession along the Panathenaic
          Way (Map 6.56, inset) to the temple of
          Athena (Parthenon) on the Acropolis
          (Map 6.56, inset).

6.59
514
17th Year/Summer
ATHENS
Hippias ruled harshly for
four more years before
the Spartans and exiled
Alcmeonidae deposed him.
He went into exile and later
accompanied the Persian
expedition to Marathon.

In this way offended love first led Harmodius and Aristogiton to conspire, and the alarm of the moment to commit the rash action recounted. [2] After this the tyranny pressed harder on the Athenians, and Hippias, now grown more fearful, put to death many of the citizens, and at the same time began to turn his eyes abroad for a refuge in case of revolution. [3] Thus, although an Athenian, he gave his daughter, Archedice, to a Lampsacene, Aeantides, son of the tyrant of Lampsacus,[3a] seeing that they had great influence with Darius.[3b] And there is her tomb in Lampsacus with this inscription:

> Archedice lies buried in this earth,
> Hippias her sire, and Athens gave her birth;
> Unto her bosom pride was never known,
> Though daughter, wife, and sister to the throne.

[4] Hippias, after reigning three years longer over the Athenians, was deposed in the fourth by the Spartans and the banished Alcmaeonidae,[4a] and went with a safe conduct to Sigeum,[4b] and to Aeantides at Lampsacus, and from thence to King Darius; from whose court he set out twenty years after, in his old age, and came with the Persians to Marathon.[4c]

6.60
415
17th Year/Summer
ATHENS
Memories of earlier
tyranny convinced many at
Athens that the Hermae and
Mysteries affairs were
connected to oligarchic
plots. They grew savage in
their search for the guilty.
One imprisoned suspect
accused some Athenians in
exchange for immunity, and
many of them were
executed.

With these events in their minds, and recalling everything they knew by hearsay on the subject, the Athenian people grew uneasy and suspicious of the persons charged in the affair of the Mysteries, and became convinced that all that had taken place was part of an oligarchic and monarchical conspiracy. [2] In the state of agitation thus produced, many persons of considerable status had already been thrown into prison, and far from showing any signs of abating, public feeling grew daily more savage, and more arrests were made; until at last one of those in custody, thought to be the most guilty of all, was induced by a fellow prisoner to give information, whether true or not is a matter on which there are two opinions, no one having been able, either then or since, to say for certain who did the deed.[2a] [3] However this may be, the other found arguments to persuade him, that even if he had not done it, he ought to save himself by gaining a promise of impunity, and free the state of its present suspicions; as he would be surer of safety if he confessed after promise of impunity than if he denied and were brought to trial. [4] He accordingly made a confession implicating himself and others in the affair of the Hermae; and the Athenian people, glad at last to get at what they supposed was the truth, and furious until then at not being able to discover those who had conspired against the ma-

6.59.3a Lampsacus: Map 6.56.
6.59.3b Darius, King of Persia.
6.59.4a The Alcmeonidae was a powerful clan easier to banish because of its role in the curse of the goddess; see 1.126–7.
6.59.4b Sigeum: Map 6.56.
6.59.4c Marathon, the Attic site of a famous Athenian victory over the invading Persians in 490: Map 6.56. Also see Appendix E, The Persians, §4.

6.60.2a As Andocides' existing oration *On the Mysteries* shows, Andocides himself was the "one in custody."

jority, at once let go the informer and all the rest whom he had not denounced, and bringing the accused to trial, executed as many as were apprehended, and condemned to death such as had fled and set a price upon their heads. [5] In this it was, after all, not clear whether the sufferers had been punished unjustly, and in any case the rest of the city received immediate and manifest relief.

To return to Alcibiades: public feeling was very hostile to him, being worked on by the same enemies who had attacked him before he went out; and now that the Athenians fancied that they had got at the truth of the matter of the Hermae, they believed more firmly than ever that the affair of the Mysteries also, in which he was implicated, had been contrived by him in the same intention and was connected with the plot against the democracy. [2] Meanwhile it so happened that, just at the time of this agitation, a small force of Spartans had advanced as far as the Isthmus,[2a] in pursuance of some scheme with the Boeotians.[2b] It was now thought that they had come by prior arrangement and at his instigation, and not on account of the Boeotians, and that if the citizens had not acted on the information received and forestalled them by arresting the prisoners, the city would have been betrayed. [3] The citizens went so far as to sleep one night armed in the temple of Theseus within the walls.[3a] Also, and just at this time, the friends of Alcibiades at Argos[3b] were suspected of a design to attack the Argive People, so the Argive hostages deposited in the islands[3c] were given up by the Athenians to the Argive People to be put to death upon that account: [4] in short, everywhere something was found to create suspicion against Alcibiades. It was therefore decided to bring him to trial and execute him, and the *Salaminia*[4a] was sent to Sicily for him and the others named in the information, with instructions to order him to return and answer the charges against him, [5] but not to arrest him, because they wished to avoid causing any agitation in the army or among the enemy in Sicily, and above all to retain the services of the Mantineans[5a] and Argives, who, it was thought, had been induced to join by his influence. [6] Alcibiades, with his own ship and his fellow accused, accordingly sailed off with the *Salaminia* from Sicily, as though to return to Athens, and went with her as far as Thurii,[6a] and there they left the ship and disappeared, being afraid to go home for trial with such a prejudice existing against them. [7] The crew of the *Salaminia* stayed some time looking for Alcibiades and his companions, and at length, as they were nowhere to be found, set sail and departed. Alcibiades, now an outlaw, crossed in a boat not long after from Thurii to the Peloponnesus; and the Athenians passed

6.61
415
17th Year/Summer
ITALY
These investigations and other developments convince many Athenians that Alcibiades has plotted against the democracy. He is recalled to stand trial. He sails for home in his own ship but disappears at Thurii in Italy, and later reaches the Peloponnesus. He is condemned to death in absentia at Athens.

6.61.2a Isthmus (of Corinth): Map 6.56.
6.61.2b Boeotia: Map 6.56.
6.61.3a The site of this temple of Theseus is unknown. Pausanias (1.17.2) says it lay southeast of the *agora*. Map 6.56, inset, shows a possible location.
6.61.3b Argos: Map 6.56.
6.61.3c These were probably the same hostages that Alcibiades and his twenty ships seized and deposited in the various is-

lands of the empire, as described in 5.84.
6.61.4a The *Salaminia* and her sister ship the *Paralus* were special state triremes used on sacred embassies and official business. Thucydides mentions them several times in the course of his narrative. See note 6.53.1a.
6.61.5a Mantinea: Map 6.56.
6.61.6a Thurii: Map 6.64, locator.

ILLUSTRATION 6.61 FRAGMENT OF AN ATTIC STELA WITH AN INSCRIBED NOTICE OF
SALE OF ALCIBIADES' PROPERTY AFTER HIS CONDEMNATION IN CONNECTION WITH THE
MOCK MYSTERIES AND THE MUTILATION OF THE HERMAE

6.62
415
17th Year/Summer
SICILY
The Athenians accomplish
little while sailing along the
coast of Sicily. Hyccara is
taken and its people sold as
slaves, but Himera refuses
them entrance and they fail
to take Hybla.

sentence of death by default upon him and those in his company.

The Athenian generals left in Sicily now divided the armament into two
parts, and each taking one by lot, sailed with the whole for Selinus and
Egesta,[1a] wishing to know whether the Egestaeans would give the money,
and to look into the question of Selinus and ascertain the state of the
quarrel between her and Egesta. [2] Coasting along Sicily, with the shore
on their left, on the side toward the Tyrrhenian Sea,[2a] they touched at
Himera,[2b] the only Hellenic city in that part of the island, and being refused admission resumed their voyage. [3] On their way they took Hyccara,[3a] a petty Sicanian seaport nevertheless at war with Egesta, and making
slaves of the inhabitants gave up the city to the Egestaeans, some of whose
horse had joined them; after which the army proceeded through the territory of the Sicels until it reached Catana,[3b] while the fleet sailed along the
coast with the slaves on board. [4] Meanwhile Nicias sailed straight from
Hyccara along the coast and went to Egesta, and after transacting his other

6.62.1a   Selinus, Egesta: Map 6.64.
6.62.2a   Tyrrhenian sea: Map 6.64.
6.62.2b   Himera: Map 6.64.
6.62.3a   Hyccara: Map 6.64.
6.62.3b   Catana: Map 6.64.

business and receiving thirty talents, rejoined the forces. They now sold their slaves for the sum of one hundred and twenty talents, [5] and sailed round to their Sicel allies to urge them to send troops; and meanwhile went with half their own force to the hostile city of Hybla in the territory of Gela,[5a] but did not succeed in taking it.

Summer was now over.

The winter following, the Athenians at once began to prepare for moving on Syracuse, and the Syracusans on their side for marching against them. [2] From the moment when the Athenians failed to attack them instantly as they at first feared and expected, every day that passed did something to revive their courage; and when they saw them sailing far away from them on the other side of Sicily, and going to Hybla only to fail in their attempts to storm it, they thought less of them than ever, and called upon their generals, as the multitude is apt to do in moments of confidence, to lead them to Catana,[2a] since the enemy would not come to them. [3] Parties also of the Syracusan horse employed in reconnoitering constantly rode up to the Athenian armament, and among other insults asked them whether they had not really come to settle alongside the Syracusans in a foreign country rather than to resettle the Leontines in their own.

Aware of this, the Athenian generals determined to draw them out in mass as far as possible from the city, and themselves in the meantime to sail by night along shore, and take up at their leisure a convenient position. This they knew they could not do so well if they had to disembark from their ships in front of a force prepared for them, or to go by land openly. The numerous cavalry of the Syracusans (a force which they were themselves without) would then be able to do the greatest harm to their light troops and the crowd that followed them; but this plan would enable them to take up a position in which the horse could do them no hurt worth speaking of, some Syracusan exiles with the army having told them of the spot near the Olympieum,[1a] which they afterwards occupied. In pursuance of their idea, the generals devised the following stratagem. [2] They sent to Syracuse[2a] a man devoted to them, and by the Syracusan generals thought to be no less in their interest; he was a native of Catana,[2b] and said he came from persons in that place, whose names the Syracusan generals were acquainted with, and whom they knew to be among the members of their party still left in the city. [3] He told them that the Athenians passed the night in the city, at some distance from their arms, and that if the Syracusans would name a day and come with all their people at daybreak to attack the armament, they, their friends, would close the gates upon the troops in the city, and set fire to the vessels, while the Syracusans would easily take

6.63
415/4
17th Year/Winter
SICILY
Athenian inactivity for the rest of the summer leads the Syracusans to despise them and to beg their generals to lead them against the invaders.

6.64
415/4
17th Year/Winter
CATANA
The Athenian generals employ a stratagem to trick the Syracusans into marching to Catana.

6.62.5a   The only known Hybla (Map 6.64) can
hardly be said to lie in the territory of
Gela; see Map 6.64. Perhaps Thucydides
is mistaken or refers here to another town
of the same name whose location is unknown.

6.63.2a   Catana: Map 6.64.
6.64.1a   Olympieum, a temple built on the
heights southwest of Syracuse: Map 6.68.
6.64.2a   Syracuse: Map 6.64.
6.64.2b   Catana: Map 6.64.

MAP 6.64

LATER ATHENIAN MILITARY OPERATIONS IN 415 AND IN THE WINTER OF 415/4

6.65
415/4
17th Year/Winter
SYRACUSE
As the Syracusans approach Catana by land, the Athenians sail off to Syracuse. Finding the Athenians gone, the Syracusans have to hurry back to their city.

the camp by an attack upon the stockade. In this they would be aided by many of the Catanians, who were already prepared to act, and from whom he himself came.

The generals of the Syracusans, who did not lack confidence, and who had intended even without this information to march on Catana, believed the man without any sufficient inquiry, fixed at once a day upon which they would be there, and dismissed him; and the Selinuntines[1a] and others of their allies having now arrived, they gave orders for all the Syracusans to march out in full force. Their preparations completed, and the time fixed for their arrival being at hand, they set out for Catana, and passed the night upon the river Symaethus,[1b] in the Leontine[1c] territory. [2] Meanwhile the Athenians no sooner knew of their approach than they took all their forces and such of the Sicels or others as had joined them, put them on board their ships and boats, and sailed by night to Syracuse. [3] Thus, when morning broke the Athenians were landing opposite the Olympieum[3a] ready to seize their camping ground, and the Syracusan horse having ridden up first to Catana and found that all the armament had put to sea, wheeled back and told the infantry, and then all turned back together and went to the relief of the city.

6.66
415/4
17th Year/Winter
SYRACUSE
The Athenians occupy favorable positions near Syracuse and await the Syracusans who return and camp for the night.

In the meantime, as the march before the Syracusans was a long one, the Athenians quietly established their army in a convenient position, where they could begin an engagement when they pleased, and where the Syracusan cavalry would have least opportunity of harassing them, either before or during the action, being flanked on one side by walls, houses, trees, and by

6.65.1a   Selinus: Map 6.64.
6.65.1b   Symaethus river: Map 6.64.
6.65.1c   Leontini: Map 6.64.
6.65.3a   Olympieum sanctuary: Map 6.68.

a marsh, and on the other by cliffs. [2] They also felled the neighboring trees and carried them down to the sea, and formed a palisade alongside of their ships, and with stones (which they picked up) and wood, hastily raised a fort at Daskon,[2a] the most vulnerable point of their position, and broke down the bridge over the Anapus.[2b] [3] These preparations were allowed to go on without any interruption from the city; the first hostile force to appear being the Syracusan cavalry, followed afterwards by all the infantry together. They first marched close up to the Athenian army and then, finding that it did not offer to engage, crossed the Helorine road[3a] and camped for the night.

The next day the Athenians and their allies prepared for battle, their dispositions being as follows:—Their right wing was occupied by the Argives and Mantineans, the center by the Athenians, and the rest of the field by the other allies. Half their army was drawn up eight deep in advance, half close to their tents in a hollow square, formed also eight deep, which had orders to look out and be ready to go to the support of the troops hardest pressed. The camp followers were placed inside this reserve. [2] The Syracusans, meanwhile, formed their hoplites sixteen deep, consisting of the mass levy of their own people, and such allies as had joined them, the strongest contingent being that of the Selinuntines; next to them the cavalry of the Geloans, numbering two hundred in all, with about twenty horse and fifty archers from Camarina.[2a] The cavalry, full twelve hundred strong, was posted on their right, and next to it the darters. [3] As the Athenians were about to begin the attack, Nicias went along the lines, and addressed these words of encouragement to the army and the nations composing it:

6.67
415/4
17th Year/Winter
SYRACUSE
The battle order of both armies is described. Nicias speaks to his army.

"Soldiers, a long exhortation is little needed by men like ourselves, who are here to fight in the same battle, the force itself being, to my thinking, more fit to inspire confidence than a fine speech with a weak army. [2] Where we have Argives, Mantineans, Athenians, and the first of the islanders in the ranks together, it were strange indeed, with so many and so brave companions in arms, if we did not feel confident of victory; especially when we have mass levies opposed to our picked troops, and what is more, Sicilians, who may disdain us but will not stand against us, their skill not being at all commensurate to their rashness. [3] You may also remember that we are far from home and have no friendly land near, except what your own swords shall win you; and here I put before you a motive just the reverse of that to which the enemy are appealing; their cry being that they shall fight for their country, mine that we shall fight for a

6.68
415/4
17th Year/Winter
SYRACUSE
After deprecating the enemy, Nicias warns that Athens and her allies must win a place in Sicily by the sword, and that the enemy's superior cavalry will make retreat impossible.

6.66.2a   Fort Daskon: Map 6.68.
6.66.2b   Anapus River: Map 6.68.
6.66.3a   Helorine Road, the road connecting
             Syracuse and Helorus: Map 6.68.
6.67.2a   Selinus, Gela, Camarina: Map 6.64.

Map 6.68 The Battle at the Anapus River

country that is not ours, where we must conquer or hardly get away, as we shall have their horse upon us in great numbers. [4] Remember, therefore, your renown, and go boldly against the enemy, thinking the present difficulty and necessity more terrible than they."

6.69
415/4
17th Year/Winter
SYRACUSE
An Athenian advance takes the Syracusans by surprise but they form lines to meet it. They lack practice but not zeal or courage. Thucydides describes the motivations of both forces.

After this address Nicias at once led on the army. The Syracusans were not at that moment expecting an immediate engagement, and some had even gone away to the city, which was close by; these now ran up as fast as they could, and though late, took their places here or there in the main body as they joined it. Lack of zeal or daring was certainly not the fault of the Syracusans, either in this or the other battles, but although not inferior in courage for as long as their military science proved adequate, when this failed them, they were compelled to give up their resolution also. On the present occasion, although they had not supposed that the Athenians would begin the attack, and although constrained to stand upon their defense at short notice, they at once took up their arms and advanced to meet them. [2] First, the stone-throwers, slingers, and archers of either army began skirmishing, and routed or were routed by one another, as might be expected between light troops; next, soothsayers brought forward the usual victims, and trumpeters urged on the hoplites to the charge; [3] and thus they advanced, the Syracusans to fight for their country, and each individual for his safety that day and liberty hereafter. In the enemy's army, the Athenians sought to make another's country theirs and to save their own from suffering by their defeat; the Argives and independent allies aimed to help them in getting what they came for, and to earn by victory another sight of the country they had left behind; while the subject allies owed most of their ardor to the desire for self-preservation, which they could only hope for if victorious and, as a secondary motive, for the chance of serving on easier terms after helping the Athenians to a fresh conquest.

The armies now came to close quarters, and for a long while fought without either giving ground. Meanwhile there occurred some claps of thunder with lightning and heavy rain, which did not fail to add to the fears of the party fighting for the first time, and very little acquainted with war; while to their more experienced adversaries these phenomena appeared to be produced by the time of year, and much more alarm was felt at the continued resistance of the enemy. [2] At last the Argives drove in the Syracusan left, and after them the Athenians routed the troops opposed to them, and the Syracusan army was thus cut in two and betook itself to flight. [3] The Athenians did not pursue far, being held in check by the numerous and undefeated Syracusan horse, who attacked and drove back any of their hoplites whom they saw pursuing in advance of the rest; in spite of which the victors followed as far as was safe in a body, and then went back and set up a trophy.[3a] [4] Meanwhile the Syracusans rallied at the Helorine road,[4a] where they reformed as well as they could under the circumstances, and even sent a garrison of their own citizens to the Olympieum,[4b] fearing that the Athenians might lay hands on some of the treasures there. The rest returned to the city.

The Athenians, however, did not go to the temple, but collected their dead and laid them upon a pyre, and passed the night upon the field. The next day they gave the enemy back their dead under truce,[1a] to the number

6.70 415/4 17th Year/Winter SYRACUSE The battle goes evenly until a thunderstorm disconcerts the inexperienced Syracusans, who are pushed back and then routed. Syracusan cavalry prevents pursuit.	

6.71
415/4
17th Year/Winter
CATANA
After returning the enemy dead under truce, the Athenians sail to Catana and make preparations for a spring campaign against Syracuse.

6.70.3a   A trophy was set up by the victors after an ancient Greek battle. It usually consisted of a set of captured armor arranged on a pole that was raised on or near the battlefield.
6.70.4a   Helorine Road, the road connecting Syracuse and Helorus: Map 6.68.
6.70.4b   Olympieum sanctuary: Map 6.68.
6.71.1a   After a battle in ancient Greece, the vic-

tors would gather up their dead, strip those of the enemy, and raise a trophy. The defeated would collect the bodies of their fallen during a truce that they would explicitly request and be granted for that purpose. In this way, appropriate reverence was shown and proper burial was accorded to all war dead. See Appendix F, *Land Warfare,* §6.

of about two hundred and sixty, Syracusans and allies, and gathered together the bones of their own, some fifty, Athenians and allies, and taking the spoils of the enemy, sailed back to Catana.[1b] [2] It was now winter; and it did not seem possible for the moment to carry on the war so near Syracuse[2a] until cavalrymen had been sent for from Athens[2b] and levied among the allies in Sicily[2c]—to do away with their utter inferiority in cavalry—and money had been collected in the country and received from Athens; and until some of the cities, which they hoped would now be more disposed to listen to them after the battle, had been brought over, and grain and all other necessities provided for a campaign in the spring against Syracuse.

With this intention they sailed off to Naxos and Catana[1a] for the winter. Meanwhile the Syracusans burned their dead, and then held an assembly, [2] in which Hermocrates son of Hermon, a man who with a general ability of the first order had given proofs of military capacity and brilliant courage in the war, came forward and encouraged them, and told them not to let what had occurred make them give way, [3] since their spirit had not been conquered, but their want of discipline had done the mischief. Still they had not been beaten by so much as might have been expected, especially as they were, one might say, novices in the art of war, an army of artisans opposed to the most experienced soldiers in Hellas. [4] What had also done great harm was the number of the generals (there were fifteen of them) and the quantity of orders given, combined with the disorder and insubordination of the troops. But if they were to have a few skillful generals, and used this winter in preparing their hoplites, finding arms for such as had not got any so as to make them as numerous as possible, and forcing them to attend to their training generally, they would have every chance of beating their adversaries, courage being already theirs and discipline in the field having thus been added to it. Indeed, both these qualities would improve, since danger would exercise them in discipline, while their courage would be led to surpass itself by the confidence which skill inspires. [5] The generals should be few and elected with full powers, and an oath should be taken to leave them entire discretion in their command: if they adopted this plan, their secrets would be better kept, all preparations would be properly made, and there would be no room for excuses.

The Syracusans heard him, and voted everything as he advised, and elected three generals, Hermocrates himself, Heraclides son of Lysimachus, and Sicanus son of Execestes. [2] They also sent envoys to Corinth and

6.72
415/4
17th Year/Winter
SYRACUSE
Speaking to a Syracusan assembly, Hermocrates says the army had done unexpectedly well against the Athenians, and will improve with better arms and training. He calls for a reform of the army's command structure.

6.73
415/4
17th Year/Winter
SYRACUSE
Syracuse requests aid from Corinth and Sparta.

6.71.1b   Catana, Sicily: Map 6.75.
6.71.2a   Syracuse, Sicily: Map 6.75 and inset.
6.71.2b   Athens: Map 6.75.
6.71.2c   Sicily: Map 6.75.
6.72.1a   Naxos and Catana, Sicily: Map 6.75.

Sparta to procure a force of allies to join them, and to induce the Spartans for their sakes to address themselves more seriously to the war against the Athenians, that they might either have to leave Sicily or be less able to send reinforcements to their army there.

The Athenian forces at Catana now at once sailed against Messana[1a] in the expectation that it would be betrayed to them. The intrigue, however, came to nothing, for Alcibiades, who had known the secret when he left his command upon the summons from home, foreseeing that he would be outlawed, gave information about the plot to the friends of the Syracusans in Messana, who had at once put to death its authors, and now rose in arms with those who supported them against the opposing faction and succeeded in preventing the admission of the Athenians. [2] The latter waited for thirteen days, and then, as they were exposed to the weather and without provisions, and met with no success, went back to Naxos,[2a] where they made places for their ships to lie in, erected a palisade round their camp, and retired into winter quarters; meanwhile they sent a trireme to Athens asking that money and cavalrymen be sent to them in the spring. [6.75.1] During the winter the Syracusans built a wall onto the city,[1a] so as to enclose the statue of Apollo Temenites,[1b] all along the side facing Epipolae,[1c] in order to make the task of circumvallation[1d] longer and more difficult, in case of their being defeated. They also erected a fort at Megara[1e] and another in the Olympieum,[1f] and stuck palisades along the sea wherever there was a landing place. [2] Meanwhile, as they knew that the Athenians were wintering at Naxos,[2a] they marched with all their people to Catana[2b] and ravaged the land and set fire to the tents and encampment of the Athenians, and so returned home. [3] Learning also that the Athenians were sending emissaries to Camarina[3a] on the strength of the alliance that had been concluded in the time of Laches,[3b] in order to gain that city, if possible, they also sent envoys from Syracuse to oppose them. They had a shrewd suspicion that the Camarinaeans had not provided the aid they did send for the first battle very willingly; and they now feared that they would refuse to assist them at all in future, after seeing the success of the Athenians in the action, and would join the latter on the strength of their old friendship. [4] Hermocrates, with some others, accordingly arrived at Camarina from Syracuse, and Euphemus and others from the Athenians; and an assembly of the Camarinaeans having been convened, Hermocrates spoke as follows, in the hope of prejudicing them against the Athenians:

6.74
415/4
17th Year/Winter
MESSANA
A plot to betray Messana to the Athenians is revealed by Alcibiades, and fails. The Athenians winter in Naxos and send to Athens for cavalry and money.

6.75
415/4
17th Year/Winter
SYRACUSE
The Syracusans extend their city walls and fortify key places.
CAMARINA
Learning that the Athenians are sending envoys to Camarina, the Syracusans send Hermocrates there to speak on their behalf to the assembly.

6.74.1a   Catana and Messana, Sicily: Map 6.75.
6.74.2a   Naxos, Sicily: Map 6.75.
6.75.1a   Approximate location of new wall built in the winter of 415/4: Map 6.75, inset.
6.75.1b   Temenites district of Syracuse: Map 6.75, inset.
6.75.1c   Epipolae, a plateau overlooking Syracuse: Map 6.75, inset.
6.75.1d   Circumvallation: the building of a wall to surround or isolate a city by land.
6.75.1e   Megara Hyblaea, Sicily: Map 6.75.

6.75.1f   Olympieum sanctuary: Map 6.75, inset.
6.75.2a   Naxos, Sicily: Map 6.75.
6.75.2b   Catana, Sicily: Map 6.75.
6.75.3a   Camarina, Sicily: Map 6.75.
6.75.3b   For operations while Laches was in Sicily, see 3.86.1, 3.90.2, and 3.115.2; Thucydides mentions no treaties of alliance, although he writes in 5.5.3 that all the allies of Syracuse, except the Locrians, made peace with Athens when the reconciliation between the Sicilians took place.

MAP 6.75 FURTHER MILITARY OPERATIONS, WINTER OF 415/4 [4a]

6.76
415/4
17th Year/Winter
CAMARINA
Hermocrates warns the
Camarinaeans that the
Athenians are not in Sicily to
return the Leontines as they
say, but to expand their rule
in the west by the same
methods they employed to
develop their empire in Ionia
and Hellas.

"Camarinaeans, we did not come on this embassy because we were afraid of your being frightened by the actual forces of the Athenians, but rather of your being won over by what they would say to you before you heard anything from us. [2] They have come to Sicily with the pretext that you know, and the intention which we all suspect, in my opinion less to restore the Leontines[2a] to their homes than to oust us from ours; as it is beyond all reason that they should restore in Sicily the cities that they lay waste in Hellas, or should cherish the Leontine Chalcidians because of their Ionian blood, and keep in servitude the Euboean[2b] Chalcidians, of whom the Leontines are a colony. [3] No; it is the very same policy which has proved so successful in Hellas that is now being tried in Sicily. After being chosen as the leaders of the Ionians and of the other allies of Athenian origin in the struggle to punish the Persians, the Athenians accused some allies of failure in military service, some of fighting against each other, and others, as the case might be, upon any specious pretext that could be found, until they thus subdued them all. [4] In short, in the struggle against the Persian, the Athenians did not fight for the liberty of the Hellenes, or the Hellenes for their own liberty, but the former to make their countrymen serve them instead of him, the

6.75.4a The new Syracusan wall in Map 6.75,
         inset, basically follows the interpretation
         of Peter Green in *Armada from Athens*
         (Hodder and Stoughton, 1971), passim.
         The reader should be aware that many
         scholars follow the quite different views

expressed in A.W. Gomme, A. Andrewes,
and K.J. Dover, *A Historical Commentary on Thucydides*, iv (Oxford, 1970),
466 ff.
6.76.2a Leontini, Sicily: Map 6.75.
6.76.2b Euboea, Map 6.75.

latter to change one master for another, wiser indeed than the first, but wiser for evil."

"But we have not now come to declare to an audience familiar with them the misdeeds of a state so open to accusation as is the Athenian, but much rather to blame ourselves, who, with the warnings we possess in the Hellenes in those parts that have been enslaved through not supporting each other, and seeing the same sophisms being now tried upon ourselves—such as restorations of Leontine kinsfolk and support of Egestaean[1a] allies—do not stand together and resolutely show them that here are no Ionians, or Hellespontines, or islanders, who change continually, but always serve a master, sometimes the Mede[1b] and sometimes some other, but free Dorians from the independent Peloponnesus, dwelling in Sicily.[1c] [2] Or, are we waiting until we be taken in detail, one city after another; knowing as we do that in no other way can we be conquered, and seeing that they turn to this plan, so as to divide some of us by words, to draw some by the bait of an alliance into open war with each other, and to ruin others by such flattery as different circumstances may render acceptable? And do we suppose when destruction first overtakes a distant fellow countryman that the danger will not come to each of us also, or that he who suffers before us will suffer himself alone?"

"As for the Camarinaean who says that it is the Syracusan, not he, who is the enemy of the Athenian, and thinks it awful to have to encounter risk on behalf of my country, I would have him bear in mind that he will fight in my country not more for mine than for his own, and will do so much more safely in that he will enter the struggle not alone, after the way has been cleared by my ruin, but with me as his ally; and that the object of the Athenian is not so much to punish the enmity of the Syracusan as to use me as an excuse to secure the friendship of the Camarinaean. [2] As for him who envies or even fears us (and envied and feared great powers must always be), and who on this account wishes Syracuse to be humbled to teach us a lesson, but would still have her survive in the interest of his own security, the wish that he indulges is not humanly possible. A man can control his own desires but he cannot likewise control circumstances; and in the event of his calculations proving mistaken, he may live to bewail his own misfortune, and wish to be again envying my prosperity. [3] An idle wish, if he now sacrifice us and refuse to take his share of perils which are the same in reality, though not in name, for him

6.77
415/4
17th Year/Winter
CAMARINA
Hermocrates blames the Sicilians for not uniting against an obvious foreign threat, and thus permitting Athens to hope to conquer them one by one.

6.78
415/4
17th Year/Winter
CAMARINA
Addressing those Camarinaeans who envy or resent Syracuse, Hermocrates points out that by aiding Syracuse against the Athenians, Camarina will be defending itself against the same enemy, who if strengthened by the fall of Syracuse will soon come against them.

6.77.1a   Egesta, Sicily: Map 6.75.
6.77.1b   The "Mede" here is the Persians; see Appendix E, §1.
6.77.1c   For the Ionians and the Dorians, see Appendix H, Dialects and Ethnic Groups, §8.

as for us; what is nominally the preservation of our power being really his own salvation. [4] It was to be expected that you, of all people in the world, Camarinaeans, being our immediate neighbors and the next in danger, would have foreseen this, and instead of supporting us in the lukewarm way that you are now doing, would rather have come to us of your own accord and be now offering at Syracuse the aid which you would have asked of us for Camarina[4a] (if the Athenians had first come to Camarina), in order to encourage us to resist the invader. Neither you, however, nor the rest have as yet bestirred yourselves in this direction."

"Fear perhaps will make you seek to do right both by us and by the invaders, and plead that you have an alliance with the Athenians. But you made that alliance, not against your friends, but against the enemies that might attack you, and to help the Athenians when they were wronged by others, not when as now they are wronging their neighbors. [2] Even the Rhegians,[2a] Chalcidians though they be, refuse to help to restore the Chalcidian Leontines;[2b] and it would be strange if, while they suspect the truth behind this fine pretense and are wise without reason, you, with every reason on your side, should yet choose to assist your natural enemies, and should join with their direst foes in undoing those whom nature has made your own kinsfolk. [3] This is not right; you should help us without fear of their armament, which has no terrors if we hold together, but only if we let them succeed in their endeavors to separate us; indeed, even after attacking us by ourselves and being victorious in battle, they had to go off without accomplishing their purpose."

"United, therefore, we have no cause to despair, but rather new encouragement to league together; especially as help will come to us from the Peloponnesians, who are in military matters the undoubted superiors of the Athenians. And you need not think that your prudent policy of taking sides with neither, because allies of both, is either safe for you or fair to us. [2] Practically it is not as fair as it pretends to be. If the vanquished be defeated, and the victor conquer, through your refusing to join, what is the effect of your abstention but to leave the former to perish unaided, and to allow the latter to offend unhindered? And yet it were more honorable to join those who are not only the injured party, but your own kindred, and by doing so to defend the common interests of Sicily and save your friends the Athenians from doing wrong."

"[3] In conclusion, we Syracusans say that it is useless for us to demonstrate either to you or to the rest what you know already as

6.79
415/4
17th Year/Winter
CAMARINA
Hermocrates says it would be unnatural for Camarina to support Chalcidians when other Sicilian Chalcidians will not do so, and to maintain a neutrality harmful to Syracuse. He reminds them that last year Syracuse beat off the Athenians by herself.

6.80
415/4
17th Year/Winter
CAMARINA
Hermocrates concludes by saying that a neutrality that harms one side is not necessarily a fair or safe policy; that Camarina's failure to help Syracuse will lead to permanent Syracusan enmity; and that continued neutrality will result in Camarina's submission to Athenian rule. He entreats the Camarinaeans to assist Syracuse now.

6.78.4a Camarina, Sicily: Map 6.75.
6.79.2a Rhegium, Sicily: Map 6.75.
6.79.2b Leontini, Sicily: Map 6.75.

well as we do; but we entreat, and if our entreaty fail, we protest that we are menaced by our eternal enemies the Ionians, and are betrayed by you our fellow Dorians.[3a] [4] If the Athenians reduce us, they will owe their victory to your decision, but in their own name will reap the honor, and will receive as the prize of their triumph the very men who enabled them to gain it. On the other hand, if we are the conquerors, you will have to pay for having been the cause of our danger. Consider, therefore; and now make your choice between the security which present servitude offers and the prospect of conquering with us and thereby escaping disgraceful submission to an Athenian master and avoiding the lasting enmity of Syracuse."

Such were the words of Hermocrates; after whom Euphemus, the Athenian ambassador, spoke as follows:

"Although we came here only to renew the former alliance,[1a] the attack of the Syracusans compels us to speak of our empire and of the good right we have to it. [2] The best proof of this the speaker himself furnished, when he called the Ionians eternal enemies of the Dorians. That is true; and since the Peloponnesian Dorians are our superiors in numbers and near neighbors, we Ionians looked out for the best means of escaping their domination. [3] After the Persian war we had a fleet, and so got rid of the empire and the supremacy of the Spartans, who had no right to give orders to us more than we to them, except that of being the strongest at that moment; and we being appointed leaders of the King's[3a] former subjects, and continuing to be so, think that we are least likely to fall under the dominion of the Peloponnesians if we have sufficient force with which to defend ourselves. And in strict truth having done nothing unfair in reducing to subjection the Ionians and islanders, the kinsfolk whom the Syracusans say we have enslaved. [4] They, our kinsfolk, came against their mother country, that is to say against us, together with the Mede, and instead of having the courage to revolt and sacrifice their property as we did when we abandoned our city, chose to be slaves themselves, and to try to make us slaves too."

"We, therefore, deserve to rule because we placed the largest fleet and an unflinching patriotism at the service of the Hellenes, and because these, our subjects, did us harm by their ready subservience to the Persians; and, quite apart from that we seek to strengthen ourselves against the Peloponnesians. [2] We make no fine professions of having a right to rule because we overthrew the barbarian single-

6.81

6.82
415
17th Year/Winter
CAMARINA
The Athenian Euphemus responds to Hermocrates by describing the Athenian empire as an Ionian defense against a stronger Dorian confederacy. He defends Athens' hegemony as a just reward for having risked all against Persia.

6.83
415/4
17th Year/Winter
CAMARINA
Euphemus says Athens has come to Sicily to increase its security, which coincides with Camarina's interests; and argues that fear of domination has led Athens to empire and to Sicily, not a desire to enslave others.

6.80.3a   Although this speech seems to suggest that there was a sharp ethnic division between the combatants, with Athens allied with Ionians, and Syracuse allied with Dorians, Thucydides will later (7.57–58)

emphasize the ethnic paradoxes of the contending armies in Sicily. See Appendix H, Dialects and Ethnic Groups, §7, 9.
6.82.1a   Former alliance: see note 6.75.3b.
6.82.3a   The Persian King: see Appendix E, §2.

handed, or because we risked what we did risk for the freedom of the subjects in question any more than for that of all, and for our own: no one can be censured for providing for his own safety. If we are now here in Sicily, it is equally in the interest of our security, with which we perceive that your interest also coincides. [3] We prove this from the conduct which the Syracusans cast against us and which you somewhat too fearfully suspect; knowing that those whom fear has made suspicious, may be carried away by the charm of eloquence for the moment, but when they come to act follow their interests."

[4] "Now, as we have said, fear makes us hold our empire in Hellas, and fear makes us now come, with the help of our friends, to safely order matters in Sicily, and not to enslave any but rather to prevent any from being enslaved. [6.84.1] Meanwhile, let no one imagine that it is none of our business to be interested in you, seeing that if you are preserved and able to hold out against the Syracusans, they will be less likely to harm us by sending troops to the Peloponnesians. [2] In this way you have everything to do with us, and on this account it is perfectly reasonable for us to restore the Leontines,[2a] and to make them, not subjects like their kinsmen in Euboea,[2b] but as powerful as possible, to help us by causing trouble for the Syracusans from their frontier. [3] In Hellas we are alone a match for our enemies; and as for the assertion that it is beyond all reason that we should free the Sicilian, while we enslave the Chalcidian, the fact is that the latter is useful to us by being without arms and contributing money only; while the former, the Leontines and our other friends, cannot be too independent."

"Besides, for tyrants and imperial cities nothing is unreasonable if expedient, no one a kinsman unless sure; but friendship or enmity is everywhere a matter of time and circumstance. Here, in Sicily, our interest is not to weaken our friends, but by means of their strength to cripple our enemies. Why doubt this? In Hellas we treat our allies as we find them useful. [2] The Chians[2a] and Methymnians[2b] govern themselves and furnish ships; most of the rest have harder terms and pay tribute in money; while others, although islanders who would be easy for us to take, are free altogether, because they occupy convenient positions round the Peloponnesus.[2c] [3] In our settlement of the states here in Sicily, we should, therefore, naturally be guided by our interest, and by fear, as we say, of the Syracusans.[3a] Their ambition is to rule you, their plan is to use the suspicions that we excite to

---

6.84
415/4
17th Year/Winter
CAMARINA
Euphemus asserts that Athens supports all Sicilians hostile to Syracuse because their independence will preoccupy her and prevent her from aiding the Peloponnesians.

6.85
415/4
17th Year/Winter
CAMARINA
Euphemus insists that expedience determines friendship for hegemonic powers. As she does in Hellas, Athens will build up independent states here to prevent Syracuse from achieving hegemony.

6.84.2a Leontini: Map 6.88.
6.84.2b Euboea: Map 6.91.
6.85.2a Chios: Map 6.56.
6.85.2b Methymna, a city on the island of Lesbos: Map 6.56. The other cities on the island of Lesbos revolted from Athens in 428, were conquered, and reduced to subject status; see 3.2–19, 3.26–50.

6.85.2c Peloponnesus: Map 6.91. The free islands mentioned here are Zacynthus, Cephallenia, and Corcyra, Map 6.95, Hellas inset.
6.85.3a Syracuse: Map 6.88.

unite you, and then, when we have gone away without effecting anything, by force or through your isolation, to become the masters of Sicily. And masters they must become, if you unite with them; as a force of that magnitude would no longer be easy for us to deal with united, and they would be more than a match for you as soon as we were away."

"Any other view of the case is condemned by the facts. When you first asked us over,[1a] the fear which you held out was that of danger to Athens if we let you come under the dominion of Syracuse; [2] and it is not right now to mistrust the very same argument by which you claimed to convince us, or to give way to suspicion because we have come with a larger force against the power of that city. Those whom you should really distrust are the Syracusans. [3] We are not able to stay here without you, and if we proved perfidious enough to bring you into subjection, we should be unable to keep you in bondage, owing to the length of the voyage and the difficulty of guarding large, and in a military sense mainland, cities. The Syracusans live close to you, not in a camp, but in a city greater than the force we have with us. They plot always against you, never let slip an opportunity once offered, [4] as they have shown in the case of the Leontines and others; and now they have the effrontery just as if you were fools, to invite you to aid them against the power that hinders this, and that has thus far maintained Sicily independent. [5] We, as against them, invite you to a much more real safety, when we beg you not to betray that common security that we provide for each other and to reflect that they, even without allies, will, by their numbers, always have the way open to you, while you will not often have the opportunity of defending yourselves with such numerous auxiliaries; if, through your suspicions, you once let us go away unsuccessful or defeated, you will wish to see us back again, if only a handful, when the day is past in which our presence could do anything for you."

"But we hope, Camarinaeans,[1a] that the calumnies of the Syracusans will not be allowed to succeed either with you or with the rest: we have told you the whole truth upon the things we are suspected of, and will now briefly recapitulate, in the hope of convincing you. [2] We assert that we are rulers in Hellas in order not to be subjects; liberators in Sicily that we may not be harmed by the Sicilians; that we are compelled to interfere in many things, because we have many

6.86
415/4
17th Year/Winter
CAMARINA
Euphemus points out that Athens is far from Sicily and would be unable to hold Sicilian cities subject, whereas Syracuse is a near, powerful, and constant threat. Thus alliance with Athens is the natural and correct course for Camarina, despite the large force that Athens has sent to Sicily.

6.87
415/4
17th Year/Winter
CAMARINA
Euphemus concludes that Athens' actions are defensive only—intended to guard and protect itself—and that this policy is in the interest of free Greeks everywhere as it restrains aggression by such potential hegemonists as Syracuse.

6.86.1a   In 427: see 3.86.2.
6.87.1a   Camarina: Map 6.88.

things to guard against; and that now, as before, we are come as allies to those of you who suffer wrong in this island, not without invitation but upon invitation. [3] Accordingly, instead of making yourselves judges or censors of our conduct, and trying to turn us (which it were now difficult to do), so far as there is anything in our interfering policy or in our character, that accords with your interest, this take and make use of it; and be sure that far from being injurious to all alike, to most of the Hellenes that policy is even beneficial. [4] Thanks to it, all men in all places, even where we are not, who either fear or plan aggression, from the near prospect before them, in the one case, of obtaining our intervention in their favor, in the other, of our arrival making the venture dangerous, find themselves constrained, respectively, to be moderate against their will, and to be preserved without effort of their own. [5] Do not you reject this security that is open to all who desire it, and is now offered to you; but do like others, and instead of being always on the defensive against the Syracusans, unite with us, and in your turn at last threaten them."

6.88
415/4
17th Year/Winter
CAMARINA
Camarina decides to remain neutral, but to give limited aid to Syracuse in fear that she is nearby and will win.
CATANA
The Athenians obtain support and some new allies among the Sicels. They transfer their winter base to Catana.
PELOPONNESUS
The Syracusans send for help to the Italians, the Corinthians, and the Spartans. Corinth responds enthusiastically but Sparta refuses aid. Alcibiades, having just arrived, speaks to the Spartans to urge them to act.

Such were the words of Euphemus. What the Camarinaeans felt was this. They sympathized with the Athenians, except insofar as they might be afraid of their subjugating Sicily, and they had always been at enmity with their neighbor Syracuse. From the very fact, however, that they were their neighbors, they feared the Syracusans most of the two, and being apprehensive that the Syracusans might win even without their help, both sent them in the first instance the few horsemen mentioned[1a] and for the future determined to support them most in fact, although as sparingly as possible; but for the moment in order not to seem to slight the Athenians, especially as they had been successful in the engagement, to answer both alike. [2] In accordance with this resolution they answered that as both the contending parties happened to be allies of theirs, they thought it most consistent with their oaths, at present, to side with neither; with which answer the ambassadors of each party departed.

[3] In the meantime, while Syracuse pursued her preparations for war, the Athenians were encamped at Naxos,[3a] and tried by negotiation to gain as many of the Sicels as possible. [4] Those more in the lowlands, and subjects of Syracuse, mostly held aloof; but the peoples of the interior who had never been otherwise than independent, with few exceptions, at once joined the Athenians, and brought down grain to the army, and in some cases even money. [5] The Athenians marched against those who refused to join, and forced some of them to do so; in the case of others they were stopped by the Syracusans sending garrisons and reinforcements. Mean-

6.88.1a Thucydides wrote in 6.67.2 that Camarina had sent about twenty horse and fifty archers to Syracuse.

6.88.3a Naxos: Map 6.88.

MAP 6.88 FINAL MILITARY OPERATIONS, WINTER OF 415/4

while the Athenians moved their winter quarters from Naxos to Catana,[5a] and reconstructed the camp burnt by the Syracusans, and stayed there the rest of the winter. [6] They also sent a trireme to Carthage,[6a] with offers of friendship, on the chance of obtaining assistance, and another to Tyrrhenia;[6b] some of the cities there having spontaneously offered to join them in the war. They also sent round to the Sicels and to Egesta,[6c] desiring them to send them as many horses as possible, and meanwhile prepared bricks, iron, and all other things necessary for the work of circumvallation,[6d] intending by the spring to begin hostilities.

6.88.5a Catana: Map 6.88.
6.88.6a Carthage: Map 6.88.
6.88.6b Tyrrhenia (Etruria): Map 6.88.

6.88.6c Egesta: Map 6.88.
6.88.6d Circumvallation: the building of a wall to surround or isolate a city by land.

[7] In the meantime the Syracusan envoys that had been dispatched to Corinth and Sparta[7a] tried as they passed along the coast to persuade the Italians to interfere with the proceedings of the Athenians which, they argued, threatened Italy quite as much as Syracuse, and having arrived at Corinth made a speech calling on the Corinthians to assist them on the ground of their common origin. [8] The Corinthians voted at once to aid them unstintingly themselves, and then sent on envoys with them to Sparta, to help them to persuade her also to prosecute the war with the Athenians more openly at home and to send assistance to Sicily. [9] The envoys from Corinth having reached Sparta found Alcibiades there with his fellow refugees, who had without delay crossed over in a trading vessel from Thurii, first to Cyllene in Elis,[9a] and afterwards from there to Sparta; upon the Spartans' own invitation, after first obtaining a safe conduct, as he feared them for the part he had taken in the affair of Mantinea.[9b] [10] The result was that the Corinthians, Syracusans, and Alcibiades, all pressing the same request in the assembly of the Spartans, succeeded in persuading them; but as the *ephors* and the authorities,[10a] although resolved to send envoys to Syracuse to prevent them surrendering to the Athenians, showed no inclination to send them any assistance, Alcibiades now came forward and inflamed and stirred the Spartans by speaking as follows:

6.89
415/4
17th Year/Winter
SPARTA
Alcibiades addresses his Spartan critics and justifies his past actions against Sparta. He explains his role in Athenian politics. He agrees that democracy is absurd, but that it was successful at Athens, that he had inherited it there, and that it could not be altered in the face of Spartan pressure.

"I am forced first to speak to you of the prejudice with which I am regarded, in order that suspicion may not make you disinclined to listen to me upon public matters. [2] The connection with you as your *proxeni*[2a] which the ancestors of our family by reason of some discontent renounced, I personally tried to renew by my good offices toward you, in particular upon the occasion of the disaster at Pylos.[2b] But although I maintained this friendly attitude, you yet chose to negotiate the peace with the Athenians through my enemies, and thus to strengthen them and to discredit me. [3] You had therefore no right to complain if I turned to the Mantineans and Argives, and seized other occasions of thwarting and injuring you; and the time has now come when those among you, who in the bitterness of the moment may have been then unfairly angry with me, should look at the matter in its true light, and take a different view. Those again who judged me unfavorably, because I leaned rather to the side of The People must not think that their dislike is any better founded. [4] We have always been hostile to tyrants, and all who oppose arbitrary power are called The People; hence we continued to act as

6.88.7a The dispatch of these envoys was mentioned in 6.73.2.
6.88.9a He sailed from Thurii, Italy (Map 6.88) to Cyllene in Elis (Map 6.91). See also Map 6.64, locator.
6.88.9b Mantinea: Map 6.91. The "affair" is the campaign and battle described by Thucydides in 5.61–75.

6.88.10a For the Spartan assembly and *ephors*, see Appendix C, Spartan Institutions, §5–6.
6.89.2a A *proxenus*, although a citizen and resident of his own state, served as a "friend or representative" (much like a modern honorary consul) of a foreign state.
6.89.2b Pylos: Map 6.91. The Spartan "disaster at Pylos" is described by Thucydides in 4.2–41.

leaders of the multitude; besides which, as democracy was the government of the city, it was necessary in most things to conform to established conditions. [5] However, we endeavored to be more moderate than the licentious temper of the times; and while there were others, formerly as now, who tried to lead the multitude astray (the same who banished me), [6] our party was that of the whole people, our creed being to do our part in preserving the form of government under which the city enjoyed the utmost greatness and freedom, and which we had found existing. As for democracy, the men of sense among us knew what it was, and I perhaps as well as any, as I have more cause to complain of it; but there is nothing new to be said of a patent absurdity—meanwhile we did not think it safe to alter it under the pressure of your hostility."

"So much then for the prejudices with which I am regarded: I now can call your attention to the questions you must consider, and upon which superior knowledge perhaps permits me to speak. [2] We sailed to Sicily first to conquer, if possible, the Sicilians, and after them the Italians also, and finally to assail the empire and city of Carthage.[2a] [3] In the event of all or most of these schemes succeeding, we were then to attack the Peloponnesus, bringing with us the entire force of the Hellenes lately acquired in those parts, and taking a number of barbarians into our pay, such as the Iberians[3a] and others in those countries, recognized as the most warlike known, and building numerous triremes in addition to those which we had already (timber being plentiful in Italy); and with this fleet blockading the Peloponnesus from the sea and assailing it with our armies by land, taking some of the cities by storm, and besieging others, we hoped without difficulty to defeat them completely and after this to rule the whole of the Hellenic world. [4] Money and grain for the better execution of these plans were to be supplied in sufficient quantities by the newly acquired places in those countries, independently of our revenues here at home."

"You have thus heard the history of the present expedition from the man who most exactly knows what our intentions were; and the remaining generals will, if they can, carry these out just the same. But that the states in Sicily must succumb if you do not help them, I will now show. [2] Although the Sicilians, with all their inexperience, might even now be saved if their forces were united, the Syracusans alone, beaten already in one battle with all their people and block-

6.90.2a   Carthage: Map 6.88.
6.90.3a   Iberia: Map 6.4, locator.

6.90
415/4
17th Year/Winter
SPARTA
Alcibiades says that Athens' true purpose in Sicily is the conquest of all the Hellenes. She intends to use the resources gained by the conquest of Sicily and Italy, and from alliances with others, to return to the Peloponnesus in overwhelming force to reduce it city by city.

6.91
415/4
17th Year/Winter
SPARTA
Alcibiades reiterates that Sparta should act for Peloponnesian interests by preventing the fall of Syracuse. He urges the Spartans to fortify Decelea in Attica and to send troops and a general to Syracuse to lead a professional defense.

MAP 6.91 ALCIBIADES' FLIGHT AND SPEECH

aded from the sea, will be unable to withstand the Athenian armament that is now there. [3] But if Syracuse falls, all Sicily falls also,
and Italy immediately afterwards; and the danger which I just now
spoke of from that quarter will before long be upon you. [4] None
need therefore imagine that only Sicily is in question; the Peloponnesus will be so also, unless you speedily do as I tell you, and send on
board ship to Syracuse troops that shall be able to row their ships
themselves,[4a] and serve as hoplites the moment that they land; and
what I consider even more important than the troops, a *Spartiate*[4b]
as commanding officer to discipline the forces already on foot and to
compel shirkers to serve. The friends that you have already will thus

6.91.4a   Oarsmen were not often soldiers also, but
     sometimes (see 3.18.4) it made economic
     and/or military sense to man a ship with
     those who could both row at sea and
     fight as hoplites on land.

6.91.4b   A *Spartiate* is a full citizen of Sparta and a
     member of the highest Spartan military
     caste.

become more confident, and the waverers will be encouraged to join
you. [5] Meanwhile you must carry on the war here more openly, so
that the Syracusans, seeing that you do not forget them, may put
heart into their resistance, and that the Athenians may be less able to
reinforce their armament. [6] You must fortify Decelea in Attica,[6a]
the blow of which the Athenians are always most afraid and the only
one that they think they have not experienced in the present war; the
surest method of harming an enemy being to find out what he most
fears, and to choose this means of attacking him, since everyone naturally knows best his own weak points and fears accordingly. [7] The
fortification in question, while it benefits you, will create difficulties
for your adversaries, of which I shall pass over many, and shall only
mention the chief. Whatever property there is in the country will
most of it become yours, either by capture or surrender; and the
Athenians will at once be deprived of their revenues from the silver
mines at Laurium,[7a] of their present gains from their land and from
the law courts, and above all of the revenue from their allies, which
will be paid less regularly, as they lose their awe of Athens and see
you addressing yourselves with vigor to this war. [6.92.1] The zeal
and speed with which all this shall be done depends, Spartans, upon
yourselves; as to its possibility, I am quite confident, and I have little
fear of being mistaken."

[2] "Meanwhile I hope that none of you will think any the worse
of me if after having hitherto passed as a lover of my country, I now
actively join its worst enemies in attacking it, or will suspect what I
say as the fruit of an outlaw's enthusiasm. [3] I am an outlaw from
the iniquity of those who drove me forth, not, if you will be guided
by me, from your service: my worst enemies are not you who only
harmed your foes, but they who forced their friends to become enemies; [4] and love of country is what I do not feel when I am
wronged, but what I felt when secure in my rights as a citizen. Indeed I do not consider that I am now attacking a country that is still
mine; I am rather trying to recover one that is mine no longer; and
the true lover of his country is not he who consents to lose it unjustly rather than attack it, but he who longs for it so much that he
will go to all lengths to recover it. [5] For myself, therefore, Spartans, I beg you to use me without scruple for danger and trouble of
every kind, and to remember the argument in everyone's mouth,
that if I did you great harm as an enemy, I could likewise do you
good service as a friend, inasmuch as I know the plans of the Athenians, while I only guessed yours. For yourselves I entreat you to be-

6.92
415/4
17th Year/Winter
SPARTA
Alcibiades argues that he is
not a traitor because he
cannot betray a country from
which he was wrongfully
driven and which is no longer
his. Moreover, he adds, a true
patriot will go to any length,
even to aid his country's
enemies, in order to recover
it. He concludes by asking
the Spartans to use his
knowledge of Athens and
Athenian plans to their best
advantage.

6.91.6a   Decelea, in Attica: Map 6.91.
6.91.7a   Laurium, in Attica: Map 6.91.

lieve that your most vital interests are now under consideration; and I urge you to send without hesitation the expeditions to Sicily and Attica; by the presence of a small part of your forces you will save important cities in that island, and you will destroy the power of Athens both present and prospective; after this you will dwell in security and enjoy the supremacy over all Hellas, resting not on force but upon consent and affection."

6.93
415/4
17th Year/Winter
SPARTA
Moved by Alcibiades, the Spartans vote to aid the Sicilians and send Gylippus to take command there. They prepare to fortify Decelea in Attica.
ATHENS
Athens votes to send funds and reinforcements to their forces in Sicily.

Such were the words of Alcibiades. The Spartans, who had previously intended to march against Athens themselves, but were still waiting and looking about them, at once became much more serious when they received this particular information from Alcibiades, and considered that they had heard it from the man who best knew the truth of the matter. [2] Accordingly they now turned their attention to fortifying Decelea[2a] and sending immediate aid to the Sicilians; and naming Gylippus son of Cleandridas to the command of the Syracusans, instructed him to consult with that people and with the Corinthians[2b] and arrange for help to reach the island in the best and speediest way possible under the circumstances. [3] Gylippus requested the Corinthians to send him at once two ships to Asine,[3a] and to prepare the rest that they intended to send, and to have them ready to sail at the proper time. Having settled this, the envoys departed from Sparta.

[4] In the meantime the Athenian trireme from Sicily sent by the generals for money and cavalry arrived at Athens; and the Athenians, after hearing what they wanted, voted to send the supplies for the armament and the cavalry. And the winter ended, and with it ended the seventeenth year of the present war of which Thucydides is the historian.

6.94
414
18th Year/Summer
SICILY
The Athenians in early spring pillage some cities and coerce others to join them. At Catana, they find reinforcements of funds and horsemen sent from Athens.

The next summer, at the very beginning of the season, the Athenians in Sicily put out from Catana,[1a] and sailed along shore to Megara in Sicily, from which, as I have mentioned above, the Syracusans expelled the inhabitants in the time of their tyrant Gelon,[1b] themselves occupying the territory. [2] Here the Athenians landed and laid waste the country, and after an unsuccessful attack upon a fort of the Syracusans, went on with the fleet and army to the river Terias,[2a] and advancing inland laid waste the plain and set fire to the grain; and after killing some of a small Syracusan party which they encountered, and setting up a trophy, went back again to their ships. [3] They now sailed to Catana and took in provisions there, and going with their whole force against Centoripa,[3a] a city of the Sicels, acquired it by capitulation, and departed, after also burning the grain of the Inessaeans and Hybleans.[3c] [4] Upon their return to Catana they found the horsemen arrived from Athens, to the number of two hundred and fifty (with their

6.93.2a Decelea, in Attica: Map 6.91.
6.93.2b Corinth: Map 6.91.
6.93.3a Asine, probably in Messenia: Map 6.91.
6.94.1a Catana: Map 6.95, Sicily.
6.94.1b This expulsion by Gelon is mentioned in

6.4.2. Megara (Hyblaea): Map 6.95, Sicily.
6.94.2a Terias river: Map 6.95, Sicily.
6.94.3a Centoripa: Map 6.95, Sicily.
6.94.3c Inessa, Hybla, possible location: Map 6.95, Sicily.

MAP 6.95 MILITARY OPERATIONS IN SPRING 414

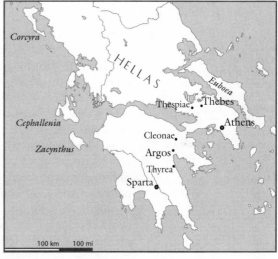

equipment, but without their horses which were to be procured upon the spot), and thirty mounted archers and three hundred talents of silver.[4a]

The same spring the Spartans marched against Argos and went as far as Cleonae,[1a] when an earthquake occurred and caused them to return. After this the Argives invaded the territory of Thyrea,[1b] which is on their border, and took much booty from the Spartans, which was sold for no less than twenty-five talents. [2] The same summer, not long after, the popular party in Thespiae made an attack upon the party in office, which was not successful, but help arrived from Thebes, and some were caught, while others took refuge at Athens.[2a]

The same summer the Syracusans learned that the Athenians had been joined by their cavalry and were on the point of marching against them; and seeing that without becoming masters of Epipolae,[1a] a precipitous spot situated exactly over the city, the Athenians could not, even if victorious in battle, easily invest them, they determined to guard its approaches in order

6.95
414
18th Year/Summer
HELLAS
Thucydides reports military raids and uprisings in Argos, Thyrea, and Boeotia.

6.96
414
18th Year/Summer
SYRACUSE
Syracuse decides that control of Epipolae is vital to its defense and selects six hundred picked troops to guard it.

6.94.4a   The talent was a unit of weight and of money; see Appendix J, Classical Greek Currency, §5.
6.95.1a   Argos, Cleonae: Map 6.95, Hellas.
6.95.1b   Thyrea: Map 6.95, Hellas.

6.95.2a   Thespiae, Thebes, Athens: Map 6.95, Hellas.
6.96.1a   Epipolae: Map 6.99, AX.

that the enemy might not ascend unobserved by these, the only ways by which ascent was possible, [2] as the remainder is lofty ground, and falls right down to the city, and can all be seen from inside; and as it lies above the rest the place is called by the Syracusans Epipolae, or Overtown.

[3] They accordingly went out in mass at daybreak into the meadow along the river Anapus,[3a] their new generals, Hermocrates and his colleagues, having just come into office, and held a review of their hoplites, from whom they first selected a picked body of six hundred, under the command of Diomilus, an exile from Andros,[3b] to guard Epipolae, and to be ready to muster at a moment's notice to help wherever help should be required.

Meanwhile the Athenians, the very same morning, were holding a review, having already made land unobserved with all the armament from Catana,[1a] opposite a place called Leon,[1b] not much more than half a mile from Epipolae,[1c] where they disembarked their army. They anchored their fleet at Thapsus,[1d] a peninsula running out into the sea with a narrow isthmus, and not far from the city of Syracuse either by land or water. [2] While the naval force of the Athenians threw a stockade across the isthmus and remained quiet at Thapsus, the army immediately went on at a run to Epipolae, and succeeded in getting up by Euryelus[2a] before the Syracusans perceived them, or could come up from the meadow and the review. [3] Diomilus with his six hundred and the rest advanced as quickly as they could, but they had nearly three miles to go from the meadow before reaching them. [4] Attacking in this way in considerable disorder, the Syracusans were defeated in battle at Epipolae and retired to the city, with a loss of about three hundred killed, and Diomilus among the number. [5] After this the Athenians set up a trophy and restored to the Syracusans their dead under truce, and next day descended to Syracuse itself; and no one coming out to meet them, reascended and built a fort at Labdalum,[5a] upon the edge of the cliffs of Epipolae, looking toward Megara,[5b] to serve as a storehouse for their baggage and money, whenever they advanced to give battle or to work at the lines.

Not long afterwards three hundred cavalry came to them from Egesta,[1a] and about a hundred from the Sicels, Naxians,[1b] and others; and thus, with the two hundred and fifty from Athens, for whom they had got horses from the Egestaeans and Catanians,[1c] besides others that they bought, they now mustered six hundred and fifty cavalry in all. [2] After posting a garrison in Labdalum,[2a] they advanced to Syca,[2b] where they halted and quickly built the Circle[2c] or center of their wall of circumvallation. The Syracusans,

MAP 6.99
THE ATHENIANS ATTACK
SYRACUSE, 414

appalled at the rapidity with which the work advanced, determined to go out against them and give battle and interrupt it; [3] and the two armies were already in battle array when the Syracusan generals observed that their troops found such difficulty in getting into line, and were in such disorder, that they led them back into the city, except part of the cavalry. These remained and hindered the Athenians from carrying stones or dispersing to any great distance, [4] until a tribe[4a] of the Athenian hoplites, with all the cavalry, charged and routed the Syracusan horse with some loss; after which they set up a trophy for the cavalry action.

The next day the Athenians began building the wall to the north of the Circle, at the same time collecting stone and timber, which they kept laying down toward Trogilus[1a] along the shortest line for their works from the Great Harbor to the sea; [2] while the Syracusans, guided by their generals,

6.99
414
18th Year/Summer
SYRACUSE
Athenian wall construction proceeds rapidly from the Circle fort on Epipolae. The Syracusans build a counter-wall to cut the line of the enemy's wall.

6.98.4a   Citizens were organized into ten tribes at Athens, and the Athenian army was also organized in tribal regiments. This was also true of the Syracusan army; see 6.100.1.

6.99.1a   Trogilus, probable location: Map 6.99, AY. This map basically follows the interpretation of Peter Green in *Armada from Athens* (London, Hodder and Stoughton, 1971), passim, particularly in the location

of Trogilus and the Lysimeleia marsh (Map 7.39). The reader should be aware, however, that many scholars follow the view adopted by K. J. Dover, as described in A.W. Gomme, A. Andrewes, and K.J. Dover, *A Historical Commentary on Thucydides,* iv (Oxford, 1970), 466 ff., which locates Trogilus in a more northerly cove shown as "Trogilus A?" on Map 6.99, AY.

and above all by Hermocrates, instead of risking any more general engagements, determined to build a counterwall in the direction in which the Athenians were going to carry their wall. If this could be completed in time the enemy's lines would be cut; and meanwhile, if he were to attempt to interrupt them by an attack, they would send a part of their forces against him, and would secure the approaches beforehand with their stockade, while the Athenians would have to leave off working with their whole force in order to attend to them. [3] They accordingly sallied forth and began to build, starting from their city, running a cross wall below the Athenian Circle,[3a] at the same time cutting down the olive trees and erecting wooden towers. [4] As the Athenian fleet had not yet sailed round into the Great Harbor,[4a] the Syracusans still commanded the sea coast, and the Athenians brought their provisions by land from Thapsus.[4b]

6.100
414
18th Year/Summer
SYRACUSE
In a surprise attack, the
Athenians take the Syracusan
counterwall and destroy it.

The Syracusans now thought the stockades and stonework of their counterwall sufficiently far advanced; and as the Athenians, afraid of being divided and so fighting at a disadvantage, and intent upon their own wall, did not come out to interrupt them, they left one tribe to guard the new work and went back into the city. Meanwhile the Athenians destroyed the underground pipes that carried drinking water into the city; and watching until the rest of the Syracusans were in their tents at midday (and some even gone away into the city), and those in the stockade keeping but indifferent guard, they appointed three hundred picked men of their own, and some men selected from the light troops who were appropriately armed for the purpose to run suddenly as fast as they could to the counterwall, while the rest of the army advanced in two divisions, one with one of the generals to the city in case of a sortie, the other with the other general to the stockade by the postern gate. [2] The three hundred attacked and took the stockade, abandoned by its garrison, who took refuge in the outworks round the statue of Apollo Temenites.[2a] Here the pursuers burst in with them, and after getting in were beaten out by the Syracusans, and some few of the Argives and Athenians slain; [3] after which the whole army retired, and having demolished the counterwall and pulled up the stockade, carried away the stakes to their own lines, and set up a trophy.

6.101
414
18th Year/Summer
SYRACUSE
A second Syracusan counterwall is also captured by the
Athenians. In a confused
battle the Syracusans are
defeated but the Athenian
general Lamachus is killed.

The next day the Athenians from the Circle[1a] proceeded to fortify the cliff above the marsh which on this side of Epipolae looks toward the Great Harbor; this being also the shortest line for their wall to go down across the plain and the marsh to the harbor. [2] Meanwhile the Syracusans marched out and began a second stockade, starting from the city, across the middle of the marsh, digging a trench alongside to make it impossible for the Athenians to carry their wall down to the sea. [3] As soon as the Athenians had finished their work at the cliff they again attacked the stockade

6.99.3a   Circle fort: Map 6.99, AX.
6.99.4a   Great Harbor: Map 6.99, BY.
6.99.4b   Thapsus: Map 6.95, Sicily.
6.100.2a Temenites district: Map 6.99, AY.
6.101.1a Circle fort: Map 6.99, AX.

and ditch of the Syracusans. Ordering the fleet to sail round from Thapsus[3a] into the Great Harbor of Syracuse,[3b] they descended at about dawn from Epipolae[3c] into the plain, and laying doors and planks over the marsh where it was muddy and firmest, crossed over on these, and by daybreak took the ditch and the stockade, except for a small portion which they captured afterwards. [4] A battle now ensued, in which the Athenians were victorious, the right wing of the Syracusans fleeing to the city and the left to the river. The three hundred picked Athenians, wishing to cut off their passage, pressed on at a run to the bridge, [5] when the alarmed Syracusans, who had with them most of their cavalry, closed and routed them, hurling them back upon the Athenian right wing, the first tribe[5a] of which was thrown into a panic by the shock. [6] Seeing this, Lamachus came to their aid from the Athenian left with a few archers and with the Argives, and crossing a ditch, was left alone with a few that had crossed with him, and was killed with five or six of his men. These the Syracusans managed immediately to snatch up in haste and get across the river into a place of security, themselves retreating as the rest of the Athenian army now came up.

Meanwhile those who had at first fled for refuge to the city, seeing the turn affairs were taking, now rallied from the city and formed against the Athenians in front of them, sending also a part of their number to the Circle on Epipolae,[1a] which they hoped to take while denuded of its defenders. [2] These took and destroyed the Athenian outwork of a thousand feet, the Circle itself being saved by Nicias, who happened to have been left in it through illness, and who now ordered the servants to set fire to the machines and timber that had been thrown down before the wall; lack of men, as he was aware, made all other means of survival impossible. [3] This step was justified by the result, as the Syracusans came no further on account of the fire, but retreated. Meanwhile help was coming up from the Athenians below, who had put to flight the troops opposed to them; and the fleet also, according to orders, was sailing from Thapsus[3a] into the Great Harbor.[3b] [4] Seeing this, the Syracusan troops on the heights retired in haste, and the whole army reentered the city, thinking that with their present force they would no longer be able to hinder the wall reaching the sea.

After this the Athenians set up a trophy and restored to the Syracusans their dead under truce, receiving in return Lamachus and those who had fallen with him. The whole of their forces, naval and military, being now with them, they began from Epipolae[1a] and the cliffs and enclosed the Syracusans with a double wall down to the sea. [2] Provisions were now brought in for the armament from all parts of Italy; and many of the Sicels, who had hitherto been looking to see how things went, came as allies to the Athenians: there also arrived three ships of fifty oars from Tyrrhenia.[2a]

6.102
414
18th Year/Summer
SYRACUSE
The Syracusans attack the enemy in the plain and at the Circle fort on Epipolae. Nicias saves the Circle by burning timber and war engines so that the fire holds off the enemy until reinforcements arrive. The defeated Syracusans return to their city.

6.103
414
18th Year/Summer
SYRACUSE
The Athenians extend their wall against the city. Provisions are secured from Italy. Some Tyrrhenians and many Sicels now join their forces. The Syracusans despair, divide into factions, replace their generals, and begin to discuss surrender terms.

6.101.3a Thapsus: Map 6.95, Sicily.
6.101.3b Great Harbor: Map 6.99, BY.
6.101.3c Epipolae: Map 6.99, AX.
1.101.5a For the tribal organization of the Athen-
    ian army, see note 6.98.4a.

6.102.1a Circle fort: Map 6.99, AX.
6.102.3a Thapsus: Map 6.95, Sicily.
6.102.3b Great Harbor: Map 6.99, BY.
6.103.1a Epipolae: Map 6.99, AX.
6.103.2a Tyrrhenia: Map 6.104, locator.

Meanwhile everything else progressed favorably for their hopes. [3] The Syracusans began to despair of finding safety in arms, no relief having reached them from the Peloponnesus, and were now proposing terms of capitulation among themselves and to Nicias, who after the death of Lamachus was left sole commander. [4] No decision was reached, but as was natural with men in difficulties and besieged more severely than before, there was much discussion with Nicias and still more in the city. Their present misfortunes had also made them suspicious of one another; and the blame of their disasters was thrown upon the ill-fortune or treachery of the generals under whose command they had happened; and these were deposed and others, Heraclides, Eucles, and Tellias, elected in their stead.

Meanwhile the Spartan Gylippus and the ships from Corinth[1a] were now off Leucas,[1b] intent upon going with all haste to the relief of Sicily. The news that reached them being of an alarming kind, and all agreeing in a false report that the siege line around Syracuse was already complete. Gylippus abandoned all hope for Sicily, and wishing to save Italy, rapidly crossed the Ionian Sea[1c] to Tarentum[1d] with the Corinthian, Pythen, in two Laconian, and two Corinthian vessels, leaving the Corinthians to follow him after manning, in addition to their own ten, two Leucadian and two Ambraciot[1e] ships. [2] From Tarentum Gylippus first went on a mission to Thurii,[2a] and claimed anew the rights of citizenship which his father had enjoyed, but failing to bring over the townspeople, he weighed anchor and coasted along Italy. Opposite the Terinaean gulf[2b] he was caught by the wind which blows violently and steadily from the north in that quarter, and was carried out to sea; and after experiencing very rough weather, made it back to Tarentum where he hauled ashore and refitted such of his ships as had suffered most from the tempest. [3] Nicias heard of his approach, but, like the Thurians, scorned the scanty number of his ships, and set down piracy as the only probable purpose of the voyage, and so took no precautions for the present.

About the same time in this summer, the Spartans invaded Argos[1a] with their allies, and laid waste most of the country. The Athenians went with thirty ships to the relief of the Argives, thus breaking their treaty with the Spartans in the most overt manner. [2] Up to this time incursions from Pylos[2a] and descents on the coasts of the rest of the Peloponnesus, instead of on the Laconian, had been the extent of their cooperation with the Ar-

6.104.1a Corinth: Map 6.104.
6.104.1b Leucas: Map 6.104.
6.104.1c Ionian sea: Map 6.104, locator.
6.104.1d Tarentum: Map 6.104, locator.
6.104.1e Ambracia: Map 6.104.
6.104.2a Thurii: Map 6.104, locator.
6.104.2b Terinaean gulf, possible location: Map 6.104, locator. Perhaps Thucydides makes a geographic error here. The city of Terina is located on the west coast of Bruttium (as shown in Map 6.104, loca-

tor), but a north wind there would hardly blow a ship out to sea, nor would Gylippus' ships be likely to return to Tarentum from the Tyrrhenian Sea west of Italy. A location on the south coast of Italy between Croton and Rhegium is certainly a more plausible location for this possibly misnamed gulf.
6.105.1a Argos: Map 6.104.
6.105.2a Pylos: Map 6.104.

MAP 6.104 MILITARY OPERATIONS IN SUMMER, 414

gives and Mantineans;[2b] and although the Argives had often begged them to land, if only for a moment, with their hoplites in Laconia,[2c] lay waste ever so little of it with them, and depart, they had always refused to do so. Now, however, under the command of Pythodorus, Laespodius, and Demaratus, they landed at Epidaurus Limera,[2d] Prasiae,[2e] and other places, and plundered the country; and thus furnished the Spartans with a better pretext for hostilities against Athens. [3] After the Athenians had retired from Argos with their fleet, and the Spartans also, the Argives made an incursion into the territory of Phlius,[3a] and returned home after ravaging the land and killing some of the inhabitants.

6.105.2b Mantinea: Map 6.104.
6.105.2c Laconia: Map 6.104.
6.105.2d Epidaurus Limera: Map 6.104.
6.105.2e Prasiae: Map 6.104.
6.105.3a Phlius: Map 6.104.

BOOK SEVEN

A fter refitting their ships, Gylippus and Pythen coasted along from Tarentum[1a] to Epizephyrian Locri.[1b] They now received the more correct information that the siege works at Syracuse[1c] were not yet complete, and that it was still possible for an army arriving by Epipolae[1d] to effect an entrance; they considered, accordingly, whether they should keep Sicily on their right and risk sailing in by sea, or leaving it on their left, should first sail to Himera,[1e] and taking with them the Himeraeans and any others that might agree to join them, go to Syracuse by land. [2] Finally they decided to sail for Himera, especially as the four Athenian ships which Nicias had at last sent off, on hearing that they were at Locri, had not yet arrived at Rhegium.[2a] Accordingly, before these reached their post, the Peloponnesians crossed the strait and after touching at Rhegium and Messana,[2b] came to Himera. [3] There they persuaded the Himeraeans to join in the war, and not only to go with them themselves but to provide arms for the seamen from their vessels which they had drawn ashore at Himera; and they sent and appointed a place for the Selinuntines[3a] to meet them with all their forces. [4] A few troops were also promised by the Geloans[4a] and by some of the Sicels, who were now ready to join them with much greater alacrity, owing to the recent death of Archonidas, a powerful Sicel king in that neighborhood and friendly to Athens, and owing also to the vigor shown by Gylippus in coming from Sparta.[4b] [5] Gylippus now took with him about seven hundred of his sailors and marines (that number only having arms), a thousand *hoplites*[5a] and light troops from Himera with a body of a hundred horse, some light troops and cavalry from Selinus, a few Geloans, and Sicels numbering a thousand in all, and set out on his march for Syracuse.

Hearing that Syracuse might still be saved, Gylippus sails to Himera where he gathers allies before marching overland to Syracuse.

7.1.1a Tarentum, Italy, Map 7.1.
7.1.1b Locri (Epizephyrian), Italy: Map 7.1.
7.1.1c Syracuse: Map 7.1.
7.1.1d Epipolae: Map 7.4, AX.
7.1.1e Himera: Map 7.1.
7.1.2a Rhegium: Map 7.1.
7.1.2b Messana: Map 7.1.
7.1.3a Selinus: Map 7.1.

7.1.4a Gela: Map 7.1.
7.1.4b Sparta: Map 7.1.
7.1.5a *Hoplite* is the Greek word for a heavily armed infantryman. See Glossary and Appendix F, Land Warfare, §2. Marines were hoplites trained to fight from the decks of triremes; see Appendix G, Trireme warfare, §8, §11, §14.

MAP 7.1 REINFORCEMENTS FOR SYRACUSE

7.2
414
18th Year/Summer
SYRACUSE
Just as the Athenians are
about to close their siege
walls, and the Syracusans
are losing hope, Gongylus
arrives with news that
reinforcements from the
Peloponnesus are coming.
The arrival of Gylippus
restores Syracusan morale.

Meanwhile the Corinthian[1a] fleet from Leucas[1b] made all haste to arrive; and one of their commanders, Gongylus, starting last with a single ship, was the first to reach Syracuse, a little before Gylippus. Gongylus found the Syracusans on the point of holding an assembly to consider whether they should not put an end to the war. This he prevented, and reassured them by telling them that more vessels were still to arrive, and that Gylippus son of Cleandridas had been despatched by the Spartans to take the command. [2] Upon this the Syracusans took courage, and immediately marched out with all their forces to meet Gylippus, who they found was now close at hand. [3] Meanwhile Gylippus, after taking Ietae,[3a] a fort of the Sicels, on his way, formed his army in order of battle, and so arrived at Epipolae, and ascending by Euryelus,[3b] as the Athenians had done at first, now advanced with the Syracusans against the Athenian lines. [4] By chance, he had arrived at a critical moment. The Athenians had already finished a double wall of almost a mile[4a] to the Great Harbor, with the exception of a small portion next to the sea, which they were still engaged upon; and in the remainder of the circle toward Trogilus[4b] on the other sea, stones had been laid ready for building for the greater part of the distance, and some points had been left half finished, while others were entirely completed. The danger of Syracuse had indeed been great.

7.2.1a   Corinth: Map 7.1.
7.2.1b   Leucas: Map 7.1.
7.2.3a   Ietae: site unknown.
7.2.3b   Euryelus on Epipolae: Map 7.4, AX.
7.2.4a   Thucydides actually wrote six or seven
         stades: the Attic stade was 607 feet, the
         Olympic stade 630.8 feet. Complete and
         incomplete Athenian walls: Map 7.4.

7.2.4b   Trogilus: Map 7.4, AY. For another the-
         ory as to its location, see note 6.99.1a.

Meanwhile the Athenians, recovering from the confusion into which they had been at first thrown by the sudden approach of Gylippus and the Syracusans, formed in order of battle. Gylippus halted at a short distance off and sent on a herald[1a] to tell them that if they would evacuate Sicily with bag and baggage within five days' time, he was willing to make a truce accordingly. [2] The Athenians treated this proposition with contempt, and dismissed the herald without an answer. After this both sides began to prepare for action. [3] Gylippus, observing that the Syracusans were in disorder and did not easily fall into line, drew off his troops more into the open ground, while Nicias did not lead on the Athenians but lay still by his own wall. When Gylippus saw that they did not come on, he led off his army to the citadel of the quarter of Apollo Temenites,[3a] and passed the night there. [4] On the following day he led out the main body of his army, and drawing them up in order of battle before the walls of the Athenians to prevent their going to the relief of any other quarter, dispatched a strong force against Fort Labdalum[4a] and took it, and put all whom he found in it to the sword, the place not being within sight of the Athenians. [5] On the same day an Athenian *trireme*[5a] that lay moored off the harbor was captured by the Syracusans.

After this the Syracusans and their allies began to build a single wall, starting from the city, in a slanting direction up Epipolae, in order to prevent the Athenians, unless they could hinder the work, from extending and completing their siege wall. [2] Meanwhile the Athenians, having now finished their wall down to the sea, had come up to the heights; and part of their wall being weak, Gylippus drew out his army by night and attacked it. [3] However, the Athenians who happened to be bivouacking outside realized what was happening and came out to meet him, upon seeing which he quickly led his men back again. The Athenians now built their wall higher, and in future kept guard at this point themselves, disposing their confederates along the remainder of the works, at the stations assigned to them. [4] Nicias also determined to fortify Plemmyrium,[4a] a promontory opposite the city, which juts out and narrows the mouth of the Great Harbor. He thought that the fortification of this place would make it easier to bring in supplies, as they would be able to carry on their blockade from a shorter distance, and near the port used by the Syracusans; instead of being obliged, upon every movement of the enemy's navy, to sail out against them from the bottom of the Great Harbor. Besides this, he now began to pay more attention to the war by sea, seeing that the coming of Gylippus had diminished their hopes by land. [5] Accordingly, he conveyed over his

7.3
414
18th Year/Summer
EPIPOLAE
The two armies form up but neither will attack. While they confront each other, Gylippus sends out a force that captures the Athenian fort of Labdalum.

7.4
414
18th Year/Summer
SYRACUSE
The Syracusans begin to construct a counterwall. Nicias fortifies Plemmyrium and other sites, and dispatches a squadron to intercept the approaching Corinthian ships.

7.3.1a   Heralds, already a venerable Greek institution in Thucydides' day, operated under the protection of the god Hermes, and were easily identified by the staff they carried. They alone could travel unmolested between states or armies during wartime in order to deliver messages, take back replies, and make perfunctory arrangements.

7.3.3a   Temenites district of Syracuse: Map 7.4, AY.
7.3.4a   Fort Labdalum: Map 7.4, AX.
7.3.5a   *Triremes* were the standard warship of this period; see Appendix G, §4–7.
7.4.4a   Plemmyrium: Map 7.4, BY.

MAP 7.4 GYLIPPUS' FIRST BATTLES AT SYRACUSE[5a]

ships and some troops, and built three forts in which he placed most of his baggage, and moored there for the future the larger craft and warships. [6] This was the first and chief occasion of the losses which the crews experienced. The water which they used was scarce and had to be fetched from far away, and the sailors could not go out for firewood without being cut off by the Syracusan horse, who were masters of the country; a third of the enemy's cavalry being stationed at the little town of Olympieum,[6a] to prevent plundering incursions on the part of the Athenians at Plemmyrium. [7] Meanwhile Nicias learned that the rest of the Corinthian fleet was approaching, and sent twenty ships to watch for them, with orders to be on the lookout for them in the vicinity of Locri and Rhegium[7a] and the approaches to Sicily.

7.4.5a   Map 7.4 basically follows the interpreta-
          tion of Peter Green in *Armada from
          Athens* (London: Hodder and Stoughton,
          1971), passim, particularly regarding the
          locations of Trogilus (Map 7.4, AY) and
          the Lysimeleia marsh (Map 7.41, BY).
          The reader should be aware, however,
          that many scholars follow the views of K.

          J. Dover as set out in A.W. Gomme, A.
          Andrewes, and K.J. Dover, *A Historical
          Commentary on Thucydides*, iv (Oxford,
          1970), 466 ff. See note 6.99.1a.
7.4.6a   Olympieum: Map 7.4, BX.
7.4.7a   Locri (Epizephyrian) and Rhegium: Map
          7.1.

Gylippus, meanwhile, went on with the wall[1a] across Epipolae, using the stones which the Athenians had laid down for their own wall, and at the same time constantly led out the Syracusans and their allies, and formed them in order of battle in front of the lines, the Athenians forming against him. [2] At last he thought that the moment had come, and began the attack; and a hand-to-hand fight ensued between the lines, where the Syracusan cavalry could be of no use; [3] and the Syracusans and their allies were defeated and took up their dead under truce,[3a] while the Athenians erected a trophy. After this Gylippus called the soldiers together, and said that the fault was not theirs but his; he had kept their lines too much within the works, and had thus deprived them of the services of their cavalry and darters. [4] He would now, therefore, lead them on a second time. He begged them to remember that in material force they would be fully a match for their opponents, while with respect to moral advantages, it were intolerable if Peloponnesians and Dorians should not feel confident of overcoming Ionians and islanders with the motley rabble that accompanied them, and of driving them out of the country.[4a]

After this he embraced the first opportunity that arose of again leading them against the enemy. Now Nicias and the Athenians were of the opinion that even if the Syracusans should not wish to offer battle, it was necessary for them to prevent the building of the cross wall, as it already almost overlapped the extreme point of their own, and if it went any further it would from that moment make no difference whether they fought ever so many successful actions, or never fought at all. They accordingly came out to meet the Syracusans. [2] Gylippus led out his hoplites further from the fortifications than on the former occasion, and so joined battle; posting his horse and darters upon the flank of the Athenians in the open space, where the works of the two walls terminated. [3] During the engagement the cavalry attacked and routed the left wing of the Athenians, which was opposed to them; and the rest of the Athenian army was in consequence defeated by the Syracusans and driven headlong within their lines. [4] The night following the Syracusans extended their wall up to the Athenian works and passed them, thus putting it out of their power any longer to stop them, and depriving them, even if victorious in the field, of all chance of investing the city for the future.

After this the remaining twelve vessels of the Corinthians, Ambraciots,[1a] and Leucadians[1b] sailed into the harbor under the command of the Corinthian Erasinides, having eluded the Athenian ships on guard, and helped the Syracusans in completing the remainder of the cross wall. [2]

7.5
414
18th Year/Summer
EPIPOLAE
Because Gylippus orders an attack in a constricted area where the Syracusan cavalry cannot be used, the Syracusans are defeated. Gylippus accepts blame for the defeat and promises a second effort with better results.

7.6
414
18th Year/Summer
EPIPOLAE
Gylippus orders another attack. This time he uses his cavalry effectively and defeats the Athenians. The Syracusans then carry their counterwall past the Athenian works and prevent Athenian investment of the city.

7.7
414
18th Year/Summer
SYRACUSE
Eluding the Athenians, the Corinthian ships arrive safely. Gylippus leaves to raise Sicilian forces. Both sides request reinforcements and the Syracusans begin to exercise their fleet.

7.5.1a   Syracusan counterwall: Map 7.4, AY.
7.5.3a   According to the ritual of hoplite warfare;
          see Appendix F, Land Warfare, §6.
7.5.4a   This is another expression of Dorian con-
          tempt for Ionian prowess; see Appendix
          H, Dialects and Ethnic Groups, §8.
7.7.1a   Ambracia: Map 7.9.
7.7.1b   Leucas: Map 7.9.

Meanwhile Gylippus went into the rest of Sicily to raise land and naval forces, and also to bring over any of the cities that either were lukewarm in the cause or had until then kept out of the war altogether. [3] Syracusan and Corinthian envoys were also dispatched to Sparta and Corinth to get a fresh force sent over, in any way possible, either in merchant vessels or transports, or in any other manner likely to prove successful, as the Athenians too were sending for reinforcements; [4] while the Syracusans proceeded to man and train a fleet,[4a] intending to try their fortune in this way also, and generally became exceedingly confident.

Nicias perceiving this, and seeing the strength of the enemy and his own difficulties daily increasing, himself also sent to Athens. He had before sent frequent reports of events as they occurred, and felt it especially incumbent upon him to do so now, as he thought that they were in a critical position, and that unless speedily recalled or strongly reinforced from home, they had no hope of safety. [2] He feared, however, that the messengers, either through inability to speak, or through failure of memory, or from a wish to please the multitude, might not report the truth, and so thought it best to write a letter, to insure that the Athenians should know his own opinion without its being lost in transmission, and be able to decide upon the real facts of the case. [3] His emissaries, accordingly, departed with the letter and the requisite verbal instructions; and he attended to the affairs of the army, making it his aim now to keep on the defensive and to avoid any unnecessary danger.

At the close of the same summer the Athenian general Euetion marched in concert with Perdiccas[1a] with a large body of Thracians against Amphipolis,[1b] and failing to take it brought some triremes round into the Strymon,[1c] and blockaded the city from the river, having his base at Himeraeum.[1d]

Summer was now over.

The winter ensuing, the persons sent by Nicias, reaching Athens, gave the verbal messages which had been entrusted to them, and answered any questions that were asked them, and delivered the letter. The secretary of the city now came forward and read out to the Athenians the letter, which was as follows:

"Our past operations, Athenians, have been made known to you by many other letters; it is now time for you to become equally familiar with our present condition, and to take your measures accordingly. [2] We had defeated the Syracusans, against whom we were sent, in most of our engagements with them, and we had built

7.7.4a   For training a fleet, see Appendix G, Trireme Warfare, §11–15.
7.9.1a   Perdiccas was the king of nearby Macedonia, Map 7.9.
7.9.1b   Amphipolis: Map 7.9. The previous attempt by Athens to capture Amphipolis had been organized in the winter of

417/6, and was to have been led by Nicias, but was aborted when Perdiccas joined the Spartan-Argive alliance and refused to assist Athens; see 5.83.
7.9.1c   Strymon river: Map 7.9.
7.9.1d   Himeraeum: location unknown.

MAP 7.9 END OF SUMMER, 414

the works which we now occupy, when Gylippus arrived from Sparta with an army obtained from the Peloponnesus and from some of the cities in Sicily. In our first battle with him we were victorious; in the battle on the following day we were overpowered by a multitude of cavalry and darters, and compelled to retire within our lines. [3] We have now, therefore, been forced by the numbers of those opposed to us to discontinue the work of circumvallation,[3a] and to remain inactive; being unable to make use even of all the force we have, since a large portion of our hoplites are absorbed in the defense of our lines. Meanwhile the enemy have carried a single wall past our lines, thus making it impossible for us to invest them in future, until this cross wall is attacked by a strong force and captured. [4] So that the besieger in name has become, at least from the land side, the besieged in reality; as we are prevented by their cavalry from even going for any distance into the country."

"Besides this, an embassy has been dispatched to the Peloponnesus to procure reinforcements, and Gylippus has gone to the cities in Sicily, partly in the hope of inducing those that are at present neutral to join him in the war, partly of bringing from his allies additional contingents for the land forces and material for the navy. [2] For I understand that they contemplate a combined attack upon our

7.12
414/3
18th Year/Winter
ATHENS
Nicias warns that the enemy is raising larger forces and is preparing to fight at sea, exploiting the deterioration that time has wreaked on Athenian ships and crews.

7.11.3a Circumvallation: the building of a wall to completely isolate a city by land.

lines with their land forces and with their fleet by sea. [3] You must none of you be surprised that I say by sea also. They have discovered that the length of time we have now been in commission has rotted our ships and wasted our crews, and that with the completeness of our crews and the soundness of our ships the pristine efficiency of our navy has departed. [4] For it is impossible for us to haul our ships ashore and dry them out[4a] because the enemy's vessels being as many or more than our own, we are constantly anticipating an attack. [5] Indeed, they may be seen exercising, and it lies with them to take the initiative; and not having to maintain a blockade, they have greater facilities for drying their ships."

"This we should scarcely be able to do, even if we had plenty of ships to spare, and were freed from our present necessity of exhausting all our strength upon the blockade. For it is already difficult to carry in supplies past Syracuse; and were we to relax our vigilance in the slightest degree it would become impossible. [2] The losses which our crews have suffered and still continue to suffer arise from the following causes. Expeditions for fuel and for forage, and the distance from which water has to be fetched, cause our sailors to be cut off by the Syracusan cavalry; the loss of our previous superiority emboldens our slaves to desert; our foreign seamen are impressed by the unexpected appearance of a navy against us, and the strength of the enemy's resistance; such of them as were pressed into the service take the first opportunity of departing to their respective cities; such as were originally seduced by the temptation of high pay, and expected little fighting and large gains, leave us either by desertion to the enemy or by availing themselves of one or other of the various facilities of escape which the magnitude of Sicily affords them. Some even engage in trade themselves and prevail upon the captains to take Hyccaric[2a] slaves on board in their place; thus they have ruined the efficiency of our navy."

"Now I need not remind you that the time during which a crew is in its prime is short, and that the number of sailors who can start a ship on her way and keep the rowing in time is small.[1a] [2] But by far my greatest trouble is that holding the post which I do, I am prevented by the natural indiscipline of the Athenian seaman from putting a stop to these evils; and that meanwhile we have no source from which to recruit our crews, which the enemy can do from many quarters, but are compelled to depend both for supplying the crews in service and for making good our losses upon the men whom we

7.13
414/3
18th Year/Winter
ATHENS
Nicias elaborates on the reasons for the decline of his fleet's strength and efficiency.

7.14
414/3
18th Year/Winter
ATHENS
Nicias reports that he can neither remedy these problems nor recruit local reinforcements. If Italian markets are closed to the Athenians, which might occur in the absence of further support, the Athenians will have to evacuate Sicily. Nicias emphasizes that his report offers the unvarnished truth.

7.12.4a   For the importance of regularly beaching triremes to dry their hulls, see Appendix G, Trireme Warfare, §6.
7.13.2a   The capture of Hyccara and the enslavement of its inhabitants was described in 6.62.

7.14.1a   For the significance of crew discipline and efficiency, see Appendix G, Trireme Warfare, §11–15 and the speech of the Athenian Phormio to his troops before battle in 2.89.9.

brought with us. For our present allies, Naxos and Catana,[2a] are incapable of supplying us. [3] There is only one thing more that our opponents lack, I mean the loss of our Italian markets. If the Italians were to see you neglect to relieve us from our present condition, and were to go over to the enemy, famine would compel us to evacuate, and Syracuse would finish the war without a blow."

[4] "I might, it is true, have written to you something different and more agreeable than this, but nothing certainly more useful, if it is desirable for you to know the real state of things here before taking your measures. Besides I know that it is your nature to love to be told the best side of things, and then to blame the teller if the expectations which he has raised in your minds are not answered by the result; and I therefore thought it safest to declare to you the truth."

"Now you are not to think that either your generals or your soldiers have ceased to be a match for the forces originally opposed to them. But you are to reflect that a general Sicilian coalition is being formed against us; that a fresh army is expected from the Peloponnesus, while the force we have here is unable to cope even with our present antagonists; and you must promptly decide either to recall us or to send out to us another fleet and army as numerous again, with a large sum of money, and someone to succeed me, as a disease in the kidneys renders me unfit to retain my post. [2] I have, I think, some claim on your indulgence, as while I was in my prime I did you much good service in my commands. But whatever you mean to do, do it at the commencement of spring and without delay as the enemy will obtain his Sicilian reinforcements shortly, those from the Peloponnesus after a longer interval; and unless you attend to the matter the former will be here before you, while the latter will elude you as they have done before."

7.15
414/3
18th Year/Winter
ATHENS
Nicias closes by asking that the Athenian response, whether to recall or to reinforce the expedition, be made rapidly. He also asks to resign his command for reasons of health.

[1] Such were the contents of Nicias' letter. When the Athenians had heard it they refused to accept his resignation, but chose him two colleagues, naming Menander and Euthydemus, two of the officers in Sicily, to fill their places until their arrival, that Nicias might not be left alone in his sickness to bear the whole weight of affairs. They also voted to send out another army and navy, drawn partly from the Athenians on the muster roll, partly from the allies. [2] The colleagues chosen for Nicias were Demosthenes son of Alcisthenes, and Eurymedon son of Thucles. Eurymedon was sent off at once, about the time of the winter solstice, with ten ships, a hundred and twenty *talents* of silver, and instructions to tell the

7.16
414/3
18th Year/Winter
ATHENS
The Athenians want Nicias to retain his command. They decide to send new generals to assist him and a new expedition to reinforce the Athenians at Syracuse.

7.14.2a   Naxos and Catana: Map 7.9.
7.16.2a   A *talent* is a unit of weight and money. See Appendix J, Classical Greek Currency, §5.

7.17
414/3
18th Year/Winter
ATHENS
The Athenians decide to
send the expedition in the
spring. Athenian triremes
are sent to block enemy
reinforcements from
reaching Sicily. The
Corinthians plan to
challenge the Athenian
squadron at Naupactus.

army that reinforcements would arrive, and that care would be taken of
them; [7.17.1] but Demosthenes stayed behind to organize the expedition,
meaning to start as soon as it was spring, and sent for troops to the allies,
and meanwhile got together money, ships, and hoplites at home.

[2] The Athenians also sent twenty vessels round the Peloponnesus to
prevent anyone crossing over to Sicily from Corinth or the Peloponnesus.
[3] For the Corinthians, filled with confidence by the favorable alteration
in Sicilian affairs which had been reported by the envoys upon their arrival,
and convinced that the fleet which they had before sent out had not been
without use, were now preparing to despatch a force of hoplites in merchant vessels to Sicily, while the Spartans did the same for the rest of the
Peloponnesus. [4] The Corinthians also manned a fleet of twenty-five vessels, intending to try the result of a battle with the squadron on guard at
Naupactus,[4a] and meanwhile to make it less easy for the Athenians there to
hinder the departure of their merchant vessels by obliging them to keep an
eye upon the triremes thus arrayed against them.

7.18
414/3
18th Year/Winter
SPARTA
The Spartans prepare to
invade Attica, to fortify
Decelea (as Alcibiades
advised), and thus to force a
second front upon the
Athenians. They were
encouraged by their
perception that they no
longer carried the legal and
moral opprobrium of
refusing arbitration which
they had borne when the war
began.

In the meantime the Spartans prepared for their invasion of Attica,[1a] in
accordance with their own previous resolve, and at the instigation of the
Syracusans and Corinthians, who wished for an invasion to prevent the reinforcements which they heard that Athens was about to send to Sicily. Alcibiades also urgently advised the fortification of Decelea,[1b] and a vigorous
prosecution of the war. [2] But the Spartans derived most encouragement
from the belief that Athens, with two wars on her hands, against themselves
and against the Sicilians, would be more easy to subdue, and from the conviction that she had been the first to violate the truce. In the former war,
they considered that the offense had been more on their own side, both on
account of the attack of the Thebans on Plataea[2a] in time of peace, and also
of their own refusal to listen to the Athenian offer of arbitration, in spite of
the clause in the former treaty that where arbitration[2b] should be offered
there should be no appeal to arms. For this reason they thought that they
deserved their misfortunes, and took to heart seriously the disaster at
Pylos[2c] and whatever else had befallen them. [3] But when, besides the ravages from Pylos,[3a] which went on without any intermission, the thirty
Athenian ships came out from Argos[3b] and wasted part of Epidaurus,[3c]
Prasiae,[3d] and other places; when upon every dispute that arose as to the interpretation of any doubtful point in the treaty, their own offers of arbitration were always rejected by the Athenians—the Spartans at length decided
that Athens had now committed the very same offense as they had before

7.17.4a   Naupactus: Map 7.18, AX.
7.18.1a   Attica: Map 7.18, AX.
7.18.1b   Decelea: Map 7.18, AX.
7.18.2a   Thucydides describes the Theban assault
          on Plataea in 2.2–6.
7.18.2b   Pericles appeals to the arbitration clause
          in the treaty establishing the Thirty Years'
          Peace in 1.144.2, and the Athenians for-
          mally challenge the Spartans to submit
          their complaint to arbitration in 1.145.

7.18.2c   Pylos: Map 7.18, BX. Thucydides de-
          scribes the Spartan defeat at Pylos in
          4.2–6, 4.8–23, and 4.26–41.
7.18.3a   For the incursions from Pylos, see
          6.105.2.
7.18.3b   Argos: Map 7.18, BX.
7.18.3c   Epidaurus: Map 7.18, BX.
7.18.3d   Prasiae: Map 7.18, BX.

MAP 7.18 WINTER 414

done, and had become the guilty party; and they began to be full of enthusiasm for the war. [4] They spent this winter in sending round to their allies
for iron, and in getting ready the other implements for building their fort;
and meanwhile began raising at home, and also by forced requisitions in
the rest of the Peloponnesus, a force to be sent out in the merchant ships
to their allies in Sicily. Winter thus ended, and with it the eighteenth year of
this war of which Thucydides is the historian.

    In the first days of the following spring, at an earlier period than usual,
the Spartans and their allies invaded Attica, under the command of Agis
son of Archidamus, king of the Spartans. They began by devastating the
parts bordering upon the plain, and next proceeded to fortify Decelea, dividing the work among the different cities. [2] Decelea is about thirteen or
fourteen miles from the city of Athens, and the same distance or not much
further from Boeotia;[2a] and the fort was intended to damage the plain and
the richest parts of the country, being in sight of Athens. [3] While the

7.19.2a Boeotia: Map 7.18, AX.

7.19
413
19th Year/Summer
ATTICA
The Spartans invade Attica
and fortify Decelea.
PELOPONNESUS
Peloponnesian
reinforcements leave for
Sicily. A Corinthian
squadron successfully
prevents intervention by the
Athenian ships at Naupactus.

Peloponnesians and their allies in Attica were engaged in the work of fortification, their countrymen at home sent off, at about the same time, the hoplites in the merchant vessels to Sicily; the Spartans furnishing a picked force of Helots[3a] and *neodamodeis*,[3b] six hundred hoplites in all, under the command of Eccritus, a *Spartiate*; and the Boeotians three hundred hoplites, commanded by two Thebans, Xenon and Nicon, and by Hegesander, a Thespian. [4] These were among the first to put out into the open sea, starting from Taenarum[4a] in Laconia.[4b] Not long after their departure the Corinthians sent off a force of five hundred hoplites, consisting partly of men from Corinth[4c] itself, and partly of Arcadian[4d] mercenaries, placed under the command of Alexarchus, a Corinthian. The Sicyonians[4e] also sent off two hundred hoplites at the same time as the Corinthians, under the command of Sargeus, a Sicyonian. [5] Meantime the five-and-twenty vessels manned by Corinth during the winter lay confronting the twenty Athenian ships at Naupactus[5a] until the hoplites in the merchant ships were fairly on their way from the Peloponnesus; thus fulfilling the object for which they had been manned originally, which was to divert the attention of the Athenians from the merchant ships to the triremes.

During this time the Athenians were not idle. Simultaneously with the fortification of Decelea,[1a] at the very beginning of spring, they sent thirty ships round the Peloponnesus, under Charicles son of Apollodorus, with instructions to call at Argos[1b] and demand a force of their hoplites for the fleet, in agreement with the alliance. At the same time they dispatched Demosthenes to Sicily, [2] as they had intended, with sixty Athenian and five Chian[2a] vessels, twelve hundred Athenian hoplites from the enlistment roll, and as many of the islanders as could be raised in the different quarters, drawing upon the other subject allies for whatever they could supply that would be of use for the war. Demosthenes was instructed first to sail round with Charicles and to operate with him upon the coasts of Laconia, [3] and accordingly sailed to Aegina[3a] and there waited for the remainder of his force, and for Charicles to fetch the Argive troops.

In Sicily about the same time in this spring, Gylippus came to Syracuse with as many troops as he could bring from the cities which he had persuaded to join. [2] Calling the Syracusans together, he told them that they must man as many ships as possible, and try their hand at a sea fight, by

7.20
413
19th Year/Summer
ATHENS
Athenian hoplites are joined by Argives and other allies. As Demosthenes prepares to leave, another squadron departs to raid the Peloponnesus.

7.21
413
19th Year/Summer
SYRACUSE
Gylippus urges the Syracusans to build and man a fleet to challenge the Athenians at sea. Hermocrates supports him, saying that such audacity will unnerve the Athenians and lead to victory. The Syracusans agree to try.

7.19.3a For a discussion of Sparta's Helots, see Appendix C, Spartan Institutions, §3.
7.19.3b The first mention of the class of *neodamodeis* is in 4.21 when they are settled on the border of Elis alongside the Helots which Brasidas took to Thrace. The name would appear to signify "newly put in the damos" ("newly made citizens") but their precise status is still debated. They were used by Sparta more and more as the war progressed; see 5.67.1 (at the battle of Mantinea), 7.58.3 (in Sicily), and frequently in large numbers in the early decades of the fourth century. A *Spartiate* is a full citizen

of Sparta, a member of its highest military caste.
7.19.4a Taenarum: Map 7.18, BX.
7.19.4b Laconia: Map 7.18, BX.
7.19.4c Corinth: Map 7.18, AX.
7.19.4d Arcadia: Map 7.18, BX.
7.19.4e Sicyon: Map 7.18, AX.
7.19.5a Naupactus: Map 7.18, AX.
7.20.1a Decelea: Map 7.18, AX.
7.20.1b Argos: Map 7.18, BX.
7.20.2a Chios: Map 7.18, AY.
7.20.3a Aegina: Map 7.18, BX. The narrative of Demosthenes' expedition continues in 7.26.

which he hoped to achieve an advantage in the war not unworthy of the risk. [3] With him Hermocrates actively joined in trying to encourage his countrymen to attack the Athenians at sea, saying that the latter had not inherited their naval prowess nor would they retain it forever; they had been landsmen even to a greater degree than the Syracusans, and had only become a maritime power when obliged by the Mede.[3a] Besides, to daring spirits like the Athenians, a daring adversary would seem the most formidable; and the Athenian plan of paralyzing by the boldness of their attack a neighbor often not their inferior in strength, could now be used against them with as good effect by the Syracusans. [4] He was convinced also that the unlooked-for spectacle of Syracusans daring to face the Athenian navy would cause a terror to the enemy, the advantages of which would far outweigh any loss that Athenian science might inflict upon their inexperience. He accordingly urged them to throw aside their fears and to try their fortune at sea; [5] and the Syracusans, under the influence of Gylippus and Hermocrates, and perhaps some others, made up their minds for the sea fight and began to man their vessels.

When the fleet was ready, Gylippus led out the whole army by night; his plan being to assault in person the forts of Plemmyrium[1a] by land, while thirty-five Syracusan triremes sailed according to an agreed plan against the enemy from the Great Harbor,[1b] and the forty-five remaining came round from the Lesser Harbor,[1c] where they had their arsenal, in order to join up with those inside and simultaneously to attack Plemmyrium, and thus to distract the Athenians by assaulting them on two sides at once. [2] The Athenians quickly manned sixty ships, and with twenty-five of these engaged the thirty-five of the Syracusans in the Great Harbor, sending the rest to meet those sailing round from the arsenal; and an action now ensued directly in front of the mouth of the Great Harbor, maintained with equal tenacity on both sides; the one wishing to force the passage, the other to prevent them.

In the meantime, while the Athenians in Plemmyrium were down at the sea, attending to the engagement, Gylippus made a sudden attack on the forts in the early morning and took the largest first, and afterwards the two smaller, whose garrisons did not wait for him, seeing the largest so easily taken. [2] At the fall of the first fort, the men from it who succeeded in taking refuge in their boats and merchant ships, found great difficulty in reaching the camp, as the Syracusans were having the best of it in the engagement in the Great Harbor, and sent a fast sailing trireme to pursue them. But when the two others fell, the Syracusans were now being de-

7.22
413
19th Year/Summer
SYRACUSE
Gylippus plans a combined land and sea attack on Plemmyrium. His fleet attempts to unite in the Great Harbor and the Athenians man ships to engage them.

7.23
413
19th Year/Summer
SYRACUSE
As the naval battle develops, a surprise attack by the Syracusan land forces captures the Athenian forts at Plemmyrium. Confusion among the inexperienced Syracusan ships finally permits the Athenians to gain a naval victory.

7.21.3a   By the Mede here, Thucydides means the
          Persians; see note 1.18.1d and Appendix
          E, The Persians, §1.
7.22.1a   Plemmyrium: Map 7.25, inset.
7.22.1b   Great Harbor: Map 7.25, inset.
7.22.1c   Lesser Harbor: Map 7.25, inset.

feated; and the fugitives from these sailed along shore with more ease. [3] The Syracusan ships fighting off the mouth of the harbor forced their way through the Athenian vessels and sailing in without any order fell foul of one another, and transferred the victory to the Athenians; who not only routed the squadron in question, but also that by which they were at first being defeated in the harbor, [4] sinking eleven of the Syracusan vessels and killing most of the men, except the crews of three ships whom they made prisoners. Their own loss was confined to three vessels; and after hauling ashore the Syracusan wrecks and setting up a trophy upon the islet in front of Plemmyrium, they retired to their own camp.

Unsuccessful at sea, the Syracusans had nevertheless the forts in Plemmyrium,[1a] for which they set up three trophies. One of the two last taken they razed, but put in order and garrisoned the two others. [2] In the capture of the forts a great many men were killed and made prisoners, and a great quantity of property was taken in all. As the Athenians had used them as warehouses, there was a large stock of goods and grain of the merchants inside, and also a large stock belonging to the captains; the masts and other equipment of forty triremes being taken,[2a] besides three triremes which had been drawn up on shore. [3] Indeed the first and foremost cause of the ruin of the Athenian army was the capture of Plemmyrium; even the entrance of the harbor being now no longer safe for carrying in provisions, as the Syracusan vessels were stationed there to prevent it, and nothing could be brought in without fighting; besides the general impression of dismay and discouragement produced upon the army.

After this the Syracusans sent out twelve ships under the command of Agatharchus, a Syracusan. One of these went to the Peloponnesus with ambassadors to describe the hopeful state of their affairs, and to incite the Peloponnesians to prosecute the war there even more actively than they were now doing, while the eleven others sailed to Italy, hearing that vessels laden with stores were on their way to the Athenians. [2] After falling in with and destroying most of the vessels in question, and burning in the Caulonian territory[2a] a quantity of timber for shipbuilding, which had been gathered for the Athenians, [3] the Syracusan squadron went to Locri,[3a] and while they were at anchor there, one of the merchant ships from the Peloponnesus came in, carrying Thespian[3b] hoplites; [4] these they took on board and sailed along shore toward home. The Athenians were on the lookout for them with twenty ships at Megara,[4a] but were only able to take one vessel with its crew; the rest getting clear off to Syracuse. [5] There was also some skirmishing in the harbor about the piles which the Syracusans had driven in the sea in front of the old docks, to allow their ships to

---

7.24.1a Plemmyrium and Nicias' forts: Map 7.4, BY, and Map 7.4, inset.
7.24.2a Regarding the loss of "masts and other equipment," see note 6.34.5a, 8.28.1, and 8.43.1, and Appendix G, Trireme Warfare, §8.

7.25.2a Caulonia: Map 7.25, BX.
7.25.3a Locri (Epizephyrian): Map 7.25, BX.
7.25.3b Thespiae: Map 7.25, BY.
7.25.4a Megara (Hyblaea), Sicily: Map 7.25, BX.

MAP 7.25 OPENING MOVES OF THE SUMMER OF 413

lie at anchor inside, without being hurt by the Athenians sailing up and running them down. [6] The Athenians brought up to them a ship of ten thousand talents'[6a] burden furnished with wooden turrets and screens, and fastened ropes round the piles from their boats, wrenched them up and broke them, or dived down and sawed them in two. Meanwhile the Syracusans plied them with missiles from the docks, to which they replied from their large vessel; until at last most of the piles were removed by the Athenians. [7] But the most difficult part of the stockade was the part out of sight: some of the piles which had been driven in did not appear above water, so that it was dangerous to sail up, for fear of running the ships upon them, just as upon a reef, through not seeing them. However divers went down and sawed off even these for reward; although the Syracusans drove in others. [8] Indeed there was no end to the contrivances to which they resorted against each other, as might be expected between two hostile armies confronting each other at such a short distance; skirmishes and all kinds of other attempts were constant occurrences. [9] Meanwhile the Syracusans sent embassies composed of Corinthians, Ambraciots,[9a] and Spartans to the cities to tell them of the capture of Plemmyrium, and that their defeat in the sea fight was due less to the strength of the enemy than to their own disorder; and generally, to let them know that they were full of hope, and to ask them to come to their help with ships and troops, as

7.25.6a   The talent as a unit of weight varied over
          time and place between sixty and eighty
          pounds, which would make the burden of
          this vessel somewhere between three and
          four hundred tons.
7.25.9a   Ambracia: Map 7.25, AY.

441

the Athenians were expected with a fresh army, and if the one already there could be destroyed before the other arrived, the war would be at an end.

While the contending parties in Sicily were thus engaged, Demosthenes, having now got together the armament with which he was to go to that island, put out from Aegina,[1a] and making sail for the Peloponnesus, joined Charicles and the thirty ships of the Athenians. Taking on board the hoplites from Argos[1b] they sailed to Laconia,[1c] [2] and after first plundering part of Epidaurus Limera,[2a] landed on the coast of Laconia, opposite Cythera,[2b] where the temple of Apollo stands, and laying waste part of the country, fortified a sort of isthmus,[2c] to which the Helots[2d] of the Spartans might desert, and from which plundering raids might be made as from Pylos.[2e] [3] Demosthenes helped to occupy this place, and then immediately sailed on to Corcyra[3a] to take up some of the allies in that island, and so to proceed without delay to Sicily; while Charicles waited until he had completed the fortification of the place, and leaving a garrison there, returned home subsequently with his thirty ships and the Argives also.

This same summer thirteen hundred *peltasts,* Thracian swordsmen of the tribe of the Dii,[1a] who were to have sailed to Sicily with Demosthenes, arrived at Athens. [2] Since they had come too late, the Athenians determined to send them back to Thrace, from where they had come; to keep them for the Decelean war seemed too expensive, as the pay of each man was a *drachma* a day.[2a] [3] Indeed since Decelea[3a] had been first fortified by the whole Peloponnesian army during this summer, and then occupied for the continuous harassment of the country—the garrisons from the cities relieving each other at stated intervals—it had been causing great harm to the Athenians. In fact this occupation, by the destruction of property and loss of men which resulted from it, was one of the principal causes of their ruin. [4] Previously the invasions were short, and did not prevent them from making use of their land during the rest of the time: the enemy was now permanently fixed in Attica; at one time it was an attack in force, at another it was the regular garrison overrunning the country and making forays for its subsistence, and the Spartan king, Agis, was in the field and diligently prosecuting the war; great damage was therefore done to the Athenians. [5] They were deprived of their whole country: more than twenty thousand slaves had deserted,[5a] a great part of them artisans, and all their sheep and beasts of burden were lost; and as the cavalry rode out daily upon ex-

---

7.26.1a Aegina: Map 7.25, BY, and Map 7.29.
7.26.1b Argos: Map 7.25, BY.
7.26.1c Laconia: Map 7.25, BY.
7.26.2a Epidaurus Limera: Map 7.25, BY.
7.26.2b Cythera: Map 7.25, BY.
7.26.2c Isthmus opposite Cythera: site unknown.
7.26.2d For more on the Spartan Helots, see Appendix C, Spartan Institutions, §3–4.
7.26.2e Pylos: Map 7.25, BY.
7.26.3a Corcyra: Map 7.25, AY.
7.27.1a Territory of the Dii: Map 7.29, locator. *Peltasts* were lightly armed troops who could move much more quickly than the

heavily and expensively armed hoplites.
7.27.2a For the *drachma,* See Appendix J, Classical Greek Currency, §3.
7.27.3a Decelea: Map 7.29.
7.27.5a Presumably Thucydides refers not just to the losses of slaves in the first few months of the Decelean War but to losses sustained during the whole Decelean War. The figure of twenty thousand may have been a "late" addition. For slavery in Athens, see Appendix A, The Athenian Government, §2.

cursions to Decelea and to guard the country, their horses were either lamed by being constantly worked upon rocky ground, or wounded by the enemy.

Besides, the transport of provisions from Euboea,[1a] which had before been carried on so much more quickly over land by Decelea from Oropus,[1b] was now effected at great cost by sea round Cape Sunium;[1c] everything the city required had to be imported from abroad, and instead of a city it became a fortress. [2] Summer and winter the Athenians were worn out by having to keep guard on the fortifications, during the day by turns, by night all together, the cavalry excepted, at the different military posts or upon the wall. [3] But what most oppressed them was that they had two wars at once, and had thus reached a pitch of frenzy which no one would have believed possible if he had heard of it before it had come to pass. For could anyone have imagined that even when besieged by the Peloponnesians entrenched in Attica, they would still, instead of withdrawing from Sicily, stay on there besieging in like manner Syracuse, a city (taken as a city) in no way inferior to Athens, or would so thoroughly upset the Hellenic estimate of their strength and audacity, as to give the spectacle of a people which, at the beginning of the war, some thought might hold out one year, some two, none more than three, if the Peloponnesians invaded their country, now seventeen years after the first invasion, after having already suffered from all the evils of war, going to Sicily and undertaking a new war nothing inferior to that which they already had with the Peloponnesians? [4] These causes, the great losses from Decelea, and the other heavy charges that fell upon them, produced their financial distress; and it was at this time that they imposed upon their subjects, instead of the tribute,[4a] the tax of a twentieth upon all imports and exports by sea, which they thought would raise more money for them; their expenditure being now not the same as at first, but having grown with the war while their revenues decayed.

Accordingly, not wishing to incur expense in their present want of money, they sent back at once the Thracians who came too late for Demosthenes, under the conduct of Diitrephes, who was instructed, as they were to pass through the Euripus,[1a] to make use of them if possible in the voyage along shore to injure the enemy. [2] Diitrephes first landed them at Tanagra[2a] and hastily snatched some booty; he then sailed across the Euripus in the evening from Chalcis in Euboea[2b] and disembarking in Boeotia led them against Mycalessus.[2c] [3] He passed the night unobserved near the temple of Hermes, not quite two miles from Mycalessus, and at daybreak assaulted and took the city, which is not a large one; the inhabitants being

7.28
413
19th Year/Summer
ATTICA
All Athenian provisions now had to come by sea. The stresses of the double war at home and at Syracuse began to exhaust the Athenians, whose endurance had thus far exceeded earlier estimates. They now replaced the tribute system with taxes on imports and exports to increase revenues.

7.29
413
19th Year/Summer
MYCALESSUS
On their return to Thrace, the Dii stop in Boeotia to launch a surprise dawn attack on the city of Mycalessus. They sack the city and massacre its inhabitants—a disaster unsurpassed in suddenness and horror.

7.28.1a	Euboea: Map 7.29.	and 3.19.1.
7.28.1b	Oropus: Map 7.29.	7.29.1a Euripus, the narrowest portion of the
7.28.1c	Cape Sunium: Map 7.29.	strait lying between Euboea and the
7.28.4a	For more on the annual tribute that	mainland: Map 7.29.
	Athens collected from subject states, see	7.29.2a Tanagra: Map 7.29.
	Appendix B, The Athenian Empire, §2,	7.29.2b Chalcis, Euboea: Map 7.29.
	10. Also see 1.96.2, 2.13.4–5, 2.69.1,	7.29.2c Mycalessus: Map 7.29.

Map 7.29 Mycalessus

off their guard and not expecting that anyone would ever come up so far from the sea to molest them, the wall too being weak, and in some places having tumbled down, while in others it had not been built to any height, and the gates also being left open through their feeling of security. [4] The Thracians bursting into Mycalessus sacked the houses and temples, and butchered the inhabitants, sparing neither youth nor age but killing all they fell in with, one after the other, children and women, and even beasts of burden, and whatever other living creatures they saw; the Thracian people, like the bloodiest of the barbarians, being ever most murderous when it has nothing to fear. [5] Everywhere confusion reigned and death in all its shapes; and in particular they attacked a boys' school, the largest that there was in the place, into which the children had just gone, and massacred them all. In short, the disaster falling upon the whole city was unsurpassed in magnitude, and unapproached by any in suddenness and in horror.

Meanwhile the Thebans[1a] heard of it and marched to the rescue, and overtaking the Thracians before they had gone far, recovered the plunder and drove them in panic to the Euripus and the sea, where the vessels which brought them were lying. [2] The greatest slaughter took place while they were embarking, as they did not know how to swim, and those in the vessels on seeing what was going on shore moored them out of bow-shot: in the rest of the retreat the Thracians made a very respectable defense against the Theban horse, by which they were first attacked, dashing out and closing their ranks according to the tactics of their country, and lost only a few men in that part of the affair. A good number who were after plunder were actually caught in the city and put to death. [3] Alto-

7.30
413
19th Year/Summer
MYCALESSUS
Theban cavalry drive the Dii to their ships, inflicting casualties. Mycalessus loses a large proportion of its population.

7.30.1a Thebes: Map 7.29.

gether the Thracians had two hundred and fifty killed out of thirteen hundred, the Thebans and the rest who came to the rescue about twenty, troopers and hoplites, with Scirphondas, one of the *boeotarchs*.[3a] The Mycalessians lost a large proportion of their population.

While Mycalessus thus experienced a calamity, for its extent, as lamentable as any that happened in the war, [7.31.1] Demosthenes, who was at that time sailing to Corcyra[1a] after building the fort in Laconia,[1b] found a merchant ship lying at Pheia in Elis,[1c] in which the Corinthian hoplites were to cross to Sicily. The ship he destroyed, but the men escaped and subsequently got another in which they pursued their voyage.[1d] [2] After this, arriving at Zacynthus[2a] and Cephallenia,[2b] he took a body of hoplites on board, and sending for some of the Messenians from Naupactus,[2c] crossed over to the opposite coast of Acarnania,[2d] to Alyzia,[2e] and to Anactorium[2f] which was held by the Athenians. [3] While he was in these parts he was met by Eurymedon returning from Sicily, where he had been sent during the winter, with the money for the army, who told him the news, and also that he had heard, while at sea, that the Syracusans had taken Plemmyrium. [4] Here, also, Conon the commander at Naupactus came to them with news that the twenty-five Corinthian ships stationed opposite to him, far from refraining from war, were meditating an engagement; and he therefore begged them to send him some ships, as his own eighteen were not a match for the enemy's twenty-five. [5] Demosthenes and Eurymedon, accordingly, sent ten of their fastest triremes with Conon to reinforce the squadron at Naupactus, and meanwhile prepared for the assembly of their forces; Eurymedon, who was now the colleague of Demosthenes, and had turned back in consequence of his appointment, sailed to Corcyra to tell them to man fifteen ships and to enlist hoplites while Demosthenes raised slingers and darters from the parts about Acarnania.[5a]

Meanwhile the envoys[1a] who had gone from Syracuse to the cities after the capture of Plemmyrium had succeeded in their mission, and were about to bring the army that they had collected to Syracuse, when Nicias got wind of it, and sent to ask the Centoripae and Alicyae[1b] and other friendly Sicels who held the passes, not to let the enemy through, but to combine to prevent their passing, there being no other way by which they could even attempt it, as the Agrigentines[1c] would not give them a passage through their country. [2] In response to this request the Sicels laid a triple

7.31
413
19th Year/Summer
ACARNANIA
Demosthenes sails to Acarnania, gathering forces along the way. Eurymedon and Conon join him there, the latter requesting more triremes for Naupactus with which to face the threatening Corinthian fleet.

7.32
413
19th Year/Summer
SICILY
Hearing that reinforcements were approaching Syracuse by land, Nicias asks friendly Sicels for help. They ambush the enemy and inflict large casualties.

7.30.3a *Boeotarchs* were chief magistrates of the Boeotian federal government. See note 5.38.2a.
7.31.1a Corcyra: Map 7.32, AY.
7.31.1b Laconia: Map 7.32, BY. Construction of this fort was mentioned in 7.26.3.
7.31.1c Pheia, in Elis: Map 7.32, BY.
7.31.1d Possibly these are the hoplites blown by a storm to Libya who turn up in Syracuse in 7.50.1.
7.31.2a Zacynthus: Map 7.32, BY.
7.31.2b Cephallenia: Map 7.32, BY.
7.31.2c Naupactus: Map 7.32, BY.
7.31.2d Acarnania: Map 7.32, AY.
7.31.2e Alyzia: Map 7.32, AY.
7.31.2f Anactorium: Map 7.32, AY.
7.31.5a Thucydides apparently omitted reporting that Eurymedon was ordered in 7.16 to return to the main force after delivering the money, but it must be so.
7.32.1a These envoys went to the cities in 7.25.9.
7.32.1b Alicyae and Centoripae: the latter presumably inhabiting the territory around Centoripa (Map 7.32, BX).
7.32.1c Agrigentum: Map 7.32, BX.

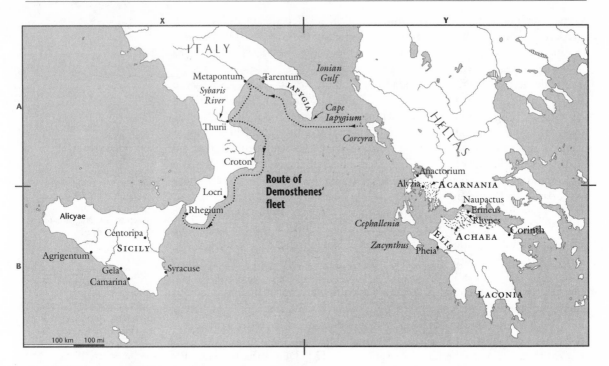

MAP 7.32 OPENING MOVES AND COUNTERMOVES IN 413

7.33
413
19th Year/Summer
SICILY-ITALY
While all Sicily (except for Agrigentum) now actively sends assistance to Syracuse, Demosthenes and his expedition cross to Italy and advance via Metapontum to Thurii.

ambush for the Sicilians on their march, and attacking them suddenly, while off their guard, killed about eight hundred of them and all the envoys except the Corinthian by whom fifteen hundred who escaped were conducted to Syracuse.

About the same time the Camarinaeans[1a] also came to the assistance of Syracuse with five hundred hoplites, three hundred darters, and as many archers, while the Geloans[1b] sent crews for five ships, four hundred darters, and two hundred horse. [2] Indeed almost the whole of Sicily, except the Agrigentines, who were neutral, now ceased merely to watch events as it had previously been doing, and actively joined Syracuse against the Athenians.

[3] While the Syracusans after the Sicel disaster put off any immediate attack upon the Athenians, Demosthenes and Eurymedon, whose forces from Corcyra[3a] and the mainland were now ready, crossed the Ionian gulf [3b] with all their armament to the Iapygian promontory,[3c] [4] and starting from thence touched at the Choerades Isles[4a] lying off Iapygia,[4b] where

7.33.1a   Camarina: Map 7.32, BX.
7.33.1b   Gela: Map 7.32, BX.
7.33.3a   Corcyra: Map 7.32, AY.
7.33.3b   Ionian gulf: Map 7.32, AY.
7.33.3c   Iapygian promontory (Cape Iapygium): Map 7.32, AY.
7.33.4a   Choerades Isles, thought to be small islands lying off the harbor of Tarentum,

Italy: Map 7.32, AX. See A. W. Gomme, A. Andrewes, and K.J. Dover, *A Historical Commentary on Thucydides,* iv (Oxford, 1970), 413.
7.33.4b   Iapygia: Map 7.32, AX.

they took on board a hundred and fifty Iapygian darters of the Messapian tribe, and after renewing an old friendship with Artas the chief, who had furnished them with the darters, arrived at Metapontum[4c] in Italy. [5] Here they persuaded their allies the Metapontines to send with them three hundred darters and two triremes, and with this reinforcement coasted on to Thurii,[5a] where they found the party hostile to Athens recently expelled by a revolution, [6] and accordingly remained there to muster and review the whole army, to see if any had been left behind, and to prevail upon the Thurians resolutely to join them in their expedition, and in the circumstances in which they found themselves to conclude a defensive and offensive alliance with the Athenians.

About the same time the Peloponnesians in the twenty-five ships stationed opposite to the squadron at Naupactus in order to protect the passage of the transports to Sicily, had prepared for battle, and manning some additional vessels, so as to be numerically little inferior to the Athenians, anchored off Erineus in Achaea in the Rhypic[1a] country. [2] The place off which they lay being in the form of a crescent, the land forces furnished to them by the Corinthians and their allies on the spot came up and ranged themselves upon the projecting headlands on either side, while the fleet, under the command of Polyanthes the Corinthian, held the intervening space and blocked up the entrance. [3] The Athenians under Diphilus now sailed out against them with thirty-three ships from Naupactus [4] and the Corinthians, at first not moving, at length thought they saw their opportunity, raised the signal, and advanced and engaged the Athenians. [5] After an obstinate struggle, the Corinthians lost three ships, and without sinking any altogether, disabled seven of the enemy, which were struck prow to prow and had their outriggers smashed by the Corinthian vessels, whose catheads had been strengthened for this very purpose.[5a] [6] After an action of this even character, in which either party could claim the victory (although the Athenians became masters of the wrecks through the wind driving them out to sea, the Corinthians not putting out again to meet them), the two combatants parted. No pursuit took place, and no prisoners were made on either side; the Corinthians and Peloponnesians who were fighting near the shore escaping with ease, and none of the Athenian vessels having been sunk. [7] The Athenians now sailed back to Naupactus, and the Corinthians immediately set up a trophy as victors, because they had disabled a greater number of the enemy's ships. Moreover they held that they had not been defeated, for the very same reason that their opponent held that he had not been victorious; the Corinthians considering that they were conquerors, if not decidedly conquered, and the Athenians thinking

7.34
413
19th Year/Summer
ACHAEA
In an inconclusive naval battle off Erineus structurally braced Corinthian triremes cause extensive damage to seven Athenian ships, while losing three of their own number. Both sides erect trophies but the Corinthians claim victory for having avoided defeat and the Athenians are reluctant to claim victory for not having won decisively.

7.33.4c Metapontum, Italy: Map 7.32, AX.
7.33.5a Thurii, Italy: Map 7.32, AX.
7.34.1a Erineus and Rhypes, Achaea: Map 7.32, BY.
7.34.5a The outriggers, in which the topmost oarsmen were seated, projected out from the sides of the ship and so were very vulnerable to attack. The Corinthians seem

to have reinforced at least the front faces of their own outriggers with strong bow timbers ("catheads"). This allowed them to ram their opponents' ships head on, thereby smashing the enemy's outriggers without causing damage to their own. See 7.36.1a and Appendix G, Trireme Warfare, §14.

themselves vanquished, because not decidedly victorious. [8] However, when the Peloponnesians sailed off and their land forces had dispersed, the Athenians also set up a trophy as victors in Achaea, about two miles and a quarter from Erineus, the Corinthian station. This was the termination of the action at Naupactus.

To return to Demosthenes and Eurymedon: the Thurians[1a] having now got ready to join in the expedition with seven hundred hoplites and three hundred darters, the two generals ordered the ships to sail along the coast to the Crotonian[1b] territory, and meanwhile held a review of all the land forces upon the river Sybaris,[1c] and then led them through the Thurian country. [2] Arrived at the river Hylias,[2a] they here received a message from the Crotonians, saying that they would not allow the army to pass through their country; upon which the Athenians descended toward the shore, and bivouacked near the sea and the mouth of the Hylias, where the fleet also met them, and the next day embarked and sailed along the coast touching at all the cities except Locri,[2b] until they came to Petra in the Rhegian territory.[2c]

Meanwhile the Syracusans hearing of their approach resolved to make a second attempt with their fleet and their other forces on shore, which they had been collecting for this very purpose in order to do something before their arrival. [2] In addition to other improvements suggested by the recent sea fight which they now adopted in the equipment of their navy, they cut down their prows to a smaller compass to make them more solid and made their catheads stronger, and from these let support beams into the vessel's sides for a length of six cubits within and without, in the same way as the Corinthians had altered their prows before engaging the squadron at Naupactus.[2a] [3] The Syracusans thought that they would thus have an advantage over the Athenian vessels, which were not constructed with equal strength, but were slight in the bows, from their being more used to sail round and charge the enemy's side than to meet him prow to prow, and that the battle being in the Great Harbor, with a great many ships in not much room, was also a fact in their favor. Charging prow to prow, they would stave in the enemy's bows, by striking with solid and stout beaks against hollow and weak ones; [4] and secondly, the Athenians for want of room would be unable to use their favorite maneuver of breaking the line or of sailing round, as the Syracusans would do their best not to let them do the one, and want of room would prevent their doing the other.[4a] [5] This charging prow to prow which had up till then been thought lack of skill in a helmsman, would be the Syracusans' chief maneuver, as being that which they should find most useful, since

7.35
413
19th Year/Summer
ITALY
Demosthenes' force, reinforced by Thurian hoplites, sails along the Italian coast to Petra in Rhegian territory.

7.36
413
19th Year/Summer
SYRACUSE
Following the Corinthian model, the Syracusans strengthen their ships to prepare them for head on ramming. They intend to engage the Athenians again, counting on the lack of room in the harbor and their control of the shore to prevent the Athenians from exploiting their superior maneuvering skills.

7.35.1a Thurii, Italy: Map 7.32, AX.
7.35.1b Croton, Italy: Map 7.32, AX.
7.35.1c Sybaris river: Map 7.32, AX.
7.35.2a Hylias river: site unknown.
7.35.2b Locri (Epizephyrian), Italy: Map 7.32, BX.
7.35.2c Petra, in Rhegian territory: site unknown.

Rhegium: Map 7.32, BX.
7.36.2a See note 7.34.5a and Appendix G, Trireme Warfare, §14.
7.36.4a For these maneuvers, see Phormio's speech on naval tactics in 2.89, and Appendix G, Trireme Warfare, §11–14.

the Athenians, if repulsed, would not be able to back water in any direction except toward the shore, and that only for a little way, and in the little space in front of their own camp. The rest of the harbor would be commanded by the Syracusans; [6] and the Athenians, if hard pressed and crowded together in a small space, would run foul of one another and fall into disorder, which was in fact what did the Athenians most harm in all the sea fights, since they had not, like the Syracusans, the whole harbor available for retreat. As to their sailing round into the open sea, this would be impossible with the Syracusans in possession of the way in and out, especially as Plemmyrium[6a] would be hostile to them and the mouth of the harbor was not large.

With these contrivances to suit their skill and ability, and now more confident after the previous sea fight, the Syracusans attacked by land and sea at once. [2] Gylippus led out the city force a little before and brought it up to the wall of the Athenians, where it looked toward the city, while the force from the Olympieum,[2a] that is to say, the hoplites that were there with the horse and the light troops of the Syracusans, advanced against the wall from the opposite side; the ships of the Syracusans and allies sailing out immediately afterwards. [3] The Athenians at first supposed that they were to be attacked by land only, and it was not without alarm that they saw the fleet suddenly approaching as well; and while some were forming upon the walls and in front of them against the advancing enemy, and some marching out in haste against the numbers of horse and darters coming from the Olympieum and from outside, others manned the ships or rushed down to the beach to oppose the enemy, and when the ships were manned put out with seventy-five sail against about eighty of the Syracusans.

After spending a great part of the day in advancing and retreating and skirmishing with each other, without either being able to gain any advantage worth speaking of, except that the Syracusans sank one or two of the Athenian vessels, they parted, the land force at the same time retiring from the lines. [2] The next day the Syracusans remained quiet, and gave no signs of what they were going to do; but Nicias, seeing that the battle had been a drawn one, and expecting that they would attack again, compelled the captains to refit any of the ships that had suffered, and moored merchant vessels before the stockade which they had driven into the sea in front of their ships, [3] to serve instead of an enclosed harbor,[3a] at about two hundred feet from each other, in order that any ship that was hard pressed might be able to retreat in safety and sail out again at leisure. These preparations occupied the Athenians all day until nightfall.

7.36.6a   Plemmyrium and the harbor mouth: Map
          7.44, BY.
7.37.2a   Olympieum: Map 7.44, BX.
7.38.3a   Nicias' substitute for an enclosed harbor,
          probable location: Map 7.44, BY.

7.39
413
19th Year/Summer
SYRACUSE
The Syracusans attack again,
planning to surprise the
Athenians by a second,
sudden attack after breaking
off for a hasty meal.

7.40
413
19th Year/Summer
SYRACUSE
The Syracusans retire to their
docks, where the market has
been relocated so that they
may eat quickly and attack
again. Taken by surprise, the
Athenians man their ships and
advance. The reinforced
Syracusan ships stave in the
bows of many of the Athenian
vessels.

7.41
413
19th Year/Summer
SYRACUSE
The Athenians flee to their
harbor, pursued by the
victorious and now confident
Syracusans.

The next day the Syracusans began operations at an earlier hour, but with the same plan of attack by land and sea. [2] A great part of the day the rivals spent as before, confronting and skirmishing with each other; until at last Ariston son of Pyrrhicus, a Corinthian, the ablest helmsman in the Syracusan service, persuaded their naval commanders to send to the officials in the city, and tell them to move the market as quickly as they could down to the sea, and oblige everyone to bring whatever edibles he had and sell them there, thus enabling the commanders to land the crews and dine at once close to the ships,[2a] and shortly afterwards, the same day, to attack the Athenians again when they were not expecting it.

In compliance with this advice a messenger was sent and the market got ready, upon which the Syracusans suddenly backed water and withdrew to the city, and immediately landed and took their dinner upon the spot; [2] while the Athenians, supposing that they had returned to the city because they felt they were beaten, disembarked at their leisure and set about getting their dinners and about their other occupations, under the impression that they had done with fighting for that day. [3] Suddenly the Syracusans manned their ships and again sailed against them; and the Athenians, in great confusion and most of them hungry, got on board, and with great difficulty put out to meet them. [4] For some time both parties remained on the defensive without engaging, until the Athenians at last resolved not to let themselves be worn out by waiting where they were, but to attack without delay, and giving a cheer, went into action. [5] The Syracusans received them, and charging prow to prow as they had intended, stove in a great part of the Athenian outriggers by the strength of their beaks; the darters on the decks also did great damage to the Athenians, but still greater damage was done by the Syracusans who went about in small boats, ran in upon the oars of the Athenian triremes, and sailed against their sides, and from there threw their javelins at the sailors.

At last, fighting hard in this fashion, the Syracusans gained the victory, and the Athenians turned and fled between the merchant ships to their own station. [2] The Syracusan ships pursued them as far as the merchant ships, where they were stopped by the beams armed with dolphins suspended from those vessels over the passage.[2a] [3] Two of the Syracusan vessels went too near in the excitement of victory and were destroyed, one of them being taken with its crew. [4] After sinking seven of the Athenian ves-

---

7.39.2a Greek soldiers and sailors at this time had to purchase their food from local markets, so the speed with which a trireme crew's meal could be prepared and eaten would be significantly effected by the proximity of markets to the boat. See also 8.95.4, where the Athenians had to disperse to the outskirts of Eretria to purchase food because nothing was for sale in the *agora*, and thus were unable to quickly man and deploy their ships to meet an enemy attack.

7.41.2a These "dolphins" were heavy lead weights which were suspended from the main yardarms of the merchant ships that had been anchored to form a stockade harbor and refuge for the Athenians. The sail of an ancient ship was suspended from a long spar that, when squared (set perpendicular to its axis), extended far beyond its hull. Dolphins heavy enough to pierce a ship's deck and hull were hung from the end of the spar and dropped on any enemy boat that ventured too close.

sels and disabling many, and taking most of the men prisoners and killing others, the Syracusans retired and set up trophies for both the engagements, being now confident of having a decided superiority by sea, and by no means despairing of equal success by land.

In the meantime, while the Syracusans were preparing for a second attack by both land and sea, Demosthenes and Eurymedon arrived with the reinforcements from Athens, consisting of about seventy-three ships, including the foreigners; nearly five thousand hoplites, Athenian and allied; a large number of darters, Hellenic and barbarian, and slingers and archers and everything else upon a corresponding scale. [2] The Syracusans and their allies were for the moment not a little dismayed at the idea that there was to be no term or end to their dangers, seeing, in spite of the fortification of Decelea,[2a] a new army arrive nearly equal to the former, and the power of Athens proving so great in every quarter. On the other hand, the first Athenian armament regained a certain confidence in the midst of its misfortunes. [3] Demosthenes, seeing how matters stood, felt that he could not drag on and fare as Nicias had done, who by wintering in Catana[3a] instead of at once attacking Syracuse had allowed the terror of his first arrival to evaporate in contempt, and had given time to Gylippus to arrive with a force from the Peloponnesus, which the Syracusans would never have sent for if he had attacked immediately; for they thought that they were a match for him by themselves, and would not have discovered their inferiority until they were already under siege, and even if they then sent for help they would no longer have been equally able to profit by its arrival. Recollecting this, and well aware that it was now on the first day after his arrival that he like Nicias was most formidable to the enemy, Demosthenes determined to lose no time in drawing the utmost profit from the consternation at the moment inspired by his army; [4] and seeing that the counterwall of the Syracusans,[4a] which hindered the Athenians from investing them, was a single one, and that he who should become master of the way up to Epipolae,[4b] and afterwards of the camp there, would find no difficulty in taking it, as no one would even wait for his attack, made all haste to attempt the enterprise. [5] This he took to be the shortest way of ending the war, as he would either succeed and take Syracuse, or would lead back the armament instead of frittering away the lives of the Athenians engaged in the expedition and the resources of the country at large.

7.42
413
19th Year/Summer
SYRACUSE
Demosthenes' relief expedition arrives, dismaying the Syracusans and raising the spirits of the Athenians. Demosthenes decides to attack and either achieve decisive success immediately or to withdraw the Athenians from their present difficult position.

7.42.2a   Decelea, in Attica: Map 7.29.
7.42.3a   Catana: Map 7.49. See 6.71 for the
          Athenian decision to winter at Catana in
          415/4.
7.42.4a   Syracusan crosswall, probable location:
          Map 7.44, AX.
7.42.4b   Epipolae: Map 7.44, AX.

7.43
413
19th Year/Summer
SYRACUSE
After failing to take the
Syracusan counterwall by
seige engine and assault,
Demosthenes attempts a
night attack on Epipolae. It
proves initially successful,
but increasing Athenian
disorganization and a
determined stand by the
Boeotians turn victory into
defeat.

[6] First therefore the Athenians went out and laid waste the lands of the Syracusans about the Anapus[6a] and carried all before them as at first by land and by sea, the Syracusans not offering to oppose them upon either element, unless it were with their cavalry and darters from the Olympieum.[6b]

Next Demosthenes resolved to make an attempt on the counterwall first by means of siege engines. As however the engines that he brought up were burnt by the enemy fighting from the wall, and the rest of the forces repulsed after attacking at many different points, he determined to delay no longer, and having obtained the consent of Nicias and his fellow commanders, proceeded to put into execution his plan of attacking Epipolae. [2] As by day it seemed impossible to approach and get up without being observed, he ordered provisions for five days, took all the masons and carpenters, and other things such as arrows, and everything else that they could want for the work of fortification if successful; and after the first watch set out with Eurymedon and Menander and the whole army for Epipolae, Nicias being left behind in the lines. [3] Having come up by the hill of Euryelus[3a] (where the former army had ascended at first), unobserved by the enemy's guards, they went up to the fort which the Syracusans had there, and took it, and put to the sword part of the garrison. [4] The greater number, however, escaped at once and gave the alarm to the camps, of which there were three upon Epipolae, defended by outworks, one of the Syracusans, one of the other Sicilians, and one of the allies; and also to the six hundred Syracusans forming the original garrison for this part of Epipolae. [5] These at once advanced against the assailants, and encountering Demosthenes and the Athenians, were routed by them after a sharp resistance, the victors immediately pushing on, eager to achieve the objects of the attack without giving time for their ardor to cool; meanwhile others from the very beginning were taking the counterwall of the Syracusans, which was abandoned by its garrison, and pulling down the battlements. [6] The Syracusans and the allies, and Gylippus with the troops under his command, advanced to the rescue from the outworks, but engaged with some consternation (a night attack being a piece of audacity which they had never expected), and were at first compelled to retreat. [7] But while the Athenians, flushed with their victory, now advanced with less order, wishing to make their way as quickly as possible through the whole force of the enemy not yet engaged, without relaxing their attack or giving them time to rally, the Boeotians[7a] made the first stand against them, attacked them, routed them, and put them to flight.

7.42.6a Anapus River: Map 7.44, BX.
7.42.6b Olympieum: Map 7.44, BX.
7.43.3a Euryelus: Map 7.44, AX.
7.43.7a Boeotia: Map 7.29.

The Athenians now fell into great disorder and perplexity, so that it was not easy to get from one side or the other any detailed account of the affair. By day certainly the combatants have a clearer notion, though even then by no means of all that takes place, no one knowing much of anything that does not go on in his own immediate neighborhood; but in a night engagement (and this was the only one that occurred between great armies during the war) how could anyone know anything for certain? [2] Although there was a bright moon they saw each other only as men do by moonlight, that is to say, they could distinguish the form of the body, but could not tell for certain whether it was a friend or an enemy. Both had great numbers of hoplites moving about in a small space. [3] Some of the Athenians were already defeated, while others were coming up yet unconquered for their first attack. A large part also of the rest of their forces either had only just got up, or were still ascending, so that they did not know which way to march. Owing to the rout that had taken place all in front was now in confusion, and the noise made it difficult to distinguish anything. [4] The victorious Syracusans and allies were cheering each other on with loud cries, by night the only possible means of communication, and meanwhile receiving all who came against them; while the Athenians were seeking for one another, taking all in front of them for enemies, even though they might be some of their now flying friends; and by constantly asking for the watchword, which was their only means of recognition, not only caused great confusion among themselves by asking all at once, but also made it known to the enemy, [5] whose own they did not so readily discover, as the Syracusans were victorious and not scattered, and thus less easily mistaken. The result was that if the Athenians fell in with a party of the enemy that was weaker than they, it escaped them through knowing their watchword; while if they themselves failed to answer they were put to the sword. [6] But what hurt them as much, or indeed more than anything else, was the singing of the *paean*,[6a] from the perplexity which it caused by being nearly the same on either side: the Argives and Corcyraeans and any other Dorian peoples in the [Athenian] army struck terror into the Athenians whenever they raised their paean, no less than did the enemy. [7] Thus, after being once thrown into disorder, they ended by coming into collision with each other in many parts of the field, friends with friends, and citizens with citizens, and not only terrified one another, but even came to blows and could only be parted with difficulty. [8] In the pursuit many perished by throwing themselves down the cliffs, the way down from Epipolae being narrow; and of those who got down safely into the plain, although many,

7.44
413
19th Year/Summer
SYRACUSE
Despite bright moonlight, the participants could perceive little of the battle. Athenian forces became scattered; they were confused by the *paean* of their Dorian allies, which was so like that of their Dorian foes. Many Athenians became lost in the rout that followed.

7.44.6a   The *paean* was the war chant sung by troops going into battle. Apparently, among other Dorian cultural elements, there was a distinctive Dorian paean, see Appendix H, Dialects and Ethnic Groups, §9.

MAP 7.44 FIGHTING AT SYRACUSE IN 413[8a]

especially those who belonged to the first armament, escaped through their better acquaintance with the locality, some of the newcomers lost their way and wandered over the country, and were cut off in the morning by the Syracusan cavalry and killed.

7.45
413
19th Year/Summer
SYRACUSE
The Syracusans erect trophies and return the dead. Athenian losses are high.

The next day the Syracusans set up two trophies, one upon Epipolae where the ascent had been made, and the other on the spot where the first check was given by the Boeotians; and the Athenians took back their dead under truce. [2] A great many of the Athenians and allies were killed, although still more arms were taken than could be accounted for by the number of the dead, as some of those who were obliged to leap down from the cliffs without their shields escaped with their lives and did not perish like the rest.

7.46
413
19th Year/Summer
SYRACUSE
Their victory restores Syracusan morale.

After this the Syracusans, recovering their old confidence at such an unexpected stroke of good fortune, despatched Sicanus with fifteen ships to Agrigentum[1a] where there was a revolution, to induce if possible the city to join them; while Gylippus again went by land into the rest of Sicily to bring up reinforcements, being now in hope of taking the Athenian lines by storm, after the result of the affair on Epipolae.

7.44.8a   Map 7.44 follows the interpretation of   7.46.1a   Agrigentum: Map 7.49.
          Peter Green in *Armada from Athens;* see
          note 7.4.7c.

In the meantime the Athenian generals consulted upon the disaster which had happened, and the general weakness of the army. They saw themselves unsuccessful in their enterprises, and the soldiers disgusted with their stay; [2] disease being rife among them owing to its being the sickly season of the year, and to the marshy and unhealthy nature of the spot in which they were encamped; and the state of their affairs generally being thought desperate. [3] Accordingly, Demosthenes was of opinion that they ought not to stay any longer; but consistent with his original idea[3a] in risking the attempt upon Epipolae, now that this had failed, he gave his vote for going away without further loss of time, while the sea might yet be crossed, and their late reinforcement might give them the superiority at all events on that element. [4] He also said that it would be more profitable for the state to carry on the war against those who were building fortifications in Attica, than against the Syracusans whom it was no longer easy to subdue; besides which it was not right to squander large sums of money to no purpose by going on with the siege.

This was the opinion of Demosthenes. Nicias, without denying the bad state of their affairs, was unwilling to admit their weakness, or to have it reported to the enemy that the Athenians in full council were openly voting for retreat; for in that case they would be much less likely to accomplish it when they wanted without discovery. [2] Moreover, his own particular information still gave him reason to hope that the affairs of the enemy would soon be in a worse state than their own, if the Athenians persevered in the siege; as they would wear out the Syracusans by lack of money, especially with the more extensive command of the sea now given them by their present navy. Besides this, there was a party in Syracuse who wished to betray the city to the Athenians, and kept sending him messages and telling him not to raise the siege.[2a] [3] Accordingly, knowing this and really waiting because he hesitated between the two courses and wished to see his way more clearly, in his public speech on this occasion he refused to lead off the army, saying he was sure the Athenians would never approve of their returning without a vote of theirs. Those who would vote upon their conduct, instead of judging the facts as eyewitnesses like themselves and not from what they might hear from hostile critics, would simply be guided by the calumnies of the first clever speaker; [4] while many, indeed most, of the soldiers on the spot, who now so loudly proclaimed the danger of their position, when they reached Athens would proclaim just as loudly the opposite, and would say that their generals had been bribed to betray them and return. For himself, therefore, who knew the Athenian temper, sooner than perish under a dishonorable charge and by an unjust sentence at the hands of the Athenians, he would rather take his chance and die, if die he must, a soldier's death at the hand of the enemy. [5] Besides, after all, the Syracusans were in a worse case than themselves. What with paying merce-

7.47
413
19th Year/Summer
SYRACUSE
Demosthenes urges an immediate withdrawal while his expedition's forces maintain their naval superiority, arguing that Athens had greater need of them at home.

7.48
413
19th Year/Summer
SYRACUSE
Nicias disagrees, arguing from information received from Syracusan informants that the enemy is running out of funds with which to pay mercenaries and sailors, and may soon financially collapse. He also fears Athenian blame for defeat and prefers a soldier's honorable death in the field to dishonorable execution in Athens.

7.47.3a Demosthenes' original plan was described   7.48.2a For the pro-Athenian faction in Syracuse,
          in 7.42.3–5.   see 6.103.3–4 and 7.73.3.

naries, spending upon fortified posts, and now for a full year maintaining a large navy, they were already at a loss and would soon be at a standstill: they had already spent two thousand talents and incurred heavy debts besides, and could not lose even ever so small a fraction of their present force through not paying it, without ruin to their cause; depending as they did more upon mercenaries than upon soldiers obliged to serve, like their own. [6] He therefore said that they ought to stay and carry on the siege, and not depart defeated in point of money, in which they were much superior.

Nicias spoke positively because he had exact information of the financial distress at Syracuse, and also because of the strength of the pro-Athenian party there which kept sending him messages not to raise the siege; besides which he had more confidence than before in his fleet, and felt sure at least of its success. [2] Demosthenes, however, would not hear for a moment of continuing the siege, but said that if they could not lead off the army without a decree from Athens, and if they were obliged to stay on, they ought to remove to Thapsus[2a] or Catana;[2b] where their land forces would have a wide extent of country to overrun, and could live by plundering the enemy, and would thus do them damage; while the fleet would have the open sea to fight in, that is to say, instead of a narrow space which was all in the enemy's favor, a wide sea room where their skills would be of use, and where they could retreat or advance without being confined or circumscribed either when they put out or put in. [3] In any case he was altogether opposed to their staying on where they were, and insisted on removing at once, as quickly and with as little delay as possible; and in this judgment Eurymedon agreed. [4] Nicias however still objecting, a certain diffidence and hesitation came over them, with a suspicion that Nicias might have some further information to make him so positive.

While the Athenians lingered on in this way without moving from where they were, Gylippus and Sicanus now arrived at Syracuse. Sicanus had failed to win over Agrigentum, the party friendly to the Syracusans having been driven out while he was still at Gela; but Gylippus was accompanied not only by a large number of troops raised in Sicily, but by the hoplites sent off in the spring from the Peloponnesus in the merchant vessels that had arrived at Selinus[1a] from Libya.[1b] [2] They had been carried to Libya by a storm, and having obtained two triremes and pilots from the Cyrenians,[2a] on their voyage along shore had taken sides with the Euesperitae[2b] and had defeated the Libyans who were besieging them, and from thence coasting on to Neapolis,[2c] a Carthaginian[2d] trading post, and the nearest point to Sicily, from which it is only two days' and a night's voyage, there crossed over and came to Selinus. [3] Immediately upon their arrival the Syracusans prepared to attack the Athenians again by land

---

7.49.2a   Thapsus: Map 7.49.
7.49.2b   Catana: Map 7.49.
7.50.1a   Syracuse, Agrigentum, Gela, and Selinus:
       Map 7.49.
7.50.1b   Libya: Map 7.49. These hoplites were
       possibly the Corinthian hoplites men-
       tioned in 7.31.1.

7.50.2a   Cyrene, in Libya: Map 7.49.
7.50.2b   Euesperides, in Libya: Map 7.49.
7.50.2c   Neapolis: Map 7.49.
7.50.2d   Carthage: Map 7.49.

MAP 7.49 MORE REINFORCEMENTS FOR SYRACUSE

and sea at once. The Athenian generals seeing a fresh army come to the aid of the enemy, and that their own circumstances, far from improving, were becoming daily worse, and above all distressed by the sickness of the soldiers, now began to repent of not having departed before; and Nicias no longer offering the same opposition, except by urging that there should be no open voting, they gave orders as secretly as possible for all to be prepared to sail out from the camp at a given signal. [4] All was at last ready, and they were on the point of sailing away when an eclipse of the moon,[4a] which was then at the full, took place. Most of the Athenians, deeply impressed by this occurrence, now urged the generals to wait; and Nicias, who was somewhat overaddicted to divination and practices of that kind, refused from that moment even to take the question of departure into consideration, until they had waited the thrice nine days prescribed by the soothsayers.

The besiegers were thus condemned to stay in the country; [7.51.1] and the Syracusans getting wind of what had happened, became more eager than ever to press the Athenians, who had now themselves acknowledged that they were no longer their superiors either by sea or by land, as otherwise they would never have planned to sail away. Besides which the Syracusans did not wish them to settle in any other part of Sicily, where they would be more difficult to deal with, but desired to force them to fight at sea as quickly as possible, in a position favorable to themselves. [2] Accordingly they manned their ships and practiced for as many days as they thought sufficient. When the moment arrived they assaulted on the first day the Athenian lines, and upon a small force of hoplites and horse sallying out against them by certain gates, cut off some of the former and routed and pursued them to the lines, where, as the entrance was narrow, the Athenians lost seventy horses and a few hoplites.

Drawing off their troops for this day, on the next the Syracusans went out with a fleet of seventy-six sail, and at the same time advanced with their land forces against the lines. The Athenians put out to meet them with eighty-six ships, came to close quarters, and engaged. The Syracusans and their allies first defeated the Athenian center, [2] and then caught Eurymedon, the commander of the right wing, who was sailing out from the line more toward the land in order to surround the enemy, in the hollow and recess of the harbor,[2a] and killed him and destroyed the ships accompanying him; after which they now chased the whole Athenian fleet before them and drove them ashore.

Gylippus seeing the enemy's fleet defeated and carried ashore beyond their stockades and camp, ran down to the breakwater[1a] with some of his troops, in order to cut off the men as they landed and make it easier for the Syracusans to tow off the vessels by the shore being friendly ground. [2] The Tyrrhenians[2a] who guarded this point for the Athenians seeing them come on in disorder, advanced out against them and attacked and routed their van, hurling it into the marsh of Lysimeleia.[2b] [3] Afterwards the Syracusan and allied troops arrived in greater numbers, and the Athenians fearing for their ships came up also to the rescue and engaged them, and defeated and pursued them for some distance and killed a few of their

7.51
413
19th Year/Summer
SYRACUSE
The Syracusans, eager to deal with the Athenians in their present location, renew their training at sea and attack the Athenians on land.

7.52
413
19th Year/Summer
SYRACUSE
The Syracusans decisively win a naval battle in the harbor. Eurymedon is killed.

7.53
413
19th Year/Summer
SYRACUSE
Gylippus attempts to capture some Athenian ships but is thwarted by the Athenians, who also stop a Syracusan fireship before it causes harm.

7.50.4a This eclipse took place on August 27, 413.
7.52.2a Recess of the great harbor, probable location: Map 7.44, BY.
7.53.1a The "breakwater" was probably a narrow spit of high ground lying north of the Athenian camp between the waters of the great harbor and the marsh of Lysimeleia; see Map 7.44, BY.
7.53.2a "Tyrrhenians" is Thucydides' name for the Etruscans from Etruria (Thucydides' Tyrrhenia) in central Italy; see Map 7.49.
7.53.2b Marsh of Lysimeleia, probable location: Map 7.44, BY; see note 6.99.1a.

hoplites. They succeeded in rescuing most of their ships and brought them down by their camp; eighteen however were taken by the Syracusans and their allies, and all the men killed. [4] The rest the enemy tried to burn by means of an old cargo ship which they filled with brush and pinewood, set on fire, and let drift down the wind which blew full on the Athenians. The Athenians, however, alarmed for their ships, contrived means for stopping it and putting it out, and checking the flames and the nearer approach of the merchant ship, thus escaped the danger.

After this the Syracusans set up a trophy for the sea fight and for the hoplites whom they had cut off up at the lines, where they took the horses; and the Athenians for the rout of the foot driven by the Tyrrhenians into the marsh, and for their own victory with the rest of the army.

7.54
413
Each side erects trophies.

The Syracusans had now gained a decisive victory at sea, where until now they had feared the reinforcement brought by Demosthenes, and deep, in consequence, was the despondency of the Athenians, and great their disappointment, and greater still their regret for having come on the expedition. [2] These were the only cities that they had yet encountered, similar to their own in character, under democracies like themselves, which had ships and horses, and were of considerable magnitude. They had been unable to divide and bring them over by holding out the prospect of changes in their governments, or to crush them by their great superiority in force, and had failed in most of their attempts, and being already in perplexity, had now been defeated at sea, where defeat could never have been expected, and were thus plunged deeper into bewilderment than ever.

7.55
413
19th Year/Summer
SYRACUSE
Naval defeat causes despair among the Athenians, who realize that they had never fought a city like Syracuse, which could not be suborned, overpowered, or persuaded to ally.

Meanwhile the Syracusans immediately began to sail freely along the harbor, and determined to close up its mouth, so that the Athenians might not be able to steal out in future, even if they wished. [2] Indeed, the Syracusans no longer thought only of saving themselves, but also how to hinder the escape of the enemy; thinking, and thinking rightly, that they were now much the strongest, and that to conquer the Athenians and their allies by land and sea would win them great glory in Hellas. The rest of the Hellenes would thus immediately be either freed or released from apprehension, as the remaining forces of Athens would be henceforth unable to sustain the war that would be waged against her; while they, the Syracusans, would be regarded as the authors of this deliverance, and would be held in high admiration, not only with all men now living but also with posterity. [3] Nor were these the only considerations that gave dignity to the struggle. They would thus conquer not only the Athenians but also their numerous allies, and conquer not alone, but with their companions-in-arms, commanding side by side with the Corinthians and Spartans, having offered their city to stand in the van of danger, and having been in a great measure the pioneers of naval success.

[4] Indeed, there were never so many peoples assembled before a single city, if we except the grand total gathered together in this war under Athens and Sparta.

7.56
413
19th Year/Summer
SYRACUSE
The Syracusans perceive their superiority, and begin to close the harbor mouth to prevent an Athenian escape. They are now ambitious to win glory from the defeat and capture of such an expedition, and the consequent liberation of Hellas.

MAP 7.56 EASTERN CONTRIBUTORS TO ATHENIAN FORCES AT SYRACUSE

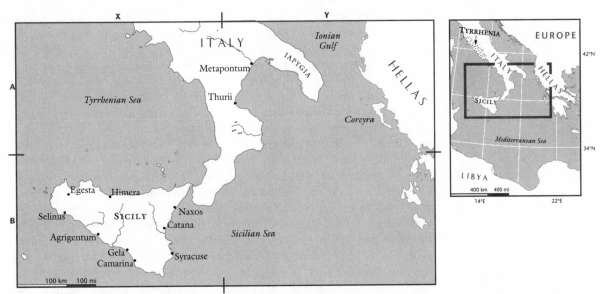

MAP 7.57 WESTERN CONTRIBUTORS TO ATHENIAN AND SYRACUSAN FORCES

The following were the states on either side who came to Syracuse to fight for or against Sicily, to help to conquer or defend the island. Right or community of blood was not the bond of union between them, so much as interest or compulsion as the case might be. [2] The Athenians themselves being Ionians went against the Dorians of Syracuse of their own free will; and the peoples still speaking Attic and using the Athenian laws, the Lemnians, Imbrians,[2a] and Aeginetans, that is to say, the then occupants of Aegina, being their colonists, went with them. To these must be also added the Histiaeans dwelling at Histiaea in Euboea.[2b] [3] Of the rest some joined in the expedition as subjects of the Athenians, others as independent allies, others as mercenaries. [4] To the number of the subjects paying tribute belonged the Eretrians, Chalcidians, Styrians, and Carystians[4a] from Euboea; the Ceans, Andrians, and Tenians[4b] from the islands; and the Milesians, Samians, and Chians from Ionia.[4c] The Chians, however, joined as independent allies, paying no tribute, but furnishing ships. Most of these were Ionians and descended from the Athenians, except the Carystians, who are Dryopes, and although subjects and obliged to serve, were still Ionians fighting against Dorians. [5] Besides these there were men of Aeolic race, the Methymnians,[5a]

7.57
413
19th Year/Summer
SYRACUSE
Thucydides lists all participants in the Athenian force, recounting their ethnicity, their status, and the circumstances that led to their inclusion in the expedition.

7.57.2a   Lemnos and Imbros: Map 7.56, AY. For
           Ionians against Dorians, see Appendix H,
           Dialects and Ethnic Groups, §8.
7.57.2b   Aegina (Map 7.56, BX) was colonized by
           Athens in 431; see 2.27: Histiaea, Eu-
           boea (Map 7.56, AX), was colonized in
           446; see 1.114.2. Some have argued from
           the phrase "the then occupants" that
           Thucydides wrote these words after 404.
7.57.4a   Eretria and Chalcis: Map 7.56, AX; Styria

and Carystus: Map 7.56, AY; all are cities
           in Euboea.
7.57.4b   Ceos, Andros, and Tenos: Map 7.56, BY.
7.57.4c   Chios, in Ionia: Map 7.56, AY; Miletus
           and Samos: Map 7.56, BY.
7.57.5a   Methymna, on Lesbos: Map 7.56, AY.
           Methymna was the only city of Lesbos
           not involved in the revolt of 427; see
           3.2.1, 3.5.1, and 3.18.1.

subjects who provided ships, not tribute, and the Tenedians and Aenians who paid tribute. These Aeolians[5b] fought against their Aeolian founders, the Boeotians in the Syracusan army, because they were obliged, while the Plataeans,[5c] the only native Boeotians opposed to Boeotians, did so upon a just quarrel. [6] Of the Rhodians[6a] and Cytherians,[6b] both Dorians, the latter, Spartan colonists, fought in the Athenian ranks against their Spartan countrymen with Gylippus; while the Rhodians, Argives by race, were compelled to bear arms against the Dorian Syracusans and their own colonists, the Geloans,[6c] serving with the Syracusans. [7] Of the islanders round the Peloponnesus, the Cephallenians and Zacynthians[7a] accompanied the Athenians as independent allies, although their insular position really left them little choice in the matter, owing to the maritime supremacy of Athens, while the Corcyraeans,[7b] who were not only Dorians but Corinthians,[7c] were openly serving against Corinthians and Syracusans, although colonists of the former and of the same race as the latter, ostensibly under compulsion, but really out of free will through hatred of Corinth. [8] The Messenians, as they are now called in Naupactus and from Pylos,[8a] then held by the Athenians, were taken with them to the war. There were also a few Megarian[8b] exiles, whose fate it was to be now fighting against the Megarian Selinuntines.[8c]

[9] The engagement of the rest was more of a voluntary nature. It was less the alliance than hatred of the Spartans and the immediate private advantage of each individual that persuaded the Dorian Argives to join the Ionian Athenians in a war against Dorians; while the Mantineans and other Arcadian[9a] mercenaries, accustomed to go against the enemy pointed out to them at the moment, were led by interest to regard the Arcadians serving with the Corinthians as just as much their enemies as any others. The Cretans[9b] and Aetolians[9c] also served for hire, and the Cretans who had joined the Rhodians in founding Gela thus came to consent to fight for pay against, instead of for, their colonists. [10] There were also some Acarnanians[10a] paid to serve, although they came chiefly for love of Demosthenes and out of goodwill to the Athenians whose allies they were. These all lived on the Hellenic side of the Ionian gulf.[10b] [11] Of the Italians, there were the Thurians and Metapontines,[11a] dragged into the quarrel by the stern necessities of a time of revolution; of the Sicilians, the Naxians and the Catanians;[11b] and of the barbarians, the Egestaeans,[11c] who called in the Athenians, most of the

7.57.5b   Aenus, Tenedos, and Aeolis: Map 7.56, AY.
7.57.5c   Plataea, in Boeotia: Map 7.56, AX. For the Aeolians from Boeotia and Lesbos, see Appendix H, Dialects and Ethnic Groups, §6.
7.57.6a   Rhodes: Map 7.56, BY.
7.57.6b   Cythera: Map 7.56, BX.
7.57.6c   Gela: Map 7.57, BX.
7.57.7a   Cephallenia: Map 7.56, AX; Zacynthus: Map 7.56, BX.
7.57.7b   Corcyra: Map 7.56, AX, and Map 7.57, AY.
7.57.7c   Corinth: Map 7.56, BX.
7.57.8a   Messenia and Pylos: Map 7.56, BX; Naupactus: Map 7.56, AX.

7.57.8b   Megara: Map 7.56, BX.
7.57.8c   Selinus: Map 7.57, BX.
7.57.9a   Argos, Mantinea, and Arcadia: Map 7.56, BX.
7.57.9b   Crete: Map 7.56, BY.
7.57.9c   Aetolia: Map 7.56, AX.
7.57.10a   Acarnania: Map 7.56, AX.
7.57.10b   Ionian gulf: Map 7.57, AY.
7.57.11a   Thurii and Metapontum: Map 7.57, AY.
7.57.11b   Naxos and Catana: Map 7.57, BX.
7.57.11c   Egesta: Map 7.57, BX. See 6.2.3 and 6.11.7, where Egesta is declared to be an Elymian (i.e., non-Greek) city.

Sicels, and outside Sicily some Tyrrhenian[11d] enemies of Syracuse and Iapygian[11e] mercenaries. Such were the peoples serving with the Athenians.

Against these the Syracusans had the Camarinaeans their neighbors, the Geloans who live next them, and then passing over the neutral Agrigentines, the Selinuntines[1a] settled on the farther side of the island. [2] These inhabit the part of Sicily looking toward Libya;[2a] the Himeraeans[2b] came from the side toward the Tyrrhenian sea,[2c] being the only Hellenic inhabitants in that quarter, and the only people that came from thence to the aid of the Syracusans. [3] Of the Hellenes in Sicily the above peoples joined in the war, all Dorians and independent, and of the barbarians the Sicels only, that is to say, such as did not go over to the Athenians. Of the Hellenes outside Sicily there were the Spartans, who provided a Spartan to take the command, and a force of *neodamodeis*[3a] and of Helots;[3b] the Corinthians,[3c] who alone joined with naval and land forces, with their Leucadian and Ambraciot[3d] kinsmen; some mercenaries sent by Corinth from Arcadia;[3e] some Sicyonians[3f] forced to serve, and from outside the Peloponnesus the Boeotians.[3g] [4] In comparison, however, with these foreign auxiliaries, the great Sicilian cities furnished more in every department—numbers of hoplites, ships and horses, and an immense multitude besides having been brought together; while in comparison, again, one may say, with all the rest put together, more was provided by the Syracusans themselves, both from the greatness of the city and from the fact that they were in the greatest danger.

Such were the auxiliaries brought together on either side, all of which had by this time assembled, neither party receiving any further support. [2] It was no wonder, therefore, if the Syracusans and their allies thought that it would win them great glory if they could follow up their recent victory in the sea fight by the capture of the whole Athenian armada, without letting it escape either by sea or by land. [3] They began at once to close up the Great Harbor by means of boats, merchant vessels, and triremes moored broadside across its mouth, which is nearly a mile wide,[3a] and made all their other arrangements for the event of the Athenians again venturing to fight at sea. There was, in fact, nothing small either in their plans or their ideas.

The Athenians, seeing them closing up the harbor and informed of their further designs, called a council of war. [2] The generals and other commanders assembled and discussed the difficulties of the situation; the point

7.58
413
19th Year/Summer
SYRACUSE
Thucydides lists the nationality, tribe, status, and circumstances of all participants in the force defending Syracuse against the Athenians.

7.59
413
19th Year/Summer
SYRACUSE
The Syracusans begin to close the Great Harbor with moored boats, intending to capture the entire Athenian force.

7.60
413
19th Year/Summer
SYRACUSE
Seeing the Syracusan efforts, the Athenians decide to reduce their lines to just a harbor fort, to man the largest fleet possible in order to defeat the enemy, and to withdraw to Catana. If defeated at sea, they plan to march to the nearest friendly city.

7.57.11d Tyrrhenia (Etruria): Map 7.57, locator.
7.57.11e Iapygia: Map 7.57, AY.
7.58.1a Camarina, Gela, Agrigentum, and Selinus: Map 7.57, BX.
7.58.2a Libya: Map 7.49.
7.58.2b Himera: Map 7.57, BX.
7.58.2c Tyrrhenian Sea: Map 7.57, AX.
7.58.3a For the *neodamodeis,* see note 7.19.3a.
7.58.3b For Helots, see Appendix C, Spartan Institutions, §3–4.
7.58.3c Corinth: Map 7.56, BX.
7.58.3d Leucas and Ambracia: Map 7.56, AX.
7.58.3e Arcadia: Map 7.56, BX.
7.58.3f Sicyon: Map 7.56, BX.
7.58.3g Boeotia: Map 7.56, AX.
7.59.3a Syracusan harbor barrier, general location: Map 7.44, BY.

which pressed most being that they no longer had provisions for immediate use (having sent on to Catana[2a] to tell them not to send any, in the belief that they were going away), and that they would not have any in future unless they could command the sea. They therefore determined to evacuate their upper lines, to enclose with a crosswall and garrison a small space close to the ships, only just sufficient to hold their stores and sick, and manning all the ships, seaworthy or not, with every man that could be spared from the rest of their land forces, to fight it out at sea, and if victorious, to go to Catana, but if not, to burn their vessels, form in close order, and retreat by land to the nearest friendly place they could reach, Hellenic or barbarian. [3] This was no sooner settled than carried into effect: they descended gradually from the upper lines and manned all their vessels, compelling all to go on board who were of age to be in any way of use. [4] They thus succeeded in manning about one hundred and ten ships in all, on board of which they embarked a number of archers and darters taken from the Acarnanians[4a] and from the other foreigners, making all other provisions allowed by the nature of their plan and by the necessities which imposed it. [5] All was now nearly ready, and Nicias, seeing the soldiery disheartened by their unprecedented and decided defeat at sea, and by reason of the scarcity of provisions eager to fight it out as soon as possible, called them all together, and first addressed them speaking as follows:

7.61
413
19th Year/Summer
SYRACUSE
Nicias reminds his men that victory will permit them to see again their native cities. He calls upon them to act like veterans.

"Soldiers of the Athenians and of the allies, we have all an equal interest in the coming struggle, in which life and country are at stake for us quite as much as they can be for the enemy; since if our fleet wins the day, each can see his native city again, wherever that city may be. [2] You must not lose heart, or be like men without any experience, who fail in a first attempt, and ever afterwards fearfully expect a future as disastrous. [3] But let the Athenians among you who have already had experience of many wars, and the allies who have joined us in so many expeditions, remember the surprises of war, and with the hope that fortune will not be always against us, prepare to fight again in a manner worthy of the number which you see yourselves to be."

7.62
413
19th Year/Summer
SYRACUSE
Nicias lists the many steps they have taken in order to win the upcoming naval battle, which should give them confidence.

"Now, whatever we thought would be of service against the crush of vessels in such a narrow harbor, and against the force upon the decks of the enemy, from which we suffered before, has all been considered with the helmsmen, and, as far as our means allowed, provided. [2] A number of archers and darters will go on board, and a multitude that we should not have employed in an action in the open sea, where our science would be crippled by the weight of the vessels; but in the present land fight that we are forced to make from shipboard all this will be useful. [3] We have also discovered the changes

7.60.2a   Catana: Map 7.57, BX.
7.60.4a   Acarnania: Map 7.56, AX.

in construction that we must make to meet theirs; and against the thickness of their cheeks, which did us the greatest mischief, we have provided grappling irons,[3a] which will prevent an assailant backing water after charging, if the marines on deck here do their duty; [4] since we are absolutely compelled to fight a land battle from the fleet, and it seems to be our interest neither to back water ourselves, nor to let the enemy do so, especially as the shore, except so much of it as may be held by our troops, is hostile ground."

"You must remember this and fight on as long as you can, and must not let yourselves be driven ashore, but once alongside must make up your minds not to part company until you have swept the hoplites from the enemy's deck. [2] I say this more for the hoplites than for the seamen, as it is more the business of the men on deck; and our land forces are even now on the whole the strongest. [3] The sailors I advise, and at the same time implore, not to be too much daunted by their misfortunes, now that we have our decks better armed and a greater number of vessels. Bear in mind how well worth preserving is the pleasure felt by those of you who through your knowledge of our language and imitation of our manners were always considered Athenians, even though not so in reality, and as such were honored throughout Hellas, and had your full share of the advantages of our empire, and more than your share in the respect of our subjects and in protection from ill treatment. [4] You, therefore, with whom alone we freely share our empire, we now justly require not to betray that empire in its extremity, and in scorn of Corinthians, whom you have often conquered, and of Sicilians, none of whom so much as presumed to stand against us when our navy was in its prime, we ask you to repel them, and to show that even in sickness and disaster your skill is more than a match for the fortune and vigor of any other."

"For the Athenians among you I add once more this reflection: you left behind you no more such ships in your docks to compare with these, no more hoplites in their flower; if you do other than conquer, our enemies here will immediately sail thither, and those that are left of us at Athens will become unable to repel their home assailants, reinforced by these new allies. Here you will fall at once into the hands of the Syracusans—I need not remind you of the intentions with which you attacked them—and your countrymen at home will fall into those of the Spartans. [2] Since the fate of both thus hangs upon this single battle—now, if ever, stand firm, and remember, each and all, that you who are now going on board are the army and navy of the Athenians, and all that is left of the state and the great name of Athens, in whose defense if any man has any ad-

7.63
413
19th Year/Summer
SYRACUSE
Nicias begs the seamen not to be daunted by recent reverses; he reminds them of the many privileges they enjoy under the empire; and he calls upon them to fight now in order to preserve themselves and it.

7.64
413
19th Year/Summer
SYRACUSE
Nicias tells the Athenians that Athens has no military resources in reserve and concludes that failure here will lead to Athens' quick defeat by Syracuse and Sparta.

7.62.3a By the use of grappling irons, the Athenians have clearly adopted the tactics of combat at close quarters to counteract the enemy's new battle strategies (see 7.34.5a). See 4.25.4a and Appendix G, Trireme Warfare, §14.

vantage in skill or courage, now is the time for him to show it, and thus serve himself and save all."

After this address[1a] Nicias at once gave orders to man the ships. Meanwhile Gylippus and the Syracusans could perceive by the preparations which they saw going on that the Athenians meant to fight at sea. They had also received intelligence of the grappling irons, [2] against which they specially provided by stretching hides over the prows and much of the upper part of their vessels, in order that the irons when thrown might slip off without taking hold. [3] All being now ready, the generals and Gylippus addressed them in the following terms:

"Syracusans and allies, the glorious character of our past achievements and the no less glorious results at issue in the coming battle are, we think, understood by most of you, or you would never have thrown yourselves with such ardor into the struggle; and if there be anyone not as fully aware of the facts as he ought to be, we will declare them to him. [2] The Athenians came to this country first to conquer Sicily, and after that, if successful, the Peloponnesus and the rest of Hellas, possessing already the greatest empire yet known, of present or former times, among the Hellenes. Here for the first time they found in you men who faced their navy which made them masters everywhere; you have already defeated them in the previous sea fight, and will in all likelihood defeat them again now. [3] When men are once checked in what they consider their special excellence, their whole opinion of themselves suffers more than if they had not at first believed in their superiority, the unexpected shock to their pride causing them to give way more than their real strength warrants; and this is probably now the case with the Athenians."

"With us it is different. The original estimate of ourselves which gave us courage in the days of our unskillfulness has been strengthened, while the conviction added to it that we must be the best seamen of the time, if we have conquered the best, has given a double measure of hope to every man among us; and, for the most part, where there is the greatest hope, there is also the greatest ardor for action. [2] The means to combat us which they have tried to find in copying our armament are familiar to our warfare, and will be countered by appropriate measures; while they will never be able to have a number of hoplites on their decks, contrary to their custom, and a number of darters—born landsmen, one may say, Acarnanians and others, embarked afloat, who will not know how to discharge their weapons when they have to keep still, without hampering their vessels and falling all into confusion among themselves through fighting

7.65.1a   See the Introduction (sect. II.v) for a discussion of the speeches in Thucydides.

not according to their own tactics.[2a] [3] For they will gain nothing by the number of their ships—I say this to those of you who may be alarmed by having to fight against odds—as a quantity of ships in a confined space will only be slower in executing the movements required, and most exposed to injury from our means of offense. [4] Indeed, if you would know the plain truth, as we are credibly informed, the excess of their sufferings and the necessities of their present distress have made them desperate; they have no confidence in their force, but wish to try their fortune in the only way they can, and either to force their passage and sail out, or after this to retreat by land, it being impossible for them to be worse off than they are."

"The fortune of our greatest enemies having thus betrayed itself, and their disorder being what I have described, let us engage in anger, convinced that nothing is more legitimate between adversaries than to claim to satisfy the whole wrath of one's soul in punishing the aggressor, and nothing more sweet, as the proverb has it, than the vengeance upon an enemy which it will now be ours to take. [2] That enemies they are and mortal enemies you all know, since they came here to enslave our country, and if successful had in reserve for our men all that is most dreadful, and for our children and wives all that is most dishonorable, and for the whole city the name which conveys the greatest reproach. [3] None should therefore relent or think it gain if they go away without further danger to us. This they will do just the same, even if they get the victory; while if we succeed, as we may expect, in chastising them, and in handing down to all Sicily her ancient freedom strengthened and confirmed, we shall have achieved no mean triumph. And the rarest dangers are those in which failure brings little loss and success the greatest advantage."

After the above address to the soldiers on their side, the Syracusan generals and Gylippus now perceived that the Athenians were manning their ships, and immediately proceeded to man their own also. [2] Meanwhile Nicias, appalled by the state of affairs, realizing the greatness and the nearness of the danger now that they were on the point of putting out from shore, and thinking, as men are apt to think in great crises, that when all has been done they have still something left to do, and when all has been said that they have not yet said enough, again called on the captains one by one, addressing each by his father's name and by his own, and by that of his tribe, and beseeched them not to be false to their own personal renown, or to obscure the hereditary virtues for which their ancestors were illustrious; he reminded them of their country, the freest of the free, and of the unfettered discretion allowed to all in it to live as they pleased; and added other arguments such as men would use at such a crisis, and which, with lit-

7.68
413
19th Year/Summer
SYRACUSE
Gylippus urges the Syracusans to take revenge and accept nothing less than total victory, asserting that failure will bring little loss and success great advantage.

7.69
413
19th Year/Summer
SYRACUSE
After both sides manned their ships, Nicias, feeling the crisis keenly, continued to speak, calling on captains by name and tribe to remember their ancestors, country, families, and gods, in hope of inciting them to greater efforts.

7.67.2a Gylippus and the generals refer here to the proper fighting tactics for trireme marines to employ while the ship was under way.

7.69.4a Syracusan harbor barrier, general location: Map 7.44, BY.

tle alteration, are made to serve on all occasions alike—appeals to wives, children, and national gods—without caring whether they are thought commonplace, but loudly invoking them in the belief that they will be of use in the consternation of the moment. [3] Having thus admonished them, not, he felt, as he would, but as he could, Nicias withdrew and led the troops to the sea, and arranged them in as long a line as he was able, in order to sustain as far as possible the courage of the men afloat; [4] while Demosthenes, Menander, and Euthydemus, who took the command on board, put out from their own camp and sailed straight to the barrier across the mouth of the harbor and to the passage left open, to try to force their way out.[4a]

7.70
413
19th Year/Summer
SYRACUSE
The Syracusans take stations around the harbor as the Athenians charge the barrier at its mouth. After the first shock a general mêlée occurs in which crowding prevents maneuver, so that much chaotic fighting amid noise and confusion takes place, with both sides displaying great zeal for battle.

The Syracusans and their allies had already set out with about the same number of ships as before, a part of which kept guard at the outlet, and the remainder all round the rest of the harbor, in order to attack the Athenians on all sides at once; while the land forces held themselves in readiness at the points at which the vessels might put into the shore. The Syracusan fleet was commanded by Sicanus and Agatharchus, who each had a wing of the whole force, with Pythen and the Corinthians in the center. [2] When the rest of the Athenians came up to the barrier, with the first shock of their charge they overpowered the ships stationed there, and tried to undo the fastenings; after this, as the Syracusans and allies bore down upon them from all quarters, the action spread from the barrier over the whole harbor, and was more obstinately disputed than any of the preceding ones. [3] On either side the rowers showed great zeal in bringing up their vessels at the boatswains' orders, and the helmsmen great skill in maneuvering, and great emulation one with another; and once the ships were alongside each other, the marines on board did their best not to let the service on deck be outdone by the others; in short, every man strove to prove himself the first in his particular department. [4] And as many ships were engaged in a small compass (for these were the largest fleets fighting in the narrowest space ever known, being together little short of two hundred), the regular attacks with the beak were few, there being no opportunity of backing water or of breaking the line; while the collisions caused by one ship chancing to run foul of another, either in flying from or attacking a third, were more frequent. [5] So long as a vessel was coming up to the charge the men on the decks rained darts and arrows and stones upon her; but once alongside, the marines tried to board each other's vessel, fighting hand to hand. [6] In many quarters also it happened, by reason of the narrow room, that a vessel was charging an enemy on one side and being charged herself on another, and that two, or sometimes more ships, had perforce got entangled round one, obliging the helmsmen to attend to defense here, offense there, not to one thing at once, but to many on all sides; while the huge din caused by the number of ships crashing together not only spread terror, but made the orders of the boatswains inaudible. [7] The boatswains on either side in the

7.69.4a   Syracusan harbor barrier, general location: Map 7.44, BY.

discharge of their duty and in the heat of the conflict incessantly shouted orders and appeals to their men; the Athenians they urged to force the passage out, and now if ever to show their mettle and lay hold of a safe return to their country; to the Syracusans and their allies they cried that it would be glorious to prevent the escape of the enemy, and conquering, to exalt the countries that were theirs. [8] The generals, moreover, on either side, if they saw in any part of the battle backing ashore without being forced to do so, called out to the captain by name and asked him—the Athenians, whether they were retreating because they thought the thrice hostile shore more their own than that sea which had cost them so much labor to win—the Syracusans, whether they were fleeing from the fleeing Athenians, whom they well knew to be eager to escape in whatever way they could.

Meanwhile the two armies on shore, while victory hung in the balance, were a prey to the most agonizing and conflicting emotions; the natives thirsting for more glory than they had already won, while the invaders feared to find themselves in even worse plight than before. [2] The fate of the Athenians being placed in their fleet, their fear for the event was like nothing they had ever felt; while their view of the struggle was necessarily as checkered as the battle itself. [3] Close to the scene of action and not all looking at the same point at once, some saw their friends victorious and took courage, and fell to calling upon heaven not to deprive them of salvation, while others who had their eyes turned upon those who were losing, wailed and cried aloud, and, although spectators, were more overcome than the actual combatants. Others, again, were gazing at some spot where the battle was evenly disputed; as the strife was protracted without decision, their swaying bodies reflected the agitation of their minds, and they suffered the worst agony of all, ever just within reach of safety or just on the point of destruction. [4] In short, in that one Athenian army as long as the sea fight remained doubtful there was every sound to be heard at once, shrieks, cheers, "We win," "We lose," and all the other manifold exclamations that a great host would necessarily utter in great peril; [5] and with the men in the fleet it was nearly the same; until at last the Syracusans and their allies, after the battle had lasted a long while, put the Athenians to flight, and with much shouting and cheering chased them in open rout to the shore. [6] The naval force, one one way, one another, as many as were not taken afloat, now ran ashore and rushed from on board their ships to their camp; while the army, no more divided, but carried away by one impulse, all with shrieks and groans deplored the event, and ran down, some to help the ships, others to guard what was left of their wall, while the remaining and most numerous part already began to consider how they should save themselves. [7] Indeed, the panic of the present moment had never been surpassed. They now suffered very nearly what they had inflicted at Pylos;[7a] as then the Spartans with the loss of

7.71
413
19th Year/Summer
SYRACUSE
Thucydides describes the varied emotions, cries, exaltation, and anguish of the armies watching from shore as the sea battle rages. Finally as the Athenian ships are routed, the Athenians give way to panic and despair, with many wondering how they will save themselves.

7.71.7a   Pylos: Map 7.56, BX. For a description of
        the Pylos campaign, see 4.2–41.

their fleet lost also the men who had crossed over to the island, so now the Athenians had no hope of escaping by land, without the help of some extraordinary accident.

The sea fight having been a severe one, and many ships and lives having been lost on both sides, the victorious Syracusans and their allies now picked up their wrecks and dead, and sailed off to the city and set up a trophy. [2] The Athenians, overwhelmed by their misfortune, never even thought of asking leave to take up their dead or wrecks, but wished to retreat that very night. [3] Demosthenes, however, went to Nicias and gave it as his opinion that they should man the ships they had left and make another effort to force their passage out next morning; saying that they had still left more ships fit for service than the enemy, the Athenians having about sixty remaining as against less than fifty of their opponents. [4] Nicias was quite in agreement; but when they wished to man the vessels, the sailors refused to go on board, being so utterly overcome by their defeat as no longer to believe in the possibility of success.

Accordingly they all now made up their minds to retreat by land. Meanwhile the Syracusan Hermocrates, suspecting their intention and impressed by the danger of allowing a force of that magnitude to retire by land, establish itself in some other part of Sicily, and from there to renew the war, went and stated his views to the authorities, and pointed out to them that they ought not to let the enemy get away by night, but that all the Syracusans and their allies should at once march out and block up the roads and seize and guard the passes. [2] The authorities were entirely of his opinion, and thought that it ought to be done, but on the other hand felt sure that the people, who had given themselves over to rejoicing and were taking their ease after a great battle at sea, would not be easily brought to obey; besides, they were celebrating a festival, having on that day a sacrifice to Heracles, and most of them in their rapture at the victory had fallen to drinking at the festival, and would probably consent to anything sooner than to take up their arms and march out at that moment. [3] For these reasons the thing appeared impracticable to the magistrates; and Hermocrates, finding himself unable to do anything further with them, had now recourse to the following stratagem of his own. What he feared was that the Athenians might quietly get ahead of them by passing the most difficult places during the night; and he therefore sent, as soon as it was dusk, some friends of his own to the camp with some horsemen who rode up within earshot and called out to some of the men, as though they were well-wishers of the Athenians, and told them to tell Nicias (who had in fact some contacts who informed him of what went on inside the city),[3a] not to lead off the army by night as the Syracusans were guarding the roads, but to make his preparations at his leisure and to retreat by day. [4] After saying this they departed; and their hearers informed the Athenian generals,

413
19th Year/Summer
SYRACUSE
The defeated Athenians are so stunned that they forget to ask for their dead. Demosthenes and Nicias agree to mount a second attack, but the demoralized Athenian sailors refuse to man the triremes.

7.73
413
19th Year/Summer
SYRACUSE
The Athenians now plan to retreat by land this very night. Hermocrates, afraid they might escape, sends messengers to deceive the Athenian generals by warning them not to leave immediately because the roads are guarded. The Athenians follow this advice.

7.73.3a For Nicias' Syracusan contacts, see
6.103.3–4 and 7.49.1.

[7.74.1] who put off going for that night on the strength of this message, not doubting its sincerity.

Since after all they had not set out at once, they now determined to stay also the following day to give time to the soldiers to pack up as well as they could the most useful articles, and, leaving everything else behind, to start only with what was strictly necessary for their personal subsistence. [2] Meanwhile the Syracusans and Gylippus marched out and blocked the roads through the country by which the Athenians were likely to pass, and kept guard at the fords of the streams and rivers, posting themselves so as to receive them and stop the army where they thought best; while their fleet sailed up to the beach and towed off the ships of the Athenians. Some few were burned by the Athenians themselves as they had intended; the rest the Syracusans lashed on to their own at their leisure as they had been thrown up on shore, without anyone trying to stop them, and conveyed to the city.

After this, Nicias and Demosthenes now thinking that enough had been done in the way of preparation, the departure of the army took place upon the second day after the sea fight. [2] It was a lamentable scene, not merely from the single circumstance that they were retreating after having lost all their ships, their great hopes gone, and themselves and their state in peril; but also in leaving the camp there were things most grievous for every eye and heart to contemplate. [3] The dead lay unburied, and each man as he recognized a friend among them shuddered with grief and horror; while the living whom they were leaving behind, wounded or sick, were to the living far more shocking than the dead, and more to be pitied than those who had perished. [4] These fell to entreating and bewailing until their friends knew not what to do, begging them to take them and loudly calling to each individual comrade or relative whom they could see, hanging upon the necks of their tent-fellows in the act of departure, and following as far as they could, and when their bodily strength failed them, calling again and again upon heaven and shrieking aloud as they were left behind. So that the whole army being filled with tears and in a distraught state, found it not easy to go, even from an enemy's land, where they had already suffered evils too great for tears and in the unknown future before them feared to suffer more. [5] Dejection and self-condemnation were also rife among them. Indeed they could only be compared to a starved-out city, and that no small one, escaping; the whole multitude upon the march being not less than forty thousand men. All carried anything they could which might be of use, and the hoplites and troopers, contrary to their custom while under arms, carried their own provisions, in some cases for lack of servants, in others through not trusting them; as they had long been deserting and now did so in greater numbers than ever. Yet even thus they did not carry enough, as there was no longer food in the camp. [6]

7.74
413
19th Year/Summer
SYRACUSE
The Athenians allow their soldiers one day to pack, and the Syracusans use this time to occupy strategic points on possible escape routes, and to tow off Athenian ships without opposition.

7.75
413
19th Year/Summer
SYRACUSE
Saddened and shamed by the necessity to leave the unburied dead and their sick and wounded comrades, the forty thousand Athenians finally march out. Having already absorbed reverses greater than those suffered by any Hellenic army, they march in fear of capture and enslavement, their initial glory turned to humiliation.

Moreover their disgrace generally, and the universality of their sufferings, although to a certain extent alleviated by being borne in company, were still felt at the moment a heavy burden, especially when they contrasted the splendor and glory of their setting out with the humiliation in which it had ended. [7] For this was by far the greatest reverse that ever befell an Hellenic army. They had come to enslave others, and were departing in fear of being enslaved themselves: they had sailed out with prayer and paeans, and now started to go back with omens directly contrary; traveling by land instead of by sea, and trusting not in their fleet but in their hoplites. Nevertheless the greatness of the danger still impending made all this appear tolerable.

Nicias seeing the army dejected and greatly altered, passed along the ranks and encouraged and comforted them as far as was possible under the circumstances, raising his voice still higher and higher as he went from one company to another in his earnestness, and in his anxiety that the benefit of his words might reach as many as possible:

"Athenians and allies, even in our present position we must still hope on, since men have before now been saved from worse straits than this; and you must not condemn yourselves too severely either because of your disasters or because of your present unmerited sufferings. [2] I myself who am not superior to any of you in strength—indeed you see how I am in my sickness—and who in the gifts of fortune am, I think, whether in private life or otherwise, the equal of any, am now exposed to the same danger as the meanest among you; and yet my life has been one of much devotion toward the gods, and of much justice and without offense toward men. [3] I have, therefore, still a strong hope for the future, and our misfortunes do not terrify me as much as they might. Indeed we may hope that they will be lightened: our enemies have had good fortune enough; and if any of the gods was offended at our expedition, we have already been amply punished. [4] Others before us have attacked their neighbors and have done what men will do without suffering more than they could bear; and we may now justly expect to find the gods more kind, for we have become fitter objects for their pity than their jealousy. And then look at yourselves, mark the numbers and efficiency of the hoplites marching in your ranks, and do not give way too much to despondency, but reflect that you are yourselves at once a city wherever you sit down, and that there is no other in Sicily that could easily resist your attack, or expel you when once established. [5] The safety and order of the march is for yourselves to attend to; the one thought of each man being that the spot on which he may be forced to fight must be conquered and held as his country and stronghold. [6] Meanwhile we shall hasten on our way night and day alike, as our provisions are scanty; and if we can reach some friendly place of the Sicels, whom fear of the Syracusans still keeps true to us, you may from then on consider yourselves safe. A message has been sent on to them with directions to meet us with supplies of food. [7] To sum up, be convinced, soldiers, that you must be brave, as there is no place near for your cowardice to take refuge in, and that if you now escape from the enemy, you may all see again what your hearts desire, while those of you who are Athenians will raise up again the great power of the state, fallen though it be. Men make the city and not walls or ships without men in them."

As he made this address, Nicias went along the ranks, and brought back to their place any of the troops that he saw straggling out of the line; while Demosthenes did as much for his part of the army, addressing them in words very similar. [2] The army marched in a hollow square, the division under Nicias leading, and that of Demosthenes following, the hoplites being outside and the baggage carriers and the bulk of the army in the middle. [3] When they arrived at the ford of the river Anapus[3a] they there found drawn up a body of the Syracusans and allies, and routing these, made good their passage and pushed on, harassed by the charges of the Syracusan horse and by the missiles of their light troops. [4] On that day they advanced about four miles and a half, halting for the night upon a certain hill. On the next they started early and got on about two miles further, and descended into a place in the plain and there encamped[4a] in order to procure some edibles from the houses, as the place was inhabited, and to carry with them water from there, as for many miles in front, in the direction in which they were going, it was not plentiful. [5] The Syracusans meanwhile went on and fortified the pass in front, where there was a steep hill with a rocky ravine on each side of it, called the Acraean cliff.[5a] [6] The next day the Athenians advancing found themselves impeded by the missiles and charges of the horse and darters, both very numerous, of the Syracusans and allies; and after fighting for a long while, at length retired to the same camp, where they no longer had provisions as before, it being impossible to leave their position by reason of the cavalry.

Early next morning they started afresh and forced their way to the hill, which had been fortified, where they found before them the enemy's infantry drawn up many shields deep to defend the fortification, the pass being narrow. [2] The Athenians assaulted the work, but were greeted by a storm of missiles from the hill, which told with the greater effect through its being a steep one, and unable to force the passage, retreated again and rested. [3] Meanwhile occurred some claps of thunder and rain, as often

7.78
413
19th Year/Summer
SYRACUSE
The Athenians make slow progress on the march, crossing the Anapus and camping where they hope to find food. Halted by the Syracusans and prevented from foraging by enemy cavalry, they begin to run low on provisions.

7.79
413
19th Year/Summer
SYRACUSE
The Athenians fail to pierce the Syracusan defense and a thunderstorm is seen by them as an omen of ruin. The next day they are attacked on every side by cavalry and infantry, and make very little progress.

7.78.3a   Anapus river: Map 7.81. The site of the particular ford referred to is unknown.
7.78.4a   First Athenian camp, possible location: Map 7.81.
7.78.5a   Acraean cliff and pass, possible location: Map 7.81.

happens toward autumn, which still further disheartened the Athenians, who thought all these things to be omens of their approaching ruin.[3a] [4] While they were resting Gylippus and the Syracusans sent a part of their army to throw up works in their rear on the way by which they had advanced; however, the Athenians immediately sent some of their men and prevented them; [5] after which they retreated more toward the plain and halted for the night. When they advanced the next day the Syracusans surrounded and attacked them on every side, and disabled many of them, falling back if the Athenians advanced and coming on if they retired, and in particular assaulting their rear, in the hope of routing them in detail, and thus striking a panic into the whole army. [6] For a long while the Athenians persevered in this fashion, but after advancing for about a half a mile, halted to rest in the plain,[6a] the Syracusans also withdrawing to their own camp.

During the night Nicias and Demosthenes, seeing the wretched condition of their troops, now in want of every kind of necessity, and numbers of them disabled in the numerous attacks of the enemy, determined to light as many fires as possible, and to lead off the army, no longer by the same route as they had intended, but toward the sea in the opposite direction to that guarded by the Syracusans. [2] This route led the army not to Catana but to the other side of Sicily, toward Camarina, Gela,[2a] and the other Hellenic and barbarian cities in that quarter. [3] They accordingly lit a number of fires and set out by night. Now all armies, and the greatest most of all, are liable to fears and alarms, especially when they are marching by night through an enemy's country and with the enemy near; and the Athenians now fell into one of these panics;[3a] [4] the leading division, that of Nicias, kept together and got on a good way in front, while that of Demosthenes, comprising rather more than half the army, became separated and marched on in some disorder. [5] By morning, however, they reached the sea, and getting onto the Helorine road,[5a] pushed on to reach the river Cacyparis[5b] in order to follow that stream up into the interior, where they hoped to be met by the Sicels whom they had sent for. [6] When they arrived at the river, they found there also a Syracusan party engaged in barring the passage of the ford with a wall and a palisade, and forcing this guard, crossed the river and went on to another called the Erineus,[6a] according to the advice of their guides.

Meanwhile, when day came and the Syracusans and allies found that the Athenians were gone, most of them accused Gylippus of having let them escape on purpose, and hastily pursuing by the road that they had taken (which they had no difficulty finding), overtook them about dinnertime. [2] They first came up with the troops under Demosthenes, who were be-

7.79.3a   Compare this reaction with the impact of a thunderstorm on the Syracusans in 6.70.1.
7.79.6a   Second Athenian camp, possible location: Map 7.81.
7.80.2a   Catana, Camarina, and Gela: Map 7.81, locator.

7.80.3a   Compare this panic with the panic of the Macedonians in 4.125.1.
7.80.5a   Helorine road: Map 7.81.
7.80.5b   Cacyparis river: Map 7.81.
7.80.6a   Erineus river, possible location: Map 7.81.

MAP 7.81
THE ATHENIAN RETREAT
AND SURRENDER[2a]

hind and marching somewhat slowly and in disorder, owing to the night panic above referred to, and at once attacked and engaged them, the Syracusan horse surrounding them with more ease now that they were separated from the rest, and hemming them in on one spot. [3] The division of Nicias was five or six miles on in front, as he led them more rapidly, thinking that under the circumstances their safety lay not in staying and fighting, unless obliged, but in retreating as fast as possible, and only fighting when forced to do so. [4] On the other hand, Demosthenes was, generally speaking, harassed more incessantly, as his post in the rear left him the first exposed to the attacks of the enemy; and now, finding that the Syracusans were in pursuit, he ceased to push on, in order to form his men for battle, and so lingered until he was surrounded by his pursuers and himself and

7.81.2a Locations in this map are based primarily
          on Donald Kagan, *The Peace of Nicias
          and the Sicilian Expedition* (Ithaca, N.Y.:
          Cornell University Press, 1981), Map 12,
          p. 341.

the Athenians with him placed in the most distressing position, being huddled into an enclosure with a wall all round it, a road on this side and on that, and olive trees in great number, where missiles were showered in upon them from every quarter.[4a] [5] This mode of attack the Syracusans had with good reason adopted in preference to fighting at close quarters, as to risk a struggle with desperate men was now more to the advantage of the Athenians than to their own; besides, their success had now become so certain that they began to spare themselves a little in order not to be killed in the moment of victory, thinking too that they would in any case be able in this way to subdue and capture the enemy.

In fact, after plying the Athenians and allies all day long from every side with missiles, they at length saw that they were worn out with their wounds and other sufferings; and Gylippus and the Syracusans and their allies made a proclamation, offering their liberty to any of the islanders who chose to come over to them; and some few cities went over. [2] Afterwards a capitulation was agreed upon for all the rest with Demosthenes, to lay down their arms on condition that no one was to be put to death either by violence or imprisonment or want of the necessaries of life.[2a] [3] Upon this they surrendered to the number of six thousand in all, laying down all the money in their possession, which filled the hollows of four shields, and were immediately conveyed by the Syracusans to the city.[3a]

Meanwhile Nicias with his division arrived that day at the river Erineus, crossed over, and posted his army upon some high ground upon the other side. [7.83.1] The next day the Syracusans overtook him and told him that the troops under Demosthenes had surrendered, and invited him to follow their example. Incredulous of the fact, Nicias asked for a truce to send a horseman to see, [2] and upon the return of the messenger with the tidings that they had surrendered, sent a herald to Gylippus and the Syracusans, saying that he was ready to agree with them on behalf of the Athenians to repay whatever money the Syracusans had spent upon the war if they would let his army go; and offered until the money was paid to give Athenians as hostages, one for every talent. [3] The Syracusans and Gylippus rejected this proposition, and attacked this division as they had the other, standing all round and plying them with missiles until the evening. [4] Food and necessaries were as miserably wanting to the troops of Nicias as they had been to their comrades; nevertheless they watched for the quiet of the night to resume their march. But as they were taking up their arms the Syracusans perceived it and raised their paean, [5] upon which the Athenians, finding that they were discovered, laid them down again, except about three hundred men who forced their way through the guards and went on during the night as they were able.

7.82
413
19th Year/Summer
SYRACUSE
The Syracusans offer liberty to islanders who surrender, but only a few go over. Then Demosthenes agrees to capitulate on condition that no one will be killed; six thousand Athenians surrender.

7.83
413
19th Year/Summer
SYRACUSE
When the Syracusans inform Nicias of Demosthenes' surrender, Nicias offers to pay for his army's liberty. The Syracusans refuse his offer and attack his men from all sides with missiles. An attempt by Nicias to march off by night is thwarted.

7.81.4a   The plight of the Athenians here parallels that of the Corinthians in 1.106.
7.82.2a   Terms that the Syracusans did not carry out, see 7.86–7.

7.82.3a   Possible site of Demosthenes' surrender: Map 7.81.

As soon as it was day Nicias put his army in motion, pressed as before, by the Syracusans and their allies, pelted from every side by their missiles, and struck down by their javelins. [2] The Athenians pushed on for the Assinarus,[2a] impelled by the attacks made upon them from every side by a numerous cavalry and the swarm of other arms, supposing that they should breathe more freely if once across the river, and driven on also by their exhaustion and craving for water. [3] Once there they rushed in, and all order was at an end, each man wanting to cross first, and the attacks of the enemy making it difficult to cross at all; forced to huddle together, they fell against and trampled one another, some dying immediately upon the javelins, others getting entangled together and stumbling over the articles of baggage, without being able to rise again. [4] Meanwhile the opposite bank, which was steep, was lined by the Syracusans, who showered missiles down upon the Athenians, most of them drinking greedily and heaped together in disorder in the hollow bed of the river. [5] The Peloponnesians also came down and butchered them, especially those in the water, which was thus immediately spoiled, but which they went on drinking just the same, mud and all, bloody as it was, most even fighting to have it.

At last, when many dead now lay piled one upon another in the stream, and part of the army had been destroyed at the river, and the few that escaped from there had been cut off by the cavalry, Nicias surrendered himself to Gylippus, whom he trusted more than he did the Syracusans, and told him and the Spartans to do what they liked with him, but to stop the slaughter of the soldiers. [2] Gylippus, after this, immediately gave orders to take prisoners; upon which the rest were assembled alive, except a large number secretly kept by the soldiery, and a party was sent in pursuit of the three hundred who had got through the guard during the night, and who were now taken with the rest. [3] The number of the enemy collected as public property was not considerable; but that taken privately[3a] was very large, and all Sicily was filled with them, no agreement having been made in their case as for those taken with Demosthenes. [4] Besides this, a large portion were killed outright, the carnage being very great, and not exceeded by any in this Sicilian war. In the numerous other encounters upon the march, not a few also had fallen. Nevertheless many escaped, some at the moment, others served as slaves, and then ran away subsequently. These found refuge at Catana.[4a]

The Syracusans and their allies now mustered and took up the spoils and as many prisoners as they could, and went back to the city. [2] The rest of their Athenian and allied captives were deposited in the quarries, this seeming the safest way of keeping them; but Nicias and Demosthenes were butchered, against the will of Gylippus, who thought that it would be the

7.84
413
19th Year/Summer
SYRACUSE
Under attack all the way, the Athenians march to the Assinarus river, driven by thirst and the hope that they would be safe there. When they arrive, they find the Syracusans waiting for them. All order is lost as men rush to drink even the foul water in which they are being butchered.

7.85
413
19th Year/Summer
SYRACUSE
Nicias surrenders to Gylippus, who then orders that prisoners be taken. Although more men died on this march than in any action of the Sicilian war, many escaped or were enslaved and escaped later to Catana.

7.86
413
19th Year/Summer
SYRACUSE
The Athenian and allied prisoners are held in quarries. Demosthenes and Nicias are executed. Thucydides remarks that Nicias did not deserve this fate.

7.84.2a   Assinarus river: Map 7.81.
7.85.3a   Prisoners and other property taken in war
           were deemed to belong to the state, not
           to those who captured it.

7.85.4a   Catana: Map 7.81, locator.

crown of his triumph if he could take the enemy's generals to Sparta. [3] One of them, as it happened, Demosthenes, was one of her greatest enemies, on account of the affair of the island and of Pylos;[3a] while the other, Nicias, was for the same reasons one of her greatest friends, owing to his exertions to procure the release of the prisoners by persuading the Athenians to make peace. [4] For these reasons the Spartans felt kindly toward him; and it was in this that Nicias himself mainly confided when he surrendered to Gylippus. But some of the Syracusans who had been in correspondence with him were afraid, it was said, of his being put to the torture and troubling their success by his revelations; others, especially the Corinthians, of his escaping by means of bribes (as he was wealthy), and living to do them further harm; and these persuaded the allies and put him to death. [5] This or the like was the cause of the death of a man who, of all the Hellenes in my time, least deserved such a fate, seeing that the whole course of his life had been regulated with strict attention to virtue.

The prisoners in the quarries were at first harshly treated by the Syracusans. Crowded in a narrow hole, without any roof to cover them, the heat of the sun and the stifling closeness of the air tormented them during the day, and then the nights which came on autumnal and chilly made them ill by the violence of the change; [2] besides, as they had to do everything in the same place for want of room, and the bodies of those who died of their wounds or from the variation in the temperature, or from similar causes, were left heaped together one upon another, intolerable stenches arose; while hunger and thirst never ceased to afflict them, each man during eight months having only half a pint of water and a pint of grain given him daily. In short, no single suffering to be apprehended by men thrust into such a place was spared them. [3] For some seventy days they thus lived all together, after which all, except the Athenians and any Siceliots or Italians who had joined in the expedition, were sold. [4] The total number of prisoners taken it would be difficult to state exactly, but it could not have been less than seven thousand.

[5] This was the greatest Hellenic achievement of any in this war, or, in my opinion, in Hellenic history; at once most glorious to the victors, and most calamitous to the conquered. [6] They were beaten at all points and altogether; all that they suffered was great; they were destroyed, as the saying is, with a total destruction, their fleet, their army—everything was destroyed, and few out of many returned home. Such were the events in Sicily.

7.87
413
19th Year/Summer
SYRACUSE
Thucydides describes the torments of the seven thousand or more captives who endured the crowded quarries for eight months before being sold as slaves. Many died. Thucydides calls the Syracusan victory the greatest of the war, and the Athenian defeat the most calamitous and total.

7.86.3a Pylos: Map 7.56, BX. For a description of the Pylos campaign, see 4.2–41.

BOOK EIGHT

When the news was brought to Athens,[1a] for a long while they disbelieved even the most respectable of the soldiers who had themselves escaped from the scene of action and clearly reported the matter, a destruction so complete not being thought credible. When the conviction was forced upon them, they were angry with the orators who had joined in promoting the expedition, just as if they had not themselves voted it, and were enraged also with the reciters of oracles and soothsayers, and all other omenmongers of the time who had encouraged them to hope that they should conquer Sicily. [2] Already distressed at all points and in all quarters, after what had now happened they were seized by a fear and consternation quite without precedent. It was grievous enough for the state and for every man in his proper person to lose so many *hoplites*,[2a] cavalry, and able-bodied troops, and to see none left to replace them; but when they saw, also, that they had not sufficient ships in their docks, or money in the treasury, or crews for the ships, they began to despair of salvation. They thought that their enemies in Sicily would immediately sail with their fleet against the Piraeus,[2b] inflamed by so great a victory; while their adversaries at home, redoubling all their preparations, would vigorously attack them by sea and land at once, aided by their own revolted confederates. [3] Nevertheless, with such means as they had, it was determined to resist to the last, and to provide timber and money, and to equip a fleet as they best could, to take steps to secure their confederates and above all Euboea,[3a] to reform things in the city upon a more economical footing, and to elect a board of elders to advise upon the state of affairs as occasion should arise. [4] In short, as is the way of a democracy, in the panic of the moment they were ready to be as prudent as possible. These resolves were carried into effect at once. Summer was now over.

8.1
413
19th Year/Summer
ATHENS
The Athenians are shocked by the disaster in Sicily and discouraged by their lack of resources with which to carry on the war. Yet they decide to resist and take steps to build ships and secure their hold on their allies.

8.1.1a   Athens: Map 8.3, AY.
8.1.2a   *Hoplite* is the Greek word for a heavily armed infantryman. See Appendix F, Land Warfare, §2.
8.1.2b   Piraeus: Map 8.3, AY.
8.1.3a   Euboea: Map 8.3, AY.

8.2
413/2
19th Year/Winter
HELLAS
Peloponnesians, neutrals, and restive Athenian subjects plan a decisive effort, confident now that Athens cannot long resist their combined forces. The Spartans look forward to securing hegemony in Hellas.

The following winter saw all Hellas stirring under the impression of the great Athenian disaster in Sicily. Neutrals now felt that even if uninvited they no longer ought to stand aloof from the war, but should volunteer to march against the Athenians, who, as each city reflected, would probably have come against them if the Sicilian campaign had succeeded. Besides, they believed that the war would now be short, and that it would be creditable for them to take part in it. Meanwhile the allies of the Spartans felt all the more anxious than ever to see a speedy end to their heavy labors. [2] But above all, the subjects of the Athenians showed a readiness to revolt even beyond their ability, judging the circumstances with passion and refusing even to hear of the Athenians being able to last out the coming summer. [3] Beyond all this, Sparta was encouraged by the near prospect of being joined in great force in the spring by her allies in Sicily, lately forced by events to acquire their navy. [4] With these reasons for confidence in every quarter, the Spartans now resolved to throw themselves without reserve into the war considering that, once it was happily terminated, they would be finally delivered from such dangers as that which would have threatened them from Athens, if she had become mistress of Sicily, and that the overthrow of the Athenians would leave them in quiet enjoyment of the supremacy over all Hellas.

8.3
413/2
19th Year/Winter
HELLAS
Agis takes hostages and secures funds in the Malian Gulf area. Sparta allots quotas of ships to be built by various allies for the creation of a new fleet.

Their king, Agis, accordingly set out at once during this winter with some troops from Decelea,[1a] and levied from the allies contributions for the fleet, and turning toward the Malian gulf[1b] exacted a sum of money from the Oetaeans[1c] by carrying off most of their cattle in reprisal for their old hostility, and, in spite of the protests and opposition of the Thessalians,[1d] forced the Achaeans of Phthiotis[1e] and the other subjects of the Thessalians in those parts to give him money and hostages, and deposited the hostages at Corinth,[1f] and tried to bring their countrymen into the confederacy. [2] The Spartans now issued a requisition to the cities[2a] for building a hundred ships, fixing their own quota and that of the Boeotians at twenty-five each; that of the Phocians and Locrians[2b] together at fifteen; that of the Corinthians at fifteen;[2c] that of the Arcadians,[2d] Pellenians,[2e] and Sicyonians[2f] together at ten; and that of the Megarians, Troezenians, Epidaurians, and Hermionians[2g] together at ten also; and meanwhile made every other preparation for commencing hostility by the spring.

8.3.1a   Decelea: Map 8.3, AY.
8.3.1b   Malian Gulf: Map 8.3, AX.
8.3.1c   Oetae, general location of their territory: Map 8.3, AX.
8.3.1d   Thessaly: Map 8.3, AX.
8.3.1e   Phthiotis: Map 8.3, AX.
8.3.1f   Corinth: Map 8.3, AX.
8.3.2a   The "cities" in this case, as in 5.17.2, are the members of the Peloponnesian League; see Appendix D, The Peloponnesian League, §3.

8.3.2b   Boeotia: Map 8.3, AY; Phocis and Opuntian Locris: Map 8.3, AX.
8.3.2c   This requisition, when compared to the seventy-five triremes launched by Corinth in 435 (1.29.1), may indicate how severely Corinth had been impoverished by the war.
8.3.2d   Arcadia: Map 8.3, BX.
8.3.2e   Pellene: Map 8.3, AX.
8.3.2f   Sicyon: Map 8.3, AX.
8.3.2g   Megara: Map 8.3, AY; Troezen, Epidaurus, and Hermione: Map 8.3, BY.

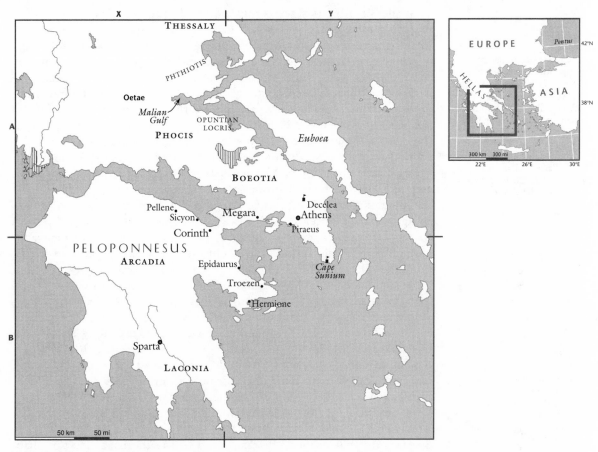

MAP 8.3 BOTH SIDES PREPARE FOR RENEWED WARFARE

In the meantime the Athenians were not idle. During this same winter, as they had intended, they contributed timber and got on with their ship-building, and fortified Sunium[1a] to enable their grain ships to round it in safety, and evacuated the fort in Laconia[1b] which they had built on their way to Sicily; while they also, for economy, reduced any other expenses that seemed unnecessary, and above all kept a careful lookout against the revolt of their allies.

8.4
413/2
19th Year/Winter
ATHENS
Athens also builds ships and prepares to carry on the war.

8.4.1a   Cape Sunium: Map 8.3, BY.
8.4.1b   Laconia: Map 8.3, BX. The exact location
         of this fort, whose construction was
         described in 7.26.1, is unknown.

483

8.5
413/2
19th Year/Winter
EUBOEA
Agis at Decelea agrees to
support a Euboean uprising
but delays action because . . .
LESBOS
The Lesbians, with Boeotian
support, convince Agis to
assist their revolt first.
CHIOS
The Chians, supported by
the Persian Tissaphernes,
apply at Sparta for aid for
their prospective revolt.

While both parties were thus engaged, and were as intent upon preparing for the war as they had been at the outset, the Euboeans first of all sent envoys during this winter to Agis to consult about their revolting from Athens. Agis accepted their proposals, and sent for Alcamenes son of Sthenelaidas,[1a] and Melanthus from Sparta to take the command in Euboea.[1b] These accordingly arrived with some three hundred *neodamodeis*,[1c] and Agis began to arrange for their crossing over. [2] But in the meantime some Lesbians[2a] arrived who also wished to revolt; and these being supported by the Boeotians,[2b] Agis was persuaded to defer acting in the matter of Euboea, and made arrangements for the revolt of the Lesbians, giving them Alcamenes, who was to have sailed to Euboea, as governor, and himself promising them ten ships, and the Boeotians the same number. [3] All this was done without instructions from home, as Agis while at Decelea[3a] with the army that he commanded had power to send troops to whatever quarter he pleased, and to levy men and money. During this period, one might say, the allies obeyed him much more than they did the Spartans in the city, as the force he had with him made him feared at once wherever he went. [4] While Agis was engaged with the Lesbians, the Chians and Erythraeans,[4a] who were also ready to revolt, applied not to him but at Sparta; where they arrived accompanied by an ambassador from Tissaphernes, the commander of King Darius son of Artaxerxes, [5] in the maritime districts,[5a] who invited the Peloponnesians to come over, and promised to maintain their army. The King had lately called upon him for the tribute from his province, for which he was in arrears, because the Athenians prevented him from collecting it from the Hellenic cities. He therefore calculated that by weakening the Athenians he could better obtain that tribute, and would also draw the Spartans into alliance with the King; and by this means, as the King had commanded him, take dead or alive Amorges the bastard son of Pissuthnes,[5b] who was in rebellion on the coast of Caria.[5c]

8.5.1a   This may be the same Sthenelaidas who as ephor spoke so strongly for war twenty years earlier in 1.86.
8.5.1b   Euboea: Map 8.3, AY.
8.5.1c   When Brasidas took the 700 helots to fight in Thrace (4.80) he inaugurated the radical policy change at Sparta of using helots for military purposes rather than keeping them all in bitter subjection. Sparta further developed that policy by creating a special class of Neodamodeis whose numbers seem to increase steadily in the succeeding half century (cf. 7.19.3). Their precise status remains unknown, and although the name implies that they were made part of the citizen body, most scholars reject this notion. See Appendix C, §9.
8.5.2a   Lesbos: Map 8.7, Asia.
8.5.2b   Boeotia: Map 8.3, AY, and Map 8.7, Hellas.
8.5.3a   Decelea: Map 8.3, AY, and Map 8.7, Hellas.
8.5.4a   Chios and Erythrae: Map 8.7, Asia.

8.5.5a   Tissaphernes, Persian satrap (governor) of the "maritime districts," governed his large province from Sardis (Map 8.7, Asia), the capital of the province or satrapy of Lydia.
8.5.5b   This Pissuthnes, son of Hystaspes, is mentioned by Thucydides as supporting the Samian Revolt of 440 (see 1.115). Pissuthnes had revolted from Darius II— precisely when or why is not known—and had been brutally executed. The rebellion of his son, Amorges, may have followed shortly after, though the date is quite unsure—415/4 is possible. He appears to have requested and received Athenian help, which, if true, may prove to be another event of perhaps great importance that is entirely omitted by Thucydides, although we can indirectly infer the existence of an alliance between Amorges and the Athenians from his text at 8.19.1, 8.28.2, and especially 8.54.3.

(continued on next page)

While the Chians and Tissaphernes thus joined to effect a common purpose, about the same time Calligeitus son of Laophon, a Megarian,[1a] and Timagoras son of Athenagoras, a Cyzicene,[1b] both of them exiles from their country and living at the court of Pharnabazus son of Pharnaces, arrived at Sparta upon a mission from Pharnabazus to procure a fleet for the Hellespont;[1c] by means of which, if possible, he might himself accomplish Tissaphernes' ambition, and cause the cities in his province to revolt from the Athenians, and thereby receive the tribute from them, and by his own agency obtain for the King the alliance of the Spartans.[1d]

[2] As the emissaries of Pharnabazus and Tissaphernes negotiated separately, a keen competition now ensued at Sparta as to whether a fleet and army should be sent first to Ionia[2a] and Chios, or to the Hellespont. [3] The Spartans, however, decidedly favored the Chians and Tissaphernes, who were supported by Alcibiades, the family friend of Endius who was one of the *ephors* for that year.[3a] Indeed, this is how their house got its Laconic name, Alcibiades being the family name of Endius. [4] Nevertheless the Spartans first sent to Chios Phrynis, one of the *perioikoi*,[4a] to see whether they had as many ships as they said, and whether their city generally was as great as was reported; and upon his bringing word that they had been told the truth, immediately entered into alliance with the Chians and Erythraeans,[4b] and voted to send them forty ships, there being already, according to the statement of the Chians, not less than sixty in the island. [5] At first the Spartans meant to send ten of these forty themselves, with Melanchridas their admiral; but afterwards, an earthquake having occurred, they sent Chalcideus instead of Melanchridas, and instead of the ten ships equipped only five in Laconia.[5a] And the winter ended, and with it ended also the nineteenth year of this war of which Thucydides is the historian.

8.6
413/2
19th Year/Winter
SPARTA
Envoys from the Persian satrap Pharnabazus arrive at Sparta to request that a fleet be sent to the Hellespont, not to Chios. Sparta decides to send forces to Chios but due to an earthquake and other problems sends only five triremes.

(continued from previous page)

Since the connection with Amorges may have led directly to a breach between Athens and Persia, and so to the Persian alliance with Sparta which ultimately caused the defeat of Athens, Thucydides' silence here has caused much scholarly puzzlement and distress. Some scholars have concluded, however, that the omission is less an indication of a lack of knowledge or interest on his part than it is evidence of the incompleteness of his work. Amorges is next mentioned in 8.19.2. See Appendix E, The Persians, §6–8.

8.5.5c   Caria: Map 8.7, Asia.
8.6.1a   Megara: Map 8.7, Hellas.
8.6.1b   Cyzicus: Map 8.7, Asia.
8.6.1c   Hellespont: Map 8.7, Asia. Pharnabazus son of Pharnaces was the Persian governor of the Hellespont region.
8.6.1d   For the rivalry between Tissaphernes, Persian governor (satrap) of Sardis (Map

8.7, Asia), and Pharnabazus, Persian governor of the Hellespont (Map 8.7, Asia), see 8.109.1 and Appendix E, The Persians, §7.
8.6.2a   Ionia: Map 8.7, Asia.
8.6.3a   Endius was one of the three envoys sent to Athens eight years earlier who were then "known to be well disposed to the Athenians" (5.44.3), and who were duped by Alcibiades in the assembly (5.45). As a Spartan ephor, Endius was now a powerful government official. See Appendix C, Spartan Institutions, §5–6.
8.6.4a   For *perioikoi*, see the Glossary and Appendix C, Spartan Institutions, §9.
8.6.4b   Erythrae: Map 8.7, Asia.
8.6.5a   Laconia: Map 8.3. BX.

ILLUSTRATION 8.7
COINS WITH PORTRAIT HEADS
OF PHARNABAZUS (LEFT) AND
TISSAPHERNES

ILLUSTRATION 8.8
TRACKWAY FOR CARTS (*DIOLKOS*)
FOR HAULING BOATS ACROSS THE
ISTHMUS OF CORINTH

MAP 8.7 PROSPECTIVE REVOLTS OF
EUBOEA, LESBOS, AND CHIOS

At the beginning of the next summer the Chians were urging that the fleet should be sent off, being afraid that the Athenians, from whom all these embassies were kept a secret, might find out what was going on, and the Spartans at once sent three *Spartiates*[1a] to Corinth to haul the ships as quickly as possible across the Isthmus[1b] from the other sea to that on the side of Athens, and to order them all to sail to Chios,[1c] including those which Agis was equipping for Lesbos[1d] not excepted. The number of ships from the allied states was thirty-nine in all.

Meanwhile Calligeitus and Timagoras did not join on behalf of Pharnabazus in the expedition to Chios or give the money—twenty-five *talents*[1a]—which they had brought with them to help in dispatching a force, but determined to sail afterwards with another force by themselves. [2] Agis, on the other hand, seeing the Spartans bent upon going to Chios first, himself came to the same view; and the allies assembled at Corinth and held a council, in which they decided to sail first to Chios under the command of Chalcideus, who was equipping the five vessels in Laconia, then to Lesbos, under the command of Alcamenes, the same whom Agis had chosen, and lastly to go to the Hellespont,[2a] where the command was

8.7
412
20th Year/Summer
CORINTH
Sparta plans to haul thirty-nine Peloponnesian warships across the Isthmus and to send them to Chios.

8.8
412
20th Year/Summer
CORINTH
In assembly at Corinth, the Peloponnesians agree to send a fleet first to Chios, then to Lesbos, and finally to the Hellespont. Twenty-one triremes are prepared for immediate departure. Athens as yet has no fleet at sea.

8.7.1a A 'Spartiate' is a full citizen of Sparta and a member of the highest Spartan military caste.
8.7.1b At the Isthmus of Corinth, (Map 8.7, Hellas) remains of an ancient trackway on which specially made carts hauled ships across the Isthmus to avoid the long and sometimes difficult voyage around the

Peloponnesus can still be seen today; see Illustration 8.8.
8.7.1c Chios: Map 8.7, Asia.
8.7.1d Lesbos: Map 8.7, Asia.
8.8.1a A *talent* is a large unit of money; see Appendix J, Classical Greek Currency, §5.
8.8.2a Hellespont: Map 8.7, Asia. Alcamenes' selection by Agis was mentioned in 8.5.1.

given to Clearchus son of Ramphias. [3] Meanwhile they would take only half the ships across the Isthmus first, and let these sail off at once, in order that the Athenians might less notice this departing squadron than those who would be taken across afterward, [4] for no care had been taken to keep this voyage secret through contempt of the impotence of the Athenians, who had as yet no fleet of any account upon the sea. In accordance with this decision, twenty-one vessels were conveyed across the Isthmus at once.

They were now impatient to set sail, but the Corinthians were not willing to accompany them until they had celebrated the Isthmian festival,[1a] which fell at that time. Upon this Agis proposed to them to respect their scruples about breaking the Isthmian truce by taking the expedition upon himself. [2] The Corinthians did not consent to this, and a delay ensued, during which the Athenians began to suspect what was being prepared at Chios,[2a] and sent Aristocrates, one of their generals, who accused them of planning to revolt and, upon the denial of the Chians, ordered them as faithful allies to send with them a contingent of ships. Seven Chian ships were sent accordingly. [3] The reason for the dispatch of the ships was that the mass of the Chians were not privy to the negotiations, while the few who were in on the secret did not wish to break with the multitude until they had something positive to lean upon, and no longer expected the Peloponnesians to arrive by reason of their delay.

In the meantime the Isthmian games took place, and the Athenians, who had also been invited, went to attend them, and there perceiving more clearly the designs of the Chians, took measures as soon as they returned to Athens to prevent the enemy fleet from setting out from Cenchreae[1a] without their knowledge. [2] After the festival the Peloponnesians set sail with twenty-one ships for Chios, under the command of Alcamenes. The Athenians first sailed against them with an equal number, drawing off toward the open sea. When the enemy, however, turned back before he had followed them far, the Athenians turned back also, not trusting the seven Chian ships which formed part of their number, [3] and afterwards manned thirty-seven vessels in all and chased the enemy fleet as it passed along shore into Spiraeum,[3a] a deserted Corinthian port on the edge of the Epidaurian[3b] frontier. After losing one ship out at sea, the Peloponnesians got the rest together and brought them to anchor. [4] The Athenians now attacked not only from the sea with their fleet, but also disembarked upon the coast; and a mêlée ensued of the most confused and violent kind, in which the Athenians disabled most of the enemy's vessels and killed Alcamenes their commander, losing also a few of their own men.

8.9
412
20th Year/Summer
CORINTH-CHIOS
Corinth's determination to celebrate the Isthmian festival delays the fleet's departure. The Athenians become suspicious and demand that Chios send ships to Athens, and seven are sent, since most Chians were ignorant of the negotiations with the Spartans.

8.10
412
20th Year/Summer
CORINTH
After learning more at the Isthmian Games about Chian intrigues, the Athenians man their fleet and, intercepting the twenty-one enemy triremes, force them into port. The Athenians attack the enemy ships there and disable most of them.

8.9.1a   The Isthmian festival was one of the main ceremonies involving all Greeks. A general truce was declared so that all Greeks could travel to and participate in the festival. See 5.49, for a description of Sparta's alleged violation of the Olympic truce, and Appendix I, Religious Festivals, §5–7.
8.9.2a   Chios: Map 8.7, Asia. For the fate of these ships, see 8.15.2.
8.10.1a   Cenchreae: Map 8.7, Hellas.
8.10.3a   Spiraeum: Map 8.7, Hellas.
8.10.3b   Epidaurus: Map 8.7, Hellas.

After this they separated, and the Athenians, detaching a sufficient number of ships to blockade those of the enemy, anchored with the rest at the small island adjacent, upon which they proceeded to encamp, and sent to Athens for reinforcements; [2] the Peloponnesians having been joined on the day after the battle by the Corinthians, who came to help the ships, and by the other inhabitants in the vicinity not long afterwards. These saw the difficulty of keeping guard in a desert place, and in their perplexity at first thought of burning the ships, but finally resolved to haul them up on shore and sit down and guard them with their land forces, until a convenient opportunity for escaping should present itself. Agis also, on being informed of the disaster, sent them a Spartiate by the name of Thermon. [3] The Spartans first received the news of the fleet having put out from the Isthmus,[3a] Alcamenes having been ordered by the ephors to send off a horseman when this took place, and immediately resolved to dispatch their own five vessels under Chalcideus, and Alcibiades with him. But while they were full of this resolution came the second news of the fleet having taken refuge in Spiraeum; and disheartened at their first step in the Ionian war proving a failure, they laid aside the idea of sending the ships from their own country, and even wished to recall some that had already sailed.

Perceiving this, Alcibiades again persuaded Endius and the other ephors to persevere in the expedition, saying that the voyage would be made before the Chians heard of the fleet's misfortune, and that as soon as he set foot in Ionia,[1a] he should, by assuring them of the weakness of the Athenians and the zeal of Sparta, have no difficulty in persuading the cities to revolt, as they would readily believe his testimony. [2] He also represented to Endius himself in private that it would be glorious for him to be the means of making Ionia revolt and the King become the ally of Sparta, instead of that honor being left to Agis, for Agis (it must be remembered) was the enemy of Alcibiades;[2a] and [3] Endius and his colleagues thus persuaded, put to sea with the five ships and the Spartan Chalcideus, and made all haste upon the voyage.[3a]

About this same time the sixteen Peloponnesian ships from Sicily, which had served through the war with Gylippus, were caught on their return off Leucas[1a] and roughly handled by the twenty-seven Athenian vessels under Hippocles son of Menippus, on the lookout for the ships from Sicily. After losing one of their number the rest escaped from the Athenians and sailed into Corinth.

Meanwhile Chalcideus and Alcibiades seized all they met with on their voyage, to prevent news of their coming, and let them go at Corycus,[1a] the first point which they touched at on the mainland. Here they were vis-

8.11
412
20th Year/Summer
SPIRAEUM
The Athenians blockade the Peloponnesian fleet, whose ships are now drawn up on shore and guarded. News of the defeat discourages the Spartans.

8.12
412
20th Year/Summer
SPARTA
Alcibiades persuades Endius and the other ephors to let him sail with five ships to Chios so that it will be Endius and not Agis who starts the revolt and thus brings Persia into alliance with Sparta.

8.13
412
20th Year/Summer
LEUCAS
There is a naval skirmish off Leucas.

8.14
412
20th Year/Summer
CHIOS
Alcibiades arrives in Chios. Saying nothing of the recent Peloponnesian defeat, he persuades Chios, Erythrae, and Clazomenae to revolt from Athens.

8.11.3a   Isthmus of Corinth: Map 8.7, Hellas.
8.12.1a   Ionia: Map 8.7, Asia.
8.12.2a   According to Plutarch ("Alcibiades," 23), Alcibiades fathered a son by Agis' wife.
8.12.3a   This squadron was apparently seen and pursued by the Athenian Strombichides,

but not overtaken; see 8.15.1.
8.13.1a   Leucas: Map 8.15, Hellas.
8.14.1a   Corycus, presumably near Mount Corycus: Map 8.15, Asia.

ited by some of their Chian correspondents, and being urged by them to sail up to the city without announcing their coming, arrived suddenly before Chios.[1b] [2] The multitude were amazed and confounded, while The Few had so arranged it that the council should be sitting at the time; and after speeches from Chalcideus and Alcibiades stating that many more ships were sailing up, but saying nothing of the fleet being blockaded in Spiraeum,[2a] the Chians revolted from the Athenians, and the Erythraeans[1b] immediately afterwards. [3] After this three vessels sailed over to Clazomenae,[3a] and made that city revolt also; and the Clazomenians immediately crossed over to the mainland and began to fortify Polichna,[3b] in order to retreat there in case of necessity, from the island where they dwelt.

8.15
412
20th Year/Summer
ATHENS
The Athenians, alarmed by news of the Chian revolt, employ their emergency funds to assemble a fleet to send to Chios.

While the places that had revolted were all engaged in fortifying and preparing for the war, news of Chios speedily reached Athens. The Athenians thought the danger by which they were now menaced was great and unmistakable, and that the rest of their allies would not consent to keep quiet after the secession of the greatest of their number. In the consternation of the moment they at once canceled the penalty imposed on whoever proposed or put to the vote a proposal for using the thousand talents which they had jealously avoided touching throughout the whole war,[1a] and voted to employ them to man a large number of ships, and to send off at once under Strombichides son of Diotimus the eight vessels that formed part of the blockading fleet at Spiraeum,[1b] but which had left the blockade and had returned after pursuing and failing to overtake the vessels with Chalcideus. These were to be followed shortly afterwards by twelve more under Thrasycles, also taken from the blockade. [2] They also recalled the seven Chian vessels forming part of their squadron blockading the fleet in Spiraeum, and giving the slaves on board their liberty,[2a] put the freemen in confinement, and speedily manned and sent out ten fresh ships to blockade the Peloponnesians in the place of all those that had departed, and decided to man thirty more. Zeal was not lacking, and no effort was spared to send relief to Chios.

8.16
412
20th Year/Summer
TEOS
The Peloponnesian fleet sails from Chios to Teos, chasing away an Athenian squadron. Teos accepts the Peloponnesians.

In the meantime Strombichides with his eight ships arrived at Samos,[1a] and taking one Samian vessel, sailed to Teos[1b] and required the Teians to remain quiet. Chalcideus also set sail for Teos from Chios[1c] with twenty-three ships, the land forces of the Clazomenians[1d] and Erythraeans[1e] moving along shore to support him. [2] Informed of this in time, Strombichides put out from Teos before their arrival, and while out at sea, seeing the number of the ships from Chios, fled toward Samos, chased by the enemy. [3] The Teians at first would not receive the land forces, but upon the flight of the Athenians took them into the city. There they waited

8.14.1b   Chios: Map 8.15, Asia.
8.14.2a   Spiraeum: Map 8.15, Hellas.
8.14.1b   Erythrae: Map 8.15, Asia.
8.14.3a   Clazomenae: Map 8.15, Asia.
8.14.3b   Polichna: exact site unknown.
8.15.1a   This fund was set aside in 431; see 2.24.1.
8.15.1b   Spiraeum: Map 8.15, Hellas.
8.15.2a   These were the Chian vessels demanded in 8.9.2–3. The Chians apparently used

slaves in the crews of these ships. See note 1.55.1b, 7.13.2, and Appendix G, Trireme Warfare, §12.
8.16.1a   Samos: Map 8.15, Asia.
8.16.1b   Teos: Map 8.15, Asia.
8.16.1c   Chios: Map 8.15, Asia.
8.16.1d   Clazomenae: Map 8.15, Asia.
8.16.1e   Erythrae: Map 8.15, Asia.

MAP 8.15 NAVAL ACTION OFF LEUCAS; PELOPONNESIAN FLEET SAILS TO CHIOS

for some time for Chalcideus to return from the pursuit, and as time went on without his appearing, began themselves to demolish the wall which the Athenians had built on the land side of the city of the Teians, being assisted by a few of the barbarians[3a] who had come up under the command of Stages, the lieutenant of Tissaphernes.

Meanwhile Chalcideus and Alcibiades, after chasing Strombichides into Samos, armed the crews of the ships from the Peloponnesus[1a] and left them at Chios, and filling their places with substitutes from Chios and manning twenty others, sailed off to bring about the revolt of Miletus.[1b] [2] The wish of Alcibiades, who had friends among the leading men of the Milesians, was to bring over the city before the arrival of the ships from the

8.16.3a   The barbarians in this case are Persians.
8.17.1a   Peloponnesus: Map 8.15, Hellas.
8.17.1b   Miletus: Map 8.15, Asia.

8.17
412
20th Year/Summer
MILETUS
Led by Alcibiades, the Peloponnesians reach Miletus just ahead of an Athenian fleet. The ensuing revolt of Miletus is followed by an alliance between the Persians and the Peloponnesians.

491

Peloponnesus, and thus, by causing the revolt of as many cities as possible with the help of the Chian power and of Chalcideus, to secure the honor for the Chians and himself and Chalcideus, and, as he had promised, for Endius who had sent them out. [3] Not discovered until their voyage was nearly completed, they arrived a little before Strombichides and Thrasycles (who had just come with twelve ships from Athens, and had joined Strombichides in pursuing them), and brought about the revolt of Miletus. The Athenians sailing up close on their heels with nineteen ships found Miletus closed against them, and took up their station at the adjacent island of Lade.[3a] The first alliance between the King and the Spartans[4a] was now concluded immediately upon the revolt of the Milesians, by Tissaphernes and Chalcideus, and was as follows:

8.18
412
20th Year/Summer
MILETUS
Thucydides offers the text of the first treaty of alliance between the Persians and the Peloponnesians.

The Spartans and their allies made a treaty with the King and Tissaphernes upon the terms following:

• Whatever country or cities the King has, or the King's ancestors had, shall be the King's; and whatever came in to the Athenians from these cities, either money or any other thing, the King and the Spartans and their allies shall jointly hinder the Athenians from receiving either money or any other thing.

• [2] The war with the Athenians shall be carried on jointly by the King and by the Spartans and their allies; and it shall not be lawful to make peace with the Athenians unless both agree, the King on his side and the Spartans and their allies on theirs.

• [3] If any revolt from the King they shall be the enemies of the Spartans and their allies. And if any revolt from the Spartans and their allies they shall be the enemies of the King in like manner.

8.19
412
20th Year/Summer
IONIA
A Chian squadron is chased into Teos and four of its ships are taken by an Athenian flotilla. More cities revolt from Athens.

This was the alliance. After this the Chians immediately manned ten more vessels and sailed for Anaia,[1a] in order to gain intelligence of those in Miletus,[1b] and also to make the cities revolt. [2] A message, however, reaching them from Chalcideus to tell them to go back again, and that Amorges was near at hand with an army by land, they sailed to the temple of Zeus,[2a] and there sighting ten more ships sailing up with which Diomedon had started from Athens after Thrasycles,[2b] [3] they fled, one ship to Ephesus,[3a] the rest to Teos.[3b] The Athenians took four of their ships empty, the men finding time to escape ashore; the rest took refuge in the city of

8.17.3a Lade: Map 8.15, Asia. This force is next mentioned in 8.24.1.
8.17.4a This "First Alliance" is probably the first of three drafts (see 8.37 and 8.58) of the eventual alliance agreement; see note 8.57.2a.
8.19.1a Anaia: Map 8.15, Asia. Anaia was the base of anti-Athenian Samian exiles; see 3.19.2, 3.32.2, and 4.75.1.
8.19.1b Miletus: Map 8.15, Asia.
8.19.2a The location of this temple is not known. Amorges was the bastard son of Pis-

suthnes, the previous Persian governor at Sardis (Map 8.15, Asia), who was now in rebellion against Tissaphernes and the Persians. He had probably received assistance from the Athenians, although Thucydides does not directly say so. See 1.115.4, 8.5.5, 8.28.2, and 8.54.3. Also see Appendix E, The Persians, §7–8.
8.19.2b For Thrasycles, see 8.15.1 and 8.17.3.
8.19.3a Ephesus: Map 8.15, Asia.
8.19.3b Teos: Map 8.15, Asia.

the Teians; after which the Athenians sailed off to Samos,[3c] [4] while the Chians put to sea with their remaining vessels, accompanied by the land forces, and caused Lebedos[4a] and after it Aerae[4b] to revolt. After this both the fleet and the army returned home.

About the same time the twenty ships of the Peloponnesians in Spiraeum,[1a] which had been chased to land and blockaded by an equal number of Athenians, suddenly sallied out and defeated the blockading squadron, took four of their ships and, sailing back to Cenchreae,[1b] prepared again for the voyage to Chios[1c] and Ionia.[1d] Here they were joined by Astyochus as admiral from Sparta, henceforth invested with the supreme command at sea. [2] The land forces now withdrawing from Teos,[2a] Tissaphernes marched there in person with an army, completed the demolition of anything that was left of the wall, and left. Not long after his departure Diomedon arrived with ten Athenian ships, and having made a convention by which the Teians admitted him as they had the enemy, coasted along to Aerae and, failing in an attempt upon the city, sailed back again.

About this time took place the rising of The People at Samos[1a] against those in power, in concert with some Athenians who were there in three vessels. The Samian popular party put to death some two hundred in all of the most powerful, banished four hundred more, and themselves took their land and houses; after which the Athenians decreed their independence, being now sure of their fidelity, and the popular party henceforth governed the city, excluding the landholders from all share in affairs, and forbidding any of The People to give his daughter in marriage to them or to take a wife from them in future.

After this, during the same summer, the Chians,[1a] whose zeal continued as active as ever, and who even without the Peloponnesians found themselves in sufficient force to bring about the revolt of the cities and who also wished to have as many companions in peril as possible, made an expedition with thirteen ships of their own to Lesbos;[1b] following the instructions from Sparta, which were to go to that island next, and from there to the Hellespont.[1c] Meanwhile the land forces of the Peloponnesians who were with the Chians and those of the allies on the spot, moved along shore toward Clazomenae[1d] and Cyme,[1e] under the command of Eualas, a Spartiate; at the same time the fleet under Diniades, one of the *perioikoi*,[1f] [2] first sailed up to Methymna[2a] and caused it to revolt, and, leaving four ships there, with the rest procured the revolt of Mytilene.[2b]

8.20
412
20th Year/Summer
SPIRAEUM
The Peloponnesian ships defeat the blockaders and escape. Astyochus takes command.
TEOS
Tissaphernes demolishes the Teian wall.

8.21
412
20th Year/Summer
SAMOS
The Samian People, with some Athenians, overthrow the upper classes and take over the government.

8.22
412
20th Year/Summer
IONIA
The Chians and Peloponnesians incite the revolt of Methymna and Mytilene on Lesbos. Peloponnesian troops march against Clazomenae and Cyme.

8.19.3c   Samos: Map 8.15, Asia.
8.19.4a   Lebedos: Map 8.15, Asia.
8.19.4b   Aerae: Map 8.15, Asia.
8.20.1a   Spiraeum: Map 8.15, Hellas; Map 8.25, Hellas.
8.20.1b   Cenchreae: Map 8.25, Hellas.
8.20.1c   Chios: Map 8.25, BX.
8.20.1d   Ionia: Map 8.25, BY.
8.20.2a   Teos: Map 8.25, BY.
8.21.1a   Samos: Map 8.25, BY.
8.22.1a   Chios: Map 8.25, BX.
8.22.1b   Lesbos: Map 8.25, AX.

8.22.1c   Hellespont: Map 8.25, AX. For Spartan instructions, see 8.8.2.
8.22.1d   Clazomenae: Map 8.25, BY.
8.22.1e   Cyme: Map 8.25, BY.
8.22.1f   *Perioikoi*: see the Glossary and Appendix C, Spartan Institutions, §9.
8.22.2a   Methymna, Lesbos: Map 8.25, AX.
8.22.2b   Mytilene, Lesbos: Map 8.25, AY.

8.23
412
20th Year/Summer
LESBOS-CHIOS
The Spartan Astyochus reaches Lesbos too late to save the island from an Athenian counterattack. The Peloponnesians retire to Chios.

In the meantime Astyochus, the Spartan admiral, set sail from Cenchreae[1a] with four ships, as he had intended, and arrived at Chios.[1b] On the third day after his arrival the Athenian ships, twenty-five in number, sailed to Lesbos under Diomedon and Leon, who had recently arrived with a reinforcement of ten ships from Athens. [2] Late in the same day Astyochus put to sea, and taking one Chian vessel with him sailed to Lesbos to render what assistance he could. Arrived at Pyrrha,[2a] and from there the next day at Eresus,[2b] he there learned that Mytilene had been taken, almost without a blow, by the Athenians, [3] who had sailed up and unexpectedly entered the harbor, had beaten the Chian ships, and landing and defeating the troops opposed to them, had become masters of the city. [4] Informed of this by the Eresians and the Chian ships, which had been left with Eubulus at Methymna and which had fled upon the capture of Mytilene, and three of which he now fell in with (one having been taken by the Athenians), Astyochus did not go on to Mytilene, but raised and armed Eresus; and sending the hoplites from his own ships by land under Eteonicus to Antissa[4a] and to Methymna, he himself proceeded there along shore with the ships which he had with him and with the three Chians, in the hope that the Methymnians upon seeing them would be encouraged to persevere in their revolt. [5] As, however, everything went against him in Lesbos, he took up his own force and sailed back to Chios; the land forces which were to have gone to the Hellespont being also conveyed on board back to their different cities. After this six of the allied Peloponnesian ships at Cenchreae joined the forces at Chios. [6] The Athenians, after restoring matters to their former state in Lesbos, set sail from there and took Polichna,[6a] the place that the Clazomenians were fortifying on the continent, and carried the inhabitants back to their city upon the island, except for the authors of the revolt, who withdrew to Daphnus;[6b] and thus Clazomenae became once more Athenian.

8.24
412
20th Year/Summer
CHIOS
Leaving a squadron to blockade Miletus, the Athenians sail to Chios. They defeat the Chians several times and force them to retire behind their walls. Thucydides praises the prudence and wisdom of the Chians, but admits that they, like many others, underestimated the ability of Athens to carry on the war.

The same summer the Athenians in the twenty ships at Lade[1a] blockading Miletus[1b] made a descent at Panormus[1c] in the Milesian territory, and killed Chalcideus the Spartan commander, who had come with a few men against them, and the third day after sailed over and set up a trophy,[1d] which, as they were not masters of the country, was however pulled down by the Milesians. [2] Meanwhile Leon and Diomedon with the Athenian fleet from Lesbos[2a] sailed out from the Oenoussae,[2b] the islands off Chios, and from their forts of Sidoussa and Pteleum in the territory of Erythrae,[2c] and from Lesbos, and carried on the war against the Chians from their ships, having on board hoplites from the enlistment rolls required to

8.23.1a   Cenchreae: Map 8.25, Hellas.
8.23.1b   Chios: Map 8.25, BX.
8.23.2a   Pyrrha, Lesbos: Map 8.25, AX.
8.23.2b   Eresus, Lesbos: Map 8.25, AX.
8.23.4a   Antissa, Lesbos: Map 8.25, AX.
8.23.6a   Polichna: exact location unknown.
8.23.6b   Daphnus: exact location unknown.
8.24.1a   Lade: Map 8.25, BY. This force took up
         station at Lade in 8.17.3.
8.24.1b   Miletus: Map 8.25, BY.

8.24.1c   Panormus: Map 8.25, BY.
8.24.1d   A trophy was a set of captured armor
         arranged on a pole and raised at or near
         the battlefield by the victors.
8.24.2a   Lesbos: Map 8.25, AX.
8.24.2b   Oenoussae Islands: Map 8.25, BX.
8.24.2c   The locations of Sidoussa and Pteleum
         are unknown. For the location of Ery-
         thrae, see Map 8.25, BY.

serve as marines. [3] Landing in Cardamyle[3a] and in Bolissus[3b] they defeated with heavy loss the Chians that took the field against them, and laying desolate the places in that neighborhood, defeated the Chians again in another battle at Phanae,[3c] and in a third at Leuconium.[3d] After this the Chians ceased to meet them in the field, while the Athenians devastated the country, which was beautifully stocked and had remained undamaged ever since the Persian wars.[3e] [4] Indeed, after the Spartans, the Chians are the only people that I have known who knew how to be wise in prosperity, and who ordered their city the more securely the greater it grew. [5] Nor was this revolt, in which they might seem to have erred on the side of rashness, ventured upon until they had numerous and gallant allies to share the danger with them, and until they perceived that the Athenians after the Sicilian disaster were themselves no longer denying the thoroughly desperate state of their affairs. And if they were tripped up by one of the surprises which upset human calculations, they found out their mistake in company with many others who had believed, like them, in the speedy collapse of the Athenian power. [6] While they were thus blockaded from the sea and plundered by land, some of the citizens undertook to bring the city over to the Athenians. Learning of this, the authorities took no action themselves, but brought Astyochus the admiral from Erythrae,[6a] with four ships that he had with him, and considered how they could most quietly, either by taking hostages or by some other means, put an end to the conspiracy.

While the Chians were thus engaged, a thousand Athenian hoplites and fifteen hundred Argives[1a] (five hundred of whom were *peltasts*[1b] furnished with armor by the Athenians), and one thousand of the allies, toward the close of the same summer sailed from Athens in forty-eight ships, some of which were transports, under the command of Phrynichus, Onomacles, and Scironides, and putting in to Samos[1c] crossed over and encamped at Miletus. [2] Upon this the Milesians came out to the number of eight hundred hoplites, with the Peloponnesians who had come with Chalcideus, and some foreign mercenaries of Tissaphernes, along with Tissaphernes himself and his cavalry, and engaged the Athenians and their allies. [3] While the Argives rushed forward on their own wing with the careless disdain of men advancing against Ionians who would never stand their charge, and were defeated by the Milesians with a loss little short of three hundred men, [4] the Athenians first defeated the Peloponnesians, and driving before them the barbarians and the rump of the army, without engaging the Milesians, who after the rout of the Argives retreated into the city upon seeing their comrades

8.25
412
20th Year/Summer
MILETUS
The Athenians, with Argive support, engage the Milesian and Peloponnesian forces. Ionians defeat Dorians on both sides; the Athenians drive the enemy within their walls and consider mounting a siege against Miletus.

8.24.3a Cardamyle, Chios: Map 8.25, BX.
8.24.3b Bolissus, Chios: Map 8.25, BX.
8.24.3c Cape Phanae, Chios: Map 8.25, BX.
8.24.3d Leuconium: location unknown.
8.24.3e Thucydides is here including in the term "the Persian wars" the events of the Ionian Revolt of 499–94 B.C. See Appendix E, The Persians, §3.
8.24.6a Erythrae: Map 8.25, BY. We next hear of Astyochus at Chios in 8.31.1.

8.25.1a Argos: Map 8.25, Hellas.
8.25.1b *Peltasts* furnished with hoplite armor: peltasts were normally armed only with a small, light shield, a javelin, and a short sword. Unhindered by body armor, they could move much more quickly than the fully armed hoplite.
8.25.1c Samos: Map 8.25, Hellas.

MAP 8.25
OPERATIONS IN LESBOS, CHIOS, SAMOS, AND MILETUS

defeated, crowned their victory by grounding their arms under the very walls of Miletus. [5] Thus, in this battle, the Ionians on both sides overcame the Dorians,[5a] the Athenians defeating the Peloponnesians opposed to them, and the Milesians the Argives. After setting up a trophy, the Athenians prepared to draw a wall round the place, which stood upon an isthmus; thinking that if

8.25.5a Thucydides obviously believed that a
double victory of Ionians over Dorians
was striking enough to warrant special

mention. See Appendix H, Dialects and
Ethnic Groups, §8.

they could gain Miletus, the other cities also would easily come over to them.

Meanwhile about dusk word reached them that the fifty-five ships from the Peloponnesus and Sicily might be expected at any moment. Of these the Sicilians, urged principally by the Syracusan Hermocrates[1a] to join in giving the finishing blow to the power of Athens, furnished twenty-two—twenty from Syracuse, and two from Selinus;[1b] and the ships that were preparing in the Peloponnesus being now ready, both squadrons had been entrusted to Therimenes, a Spartan, to take to Astyochus, the admiral. They now put in first at Leros,[1c] the island off Miletus, [2] and from there, discovering that the Athenians were before the city, sailed into the Iasic gulf,[2a] in order to learn how matters stood at Miletus. [3] Meanwhile Alcibiades came on horseback to Teichioussa[3a] in the Milesian territory, the point of the gulf in which they had put in for the night, and told them of the battle, in which he had fought in person by the side of the Milesians and Tissaphernes, and advised them, if they did not wish to sacrifice Ionia and their cause, to hurry to the relief of Miletus and hinder its investment.

Accordingly they resolved to relieve it the next morning. Meanwhile Phrynichus, the Athenian commander, had received precise intelligence of the fleet from Leros, and when his colleagues expressed a wish to remain at sea and fight it out, flatly refused either to stay himself or to let them or anyone else do so if he could help it. [2] Where they could hereafter contend after full and undisturbed preparation, with an exact knowledge of the number of the enemy's fleet and of the force with which they could confront him, he would never allow the reproach of disgrace to drive him into a risk that was unreasonable. [3] It was no disgrace for an Athenian fleet to retreat when it suited them: put it as they would, it would be more disgraceful to be defeated, and to expose the city not only to disgrace but to the most serious danger. After its late misfortunes the city could hardly be justified in voluntarily taking the offensive even with the strongest force, except in a case of absolute necessity: much less then without compulsion could it rush upon peril of its own seeking. [4] He told them to take up their wounded as quickly as they could and the troops and stores which they had brought with them, and leaving behind what they had taken from the enemy's country in order to lighten the ships, to sail off to Samos[4a] and there concentrate all their ships to attack as opportunity arose. [5] As he spoke so he acted; and thus not now more than afterwards, nor in this alone but in all that he had to do with, did Phrynichus show himself to be a man of sense.[5a] [6] In this way that very evening the Athenians broke camp from before Miletus, leaving their victory incomplete and the Argives, mortified at their disaster, promptly sailed off home from Samos.

8.26
412
20th Year/Summer
MILETUS
A combined Sicilian and Peloponnesian fleet now arrives at Miletus. Alcibiades advises them to quickly relieve the city.

8.27
412
20th Year/Summer
MILETUS
Phrynichus, the Athenian commander, receives word of the enemy fleet's approach and prudently decides, against the objections of others, to avoid battle and retire immediately from Miletus to Samos, winning Thucydides' approval for his wisdom.

8.26.1a   Hermocrates son of Hermon is the states-
          man and general from Syracuse (Map
          8.37, locator); cf. Books 6 and 7.
8.26.1b   Selinus: Map 8.37, locator.
8.26.1c   Leros (Map 8.25, BY) is forty miles from
          Miletus (Map 8.25, BY), but could be

          described as "on the way" to Miletus.
8.26.2a   Gulf of Iasus: Map 8.25, BY.
8.26.3a   Teichioussa: Map 8.25, BY.
8.27.4a   Samos: Map 8.25, BY.
8.27.5a   Phrynichus reenters the narrative in
          8.48.4.

8.28
412
20th Year/Summer
IASUS
At the request of the
Persian Tissaphernes, the
Peloponnesian fleet attacks
Iasus and takes it, capturing
the Persian rebel Amorges.

As soon as it was morning the Peloponnesians set out from Teichioussa and put into Miletus[1a] after the departure of the Athenians; they stayed one day, and on the next took with them the Chian vessels originally chased into port with Chalcideus,[1b] and resolved to sail back for the tackle[1c] which they had put on shore at Teichioussa. [2] Upon their arrival Tissaphernes came to them with his land forces and induced them to sail to Iasus,[2a] which was held by his enemy Amorges. Accordingly they suddenly attacked and took Iasus, whose inhabitants never imagined that the ships could be other than Athenian. The Syracusans distinguished themselves most in the action. [3] Amorges, a bastard of Pissuthnes and a rebel from the King, was taken alive and handed over to Tissaphernes, to carry to the King, if he chose, according to his orders: Iasus was sacked by the army, who found a very great booty there, the place being wealthy from ancient date. [4] The Peloponnesians received the mercenaries serving with Amorges and enrolled them in their army without doing them any harm, since most of them came from the Peloponnesus, and handed over the city to Tissaphernes with all the captives, bond or free, at the stipulated price of one Daric *stater*[4a] a head; after which they returned to Miletus. [5] Pedaritus son of Leon, who had been sent by the Spartans to take the command at Chios,[5a] they dispatched by land as far as Erythrae[5b] with the mercenaries taken from Amorges; appointing Philip to remain as governor of Miletus.

8.29
412/1
20th Year/Winter
MILETUS
Tissaphernes pays the
Peloponnesian fleet as he had
promised, but decides that
future payments will be
made at a lower scale.

Summer was now over. The following winter Tissaphernes put Iasus in a state of defense, and passing on to Miletus distributed a month's pay to all the ships as he had promised at Sparta, at the rate of an Attic drachma a day for each man. In future, however, he was resolved not to give more than three *obols*,[1a] until he had consulted the King when, if the King should so order, he would give, he said, the full drachma. [2] However, upon the protest of the Syracusan general Hermocrates (for as Therimenes was not admiral, but only accompanied them in order to hand over the ships to Astyochus, he made little difficulty about the pay), it was agreed that the amount of five ships' pay should be given over and above the three obols a day for each man; Tissaphernes paying thirty talents a month for fifty-five ships, and to the rest, for as many ships as they had beyond that number, at the same rate.

8.30
412/1
20th Year/Summer
MILETUS-CHIOS
The arrival of reinforcements
permits the Athenians to
blockade Miletus and to
attack Chios.

The same winter the Athenians in Samos[1a] having been joined by thirty-five more vessels from home under Charminus, Strombichides, and Euctemon, called back their squadron at Chios[1b] and all the rest, intending to blockade Miletus[1c] with their navy, and to send a fleet and an army against

8.28.1a Teichioussa and Miletus: Map 8.31, BY.
8.28.1b For Chalcideus and the Chian ships' arrival at Miletus, see 8.17.
8.28.1c They had left the ships' tackle at Teichioussa in order to lighten their ships in preparation for battle off Miletus. See 6.34.5, 7.24.2, and Appendix G, Trireme Warfare, §8.
8.28.2a Iasus: Map 8.31, BY. The base of Amorges was last mentioned in 8.19.2; see also 8.5.5 (note 8.5.5b) and 8.54.3.
8.28.4a Doric *stater:* a unit of money; see Appendix J, Classical Greek Currency, §4.

8.28.5a Chios: Map 8.31, AX.
8.28.5b Erythrae: Map 8.31, BY. Pedaritus arrives here in 8.32.2.
8.29.1a This is a 50 percent reduction, as six obols equal one drachma; see Appendix J, Classical Greek Currency, §3. As we learn in 8.45.2, Alcibiades had advised Tissaphernes to reduce the pay.
8.30.1a Samos: Map 8.31, BY.
8.30.1b Chios: Map 8.31, AX.
8.30.1c Miletus: Map 8.31, BY.

MAP 8.31 FIGHTING IN IONIA

Chios; drawing lots for the respective services. This intention they carried into effect; [2] Strombichides, Onomacles, and Euctemon sailing against Chios, which fell to their lot, with thirty ships and a part of the thousand hoplites who had come to Miletus in transports;[2a] while the rest remained masters of the sea with seventy-four ships at Samos, and advanced upon Miletus.

Meanwhile Astyochus, who at that time was at Chios collecting the hostages required in consequence of the conspiracy,[1a] stopped upon learning that the fleet with Therimenes had arrived, and that the affairs of the alliance were in a more flourishing condition, and put out to sea with ten Peloponnesian and as many Chian vessels. [2] After a futile attack upon Pteleum,[2a] he coasted on to Clazomenae[2b] and ordered the pro-Athenian party to move inland to Daphnus,[2c] and to join the Peloponnesians—an

8.31
412/1
20th Year/Winter
IONIA
The Spartan admiral Astyochus sails from Chios, attacks various places without success, and is blown to Phocaea by a gale.

8.30.2a   The arrival of these thousand Athenian hoplites was described in 8.25.1.
8.31.1a   Conspiracy at Chios: see 8.24.6, and perhaps 8.38.3.

8.31.2a   Pteleum: location unknown.
8.31.2b   Clazomenae: Map 8.31, AY.
8.31.2c   Daphnus: location unknown.

order in which he was joined by Tamos, the King's lieutenant in Ionia. [3] This order being disregarded, Astyochus made an attack upon the city, which was unwalled, and having failed to take it was himself carried off by a strong gale to Phocaea and Cyme,[3a] while the rest of the ships put in at the islands adjacent to Clazomenae—Marathoussa, Pele,[3b] and Drymoussa.[3c] [4] Here they were detained eight days by the winds, and plundering and consuming all the property of the Clazomenians deposited there, put the rest on shipboard and sailed off to Phocaea and Cyme to join Astyochus.

While he was there, envoys arrived from the Lesbians[1a] who wished to revolt again. With Astyochus they were successful; but the Corinthians[1b] and the other allies being averse to it by reason of their former failure, he weighed anchor and set sail for Chios,[1c] where they eventually arrived from different quarters, the fleet having been scattered by a storm. [2] After this Pedaritus, who was then marching along the coast from Miletus,[2a] arrived at Erythrae,[2b] and from there crossed over with his army to Chios, where he found also about five hundred soldiers with their arms who had been left there by Chalcideus from the five ships.[2c] [3] Meanwhile as some Lesbians made offers to revolt, Astyochus sought to persuade Pedaritus and the Chians that they ought to go with their ships and bring about a revolt of Lesbos and so increase the number of their allies or, if not successful, at all events harm the Athenians. The Chians, however, turned a deaf ear to this, and Pedaritus flatly refused to give up to him the Chian vessels.[3a]

Upon this Astyochus took five Corinthian and one Megarian[1a] vessel, with another from Hermione,[1b] and the ships which had come with him from Laconia,[1c] and set sail for Miletus[1d] to assume his command as admiral; after telling the Chians[1e] with many threats that he would certainly not come and help them if they should be in need. [2] At Corycus[2a] in the territory of Erythrae,[2b] he went ashore for the night; the Athenian armament sailing from Samos[2c] against Chios being separated from him only by a hill, upon the other side of which it had stopped, so that neither perceived the other. [3] But when a letter arrived in the night from Pedaritus to say that some liberated Erythraean prisoners had come from Samos to betray Erythrae, Astyochus at once put back to Erythrae, and so just escaped falling in with the Athenians. [4] Here Pedaritus sailed over to join him; and after inquiry into the pretended treachery, finding that the whole story had been made up to procure

8.31.3a Phocaea and Cyme: Map 8.31, AY.	8.32.3a Pedaritus could refuse because he had
8.31.3b Marathoussa and Pele: locations unknown.	been sent from Sparta to command at
8.31.3c Drymoussa: Map 8.31, AX.	Chios (8.28.5).
8.32.1a Lesbos: Map 8.31, AX.	8.33.1a Megara: Map 8.31, Hellas.
8.32.1b Corinth: Map 8.31, Hellas.	8.33.1b Hermione: Map 8.31, Hellas.
8.32.1c Chios: Map 8.31, AX.	8.33.1c Laconia: Map 8.31, Hellas. Astyochus
8.32.2a Miletus: Map 8.31, BY. Pedaritus set out	crossed over with four ships in 8.23.1.
from here in 8.28.5.	8.33.1d Miletus: Map 8.31, BY.
8.32.2b Erythrae: Map 8.31, BY.	8.33.1e Chios: Map 8.31, AX.
8.32.2c These were the five ships that Alcibiades	8.33.2a Mount Corycus: Map 8.31, BY.
persuaded Endius and the other ephors	8.33.2b Erythrae: Map 8.31, BY.
to send in 8.12.1–3.	8.33.2c Samos: Map 8.31, BY.

the escape of the men from Samos, they acquitted them of the charge, and sailed away, Pedaritus to Chios and Astyochus to Miletus, as he had intended.

Meanwhile the Athenian armament sailing round Corycus[1a] fell in with three Chian triremes off Arginus,[1b] and gave immediate chase. A great storm coming on, the Chians with difficulty took refuge in the harbor; the three Athenian vessels most forward in the pursuit being wrecked and blown ashore near the city of Chios, and the crews slain or taken prisoners. The rest of the Athenian fleet took refuge in the harbor called Phoenicus,[1c] under Mount Mimas,[1d] and from there they later put into Lesbos[1e] and prepared for the work of fortification.

The same winter the Spartan Hippocrates sailed out from the Peloponnesus with ten Thurian[1a] ships (under the command of Dorieus son of Diagoras, and two colleagues), and one Laconian and one Syracusan vessel, and arrived at Cnidus,[1b] which had already revolted at the instigation of Tissaphernes. [2] When their arrival was known at Miletus,[2a] orders came to them to leave half their squadron to guard Cnidus, and with the rest to cruise round Triopium[2b] and seize all the merchant ships arriving from Egypt.[2c] Triopium is a promontory of Cnidus and sacred to Apollo. [3] This coming to the knowledge of the Athenians, they sailed from Samos[3a] and captured the six ships on the watch at Triopium, the crews escaping out of them. After this the Athenians sailed into Cnidus and made an assault upon the city, which was unfortified, and all but took it; [4] and the next day assaulted it again, but with less effect, as the inhabitants had improved their defenses during the night, and had been reinforced by the crews escaped from the ships at Triopium. The Athenians now withdrew, and after plundering the Cnidian territory sailed back to Samos.

About the same time Astyochus came to the fleet at Miletus.[1a] The Peloponnesian camp was still plentifully supplied, being in receipt of sufficient pay, and the soldiers having still in hand the large booty taken at Iasus.[1b] The Milesians also showed great ardor for the war. [2] Nevertheless the Peloponnesians thought the first agreement[2a] with Tissaphernes, made with Chalcideus, defective, and more advantageous to him than to them, and consequently while Therimenes was still there concluded another, which was as follows:

8.34
412/1
20th Year/Winter
CHIOS
An Athenian pursuit of three Chian ships in a gale leads to the shipwreck of three of their own ships.

8.35
412/1
20th Year/Winter
CNIDUS
A Peloponnesian squadron at Cnidus is captured by Athenian ships, who then attack and almost succeed in taking the city before retiring to Samos.

8.36
412/1
20th Year/Winter
MILETUS
Sparta concludes a new and more equitable treaty with Persia.

8.34.1a Mount Corycus: Map 8.31, BY.
8.34.1b Cape Arginus: Map 8.31, BX.
8.34.1c Phoenicus: exact location unknown.
8.34.1d Mount Mimas: Map 8.31, AX.
8.34.1e Lesbos: Map 8.31, AX.
8.35.1a Thurii: Map 8.37, locator.
8.35.1b Cnidus: Map 8.37, BY.
8.35.2a Miletus: Map 8.37, BY.
8.35.2b Cape Triopium: Map 8.37, BY.
8.35.2c Egypt: Map 8.37, locator.
8.35.3a Samos: Map 8.37, BY.
8.36.1a Miletus: Map 8.37, BY.

8.36.1b Iasus: Map 8.37, BY. See 8.28.3–4.
8.36.2a Thucydides refers to the first of three agreements or three drafts of an agreement (8.18, 8.37, and 8.58); see note at 8.57.2.

8.37
412/1
20th Year/Winter
MILETUS
Thucydides offers the text of
the new treaty between
Sparta and Persia.

The agreement of the Spartans and the allies with King Darius and the sons of the King, and with Tissaphernes, for a treaty and friendship, as follows:

• [2] Neither the Spartans nor the allies of the Spartans shall make war against or otherwise injure any country or cities that belong to King Darius or did belong to his father or to his ancestors: neither shall the Spartans nor the allies of the Spartans exact tribute from such cities. Neither shall King Darius nor any of the subjects of the King make war against or otherwise injure the Spartans or their allies.

• [3] If the Spartans or their allies should require any assistance from the King, or the King from the Spartans or their allies, whatever they both agree upon they shall be right in doing.

• [4] Both shall carry on jointly the war against the Athenians and their allies; and if they make peace, both shall do so jointly.

• The expense of all troops in the King's country, sent for by the King, shall be borne by the King.

• [5] If any of the states which made this agreement with the King attack the King's country, the rest shall stop them and aid the King to the best of their power. And if any in the King's country or in the countries under the King's rule attack the country of the Spartans or their allies, the King shall stop it and help them to the best of his power.

8.38
412/1
20th Year/Winter
CHIOS
After an oligarchy is imposed
upon the Chians, they fall
out among themselves and,
lacking confidence in their
unity and power, request
more aid from Astyochus.
He refuses them.

After this convention Therimenes handed over the fleet to Astyochus, sailed off in a small boat, and was lost. [2] The Athenian armament had now crossed over from Lesbos[2a] to Chios,[2b] and being master on land and sea began to fortify Delphinium, a place naturally strong on the land side, provided with more than one harbor, and also not far from the city of Chios.[2c] [3] Meanwhile the Chians remained inactive. Already defeated in so many battles, they were now also at discord among themselves; the execution of the party of Tydeus son of Ion,[3a] by Pedaritus upon the charge of Atticism, followed by the forcible imposition of an oligarchy upon the rest of the city, having made them suspicious of one another; and they therefore thought neither themselves nor the mercenaries under Pedaritus a match for the enemy. [4] They sent, however, to Miletus[4a] to beg Astyochus to assist them, which he refused to do, and for which he was denounced at Sparta by Pedaritus as a traitor. [5] Such was the state of the Athenian affairs at Chios; while their fleet at Samos[5a] kept sailing out against the enemy in Miletus until they found that he would not accept their challenge, and then would retire again to Samos and remain quiet.

8.38.2a   Lesbos: Map 8.37, AX; where the
          Athenian ships went to prepare for the
          work of fortification, 8.34.1.
8.38.2b   Chios: Map 8.37, AX.
8.38.2c   Delphinium and the city of Chios: Map
          8.37, AX.

8.38.3a   Party of Ion: probably the authors of the
          conspiracy on Chios mentioned in 8.24.6
          and 8.31.1.
8.38.4a   Miletus: Map 8.37, BY.
8.38.5a   Samos: Map 8.37, BY.

MAP 8.37 FURTHER FIGHTING IN THE WINTER OF 412/1

In the same winter the twenty-seven ships equipped by the Spartans for Pharnabazus[1a] through the agency of the Megarian[1b] Calligeitus, and the Cyzicene[1c] Timagoras, put out from the Peloponnesus and sailed for Ionia[1d] about the time of the solstice, under the command of Antisthenes, a Spartiate. [2] With them the Spartans also sent eleven Spartiates as advisers to Astyochus; Lichas son of Arcesilaus being among the number. Arrived at Miletus, their orders were to aid in generally superintending the good conduct of the war; to send off the above ships or a greater or lesser number to the Hellespont to Pharnabazus, if they thought proper, appointing Clearchus son of Ramphias, who sailed with them, to the command; and further, if they thought proper, to make Antisthenes admiral, dismissing Astyochus, whom the letters of Pedaritus had caused to be regarded with suspicion. [3] Sailing accordingly from Malea[3a] across the

8.39
412/1
20th Year/Winter
AEGEAN
A fleet of Peloponnesian reinforcements for the Hellespont with new leaders sails to Miletus via Melos, Crete, and Caunus.

8.39.1a Pharnabazus was the Persian governor (satrap) of the Hellespont region (Map 8.37, AX). See Appendix E, The Persians, §2, 7.
8.39.1b Megara: Map 8.31, Hellas. Calligeitus and Timagorus appear also in 8.6.1 and 8.8.1.
8.39.1c Cyzicus: Map 8.37, AY.
8.39.1d Ionia: Map 8.37, BY.
8.39.3a Cape Malea of the Peloponnesus: Map 8.37, locator, and Map 8.45, BX.

open sea, the squadron touched at Melos[3b] and there fell in with ten Athenian ships, three of which they took empty and burned. After this, being afraid that the Athenian vessels escaped from Melos might, as they in fact did, give information of their approach to the Athenians at Samos, they sailed to Crete,[3c] and having lengthened their voyage by way of precaution made land at Caunus[3d] in Asia [4] from where, considering themselves in safety, they sent a message to the fleet at Miletus for a convoy along the coast.

8.40
412/1
20th Year/Winter
CHIOS
The Chians continue to press Astyochus to help them, citing the desertion of their slaves and the impending completion of the Athenian siege works. Astyochus now prepares to go to their assistance.

Meanwhile the Chians[2a] and Pedaritus, undeterred by the delays of Astyochus, went on sending messengers pressing him to come with all the fleet to assist them against their besiegers, and not to leave the greatest of the allied states in Ionia to be shut up by sea and overrun and pillaged by land. [2] There were more slaves at Chios than in any one other city except Sparta,[2b] and being also by reason of their numbers punished more rigorously when they offended, most of them when they saw the Athenian armament firmly established in the island with a fortified position, immediately deserted to the enemy, and through their knowledge of the country did the greatest harm. [3] The Chians therefore urged upon Astyochus that it was his duty to assist them, while there was still a hope and a possibility of stopping the enemy's progress, while Delphinium[3a] was still in process of fortification and unfinished, and before the completion of a higher rampart which was being added to protect the camp and fleet of their besiegers. Astyochus now saw that the allies also wished it and prepared to go, in spite of his intention to the contrary owing to the threat already referred to.[3b]

8.41
412/1
20th Year/Winter
CARIA-LYCIA
Hearing of the new Peloponnesian fleet at Caunus, Astyochus postpones action at Chios and sails to Caunus, seeking an Athenian squadron off the coast of Lycia.

In the meantime news came from Caunus[1a] of the arrival of the twenty-seven ships with the Spartan commissioners; and Astyochus postponing everything to the duty of convoying a fleet of that importance, in order to be more able to command the sea, and to the safe conduct of the Spartans sent as spies over his behavior, at once gave up going to Chios[1b] and set sail for Caunus. [2] As he coasted along he landed at the Meropid Cos[2a] and sacked the city, which was unfortified and had been lately laid in ruins by an earthquake, by far the greatest in living memory, and, as the inhabitants had fled to the mountains, overran the country and made booty of all it contained, letting go, however, the free men. [3] From Cos arriving in the night at Cnidus[3a] he was compelled by the urgent pleas of the Cnidians not to disembark the sailors, but to sail immediately against the twenty Athen-

8.39.3b Melos: Map 8.37, BX.
8.39.3c Crete: Map 8.37, locator.
8.39.3d Caunus: Map 8.37, BY.
8.40.2a Chios: Map 8.37, AX.
8.40.2b Thucydides is probably thinking in terms of the proportion of slaves to free men in Chios in comparison to the ratio of Helots to free citizens in Sparta. Although a large and rich island, it is most unlikely that there would have been a larger absolute number of slaves at Chios

than at Athens, or of Helots at Sparta.
8.40.3a Delphinium, Chios: Map 8.37, AX.
8.40.3b Astyochus had threatened to withhold aid from the Chians when they refused to assist the Lesbians; see 8.33.1.
8.41.1a Caunus: Map 8.45, BY. The departure and circuitous voyage of this fleet was described in 8.39.
8.41.1b Chios: Map 8.45, AY.
8.41.2a Cos: Map 8.45, BY.
8.41.3a Cnidus: Map 8.45, BY.

ian vessels, which with Charminus, one of the commanders at Samos,[3b] were on the watch for the very twenty-seven ships from the Peloponnesus[3c] which Astyochus was himself sailing to join; [4] the Athenians in Samos having heard from Melos[4a] of their approach, and Charminus being on the lookout off Syme, Chalce, Rhodes, and Lycia,[4b] as he now heard that they were at Caunus.

Astyochus accordingly sailed as he was to Syme,[1a] before he was heard of, in the hope of catching the enemy somewhere out at sea. He encountered rain and foggy weather, however, that caused his ships to straggle and get into disorder in the dark. [2] In the morning his fleet had become separated and was most of it still straggling round the island, so that as the left wing only came in sight of Charminus and the Athenians, they took it for the squadron which they were watching for from Caunus,[2a] and hastily put out against it with only part of their twenty vessels. [3] Attacking immediately, they sank three ships and disabled others, and had the advantage in the action until the main body of the fleet unexpectedly hove in sight, when they were surrounded on every side. [4] Upon this they took to flight, and after losing six ships, the rest escaped to the island of Teutloussa[4a] and from there to Halicarnassus.[4b] After this the Peloponnesians put into Cnidus,[4c] and being joined by the twenty-seven ships from Caunus, sailed all together and set up a trophy in Syme, and then returned to anchor at Cnidus.

As soon as the Athenians knew of the sea fight they sailed with all the ships at Samos to Syme, and without attacking or being attacked by the fleet at Cnidus,[1a] took the ships' tackle[1b] left at Syme, and touching at Loryma[1c] on the mainland sailed back to Samos. [2] Meanwhile the Peloponnesian ships being now all at Cnidus, underwent such repairs as were needed; while the eleven Spartan commissioners conferred with Tissaphernes, who had come to meet them, upon the points which did not satisfy them in the past transactions, and upon the best and mutually most advantageous manner of conducting the war in future. [3] The severest critic of the present proceeding was Lichas, who said that neither of the treaties could stand, neither that of Chalcideus, nor that of Therimenes; it being monstrous that the King should at this date pretend to the possession of all country formerly ruled by himself or by his ancestors—a pretension which implicitly put back under the yoke all the islands, Thessaly,[3a] Locris,[3b] and everything as far as Boeotia,[3c] and made the Spartans give to the Hellenes instead of liberty a Median[3d] master. [4] He therefore invited

8.42
412/1
20th Year/Winter
SYME
The Athenians attack the vanguard of Astyochus' fleet off Syme with success, but are driven off with losses when the rest of the Peloponnesian fleet joins the fray. Astyochus' ships and the new fleet from the Peloponnesus link up at Cnidus.

8.43
412/1
20th Year/Winter
CNIDUS
Newly arrived Spartan commissioners reject the previous treaty as too generous to Persia and insist on a more equitable agreement. This demand angers Tissaphernes, who leaves in a rage.

8.41.3b   Samos: Map 8.45, AY.
8.41.3c   Peloponnesus: Map 8.45, BX.
8.41.4a   Melos: Map 8.45, BX. See 8.39.3.
8.41.4b   Syme, Chalce, Rhodes, and Lycia: Map 8.45, BY.
8.42.1a   Syme: Map 8.45, BY.
8.42.2a   Caunus: Map 8.45, BY.
8.42.4a   Teutloussa: Map 8.45, BY.
8.42.4b   Halicarnassus: Map 8.45, BY.
8.42.4c   Cnidus: Map 8.45, BY.
8.43.1a   Syme and Cnidus: Map 8.45, BY.

8.43.1b   Ships' tackle: see 6.34.5, 7.24.2, 8.28.1, and Appendix G, Trireme Warfare, §8.
8.43.1c   Loryma: Map 8.45, BY.
8.43.3a   Thessaly: Map 8.45, AX.
8.43.3b   Locris (Opuntian): Map 8.45, AX.
8.43.3c   Boeotia: Map 8.45, AX.
8.43.3d   The Greeks regularly referred to the Persians as "the Mede," or "the Medes," and to the Persian wars as the "Median wars," although the Medes and Persians were distinct peoples. See Appendix E, §1.

Tissaphernes to conclude another and a better treaty, as they certainly would not recognize those existing and did not want any of his pay upon such conditions. This offended Tissaphernes so much that he went away in a rage without settling anything.

The Peloponnesians now determined to sail to Rhodes,[1a] upon the invitation of some of the principal men there, hoping to gain an island powerful by the number of its seamen and by its land forces, and also thinking that they would be able to maintain their fleet from their own allies without having to ask for money from Tissaphernes. [2] They accordingly at once set sail that same winter from Cnidus,[2a] and first put in with ninety-four ships at Camirus[2b] in the Rhodian country, to the great alarm of the mass of the inhabitants, who were not privy to the intrigue, and who consequently fled, especially as the city was unfortified. They were afterwards, however, assembled by the Spartans together with the inhabitants of the two other cities of Lindus and Ialysus;[2c] and the Rhodians were persuaded to revolt from the Athenians and the island went over to the Peloponnesians. [3] Meanwhile the Athenians had received the alarm and set sail with the fleet from Samos[3a] to forestall them, and came within sight of the island, but being a little too late sailed off for the moment to Chalce, and from thence to Samos, and subsequently waged war against Rhodes, sailing from Chalce, Cos,[3b] and Samos. [4] The Peloponnesians now levied a contribution of thirty-two talents from the Rhodians, after which they hauled their ships ashore and for eighty days remained inactive.

During this time, and even earlier, before they went to Rhodes, the following intrigues took place. After the death of Chalcideus and the battle at Miletus,[1a] Alcibiades began to be suspected by the Peloponnesians; and Astyochus received from Sparta an order from them to put him to death, he being the personal enemy of Agis,[1b] and in other respects thought unworthy of confidence. Alcibiades in his alarm first withdrew to Tissaphernes, and immediately began to do all he could with him to injure the Peloponnesian cause. [2] Henceforth becoming his adviser in everything, he cut down the pay from an Attic drachma to three obols a day,[2a] and even this not paid too regularly; and told Tissaphernes to say to the Peloponnesians that the Athenians, whose maritime experience was of an older date than their own, only gave their men three obols, not so much from poverty as to prevent their seamen being corrupted by being too well off, and spoiling their fitness by spending money upon enervating indulgences, and also paid their crews irregularly in order to have a security against their deserting in the arrears which they would leave behind them. [3] He also told Tissaphernes to bribe the captains and generals of the cities, and

---

8.44
412/1
20th Year/Winter
RHODES
The Peloponnesian fleet sails to Rhodes and incites its cities to revolt from the Athenians, who arrive too late to prevent the uprising. The Spartans levy a contribution from Rhodes.

8.45
412/1
20th Year/Winter
MAGNESIA?
Alcibiades, already condemned to death by the Spartans, had joined Tissaphernes. He advises him to reduce the Spartan sailors' pay, to pay them irregularly, and to refuse to contribute to defending Chios and other cities that had revolted from Athens.

8.44.1a   Rhodes: Map 8.45, BY.
8.44.2a   Cnidus: Map 8.45, BY.
8.44.2b   Camirus, Rhodes: Map 8.45, BY.
8.44.2c   Lindus and Ialysus on Rhodes: Map 8.45, BY.
8.44.3a   Samos: Map 8.45, AY.
8.44.3b   Chalce and Cos: Map 8.45, BY.

8.45.1a   The battle at Miletus (Map 8.45, BY) was described in 8.25.
8.45.1b   For Agis' enmity with Alcibiades, see note 8.12.2a.
8.45.2a   Six *obols* equals one *drachma;* see Appendix J, Classical Greek Currency, §3.

MAP 8.45 FIGHTING IN LYCIA; ALCIBIADES LEAVES THE SPARTANS

so to obtain their agreement—an expedient which succeeded with all except the Syracusans, Hermocrates alone opposing him on behalf of the whole alliance.[3a] [4] Meanwhile Alcibiades sent away the cities that were asking for money, telling them, in the name of Tissaphernes, that it was great impudence in the Chians,[4a] the richest people in Hellas, not content with being defended by a foreign force, to expect others to risk not only their lives but their money as well on behalf of their freedom; [5] while

8.45.3a   This move by Tissaphernes to reduce the
          pay of the Peloponnesian sailors, and
          Hermocrates' opposition to it, was previ-
          ously described in 8.29.1–2.
8.45.4a   Chios: Map 8.45, AY.

the other cities, he said, had to pay largely to Athens before their rebellion, and could not justly refuse to contribute as much or even more now for their own defense. [6] He also pointed out that Tissaphernes was at present carrying on the war at his own expense, and had good cause for economy, but that as soon as he received remittances from the King he would give them their pay in full, and do what was reasonable for the cities.

Alcibiades further advised Tissaphernes not to be in too great a hurry to end the war, or to let himself be persuaded to bring up the Phoenician[1a] fleet which he was equipping, or to provide pay for more Hellenes, and thus put the power by land and sea into the same hands; but to leave each of the contending parties in possession of one element, thus enabling the King when he found one party troublesome to call in the other. [2] For if the command of the sea and land were united in one hand, he would not know where to turn for help to overthrow the dominant power; unless he at last chose to stand up himself and go through with the struggle at great expense and danger. The cheapest plan was to let the Hellenes wear each other out, at a small share of the expense and without risk to himself. [3] Besides, he would find the Athenians the most convenient partners in empire as they did not aim at conquests on shore, and carried on the war upon principles and with a practice most advantageous to the King; being prepared to combine to conquer the sea for Athens, and for the King all the Hellenes inhabiting his country, whom the Peloponnesians, on the contrary, had come to liberate. On the other hand, it was not likely that the Spartans would free the Hellenes from the Hellenic Athenians, without freeing them also from the barbarian Persians, unless overthrown by him in the meantime. [4] Alcibiades therefore urged him to wear them both out at first, and after reducing the Athenian power as much as he could, forthwith to rid the country of the Peloponnesians. [5] On the whole, Tissaphernes approved of this policy, at least so far as could be conjectured from his behavior; since he now gave his confidence to Alcibiades in recognition of his good advice, and kept the Peloponnesians short of money, and would not let them fight at sea, but ruined their cause by pretending that the Phoenician fleet would arrive, and that they would thus be enabled to wage war with the odds in their favor, and so made their navy lose its efficiency, which had been very remarkable, and generally betrayed a coolness in the war that was too plain to be mistaken.

Alcibiades gave this advice to Tissaphernes and the King, with whom he then was, not merely because he thought it really the best, but because he was seeking means to bring about his restoration to his country, well knowing that if he did not destroy it he might one day hope to persuade the Athenians to recall him, and thinking that his best chance of persuading them lay in letting them see that he possessed the favor of Tissaphernes. [2] The event

8.46.1a   Phoenicia, Map 8.45, locator. The
Phoenician fleet was a major component
of Persian naval power.

proved him to be right. When the Athenians at Samos[2a] found that he had influence with Tissaphernes, principally of their own motion (though partly also through Alcibiades himself sending word to their chief men to tell the best men in the army that if only there were an oligarchy in the place of the corrupt democracy that had banished him, he would be glad to return to his country and to make Tissaphernes their friend), the captains and chief men in the armament at once embraced the idea of subverting the democracy.

This plan was first raised in the camp, and afterwards from there reached the city. Some persons crossed over from Samos and had an interview with Alcibiades, who immediately offered to make first Tissaphernes, and afterwards the King, their friend, if they would give up the democracy, and make it possible for the King to trust them. The most powerful citizens, who also suffered most severely from the war, now had great hopes of getting the government into their own hands and of triumphing over the enemy. [2] Upon their return to Samos the emissaries formed their partisans into a cabal, and openly told the army generally that the King would be their friend and would provide them with money if Alcibiades were restored and the democracy abolished. [3] The multitude, if at first irritated by these intrigues, were nevertheless kept quiet by the advantageous prospect of the pay from the King; and the oligarchic conspirators, after making this communication to the people, now reexamined the proposals of Alcibiades among themselves, with most of their associates. [4] Unlike the rest, who thought them advantageous and trustworthy, Phrynichus,[4a] who was still general, by no means approved of the proposals. Alcibiades, he rightly thought, cared no more for an oligarchy than for a democracy, and only sought to change the institutions of his country in order to get himself recalled by his associates; while for themselves their one purpose should be to avoid civil discord. He thought it would not be in the King's interest, when the Peloponnesians were now their equals at sea, and in possession of some of the chief cities in his empire, to go out of his way to side with the Athenians whom he did not trust, when he might make friends of the Peloponnesians who had never injured him. [5] And as for the allied states to whom oligarchy was now offered, because the democracy was to be put down at Athens, he well knew that this would not make the rebels come back any the sooner, or confirm the loyal in their allegiance; as the allies would never prefer servitude with an oligarchy or democracy to freedom with the constitution which they currently lived under, to whichever type it belonged. [6] Besides, the cities of the empire thought that the so-called "best people" would prove just as oppressive as The People, since it was they who originated, proposed, and for the most part benefited from the acts of The People that were injurious to the allies. Indeed, if it depended on the "best people," the citizens of the allied states would be put to death without trial and with violence; while The People was their

8.48
412/1
20th Year/Winter
SAMOS
Alcibiades' ideas prove attractive to some Athenians at Samos, who form a cabal to promote them. The general Phrynichus opposes them, arguing that Alcibiades cares only for his own recall, the King wants only the restoration of his possessions, and the allies desire only freedom from subjection. He predicts that no allies will respond to the installation of an Athenian oligarchy with greater friendship for Athens.

8.47.2a   Samos: Map 8.45, AY.

8.48.4a   Phrynichus, the "man of sense," was last heard from in 8.27.

refuge and the chastiser of these men. [7] He was certain that the cities had learned this by experience, and that such was their opinion. The propositions of Alcibiades and the intrigues now in progress could therefore never meet with his approval.

However, the members of the cabal assembled in accordance with their original intention, accepted what was proposed, and prepared to send Pisander and others on an embassy to Athens to work for the restoration of Alcibiades and the abolition of the democracy in the city, and thus to make Tissaphernes the friend of the Athenians.

Phrynichus now saw that there would be a proposal to restore Alcibiades, and that the Athenians would consent to it; and fearing after what he had said against it that Alcibiades, if restored, would revenge himself upon him for his opposition, had recourse to the following scheme. He sent a secret letter to the Spartan admiral, [2] Astyochus, who was still in the neighborhood of Miletus,[2a] to tell him that Alcibiades was ruining the Peloponnesian cause by making Tissaphernes the friend of the Athenians, and containing an explicit revelation of the rest of the intrigue, desiring to be excused if he sought to harm his enemy even at the expense of the interests of his country. [3] Astyochus, however, instead of thinking of punishing Alcibiades, who, besides, no longer ventured within his reach as formerly, went up to him and Tissaphernes at Magnesia,[3a] communicated to them the letter from Samos,[3b] and turned informer; and if report may be trusted, became the paid creature of Tissaphernes, undertaking to inform him about this and all other matters—which was also the reason why he did not object more strongly against the pay not being given in full. [4] Upon this Alcibiades instantly sent to the authorities at Samos a letter against Phrynichus, stating what he had done, and asking that he should be put to death. [5] Phrynichus distracted, and placed in the utmost peril by the denunciation, sent again to Astyochus, reproaching him with having so ill kept the secret of his previous letter, and saying that he was now prepared to give him an opportunity to destroy the whole Athenian armament at Samos, gave a detailed account of the means which he should employ—Samos being unfortified—and pleading that being in danger of his life on their account, he could not now be blamed for doing this or anything else to escape being destroyed by his mortal enemies. This also Astyochus revealed to Alcibiades.

Meanwhile Phrynichus having had timely notice that Astyochus was playing him false, and that a letter on the subject was on the point of arriving from Alcibiades, himself anticipated the news, and told the army that the enemy, seeing that Samos was unfortified and the fleet not all stationed

8.49
SAMOS
The cabal prepares to send Pisander to Athens to argue for oligarchy.

8.50
412/1
20th Year/Winter
SAMOS
To thwart Alcibiades, Phrynichus sends Astyochus a letter that accuses Alcibiades of injuring the Peloponnesian cause. Astyochus reveals this letter to Alcibiades, who quickly exposes Phrynichus' correspondence with the enemy to the Athenians at Samos. To save himself, Phrynichus writes again to Astyochus, describing the Athenian dispositions, and advising him when and how to attack the Athenian fleet.

8.51
412/1
20th Year/Winter
SAMOS
Phrynichus then orders the Athenians to prepare defenses against an enemy attack, which thwarts the intent of Alcibiades' letter to the Athenians that warns them of an attack and accuses Phrynichus of plotting with the enemy.

8.50.2a Miletus: Map 8.45, BY, and Map 8.56.
8.50.3a Magnesia: Map 8.45, AY, and Map 8.56.
8.50.3b Samos: Map 8.45, AY, and Map 8.56.

within the harbor, meant to attack the camp; that he could be certain of this intelligence, and that they must fortify Samos as quickly as possible, and generally look to their defenses. It will be remembered that he was general, and had himself authority to carry out these measures. [2] Accordingly they addressed themselves to the work of fortification, and Samos was thus fortified sooner than it would otherwise have been. Not long afterwards the letter from Alcibiades arrived, saying that the army was betrayed by Phrynichus, and the enemy about to attack it. [3] Alcibiades, however, gained no credit from this, as it was thought that he was in on the secret of the enemy's plans, and had tried out of hatred to fasten them upon Phrynichus, and to make out that he was their accomplice; and consequently far from hurting him, he rather bore witness to what Phrynichus had said by this intelligence.

After this Alcibiades set to work to persuade Tissaphernes to become the friend of the Athenians. Tissaphernes, although afraid of the Peloponnesians because they had more ships in Asia than the Athenians, was yet disposed to be persuaded if he could, especially after his quarrel with the Peloponnesians at Cnidus[1a] about the treaty of Therimenes. The quarrel had already taken place, as the Peloponnesians were by this time actually at Rhodes;[1b] and there the original argument of Alcibiades concerning the liberation of all the cities by the Spartans had been verified by the declaration of Lichas, that it was impossible to submit to a convention which made the King master of all the states at any former time ruled by himself or by his fathers.[1c]

While Alcibiades was soliciting the favor of Tissaphernes with an earnestness proportioned to the greatness of the issue, [8.53.1] the Athenian envoys who had been dispatched from Samos with Pisander arrived at Athens, and made a speech before the people, giving a brief summary of their views, and particularly insisting that if Alcibiades were recalled and the democratic constitution changed, they could have the King as their ally, and would be able to overcome the Peloponnesians. [2] A number of speakers opposed them on the question of the democracy, the enemies of Alcibiades cried out against the scandal of a restoration to be brought about by a violation of the constitution, and the *Eumolpidae* and *Ceryces*[2a] protested in behalf of the Mysteries, the cause of his banishment, and called upon the gods to avert his recall; when Pisander, in the midst of much opposition and abuse, came forward, and taking each of his opponents aside asked him the following question: In the face of the fact that the Peloponnesians had as many ships as their own confronting them at sea, more cities in alliance with them, and the King and Tissaphernes to supply

8.52
412/1
20th Year/Winter
MAGNESIA
Alcibiades tries to obtain Tissaphernes' friendship for the Athenians, which seems possible after his quarrel at Cnidus with the Spartans over the treaty.

8.53
412/1
20th Year/Winter
ATHENS
Pisander and the envoys from Samos seek to persuade the Athenians to adopt an oligarchy, arguing that only by the restoration of Alcibiades and the establishment of an oligarchy can Athens hope to obtain the King's friendship and thereby the resources with which to resist and ultimately defeat the Spartans.

8.52.1a   Cnidus: Map 8.56.
8.52.1b   The Spartans' arrival at Rhodes (Map 8.56) was described in 8.44.
8.52.1c   Although the quarrel with Lichas was described in 8.43.3–4, Alcibiades' prior advice to Tissaphernes was recounted in 8.46.1–4.
8.53.2a   The *Eumolpidae* and *Ceryces* were the

only two families from whom officials who led and conducted the Mystery rites at the shrine of Eleusis (Map 8.61, BX) could be selected. Since Alcibiades had been condemned for blaspheming against the "Mysteries" (see 6.27–29 and 6.61), they would naturally be concerned at his recall.

them with money, of which the Athenians had none left, had he any hope of saving the state unless someone could induce the King to come over to their side? [3] Upon their replying that they had not, he then plainly said to them: This we cannot have unless we have a more moderate form of government, and put the offices into fewer hands, and so gain the King's confidence, and forthwith restore Alcibiades, who is the only man living that can bring this about. The safety of the state, not the form of its government, is for the moment the most pressing question, as we can always change afterwards whatever we do not like.

The People were at first highly irritated at the mention of an oligarchy, but upon understanding clearly from Pisander that this was the only resource left, they took counsel of their fears, and promised themselves some day to change the government again, and gave way. [2] They accordingly voted that Pisander should sail with ten others and make the best arrangement that they could with Tissaphernes and Alcibiades. [3] At the same time The People, upon a false accusation of Pisander, dismissed Phrynichus from his post together with his colleague Scironides, sending Diomedon and Leon to replace them in the command of the fleet. The accusation was that Phrynichus had betrayed Iasus and Amorges;[3a] and Pisander asserted it because he thought him a man unfit for the business now in hand with Alcibiades. [4] Pisander also made the round of all the clubs[4a] already existing in the city for help in lawsuits and elections, and urged them to draw together and to unite their efforts for the overthrow of the democracy; and after taking all other measures required by the circumstances, so that no time might be lost, set off with his ten companions on his voyage to Tissaphernes.

In the same winter Leon and Diomedon, who had by this time joined the fleet, made an attack upon Rhodes.[1a] The ships of the Peloponnesians they found hauled up on shore, and after making a descent upon the coast and defeating the Rhodians who appeared in the field against them, withdrew to Chalce[1b] and made that place their base of operations instead of Cos,[1c] as they could better observe from there if the Peloponnesian fleet put out to sea. [2] Meanwhile Xenophantes, a Laconian, came to Rhodes from Pedaritus at Chios,[2a] with the news that the fortification of the Athenians was now finished,[2b] and that, unless the whole Peloponnesian fleet came to the rescue, the cause in Chios must be lost. Upon this they

8.54
412/1
20th Year/Winter
ATHENS
Bowing to necessity and hoping for a future return to democracy, the Athenians agree to alter the government, dismiss Phrynichus, and send Pisander to negotiate with Tissaphernes. Pisander solicits support for these moves from the political clubs.

8.55
412/1
20th Year/Winter
RHODES-CHIOS
The Athenians raid Rhodes. The Chians call on the Peloponnesians at Rhodes for help. A Chian attack against the Athenian siege works is initially successful, but is finally routed.

8.54.3a   Iasus: Map 8.56. This statement indicates a relationship of some sort between Amorges and Athens that could be betrayed; see note 8.5.5b.
8.54.4a   At Athens there were no political parties in the modern sense. Nonetheless, there were groups of citizens whose interests coincided. These groups even when ostensibly social in nature could be employed for political ends; indeed, they were constantly and lawfully active in the political life of the democracy. The "clubs" mentioned here are more sinister, as they are Crawley's translation of *syn-*

omosiai, a word which shows that oaths were exchanged. They were not necessarily dedicated to the subversion of the democracy, but clearly could be so used. See Appendix A, The Athenian Government, §11.
8.55.1a   Rhodes: Map 8.56.
8.55.1b   Chalce: Map 8.56.
8.55.1c   Cos: Map 8.56.
8.55.2a   Chios: Map 8.56.
8.55.2b   Progress on the Athenian fortifications on Chios at Delphinium (Map 8.37, AX) was mentioned in 8.38.2 and 8.40.3.

MAP 8.56 FIGHTING AND
DIPLOMACY AT THE END
OF WINTER IN 412/11

resolved to go to his relief. [3] In the meantime Pedaritus, with the mercenaries that he had with him and the whole force of the Chians, made an assault upon the stockade round the Athenian ships and took a portion of it, and got possession of some vessels that were hauled up on shore, when the Athenians sallied out to the rescue, and first routing the Chians, next defeated the remainder of the force round Pedaritus (who was himself killed with many of the Chians), and took a great quantity of arms.

After this the Chians were besieged even more tightly than before by land and sea, and the famine in the place was great. Meanwhile the Athenian envoys with Pisander arrived at the court of Tissaphernes, and conferred with him about the proposed agreement. [2] However, Alcibiades, not being altogether sure of Tissaphernes (who feared the Peloponnesians more than the Athenians, and besides wished to wear out both parties, as Alcibiades himself had recommended), had recourse to the following stratagem to make the treaty between the Athenians and Tissaphernes miscarry by reason of the magnitude of the latter's demands. [3] In my opinion Tissaphernes desired this result, fear being his motive; while Alcibiades, who now saw that Tissaphernes was determined not to treat on any terms, wished the Athenians to think, not that he was unable to persuade Tissaphernes, but that after the latter had been persuaded and was willing to join them, they had not conceded enough to him. [4] For the demands of

8.56
412/1
20th Year/Winter
CHIOS
The siege of Chios continues.
MAGNESIA?
The Athenians begin discussions with Tissaphernes who, not wishing to conclude an agreement, makes unacceptable demands. The Athenians finally decide that Alcibiades has deceived them and that no agreement is possible, so they angrily break off negotiations.

Alcibiades, speaking for Tissaphernes, who was present, were so extravagant that the Athenians, although for a long while they agreed to whatever he asked, yet had to bear the blame of failure: he required the cession of the whole of Ionia, next of the islands adjacent, besides other concessions, and these passed without opposition; at last, in the third interview, Alcibiades, who now feared a complete discovery of his inability, required them to allow the King to build ships and sail along his own coast wherever and with as many as he pleased.[4a] Upon this the Athenians would yield no further, and concluding that there was nothing to be done, but that they had been deceived by Alcibiades, went away in a rage and proceeded to Samos.[4b]

Immediately after this, in the same winter, Tissaphernes proceeded along shore to Caunus,[1a] desiring to bring the Peloponnesian fleet back to Miletus, and to supply them with pay, making a fresh convention upon such terms as he could get, in order not to bring matters to an absolute breach between them. He was afraid that if many of their ships were left without pay they would be compelled to engage and be defeated, or that their vessels being left without hands, the Athenians would attain their objects without his assistance. Still more he feared that the Peloponnesians might ravage the continent in search of supplies. [2] Having calculated and considered all this, according to his plan of keeping the two sides equal, he now sent for the Peloponnesians and gave them pay, and concluded with them a third treaty[2a] in words following:

In the thirteenth year of the reign of Darius, while Alexipippidas was ephor at Sparta, a treaty was concluded in the plain of the Meander by the Spartans and their allies with Tissaphernes, Hieramenes, and the sons of Pharnaces, concerning the affairs of the King and of the Spartans and their allies.

• [2] The country of the King in Asia shall be the King's, and the King shall treat his own country as he pleases.

• [3] The Spartans and their allies shall not invade or injure the King's country; neither shall the King invade or injure that of the Spartans or of their allies. [4] If any of the Spartans or their allies

8.57
412/1
20th Year/Winter
CAUNUS-MILETUS
Tissaphernes now improves relations with the Spartans, giving pay to their sailors and concluding a new treaty with them.

8.58
412/1
20th Year/Winter
MEANDER PLAIN
Thucydides offers the text of the third treaty between Sparta and the Persian Great King.

8.56.4a   Many scholars have taken this last demand of Alcibiades to imply the existence of a treaty between Athens and Persia. The movement of the royal fleet may have been restricted by nothing more than fear of the Athenians, but what prevented the King from building ships if it was not some clause of a treaty? See Appendix B, The Athenian Empire, §8; Appendix E, The Persians, §5; and note E5c.
8.56.4b   Samos: Map 8.56.
8.57.1a   Caunus: Map 8.56.
8.57.2a   Thucydides seems persuaded that there were three "treaties" between Sparta and Persia in 412/1 (8.18, 8.37, and here), but the truth seems to be that the first two were mere drafts of treaties and were

rejected by one party, which is why only the third has a formal introduction with a date and the names of the Persians involved. It was negotiated in Caunus (8.57.1), but the introduction to the treaty says the agreement was made "in the plain of the Meander" (8.58.1), that is, there was an interval in which the text could be referred to both the King and to Sparta. It is to be noted, however, that only with this third "treaty" does Thucydides use the technical term (not reproduced in Crawley's translation) signifying, literally, the pouring of a libation which was necessary to complete the accord. So perhaps Thucydides was not deceived.

invade or injure the King's country, the Spartans and their allies shall prevent it; and if any from the King's country invade or injure the country of the Spartans or of their allies, the King shall prevent it.

• [5] Tissaphernes shall provide pay for the ships now present, according to the agreement, until the arrival of the King's vessels;[5a] [6] but after the arrival of the King's vessels the Spartans and their allies may pay their own ships if they wish it. If, however, they choose to receive the pay from Tissaphernes, Tissaphernes shall furnish it; and the Spartans and their allies shall repay him at the end of the war such moneys as they shall have received.

• [7] After the King's vessels have arrived, the ships of the Spartans and of their allies and those of the King shall carry on the war jointly, according as Tissaphernes and the Spartans and their allies shall think best. If they wish to make peace with the Athenians, they shall make peace also jointly.

This was the treaty. After this Tissaphernes prepared to bring up the Phoenician[1a] fleet according to agreement, and to make good his other promises, or at all events wished to make it appear that he was so preparing.

Winter was now drawing to its close, when the Boeotians took Oropus by treachery, although it was held by an Athenian garrison. Their accomplices in this were some Oropians themselves, and some Eretrians who were plotting the revolt of Euboea,[1a] as the place was exactly opposite Eretria, and while in Athenian hands was necessarily a great threat to Eretria and the rest of Euboea. [2] Oropus being in their hands, the Eretrians now came to Rhodes[2a] to invite the Peloponnesians into Euboea. The latter, however, were set rather on the relief of the distressed Chians, and accordingly put out to sea and sailed with all their ships from Rhodes. [3] Off Triopium they sighted the Athenian fleet out at sea sailing from Chalce and as neither fleet attacked the other, the Athenians went on to Samos, the Peloponnesians to Miletus, seeing that it was no longer possible to relieve Chios[3a] without a battle. And this winter ended, and with it ended the twentieth year of this war of which Thucydides is the historian.

Early in the spring of the following summer Dercyllidas, a Spartiate, was sent with a small force by land to the Hellespont to bring about the revolt of Abydos,[1a] which is a Milesian[1b] colony; and the Chians, while Astyochus was at a loss how to help them, were compelled to fight at sea by the pressure of the siege. [2] While Astyochus was still at Rhodes they had received from Miletus, as their commander after the death of Pedaritus, a Spartiate named Leon, who had come out with Antisthenes,[2a] and twelve vessels

8.59
Tissaphernes appears to fulfill his promises.

8.60
412/1
20th Year/Winter
OROPUS
The Boeotians take Oropus by treachery and plot a revolt of Euboea.
RHODES-MILETUS
The Peloponnesians sail toward Chios, but finding they cannot relieve it without a battle, they retire to Miletus.

8.61
411
21st Year/Summer
CHIOS
Pressed by the siege, the Chians decide to give battle at sea. Although they fight well, they are forced to retire inside their walls at the end of the day.

8.58.5a   The King's vessels: the Phoenician fleet.
8.59.1a   Phoenicia: Map 8.45, locator.
8.60.1a   Boeotia and Oropus: Map 8.61, BX. Eretria and Euboea: Map 8.61, AX. For the eventual revolt of Euboea, see 8.95.
8.60.2a   Rhodes: Map 8.61, BY.
8.60.3a   Cape Triopium, Chalce, Samos, and Miletus: Map 8.61, BY; Chios, Map 8.61, AY.
8.61.1a   Abydos: Map 8.61, AY.
8.61.1b   Miletus: Map 8.61, BY.
8.61.2a   For Antisthenes' arrival, see 8.39.2.

MAP 8.61 OPENING OF SUMMER 411

which had been on guard at Miletus, five of which were Thurian,[2b] four Syracusan, one from Anaia,[2c] one Milesian, and one Leon's own. [3] Accordingly the Chians marched out in mass and took up a strong position, while thirty-six of their ships put out and engaged thirty-two of the Athenians; and after a tough fight, in which the Chians and their allies had rather the best of it, as it was now late, they retired to their city.

8.61.2b Thurii: Map 8.37 locator.
8.61.2c Anaia: Map 8.61, BY. Anaia was the city
           from which the Samian exiles operated;
           see 4.75.1.

Immediately after this Dercyllidas arrived by land from Miletus; and Abydos[1a] in the Hellespont revolted to him (and to Pharnabazus),[1b] and Lampsacus[1c] two days later. [2] Upon receipt of this news Strombichides hastily sailed from Chios[2a] with twenty-four Athenian ships, some transports carrying hoplites being in that number, and defeating the Lampsacenes who came out against him, took Lampsacus, which was unfortified, at the first assault, and making prize of the slaves and goods, restored the freemen to their homes, and went on to Abydos. [3] The inhabitants there, however, refused to capitulate, and when his assaults failed to take the place, he sailed over to the coast opposite, and made Sestos,[3a] the city in the Chersonese once held by the Persians, the center for the defense of the whole Hellespont.

In the meantime the Chians commanded the sea more than before; and the Peloponnesians at Miletus[1a] and Astyochus, hearing of the sea fight and of the departure of the squadron with Strombichides, took fresh courage. [2] Coasting along with two vessels to Chios, Astyochus took the ships from that place, and now moved with the whole fleet upon Samos,[2a] from where, however, he sailed back to Miletus, as the Athenians did not put out against him, owing to their suspicions of one another.

[3] For it was about this time, or even before, that the democracy was put down at Athens.[3a] When Pisander and the envoys returned from Tissaphernes to Samos they at once strengthened still further their control in the army itself, and induced the upper class in Samos to join them in establishing an oligarchy, the very form of government which a party of them had recently risen to avoid.[3b] [4] At the same time the Athenians at Samos, after a consultation among themselves, determined to let Alcibiades alone, since he refused to join them, and besides was not the man for an oligarchy; and now that they were once embarked on this course, to see for themselves how they could best prevent the ruin of their cause, and meanwhile to sustain the war, and to contribute without stint money and all else that might be required from their own private estates, as they would henceforth labor for themselves alone.

After encouraging each other in these resolutions, they now at once sent off half the envoys and Pisander to do what was necessary at Athens (with instructions to establish oligarchies on their way in all the subject cities which they might touch at), and dispatched the other half in different directions to the other dependencies. [2] Diitrephes[2a] also, who was in the neighborhood of Chios, and who had been elected to the command of the

8.62
411
21st Year/Summer
HELLESPONT
When Peloponnesian land forces arrive, Abydos and Lampsacus revolt from Athens. The Athenians respond quickly and recover Lampsacus.

8.63
411
21st Year/Summer
CHIOS-SAMOS
Gathering ships from Chios and Miletus, Astyochus challenges the Athenians at Samos. They refuse to fight, due to disunity caused by the fall of the democracy at Athens. The conspiracy at Samos begins to incite the local oligarchs to establish an oligarchy on Samos.

8.64
411
21st Year/Summer
AEGEAN
Envoys from the Athenian army at Samos are sent to Athens and other places to abolish democracies and install oligarchies. At Thasos, the new oligarchy plots to join the Spartans. Thucydides says that Athen's allies were more interested in securing their freedom than in changes of constitution.

8.62.1a   Abydos: Map 8.61, AY.
8.62.1b   Pharnabazus, son of Pharnaces was the Persian governor (satrap) of the Hellespont region (Map 8.61, AY).
8.62.1c   Lampsacus: Map 8.61, AY.
8.62.2a   Chios: Map 8.61, AY. Strombichides had been assigned to the siege of Chios in 8.30.1.
8.62.3a   Sestos: Map 8.61, AY. The Athenian capture of Sestos from the Persians in 479/8 was described in 1.89.2. This flotilla based at Sestos is next mentioned in

8.79.3.
8.63.1a   Miletus: Map 8.61, BY.
8.63.2a   Samos: Map 8.61, BY.
8.63.3a   Thucydides describes the actual overthrow of the Athenian democracy below, in 8.65–69.
8.63.3b   For the revolt at Samos in 412, see 8.21. The narrative of political events at Samos continues at 8.73.
8.64.2a   Presumably this is the same Diitrephes who led the Dii in the massacre at Mycalessus in 413 (7.29).

Thracian district of the empire, was sent off to his command, and arriving at Thasos[2b] abolished the democracy there. [3] Within two months of his departure, however, the Thasians began to fortify their city, being quickly tired of an aristocracy allied to Athens when they daily expected to receive freedom from Sparta. [4] Indeed there was a party of them whom the Athenians had banished with the Peloponnesians, who with their friends in the city were already making every effort to bring up a squadron, and to bring about the revolt of Thasos; and this party thus saw exactly what they most wanted done, that is to say, the reformation of the government without risk, and the abolition of the democracy which would have opposed them. [5] Things at Thasos thus turned out just the contrary to what the oligarchic conspirators at Athens expected; and the same in my opinion was the case in many of the other dependencies; as the cities no sooner got a moderate government and liberty of action, than they went on to absolute freedom without being at all seduced by the show of reform offered by the Athenians.

Pisander and his colleagues on their voyage along shore abolished, as had been determined, the democracies in the cities, and also took some hoplites from certain places as their allies, and so came to Athens. [2] Here they found most of the work already done by their associates. Some of the younger men had banded together and secretly assassinated one Androcles, the chief leader of The People, and the man mainly responsible for the banishment of Alcibiades; Androcles being singled out both because he was a popular leader, and because they sought by his death to recommend themselves to Alcibiades, who was, as they supposed, to be recalled, and to make Tissaphernes their friend. There were also some other obnoxious persons whom they secretly did away with in the same manner. [3] Meanwhile their cry in public was that no pay should be given except to persons serving in the war, and that not more than five thousand should share in the government, and those such as were most able to serve the state in person and in purse.

But this was merely a catchword for the multitude, as the authors of the revolution were really to govern. However, the assembly and the council[1a] still met notwithstanding, although they discussed nothing that was not approved of by the conspirators, who both supplied the speakers, and reviewed in advance what they were to say. [2] Fear, and the sight of the numbers of the conspirators, closed the mouths of the rest; or if any ventured to rise in opposition, he was promptly put to death in some convenient way, and there was neither search for the murderers nor justice to be had against them if suspected; but The People remained motionless, being so thoroughly cowed that men thought themselves lucky to escape violence, even when they held their tongues. [3] An exaggerated belief in the numbers of the conspirators also demoralized The People, rendered helpless by the magnitude of the city, and by their being

8.65
411
21st Year/Summer
ATHENS
The envoys from the army at Samos find the overthrow of the Athenian democracy well under way. Gangs have already assassinated the leader of The People and others.

8.66
411
21st Year/Summer
ATHENS
The assembly and the council continue to meet but they are controlled by the conspirators. Open opponents of the oligarchy are murdered. The People are cowed because they cannot unite or speak openly to find out who among them are conspirators.

8.64.2b Thrace: Map 8.61, AY; Thasos: Map 8.61, AX.

8.66.1a For the assembly and council, see Appendix A, The Athenian Government, §5–8.

uncertain about each other, and being without means of finding out what those numbers really were. [4] For the same reason it was impossible for anyone to speak his mind to a neighbor and to concert measures to defend himself, as he would have had to speak either to one whom he did not know, or whom he knew but did not trust. [5] Indeed all the popular party approached each other with suspicion, each thinking his neighbor involved in what was going on, the conspirators having in their ranks persons whom no one could ever have believed capable of joining an oligarchy; and these it was who made the many so suspicious, and so helped to procure impunity for the few, by confirming the commons in their mistrust of one another.

At this juncture Pisander and his colleagues arrived, and lost no time in completing the job. First they assembled the people, and moved to elect ten commissioners with full powers to frame a constitution, and that when this was done they should on an appointed day lay before the people their opinion as to the best mode of governing the city. [2] Afterwards, when the day arrived, the conspirators enclosed the assembly in Colonus, a temple of Poseidon, a little more than a mile outside the city;[2a] when the commissioners simply brought forward this single motion: that any Athenian might propose with impunity whatever measure he pleased, and that heavy penalties would be imposed upon any who should indict for illegality, or otherwise molest him for so doing.[2b] [3] The way thus cleared, it was now plainly declared that all tenure of office and receipt of pay under the existing institutions were at an end, and that five men must be elected as presidents who should in their turn elect one hundred, and each of the hundred three apiece; and that this body thus made up to four hundred should enter the council chamber[3a] with full powers and govern as they judged best, and should convene the five thousand whenever they pleased.

8.67
411
21st Year/Summer
ATHENS
With the arrival of the envoys from Samos, the oligarchs led by Pisander change the constitution.

The man who moved this resolution was Pisander, who was throughout the chief ostensible agent in putting down the democracy. But he who concerted the whole affair, and prepared the way for the catastrophe, and who had given the greatest thought to the matter, was Antiphon, one of the best men of his day in Athens; who, with a head to contrive measures and a tongue to recommend them, did not willingly come forward in the assembly or upon any public scene, being ill-looked upon by the multitude owing to his reputation for cleverness; and who yet was the one man best able to aid in the courts, or before the assembly, the suitors who required his opinion.[1a] [2] Indeed, when he was afterwards himself tried for his life on the charge of having been concerned in setting up this very govern-

8.68
411
21st Year/Summer
ATHENS
Thucydides describes the leaders of the oligarchs and comments that it was no small thing to deprive the Athenian people of their freedom after a century of democratic rule.

8.67.2a   Temple of Poseidon (Hippios) in Colonus, probable location: Map 8.75, inset map. Thucydides writes "ten stades"; the Attic stade was 607 feet long, the Olympic stade was 630.8 feet.

8.67.2b   A guarantee of immunity from prosecution for making proposals to change the constitution was necessary before any revolutionary changes could be made.

8.67.3a   Remains of this building (the Bouleuterion) have been located in the Athenian agora (Map 6.56, inset).

8.68.1a   See Appendix A, The Athenian Government, §10, for some light on why citizens would require assistance from experts in the courts and the assembly.

ment, when the Four Hundred were overthrown and harshly dealt with by the commons, he made what would seem to be the best defense of any known up to my time.[2a] [3] Phrynichus also went beyond all others in his zeal for the oligarchy. Afraid of Alcibiades, and assured that he was no stranger to his intrigues with Astyochus at Samos, he held that no oligarchy was ever likely to restore him, and once embarked in the enterprise, proved, where danger was to be faced, by far the staunchest of them all. [4] Theramenes son of Hagnon was also one of the foremost of the subverters of the democracy—a man as able in council as in debate. Conducted by so many and by such sagacious heads, the enterprise, great as it was, not unnaturally went forward; although it was no light matter to deprive the Athenian people of its freedom, almost a hundred years after the deposition of the tyrants, when it had been not only not subject to any during the whole of that period, but accustomed during more than half of it to rule over subjects of its own.

The assembly ratified the proposed constitution, without a single opposing voice, and was then dissolved; after which the Four Hundred were brought into the council chamber[1a] in the following way. On account of the enemy at Decelea,[1b] all the Athenians were constantly on the wall or in the ranks at the various military posts. [2] On that day the persons not in on the secret were allowed to go home as usual, while orders were given to the accomplices of the conspirators to hang about, without making any demonstration, at some little distance from the posts,[2a] and in case of any opposition to what was being done, to seize the arms and put it down. [3] There were also some Andrians and Tenians,[3a] three hundred Carystians[3b] and some of the settlers in Aegina[3c] come with their own arms for this very purpose, who had received similar instructions. [4] These dispositions completed, the Four Hundred went, each with a dagger concealed about his person, accompanied by one hundred and twenty youths, whom they employed wherever violence was needed, and appeared before the councilors chosen by lot[4a] in the council chamber, and told them to take their pay and be gone; themselves bringing it for the whole of the residue of their term of office, and giving it to them as they went out.

Upon the council withdrawing in this way without venturing any objection, and the rest of the citizens making no movement, the Four Hundred entered the council chamber, and for the present contented themselves with drawing lots for their *prytanes*,[1a] and making their prayers and sacri-

---

8.68.2a A few fragments of this speech survive, but they are insufficient to assess Thucydides' judgment of it.

8.69.1a For the council chamber, see note 8.67.3a.

8.69.1b Decelea: Map 8.75.

8.69.2a By "posts" Thucydides means locations where arms were stored.

8.69.3a Andros and Tenos: Map 8.61, BX.

8.69.3b Carystus: Map 8.61, BX.

8.69.3c Aegina: Map 8.61, BX.

8.69.4a For an explanation of the "councilors chosen by lot," see Appendix A, The Athenian Government, §5.

8.70.1a The *prytanes* were a group who acted as a standing committee for both the council and the assembly during the tenth of the year when it was their tribe's turn "to preside"; see note at 6.14.1a and Appendix A, The Athenian Government, §5.

fices to the gods upon entering office; but afterwards departed widely from the democratic system of government, and except that on account of Alcibiades they did not recall the exiles,[1b] ruled the city by force; [2] putting to death some men, though not many, whom they thought it convenient to remove, and imprisoning and banishing others. They also sent to Agis, the Spartan king at Decelea,[2a] to say that they desired to make peace, and that he might reasonably be more disposed to treat now that he had them to deal with instead of the inconstant People.

Agis, however, did not believe in the tranquillity of the city, or that the commons would thus in a moment give up their ancient liberty, but thought that the sight of a large Spartan force would be sufficient to excite them if they were not already in commotion, of which he was by no means certain. He accordingly gave to the envoys of the Four Hundred an answer which held out no hopes of an accommodation, and sending for large reinforcements from the Peloponnesus, not long afterwards, with these and his garrison from Decelea, descended to the very walls of Athens; hoping either that civil disturbances might help to subdue them to his terms, or that, in the confusion to be expected within and without the city, they might even surrender without a blow being struck; at all events he thought he would succeed in seizing the Long Walls,[1a] bared of their defenders. [2] However, the Athenians saw him come close up, without making the least disturbance within the city; and sending out their cavalry, and a number of their hoplites, light troops, and archers, shot down some of his soldiers who approached too near, and got possession of some arms and dead. Upon this Agis, at last convinced, led his army back again, [3] and remaining with his own troops in the old position at Decelea, sent the reinforcement back home after a few days' stay in Attica.[3a] After this the Four Hundred persevering sent another embassy to Agis, and now meeting with a better reception, at his suggestion dispatched envoys to Sparta to negotiate a treaty, being desirous of making peace.

They also sent ten men to Samos[1a] to reassure the army, and to explain that the oligarchy was not established to harm the city or the citizens, but to save the country as a whole; and that there were five thousand, not four hundred only, concerned; although, what with their expeditions and employments abroad, the Athenians had never yet assembled to discuss a question important enough to bring five thousand of them together. [2] The emissaries were also told what to say upon all

8.71
411
21st Year/Summer
ATHENS
Agis responds negatively to the Athenian oligarchs' first overtures with a show of force, marching his army to the walls of Athens. He finds the walls manned, and actively defended. When the oligarchs send a second embassy to him, he responds more positively.

8.72
411
21st Year/Summer
ATHENS
The oligarchs send envoys to the fleet at Samos to win acceptance for the new regime, fearing that failure to do so could lead to their overthrow.

8.70.1b   Thucydides means here that although one would expect the new government to undo the acts of the democracy and to recall all exiles, the oligarchs did not now recall the exiles because they did not wish Alcibiades to return to the city. It should be noted that Thucydides himself at this time was an exile.
8.70.2a   Decelea: Map 8.75.
8.71.1a   Long Walls of Athens: Map 8.75, inset.
8.71.3a   Attica: Map 8.75.
8.72.1a   Samos: Map 8.75.

other points, and were sent off immediately after the establishment of the new government, which feared, as it turned out correctly, that the mass of seamen would not be willing to remain under the oligarchic constitution, and, the evil beginning there, might be the means of their overthrow.

An oligarchic party is formed at Samos with the help of some Athenians, and it plots to overthrow Samos' democracy. The Samian democrats, learning of the plot, turn for help to various prodemocratic Athenian officers and the crew of the ship *Paralus.* They organize a force that helps the Samian democrats to defeat the coup.

Indeed at Samos the question of the oligarchy had already entered upon a new phase, the following events having taken place just at the time that the Four Hundred were conspiring.[1a] [2] That part of the Samian population which has been mentioned as rising against the upper class and as being the democratic party, had now turned round, and yielding to the solicitations of Pisander during his visit, and of the Athenians in the conspiracy at Samos, had bound themselves by oaths to the number of three hundred, and were about to fall upon the rest of their fellow citizens, whom they now in their turn regarded as the democratic party. [3] Meanwhile they put to death one Hyperbolus, an Athenian, a pestilent fellow who had been ostracized,[3a] not from fear of his influence or position, but because he was a scoundrel and a disgrace to the city; being aided in this by Charminus, one of the generals, and by some of the Athenians with them, to whom they had sworn friendship, and with whom they perpetrated other acts of the kind, and now determined to attack the majority. [4] The latter got wind of what was coming, and told two of the generals, Leon and Diomedon, who, on account of the credit which they enjoyed with The People, were unwilling supporters of the oligarchy; and also Thrasybulus and Thrasyllus, the former a captain of a trireme, the latter serving with the hoplites, besides certain others who had always been thought most opposed to the conspirators, appealing to them not to look on and see them destroyed, and Samos, the sole remaining stay of their empire, taken from the Athenians. [5] Upon hearing this, the persons whom they addressed now went round the soldiers one by one, and urged them to resist, especially the crew of the *Paralus,*[5a] which was made up entirely of Athenians and free men, and had always been enemies of oligarchy, even when there was no such thing existing; and Leon and Diomedon left behind some ships for their protection in case they had to sail away anywhere themselves. [6] Accordingly, when the Three Hundred attacked the people, all these came to the rescue, and foremost of all the crew of the *Paralus;* and the Samian majority gained the victory, and putting to death

8.73.1a This continues the narrative of political events at Samos from 8.63.3.

8.73.3a Hyperbolus was ostracized at some time before the Sicilian Expedition (the commonly cited date of 418/7 is ill-grounded). His was the last instance of a practice begun less than a century earlier whereby, if The People chose to have such a vote, the man who received the largest number of votes, provided that six thousand or more citizens voted, had to withdraw from Athens for ten years,

though he retained his property; see Appendix A, The Athenian Government, §8. Small shards of pottery (*ostraka*) were used on which names were written; see Illustration 1.135. For the ostracism of Themistocles, see 1.135.3.

8.73.5a The *Paralus* and her sister ship the *Salaminia* were special state triremes used on sacred embassies and official business. They appear several times in Thucydides' narrative, see note 3.33.1a.

some thirty of the Three Hundred, banishing three others of the ringleaders, accorded an amnesty to the rest, and lived together under a democratic government for the future.

The ship *Paralus,* with Chaereas son of Archestratus on board, an Athenian who had taken an active part in the revolution, was now without loss of time sent off by the Samians and the army to Athens to report what had occurred; the fact that the Four Hundred were in power not being yet known. [2] When they sailed into harbor the Four Hundred immediately arrested two or three of the *Parali,* and taking the vessel from the rest, shifted them into a troopship and set them to keep guard round Euboea.[2a] [3] Chaereas, however, managed to hide as soon as he saw how things stood, and returning to Samos, drew a picture to the soldiers of the horrors being enacted at Athens, in which everything was exaggerated; saying that all were punished with lashes, that no one could say a word against the holders of power, that the soldiers' wives and children were outraged, and that it was intended to seize and shut up the relatives of all in the army at Samos who were not of the government's way of thinking, to be put to death in case of their disobedience; and a host of other harmful inventions.

On hearing this the first thought of the army was to fall upon the chief authors of the oligarchy and upon all the rest concerned. Eventually, however, they desisted from this idea when the men of moderate views opposed it and warned them against ruining their cause with the enemy close at hand and ready for battle. [2] After this Thrasybulus son of Lycus, and Thrasyllus, the chief leaders in the revolution, now wishing in the most public manner to change the government at Samos to a democracy, bound all the soldiers by the most tremendous oaths, and those of the oligarchic party more than any, to accept a democratic government, to be united, to prosecute actively the war against the Peloponnesians, and to be enemies of the Four Hundred and to hold no communication with them. [3] The same oath was also taken by all the Samians of full age; and the soldiers associated the Samians in all their affairs and in the fruits of their dangers having the conviction that there was no way of escape for themselves or for the Samians, and that success of the Four Hundred or of the enemy at Miletus[3a] must be their ruin.

8.74
411
21st Year/Summer
ATHENS
Not yet aware of the coup at Athens, the *Paralus* arrives there with news of the failed coup at Samos; its crew is imprisoned or kept at sea. One escapes to Samos and gives an exaggerated account of events at Athens.

8.75
411
21st Year/Summer
SAMOS
The troops at Samos vow to remain united in support of democracy both at Samos and at Athens, to maintain the war against Sparta, and to have no relations with the oligarchs at Athens.

8.74.2a   Euboea: Map 8.75. We next hear of the
crew of the *Paralus* in 8.86.9.
8.75.3a   Miletus: Map 8.75.

Map 8.75 Revolution in Athens and Samos

8.76
411
21st Year/Summer
SAMOS
Athenian forces on Samos choose new officers and agree to restore democracy at Athens. They realize that Athens no longer provides them with funds or counsel, that they can carry on the war alone and inflict more harm on Athens from Samos than the oligarchs can inflict on them. Moreover, their ships could carry them to refuge if they should fail.

The struggle was now between the army trying to force a democracy upon the city, and the Four Hundred an oligarchy upon the army. [2] Meanwhile the soldiers immediately held an assembly in which they deposed the former generals and any of the captains whom they suspected, and chose new captains and generals to replace them, in addition to Thrasybulus and Thrasyllus, whom they had already selected. [3] They also stood up and encouraged one another, and among other things urged that they ought not to lose heart because the city had revolted from them, as the party seceding was smaller and in every way poorer in resources than themselves. [4] They had the whole fleet with which to compel the other cities in their empire to give them money just as if they had their base in the capital, having a city in Samos[4a] which, far from lacking strength, had

8.76.4a Samos: Map 8.75.

when at war come within an inch of depriving the Athenians of the command of the sea, while as far as the enemy was concerned they had the
same base of operations as before. Indeed, with the fleet in their hands,
they were better able to provide themselves with supplies than the government at home. [5] It was their advanced position at Samos which had
throughout enabled the home authorities to command the entrance into
Piraeus;[5a] and if they refused to give them back the constitution, they
would now find that the army was more in a position to exclude them from
the sea than they were to exclude the army. [6] Besides, the city was of little or no use in enabling them to overcome the enemy; and they had lost
nothing in losing those who had no longer either money to send them (the
soldiers having to find this for themselves), or good counsel, which entitles
cities to direct armies. On the contrary, even in this the home government
had done wrong in abolishing the institutions of their ancestors, while the
army maintained these institutions, and would try to force the home government to do likewise. So that even in point of good counsel the camp
had as good counselors as the city. [7] Moreover, they had only to grant
Alcibiades security for his person and his recall, and he would be only too
glad to procure them the alliance of the King. And above all, if they failed
completely, with the navy which they possessed, they had numbers of places
to retire to in which they would find cities and lands.

Debating together and comforting themselves in this manner, they
pushed on their war measures as actively as ever; and the ten envoys sent to
Samos by the Four Hundred, learning how matters stood while they were
still at Delos,[1a] stayed quiet there.

About this time a cry arose among the soldiers in the Peloponnesian fleet
at Miletus[1a] that Astyochus and Tissaphernes were ruining their cause. Astyochus had not been willing to fight at sea—either before, while they were
still in full vigor and the fleet of the Athenians small, or now, when the
enemy was, as they were informed, in a state of sedition and his ships not yet
united—but he kept them waiting for the Phoenician[1b] fleet from Tissaphernes, which had only a nominal existence, at the risk of wasting away in
inactivity. Yet Tissaphernes not only did not bring up the fleet in question,
but was ruining their navy by payments made irregularly, and even then not
made in full. They must therefore delay no longer, they insisted, but fight a
decisive naval engagement. The Syracusans were the most urgent of all.

The allies and Astyochus, aware of these murmurs, had already decided in
council to fight a decisive battle; and when the news reached them of the disturbance at Samos, they put to sea with all their ships, one hundred and ten
in number, and ordering the Milesians to move by land to Mycale,[1a] set sail
for that place. [2] The Athenians with the eighty-two ships from Samos were
at that moment lying at Glauce in Mycale,[2a] a point where Samos approaches
near to the continent; and seeing the Peloponnesian fleet sailing against

8.77
The envoys from Athens stop
at Delos.

8.78
411
21st Year/Summer
MILETUS
The Peloponnesian sailors
accuse Astyochus and
Tissaphernes of ruining the
fleet by refusing battle and by
irregular and insufficient pay.
They demand a decisive
battle.

8.79
411
21st Year/Summer
MILETUS-SAMOS
The Peloponnesian fleet sails
to Samos seeking battle, but
when they learn that Athenian
reinforcements have arrived
from the Hellespont, they
retire to Miletus and refuse to
engage the Athenians.

8.76.5a Piraeus: Map 8.75, inset.
8.77.1a Delos: Map 8.75. The dispatch of these
         ten envoys is described in 8.72.
8.78.1a Miletus: Map 8.75.

8.78.1b Phoenicia: Map 8.84, locator.
8.79.1a Mount Mycale: Map 8.75.
8.79.2a Glauce in Mycale: exact location
         unknown.

them, retired into Samos, not thinking themselves numerically strong enough to stake their all upon a battle. [3] Besides, they had intelligence from Miletus that the enemy wished to engage, and were expecting to be joined from the Hellespont[3a] by Strombichides (to whom a messenger had been already dispatched), with the ships that had gone from Chios[3b] to Abydos.[3c] [4] The Athenians accordingly withdrew to Samos, and the Peloponnesians put in at Mycale, and encamped with the land forces of the Milesians and the people of the neighborhood. [5] The next day they were about to sail against Samos when news reached them of the arrival of Strombichides with the squadron from the Hellespont, whereupon they immediately sailed back to Miletus. [6] The Athenians, thus reinforced, now in their turn sailed against Miletus with a hundred and eight ships, wishing to fight a decisive battle, but as no one put out to meet them, sailed back to Samos.

In the same summer, immediately after this, the Peloponnesians having refused to fight with their fleet united, through not thinking themselves a match for the enemy, and not knowing where to look for money for such a number of ships, especially as Tissaphernes proved so bad a paymaster, sent off Clearchus son of Ramphias with forty ships to Pharnabazus,[1a] in accordance with their original instructions from the Peloponnesus;[2a] [2] for Pharnabazus invited them and was prepared to furnish pay, and in addition Byzantium[2a] sent offers to revolt to them. [3] These Peloponnesian ships accordingly put out into the open sea, in order to escape the observation of the Athenians, and being overtaken by a storm, the majority with Clearchus put into Delos,[3a] and afterwards returned to Miletus,[3b] from which Clearchus proceeded by land to the Hellespont to take the command: ten of the ships, however, under the Megarian[3c] Helixus, made good their passage to the Hellespont, and brought about the revolt of Byzantium. [4] After this, the commanders at Samos[4a] were informed of it and sent a squadron against them to guard the Hellespont, and an encounter took place before Byzantium between eight vessels on either side.

Meanwhile the leaders at Samos, and especially Thrasybulus, who from the moment that he had changed the government had remained firmly resolved to recall Alcibiades, at last in an assembly brought over the mass of the soldiery, and upon their voting for his recall and amnesty, sailed over to Tissaphernes and brought Alcibiades to Samos, being convinced that their only chance of salvation lay in his bringing over Tissaphernes from the Peloponnesians to themselves. [2] An assembly was then held in

8.80
411
21st Year/Summer
HELLESPONT
The Peloponnesians send forty triremes to the Hellespont to Pharnabazus who had offered them pay, but a storm scatters the fleet and only ten arrive there. These incite Byzantium to revolt, which forces the Athenians to send a squadron north from Samos.

8.81
411
21st Year/Summer
SAMOS
Thrasybulus persuades the Athenians on Samos to recall Alcibiades in order to win the friendship of Tissaphernes, their only hope for defeating Sparta. Alcibiades arrives and makes extravagant promises as to what he can accomplish for them with Tissaphernes if Athens only will reinstate him.

8.79.3a Hellespont: Map 8.84, AY.
8.79.3b Chios: Map 8.84, BX.
8.79.3c Abydos: Map 8.84, AY. For Strombichides' triremes and mission from Chios to Abydos, see 8.62.2.
8.80.1a Pharnabazus was the Persian governor (satrap) of the Hellespont region (Map 8.84, AY). See Appendix E, The Persians, §2, 7.
8.80.2a The plan and instructions to send forces to Pharnabazus in the Hellespont after operations were begun in Chios and Lesbos were mentioned in 8.8.2 and 8.39.2.
8.80.2a Byzantium: Map 8.84, AY.
8.80.3a Delos: Map 8.84, BX.
8.80.3b Miletus: Map 8.84, BY.
8.80.3c Megara: Map 8.84, BX.
8.80.4a Samos: Map 8.84, BY.

which Alcibiades complained of and deplored his private misfortune in having been banished, and speaking at great length upon public affairs, highly incited their hopes for the future, and extravagantly magnified his own influence with Tissaphernes. His purpose in this was to make the oligarchic government at Athens afraid of him, to hasten the dissolution of the clubs,[2a] to increase his influence with the army at Samos and heighten their own confidence, and lastly to prejudice the enemy as strongly as possible against Tissaphernes, and blast the hopes which they entertained. [3] Alcibiades accordingly held out to the army such extravagant promises as the following: that Tissaphernes had solemnly assured him that if he could only trust the Athenians they should never want for supplies while he had anything left, no, not even if he should have to coin his own silver couch, and that he would bring the Phoenician[3a] fleet now at Aspendus[3b] to the Athenians instead of to the Peloponnesians; but that he could only trust the Athenians if Alcibiades were recalled to be his security for them.

Upon hearing this and much more besides, the Athenians at once elected him general together with the former ones, and put all their affairs into his hands. There was now not a man in the army who would have exchanged his present hopes of safety and vengeance upon the Four Hundred for any consideration whatever; and after what they had been told they were now inclined to disdain the enemy before them, and to sail at once for the Piraeus.[1a] [2] To the plan of sailing for the Piraeus, leaving their more immediate enemies behind them, Alcibiades opposed the most positive refusal, in spite of the numbers that insisted upon it, saying that now that he had been elected general he would first sail to Tissaphernes and coordinate with him measures for carrying on the war. [3] Accordingly, upon leaving this assembly, he immediately took his departure in order to have it thought that there was a complete trust between them, and also wishing to increase his standing with Tissaphernes, and to show that he had now been elected general and was in a position to do him good or evil as he chose; thus managing to frighten the Athenians with Tissaphernes and Tissaphernes with the Athenians.

Meanwhile the Peloponnesians at Miletus[1a] heard of the recall of Alcibiades, and being already distrustful of Tissaphernes, now became far more disgusted with him than ever. [2] Indeed after their refusal to go out and give battle to the Athenians when they appeared before Miletus, Tissaphernes had grown slacker than ever in his payments; and even

8.82
411
21st Year/Summer
SAMOS
The Athenian troops elect Alcibiades general. He insists on first consulting with Tissaphernes. Thucydides describes Alcibiades' policy as one of bluff and bluster to both the Athenians and Tissaphernes.

8.83
411
21st Year/Summer
MILETUS
After the Athenians recall Alcibiades, the Peloponnesians revile Tissaphernes and Astyochus all the more. They fear their sailors will desert unless they receive supplies or fight a decisive battle.

8.81.2a On the Athenian political clubs, see note 8.54.4a.
8.81.3a Phoenicia: Map 8.84, locator.
8.81.3b Aspendus: Map 8.84, BY.
8.82.1a Piraeus: Map 8.84, BX.
8.83.1a Miletus: Map 8.84, BY.

before this, on account of Alcibiades, his unpopularity had been on the increase. [3] Gathering together, just as before, the soldiers and some persons of importance besides the soldiers began to reckon up how they had never yet received their pay in full; that what they did receive was small in quantity, and even that had been paid irregularly, and that unless they fought a decisive battle or moved away to some station where they could get supplies, the ships' crews would desert; and that it was all the fault of Astyochus, who humored Tissaphernes for his own private advantage.

The army was engaged in these reflections when the following disturbance took place about the person of Astyochus. [2] Most of the Syracusan and Thurian[2a] sailors were free men, and these the freest crews in the armament were likewise the boldest in setting upon Astyochus and demanding their pay. The latter answered somewhat stiffly and threatened them, and when Dorieus spoke up for his own sailors even went so far as to lift his baton against him; [3] upon seeing which the mass of the men, in sailor fashion, rushed in a fury to strike Astyochus. He, however, saw them in time and fled for refuge to an altar;[3a] and they were thus parted without his being struck. [4] Meanwhile the fort built by Tissaphernes in Miletus was surprised and taken by the Milesians, and the garrison in it expelled—an act which met with the approval of the rest of the allies, and in particular of the Syracusans, [5] but which found no favor with Lichas, who said moreover that the Milesians and others in the King's realm ought to show a reasonable submission to Tissaphernes and to pay him court until the war should be happily settled. The Milesians were angry with him for this and for other things of the kind, and upon his afterwards dying of sickness, would not allow him to be buried where the Spartans with the army desired.

The discontent of the army with Astyochus and Tissaphernes had reached this pitch when Mindarus arrived from Sparta to succeed Astyochus as admiral, and assumed the command. Astyochus now set sail for home; [2] and Tissaphernes sent with him one of his confidants, Gaulites, a Carian,[2a] who spoke the two languages, to complain about the Milesians for the affair of the fort, and at the same time to defend himself against the Milesians, who were, as he was aware, on their way to Sparta chiefly to denounce his conduct and had with them Hermocrates, who was to accuse Tissaphernes of joining with Alcibiades to ruin the Peloponnesian cause and of playing a double game. [3] Indeed Hermocrates had always been at enmity with him about the pay not being restored in full; and eventually when he was banished from Syracuse,

---

8.84
411
21st Year/Summer
MILETUS
Sailors from Syracuse and Thurii demand their pay from Astyochus and attack him when he responds harshly, but he escapes to an altar. A Persian fort at Miletus is taken by the Milesians, with the approval of many Peloponnesians, but not of the Spartan Lichas.

8.85
411
21st Year/Summer
MILETUS
Mindarus, sent by the Spartans to take command of the fleet, arrives at Miletus. Astyochus, Hermocrates, and envoys of both Miletus and Tissaphernes all sail to Sparta to accuse each other.
SAMOS
Alcibiades returns to Samos.

8.84.2a   Syracuse, Sicily, and Thurii, Italy: Map 8.91. If *most* were free men, then *some* were not; see Appendix G, Trireme Warfare, §12.
8.84.3a   It would have been sacrilege to harm someone who had taken refuge at an altar; see also the "curse of the goddess,"

1.126.10–11; the supplication of the Mytilenians, 3.28.2; the excesses of the Corcyraean revolution, 3.81.5; and the flight of Thrasyllus, 5.60.6.
8.85.2a   Caria: Map 8.84, BY.

MAP 8.84
ATHENIAN, PELOPONNESIAN, AND PERSIAN POLITICAL AND MILITARY MANEUVERS

and new commanders, Potamis, Myscon, and Demarchus, had come out to Miletus to the ships of the Syracusans, Tissaphernes pressed harder than ever upon him in his exile,[3a] and among other charges against him accused him of having once asked him for money, and then pronounced himself his enemy because he failed to obtain it.

[4] While Astyochus and the Milesians and Hermocrates sailed for Sparta, Alcibiades had now crossed back from Tissaphernes to Samos.[4a]

After his return the envoys of the Four Hundred who had been sent, as has been mentioned above, to pacify and explain matters to the forces at Samos, arrived from Delos;[1a] and an assembly was held in which they attempted to speak. [2] The soldiers at first would not hear them, and cried out to put to death the subverters of the democracy, but at last, after some difficulty, calmed down and gave them a hearing. [3] Upon this the envoys

8.86
411
21st Year/Summer
SAMOS
Envoys from the Athenian oligarchs are received with anger and suspicion at Samos. Alcibiades serves Athens well by preventing the fleet from sailing to Piraeus, which would have abandoned Ionia and the Hellespont to the enemy. Alcibiades talks of reconciliation. Argive envoys arrive and promise support for democracy.

8.85.3a   Hermocrates is the leader from Syracuse (Map 8.91) who figures so prominently in Books 6 and 7. His quarrel with Tissaphernes is described in 8.29. Except for these lines in 8.85.3, Thucydides does not further describe his banishment by the new regime in Syracuse.

8.85.4a   Samos: Map 8.84, BY.
8.86.1a   Delos: Map 8.84, BX. These ten envoys, whose dispatch was described in 8.72, had stopped at Delos (see 8.77.1) when they heard of the hostile reaction of the army at Samos to the Four Hundred's overthrow of the democracy at Athens.

proceeded to inform them that the recent change had been made to save the city, and not to ruin it or to deliver it over to the enemy, for they had already had an opportunity of doing this when he invaded the country during their government;[3a] that all the Five Thousand would have their proper share in the government; and that their hearers' relatives had neither outrage, as Chaereas had slanderously reported,[3b] nor other ill treatment to complain of, but were all in undisturbed enjoyment of their property just as they had left them. [4] Besides these they made a number of other statements which had no better success with their angry audience; and amid a host of different opinions the one which found most favor was that of sailing to the Piraeus.[4a] Now it was that Alcibiades for the first time did the state a service, and one of the most outstanding kind. For when the Athenians at Samos were bent upon sailing against their countrymen, in which case Ionia and the Hellespont would most certainly at once have passed into possession of the enemy, Alcibiades it was who prevented them. [5] At that moment, when no other man would have been able to hold back the multitude, he put a stop to the intended expedition, and rebuked and turned aside the resentment felt, on personal grounds, against the envoys; [6] he dismissed them with an answer from himself, to the effect that he did not object to the government of the Five Thousand, but insisted that the Four Hundred should be deposed and the Council of Five Hundred reinstated in power: meanwhile any retrenchments for economy, by which pay might be better found for military forces, met with his complete approval. [7] Generally, he told them to hold out and show a bold face to the enemy, since if the city was saved there was good hope that the two parties might some day be reconciled, whereas if either were once destroyed, that at Samos, or that at Athens, there would no longer be anyone to be reconciled to. [8] Meanwhile envoys arrived from the Argives,[8a] with offers of support to the Athenian democrats at Samos: these were thanked by Alcibiades, and dismissed with a request to come when called upon. [9] The Argives were accompanied by the crew of the *Paralus,* who had been placed in a troopship by the Four Hundred with orders to cruise round Euboea,[9a] and who when they were being employed to carry to Sparta some Athenian envoys sent by the Four Hundred—Laespodias, Aristophon, and Melesias—laid hands upon these envoys as they sailed by Argos, and delivering them over to the Argives as the chief subverters of the democracy; themselves, instead of returning to Athens, took the Argive envoys on board and came to Samos in the trireme which had been confided to them.

8.86.3a The recent invasion by forces under Agis: see 8.71.1–3.
8.86.3b Chaereas' reports were described in 8.74.3.
8.86.4a Piraeus: Map 8.84, BX.
8.86.8a Argos: Map 8.84, BX.
8.86.9a Euboea: Map 8.84, BX. See 8.74.2 for the previous mention of the crew of the *Paralus.*

The same summer at the time that the return of Alcibiades coupled with the general conduct of Tissaphernes had carried to its height the discontent of the Peloponnesians (who no longer entertained any doubt of his having joined the Athenians), Tissaphernes wishing, it would seem, to clear himself to them of these charges, prepared to go to the Phoenician[1a] fleet at Aspendus,[1b] and invited Lichas to go with him; saying that he would appoint Tamos as his lieutenant to provide pay for the fleet during his own absence. [2] Accounts differ, and it is not easy to ascertain with what intention he went to Aspendus and did not bring the fleet after all. [3] That one hundred and forty-seven Phoenician ships came as far as Aspendus is certain; but why they did not come further has been variously accounted for. Some think that he went away in pursuance of his plan of wasting the Peloponnesian resources, since at any rate Tamos, his lieutenant, far from being any better, proved a worse paymaster than himself; others believe that he brought the Phoenicians to Aspendus to exact money from them for their discharge, having never intended to employ them; others again think that it was in view of the outcry against him at Sparta, in order that it might be said that he was not at fault, but that the ships were really manned and that he had certainly gone to fetch them. [4] To myself it seems only too evident that he did not bring up the fleet because he wished to wear out and paralyze the Hellenic forces, that is, to waste their strength by the time lost during his journey to Aspendus, and to keep them evenly balanced by not throwing his weight into either scale. Had he wished to finish the war, he could have done so, assuming of course that he made his appearance in a way which left no room for doubt; as by bringing up the fleet he would in all probability have given the victory to the Spartans, whose navy, even as it was, faced the Athenian more as an equal than as an inferior. [5] But what convicts him most clearly is the excuse which he put forward for not bringing the ships. He said that the number assembled was less than the King had ordered; but surely it would only have enhanced his credit if he spent little of the King's money and accomplished the same end at less cost. [6] In any case, whatever his intention, Tissaphernes went to Aspendus and saw the Phoenicians; and the Peloponnesians at his request sent a Spartan called Philip with two triremes to bring the fleet.[6a]

When Alcibiades discovered that Tissaphernes had gone to Aspendus, he sailed there himself with thirteen ships, promising to do a great and certain service for the Athenians at Samos, as he would either bring the Phoenician fleet to the Athenians, or at all events prevent its joining the Peloponnesians. In all probability he had long known that Tissaphernes never

Tissaphernes goes to Aspendus ostensibly to bring on the Phoenician fleet. Thucydides reports that 147 Phoenician triremes definitely were at Aspendus, and that Tissaphernes did go there. Since the intervention of that force on either side would have been decisive, Tissaphernes was still following the policy of wearing out both sides, because he did not bring the fleet to the region and his explanation why was not credible.

Alcibiades sails to Aspendus, promising to obtain favors from Tissaphernes for the Athenians at Samos.

8.87.1a   Phoenicia: Map 8.84, locator.
8.87.1b   Aspendus: Map 8.84, BY.
8.87.6a   The narrative of the Peloponnesian fleet
          picks up again at 8.99.

meant to bring the fleet at all, and wished to compromise him as much as possible in the eyes of the Peloponnesians through his apparent friendship for himself and the Athenians, and thus in a manner to oblige him to join their side.

While Alcibiades weighed anchor and sailed eastward straight for Phaselis[1a] and Caunus,[1b] [8.89.1] the envoys sent by the Four Hundred to Samos[1a] arrived at Athens. Upon their delivering the message from Alcibiades, telling them to hold out and to show a firm front to the enemy, and saying that he had great hopes of reconciling them with the army and of overcoming the Peloponnesians, the majority of the members of the oligarchy, who were already discontented and only too much inclined to be quit of the business in any safe way that they could, were at once greatly strengthened in their resolve. [2] These now banded together and strongly criticized the administration, their leaders being some of the principal generals and men in office under the oligarchy, such as Theramenes son of Hagnon, Aristocrates son of Scellias, and others; who, although among the most prominent members of the government were afraid, as they said, of the army at Samos, and especially of Alcibiades, and also feared that the envoys whom they had sent to Sparta might do the state some harm without the authority of the majority. And so without insisting on their objections to the excessive concentration of power in a few hands, they nevertheless urged that the Five Thousand must be shown to exist not merely in name but in reality, and the constitution placed upon a fairer basis. [3] But this was merely their political cry; most of them were driven by private ambition into the line of conduct so surely fatal to oligarchies that arise out of democracies. For all at once pretend to be not only equals but each the chief and master of his fellows; while under a democracy a disappointed candidate accepts his defeat more easily, because he has not the humiliation of being beaten by his equals.[3a] [4] But what most clearly encouraged the malcontents was the power of Alcibiades at Samos, and their own conviction that the oligarchy was unstable; and that it was now a race among them as to who should first become the leader of The People.

Meanwhile the leaders and members of the Four Hundred most opposed to a democratic form of government—Phrynichus who had had the quarrel with Alcibiades during his command at Samos, Aristarchus the bitter and inveterate enemy of the democracy, and Pisander and Antiphon and others who were very powerful, and who already as soon as they entered upon power, and again when the army at Samos seceded from them and declared for a democracy, had sent envoys from their own body

8.89
411
21st Year/Summer
ATHENS
The oligarchy's envoys return from Samos and deliver Alcibiades' message. This leads discontented oligarchs, many now frightened of the army, to criticize the government. Now believing that the oligarchy would not last, they were maneuvering to establish themselves as leaders of The People.

8.90
411
21st Year/Summer
ATHENS
Alarmed by the antagonism of the army and of some in their own party, the oligarchs send a new delegation to Sparta with instructions to make peace on any tolerable terms. They also push forward work on the wall in Eetionia at the Piraeus, which would permit them to control the port, both to keep the fleet from Samos out and to permit an enemy fleet to enter.

8.88.1a Phaselis: Map 8.84, BY.
8.88.1b Caunus: Map 8.84, BY.
8.89.1a Samos: Map 8.91.
8.89.3a Thucydides means that indiscriminate and chance selection in a democratic drawing by rabble, where everyone votes, is not a valid measure of a man's worth, so defeat can cause no humiliation.

to Sparta and made every effort for peace, and were building the wall in Eetionia[1a]—now redoubled their efforts when their envoys returned from Samos and they saw not only The People but their own most trusted associates turning against them. [2] Alarmed at the state of things at Athens and at Samos, they now sent off in haste Antiphon and Phrynichus and ten others with injunctions to make peace with Sparta upon any terms, no matter what, that would be at all tolerable. [3] Meanwhile they pushed on more actively than ever with the wall in Eetionia. Now the meaning of this wall, according to Theramenes and his supporters, was not so much to keep out the army of Samos in case of its trying to force its way into the Piraeus as to be able to let in, at pleasure, the fleet and army of the enemy. [4] For Eetionia is a breakwater of the Piraeus, close alongside the entrance of the harbor, and was now being fortified in connection with the wall already existing on the land side, so that a few men placed in it might be able to command the entrance; the old wall on the land side and the new one now being built within on the side of the sea both ending in one of the two towers standing at the narrow mouth of the harbor. [5] They also walled off the largest porch[5a] in the Piraeus which was connected to this wall, and kept it in their own hands, compelling all to unload there the grain that came into the harbor, and what they had in stock, and to take it out from there when they sold it.

These measures had long provoked the murmurs of Theramenes, and when the envoys returned from Sparta without having effected any general peace agreement, he affirmed that this wall was likely to prove the ruin of the state. [2] At this moment forty-two ships from the Peloponnesus,[2a] including some Sicilian[2b] and Italian[2c] vessels from Locri[2d] and Tarentum,[2e] had been invited over by the Euboeans[2f] and were already anchored off Las[2g] in Laconia[2h] preparing for the voyage to Euboea, under the command of Agesandridas son of Agesander, a Spartiate. Theramenes now asserted that this squadron was destined not so much to aid Euboea as the party fortifying Eetionia,[2i] and that unless precautions were speedily taken the city would be surprised and lost. [3] This was no mere calumny, there being really some such plan entertained by the accused. Their first wish was to have the oligarchy without giving up the empire; failing this to keep their ships and walls and be independent; while, if this also were denied them, sooner than be the first victims of the restored democracy, they were resolved to call in the enemy and make peace, give up their walls and ships, and at all costs retain possession of the government, if only their lives were assured to them.

8.90.1a   Eetionia, a site in Piraeus: Map 8.92.
8.90.5a   Crawley's translation of the Greek word *stoa* as "porch" is misleading. This *stoa* was undoubtedly a port warehouse suitably large for controlling the city's grain supply. Its possible location is shown on Map 8.92, inset.
8.91.2a   Peloponnesus: Map 8.91.
8.91.2b   Sicily: Map 8.91.

8.91.2c   Italy: Map 8.91.
8.91.2d   Locri (Epyzephyrian), in Italy: Map 8.91.
8.91.2e   Tarentum, in Italy: Map 8.91.
8.91.2f   Euboea: Map 8.91.
8.91.2g   Las, in the Peloponnesus: Map 8.91. The route of Agesandridas' voyage to Euboea is shown on Map 8.96.
8.91.2h   Laconia: Map 8.84, BX.
8.91.2i   Eetionia, in Piraeus: Map 8.92, inset.

MAP 8.91   THE PELOPONNESIANS MOVE AGAINST EUBOEA

8.92
411
21st Year/Summer
ATHENS-PIRAEUS
Phrynichus is murdered.
Failure to find the assassin
encourages the regime's
opponents, who also fear
that a Spartan fleet will
attack the Piraeus. When
hoplites at Eetionia imprison
a general, the Four Hundred
send Theramenes to the
Piraeus. He lets the hoplites
destroy the wall. Many
demand that the Five Thousand should rule, although
no one knows if that body
really exists.

For this reason they hastened the construction of their work with postern gates and entrances and means of introducing the enemy, being eager to have it finished in time. [2] Meanwhile the murmurs against them were at first confined to a few persons and went on in secret, until Phrynichus, after his return from the embassy to Sparta, was laid wait for and stabbed in the open market[2a] by one of the *peripoli*,[2b] and fell down dead before he had gone far from the council chamber.[2c] The assassin escaped; but his accomplice, an Argive,[2d] was taken and put to the torture by the Four Hundred, without their being able to extract from him the name of his employer, or anything further than that he knew of many men who used to assemble at the house of the commander of the *peripoli* and at other houses. Here the matter was allowed to drop. This so emboldened Theramenes and Aristocrates and the rest of their partisans in the Four Hundred and outside that body, that they now resolved to act. [3] For by this time the ships had sailed round from Las, and anchoring at Epidaurus had overrun Aegina;[3a] and Theramenes asserted that, being bound for Euboea, they would never have sailed in to Aegina and come back to anchor at Epidaurus, unless they had been invited to come to aid in the designs of which he had always accused the government.

8.92.2a   Athenian market (*agora*): Map 8.92, inset, and Map 6.56, inset.
8.92.2b   The *peripoli* were a special Athenian military unit, perhaps a mobile force of young recruits serving as frontier guards. They were used by Demosthenes in the surprise assault against Megara, described in 4.67.2. See note 4.67.2a.
8.92.2c   Remains of this building (the council chamber, called the Bouleuterion) have been located in the Athenian *agora*, see Map 6.56, inset, and Map 8.92, inset.
8.92.2d   Argos: Map 8.92.
8.92.3a   Epidaurus, Aegina: Map 8.92. The route of this fleet's voyage to Euboea is shown on Map 8.96.

MAP 8.92 RESISTANCE TO THE ATHENIAN OLIGARCHS

Further inaction had therefore now become impossible. [4] In the end, after a great many seditious harangues and suspicions, they set to work in real earnest. The hoplites in the Piraeus who were building the wall in Eetionia,[4a] among whom was Aristocrates, a commander having soldiers of his own tribe,[4c] laid hands upon Alexicles, a general under the oligarchy and a devoted adherent of the cabal, and took him into a house and confined him there. [5] In this they were assisted by one Hermon, commander of the *peripoli* in Munychia,[5a] and others, and above all they had the support of the great bulk of the hoplites. [6] As soon as news of this reached the Four Hundred, who happened to be sitting in the coun-

8.92.4a Eetionia, Piraeus: Map 8.92, inset.
Details of the Piraeus in this map are
derived mainly from a map labeled 3.
Eetionia, from A. W. Gomme, A.
Andrewes, and K. J. Dover, *A Historical
Commentary on Thucydides,* v (Oxford,
1981), xv.
8.92.4c Aristocrates presumably thought that

troops of his own "tribe" would be more
reliable for such work. See Appendix A,
The Athenian Government, §3–5, 7, for a
discussion of tribes in the Athenian constitution.
8.92.5a Munychia, a hill in the Piraeus: Map
8.92, inset.

535

cil chamber, all except the disaffected wished at once to go to the posts where the arms were and threatened Theramenes and his party. Theramenes defended himself, and said that he was ready immediately to go and help to rescue Alexicles; and taking with him one of the generals belonging to his party, went down to the Piraeus, followed by Aristarchus and some young men of the cavalry. [7] All was now panic and confusion. Those in the city imagined that the Piraeus was already taken and the prisoner put to death, while those in the Piraeus expected at every moment to be attacked by the party in the city. [8] The older men, however, stopped the persons running up and down the city and making for the stands of arms; and Thucydides the Pharsalian, *proxenus* of the city,[8a] came forward and threw himself between the rival factions, and appealed to them not to ruin the state while the enemy was still nearby waiting for his opportunity, and so at length succeeded in quieting them and in keeping them from attacking each other. [9] Meanwhile Theramenes came down to the Piraeus, being himself one of the generals, and raged and stormed against the hoplites, while Aristarchus and the opponents of The People were genuinely infuriated. [10] Most of the hoplites, however, went on with the business without faltering, and asked Theramenes if he thought the wall had been constructed for any good purpose, and whether it would not be better that it should be pulled down. To this he answered that if they thought it best to pull it down, he for his part agreed with them. Upon this the hoplites and a number of the people in Piraeus immediately got up on the fortification and began to demolish it. [11] Now their cry to the multitude was that all should join in the work who wished the Five Thousand to govern instead of the Four Hundred. For instead of saying in so many words "all who wished The People to govern," they still disguised themselves under the name of the Five Thousand; being afraid that these might really exist, and that they might be speaking to one of their number and get into trouble through ignorance. Indeed this was why the Four Hundred neither wished the Five Thousand to exist, nor to have it known that they did not exist; being of the opinion that to give themselves so many partners in empire would be downright democracy, while the mystery in question would make the people afraid of one another.

8.92.8a   Pharsalus, in Thessaly: Map 8.91. A *prox-enus* was the representative of a foreign state (much like a modern honorary consul) in another state of which he was a resident and citizen. This Thucydides was a citizen and resident of Pharsalia, who was the *proxenus* of Athens at Pharsalia, and happened to be in Athens during these events.

The next day the Four Hundred, although alarmed, nevertheless assembled in the council chamber[1a] while the hoplites in the Piraeus,[1b] after having released their prisoner Alexicles and pulled down the fortification, went with their arms to the theater of Dionysus[1c] close to Munychia. There they held an assembly in which they decided to march into the city, and setting forth accordingly halted in the Anaceum.[1d] [2] Here they were joined by some delegates from the Four Hundred, who reasoned with them one by one, and persuaded those whom they saw to be the most moderate to remain quiet themselves, and to restrain the rest; saying that they would make known the Five Thousand, and have the Four Hundred chosen from them in rotation, as should be decided by the Five Thousand, and meanwhile entreated them not to ruin the state or drive it into the arms of the enemy. [3] After a great many had spoken and had been spoken to, the whole body of hoplites became calmer than before, absorbed by their fears for the country at large, and now agreed to hold upon an appointed day an assembly in the theater of Dionysus for the restoration of concord.

When the day came for the assembly in the theater, and they were upon the point of assembling, news arrived that the forty-two ships under Agesandridas were sailing from Megara along the coast of Salamis.[1a] The people to a man now thought that it was just what Theramenes and his party had so often said, that the ships were sailing to the fortification, and concluded that they had done well to demolish it. [2] But though it may possibly have been by appointment that Agesandridas hovered about Epidaurus[2a] and the neighborhood, he would also naturally be kept there by the hope of an opportunity arising out of the troubles in the city. [3] In any case the Athenians, on receipt of the news, immediately ran down in mass to the Piraeus, seeing themselves threatened by the enemy with a worse war than their war among themselves, not at a distance, but close to the harbor of Athens. Some went on board the ships already afloat, while others launched fresh vessels, or ran to defend the walls and the mouth of the harbor.

Meanwhile the Peloponnesian vessels sailed by, and rounding Sunium anchored between Thoricus and Prasiae,[1a] and afterwards arrived at Oropus.[1b] [2] The Athenians, with revolution in the city, and unwilling to lose a moment in going to the relief of their most important possession (for

8.93
411
21st Year/Summer
ATHENS-PIRAEUS
While the oligarchs meet in Athens, the hoplites assemble in the Piraeus and march to Athens. They are met by envoys from the oligarchs who beg them to be calm and not to betray the city to its enemies. The hoplites agree to the convening of a new assembly to restore concord.

8.94
411
21st Year/Summer
ATHENS-PIRAEUS
As the Athenians assemble, word arrives that a Spartan fleet is approaching the Piraeus from Megara. All hasten to the port to launch the remaining ships and man its defenses.

8.95
411
21st Year/Summer
EUBOEA
The Spartan fleet sails to Euboea, forcing Athens to send ships to protect that island. A battle takes place off Eretria in which the Spartans, aided secretly by the Eretrians, surprise the Athenians and gain a great victory. All Euboea, except for Oreus, which was settled by the Athenians, revolts from Athens.

8.93.1a   For the council chamber, see note 8.92.2c.
8.93.1b   Piraeus: Map 8.92.
8.93.1c   Theater of Dionysus, The Piraeus: Map 8.92, inset.
8.93.1d   Anaceum, the temple of the Dioscuri, in Athens, possible location: Map 8.92, inset.

8.94.1a   Megara, Salamis: Map 8.96, BX. The voyage of Agesandridas' fleet to Euboea is shown in Map 8.96.
8.94.2a   Epidaurus: Map 8.96, BX.
8.95.1a   Cape Sunium, Thoricus, and Prasiae, in Attica: Map 8.96, BY.
8.95.1b   Oropus: Map 8.96, AY.

Euboea[2a] was everything to them now that they were shut out from Attica), were compelled to put to sea in haste and with untrained crews, and sent Thymochares with some vessels to Eretria.[2b] [3] These upon their arrival, with the ships already in Euboea, made up a total of thirty-six vessels, and were immediately forced to engage. For Agesandridas, after his crews had taken their dinner, put out from Oropus, which is about seven miles[3a] from Eretria by sea; [4] and the Athenians, seeing him sailing up, immediately began to man their vessels. The sailors, however, instead of being by their ships, as they supposed, were gone away to purchase provisions[4a] for their dinner in the houses in the outskirts of the city; the Eretrians having so arranged that there should be nothing on sale in the *agora*,[4b] in order that the Athenians might be a long time in manning their ships, and the enemy's attack taking them by surprise, might compel them to put to sea just as they were. A signal also was raised in Eretria to give them notice in Oropus when to put to sea.[4c] [5] The Athenians, forced to put out so poorly prepared, engaged off the harbor of Eretria, and after holding their own for some little while notwithstanding, were at length put to flight and chased to the shore. [6] Such of their number as took refuge in Eretria, which they presumed to be friendly to them, found their fate in that city, being butchered by the inhabitants; while those who fled to the Athenian fort in the Eretrian territory, and the vessels which got to Chalcis,[6a] were saved. [7] The Peloponnesians, after taking twenty-two Athenian ships, and killing or making prisoners of the crews, set up a trophy, and not long afterwards effected the revolt of the whole of Euboea (except Oreus,[7a] which was held by the Athenians themselves) and made a general settlement of the affairs of the island.

When the news of what had happened in Euboea reached Athens a panic ensued such as they had never before known. Neither the disaster in Sicily, great as it seemed at the time, nor any other, had ever so much alarmed them. [2] The fleet at Samos[2a] was in revolt; they had no more ships or men to man them; they were in conflict among themselves and might at any moment come to blows; and a disaster of this magnitude coming on top of everything else, by which they lost their fleet, and worst of all Euboea, which was of more value to them than Attica, could not occur without throwing them into the deepest despondency. [3] Meanwhile their greatest and most immediate trouble was the possibility that the enemy, emboldened by his victory, might make straight for them and sail

8.96
411
21st Year/Summer
ATHENS
The loss of Euboea promotes panic at Athens. If the enemy besieges the Piraeus, the fleet from Samos would have to defend the city, exposing the rest of the empire. Thucydides notes that the Spartans were characteristically too slow to grasp or exploit this opportunity.

8.95.2a Euboea: Map 8.96, AY. For Euboea as a major source of supplies for Athens, see 7.28.1.
8.95.2b Eretria: Map 8.96, AY.
8.95.3a Thucydides writes "sixty stades"; the Attic stade was 607 feet long, the Olympic stade was 630.8 feet.
8.95.4a Greek soldiers and sailors at this time were expected to purchase their food from local markets with their own money. Triremes had no room or facilities for preparing food and had to put in to shore to feed the crew; see Appendix G, Trireme Warfare, §7.
8.95.4b The *agora* was a classical city's principal marketplace.
8.95.4c Boeotian plotting to take Euboea was mentioned in 8.60.1.
8.95.6a Chalcis: Map 8.96, AY.
8.95.7a Oreus is another name for Histiaea, in Euboea (Map 8.96, AY), and is so represented in the army in Sicily (7.57.2). Thucydides does not explain this, but perhaps the Athenians changed the name when they replaced the original inhabitants with their own colonists in 446 (1.116.3).
8.96.2a Samos: Map 8.96, locator.

MAP 8.96 PELOPONNESIAN VICTORY AT EUBOEA

against the Piraeus,[3a] which they no longer had ships to defend; and every moment they expected the enemy to arrive. [4] This, with a little more courage, he might easily have done, in which case he would either have increased the dissensions of the city by his presence, or if he had stayed to besiege it have compelled the fleet from Ionia,[4a] although opposed to the oligarchy, to come to the rescue of their country and of their relatives, and in the meantime, the enemy would have become master of the Hellespont,[4b] Ionia, the islands, and of everything as far as Euboea, or, to speak roundly, of the whole Athenian empire. [5] But here, as on so many other occasions, the Spartans proved the most convenient people in the world for the Athenians to be at war with. The wide difference between the two characters, the slowness and want of energy of the Spartans as contrasted with the dash and enterprise of their opponents, proved of the greatest service, especially to a maritime empire like Athens. Indeed this was shown by the Syracusans, who were most like the Athenians in character, and also most successful in combating them.

8.96.3a Piraeus: Map 8.96, BY.   8.96.4b Hellespont: Map 8.100, AY.
8.96.4a Ionia: Map 8.96, locator.

539

8.97
411
21st Year/Summer
ATHENS
The Athenians react to the Euboea disaster by deposing the oligarchy, installing a new regime of the Five Thousand, and enacting reforms. They also recall Alcibiades and other exiles and urge the army at Samos to vigorously carry on the war.

Nevertheless, upon receipt of the news, the Athenians manned twenty ships and immediately called a first assembly in the Pnyx,[1a] where they had been accustomed to meet formerly, and deposed the Four Hundred and voted to hand over the government to the Five Thousand, of which body all who furnished a suit of armor were to be members, decreeing also that no one should receive pay for the discharge of any office, [2] or if he did should be held accursed. Many other assemblies were held afterwards, in which lawmakers were elected and all other measures taken to form a constitution. It was during the first period of this constitution that the Athenians appear to have enjoyed the best government that they ever did, at least in my time.[2a] For the fusion of the high and the low was accomplished with judgment, and this was what first enabled the state to raise up her head after her manifold disasters. [3] They also voted for the recall of Alcibiades and of other exiles,[3a] and sent to him and to the camp at Samos, and urged them to devote themselves vigorously to the war.

8.98
411
21st Year/Summer
ATHENS
The chief oligarchs flee to the enemy at Decelea. Aristarchus, one of their generals, tricks the garrison of the Athenian fort at Oenoe into evacuating the fort, which is then occupied by the Boeotians.

Upon this revolution taking place, the party of Pisander and Alexicles and the chiefs of the oligarchs immediately withdrew to Decelea,[1a] with the single exception of Aristarchus, one of the generals, who hastily took some of the most barbarian of the archers and marched to Oenoe.[1b] [2] This was a fort of the Athenians upon the Boeotian[2a] border, at that moment besieged by the Corinthians[2b] who were responding to the loss of a party returning from Decelea, who had been cut off by the garrison. The Corinthians had volunteered for this service, and had called upon the Boeotians to assist them. [3] After communicating with them, Aristarchus deceived the garrison in Oenoe by telling them that their countrymen in the city had settled with the Spartans, and that one of the terms of the capitulation was that they must surrender the place to the Boeotians. The garrison believed him as he was general, and besides knew nothing of what had occurred owing to the siege, and so evacuated the fort under truce. [4] In this way the Boeotians gained possession of Oenoe, and the oligarchy and the troubles at Athens ended.

8.99
411
21st Year/Summer
MILETUS
Since the Peloponnesian fleet received no pay from Tissaphernes, who also did not bring up, as promised, the Phoenician fleet, Mindarus decides to take his fleet to Pharnabazus (who promised financial support) and, after diversion by a storm, arrives at Chios.

To return to the Peloponnesians in Miletus.[1a] No pay was forthcoming from any of the agents appointed by Tissaphernes for that purpose upon his departure for Aspendus;[1b] neither the Phoenician fleet nor Tissaphernes showed any signs of appearing; and Philip, who had been sent with him, and another Spartiate, Hippocrates, who was at Phaselis,[1c] sent word to Mindarus the admiral that the ships were not coming at all, and that they

---

8.97.1a   The Pnyx, the traditional site for meetings of the assembly in Athens: Map 6.56, inset, and Map 8.92, inset.
8.97.2a   The following alternative translation is more commonly accepted. "And in no little measure the Athenians for the first time, at least in my lifetime, appear to have enjoyed good government."
8.97.3a   They recalled other exiles but not, presumably, Thucydides the author.
8.98.1a   Decelea: Map 8.96, AY.

8.98.1b   Oenoe: Map 8.96, AX. Oenoe was unsuccessfully besieged by the Peloponnesians under Archidamus during the first invasion of Attica in 431; see 2.18.1.
8.98.2a   Boeotia: Map 8.96, AX.
8.98.2b   Corinth: Map 8.96, BX.
8.99.1a   Miletus: Map 8.100, BY. This picks up the Peloponnesian fleet narrative from 8.87.
8.99.1b   Aspendus: Map 8.100, locator.
8.99.1c   Phaselis: Map 8.100, locator.

were being grossly abused by Tissaphernes. Meanwhile Pharnabazus[1d] was inviting them to come, and making every effort to get the fleet and, like Tissaphernes, to cause the revolt of the cities in his province that were still subject to Athens, founding great hopes on his success; until at length, at about this time in the summer, Mindarus yielded to his requests and, with great order and at a moment's notice, in order to elude the enemy at Samos,[1e] weighed anchor with seventy-three ships from Miletus and set sail for the Hellespont.[1f] Sixteen vessels had already preceded him there in the same summer, and had overrun part of the Chersonese.[1g] Being caught in a storm, Mindarus was compelled to run in to Icarus,[1h] and after being detained five or six days there by stress of weather, arrived at Chios.[1i]

Meanwhile Thrasyllus had heard of his having put out from Miletus,[1a] and immediately set sail with fifty-five ships from Samos, hurrying to arrive before him in the Hellespont. [2] But learning that he was at Chios, and expecting that he would stay there, he posted scouts in Lesbos[2a] and on the continent opposite to prevent the fleet moving without his knowing it, and himself sailed along the coast to Methymna,[2b] and gave orders to prepare ground barley and other necessaries, in order to attack them from Lesbos in the event of their remaining for any length of time at Chios. [3] Meanwhile he resolved to sail against Eresus,[3a] a city in Lesbos which had revolted, and to take it if he could. For some of the principal Methymnian exiles had carried over about fifty hoplites, their sworn associates from Cyme,[3b] and hiring others from the mainland so as to make up three hundred in all, chose Anaxander, a Theban,[3c] to command them, on account of the community of blood existing between the Thebans and the Lesbians, and first attacked Methymna. Thwarted in this attempt by the advance of the Athenian guards from Mytilene,[3d] and repulsed a second time in a battle outside the city, they then crossed the mountain and brought about the revolt of Eresus. [4] Thrasyllus accordingly determined to go there with all his ships and to attack the place. Meanwhile Thrasybulus had preceded him there with five ships from Samos, as soon as he heard that the exiles had crossed over, and coming too late to save Eresus, went on and anchored before the city. [5] Here they were joined also by two vessels on their way home from the Hellespont, and by the ships of the Methymnians, making a grand total of sixty-seven vessels; and the forces on board now made ready with siege engines and every other means available to do their utmost to storm Eresus.

8.100
411
21st Year/Summer
LESBOS
Learning of the Spartan move, the Athenian fleet leaves Samos for the Hellespont and takes station at Methymna on Lesbos. The general Thrasyllus decides to attack Eresus, a Lesbian city that has revolted and serves now as a base for Methymnian exiles.

8.99.1d   Pharnabazus was the Persian governor (satrap) of the Hellespont region (Map 8.100, AX).
8.99.1e   Samos: Map 8.100, BY.
8.99.1f   Hellespont: Map 8.100, AY.
8.99.1g   Chersonese (Hellespont): Map 8.100, AX.
8.99.1h   Icarus: Map 8.100, BX.
8.99.1i   Chios: Map 8.100, BX.
8.100.1a Miletus: Map 8.100, BY.
8.100.2a Lesbos: Map 8.100, AX.

8.100.2b Methymna, on Lesbos: Map 8.100, AX.
8.100.3a Eresus, on Lesbos: Map 8.100, AX.
8.100.3b Cyme: Map 8.100, BY.
8.100.3c Thebes: Map 8.96, AX.
8.100.3d Mytilene, on Lesbos, Map 8.100, AX.

MAP 8.100
FIGHTING ON LESBOS; BOTH FLEETS MOVE NORTH

8.101
411
21st Year/Summer
LESBOS
After taking pay for its sailors from the Chians, the Peloponnesian fleet leaves Chios for Lesbos, sails north between Lesbos and the mainland, and arrives at the Hellespont without encountering the Athenian fleet.

In the meantime Mindarus and the Peloponnesian fleet at Chios,[1a] after taking provisions for two days and receiving three Chian pieces of money[1b] for each man from the Chians, on the third day sailed out in haste from the island; in order to avoid falling in with the ships at Eresus.[1c] They did not make for the open sea, but keeping Lesbos on their left, sailed for the mainland. [2] After touching at the port of Carteria, in the territory of

8.101.1a Chios: Map 8.100, BX.
8.101.1b Thucydides' word for these "pieces of money" is *tessarakontas,* literally, "a fortieth"; but scholars are not sure what these were "fortieths" of, or what three of them amounted to. See Appendix J, Classical Greek Currency, §3.
8.101.1c Eresus, on Lesbos: Map 8.100, AX.

Phocaea,[2a] and having their dinner, they went on along the Cymaean[2b] coast and took supper at Arginousae,[2c] on the mainland over against Mytilene. [3] From there they continued their voyage along the coast, although it was late in the night, and arriving at Harmatus[3a] on the continent opposite Methymna, took a meal there; and swiftly passing Lectum,[3b] Larisa,[3c] Hamaxitus,[3d] and the neighboring cities, arrived a little before midnight at Rhoeteum.[3e] Here they were now in the Hellespont.[3f] Some of the ships also put in at Sigeum[3g] and at other places in the neighborhood.

Meanwhile the warnings of the fire signals and the sudden increase in the number of fires on the enemy's shore informed the eighteen Athenian ships at Sestos[1a] of the approach of the Peloponnesian fleet. That very night they set sail in haste just as they were, and hugging the shore of the Chersonese,[1b] coasted along to Elaeus,[1c] in order to sail out into the open sea away from the fleet of the enemy. [2] After passing unobserved by the sixteen ships at Abydos,[2a] (although they had been warned by their approaching friends to be on the alert to prevent their sailing out), at dawn they sighted the fleet of Mindarus, which immediately gave chase. All had not time to get away; the greater number however escaped to Imbros[2b] and Lemnos,[2c] while four of those in the rear were overtaken off Elaeus. [3] One of these was stranded opposite the temple of Protesilaus and taken with its crew, two others without their crews; the fourth was abandoned on the shore of Imbros and burned by the enemy.

After this the Peloponnesians were joined by the squadron from Abydos,[1a] which brought their fleet to a grand total of eighty-six vessels; they spent the day in unsuccessfully besieging Elaeus,[1b] and then sailed back to Abydos. [2] Meanwhile the Athenians, deceived by their scouts, and never dreaming that the enemy's fleet would go by undetected, were tranquilly besieging Eresus.[2a] As soon as they heard the news they instantly abandoned Eresus and made with all speed for the Hellespont, [3] and after taking two of the Peloponnesian ships which had been carried out too far into the open sea in the ardor of the pursuit and which now fell in their way, dropped anchor the next day at Elaeus. There they brought back the ships that had taken refuge at Imbros[3a] and for five days prepared for the coming engagement.

8.102
411
21st Year/Summer
HELLESPONT
Learning of the approach of the Spartan fleet, an Athenian squadron at Sestos attempts to flee. They are pursued, attacked, and lose four triremes off Elaeus.

8.103
411
21st Year/Summer
HELLESPONT
The Athenians at Eresus finally learn of the nearby presence of the Peloponnesian fleet and leave for Elaeus, where they prepare for battle.

8.101.2a Carteria, in Phocaean territory: precise location unknown. Phocaea: Map 8.100, BY.
8.101.2b Cyme: Map 8.100, BY.
8.101.2c Arginousae: Map 8.100, AY.
8.101.3a Harmatus: location unknown.
8.101.3b Cape Lectum: Map 8.100, AX.
8.101.3c Larisa: Map 8.100, AX.
8.101.3d Hamaxitus: Map 8.100, AX.
8.101.3e Rhoeteum: Map 8.100, AX.
8.101.3f Hellespont: Map 8.100, AY. For the route of Mindarus' fleet as described, see Map 8.100.
8.101.3g Sigeum: Map 8.100, AX.
8.102.1a Sestos: Map 8.100, AX. Sestos was estab-

lished as the Athenian naval base in the Hellespont by Strombichides in 8.62.3.
8.102.1b Chersonese (Hellespont): Map 8.100, AX, and Map 8.103, inset.
8.102.1c Elaeus: Map 8.100, AX.
8.102.2a Abydos: Map 8.100, AX. Abydos had revolted from Athens, as Thucydides writes in 8.62.1.
8.102.2b Imbros: Map 8.100, AX, and Map 8.103.
8.102.2c Lemnos: Map 8.100, AX and Map 8.103.
8.103.1a Abydos: Map 8.100, inset.
8.103.1b Elaeus: Map 8.100, inset.
8.103.2a Eresus: Map 8.100, AX.
8.103.3a Imbros: Map 8.103.

MAP 8.103
THE BATTLE IN THE HELLESPONT OFF POINT CYNOSSEMA

8.104
411
21st Year/Summer
HELLESPONT
The location, formations, and maneuvers of battle are described. The Athenian wings prevent the enemy's attempt to outflank them, but their center near Point Cynossema is thereby weakened.

After this they engaged in the following way. The Athenians formed in column and sailed close along shore to Sestos;[1a] upon perceiving which the Peloponnesians put out from Abydos to meet them. [2] Realizing that a battle was now imminent, both combatants extended their flank; the Athenians along the Chersonese[2a] from Idacus[2b] to Arrhiana[2c] with seventy-six ships; the Peloponnesians from Abydos to Dardanus[2d] with eighty-six. [3]

8.104.1a Sestos: Map 8.103, inset.
8.104.2a Chersonese (Hellespont): Map 8.103, inset.
8.104.2b Idacus: precise location unknown.

8.104.2c Arrhiana: precise location unknown.
8.104.2d Dardanus: Map 8.103, inset.

The Peloponnesian right wing was occupied by the Syracusans,[3a] their left by Mindarus in person with the best sailors in the navy; the Athenian left by Thrasyllus, their right by Thrasybulus, the other commanders being in different parts of the fleet. [4] The Peloponnesians hastened to engage first, and outflanking with their left the Athenian right sought to cut them off, if possible, from sailing out of the straits, and to drive their center upon the shore, which was not far off. The Athenians perceiving their intention extended their own (right) wing and outsailed them, [5] while their left had by this time passed the point of Cynossema.[5a] This, however, obliged them to thin and weaken their center, especially as they had fewer ships than the enemy, and as the coast round Point Cynossema formed a sharp angle which prevented their seeing what was happening on the other side of it.

The Peloponnesians now attacked their center and drove ashore the ships of the Athenians, and disembarked to follow up their victory. [2] No help could be given to the center either by the squadron of Thrasybulus on the right, on account of the number of ships attacking him, or by that of Thrasyllus on the left, from whom the point of Cynossema hid what was going on, and who was also hindered by his Syracusan and other opponents, whose numbers were fully equal to his own. At length, however, the Peloponnesians in the confidence of victory began to scatter in pursuit of the ships of the enemy, and allowed a considerable part of their fleet to get into disorder. [3] On seeing this the squadron of Thrasybulus discontinued their lateral movement and, facing about, attacked and routed the ships opposed to them, and next fell fiercely upon the scattered vessels of the victorious Peloponnesian division, and put most of them to flight without a blow. The Syracusans also had by this time given way before the squadron of Thrasyllus, and now openly took to flight upon seeing the flight of their comrades.

The rout was now complete. Most of the Peloponnesians fled for refuge first to the river Midius,[1a] and afterwards to Abydos.[1b] Only a few ships were taken by the Athenians; as owing to the narrowness of the Hellespont[1c] the enemy had not far to go to be in safety. Nevertheless nothing could have been more opportune for them than this victory. [2] Up to this time they had feared the Peloponnesian fleet, owing to a number of petty losses and the disaster in Sicily; but they now ceased to mistrust themselves or any longer to think their enemies good for anything at sea. [3] Meanwhile they took from the enemy eight Chian[3a] vessels, five Corinthian,[3b] two Ambraciot,[3c] two Boeotian,[3d] one Leucadian,[3e] Spartan, Syracusan, and Pellenian,[3f] losing fifteen of their own. [4] After setting up a trophy upon Point Cynossema,[4a] securing the wrecks, and restoring to the enemy his dead under truce, they sent off a trireme to Athens with the news of their victory. [5] The arrival of this vessel with its unhoped-for

8.105
411
21st Year/Summer
HELLESPONT
Initial Peloponnesian victory in the center leads to disorder and then defeat when the Athenian wings attack and finally put their adversaries to flight.

8.106
411
21st Year/Summer
HELLESPONT
The completeness of the victory, although the Athenians only captured twenty-one triremes and lost fifteen of their own, restores Athenian confidence in their prowess at sea.

8.104.3a Syracuse: Map 8.91.
8.104.5a Point Cynossema: Map 8.103, inset.
8.106.1a Midius River: location unknown.
8.106.1b Abydos: Map 8.103, inset.
8.106.1c Hellespont: Map 8.100, AY, and Map 8.103, inset.
8.106.3a Chios: Map 8.103.

8.106.3b Corinth: Map 8.107, BX.
8.106.3c Ambracia: Map 8.107, AX.
8.106.3d Boeotia: Map 8.107, BX.
8.106.3e Leucas: Map 8.107, AX.
8.106.3f Pellene: Map 8.107, BX.
8.106.4a Point Cynossema: Map 8.103, inset.

good news, after the recent disasters of Euboea,[5a] and during the revolution at Athens, gave fresh courage to the Athenians, and caused them to believe that if they put their shoulders to the wheel their cause might yet prevail.

On the fourth day after the sea fight the Athenians in Sestos[1a] having hastily refitted their ships, sailed against Cyzicus,[1b] which had revolted. Off Harpagium[1c] and Priapus[1d] they sighted at anchor the eight vessels from Byzantium,[1e] and sailing up and routing the troops on shore, took the ships, and then went on and recovered the city of Cyzicus, which was unfortified, and levied money from the citizens. [2] In the meantime the Peloponnesians sailed from Abydos[2a] to Elaeus,[2b] and recovered such of their captured triremes as were still uninjured, the rest having been burned by the Elaeusians, and sent Hippocrates and Epicles to Euboea to bring the squadron from that island.

About the same time Alcibiades returned with his thirteen ships from Caunus[1a] and Phaselis[1b] to Samos,[1c] bringing word that he had prevented the Phoenician[1d] fleet from joining the Peloponnesians, and had made Tissaphernes more friendly to the Athenians than before. [2] Alcibiades now manned nine more ships, and levied large sums of money from the Halicarnassians,[2a] and fortified Cos.[2b] After doing this and placing a governor in Cos, he sailed back to Samos, autumn being now at hand. [3] Meanwhile Tissaphernes, upon hearing that the Peloponnesian fleet had sailed from Miletus[3a] to the Hellespont,[3b] set off again back from Aspendus,[3c] and made all sail for Ionia.[3d]

[4] While the Peloponnesians were in the Hellespont, the Antandrians,[4a] a people of Aeolic[4b] extraction, conveyed by land across Mount Ida[4c] some hoplites from Abydos,[4d] and introduced them into the city; having been ill-treated by Arsaces, the Persian lieutenant of Tissaphernes. This same Arsaces had, upon pretense of a secret quarrel, invited the chief men of the Delians[4e] to undertake military service (these were Delians who had settled at Atramyttium[4f] after having been driven from their homes by the Athenians for the sake of purifying Delos);[4g] and after drawing them out from their city as his friends and allies, had laid wait for them at dinner, and surrounded them and caused them to be shot down by his soldiers. [5] This deed made the Antandrians fear that he might someday do them some mischief; and as he also laid upon them burdens too heavy for them to bear, they expelled his garrison from their citadel.

8.106.5a Euboea: Map 8.107, BX.
8.107.1a Sestos: Map 8.107, AY.
8.107.1b Cyzicus: Map 8.107, AY.
8.107.1c Harpagium: Map 8.107, AY.
8.107.1d Priapus: Map 8.107, AY.
8.107.1e Byzantium: Map 8.107, AY.
8.107.2a Abydos: Map 8.107, AY.
8.107.2b Elaeus: Map 8.107, AY.
8.108.1a Caunus: Map 8.107, BY.
8.108.1b Phaselis: Map 8.107, BY.
8.108.1c Samos: Map 8.107, BY.
8.108.1d Phoenicia: Map 8.107, locator.
8.108.2a Halicarnassus: Map 8.107, BY.
8.108.2b Cos: Map 8.107, BY.

8.108.3a Miletus: Map 8.107, BY.
8.108.3b Hellespont: Map 8.107, AY.
8.108.3c Aspendus: Map 8.107, BY.
8.108.3d Ionia: Map 8.107, BY.
8.108.4a Antandrus: Map 8.107, AY.
8.108.4b Aeolis: Map 8.107, AY.
8.108.4c Mount Ida: Map 8.107, AY.
8.108.4d Abydos: Map 8.107, AY.
8.108.4e Delos: Map 8.107, BY.
8.108.4f Atramyttium: Map 8.107, AY.
8.108.4g For this purification of Delos, see 3.104
          and 5.1.

MAP 8.107 AFTERMATH OF THE BATTLE OF CYNOSSEMA

8.109
411
21st Year/Summer
IONIA
Anxious to heal the breach between the Peloponnesians and himself, Tissaphernes hurries to the Hellespont to explain his actions and restore relations. He stops at Ephesus.

Tissaphernes[1a] upon hearing of this act of the Peloponnesians in addition to what had occurred at Miletus[1b] and Cnidus,[1c] where his garrisons had been also expelled, now saw that the breach between them was serious; and fearing further injury from them, and being also vexed to think that Pharnabazus[1d] should receive them, and in less time and at less cost perhaps succeed better against Athens than he had done, determined to rejoin them in the Hellespont, in order to complain of the events at Antandrus[1e] and excuse himself as best he could in the matter of the Phoenician[1f] fleet and of the other charges against him. Accordingly he went first to Ephesus[1g] and offered sacrifice to Artemis.

[When the winter after this summer is over the twenty-first year of this war will be completed.]

8.109.1a Tissaphernes was the Persian governor (satrap) of the "maritime provinces"; see note 8.5.5a and Map 8.84, BY.
8.109.1b Miletus: Map 8.107, BY.
8.109.1c Cnidus: Map 8.107, BY.
8.109.1d Pharnabazus was the Persian governor (satrap) of the Hellespont region (Map 8.107, AY, and Map 8.84, AY).

8.109.1e Antandrus: Map 8.107, AY. For the Aeolians, see Appendix H, Dialects and Ethnic Groups.
8.109.1f Phoenicia: Map 8.107, locator.
8.109.1g Ephesus: Map 8.107, BY.

EPILOGUE

§1. Thucydides' narrative breaks off in the middle of the year 411, although he returned to Athens from exile after the war ended in 404 (5.26.5) and the last years of the war clearly did leave their mark on his final revisions of the text (e.g., 2.65, 2.100, 4.81, 6.15). Unfortunately, we lack what might have been his accounts of both Athens' partial military recovery—marked by her two great naval victories at Cyzicus[1a] (410) and Arginousae[1b] (406)—and her final defeat at Aegospotami[1c] (405) where, assisted by obtuse and perhaps inexperienced Athenian commmanders,[1d] the Spartan admiral Lysander employed stealth and superior tactical skill to capture—on the beach—almost the entire Athenian fleet in the Hellespont.[1e] After that disaster, the Athenians had no means left with which to prevent Lysander from blockading their city, starving her of the grain from the Black Sea region[1f] on which she largely depended, and ultimately forcing her to sue for peace. Victorious Sparta, after initially contemplating the total destruction of her defeated adversary, finally decided that Athens would be allowed to continue to exist as a city, but demanded the surrender of what remained of her fleet, the demolition of the walls of Piraeus[1g] and the Long Walls, and the granting of complete freedom to the former subject cities of what had been the Athenian Empire. Now supreme in Greece, Sparta thus reduced Athens to a state of isolation, weakness, and dependency which must have been dreadful indeed to the writer of Pericles' Funeral Oration.

§2. In his obituary of Pericles (2.65), which Thucydides wrote after the end of the war, he acknowledged the vital role of the Persian prince Cyrus the Younger in maintaining Sparta.[2a] Yet he says little in the body of his text about the rising importance of Persia in Greek affairs. In truth, although the Persian governor at Sardis,[2b] Tissaphernes, never did honor his promises to provide a fleet to assist Sparta, his meager financial support, along with that of Pharnabazus in the Hellespont, did permit Sparta to challenge Athens in the Aegean and to bring about the revolt of many Asian Greek cities from Athenian allegiance. It was Cyrus the Younger,

1a Cyzicus: Epilogue Map, AY.
1b Arginousae Islands: Epilogue Map, AY.
1c Aegospotami: Epilogue Map, AY.
1d Now in command because most of the generals responsible for the victory at Arginousae had been exiled or executed in a postbattle fit of fratricidal, if not suicidal, political antagonism reminiscent of what

took place at Corcyra in 427 (3.69).
1e Hellespont: Epilogue Map, AY.
1f Black Sea: Epilogue Map, locator .
1g Piraeus: Epilogue Map, BX.
2a See 2.65.12.
2b Sardis: Epilogue Map, BY.

however, the successor to Tissaphernes, who demanded of his father, Darius II, that real naval support be provided to Sparta, and whose active assistance and collusion with Lysander encouraged the Spartans to persevere despite setbacks. Thus, even though Aegospotami was won without the help of a Persian fleet, Sparta found herself greatly indebted to Cyrus at the end of the war; and when Darius died in 404 and Cyrus began to assemble an army to support his claim to the throne, Sparta had no choice but to become involved, partly by her obligation of gratitude, and partly by the reflection that if Cyrus were to succeed without her aid, she would feel his wrath. So Sparta made her contribution to Cyrus' expedition and approved the creation of a mercenary force of Greek hoplites for his army. Their adventurous journey into and out of Mesopotamia was later made famous by one of its Athenian captains, Xenophon, in his book *Anabasis,* "The March of the Ten Thousand."

§3. Cyrus' army won the battle at Cunaxa near Babylon[3a] (401) but gained no victory, for Cyrus himself died on the field, and his death left Sparta, as far as the triumphant King Artaxerxes II was concerned, in an awkward position. Although efforts were made to restore amicable relations, the truth was inescapable. Alcibiades had been right when he predicted (8.46) that Sparta, having liberated the Greeks of Greece from Athens, could not refuse the entreaties of the Greeks of Asia to liberate them from Persia.[3b] When Sparta did go to their aid, she brought upon herself a war that was impossible for her to win and which irremediably damaged her supremacy and control over Greece itself; for Persia countered Sparta by encouraging (and in part financing) a new coalition of Athens, Thebes, Corinth, and Argos[3c] to oppose Spartan domination. This combined alliance waged the so-called Corinthian War (395–87) against Sparta, defeated her decisively at sea in 394—just ten years after Aegospotami—and ultimately forced her to abandon her attempt to liberate the Greeks of Asia.

§4. Certainly Sparta had no monopoly on folly. When the Athenians, bent on restoring their empire, chose to intervene in cities within the Persian King's domain, the King in turn allied with Sparta in order to thwart them, and the Athenians, faced again in 387 with the loss of their Black Sea grain supply, had to renounce their imperial goals. The general agreement of 386—known as the King's Peace—formalized the position. Both Sparta and her opponents in Greece undertook to leave the King in complete control of his domains and, with the threat of Persian support if it were needed, Sparta was established as the enforcer of the peace, the policeman of the Hellenes.

§5. In short, Sparta's total military victory over Athens in the Peloponnesian War gained her little more than a short-lived supremacy in Greece, one that ultimately could not be maintained without the support of Persia, who would not grant it to her unless she accepted conditions and limitations imposed by Persia. Thus it was the King of Persia who seems to have gained most from the war, for with the destruction of the Athenian Empire he recovered his territories in Asia at

---

3a Cunaxa and Babylon: Epilogue Map, locator.
3b Persia: Epilogue Map, locator.

3c Sparta, Athens, Thebes, Corinth, and Argos: Epilogue Map, BX.

EPILOGUE MAP

551

little cost to himself and was able to cheaply maintain his hold on them by playing off the always-contentious and now utterly disunited Greek *poleis* (city-states) against each other. Later Kings continued this policy with such success that none of them had to defend against invasion from the west until the Macedonians under Alexander the Great attacked Persia in 334.

§6. Persian dominance in Greece, exerted through, and made possible by, the continuous stalemate among Greek states—arrayed now in one, now in another balanced set of alliances—reveals the increasing inability of the traditional *polis* (city-state) to deal effectively with new problems of war, trade, and politics in a larger, Mediterranean framework. The polis, a uniquely Greek phenomenon, had developed and flowered in the particular circumstances of the eighth, seventh, and early sixth centuries when, as Thucydides noted (1.12–19), there were no great wars, powerful states, or large-scale enterprises in the Greek world. The key institutions of the polis—an agrarian economy, many owners of small plots of land, rule by a restricted list of citizen voters, and hoplite warfare—to which most Greeks remained deeply attached throughout the period—were not seriously challenged by the outside world until the encroachments and invasions of Persia in the late sixth and early fifth centuries. Although the Greeks threw back the Persians in the first half of the fifth century, they did so through leagues and alliances that proved inimical to the total autonomy, and incompatible with the local focus, that were so central to the classical polis. These inherent conflicts, perhaps first exposed in the fifth century by the Delian League's rapid transition to a tyrannous Athenian Empire, and then further revealed by Sparta's clumsy attempt to substitute her own domination for that of Athens, continued to manifest itself in the polis' essential political failure throughout the fourth century. In fact, the bankruptcy of the polis in the greater and more integrated world that was developing is nowhere more starkly revealed than in the narrow hegemonist goals that the leading Greek poleis continuously and unrealistically pursued during this period. Their myopic vision and sterile objectives embroiled the Greek cities in continuous and increasingly expensive warfare that not only impoverished them but that also allowed Persia to maintain sufficient control to neutralize, at little expense, what otherwise might have been a troublesome and dangerous region.

§7. Athens, for example, could not forego another attempt to recover her imperial assets from the fifth century. Although she was for a time checked by fear of Sparta and of provoking the Great King to intervene, she recognized and seized her opportunity when the Thebans inflicted a severe defeat upon Sparta at the battle of Leuctra[7a] in 371. When the decisive impact of that battle became clear, Athens set out to regain two of the most strategic of those assets, the city of Amphipolis[7b] (the loss of which was described by Thucydides in Book 4) and the Chersonese on the Hellespont,[7c] (which Athens under Pericles had settled, and which would protect her access to the Black Sea). When the Great King was distracted and temporarily paralyzed by the revolt of the satraps (provincial governors) of Asia[7d] between 366

7a Leuctra: Epilogue Map, BX.
7b Amphipolis: Epilogue Map, AX.

7c Chersonese on the Hellespont: Epilogue Map, AY.
7d Asia: Epilogue Map, AY.

and 359, Athens' attempt to recover her old empire became so offensive and blatant that three of her main allies turned against her and stalemated her in what is known as the Social War of 357–55. Then, when the Great King, having restored order in Asia, threatened Athens with another round of punitive action, the now nearly bankrupt city had no choice but to yield and finally to abandon her imperial ambitions for good.

§8. Sparta's aspirations to leadership in Greece were also dealt a fatal blow during this period. When the mass of Theban hoplites, arrayed in an extraordinary formation fifty-ranks deep, broke through their opposing phalanx at Leuctra, the Spartan army's reputation for military invincibility was forever shattered; and the Thebans, led by the great general Epaminondas, were not slow to exploit their new military advantage in order to make it permanent. In 369, Epaminondas marched into the Peloponnesus and invaded Laconia,[8a] inviolate for centuries, and on its borders founded and fortified the two great democratic bastions of Megalopolis and Ithome in Messenia[8b]—the inhabitants of the latter being given freedom from Sparta after centuries of degrading subjection. By the establishment of these two states, he reduced Sparta in a flash from a world power to a mere local wrangler intent for the rest of her independent existence on recovering the irrecoverable Messene on which Spartan power had depended.

§9. After the resounding victory at Leuctra, Thebes found herself the greatest military power of free Greece. The 380s and the 370s had been the decades of Spartan hegemony; in the 360s Thebes sought to take Sparta's place, and for a brief moment her prospects seemed good. But with the death of Epaminondas on the battlefield of Second Mantinea[9a] (362) and with the onset of the miserable Sacred War that embroiled Thebes with Phocis[9b] in a long and debilitating conflict, the threat of Theban power faded.

§10. A new menace to Greece now arose in Macedon, a kingdom that plays only a peripheral role in Thucydides' narrative, as it did in the Hellenic world before its first great king, Philip II (reigned 359–36). Although the Macedonians spoke Greek, they were considered boorish, primitive, and foreign by most Greeks of Thucydides' time. After all, they did not live in independent poleis like self-respecting "modern" Greeks; instead, they were citizens of loose and some of them petty kingdoms, who owed loyalty to kings who ruled and played dynastic politics of marriage and war in a style that must have reminded fifth-century Greeks of Homer's most unsophisticated chieftains. Yet the Argeadae, the royal house of Macedon, traced their ancestry to Argos, and they demonstrated their Hellenic origin sufficiently for Macedonians to be allowed to participate in the Olympic Games. By the late fifth century, they had become dominant in their region, and although Thucydides shows them as weakly seeking help, now from Athens, now from Sparta, and dropping and restoring alliances with dizzying speed, their battles in Lyncestis, and their defense against overwhelming invasion from Odrysian Thrace, gained them experience and stature. In the fourth century, under Philip II, they became a menace to all of Greece and indeed to much of the rest of the world also.

8a Laconia: Epilogue Map, BX.
8b Megalopolis and Messene: Epilogue Map, BX.

9a Mantinea: Epilogue Map, BX.
9b Phocis: Epilogue Map, BX.

§11. During the first part of his reign, Philip extended Macedonian power to Thrace,[11a] Thessaly,[11b] and the whole of northern Greece. From there, setting his eyes on the riches of Persia, he attempted to control and organize the many poleis of Greece so that they might assist him against Persia, but if they would not, to at least prevent them from joining with Persia against him when he moved east. In other words, he sought less to conquer the Greek cities than to render them impotent. He proved to be a skillful diplomat and an acute judge of his own interests. Above all, he was a resourceful general who commanded a large and superbly trained army. Although occasionally defeated in the field or checked by treaty, he tirelessly maneuvered by both war and diplomacy to increase his influence and power in Greece. The one Athenian political faction (led by the orator Demosthenes) which saw clearly that the huge Macedonian power posed a serious menace to Greek liberty achieved little more, for all its machinations and plots, than to cause Philip to delay his Asiatic plans for a few years. In the end, when Philip finally advanced into Greece proper, his opponents proved so incapable of uniting or otherwise seriously challenging him that he found himself opposed by the armies of only the two most directly threatened poleis: Athens and Thebes. When Philip defeated these armies in the decisive battle at Chaeronea[11c] in 338, all hopes of freedom for Greece from Macedonian dominion were extinguished.

§12. Philip settled affairs in Greece to his satisfaction by organizing a "League of Corinth" (337) and by establishing a few strategically placed garrisons throughout the country. Then, returning to Macedon, he prepared for his onslaught on Persia. In the spring of 336, the vanguard of his army crossed over to Asia, with Philip intending to follow shortly. By midsummer, however, he had been murdered. His son, Alexander III, succeeded him and, after a short interval, fulfilled and perhaps overfulfilled his father's ambitions. Crossing the Hellespont in 334, Alexander completely destroyed Persian military power in a series of brilliant victories in just three years. By 331, when the last Great King, Darius III, died ignominiously in flight, Alexander—known to us as Alexander the Great—began to rule over both Greece and Persia. Ten years later, when he died in Babylon, the independent polis was well on its way to oblivion, and the Hellenistic world was born.

R.B.S.

11a Thrace, now the area of modern Bulgaria and European Turkey: Epilogue Map, AY, and locator.

11b Thessaly: Epilogue Map, AX.
11c Chaeronea: Epilogue Map, BX.

THEATERS OF OPERATION
IN THE PELOPONNESIAN WAR

Year/ Season	Attica-Euboea-Boeotia	Peloponnesus Megarid, Cephallenia, Zacynthus, Melos
	BOOK ONE **Introduction** **The Archaeology**	
435		**1.24–29** Epidamnian affair. A Corinthian fleet is defeated by the Corcyraeans off Leukimme. **1.30** Corcyraeans raid Leucas and Cyllene. Corinth establishes bases at Actium and Thesprotis.
433	**1.31–45** Speeches by Corcyraeans (1.32) and Corinthians (1.37). **1.45** Athens makes a defensive alliance with Corcyra, sends 10 ships to the island. **1.50–51** Athenian ships at the battle of Sybota prevent a Corcyraean rout. **1.56** Suspicious of Potidaea, Athens prepares to send a fleet but is delayed by Potidaean envoys.	**1.31** Corinth prepares for more war with Corcyra; sends envoys to Athens to rebut the Corcyraeans. **1.37–43** Speech of the Corinthians at Athens. **1.46–55** Corinthian victory at Sybota. Corinthians take Anactorium. **1.58** Sparta promises to support a Potidaean revolt by invading Attica.
432	**1.59–65** The arriving Athenians find Potidaea already in revolt. They besiege the city.	**1.60** Corinthian volunteers go to Potidaea. **1.68** Speech of the Corinthians. **1.73** Speech of the Athenians. **1.80** Speech of Archidamus for caution and delay. **1.86** Speech of Sthenelaides. **1.87** The Spartans vote for war.
479–31 Pentecontaetia		
479–78 Pentecontaetia	**1.89** The Persians retreat; Athens rebuilds, and sends a fleet to the Hellespont. **1.90–92** Themistocles tricks the Spartans while Athens builds walls. **1.93** He fortifies the Piraeus.	**1.94** Pausanias leads an expedition against Cyprus and Byzantium.
478–77 Pentecontaetia	**1.95** The allies select Athens to lead; Sparta accepts this choice. **1.96** Delian league formed under Athenian leadership.	**1.95** Pausanias returns to Sparta; the allies choose Athens to lead them and Sparta accepts this choice.
476–67 Pentecontaetia	**1.98** The Delian League takes military actions against Scyros, Eion, Carystus, and Naxos.	
467–65? Pentecontaetia	**1.100–101** Persians defeated. Rebellion of Thasos put down. Athens' attempt to colonize Amphipolis fails.	
466–61 Pentecontaetia	**1.101–2** Athens sends troops to help Sparta defeat a Helot revolt. Sparta sends them home.	**1.101–2** An earthquake prevents Sparta from aiding Thasos and triggers a Helot revolt. Sparta requests, receives, and then rejects Athenian help. Athens renounces her alliance with Sparta.

556

Year/ Season	Attica-Euboea-Boeotia	Peloponnesus Megarid, Cephallenia, Zacynthus, Melos
457–56? Pentecontaetia	**1.103** Athens resettles the Helot rebels in Naupactus. Megara allies herself with Athens.	**1.103** Megara quarrels with Corinth and allies with Athens.
460? Pentecontaetia	**1.104** Athens sends a fleet to aid an Egyptian rebellion against Persia.	
459–58? Pentecontaetia		**1.105–6** An Athenian fleet is repelled at Halieis; another defeats the Peloponnesian fleet at Cecryphalia and besieges Aegina. A reserve army defeats the Corinthians in the Megarid.
457 Pentecontaetia	**1.107** Athens begins the Long Walls. **1.108** A Peloponnesian army defeats the Athenians at Tanagra. Athens defeats the Boeotians at Oenophyta and becomes master of Boeotia. Aegina surrenders.	**1.108** An Athenian fleet raids the Peloponnesus.
454? Pentecontaetia	**1.109–10** Athens' fleet in Egypt is defeated and destroyed	**1.111** An Athenian fleet under Pericles raids Sicyon.
451? Pentecontaetia	**1.112** Athens and Sparta sign a five-year truce. Athens defeats the Persians at Cyprus.	**1.112** Athens and Sparta sign a five-year truce. Athens defeats the Persians at Cyprus.
447–46 Pentecontaetia	**1.113** The Boeotians defeat the Athenians at Coronea, and recover their independence. **1.114–15** Megara and Euboea revolt. A Peloponnesian army invades Attica but turns back.	**1.114–15** Megara revolts, joins Peloponnesian alliance.
446 Pentecontaetia	**1.115** Athens gives up bases in the Megarid and Peloponnesus and concludes a thirty-year peace with Sparta.	**1.115** Sparta and Athens conclude a thirty-year peace treaty.
441–40 Pentecontaetia ends	**1.115–17** Samos and Byzantium revolt. Athens forces Samos to surrender; Byzantium submits.	
432/1 Winter	**1.128** Athens tells the Spartans to drive out the curse of Taenarus. **1.135–38** Flight of Themistocles. **1.139** Further Spartan demands. **1.140–44** Speech of Pericles explains how Athens can win.	**1.119** Meeting of the allies at Sparta. **1.120** Speech of the Corinthians demands action. **1.126** Sparta tells the Athenians to drive out the curse of the Goddess. **1.129–34** The tale of Pausanias and the curse of the Goddess of the Bronze House.
BOOK TWO 431 Summer	**2.1–6** War begins when Thebes launches a surprise attack on Plataea. **2.9** Athenian allies listed. **2.12–17** Athenians abandon Attica and move inside the city walls. **2.18–21** The Peloponnesians invade Attica. **2.22** Pericles prevents the Athenians from sallying out. **2.23–25** An Athenian fleet raids the Peloponnesus. **2.24** Athens sets up an emergency war fund and a reserve fleet. **2.26** An Athenian fleet is sent to protect Euboea and raid Locris; (2.32) it fortifies Atalanta. **2.27** The Athenians expel the Aeginetans and occupy Aegina themselves. **2.32** The Athenians fortify the island of Atalanta.	**2.7–8** Preparing for war, Sparta sends envoys to Persia, asks allies to construct 500 triremes. **2.9** Spartan allies listed. **2.10–11** Speech of Archidamus to the Peloponnesian army assembled at the Isthmus. **2.23** The Peloponnesian army returns home. **2.25** An Athenian fleet raids Laconia, Methone (defended by Brasidas), and Pheia in Elis. **2.27** Exiled from Aegina, the Aeginetans are settled by Sparta in Thyrea. **2.31** Pericles commands the Athenians' first invasion of Megara.
431/0 Winter	**2.34–46** Pericles' funeral oration.	**2.33** Corinthian fleet raids Acarnania and Cephallenia.

Western Hellas Acarnania, Corcyra, Ambracia, Naupactus, Epidamnus, Ionian islands	Thrace Chalcidice, Macedonia, Hellespont, Thessaly	Other Regions Asia, the Aegean, Italy-Sicily
		1.104 Athens sends a fleet to aid an Egyptian rebellion against Persia.
1.107 A Spartan army rescues Doris from Phocis		
1.111 An Athenian fleet under Pericles fails to take Oeniadae.	**1.111** Athens' attempt to install a Thessalian king fails.	**1.109–10** Athens' fleet in Egypt is defeated and destroyed.
1.112 Athens and Sparta vie for control of Delphi.		**1.112** Athens defeats the Persians in Cyprus.
	1.115–17 Byzantium revolts, but later submits to Athens.	**1.115–17** Samos revolts, assisted by Persia, but is forced to surrender after an Athenian siege.
		2.7–8 Sparta orders contributions of money and ships from her allies in Sicily and Italy, and sends an embassy to the Persian King.
		2.28 Eclipse of the sun occurs at the beginning of a new lunar month.
	2.29 The Athenians conclude alliances with Sitalces, king of Odrysian Thrace, and Perdiccas, king of Macedonia.	
2.30 An Athenian fleet raids Acarnania and brings Cephallenia into the Athenian camp without use of force.		
2.33 Acarnania and Cephallenia are aided by the Corinthians.		

Year/ Season	Attica-Euboea-Boeotia	Peloponnesus Megarid, Cephallenia, Zacynthus, Melos
430 Summer	**2.47** The Peloponnesians invade Attica. **2.47–2.54** Plague strikes Athens. **2.55** Again, Pericles prevents the Athenians from sallying out. **2.56** An Athenian fleet raids the Peloponnesus. **2.58** Athenian reinforcements at Potidaea suffer losses from the plague. **2.59** Athenian envoys to Sparta fail to make peace. **2.60–64** Speech of Pericles urges Athens to continue the war. **2.65** Athenians fine Pericles but reelect him general. Thucydides appraises Pericles.	**2.47** The Peloponnesians invade Attica again, ravaging it extensively (2.55) for 40 days before returning (2.57). **2.66** Peloponnesian fleet raids Zacynthus.
430/29 Winter		
429 Summer	**2.71–78** The Peloponnesians assault Plataea. **2.72** Archidamus offers neutrality. **2.74** Plataea decides to remain with Athens. **2.75–78** The Peloponnesian assaults are described.	
429/8 Winter	**2.94** A Peloponnesian raid against Piraeus causes panic in Athens.	**2.93–94** A Peloponnesian fleet attempts a surprise attack against Piraeus, but stops at Salamis.
BOOK THREE **428** Summer	**3.1** The Peloponnesians invade Attica. **3.3** Athens sends a fleet to Lesbos in rebellion. **3.7** An Athenian fleet raids the Peloponnesus. **3.16–7** Athens deploys 100 triremes to deter the Spartans. At this time Athens has 250 triremes at sea. **3.18** Athens sends 1,000 hoplites to besiege Mytilene. **3.19** Athenians levy a special capital tax on themselves for the siege.	**3.1** The Peloponnesians invade Attica. **3.7** Athenian ships under Asopius, son of Phormio, raid the Peloponnesus. **3.8–14** Speech of the Mytilenians to the Peloponnesians at Olympia. **3.15** Sparta allies with Mytilene and prepares a fleet to help her.
428/7 Winter	**3.24** 212 Plataeans escape to Athens.	**3.25** Sparta sends Salaethus to encourage Mytilene.
427 Summer		**3.26** The Peloponnesians invade Attica and despatch a fleet under Alcidas to Lesbos.

Western Hellas	Thrace	Other Regions
Acarnania, Corcyra, Ambracia, Naupactus, Epidamnus, Ionian islands	Chalcidice, Macedonia, Hellespont, Thessaly	Asia, the Aegean, Italy-Sicily
	2.47 Plague appears in Lemnos before Athens.	
	2.58 Athenian reinforcements at Potidaea suffer losses from plague.	
2.68 The Ambraciots attack Amphilochian Argos. Previous Athenian intervention in the area had produced an alliance between Athens and Acarnania.	**2.67** Peloponnesian envoys to the Persian King are captured in Thrace. They are executed without trial at Athens.	
2.69 Athens stations triremes at Naupactus under Phormio.	**2.70** The Potidaeans surrender. They are expelled and replaced by settlers from Athens.	
2.80–82 A Peloponnesian force is defeated at Stratus in Acarnania. **2.83–84**–Phormio's Athenian squadron defeats a Peloponnesian fleet off Patrae. **2.85–8** Speeches of Phormio and Spartan commanders. **2.90–92** Phormio defeats a Peloponnesian fleet near Naupactus.	**2.79** An Athenian expedition in Chalcidice wins a victory at Spartolus but is then defeated by peltasts and cavalry.	
2.102–3 Phormio raids hostile cities in Acarnania.		**2.95–101** Sitalces launches his Thracian army at Macedonia and Chalcidice.
3.7 The Athenian Asopius is killed leading a raid on Leucas.		**3.2–6** Lesbos revolts. Mytilene sends envoys to Sparta for help. An Athenian fleet blockades Mytilene by sea.
		3.18 Athenian hoplites arrive at Mytilene under Paches to blockade the city by land. **3.19** Troops from an Athenian squadron collecting tribute are defeated in Caria.
3.20–24 212 Plataeans break out of Peloponnesian siege works, escape to Athens.		**3.25** The Spartan Salaethus arrives at Mytilene.
		3.27–28 The Mytilenian commons, armed by Salaethus, force him to surrender the city to the Athenians. **3.29–33** A Peloponnesian fleet reaches Ionia, learns of Mytilene's fall, and flees. **3.34–35** Paches takes Notium by trick, recaptures Lesbos.

Year/ Season	Attica-Euboea-Boeotia	Peloponnesus Megarid, Cephallenia, Zacynthus, Melos
427 Summer *(cont'd)*	**3.36–50** Mytilenian debate. **3.37–40** Speech of Cleon. **3.41–48** Speech of Diodotus. **3.49** The Athenians vote to reduce the punishment of Mytilene. They send a boat which arrives (**3.50**) just in time to prevent a massacre. **3.51** The Athenians capture the island of Minoa near Megara. **3.52–68** Plataea surrenders. **3.53–60** Speech of the Plataeans. **3.61–67** Speech of the Thebans. **3.68** The Spartans condemn the Plataeans to death. **3.86** Athens sends a squadron to Rhegium in Sicily.	**3.51** The Athenians capture the island of Minoa near Megara. **3.69** The Peloponnesian fleet arrives at Cyllene, is strengthened, and sails for Corcyra.
427/6 Winter	**3.87** Plague returns to Athens.	
426 Summer	**3.89** Earthquakes in the Isthmus turn back a Peloponnesian invasion of Attica. A tidal wave occurs near Euboea. **3.91** After ravaging Melos, an Athenian fleet sails to Oropus from which its troops march to Tanagra to join other forces coming from Athens.	**3.89** Earthquakes in the Isthmus turn back a Peloponnesian invasion of Attica. **3.91** An Athenian fleet raids Melos. **3.92** Sparta founds Heraclea. ***3.100** The Aetolians send envoys to Corinth and Sparta to urge a combined attack on Naupactus.
426/5 Winter	**3.104** Athenians purify Delos. **3.114** Demosthenes returns from Amphilochia in triumph. **3.115** Athens votes to send reinforcements to Sicily.	

*Although the Aetolian-Peloponnesian assault on Naupactus (**3.101–2**) is preceded in the narrative by the description of Demosthenes' invasion of Aetolia (**3.94**), Thucydides makes it clear that the Aetolians had requested and persuaded the Peloponnesians to join in such an assault prior to Demosthenes' invasion (**3.100**). He also reports that the Aetolians were aware of Demosthenes' plan from its conception (**3.96.3**). Thus the text does not permit us to say which decision was made first; either side could plausibly have designed its move to preempt the other, and both plans could have been developed, whether independently or not, quite simultaneously.

Western Hellas	Thrace	Other Regions
Acarnania, Corcyra, Ambracia, Naupactus, Epidamnus, Ionian islands	Chalcidice, Macedonia, Hellespont, Thessaly	Asia, the Aegean, Italy-Sicily

		3.49–50 The second boat reaches Mytilene in time to prevent execution of all adult males. Athens executes 1,000 revolt leaders, destroys city walls, allots Lesbian land to Athenian holders.
3.70–73 Revolutionary civil war breaks out in Corcyra. **3.74** The oligarchs are defeated. **3.75** The Athenian Nicostratus tries to arrange a truce. **3.76–79** The Peloponnesian fleet arrives and defeats the Corcyraeans. **3.80** The Peloponnesian ships leave when warned of an approaching Athenian fleet. **3.81** The Corcyraean people massacre their domestic foes. **3.82–85** Thucydides describes the revolution.		
		3.86 The Athenians establish themselves at Rhegium.
		3.88 The Athenians raid the Aeolian islands.
3.91 Athenian triremes sail to Naupactus.		**3.90** Athenians capture Mylae and Messana in Sicily.
3.94 Demosthenes raids Leucas. *__3.94–95__ Demosthenes decides to attack Aetolia. **3.96–98** An Athenian force is routed at Aegitium in Aetolia. **3.100–1** A Peloponnesian army to help the Aetolians assembles under Eurylochus at Delphi. **3.102** Acarnanian troops arrive at Naupactus in time to thwart Eurylochus' assault.	**3.92–93** Heraclea in Trachis is founded by Sparta.	**3.99** Athenians attack Locris in Italy.
3.105–6 The Ambraciots attack Amphilochia, aided by a Peloponnesian army. **3.107–12** Acarnanians and Athenians under Demosthenes aid the Amphilochians and win battles by ambush and surprise at Olpae and Idomene. **3.114** The Amphilochians and Ambracians make peace.		**3.103** Athenians attack Inessa unsuccessfully. Later they raid Locris.
		3.115 Athenians raid Himera and Locris. **3.116** Mount Etna erupts.

563

BOOK FOUR

425 Summer	**4.2** Athens' fleet to Sicily departs with orders to stop at Corcyra and to allow Demosthenes to use the fleet as it rounds the Peloponnesus. **4.6** The Peloponnesian army in Attica marches home after learning of the Athenian fort at Pylos.	**4.2** Peloponnesians invade Attica. A Peloponnesian fleet sails to Corcyra. **4.3–5** The Athenian fleet destined for Sicily fortifies Pylos.
		4.8 Spartans arrive at Pylos to assault and blockade the fort. **4.9–12** Spartan assaults against Pylos from land and sea do not succeed. **4.13–14** The Athenian fleet returns to Pylos and routs the Peloponnesian fleet, marooning a Spartan force on Sphacteria. **4.15–16** Requesting and receiving a truce, Spartan envoys sail to Athens.
	4.17–22 Speech of the Spartan envoys from Pylos to the Athenians. **4.22** Led by Cleon, the Athenians turn down the Spartan offers.	**4.23** Negotiations fail; hostilities resume at Pylos.
	4.27–29 Cleon is chosen to command at Pylos.	**4.26** Helots bring food to the garrison.
	4.41 The Spartans fail to negotiate peace or the return of the men from Pylos. **4.42** An Athenian expedition under Nicias raids Corinth.	**4.30–40** The Athenians invade Sphacteria and defeat the Spartans, forcing them to surrender. **4.41** Messenians raid Laconia from Pylos. Spartan attempts to negotiate peace fail. **4.42–45** Corinth defends against raid by an Athenian fleet.
425/4 Winter		
424 Summer		**4.53–57** An Athenian fleet under Nicias conquers Cythera and raids Thyrea. Sparta organizes defensive units of archers and cavalry.
	4.65 The Athenian generals returning from Sicily are punished.	**4.67–72** The Athenians attack Megara by surprise and occupy Nisea, but (**4.73**) fail to attack a rapidly assembled Peloponnesian and Theban force under Brasidas. **4.74** Megara remains a Peloponnesian ally; pro-Athenian Megarians flee. Some who do not are executed.
	4.76 Athenians plot with Boeotian factions to establish democracy in Boeotia.	
	4.82 Athens declares war on Perdiccas.	**4.80** Spartan atrocities against Helots are recounted.
424/3 Winter	**4.89–90** Athens' assault against Boeotia is betrayed and goes awry, but they fortify Delium. **4.91–96** The Boeotians defeat the Athenians in the field. **4.100–101** The Boeotians retake Delium by storm.	**4.101** Demosthenes' raid on Sicyon fails.
	4.108 Athens is alarmed by the fall of Amphipolis.	**4.109** The Megarians recapture and raze their long walls.

Western Hellas Acarnania, Corcyra, Ambracia, Naupactus, Epidamnus, Ionian islands	Thrace Chalcidice, Macedonia, Hellespont, Thessaly	Other Regions Asia, the Aegean, Italy-Sicily
		4.1 Messana revolts and a Syracusan and Locrian fleet occupy the city. Locrian forces ravage Rhegium.
4.2 Civil strife on Corcyra causes famine in the city. The Peloponnesian fleet sails to Corcyra.		
4.8 The Peloponnesian fleet is recalled from Corcyra to Pylos.	**4.7** An Athenian expedition takes an unknown Eion in Thrace but is soon driven out.	
		4.24–25 Indecisive fighting at Messana, Rhegium, and Naxos.
4.46–48 Arriving at Corcyra from Pylos, Athenian forces end civil strife there by helping the popular faction to capture its domestic foes and permitting it to annihilate them. **4.49** Athenians and Acarnanians capture Anactorium by treachery.		
	4.50 A Persian envoy to Sparta is captured by Athenians at Eion in Thrace.	**4.51** Chios demolishes its new city wall at the command of Athens.
		4.52 An eclipse of the sun occurs. Lesbian exiles capture Antandrus.
		4.58 Sicilians assemble at Gela. **4.59–64** Speech of Hermocrates. The Sicilians decide to end the war in Sicily. **4.65** The Athenians sail home from Sicily.
		4.75 An Athenian squadron collecting tribute prevents Lesbian exiles from fortifying Antandrus. Another squadron loses its ships at anchor to a river flood at Heraclea on Pontus. They return through Bythinia.
4.77 The Acarnanians compel Oeniadae to join their alliance with Athens. Demosthenes subdues Agraea.	**4.79–80** Brasidas marches rapidly through Thessaly to Macedonia and Thrace.	
	4.83 Brasidas makes peace in Lyncestis. **4.84–88** Brasidas persuades Acanthus to revolt from Athens.	
	4.101 Sitalces dies. **4.102–6** Brasidas captures Amphipolis. **4.107** Thucydides saves Eion.	
	4.109 The cities of Acte submit to Brasidas. **4.110–16** Brasidas takes Torone by treachery and audacity.	

Year/Season	Attica-Euboea-Boeotia	Peloponnesus Megarid, Cephallenia, Zacynthus, Melos
423 Summer	**4.116–19** Athens and Sparta agree to a one-year truce.	**4.116–19** Sparta and Athens agree to a one-year truce.
	4.129 Athens sends an expedition to retake Mende and Scione.	
	4.133 Thebes dismantles the walls of Thespiae.	**4.133** The temple of Hera at Argos burns down.
423/2 Winter		**4.134** Mantineans and Tegeans fight at Laodicium.
BOOK FIVE **422** Summer	**5.1** The truce ends. Athens expels the Delians from Delos to Atramyttium. **5.2–3** Athens sends an expedition under Cleon to Thrace. **5.3** The Boeotians take Panactum in Attica by treachery.	**5.1** The truce ends.
422/1 Winter	**5.14–19** Sparta and Athens sign a treaty of peace. **5.21–24** Sparta and Athens sign a treaty of alliance.	**5.14–19** Sparta and Athens sign a treaty of peace. **5.21–24** Sparta and Athens sign a treaty of alliance.
421 Summer		**5.27–29** Reactions of Corinth, Argos, Mantinea, and Elis to Sparta's alliance with Athens. **5.30** Sparta complains to Corinth. **5.31** Elis allies with Corinth and Argos. **5.32** Tegea retains its Spartan alliance. Corinth fails to persuade Boeotia to ally with Argos. **5.33** Sparta liberates Arcadian subjects of Mantinea. **5.35** Athens withdraws the Messenians from Pylos.
	5.32 The Athenians retake Scione and resettle the Plataeans there. Obeying the god of Delphi, Athens permits the Delians to return to Delos. **5.35** At Spartan request, Athens withdraws the Messenians from Pylos.	
421/0 Winter	**5.36–38** After Sparta and Boeotia fail to ally with Argos, they join in a separate alliance (**5.39**). **5.39** The Boeotians raze Panactum.	**5.36–38** After Sparta and Boeotia fail to ally with Argos, they join in a separate alliance (**5.39**).
420 Summer	**5.43–47** Alcibiades outwits the Spartan envoys and creates an alliance of Athens, Argos, Mantinea, and Elis.	**5.43–47** Spartan envoys are tricked by Alcibiades, who creates an anti-Spartan alliance in the Peloponnesus. **5.49–50** Elis excludes Sparta from Olympic games because of their quarrel over Lepreum.
420/19 Winter	**5.51** Heraclea-in-Trachis is defeated by its neighbors.	
419 Summer	**5.52** Boeotians occupy Heraclea-in-Trachis. Alcibiades marches a small force through the Peloponnesus.	**5.52** Alcibiades marches through the Peloponnesus. **5.53–55** War begins between Argos and Epidaurus.
419/8 Winter	**5.56** Athens returns the Messenians to Pylos at Argive request.	**5.56** The Messenians return to Pylos. Argos tries again to take Epidaurus.
418 Summer		**5.57-60** Spartans and allies surround the Argives near Argos, but grant them a truce and go home. **5.61–63** Alcibiades persuades Argos to renounce the truce and attack Orchomenos and Tegea. **5.64–75** Sparta defeats the Argive alliance in a battle at Mantinea.

Western Hellas Acarnania, Corcyra, Ambracia, Naupactus, Epidamnus, Ionian islands	Thrace Chalcidice, Macedonia, Hellespont, Thessaly	Other Regions Asia, the Aegean, Italy-Sicily
	4.120–1 Scione revolts, joins Brasidas before he knows of the truce. **4.123** Mende revolts, is received by Brasidas though he now knows of the truce. **4.124–28** Brasidas joins the Macedonians against Lyncestis. **4.129-31** Athenians retake Mende. They defeat the Scionaeans and besiege the city. **4.132** Macedonia makes peace with Athens and prevents Spartan reinforcements from marching through Thessaly.	
	4.135 Brasidas' attempt to recapture Potidaea fails.	
		5.1 The Delians are expelled by Athens from Delos to Atramyttium.
	5.2–3 Cleon takes an Athenian army to Thrace. He recaptures Torone.	
		5.4–5 Sicily-Italy; Phaeax, Athens' envoy to Sicily and Italy, fails to create an anti-Syracusan coalition. Locris makes peace with Athens.
	5.6–11 Cleon advances to Amphipolis but is defeated by Brasidas' audacious attack. Both generals are killed. **5.12–13** Spartan reinforcements for Thrace delay at Heraclea.	
		5.20 Thucydides discusses his method of dating by year and season rather than by magistrates' names.
	5.26 Thucydides describes how he continued to write his history from exile.	
5.32 The god of Delphi orders Athens to permit the Delians to return to Delos.	**5.32** The Athenians retake Scione; they execute the adult males and enslave the women and children. The Plataeans settle Scione. **5.35** The Dians take Thyssus on Acte.	
	5.39 The Olynthians take Mecyberna from the Athenians.	
	5.52 Boeotians occupy Heraclea-in-Trachis.	

568

Western Hellas Acarnania, Corcyra, Ambracia, Naupactus, Epidamnus, Ionian islands	Thrace Chalcidice, Macedonia, Hellespont, Thessaly	Other Regions Asia, the Aegean, Italy-Sicily
	5.83 An Athenian fleet blockades Macedonia.	
	6.7 The Athenians raid Macedonia.	**6.2–5** Thucydides describes the history of the Greek settlement of Sicily. **6.6** Egestan sends envoys to request Athenian help against Selinus.
6.42 The Athenian expedition for Sicily assembles at Corcyra. **6.43** Thucydides describes its forces.		**6.33–41** Hermocrates and Athenagoras and a Syracusan general give speeches at Syracuse discussing how their city should prepare for the approaching Athenian expedition. **6.44–51** Athenian fleet gets a cool reception in Italy. It stops at Rhegium, where the discovery of Egestan poverty leads to a policy debate. It finally finds a base at Catana. **6.60–61** Alcibiades is recalled from Sicily but escapes at Thurii. **6.62** Athenians take Hyccara and sell its inhabitants into slavery.
		6.63–70 The Syracusans are enticed to Catana while the Athenians sail to Syracuse. **6.70** The Athenian army wins the battle at the Anapus river that occurs when the Syracusans return, but not decisively. The Athenians send home for reinforcements. **6.73–75** Syracuse sends to Corinth and Sparta for help, and constructs new walls and forts. **6.74** An Athenian attack on Messana is betrayed by Alcibiades and fails. **6.75–88** After speeches by Hermocrates (**6.75–80**) and Euphemus (**6.82–87**) at Camarina, Camarina decides to remain neutral.

Year/Season	Attica-Euboea-Boeotia	Peloponnesus Megarid, Cephallenia, Zacynthus, Melos
415/4 Winter *(cont'd)*	**6.93** Athens votes funds and reinforcements to Sicily.	**6.88–93** Syracusan requests for aid are approved at Corinth but initially rejected by Sparta. However, after Alcibiades' speech to them (**6.89–92**), the Spartans decide to send a general (Gylippus) to Syracuse and to renew the war with Athens by fortifying Decelea.
414 Summer	**6.95** A democratic uprising in Thespiae fails.	**6.95** Spartans invade Argos, but are turned back by an earthquake. The Argives plunder Thyrea.
	6.105 Athens joins the fighting between Argos and Sparta.	**6.105** Spartans invade Argos. The Athenians assist Argos by raiding Spartan territory, providing a pretext for Sparta to renew the war with Athens.

BOOK SEVEN

Year/Season	Attica-Euboea-Boeotia	Peloponnesus Megarid, Cephallenia, Zacynthus, Melos
414 Summer		
414/3 Winter	**7.10–15** Nicias' letter is received and debated at Athens. **7.16–17** The Athenians decide to send him large reinforcements and new generals. **7.20** As Demosthenes prepares to depart for Sicily with reinforcements, another Athenian fleet is sent to raid the Peloponnesus. **7.27–28** Athenian hardships are caused by Decelea. **7.29–30** Mycalessus is destroyed by Thracian Dii.	**7.18–19** Sparta prepares for war with Athens. Sparta invades Attica and fortifies Decelea. Peloponnesian reinforcements leave for Sicily. **7.26** Athenians fortify an isthmus of Laconia and pillage Spartan territory.
413 Summer		**7.34** An inconclusive naval battle takes place off Erineus in Achaea between a Peloponnesian fleet with reinforced prows and the Athenian squadron from Naupactus.
413 Winter		

Western Hellas	Thrace	Other Regions
Acarnania, Corcyra, Ambracia, Naupactus, Epidamnus, Ionian islands	Chalcidice, Macedonia, Hellespont, Thessaly	Asia, the Aegean, Italy-Sicily

		6.94 Operations of the Athenians in Sicily at Megara, Centoripa, Inessa, and Hybla.
		6.96–103 The Athenians sail to Syracuse. They occupy Epipolae and construct circumvallation walls. Syracusan efforts to stop them or to build counterwalls are defeated. The Syracusans begin to despair.
6.104 Gylippus leaves Leucas.		**6.104** Gylippus arrives in Italy.
		7.1–2 Gylippus marches from Himera to Syracuse, arriving just in time to save Syracuse.
		7.3 The Syracusans capture Labdalum.
		7.4–7 The Athenians fortify Plemmyrium. Gylippus and the Syracusans are defeated in the first of two battles, but by exploiting Syracusan cavalry in the second, he gains a victory. A Syracusan crosswall passes the Athenian wall and the Athenians are forced on the defensive.
	7.9 The Athenians and their allies attempt to take Amphipolis but fail.	**7.8** Nicias writes home asking for large reinforcements or for permission to withdraw.
		7.21 Gylippus persuades the Syracusans to build and train a fleet.
		7.22–25 While the Syracusan navy is fighting and losing its first battle (**7.23–24**), the army takes the Athenian forts at Plemmyrium.
7.31 Athenians sail to Acarnania gathering forces. They send triremes to reinforce Naupactus.		**7.32** Sicels ambush the Syracusan reinforcements.
		7.36–41 The Syracusans win a naval battle.
		7.42–45 Athenian reinforcements arrive. Demosthenes' night assault on Epipolae fails.
		7.47–49 Demosthenes wants an immediate withdrawal, but Nicias demurs.
		7.50 An eclipse of the moon causes the Athenians to delay their withdrawal.
		7.52 The Syracusans win another naval battle.
		7.57–58 Thucydides lists the nationality and tribe of all the participants on either side, and describes how they became involved in the struggle.
		7.61–68 Speeches of Nicias and Gylippus in preparation for a final naval battle.
		7.69–72 The Athenian fleet is decisively defeated.
		7.73–85 An Athenian attempt to march north to Catana is blocked by the Syracusans. Returning south, the Athenians are pursued, harassed, and finally forced to surrender at the Assinarus river.
		7.86–87 The prisoners are confined in quarries, where many die.

Year/ Season	Attica-Euboea-Boeotia Peloponnesus Western Hellas	Samos
BOOK EIGHT **413/2** Winter	**8.1–4** Though shocked by the Sicilian disaster, the Athenians vote to build more ships, secure their allies, and continue the war. The Peloponnesians plan a decisive effort against Athens. **8.5** The Spartan king Agis at Decelea receives envoys of Euboea and Lesbos who wish to discuss revolt. Chios and Tissaphernes sends envoys to Sparta to discuss aid for revolt against Athens. **8.6** Pharnabazus sends envoys to ask for a fleet to the Hellespont.	
412 Summer	**8.7–8** The Peloponnesians haul 21 triremes across the Isthmus to the Aegean. They make plans to conquer Athenian subjects in Asia. **8.10–11** An Athenian fleet drives a Peloponnesian fleet into Spiraeum and blockades it there. **8.13** A Peloponnesian squadron returning from Sicily loses one ship in battle with Athenian ships off Leucas. **8.15** Athens reacts strongly to the Chian revolt. The 1,000 talent reserve fund is used to equip a new fleet.	
		8.16 The first Athenian forces arrive in the area.
	8.20 The Peloponnesian fleet at Spiraeum sails out, defeats the Athenians, and returns to Cenchreae.	
		8.21 With Athenian help, the commons on Samos overthrow the upper classes.
		8.23–27 After the Athenians counter-attack at Lesbos, Chios, and Miletus, the arrival of a large enemy fleet causes the general Phrynichus to order his fleet to retire to Samos.
	8.25 1,500 Argive hoplites participate with Athenians in a battle at Miletus.	
412/1 Winter		**8.30** Receiving reinforcements, the Athenians plan to blockade both Miletus and Chios.
	8.53–54 Pro-oligarch envoys from the army at Samos try to persuade the Athenian assembly to establish an oligarchy.	
	8.60 Boeotians capture Oropus by treachery. They ask the Peloponnesians at Rhodes to assist a revolt by Euboea but the latter decide to rescue Chios first.	

Chios-Sardis	Miletus and Asia South	Lesbos, Hellespont, Other
8.5 Chios and Tissaphernes send envoys to discuss aid for a revolt against Athens.		
		8.6 Pharnabazus sends envoys to ask that a fleet be sent to the Hellespont.
8.14 Alcibiades and Chalcideus arrive in Chios and incite the island to revolt.		
8.16–19 A Peloponnesian fleet from Chios incites Teos, Lebedos, Aerae, and Miletus to revolt.	**8.16–17** As Athenian forces arrive in the area, a Peloponnesian fleet from Chios incites Miletus to revolt.	
8.20 Tissaphernes completes the demolition of Teos' wall.	**8.18** The Spartans and the Persians complete their first draft of a treaty of alliance.	**8.18** The Spartans and the Persians complete their first draft of a treaty of alliance.
8.22 A Chian-Peloponnesian squadron causes revolts at Clazomenae and Cyme.		**8.22** A Chian-Peloponnesian squadron causes revolts at Clazomenae and Cyme.
8.23–27 The Athenians counterattack and blockade Chios.		**8.23** The Athenians recover Lesbos.
	8.25 The Athenians raid Milesian territory and win a battle there, but then retire to Samos when a large Peloponnesian fleet approaches.	**8.28** At Tissaphernes' request, the Peloponnesian fleet from Miletus captures Iasus and the rebel Amorges.
	8.29 Tissaphernes pays the Peloponnesian fleet but decides in future to pay less.	
	8.35 An Athenian squadron captures six enemy triremes off Cnidus and almost takes the city before retiring to Samos.	
	8.36–37 Sparta and Persia conclude a second treaty draft.	
	8.39 27 Peloponnesian triremes reach Miletus via Melos, Crete, and Caunus.	
	8.41–42 The Peloponnesian fleet under Astyochus sails from Miletus to Cnidus, from which he defeats an Athenian squadron near Syme.	
	8.43 The Spartan commissioners quarrel with Tissaphernes.	
	8.44 The Peloponnesian fleet sails to Rhodes, whose cities revolt.	
8.47–51 Alcibiades tells the Athenians on Samos that Persia will support them if Athens becomes an oligarchy. Phrynichus objects, and he and Alcibiades duel with letters and counter-letters to the Spartans.	**8.45–6** Alcibiades escapes to Tissaphernes and advises him to let both sides exhaust each other.	
8.53–54 Pro-oligarchic envoys are sent from the army at Samos to try to persuade the Athenian assembly to establish an oligarchy.	**8.56–58** Athenian negotiations with Tissaphernes fail. Sparta and Tissaphernes conclude their treaty of alliance.	
	8.60 The Boeotians ask the Peloponnesians at Rhodes to assist a revolt by Euboea but the Peloponnesians decide to rescue Chios first.	

573

Year/ Season	Attica-Euboea-Boeotia Peloponnesus Western Hellas	Samos
411 Summer		

<table>
<tr>
<td></td>
<td></td>
<td>8.63–64 The main Athenian fleet remains at Samos. The pro-oligarchs in the army send envoys to create an oligarchy at subject cities and at Athens.</td>
</tr>
<tr>
<td></td>
<td>8.64–70 Athenian democracy falls, weakened by assassination and intimidation. The new regime of the Four Hundred rules by force; it sends envoys to Agis with notice of its desire for peace, but they are rejected.
8.71 Agis responds negatively to the overtures of the Four Hundred.</td>
<td></td>
</tr>
<tr>
<td></td>
<td></td>
<td>8.73–76 At Samos, local democrats and pro-democratic Athenians from the army defeat an oligarchic plot. After learning of the fall of the democracy at Athens, the army chooses new generals and vows to fight both the Four Hundred and the Spartans.</td>
</tr>
<tr>
<td></td>
<td></td>
<td>8.80 The Athenians send ships from Samos back to the Hellespont.
8.81–82 The Athenians on Samos recall Alcibiades and elect him general.</td>
</tr>
<tr>
<td></td>
<td></td>
<td>8.88 Alcibiades sails for Caunus.</td>
</tr>
<tr>
<td></td>
<td>8.89–94 Worried by opposition from the army in Samos, the Four Hundred send envoys to Sparta to make peace. Phrynichus is murdered in the agora. A faction of the Four Hundred led by Theramenes, fearing a betrayal to the Spartans, destroys the wall being built in Eetionia. Despite this civil strife, the Athenians unite against an approaching enemy fleet.
8.95–98 A hastily assembled Athenian fleet is defeated off Euboea by a Peloponnesian fleet assisted by Euboean treachery in Eritrea. Euboea revolts, causing panic at Athens, which leads to the restoration of the democracy. Some of the Four Hundred flee to Agis. One of them helps the Boeotians to capture the fort of Oenoe.</td>
<td></td>
</tr>
<tr>
<td></td>
<td></td>
<td>8.100 Learning of the departure of the Peloponnesian fleet, the Athenian fleet leaves Samos for the Hellespont.</td>
</tr>
<tr>
<td></td>
<td></td>
<td>8.108 Alcibiades returns to Samos, claiming to have kept the Phoenician fleet from joining the enemy.</td>
</tr>
</table>

574

8.61 The Chians attack their besiegers but fail to break out.

8.62 An Athenian fleet under Strombichides leaves Chios to counter the Peloponnesians in the Hellespont.

8.62 A Peloponnesian army reaches the Hellespont and, with Pharnabazus, captures Abydos and Lampsacus. An Athenian fleet commanded by Strombichides retakes Lampsacus.

8.78–79 Tissaphernes and Astyochus are strongly criticized by the Peloponnesian sailors at Miletus. The Peloponnesian fleet challenges the Athenians at Samos but draws back after learning Athenian reinforcements have arrived from the Hellespont.

8.79 Strombichides is summoned back to join the main fleet at Samos.

8.80 The Peloponnesians send ships to the Hellespont in response to Pharnabazus' offer to pay them.

8.80 The Peloponnesians send ships to the Hellespont in response to Pharnabazus' offer to pay them. Byzantium revolts.

8.84 Thurian and Syracusan sailors demand their pay from Astyochus.

8.87 The Phoenician fleet appears at Aspendus, where Tissaphernes joins it, promising to bring it into the struggle, but it advances no further.

8.99 The Peloponnesian fleet leaves Miletus for the Hellespont.

8.101 The Peloponnesian fleet stops at Chios before continuing north.

8.100 The Athenian fleet sails from Samos to Lesbos but misses the Peloponnesian fleet.

8.102 The Peloponnesian fleet avoids the Athenian fleet at Lesbos.

8.103–7 The Athenian fleet sails to the Hellespont where the fleets join battle off Point Cynossema. The Peloponnesian fleet is defeated, but not decisively.

8.109 Tissaphernes hurries to the Hellespont.

APPENDIX A

The Athenian Government in Thucydides

§1. Athens was the chief population center in Attica, an area about the size of Rhode Island, bounded east and south by the Aegean Sea, and north and west by Boeotia and Megara. Other centers within the state included Piraeus (the chief port), Eleusis, Acharnae, Rhamnous, Thoricus, and Marathon.[1a] Some three to four hundred thousand people lived in Attica, most of them crowded behind the walls of Athens during the Peloponnesian War but otherwise spread out in lesser centers and on individual farms. Of the total population, thirty thousand or so had full rights as citizens at the beginning of the war, which is to say they were males over thirty years of age born of two Athenian parents.

§2. A citizen belonged to one of the four classes defined and named by the law-giver Solon early in the sixth century: the criterion was annual income, expressed in terms of agricultural units or other capabilities. At the top were the *pentacosiomedimnoi,* men who had five hundred measures (wet or dry) of produce a year. Next were the *knights* (three hundred measures), who could afford to keep a horse. Below these were the *zeugitai* or yokefellows (two hundred measures), and last were the *thetes,* who even into the fourth century endured certain limitations in the recognition of their civil status. The rest of the population consisted of women; children; resident aliens (*metics*), whose numbers fluctuated between ten and forty thousand depending on how many foreigners happened to be in residence at a given time; and slaves, whose number has been estimated at 150,000. Women, even those who could be identified as fully Athenian, had no vote in courts or assemblies. Indeed, respectable women were not supposed to appear in public except in duly approved processions.[2a] Only as an heiress could a woman in some sense control property, although she could not dispose of an estate. Metics could prosper in Athens, but like women they had to have a citizen represent them if they ever had business before a court or assembly. Despite their lack of citizenship, many metics were involved in commerce and some grew rich as manufacturers, merchants, and bankers. Slaves did almost every kind of work. Some wore out their lives in painful

A1a Piraeus, Eleusis, Acharnae, Rhamnous, Thoricus, and Marathon: Appendix A Map.

A2a See Pericles' advice to war widows at 2.45.2.

577

APPENDIX A MAP

and dangerous underground work in silver mines at Laurium,[2b] others labored in the fields, and still others performed relatively light duties as household staff. Some were public functionaries, prostitutes, or teachers; more than a few were skilled artisans[2c] whose earnings might someday permit them to purchase their freedom. When a slave was dedicated to a god, he became a free man.

§3. In modern terms the granting of full citizen rights to less than 10 percent of the population would hardly qualify a constitution to be called democratic, but in the ancient Greek world the extension of the franchise to that many adult males was extraordinarily democratic. This "radical" democracy at Athens developed in the first half of the fifth century, after appointment by lot had been established for members of the council and (in 487/6) for the chief administrative officers of the state, and when (in 462) popular courts, manned by citizens who were paid to pronounce justice, had gained a wide jurisdiction. Kleisthenes, an aristocrat, prepared the way for democracy when in 507 he replaced a venerable aristocratic system of four clans with one based on a more or less arbitrarily defined set of ten tribes named after eponymous heroes. By this constitutional reform, he increased the general citizen population and weakened the power of the few.

§4. After Kleisthenes, an Athenian's civic identity was fixed in his *deme*, a geographically defined administrative district, one of 140 in Attica. A father introduced his son formally to his fellow *demesmen* when the son reached eighteen years of age, and on that occasion the son was enrolled in the deme register as a citizen. An Athenian's full official name included his own name, his father's name, and his deme name (e.g., Thucydides son of Oloros, of the deme Halimous). Besides belonging to a deme, he was a member of one of the ten tribes devised by Kleisthenes. Membership in a brotherhood called a *phratry* was desirable but probably not a necessary condition of citizenship. Citizens were landowners; resident aliens and slaves were not. A small landowner might nevertheless work his land alongside the single slave or two he could afford to own. Citizens likewise worked for equal pay alongside slaves and metics on public construction projects.

§5. The tribes were the basis of civic administration at Athens, where a council (*boule*) consisting of five hundred citizens—fifty from each tribe chosen annually by lot—would prepare an agenda for the assembly (*ekklesia*). They served for one year, and they were not permitted to serve more than twice in that office. For thirty-five or thirty-six days, that is, one tenth of the civic year, each of these bodies of fifty acted as the city's standing executive committee (the *prytany*). Each prytany was responsible for the sacred treasuries and kept watch twenty-four hours a day in the Tholos, a round building on the west side of the agora just south of the council chamber (the *Bouleuterion*) where the council conducted its meetings.[5a] Every day a different member of the prytany was chosen by lot to serve as its chairman (*epistates*). Besides preparing an agenda for meetings of the assembly, the council might interview foreign ambassadors, assign various tasks and contracts (for construction and the like), and authorize pay for services and materials.

A2b Laurium: see Appendix A Map.
A2c Cf. Thucydides' estimates in 7.27.5 that twenty thousand Athenian slaves, many of whom were skilled artisans, had deserted or escaped.

A5a The remains of the Tholos and the council chamber have been located in the Athenian *agora* (see Glossary), where they can be seen today.

§6. Generally speaking, whatever civic tasks Athenians assigned to a committee were performed by citizens who had been chosen by lot and not by special capacity or training to do that committee's work. The nine chief administrative officers (*archons*) of the city were (in the order in which they are usually listed): archon eponymous (who gives his name to the year), king, *polemarch,* and six *Thesmothetai.* The titles "king" and "polemarch," or "war magistrate," later prompted Greek writers to record tales about an early transfer of power from an attenuated line of kings to the aristocracy. The historicity of this transfer, however, is not clear. *Thesmothetai,* to judge from the name, were concerned initially with legislation and continued to act in the administration of justice. The underlying supposition behind the Athenians' unremitting use of the lot to assign tasks and responsibilities was that every citizen could do what was necessary. The tasks accordingly were made simple.

§7. Generals and treasurers, however, were appointed not by lot, but by election, as it was manifestly dangerous to simplify responsibilities so that persons of indifferent quality could be qualified to hold those offices. Ten generals, one from each tribe, were elected every year for annual terms, and they could be reelected without interruption. No order of precedence or assigned area of authority such as is attested for the fourth century is visible in the fifth century, but when two or more generals went along on an expedition, it would seem that one was designated as being in charge. A general had authority to convene extraordinary meetings of the assembly, and a decision to call or not call a meeting at critical times could be full of consequence. The means by which Pericles, for instance, prevented such a meeting from being called (2.22.1) is not clear; it may have had to do with his own personal authority.

§8. The assembly met regularly four times during each prytany,[8a] usually on a hillside called the Pnyx[8b] a little west of the agora. This gathering of six thousand or more citizens was the final arbiter of any and all business brought before it, and debated all major decisions of state such as whether or not to go to war, sign a treaty, embark on a new campaign, send an embassy, receive envoys, raise and assign forces, or levy or dispose of funds, with all that such decisions entail. One question that recurred during the fifth century at a regular interval, namely, during the sixth prytany of the year, was whether or not to hold an *ostracism.* The issue was private, personal power. A man who was felt to have amassed too much of it was "ostracized," that is, sent into honorable exile for ten years, after which he could return and reclaim his property and his political rights. Although the assembly was scheduled to meet at least four times a prytany, it could meet as often as was deemed necessary. A different president chaired the meeting every day. Motions were introduced, and speakers advocated, modified, or contested what was proposed. The speakers were citizens who for one reason or another—training, natural ability, political climate—could persuade their fellow citizens to vote as they recommended. Pericles was one such speaker, Cleon another. There was no authority higher than

A8a I.e., four times every five weeks or so, or at least forty times per year given one prytany per year for each of ten tribes.

A8b Pnyx: Map 6.56. See 8.97.1. Note, however, that certain assemblies were convened elsewhere; see 8.67.2, 8.93.3, and 8.97.1.

this assembly. The people voted by raising their hands, and their determinations were final, unless, as in the Mytilenian debate (3.36–50), they themselves reversed them.

§9. The administration of justice was likewise in the hands of citizens, who acted in most questions as *dikasts*[9a] in two separate and distinct systems. Certain officials such as generals had summary powers of judgment in some cases, and the assembly could initiate one form of prosecution called *eisangelia,* but for the most part citizens as dikasts heard trials in courts. A homicide might be tried in one of five different venues, where specially designated citizens judged. Most legal cases, however, came before one of the five popular (or *heliastic*) courts, which drew on a pool of about six thousand citizens who were selected by lot, assigned to a single court for one year, and paid to judge in panels that numbered (according to the sums involved or the seriousness of the alleged offense) two hundred, four hundred, five hundred, one thousand, or even six thousand. Athenians saw these panels as representing the city as a whole; pay for service allowed poor citizens to participate, and appointment by lot affirmed a random mix. The combination of selection by lot and voting by secret ballot helped to keep bribes, threats, and other inappropriate influences from affecting judicial decisions. Since the city was the ultimate judging body, there was no form of appeal to a higher tribunal. As a corollary to this conception, a number of prosecutions and convictions, such as that of Alcibiades (6.28.2–29.3; 6.61.1,4;), may have reflected politics or public opinion more than judiciary fairness. Trials might be won or lost by eloquence. Speeches for the prosecution and the defense were carefully timed and limited so that no trial lasted longer than a day. Votes on verdict and (when required by the lack of a statutory penalty) on punishment were by secret ballot; a simple majority determined the outcome, with ties favoring the defendant. Athenians were rightly proud of their legal system without, however, ignoring its defects and abuses.[9b] Any citizen could prosecute another for wrongdoing, and there was no publicly appointed prosecutor. As a result, extortionists could threaten or initiate lawsuits against wealthy Athenians, who would often settle for cash rather than expose themselves to the risky outcome of a panel's temperament. Or citizens could for whatever private reason take advantage of a popular mood and indict someone for a real or a fancied wrong. Socrates and Pericles are famous examples of people so indicted.

§10. Prosecutor and defendant alike were expected to speak for themselves, and yet the ordinary citizen, whose real business might be running his small farm, would not necessarily know how to begin and end a speech. But length was tightly limited, and the outcome might be literally life or death, since imprisonment was used only for temporary restraint, not for long-term punishment. Penalties were money fines, exile, or death. As a result, skilled speakers who could help friends or clients by teaching them how to speak and how to behave in a court when under the pressure of litigation were highly prized resources. Antiphon, whom Thucydides

A9a Athenian citizens organized in panels to hear evidence and determine guilt or innocence in cases brought before them.

A9b See the speech of the Athenian emissaries to the Spartan assembly, 1.76.3–77.5.

calls "the one man best able to aid in the courts, or before the assembly, the suitors who required his opinion" (8.68.1), was one such speaker.[10a]

§11. There were some Athenians who persistently criticized and sometimes even physically attacked the Athenian democratic system. Many were powerful, educated, and articulate aristocrats who saw no virtue in entrusting power to a mass of base persons.[11a] These Athenians, who wanted a narrower base of power (and who tended to admire the Spartan way of life), were styled *oligarchs*.[11b] When they modified the constitution, as happened in 411,[11c] they limited the franchise and stopped pay for service in public offices. As a result, the number of citizens entitled to vote on major questions (ostensibly) shrunk from thirty thousand to five thousand, and the actual numbers present in any given assembly were accordingly greatly diminished. A council of four hundred actually governed. The popular courts of the democracy, whose panels required numerous citizens, could not function, and all the city's various councils and committees had to be manned (if they continued in existence at all) by men who could afford to serve.

§12. Despite the opposition of domestic and foreign oligarchs, the Athenian democracy proved a vigorous institution. For over one hundred forty years, during a period that extended approximately from 462 to 320, only two short-lived oligarchic regimes managed to seat themselves, namely, the ambiguous government of the Four Hundred in 411, and the oppressive rule of the Thirty in 404/3. Thucydides could well remark in 8.68.4 that "it was no light thing to deprive the Athenian people of its freedom a hundred years after the deposition of the tyrants."

Alan L. Boegehold
Brown University
Providence, Rhode Island

A10a But note that Thucydides also says that Antiphon never came forward to speak in the assembly or any other public forum, because he was not liked by the multitude owing to his reputation for cleverness.

A11a Note Athenagoras' criticism of the "young Syracusan aristocrats" in his speech at 6.36–40, and Alcibiades' antidemocratic remarks to the Spartans at 6.89–92.

A11b See note 8.54.4a on political clubs at Athens.

A11c The success of the oligarchs is described at 8.53ff.

APPENDIX B
The Athenian Empire in Thucydides

§1. "Athenian Empire" is a phrase in conventional use, describing a system of tribute-paying states who answered in varying ways to the authority of Athens. Originally they were autonomous members of an alliance of Greek city-states and islands formed in 478 after the battles of Plataea[1a] and Mycale[1b] to defend Greeks against anticipated Persian invasions, and to avenge damage and injuries done by the Persians in the recent past. This alliance came under Athenian military leadership after the Spartan regent and general Pausanias disgraced himself and the Spartans withdrew from further participation in the struggle against Persia.[1c] States from the allied fleet asked Athens to lead them and Athens complied: she was in an advantageous position to command, employing as she did a large and active fleet and enjoying a new and singular reputation for heroism gained by her triumph at the battle of Marathon,[1d] her people's heroic evacuation of their city, and her role in the recent naval victory of Salamis.[1e]

§2. The new alliance is known as the Delian League because its members at first conducted their deliberations and established their treasury on the small centrally located island of Delos, an ancient Ionian sanctuary sacred to Apollo.[2a] Most of the island cities in the Aegean Sea and many coastal cities of Thrace and Asia Minor became members,[2b] recognizing that they were vulnerable to Persian forces and exposed to an allied Greek fleet that could either support or harry them. When the Athenian Aristides, widely known as "the Just," took command, he designed a League fund to which member states were to contribute money annually,[2c] with each paying an amount determined more or less by its size and resources. It was agreed that some nautical cities, and the major islands of Chios, Lesbos, and

B1a Plataea: Appendix B Map, BX. Site of a great land victory of the Greeks over the Persians. See also Appendix E, §4.

B1b Mycale (near Mount Mycale): Appendix B Map, BY. Site of a Greek victory over the Persians mentioned in 1.89.2. See also Appendix E, §4.

B1c Thucydides describes the disgrace of Pausanias and the withdrawal of the Spartans in 1.95.

B1d Marathon: Appendix B Map, BX. Site in Attica of a victory in 490 by the Athenians over a Persian expedition. See also Appendix E, §4.

B1e Salamis: Appendix B Map, BX. Site of the first great naval victory by the combined Greek fleet over a much larger Persian fleet in 480. See also Appendix E, §4.

B2a Delos: Appendix B Map, BY. For the religious significance of Delos, see Polycrates' consecration of Rhenea to Delos (1.13.6) and Athenian purifications of Delos (3.104.1).

B2b Melos: Appendix B Map, BX; Thera: Appendix B Map, BY. These islands in the southern Aegean, settled by Dorians, were however among the few Aegean islands that did not join the league (2.9.4).

B2c Thucydides says in 1.96.2 that the first year's tribute totaled 460 talents. The Athenian-Spartan peace treaty described by Thucydides in 5.18.5. refers to the tribute set by Aristides.

583

Samos,[2d] would contribute ships and manpower in lieu of money. All member states took an oath binding them permanently to the alliance. Although each member theoretically had an equal say in League matters, there was no major, counterbalancing force against that of Athens to attract clusters of votes in opposition. For this reason, when there was great diversity of opinion among members, any few who voted with Athens weighted the balloting enough for Athens to prevail; and there would always be some who would cooperate with her. In time the restless energy of the Athenians almost inevitably transformed their initial commanding position among equals into that of a ruling power.

§3. The genesis and duration of the Athenian Empire can be sketched in its larger outlines from several ancient written sources. Thucydides' description (1.89–118) of the years between the defeat of the Persians in 479 and the outbreak of the Peloponnesian War in 431—known as the "Pentecontaetia" by scholars, although it does not exactly comprise fifty years—is our most substantial account of this period, despite some surprising omissions. Plutarch and Diodorus Siculus also provide important information, and other details can be drawn from various surviving state documents inscribed on stone. And yet despite this comparative abundance of evidence for a short period of time, many elements of chronology and sequence continue to resist satisfactory ordering. There can be no doubt, however, that Athens' empire ceased to exist when her fleet was defeated and captured by the Peloponnesians at Aegospotami in 405.[3a]

§4. After Aristides came Cimon son of Miltiades, one of Athens' greatest generals. He assumed command of the Greek forces and vigorously and successfully set about driving the Persians out of the Aegean. By the early 460s (467?), when Cimon won his most famous victory over the Persians in a combined land and sea battle at the Eurymedon River in Pamphylia,[4a] the Delian League comprised nearly two hundred member states and controlled not only the entire Aegean Sea but also a broad coastal strip of western Asia Minor. Many of these states benefited greatly from their membership in an alliance that suppressed piracy, encouraged trade and commerce, and provided employment for the poor as rowers in the fleet. Moreover, Athens generally favored democratic factions, and when oligarchs and democrats in a given state were almost equally matched in a struggle for dominance, Athenian support could prove decisive for the democrats. Democratic regimes that owed their establishment and continued existence to Athens tended to be reliable and loyal subject allies. They might have preferred autonomy, but, for many, answering to Athens was an acceptable alternative to the rule of local oligarchs. Accordingly, despite the assurances with which Corinth predicted uprisings,[4b] subject cities were slow to revolt against Athens after the outbreak of the Peloponnesian War and only did so with any frequency in the presence of Peloponnesian troops under Brasidas in Chalcidice[4c] or after Athens' apparently crippling defeat in Sicily. Some states, however, remained allies of Athens throughout the Peloponnesian War.

§5. In time, many members of the League found their contributions of military

B2d   Lesbos, Appendix B Map, AY; Chios and Samos: Appendix B Map, BY.
B3a   Aegospotami: Appendix B Map, AY.
B4a   Eurymedon river: Appendix B Map, locator.

Thucydides mentions this victory in 1.100.1.
B4b   For Corinth's predicted uprisings, see 1.122.1.
B4c   Chalcidice: Appendix B Map, AX.

service and ships onerous, and elected to pay a cash equivalent instead. Athens used these funds to improve her own properly equipped and well-trained fleet. As a result, Athens found herself in an even better position to collect tribute from reluctant allies, and such allies found themselves less able to offer serious resistance to Athenian demands. By 431, only Lesbos and Chios[5a] continued to supply ships of their own and to enjoy the status of privileged allies rather than subjects.

§6. States who sought to leave the alliance found early on that Athens would not permit them to do so. Naxos (before 467) and Thasos (465–62) tried to break away but were besieged, defeated, and compelled to remain as members.[6a] When the large island of Samos[6b] defied Athens in 440, a major military campaign was mounted to subdue and punish her. The revolts of Lesbos in 428 and of Chios and other states in 411 were more threatening still, because they took place during the Peloponnesian War. Athens responded to these uprisings with increasingly firm and harsh measures designed to maintain and even to increase the nature and extent of her rule. Opponents were exiled or executed. Fines were levied, and in some cases land was confiscated and allocated to Athenian citizens (see §10 below). Some states that refused to become members of the alliance were compelled to join it. This odious use of imperial power, perhaps based on the presumption that those who are not with us are against us, was first employed against Carystus in Euboea around 472; it culminated in the brutal conquest of Melos in 415,[6b] and collapsed in Athens' total and calamitous failure to subjugate Syracuse two years later.

§7. Relations with Sparta began to deteriorate when Cimon, in 462, persuaded the Athenians to help the Spartans, who were besieging Messenians and Helots at Mount Ithome.[7a] When the Spartans rudely sent the Athenians home soon after they had arrived, many Athenians were offended and blamed Cimon personally. Not long afterward they ostracized him (1.102), but they recalled him before his ten-year banishment was complete so that he could again command their forces against the Persians. He died while leading a Greek fleet at Citium on the island of Cyprus[7b] around 450. Cimon's death, together with the outbreak of open conflict with Sparta and the destruction by Persia of a large Greek fleet in Egypt[7c] in 454, may well have led Athens to increase her control over the League. In any case, she moved the League treasury from Delos to Athens in 454/3, and seems thereafter to have consulted less and less with the allies about questions of policy. In her official language, she began to refer to the allies as "all the cities that Athens rules." Pericles had reason to warn his fellow citizens in 429 that their rule over the empire was a tyranny, one that it may have been wrong to take, but which by that time was very dangerous to let go.[7d]

§8. For some reason, Athenian military activity against Persia ceased shortly after Cimon's death. There is a persistent tradition in the fourth century that the Athenian Callias, son of Hipponicus, secured a formal peace with Persia around this

---

B5a Lesbos: Appendix B Map, AY; Chios, Appendix B Map, BY. The Athenians were more acutely outraged by the revolt of Lesbos because of the island's privileged status (3.36.2).

B6a Naxos: Appendix B Map, BY; Thasos: Appendix B Map, AX.

B6b Samos: Appendix B Map, BY.

B6c For Thucydides' "Melian Dialogue," see 5.85–5.113.

Carystus, Euboea, Melos: Appendix B Map, BX.

B7a Sparta, Mount Ithome: Appendix B Map, BX.

B7b Citium, Cyprus: Appendix B Map, locator.

B7c For the story of the loss of this Athenian expedition to Egypt, as well as the fleet sent by the Athenians to relieve it, see 1.104, 1.109–10.

B7d See Pericles' speech at 2.63.2 and the speech of the Athenians at Sparta, 1.75.3.

time—the mid-fifth century. By the terms of that peace, it is thought that Persia agreed that her ships would not sail west of Phaselis or out of the Black Sea,[8a] and that her *satraps* (governors of Persian provinces) would not attempt to force Athenian allies to return to Persian rule. Thucydides, however, does not mention any such peace treaty, nor do other fifth-century writers. As a result, there is wide disagreement whether such a "Peace of Callias,"[8b] which occupies a key place in modern (and authoritative) reconstruction of the course of the Athenian Empire, was actually made.

§9. Athens also exerted control over her subjects through judicial agreements. Questions of justice required agreements between states—if only to determine where complaints would be heard. Often more complex questions needed to be addressed, such as the class of offense, the kind of court, and the citizenship of the perpetrator. It was normal for a state to enter into a formal agreement with another to regulate such matters, and the two would publish their own particular rules of administration. Athenians required that a larger number and variety of cases be tried at Athens than was usual in such agreements. They believed their courts were just and fair to their subjects, and indeed they complained that despite their superior power, they abided by such agreements to their own disadvantage.[9a] It is relevant to note that after 462, when Athenian popular courts entered a new era, one in which the people adjudicated a vastly wider array of suits and prosecutions, their facilities for judging, that is, courts and personnel, functioned at a level of volume and complexity higher than anything that could be found anywhere else in the Aegean basin.

§10. Whether the allocation of legal business was consistent with perfect equity or not is a moot point. Certainly, Athens wielded various instruments of power effectively, at least during the first sixty years of its empire. An important control was her ability to modulate a robust flow of commercial traffic by sea and to pay for an abundance of goods, from basic foodstuffs to luxuries, all of which meant profit for those who did business with her. This power was used against Megara when Athens by decree barred Megarians from conducting trade in any ports of the empire or the markets of Attica. This particular prohibition proved so harmful to Megara and was considered so outrageous that its repeal was among the key Peloponnesian demands that preceded the outbreak of war.[10a] In addition, the League treasurers (*hellenotamiai*), who were all Athenians, collected the tribute and acted as enforcers when states were slow to pay. In some locations—for example, on Lemnos, Imbros, the Chersonese, as well as at Histiaea, Aegina, Lesbos and Melos[10b]—Athens settled her own citizens as colonists or lot-holders (*clerouchs*) who turned their new land into virtual extensions of Athens, and served, if only by their presence, as Athenian garrisons overseeing the local citizens.[10c] In time, Athens also imposed on her tributary allies her own silver coinage and a system of standard weights and measures.

§11. When the Athenians moved the League treasury to Athens in 454/3, they

B8a   Phaselis and the Black Sea: Appendix B Map, locator.
B8b   The "Peace of Callias" is also discussed in Appendix E, §5, and note E5c. See also note 8.56.4a.
B9a   See Thucydides, 1.77.
B10a For the Megarian Decree, see note 1.42.2a; 1.139.1–2,4; 1.140.3; and 1.144.2.
B10b Lemnos, Imbros, Chersonese, and Lesbos: Appen-

dix B Map, AY; Histiaea, Appendix B Map, AX; Aegina and Melos: Appendix B Map, BX. For the establishment of *clerouchs* on Lesbos, see 3.50.2.
B10c The taking of land by these *clerouchies* was deeply resented by the local citizens and was explicitly forbidden in the charter of a second Athenian confederacy formed briefly in the mid-fourth century.

consecrated a sum equal to one sixtieth of each year's tribute to Athena, tutelary goddess of Athens, and used that money in various ways to enhance their city; they could now pay citizens to hold many civic offices, and they could honor Athena on the Acropolis with magnificent new buildings such as the Parthenon and the Propylaia. A fragmentary record of these appropriated sums, published as lists inscribed on marble slabs, begins in 454/3 and ends possibly in 410/409.[11a] A 5 percent harbor tax imposed on the allies in 413 may have turned out to be more practicable. A major reassessment in 425, which substantially increased the annual tribute of the allies, and which is preserved on its own stele, is not mentioned at all by Thucydides.

§12. Plutarch wrote that Pericles had to respond to complaints that he should not use League contributions to beautify Athens. In reply, he said that the allies contributed nothing but money, and that as long as the Athenians did their job, which was to run the war against Persia, they did not need to present any accounting to those who gave the money. This cool assessment is in its tone quite in keeping with the chilling Athenian "realpolitik" of the Melian Dialogue:[12a] those who have power do what they like, those who do not, do what they must.

Alan L. Boegehold
Brown University
Providence, Rhode Island

B11a See Illustration 2.69, which shows a fragment of a tribute list.
B12a For the Melian Dialogue, see Thucydides, 5.85–113.

APPENDIX C
Spartan Institutions in Thucydides

Social Structure

§1. Sparta was different, "other," almost un-Greek—or so it could be made to seem from the Athenian side of the fifth-century B.C. "Great Powers" divide (1.77.5; 5.105.3–4). Only a few favored non-Spartans knew Sparta well from the inside. Conversely, unwelcome foreign visitors might find themselves summarily expelled (2.39.1). But the experience of Thucydides was probably more typical. He complains in exasperation of "the secrecy of their government" (5.68.2), and his Athenian speakers emphasize the polar opposition between themselves and their principal foes in character as in institutions (1.69.4–71; 2.39; 8.96.5). These fundamental differences can almost all be traced to two Spartan peculiarities: their educational system and their relationship with the Helots of Laconia and Messenia.

§2. Unlike all other Greek city-states, Sparta had a comprehensively, minutely, and centrally organized system of education that was prescribed as a condition of attaining full Spartan adult citizen status. Its main emphasis was military. Boys were separated early from their mothers—indeed, from all females—and educated roughly in rigidly controlled packs divided and subdivided by age. Fighting, stealing, and finally even murdering (see §4) were enjoined as integral parts of the educative process. Basic literacy was apparently taught, so some Spartans at least could presumably read the few official documents their city chose to record and display (5.18.23). Music (5.70) and dancing (5.16) were also part of the prescribed curriculum, since they were crucial to performing the major religious festivals devoted to Apollo, such as the Carneia (5.54; 5.76.1), but they were also learned in significant measure for their military benefits.[2a] Hence, too, the conscious development of a clipped, military-style form of utterance (4.17.2; 4.84.2), which is still called by us "laconic" (after the Greek adjective meaning "Spartan"), just as we still speak of a "spartan"—that is, a spare, austere, self-denying—mode of existence. Between the ages of seven and thirty Spartan males spent almost their entire lives in communal dormitories, messes, or barracks; even married men were required to make their conjugal visits furtively, briefly, and under cover of darkness.

C2a At the battle of Mantinea, the Spartans advanced slowly (and presumably in unison) into battle to the music of flute players (5.70). Mantinea: Appendix D Map, AX.

§3. The Helots, especially the more numerous portion living in Messenia to the west of Sparta on the far side of the eight-thousand-foot Taygetus mountain range,[3a] were the Spartans' enemy within, not least because they always and appreciably outnumbered their masters. Most were farmers producing the food, drink, and other basics (especially barley, pork, wine, and olive oil) that enabled all Spartans to live a barrack-style military life in Sparta instead of working for a living. But the Helots, though native Greeks, farmed the Spartans' land under a harsh yoke of servitude, so that many of them vehemently opposed the Spartan regime, yearned to regain the liberty and autonomy they imagined they had lost through earlier defeats (their name probably means "captives"), and were prepared to stake all on revolt (1.101.2; 2.27.2; 4.56.2). Spartan policy, therefore, as Thucydides starkly and accurately asserts, was "at all times . . . governed by the necessity of taking precautions against them" (4.80.2; cf. 1.132.4–5; 5.23.3—"the slave population").

§4. Precautions might exceptionally be intensified, as in 425–24, when, in response to the Athenians' exploitation of Helot disaffection following the vital loss of Pylos and Cythera[4a] (4.3.3; 4.55.1; 5.35.7), some two thousand selected troublemakers were secretly liquidated (4.80.5). But Spartans were routinely brought up, within the normal framework of their educational curriculum, to put Helots to death in peacetime. This occurred under cover of a general proclamation, repeated every autumn by each new board of *ephors* (see below), declaring war on the Helots collectively and thereby exonerating their Spartan killers in advance from the ritual pollution of homicide. There could not be a more perfect illustration of the Spartans' intense religiosity bordering on superstition that was perhaps another by-product of their military style of life.

Government Institutions

§5. The five ephors, chosen by a curious form of election from any Spartans who wished to stand, were Sparta's chief executive officials. They possessed very extensive powers in both the formulation and the execution of foreign and domestic policy (1.85.3; 1.86; 1.131.1; 2.2.1; 6.88.10). Collegiality and the majority principle did impose some constraints, but the annual oath they exchanged with the two Spartan hereditary kings indicates where the balance of authority rested: the ephors swore on behalf of the Spartans collectively to uphold the kingship so long as the kings themselves observed the laws (which the ephors interpreted and applied).

§6. Ephors, though, were annual officials, and the office could apparently be held only once. The two kings, on the other hand, and the other members of the thirty-strong Gerousia (Sparta's senate, also curiously elected, but only from men aged sixty or over who probably also had to belong to certain aristocratic families), held office for life and partly for that reason enjoyed exceptional prestige and authority. However, not even the kings' supposed direct descent from Heracles, "the demigod son of Zeus" (5.16.2), nor their hereditary right to the overall command of any Spartan army or Spartan-led allied force, prevented them from being disci-

C3a Messenia and the Taygetus range in relation to Sparta: Appendix D Map, BY.

C4a Pylos: Appendix D Map, BX; Cythera: Appendix D Map, BY.

plined (5.63.2–4), and sometimes deposed and exiled (5.16). An adroit king such as Archidamus might seek to exploit his aura of prestige and abundant opportunities for patronage to exercise a decisive and sometimes lasting influence on policy. But in 432 not even Archidamus (1.80–85) and his supporters in the Gerousia could persuade the assembly of citizen warriors, which had the final say in matters of peace and war, to vote against immediate war with Athens—in this one known instance by a formal division rather than by its usual crude procedure of shouting (1.87).

Military Organization

§7. In his account of the great battle of Mantinea[7a] in 418, Thucydides provides a privileged glimpse of Sparta's unique and complex military organization in decisive and successful action (esp. 5.66, 5.69.2–7; cf. 4.34.1; 5.9). The goal of the Spartan educational system was to produce exceptionally disciplined and efficient *hoplite* infantrymen (see Appendix F, §7); the navy was very much an inferior Spartan service (1.142.2). For almost two centuries, indeed, the Spartans suffered no major reverses of any sort. Yet partly because of the constant internal Helot threat, the Spartans did not lightly undertake aggressive foreign wars (1.118.2; cf. 5.107), and they very rarely fought without large-scale allied support.

§8. Moreover, the Spartans experienced a growing and increasingly critical shortage of citizen military manpower, caused basically by internal socioeconomic deficiencies. Each Spartan citizen had to contribute a minimum of natural produce from the land worked for him by Helots toward the upkeep of the communal "mess" in which he lived and ate, and through which he exercised his military and other civic responsibilities. But in the period after the Persian Wars the number of Spartan citizens who could contribute the required minimum declined, through a process not entirely understood today, but which probably was the result of an increasing concentration of land in fewer hands. This socioeconomic manpower shortage was aggravated by the catastrophic earthquake of the 460s (1.101.2; 1.128.1; 2.27.2; 4.56.2) and by important losses in the Peloponnesian War.

§9 The Spartans therefore drew ever more heavily on non-Spartan troops to make up their frontline infantry force. In the first place, they had regular and increasing recourse to the hoplites of the *perioikoi* (literally, "dwellers around") whom they even brigaded in the same regiments as themselves. These perioikoi were free Greeks who lived in their own semiautonomous communities, mainly along the coasts of both Laconia (e.g., Epidaurus Limera and Thyrea [4.56.2]) and Messenia[9a] (e.g., Methone [2.25.1]), but also along the vulnerable northern border with Arcadia and Argos[9b] (e.g., the Sciritae [5.67.2; 5.68.3; 5.71.2–3; 5.73.1–2; cf. 5.33.1]). The perioikoi spoke the same dialect as the Spartans and resembled them in other cultural ways, but they enjoyed no political rights at Sparta and so had no say in Sparta's foreign affairs (3.92.5; 4.8.1; 4.53.2; 5.54.1; 5.67.1; 8.6.4; 8.22.1). Secondly, and paradoxically, the Spartans also had regular and increasing

---

C7a Mantinea: Appendix D Map, AX.
C9a Epidaurus Limera: Thyrea: Appendix D Map, AY.
  Methone: Appendix D Map, BX.

C9b Arcadia: Appendix D Map, AX; Argos: Appendix D Map, AY.

military recourse to Helots and various categories of liberated Helots, of which the most privileged but still awkwardly unassimilated were the *neodamodeis* (4.21; 5.67; 7.19.3; 7.58.3). All the same, the Peloponnesian War was decided not on land but at sea, and above all by Persian money, rather than by traditional Spartan military prowess.

Paul Cartledge
Clare College
Cambridge University
Cambridge, England

APPENDIX D
The Peloponnesian League in Thucydides

Origins

§1. "Peloponnesian League," a modern term for the ancient formula "The Spartans and the Allies," invites the Voltairean comment that it was actually neither Peloponnesian nor a league (as the Holy Roman Empire was to Voltaire neither holy nor Roman nor an empire). It was not a "league" in our sense because the allies were bound individually by treaty to Sparta, not to each other, and indeed sometimes fought against each other (4.134; 5.81.1). The official name is known to us both from narrative sources such as Thucydides, who also abbreviates it to "the Peloponnesians" alone (1.105.3), and from a tiny handful of documentary inscriptions.

§2. Precisely how Sparta's original military alliances with such Peloponnesian cities as Corinth (always her most important ally), Elis, and Tegea[2a] were translated into a composite League is not known for certain, though the transformation had definitely occurred by the time of the Persian Wars of 480–79 and probably as many as twenty years before that. The turning point may well have been the fiasco of about 506, when Sparta under her wayward and autocratic king Cleomenes I lost the support of the majority of her allies on the very brink of a combined attack on Athens. Cleomenes' Spartan co-king led the defection at the prompting of the Corinthians. Thereafter only one king at a time was empowered to lead a Spartan or allied army, and Sparta required the allies' formal consent before undertaking such a League expedition (see "Mechanisms," below).

Extent

§3. Several cities within the Peloponnese, most conspicuously Argos, were never members of the League, and some cities outside, above all Megara and those of the Boeotian federation,[3a] sometimes were. At its largest, within the half century following the Peloponnesian War, the League extended as far north as Chalcidice,[3b] but never outside mainland Greece. It is useful therefore to distinguish between the wider Spartan alliance (1.31.2; 2.9.3), on the one hand, and its inner core or circle

D2a Corinth: Appendix D Map, AY; Elis, Tegea: Appendix D Map, AX.

D3a Argos, Megara, Boeotia: Appendix D Map, AY.
D3b Chalcidice: Appendix D Map, locator.

APPENDIX D MAP

comprised by the Peloponnesian League members, on the other. Occasionally there is a doubt as to the status of an ally, most conspicuously in the case of Athens after the Peloponnesian War in the years 404 and immediately following. We know that the "hegemony clause" (discussed below) was applied to Athens by Sparta, but it does not follow that Athens was incorporated fully within the League structure any more than Argos had been after the battle of Mantinea (5.79–80.1).

§4. Conversely, there were episodes, indeed whole periods, in which a Peloponnesian League ally or allies defected from or even fought an outright war against Sparta: such a period was 421–18, when Corinth, Mantinea, and Elis[4a] revolted from Sparta and allied themselves with Argos. The Boeotians and the Megarians, however, significantly refused to join the Argive-led coalition in the belief that "the Argive democracy would not agree so well with their aristocratic forms of government as the Spartan constitution" (5.31.6).

Mechanisms

§5. In technical language the Peloponnesian League was a hegemonic symmachy. Each of Sparta's allies swore to have the same friends and enemies as their *hegemon* ("leader") and to follow the Spartans wherever they might lead them. In practice, Sparta's leadership was restricted by the obligation to persuade a majority of allied delegates at a duly constituted League congress to follow her in declaring war or in making peace, and to do so on her terms. But only Sparta could summon such a congress (1.67.3; 1.87.4; 1.119–125.1), so that she could never be committed by her allies to a policy she opposed (1.88.1; 1.118.2). On the other hand, she did fail to persuade a majority on more than one occasion (e.g., 1.40.5). Allies, moreover, had one important opt-out clause: they were obligated to obey a majority congress decision "unless the gods or heroes stand in the way" (5.30.3)—unless, that is, they could legitimately invoke a prior and overriding religious obligation.

§6. Unlike Athens, Sparta did not impose on her allies tribute in cash or kind (1.19), partly because traditional hoplite-style warfare (see Appendix F) was much less expensive than maintaining a large trireme navy (see Appendix G, §12 and 13, and Appendix J, §6), but also because Sparta lacked the necessary administrative mentality or infrastructure (1.141.6). Allies were required by Sparta to contribute a certain number or proportion of their troops to a League force, and Sparta provided the officers both to levy and to command the contingents stipulated (2.75.3). Most importantly of all, however, by a variety of informal means, and chiefly through the overt or covert support of favorable oligarchic regimes in the allied cities (1.19; 1.144.2; cf. 1.18.1; 5.31.6), Sparta took great care to ensure that her League allies would routinely fulfill her wishes.

§7. For almost 150 years (c. 505–365), therefore, the Peloponnesian League quite satisfactorily realized the twin aims the *hegemon* set for it: to serve as the means whereby Sparta could behave on the international stage as one of the two (or three) great Greek powers, and to throw a protective cordon around the vulnerable

D4a Mantinea, Elis: Appendix D Map, AX.

domestic basis of all Spartan life and policy, the Helots. In 371, however, the Spartans and their allies were decisively beaten at Leuctra in Boeotia by their former allies the Thebans;[7a] the now-undisguisable shortage of Spartan citizen manpower (see Appendix C, §8) was not the least cause of their disastrous defeat. In its wake the brilliant Theban commander Epaminondas conducted a massive invasion of Laconia, the first-ever invasion of Laconia by land by a foreign power since the formation of the Spartan state some three to four centuries earlier. By freeing the Helots of Messenia, and so destroying the economic basis of the Spartan army's superiority, and by fortifying the Messenians' old stronghold on Mt. Ithome[7b] (1.101.2–3; 1.102.1–3; 1.103.1; 3.54.5) to ensure the independence of their new (or reborn) city of Messene, Epaminondas put an end to Sparta's "Great Power" status for good. The Peloponnesian League was an early casualty of Sparta's enforced weakness, simply melting away into oblivion well before Sparta's second major defeat in hoplite battle at the hands of Epaminondas, at Mantinea in 362.

> Paul Cartledge
> Clare College
> Cambridge University
> Cambridge, England

D7a Boeotia, Leuctra, Thebes: Appendix D Map, AY.
D7b Messenia, Mt. Ithome (Ithome): Appendix D Map,
    BX.

APPENDIX E
The Persians in Thucydides

§1. When Cyrus the Great overthrew the kingdom of the Medes in 550 B.C. he changed what had been a Median empire into a Persian one. Since both Medes and Persians came from the same region—Iran—and Median nobles continued to be powerful within the empire of the Persians, Greeks often used the terms "Mede" or "Medes" interchangeably with "Persian" or "Persians." Those Greeks who took the Persian side in any conflicts were said to have "Medized" or to be guilty of "Medism."

§2. Cyrus and his successors vigorously expanded their empire until, under Darius I, who ruled from 521 to 486 B.C., Persian dominion reached from Thrace in southeastern Europe to parts of India, and from southern Egypt to the Caucasus.[2a] Contemporary Greeks referred to the Persian ruler simply as "the King," there being no doubt about which monarch was thus signified. To govern so vast an empire, the King's authority had to be delegated to governors (called *satraps*) of provinces (*satrapies*) who, in turn, exercised power through subordinate officials or local dynasts. The system worked well when provincial governors, who were usually monitored by agents of the King, were loyal to him, but when central authority was weak, or when problems occurred in the royal succession, they could be tempted to act independently or even to revolt. Satrapies were linked by imperial highways and a royal messenger post whose speed and efficiency amazed the contemporary world. Trade was facilitated by common official languages and a universal Persian gold currency. To a Greek of the fifth century, even a sophisticated one whose worldview was not entirely limited to the borders and neighbors of his *polis* (city-state), Persia seemed immense in size, in wealth, and in power. It was largely through contact with Persia that the Greeks became acquainted with the accumulated knowledge of ancient Egypt, Mesopotamia, and even India, so that it is not an accident that most of the first Greek philosophers, poets, and historians came from the cities of Asia Minor that had fallen under Lydian and later Persian rule. But to the Persians, the Greeks must have seemed a troublesome, if peripheral, set of hardly civilized peoples with strange customs and enough military prowess to be

---

E2a Egypt, Caucasus: Appendix E Map, locator; Thrace:
Appendix E Map, AY.

dangerous—although fortunately self-neutralized by wars they constantly waged among themselves.

§3. In 546 B.C., Cyrus conquered Lydia[3a] in western Asia (Asia Minor), and thereby succeeded to the dominion over many Greek cities that had been earlier subdued and made tributary by the Lydians. Almost fifty years later, in 499 B.C., the Greeks of Ionia (in Asia Minor) revolted against Persian rule and requested their fellow Greeks to help them. Sparta refused, but Athens and Eretria (a city on Euboea),[3b] sent small squadrons of ships to assist them. Troops from their contingents joined a combined Greek assault against Sardis,[3c] the former capital of the kingdom of Lydia and now the seat of a Persian satrap. The Greeks captured the lower city and burned it, but thereafter Persian forces defeated them on both land and sea (the fighting spread as far away as Cyprus[3d]) and finally put down the Greek rebellion by 494.

§4. To punish the affront at Sardis, Darius sent a punitive expedition into Greece in 490 B.C., which, after sacking Eretria and carrying off its inhabitants, was defeated by the Athenians at Marathon[4a] in Attica (1.18.1; 1.73.4; 2.34.5). A decade later, a second and much larger Persian invasion of Greece was launched by Darius' successor Xerxes, who led the combined land and sea expedition in person, and clearly hoped to add the states of Greece permanently to his empire. The Persians crossed the Hellespont, advanced unhindered through Thrace and Thessaly, and met their first serious Greek opposition at the narrow pass of Thermopylae.[4b] Here a small Greek force fought effectively and checked the entire Persian army for several days; when it was finally outflanked, most of the Greeks withdrew, but a few, led by the Spartan king Leonidas with a unit of three hundred Spartan *hoplites* (see Appendix F), remained in the pass and fought gloriously until surrounded and annihilated. Xerxes then advanced through Boeotia—which Medized[4c]—crossed into Attica, and reached Athens itself. He occupied the city and destroyed it, but he captured few of the inhabitants because, in an unprecedented step, the Athenians had left their lands and hearths and evacuated by sea to the island of Salamis and other nearby parts of Greece (1.18.2; 1.73.4). Shortly thereafter, the combined Greek fleet, inspired by the leadership and stratagems of the Athenian general Themistocles, inflicted such a crushing defeat on the Persian navy at Salamis[4d] that Xerxes retired with what remained of his fleet to Persian territory. In the following year, the Persian army also withdrew from Greece after it was defeated at Plataea[4e] by the largest allied force ever assembled by the Greek city-states under the command of the Spartan Pausanias.[4f] Finally, the Persian fleet was again smashed by the Greeks at

E3a Lydia: Appendix E Map, AY.
E3b Eretria on Euboea: Appendix E Map, BX.
E3c Sardis: Appendix E Map, BY.
E3d Cyprus: Appendix E Map, locator.
E4a Marathon in Attica: Appendix E Map, BX.
E4b Hellespont, Thrace. Thessaly, Thermopylae: Appendix E Map, AX. Thucydides refers to the great Persian invasion at 1.18.2, and to the battle of Thermopylae at 4.36.3
E4c Boeotia: Appendix E Map, BX. The Plataeans remind the Spartans of the "Medism" of the Thebans in 3.56.4 and the Thebans in turn explain their defection in 3.62.
E4d Salamis: Appendix E Map, BX. Thucydides recounts Themistocles' role as both advocate for the con-

struction of an Athenian fleet (1.14.3) and as a wily restorer of Athens' walls (1.90–3); he evaluates him as a statesman and describes his ultimate flight from Athens and reception by the Persian king in 1.135–38.

E4e Plataea: Appendix E, Map BX. See 2.71.2–4, where the Plataeans seek to halt the invading Spartans by invoking the memory of Pausanias' victory over the Persians at their city, and the oaths taken later by the Spartans in appreciation of Plataea's bravery in that struggle.

E4f Pausanias' subsequent arrogance, his alleged final treason, and his death are described in 1.94–95 and 1.128–34.

APPENDIX E MAP

Mycale (1.89.2) on the coast of Ionia. The story of these events (and of many others) is told by Herodotus.[4g]

§5 Thucydides takes up the historical narrative after the Persian withdrawal from mainland Greece in a major digression in Book 1, beginning at chapter 1.89 and ending at 1.118. In these twenty-nine chapters[5a] he describes many but not all of the significant events that mark the growth of Athenian power in the Aegean in the fifty years (479–31) between the defeat of Xerxes' expedition and the outbreak of the Peloponnesian War. He briefly mentions, for example, the outstanding victory of the Athenians and their allies over Persian forces on both land and sea that took place about 467 B.C. at the Eurymedon River on the south coast of Asia Minor,[5b] but he says nothing at all about the very important peace between Athens and Persia negotiated in 449 by the Athenian Callias at the court of the Persian king.[5c] Yet that peace left Athens free to strengthen her power over the members of the Delian League and to turn that alliance further into an Athenian-controlled naval empire; it also ratified the withdrawal of Persian rule from the coastlands of western Asia Minor, and in effect ceded that region to the control of Athens. Finally, it left Athens free to confront Sparta, and it is not impossible that the Persian king realized, even at this early date, that his interest could best be served if the two leading states of Greece were to exhaust themselves in a struggle for dominance.

§6. The failure of Thucydides to mention the so-called Peace of Callias (or some treaty between Athens and Persia) either in the text at 1.112 or somewhere else, has led some scholars to question his reliability and others to infer that the historian had not yet worked out the earlier Greco–Persian diplomatic background to the struggle before he died. There can be no doubt that Thucydides had gathered much evidence concerning Persian diplomacy. He was certainly aware of the diplomatic exchanges between Pausanias and Artabazus, the Persian governor at Dascylium (1.129.1),[6a] and he was informed about the negotiations between the fugitive Themistocles and King Artaxerxes that took place soon after the accession of the latter in 464 (1.137.3). Thucydides also knew that even before hostilities broke out, the Spartans had intended to ask for Persian assistance against Athens (1.82.1; 2.7.1), that they sent at least one diplomatic mission for that purpose (2.67.1), and that on at least one occasion the Great King responded to their overtures by expressing his willingness to listen (4.50.1).

§7. Persian intervention in Aegean affairs did not become significant until after the crippling failure in 413 of the Athenian expedition to Sicily, and Athens' decision to support Amorges, the rebel governor of Caria[7a]. As Thucydides describes it,

E4g   Mycale, Ionia: Appendix Map E, BY. Herodotus (who lived c. 484–25) is the author of a major history of the wars between the Persians and Greeks that includes much other interesting information. Thucydides criticizes him without naming him in 1.20. See introduction, II, i, ii, v and IV.ii.

E5a   This section or excursus is often called the "Pentecontaetia" although the period it describes does not exactly cover fifty years. Despite Thucydides' treatment, there is much scholarly controversy over the detailed chronology of this period.

E5b   Eurymedon River: Appendix E Map, locator.

E5c   We lack definitive proof that this treaty really existed, but there is much circumstantial evidence. Thucydides provides indirect evidence for a treaty between Athens and Persia in 8.56.4, when he describes Alcibiades' demands that the King should have the right "to build ships and sail along his own coast wherever and with as many as he please." Why would these freedoms have been demanded unless they had been previously prohibited by treaty? See also Appendix B, The Athenian Empire, §8.

E6a   Dascylium: Appendix E Map, AY.

E7a   Caria: Appendix E Map, BY. Athens' relationship with Amorges is discussed in note 8.5.5b.

in 412 the two Persian governors—Tissaphernes (8.5.5) at Sardis and Pharnabazus (8.6.1) at Dascylion—began to compete with each other in obedience to a command from the King to conclude an alliance with the Spartans. The Persians expected that with their assistance the Spartans would drive the Athenians out of the region and enable the Persian governors to regain the tribute from the cities which the Athenians denied them; Tissaphernes also hoped that the Spartans would help to destroy Amorges (8.5.5).

§8. In 412, after the annihilation of Athens' expedition in Sicily, Sparta responded to Persian solicitation and Asian Greek entreaties by establishing a fleet in Ionia, but Spartan commanders found it difficult to maintain their ships on Persian financial support and supplies. Despite their success in capturing and delivering Amorges,[8a] the Spartan relationship with Tissaphernes did not run smoothly. The Persian governor turned out to be an unreliable and stingy paymaster, which led to long and acrimonious disputes over his failure to supply sufficient pay for the sailors (8.29; 8.45.2–6; 8.78; 8.80.1; 8.83.3). Three successive draft treaties between Sparta and Persia had to be negotiated in 412 and 411 before agreement was reached (8.18; 8.37; 8.58). The Spartans rejected the first two of them as unacceptable; their officer Lichas objecting particularly to the Great King's implied claim to all lands Persia had formerly held, which would have required Sparta to recognize a Persian right to govern northern and central Greece (8.43.4; 8.52). Moreover, Tissaphernes had to contend with a potentially dangerous division of opinion at Sparta itself between those who proposed sending troops and ships to him in Ionia, and others who wanted instead to dispatch those forces to Pharnabazus, his rival in the Hellespont (8.6.2). It is not surprising, then, that Tissaphernes may have come to feel easier in his dealings with the renegade Athenian aristocrat Alcibiades than with the blunt Spartans (cf. 8.46.5).

§9. When in 411 a desperate Athens tried to renew her relationship with Persia, Alcibiades (8.47.2) and Pisander (8.53.3) argued, not quite disingenuously, that an oligarchic form of government would prove more acceptable to the Great King and to Tissaphernes (8.53.3). It is clear, however, that Persia cared less about the Athenians' form of government than about Athenian activity in the eastern Aegean, and the later restoration of democracy at Athens produced no perceptible impediment to diplomatic dealings between them.

§10. Perhaps a more important development, if Thucydides reports the affair accurately, is that Alcibiades' advice to Tissaphernes may have originated what was to become Persia's new long-term policy toward Greece: that of managing her support

---

E8a See 8.28.2; Amorges established himself at Iasus in
     Caria (Appendix E Map, BY), where he was
     captured by the Peloponnesians, who also sacked
     the city and ransomed the inhabitants to replenish
     their financial resources.

so as to prevent either side from achieving victory (8.46.1–4). It is interesting to note that this policy was not followed by the Persian prince Cyrus the Younger, whose steadfast and generous assistance to the Spartans after 407 permitted the Peloponnesian fleet to recover from successive reverses until they were finally able to inflict a decisive defeat on the Athenian navy at Aegospotami in 405[10a]. Indeed, Thucydides, in a late passage written after the end of the war (2.65.12), characterized Cyrus' aid as the one cause of Sparta's success. Aegospotami led to the complete surrender of Athens and to a Spartan hegemony over Greece that proved unfavorable to Persian interests. So when Persia decided to limit Sparta's power, she financed an alliance of Greek states (including a democratic Athens) to oppose Sparta on land, and used her fleet, commanded by the Athenian Conon (see 7.31.4), to defeat the Spartan fleet at Cnidus in 394[10b]. Later, with Persian approval, Conon helped the Athenians to complete new Long Walls and to refortify Piraeus,[10c] thus restoring Athens to independence from Sparta.

§11. Ever since the peace of 449, the Aegean had been essentially a frontier problem for Persia—one of many frontier problems—and so it remained even in the time of Alcibiades' intrigues with Tissaphernes in 411. But Persia's policy in the region, which could be characterized as passive from 449 to 411, became more aggressive and interventionist thereafter. In the following decades, having learned from Prince Cyrus' error, she became adept at maneuvering politically among the Greeks, manipulating their governments, and keeping them divided into rival alliances so that, exhausted by constant warfare, they would pose no threat to herself. Finally, in 387 B.C., Persia dictated what was called the King's Peace, which ratified her reestablished control over the Greek cities of Asia Minor and effectively protected her from Greek attack for more than forty years.

R.B.S.

10a Aegospotami: Appendix E Map, AY.
10b Cnidus: Appendix E Map, BY.

10c Piraeus: Appendix E Map, BX.

APPENDIX F
Land Warfare in Thucydides

§1. Classical Greek infantry fighting in mass formation was hardly original—Mycenean and Near Eastern armies had done the same for centuries. But the Greeks of the early (700–500 B.C.) city-states refined the earlier loosely organized mob into neat lines and files, with each propertied citizen now claiming an equal slot in the phalanx, a voice in the assembly, and a plot of land in the countryside.

§2. *Hoplite* infantrymen by the late eighth century B.C. had adopted sophisticated weaponry and armor to meet the new realities of formalized shock warfare. Their helmets, breastplates, and greaves were constructed entirely of bronze, reaching a thickness of about a half inch, providing them with substantial protection from the blows of most swords, missiles, and spears. An enormous and heavy shield—the *aspis* or *hoplon*—some three feet in diameter covered half the body and completed the panoply. But the hoplite still depended on the man next to him to shield his own unprotected right side and to maintain the cohesion of the entire phalanx. Thus military service now reinforced the egalitarian solidarity of the citizenry (4.126). The shield's unique double grip allowed its oppressive weight to be held by the left arm alone, and its concave shape permitted the rear ranks to rest it on their shoulders. Because of the natural tendency of each hoplite to seek protection for his unshielded right side behind the shield of his companion on the right, the entire phalanx often drifted rightward during its advance (5.71). Outside of Sparta, the general—an amateur and elective public official—usually led his troops on the right wing to spearhead the attack; in defeat he normally perished among his men (4.44.2; 4.101.2; 5.74.3). Because of the limited tactical options open to a phalanx once battle commenced, complex maneuvers and tactics were problematic (5.66.2; 5.72) and therefore rarely attempted. Usually a phalanx simply tried to win the battle outright on the stronger right side before its own inferior left side collapsed and eroded the cohesion of the entire army (4.96; 5.72–73).

§3. Offensively, the hoplite depended on his eight-foot spear; should the shaft break, he might turn around what was left of its length to employ the reverse end, which was outfitted with a bronze spike.[3a] Each hoplite carried a small iron sword in case his spear was lost altogether. The phalanx usually stacked eight men deep (5.68.3), but only the spears of the first three rows could extend to the enemy—the rear five lines pushed on the men in front. If he kept his nerve and stayed in formation with his fellow fighters, the hoplite with his seventy pounds of armor and his long spear was practically invulnerable *on level ground* to cavalry charges and skirmishers alike—even in the most desperate circumstances impenetrable to any but other hoplites (1.63.1; 3.108.3). True, on rare occasions, heavy infantry could be defeated by mixed contingents (4.35.2–6), but almost always this turnabout was accomplished through ruse, manipulation of terrain, or ambush and encirclement (4.32.3–34.2; 5.10.3–8), not decisive engagement or shock tactics.

§4. This traditional practice of hoplite battle as Greek warfare persisted well into the fifth century B.C. Even then phalanxes continued to fight almost entirely over disputed land, usually border strips of marginal ground (1.15.2; 5.41.2), often more important to an agrarian community's national pride than to its economic survival. Preliminary devastation of fields and rural infrastructure was sometimes used to draw reluctant opponents onto the battlefield or to shame them into submission (1.82.3–6; 2.11.6–8; 4.84.1–2; 4.88.1–2). But inflicting permanent damage to agricultural land was difficult, laborious, and time-consuming (3.26.3; 7.27.4), and thus ravaging was more often a formalized part of the more general protocols between city-states that governed the time, location, and conduct of such one-day wars (5.41.2–3; 5.47) than a realistic means to starve an enemy community. Campaigning was confined to the late spring and summer months and thus synchronized with the slack periods in the agricultural year, when agrarian infantrymen and their servile attendants (3.17.3) might be free from their planting and harvesting labors (1.141.3, 5; 3.15.2; 4.6.1; cf. 4.84.1; 4.88.1–2).

§5. The contrived and ritualized nature of Greek infantry fighting should not suggest an absence of mayhem and savagery. Columns eyed each other formally across flat plains, with bronze glittering in the summer sun, and their generals shouting a few words of last-minute encouragement (4.92; 5.69.1). After divination and sacrifice by the seer (6.69.2), hoplites often advanced at a trot from about two hundred yards, singing the *paean* or war-chant (4.43.2; 4.96.1). The initial collision was horrific, as each side stumbled blindly ahead into the enemy mass, attempting to create some momentum that might shatter the opposing formation into fragments (4.96).

§6. Hearing and sight by those in the ranks was difficult if not nonexistent (4.34.2; 7.44.1). The din of clashing metal and screaming men must have been ear-splitting; dust, the crowded conditions of the battlefield, and crested helmets with small eye slots would have limited vision severely—indeed, mistaken identity was commonplace as uniforms and national insignia were usually absent (4.96.3–6; 7.44.7–8). Reports of gaping wounds to the unprotected neck and groin, involun-

F3a Such a spear-butt spike, in this case taken as spoil from the defeated Lesbians and dedicated to the Dioscuri (whose temple at Athens is mentioned as the Anaceum in 8.93), is shown in Illustration 3.48.

tary defecation and urination, and panic abound in battle descriptions in Greek literature. Weight and steadiness in formation were crucial to hoplite success: the greater the cohesion and thrust of the column, the more likely it was for a phalanx to push itself over and through the enemy (5.10.5). Perhaps after not much more than an hour, the pushing ceased as one side collapsed and fled the field, allowing the exhausted victors to gather up their own dead and to strip the armor from the dead bodies of the enemy. One set of captured armor would be arranged on a pole and raised at or near the battlefield as a trophy or monument to the victors' prowess (4.97.1; 4.134.2; 5.74); the disputed territory would usually be annexed. The vanquished would manifest their defeat by sending a herald (whose distinctive herald's staff identified him) to request a truce in which they could return to the field to gather up the bodies of their own fallen (5.11; 5.74; 6.71.1). This request was nearly always granted, for the bodies of all war dead had to be respected and accorded proper funeral rites according to Panhellenic custom. Any failure to carry out these post-battle rituals was a profound offense against both gods and man that was harshly condemned. Yet abandonment and desecration of the dead by both friend and enemy did occur in extreme circumstances. The Thebans refused to grant a truce to the defeated Athenians as long as they occupied and profaned the shrine at Delium (4.97–99); the Ambraciot herald was so shocked and appalled when he learned of the annihilation of his compatriots at Idomene that he forgot to ask for a truce (3.113); and the demoralization of the Athenians during their retreat from Syracuse was exacerbated by their inability to care properly for their dead and wounded comrades (7.75).

§7. Despite the uniformity of weaponry and tactics there were qualitative differences among Greek armies. The more professional hoplites of Sparta, notorious for their red cloaks and deliberate advance at a walk to the music of flutes, gained a reputation for military ferocity and consistently maintained military supremacy on land (4.34.1; 5.9; 5.69.2–7). It was the agrarian hoplites of Boeotia, however, who characteristically charged in deep columns who ultimately proved of all Greek armies the most formidable on the battlefield (4.96). Argive, Corinthian, and Athenian hoplites, who were less well trained and often undependable, enjoyed mixed success (4.96.5–6; 5.10.8; 5.73.1; 8.25). Gradually cities began to form elite corps to ensure uniform, well-trained contingents with high morale who might form effective spearheads in battle and offer examples for emulation by their amateur counterparts (5.67.2).

§8. Athens and Sparta during the fifth century managed to circumvent many of the rules of hoplite fighting. The presence of thousands of indentured agrarian servants in Laconia and Messenia allowed Spartan infantry to be less worried over farmwork and thus free to campaign year round if need be (see Appendix C, §3). Similarly, Athens' imperial infrastructure overseas (see Appendix B, §§ 10 and 11) supplied abundant capital and food, lessening dependence on her native ground (1.143.4–5; 2.13.1; 2.14.1; 2.21–22) and all the traditional encumbrances to ab-

solute warmaking that agrarianism had entailed (2.20.1–2.21.3; 2.59.1–2). Dur-
-ing the Peloponnesian War (431–404 B.C.) the strategic limitations of war waged
exclusively by phalanxes became unmistakable, and Thucydides clearly saw that the
inevitable collision of Athens and Sparta—atypical poleis both—would have far-
reaching effects on hoplite warfare in particular and the culture of the city-state in
general (1.2–3). Capital, not courage alone, would prove the key to the victory
(1.83.2; 1.141.5–143.2).

§9. In the new way of fighting of the Peloponnesian War battle was ubiquitous:
in rough terrain, within mountain passes, during amphibious operations, and on
long marches, cavalry, light-armed troops, and archers were needed to provide reconnaissance, cover, and pursuit against like kind (2.24–26; 3.1.2; 3.98; 6.21;
7.81–82). Peltasts (see Glossary) and other light troops—mostly highly mobile
javelin throwers unencumbered by body armor—became especially prized once
battle moved away from the plains and on to difficult ground (2.29.5; 2.79.4;
3.107–8; 4.11.1; 4.34.1–2; 4.123.4; 5.10.9). Horsemen, no longer mere ancillaries
at the peripheries of hoplite battle (4.94.1; 5.67), often became critical to military
success against a melange of enemies in a variety of locales (1.11.1; 2.31.3; 2.100;
4.44.1; 4.94.5; 6.70.2–3; 7.4.6; 7.6.2–3; 7.27.5). In the entire Peloponnesian War
there were fewer than a half dozen battles decided by the traditional collision of
phalanxes (4.43; 4.96; 4.134; 5.10–11; 5.66–73; 6.70). Far more Greeks were
killed during sieges, mass executions, ambushes, cavalry pursuits, urban street
fights, and night raids than in traditional hoplite battles.

§10. Just as often cities now chose to ride out a siege, so that the science of circumvallation—the construction of massive counterwalls to trap the citizenry within
their own fortifications—became commonplace (1.64; 3.21; 5.114; 6.99). Athens
enjoyed preeminence in storming fortifications (1.102.2) and expended enormous
sums in lengthy though ultimately successful sieges (1.104.2; 1.65.3; 2.70.2;
3.17.3–4; 4.133.4; 5.116). So in the place of agrarian protocol and phalanx fighting, city-states in search of absolute victory applied capital and technology without
ethical restraint and began to hire mercenaries, build engines, employ marines, and
rely on missile troops (4.100; 7.29–30; 7.81–82). There was no longer a clear distinction between civilians and combatants (2.5.7; 3.50; 3.68; 5.32; 5.116). The
census rubrics that had correlated civilian and military status were often ignored.
Slaves, resident aliens, and foreigners entered battle side-by-side (2.13.6; 2.31.2;
4.28.4; 5.8.2; 7.57.2); the poor and rich citizenry themselves often were employed
indistinguishably on land and sea with their participation determined solely on the
basis of military expediency (3.16.1; 3.18.3–4; 6.43.1). But the breakdown of the
old rituals—resulting in the enslavement of entire populations, the execution of
captive adversaries and the enormous capital allotted to siege works and support
troops—ensured the impoverishment of the victors and the defeated alike. Military
efficacy came at the expense of increased barbarity (1.50.1; 2.90.5; 3.50.1; 5.32.1;
5.116.4; 7.29.3–5; 7.87.3).

§11. In a social sense, the growing importance during the Peloponnesian War of horsemen, archers, slingers, skirmishers, mercenaries, and naval forces in the city-state's front ranks was antithetical to the whole idea of an agrarian community defended by its middling hoplite citizenry. So gradually military service of all types became divorced from social status and the values of an agrarian citizenry, and the original idea of the hoplites' city-state was lost. No wonder that the nostalgic Thucydides could on occasion find poignancy in the destruction of hoplite infantry on both sides during the Peloponnesian War (3.98.4; 2.42–43; 4.40.2; 7.75; 7.87).

Victor Davis Hanson
Professor of Greek
Department of Foreign Languages
and Literatures
California State University, Fresno

APPENDIX G
Trireme Warfare in Thucydides

§1. Ships, sea battles, and naval policy are key features in Thucydides' account of the Peloponnesian War. Thucydides—who served as a general and commanded a squadron of *triremes* himself (4.104.4–5; 4.106.3)—clearly viewed naval power as the key to supremacy in the Aegean (1.15); Athens' rise to empire and fall from glory was inextricably bound up with her fortunes at sea.

§2. The opening years of the Peloponnesian War saw the Athenian navy at the height of its glory: her ships were the fastest and most efficient afloat, and her oarsmen were superior in executing the complicated maneuvers by which sea battles were fought and won. But by the end of the war, the Athenian navy had collapsed: her generals had been outsmarted, her men were exhausted or dead, her ships were outmoded and defeated more than once by new tactics of naval warfare. Thucydides had a dramatic story to tell.

§3. He told it in snapshots—a moment of battle, an orator's defense of a certain naval policy, the snippet of a commander's exhortation to his men—and wrote for an audience intimately familiar with the ships, men, and often the localities and the battles themselves. These factors sometimes make it difficult for us to understand the details of what he is describing, though the general outlines are clear.

§4. The building of specialized warships already had a long history by Thucydides' day, and both warship design and naval fighting tactics had evolved substantially over the centuries. In earliest times, when fleets were used primarily for transport and the battle itself took place on land, warships were built to quickly carry as many men as possible to battle. Eventually confrontations took place at sea, but at first these earliest naval skirmishes hardly differed from the kind of fighting done on land: ships served simply as vehicles to get soldiers within close range of their enemy. Archers, javelin throwers, and hand-to-hand combat decided the outcome of battle. Gradually the ships themselves began to be used as weapons, and speed, maneuverability, and hull strength superseded the importance of transport capacity in warship design. By the time of the Peloponnesian War, naval strategy centered on the offensive capabilities of the trireme, a warship

Side view

Meters

0   5   10   15   20   25   30   35

Top view

Stern   Mid-ship   Bow

Cross-sections

Appendix G Illustration
Diagram of the modern trireme Olympias

whose main weapon was the ram mounted upon her prow. Success at sea depended on a strong crew of rowers skilled in carrying out ramming tactics.

§5. Long and sleek, with a length-to-beam ratio of 9 to 1, the trireme took its name from the arrangement of rowers. The hull enclosed two levels of rowers: the *thalamites* in the depths of the hold and the *zygites* seated on the hull's crossbeams (thwarts). A third row of oarsmen, the *thranites,* sat in outriggers mounted along the topsides of the hull. Thranites were the key members of the crew, since only they were in a position to see the oar blades enter the water. For this reason each thranite was responsible for guiding the zygite and thalamite immediately next to and below him to adjust their stroke to fit the general cadence. Thus the trireme crew worked in teams of three, and this is why the Greeks referred to these warships as *trieres,* "three-fitted." (*Trireme* is an Anglicized and Latinized version of the Greek.) This configuration packed 170 rowers into a hull only about 120 feet long and 15 feet wide, and optimized the balance of power, speed, and maneuverability: a longer boat with more rowers would have been heavier and more difficult to maneuver without gaining much in the way of increased speed; a smaller boat with fewer rowers would have lacked speed and striking power. Since ramming was the primary offensive technique, and since lightness and speed were paramount, the rest of the crew was pared down to a bare minimum. In addition to the rowers, the standard complement for an Athenian trireme during the Peloponnesian War consisted of only ten *hoplites* (marines), four archers, and about sixteen other crew to sail the boat.

§6. Like the hulls of modern racing shells, the hull of a trireme was built to be as strong but light as possible, and this is reflected in its design as well as in the techniques and materials used in its construction. The elaborate shipsheds built around the Piraeus harbors to dry-dock warships also bear eloquent testimony to the Athenians' concern for light hulls. Since a dry ship was both faster and less apt to rot than a waterlogged one, crews regularly pulled their triremes out of the water when they weren't in use. The lightweight, shallow-drafted ships were relatively easy to beach and carried rollers to help haul them onto the shore and supports to stabilize them once there. During the Sicilian expedition, when the constant danger of attack required the Athenian fleet to be ever battle-ready, drying out the hulls was of paramount concern. A note of real desperation creeps into Nicias' letter to the Athenians as he describes the impossibility of pulling his sodden ships out of the water (7.12.3–5).

§7. Because triremes were designed to maximize speed and minimize weight, almost every inch of space was used to accommodate rowers. There was hardly room for stretching, much less for sleeping or preparing and serving food. Thus, in addition to the necessity of regular beaching, triremes were constrained to travel along the coast (and put in at night so that the crew could eat and rest (1.52; 4.26; 6.44).[7a] These logistical considerations affected the strategy and tactics, the pace, and sometimes even the outcome of battles. Fighting usually ceased at sunset— sometimes even at midday—in order to rest and feed crews quickly fatigued by their exertions in the stifling heat of cramped, closely packed quarters baked under the

G7a It was this constraint that made the nonstop voyage at the second trireme to Mytilene so remarkable that Thucydides felt the need to explain how the crew did it (3.49).

Mediterranean sun. In fact, several "naval" battles were won by one fleet surprising its enemy's crews ashore while they were on dinner break (7.40). Beaches where boats could put in and the crew could disembark for eating and sleeping were so vital to naval combat that the Spartans at Pylos could plan to drive away the Athenian fleet simply by denying it access to all local landing places (4.8).

§8. A shore camp was also vital as a repository. Although a trireme carried masts and sails for long-distance travel, as well as anchors, spare oars, cooking equipment, and other supplies, when the ship entered combat all dead weight was left ashore or in an emergency jettisoned. Finally, the shore station served as both a refuge and a base from which to organize a new attack in the event of defeat. For these reasons, "naval battles" were often amphibious affairs that included fiercely fought battles on land for control of the shore (7.24). The loss of a base camp was a serious setback even for a fleet undefeated on the water.

§9. The trireme's light and slender hull can be likened to the shaft of an arrow; its point, the warship's offensive weapon, was the bronze-clad ram mounted on its prow. One such prow—the only ancient ram ever found—has been excavated off the coast of Israel, near Athlit. A warship with its buoyant wooden construction was slow to sink, and long after the battle had ended the victorious fleet scoured the waters for flooded and capsized hulls to tow off as war booty (1.54). At the very least, long timbers and the bronze ram could be salvaged and reused. The Athlit ram, although from a ship larger and later than the fifth-century triremes, provides a fascinating glimpse into the engineering and cost invested in a Greek warship. The ram itself, a hollow casing weighing half a ton, was cast in a single pouring—a feat that impresses even modern bronzesmiths. Its tip flared into fins rather than coming to a point in order to prevent it from getting wedged in the hull of its opponent, and the timbers that the bronze casing covered were carefully designed to distribute the shock of impact over the entire length of the light hull. Like our sophisticated military technology today, the ancient warship was an example of contemporary engineering at its highest level.

§10. The prow, then, with its ram and heavy buildup of timbers, was both the offensive weapon and the best protected area of the ship. The stern and sides were her vulnerable quarters. As long as a warship kept her prow toward the enemy, she was poised for both offensive and defensive action. Consequently, in the vicinity of land, the most advantageous position was a battle line drawn up parallel to the shore with prows facing seaward against the enemy (2.90). This position also had the advantage of protecting a place on the beach for the fleet to store all nonessential equipment stripped from a warship before going into battle. In open seas, a fleet achieved a defensive position by forming a circle with sterns toward the center and prows bristling outward (2.83.5; 3.78.1). A confrontation between two evenly matched fleets usually began with warships ranged in two parallel lines, prows facing one another.

§11. Only a commander with fast ships and skilled rowers could successfully take aggressive action. A commander less sure of his forces would simply wait for the attack, hoping to escape by means of evasive action. If the attacker faltered within close range, marine hoplites threw grappling irons to secure the enemy ship alongside and close-range fighting commenced between the crews of the two ships. The skilled Athenians, however, had a reputation for aggressiveness and were particularly proficient at executing two standard attack maneuvers. In the *periplous* ("sailing around") the faster Athenian ships outflanked the enemy, turned quickly, and struck from behind. Alternately, in the *diekplous* ("sailing through"), the Athenian ships broke through gaps between the enemy ships and then either immediately rammed their sides or turned quickly and battered their sterns. Ramming itself required great skill, for the enemy hull had to be hit with enough force to cause significant damage but not so much as to entangle the attacking ship in the splintered hull, preventing its crew from backing their ship away to safety. The triremes of all navies were theoretically capable of these maneuvers, but at the outset of the Peloponnesian War it seems that only Athenian crews had the expertise and discipline necessary to execute such tactics effectively.

§12. Swift confusion could descend upon even well-trained rowers once an engagement commenced and more than once turned the tide of battle (2.91, 3.77). Therefore, skilled and experienced crews were a prime commodity and rival navies competed fiercely for personnel. Rowers were generally free men hired on at decent wages; slaves were employed only in unusual circumstances (1.55; 8.15). Thucydides tells us that Athenian (6.31) and Corinthian (1.31) *trierarchs* (trireme commanders) offered substantial bonuses in an effort to lure well-trained crews, and that desertion from one navy to another was frequent (7.13). In an effort to keep her crews intact, the Athenian custom was to pay half in advance and the remainder upon completion of the voyage (8.45). The going rate in Athens was one *drachma* per day—the standard workman's wage—to row in the lower two levels of a trireme (the thalamite and zygite positions). Thranites received an additional bonus. At these rates (along with the wages of the rest of the crew), it cost about one *talent* per month to operate each trireme (for *drachma* and *talent*, see Appendix J). One major advantage of Athens' imperial income was that it allowed her to maintain fleets at sea every year and thereby bring her crews to a decisively superior level of skill in relation to those of her opponents.

§13. Their navy was an evocative symbol of the power and discipline of the democratic state for all ranks of Athenians. Even members of the upper class actively participated in the maintenance and operation of her fleet. Wealthy and powerful individuals were assigned one-year commissions as commanders (*trierarchs*) of triremes. Their appointment served as a form of tax, for while the state provided an empty ship and the crew's wages, the trierarch was responsible for outfitting and maintaining the vessel with funds from his own pocket. Their financial investment gave the upper class a powerful voice in setting naval policy, and many decisions made by Athenian commanders had at least as much to do with domestic politics as with field strategies.

§14. Of course, Thucydides, an Athenian, wrote a history of Athens, and his story is clearest in its portrayal of Athenian policy. Yet many other states—Corinth,

Syracuse, and Corcyra, among others—had powerful navies and, like Athens, their ship-of-the-line was the trireme. All triremes were basically alike in design, so that the crew of an Athenian trireme could comfortably operate a Peloponnesian or a Phoenician trireme, and vice versa. But certainly the number of warships and skilled rowers a state could muster varied greatly. At least in the early decades of the war, few could directly challenge the fleets and experienced crews of the Athenians. Thucydides' battle descriptions give us an indication of the tactics developed by Athens' enemies to counteract her superior might at sea. For example, since the classic Athenian naval maneuvers required plenty of sea room (2.89), one straight-forward measure taken by her enemies was to avoid engaging in battle on the open seas. Whenever possible, they took advantage of topography and challenged the Athenian fleet in confined waters such as the harbors of Pylos and Syracuse, where it was impossible to execute the periplous or diekplous. Confinement not only prevented the Athenians from employing their prowess at rowing but also increased the ever-present danger of ships running afoul of one another. Once fleets were locked in a standstill, fighting was reduced to hand-to-hand combat and tactics and weapons differed little from those used on land (1.48). The Corinthians (7.34) and the Syracusans (7.36) carried this strategy one step further and rebuilt their navy to suit the new demands of warfare based on strong hulls and brute force. Thucydides' description is too brief for us to understand the exact nature of the alterations, but it is clear that they redesigned their prows so that the force of collision would be aimed against the Athenians' unprotected outriggers. Rowers rather than hulls were damaged, but the effect was the same: with their wings clipped, the Athenian triremes became sitting ducks and were easily overcome by the heavily manned ships of their enemies. Over the course of the war, tactics developed to counteract Athenian rowing prowess became standard battle strategy. For navies relying on such strategies, hull strength and capacity to carry marines became more important than speed and maneuverability, and the design and operation of the classic Athenian trireme was eventually superseded by the demands of new kinds of warfare.

§15. Athens ruled the sea during the period when she alone, due to her imperial system, could finance the training, manning, and sustained operation of large numbers of triremes capable of executing sophisticated maneuvers. Thucydides eloquently described this heyday of Athenian naval might. But as the war dragged on, Athens' opponents developed new strategies and modified their ships to gain a major victory in Sicily, and then obtained financial support from Persia with which to challenge Athenian supremacy in the Aegean, and ultimately to destroy it. Almost a century would pass before the final eclipse of the trireme, but Thucydides' account heralds the beginning of the end.

Nicolle Hirschfeld
Department of Classics
University of Texas at Austin

APPENDIX H
Dialects and Ethnic Groups in Thucydides

§1. "Hellas," as the Greeks did and continue to refer to their land, was not a unified nation in Thucydides' time, but rather a country composed of hundreds of independent city-states, most of them very small. The citizens of these states all spoke Greek, but the Greek of each city-state was at least slightly different from the Greek speech of all other city-states. Athenian speech, for example, differed from that of neighboring Boeotia, and Spartan speech differed from both of these and also from that of nearby Arcadia.

§2. In general, Greeks made little comment about dialects. There was no ancient, common, Standard Greek, as there is a Modern Standard English, and it seemed natural to them that the people of different city-states had different accents. Every Greek could understand every other Greek regardless of dialect, although Thucydides does mention the Eurytanians of Aetolia whose speech was said to be exceedingly difficult to understand (3.94.5).[2a] Greek authors only occasionally took notice of dialectal differences. The Athenian comic poet Aristophanes brings Spartan, Megarian, and Boeotian characters on stage, each speaking in his native dialect[2b] to achieve comic effects; and Aeschylus, the tragic poet, has one character in the drama *The Libation Bearers* refer to speaking in "the Phocian manner"—the dialect spoken in the vicinity of Delphi. Thucydides mentions dialects several times. Although he himself writes in his native Attic with an admixture of a few Ionic forms, he does quote Dorian decrees in 5.77 and 5.79, and quotes them in a Doric dialect. The first decree must have been composed in Sparta, the second either in Sparta or in Argos. Though he might well have summarized the decrees or translated them into Attic if he had time to revise them, their presence in the text shows that he had access to Spartan decrees and could read them easily, and that later readers and scribes also could understand these dialects.

§3. Throughout antiquity the Greeks thought that all their dialects arose from three main roots: Doric, Ionic, and Aeolic. This concept must be an ancient one, for it is found in the work of the early epic poet Hesiod, who says (fragment 9) that

H2a These same people were said to eat their meat raw. Most likely Thucydides knew very little about them, but thinking them primitive, felt that their language must be primitive as well.

H2b Boeotian and Megarian characters appear in *The Acharnians,* and a Spartan woman plays an impor-

tant role in *Lysistrata*. The broad use of dialect by these characters must have delighted Athenian audiences in much the same way that modern American writers employ "yankee" or a "southern" or "western" drawl, or modern British writers use Scots or Yorkshire dialects.

from King Hellēn (= Greek) were born three sons, Dōros, Xouthos, and Aiolos. These three are the ancestors of the later Dorians, Ionians, and Aeolians—Xouthos had a son Ion, who settled in Athens and was regarded as the ancestor of the Ionians. Modern scholars accept the ancient classification, but add a fourth grouping, the Arcado-Cypriote, a dialect spoken over much of the Peloponnese before the arrival there of the Dorians.

§4. The origin of these dialectal differences is of course lost to us by time. Some scholars used to feel that the Greeks migrated into Greece in three distinct waves: first the Ionians, then the Aeolians, and finally the Dorians. And it is true at least that the Aeolic and Ionic dialects must have become differentiated long before they crossed over to Asia Minor (Ionia, 1.2.6), perhaps around 1000 B.C. The Dorian "invasion" was thought to have taken place at the very end of the Bronze Age (1200 B.C.) or later, and this date, at least for the Dorian settlement of the Peloponnese and elsewhere, must be about right. A later wave of Greek colonization (750–600) took speakers of the various dialects to Sicily, southern Italy, and the Black Sea region.

§5. Scholars no longer believe in this neat three-wave hypothesis of the arrival of the Greeks; they assume rather that dialectal differences arose among Greeks in Greece during the Bronze Age (2200–1200 B.C.). There are, however, a number of cultural differences that argue for some period of independent development of Dorians and Ionians. The names of the Dorian tribes—Hylleis, Dumanes, Pamphyleis—are common to all states whose citizens speak the Dorian dialect, but are found in no others. Each dialect group celebrates at least a few religious festivals that are peculiar to themselves and different from those of other groups. The Carneia mentioned by Thucydides (5.54; 5.75) was a uniquely Dorian festival, just as the Panionia mentioned by Herodotus (1.1.148) was a uniquely Ionic festival. Their calendars also differ in characteristic ways, as in the names of the months. Heracles, the protagonist of many tales, was the Dorian hero par excellence, and the Ionians developed myths involving the Athenian Theseus in part so as to have a native hero as powerful as Heracles.[5a]

§6. Aeolic, the dialect spoken in Boeotia, Thessaly, Lesbos and a small portion of the northern Asia Minor coast, is of little importance in Thucydides, and he rarely alludes to Aeolians (3.31.1; 8.108.4). He does say that the Lesbians are kin to the Boeotians (3.2.3; 7.57.5; 8.100.3), as indeed they are linguistically, but he also incorrectly believed that Aeolians once lived in the area around Corinth (4.42.2) and in Aetolia (3.102.5).

§7. Thucydides does make frequent references to Ionians and Dorians, however, and reports that the war between Athens and Sparta was perceived by many as a dispute between these two distinct groups, with Athens and the Ionians of the Asia Minor coast pitted against the Dorian inhabitants of the Peloponnesus and elsewhere. This view was maintained despite the fact that many Dorians fought with

H5a For Theseus, see Appendix E, §4.

Athens, and many Ionians, at least near the end of the war, fought against her. Thucydides provides a convenient list of the mixed dialectal allegiances in his description of the combatants at Syracuse (7.57–58). Rhetorically, at least, Dorians and Ionians were eternal enemies (6.80.3; 6.82.2).

§8. Thucydides makes abundantly clear that his contemporaries developed, used, and responded to distinct and pronounced stereotypes of Dorians and Ionians. Dorians were thought to be rough, hardy folk in habits—brave fighters to be sure, but rural, conservative, and a little slow. In speech they were spare, pithy, and blunt (4.17.2; 4.84.2). Ionians (and primarily Athenians), on the other hand, were cultivated in manner (1.6.3) and glib in language—clever, commercial, and adventurous: one may instance Pericles' Funeral Oration (2.36–46) as an example of Athenian developed oratory. Although some Ionians (but not Athenians) were scorned as all too ready to serve any master (6.77.2), the Athenian Ionians were feared as restless and aggressive. Many Greeks seem to have been surprised when Ionians defeated Dorians (8.25.5), as this outcome was contrary to the expectation often expressed (5.9.1; 7.5.4).

§9. The linguistic differences between the dialects were clear. Where Dorians said *dāmos* "people," as in the name of the Spartan king Archidamos, Ionians said *dēmos;* and when a Dorian said "he gives," he would say *didōti,* while an Ionian would say *didōsi.* These differences were slight, but they could sometimes be very significant. The Athenian general Demosthenes, for example, exploited the Dorian accent of the Messenians from Naupactus in order to deceive and surprise the Ambraciots at Idomene (3.112.4); and he later remarked that because their dialect was the same as that of Sparta, they would make particularly effective raiders against the Spartans (4.3.3). The Athenians, in their turn, were thrown into confusion in the night battle on Epipolae (7.44.6), when the *paean* (see Glossary) was simultaneously raised both by their Dorian allies, the Argives and Corcyraeans, and by their Dorian enemies, the Syracusans and Peloponnesians; since all these Dorians were chanting their paean in the same dialect but the Athenians could not distinguish friendly from hostile accents, the Athenians were unable to locate their allies and perceived their enemies to be on all sides, which contributed much to their bewilderment and ultimate panic.

§10. The ancients were generally more concerned with ethnic differences than with linguistic ones, and believed that language reflected character. Thucydides shared this focus, as his own interest in dialect was generally more cultural than linguistic. In this he proves a better guide to ancient attitudes toward language than to the facts of linguistic diversity.

William F. Wyatt
Classics Department
Brown University
Providence, Rhode Island

APPENDIX I

Religious Festivals in Thucydides

§1. Greek religion in Thucydides is much like the famous dog in the Sherlock Holmes tale who provided a clue because he did *not* bark in the night: Thucydides' comparative silence on Greek religious practices and institutions dramatically illustrates the rationalizing and secular nature of his work. Herodotus, for example, refers to the famous sanctuary of Apollo at Delphi more than five times as often as does Thucydides.

§2. Precisely because Thucydides' secular outlook anticipates modern inclinations, we must make an effort to understand how atypical this would have been: Socrates was, of course, executed for impiety, while the mutilation of the *Hermae* (6.27.1–3) and the profanation of the Eleusinian Mysteries described in Book 6 of Thucydides (6.28.1) brought down sentences of exile and death. An eclipse of the moon frightened the Athenians into delaying their retreat from Syracuse and led to the annihilation of the entire expedition (7.50). Thus the average fifth-century Athenian must have been far more superstitious and intolerant than one might suspect from reading Thucydides' calm and rational narrative.

§3. It is important to bear in mind two key aspects of Greek religion. First, Greeks had no religious texts comparable to the Bible or the Koran. Their religion centered around ritual practice rather than doctrine: participation in communal activities was at the heart of Greek religion, while belief was less important. Second, all Greek religious actions were, to some measure, exclusive: some religious cults were restricted to kinship groups, others were open only to citizens of a particular city-state, and the great "Panhellenic" events were restricted to those who could prove themselves to be Greek. Participation in any Greek religious activity was a sign of membership in an exclusive group, whether small or large.

§4. Scattered as they were among hundreds of small city-states from the Crimea to Spain, the Greeks desperately needed a number of central locations in which they could gather, exchange information, establish and strengthen personal contacts, and compete for a prestige that would transcend that which they had gained in their own city-states. Thucydides stresses at 1.3 that Homer has no word for the Greeks as a whole: the idea of Greece and a common Greek identity gained force only after the Greeks founded colonies throughout the Mediterranean world and came into contact with a number of different, often unfriendly, cultures.

§5. In the eighth century the local athletic contests at Olympia began to acquire an international character, as Greeks from outside the Peloponnese started competing for prizes and the admiration of their peers. The oracle of Apollo at Delphi also evolved into an international Greek institution: those who wished to found a new colony regularly consulted the god, and the oracle could, at the least, prevent two expeditions from accidentally setting off to colonize the same location. The popularity of the athletic contests at Olympia grew so great that in the first half of the sixth century games were added at Delphi (the so-called Pythian Games) as well as at Nemea and the Isthmus of Corinth. Alcibiades' speech at 6.16, which boasts of his victories at Olympia and of the credit that they conferred on Athens as a whole, provides an outstanding account of how Greeks viewed these games. Greek states took pride in the achievements of their citizens, and individual citizens could convert their athletic prestige into political power (witness the attempt by the Athenian Cylon at 1.126.3 to make himself tyrant after becoming an Olympic victor).

§6. The Greeks were extremely jealous of their independence and suspicious of any entity that acquired too much power. Panhellenic religious centers badly needed at least the appearance of neutrality if they were to maintain their authority. Unquestionably, the religious hub of the classical Greek world was the sanctuary of Apollo at Delphi. Located in the virtual center of the Greek world (it was, in fact, called the "navel of the world"), Delphi played a crucial role: it was militarily weak and thus could not translate any cultural prestige or moral authority into imperial power. Eventually, when the oracle of Apollo at Delphi took sides and reported that the god would aid the Peloponnesian side (1.118), it violated its apolitical status. Even Panhellenism had it limits: both sides assumed that the Peloponnesians would "borrow" the treasures accumulated at Delphi and Olympia (1.121; 1.143).

§7. Similarly, a universal truce was supposed to reign among Greeks during the Panhellenic athletic contests at Olympia, Delphi, Nemea, and Isthmia. When the people of Elis barred the Spartans from competing (5.49), it caused a major scandal that many feared would lead to war and undermine the cultural authority of the games. The people of Elis justified this action by accusing the Spartans of invading the territory of another Greek state during a previous Olympic truce. Thucydides reports that a truce for the Isthmian games delayed a Corinthian expedition to Chios (8.9), and that during the games themselves the Athenians gained knowledge of the Corinthian plan and were able to take preemptive action at Chios (8.10).

§8. By contrast, each Greek city-state and even many kinship groups had their own exclusive religious rituals. These included the Carneia (5.75.2) and the Hyacinthia (5.23.4) at Sparta and the Dionysia at Athens (5.23.4). Athens had pretensions to Panhellenic stature: the Eleusinian Mysteries (8.53) and the "Festival of All Athens" (Panathenaea, 6.56.2) had potential for Panhellenic stature, but the power of Athens, especially in the fifth century, made many Greeks leery of these religious institutions and limited their appeal. Contests at the religious festivals included cultural as well as athletic events—poetry, music, even orations—but it was the local festival of Dionysus at Athens that produced Greek drama, one of the most successful literary forms ever produced.

Gregory Crane
Classics Department
Tufts University
Medford, Massachusetts

APPENDIX J
Classical Greek Currency in Thucydides

§1. By the time of the Peloponnesian War, many Greek city-states, whether by themselves or organized into leagues, were minting their own coins, primarily in silver. They minted much less often in gold, a far more valuable metal, but the Persian Empire produced gold coins that the Greeks called "Daric staters."[1a] During the Peloponnesian War gold seems to have been worth about thirteen to fourteen times the value of silver. Bronze, an alloy of copper and tin, gradually became common for minting coins of small value. Most Greek coinages were used only in their own region. Only a handful of mints, Athens among them, produced coins that people were willing to accept internationally.

§2. The many different mints identified their coinages via designs and inscriptions, but they did not usually include an indication of a coin's value as money, as modern currency does. Users were expected to know how much a particular coin was worth. Greek silver and gold coinages derived perhaps as much as 95 percent of their monetary value from the intrinsic bullion value of the precious metal in each coin; the remaining value was added by the implicit guarantee that the authority issuing a coin would redeem it and thus prevent a consumer from winding up with worthless currency. Bronze coins constituted what today we call a "fiduciary coinage," whose value comes from the guarantee that its minting authority would redeem it rather than from any intrinsic value of the material from which it is made. (Almost all currency in use today is fiduciary.)

§3. Since intrinsic metallic value was so important in Greek coinages, the weight of a coin was directly related to its value. (For everyday purposes Greeks seem to have assumed that the purity of officially minted coins was essentially the same.) A Greek mint therefore produced its various denominations of coins corresponding to a system of weights. Numerous and different weight standards were in use in the Greek world. The most commonly mentioned Greek silver denomination, the *drachma* (plural = *drachmae*), weighed somewhat more than 4.3 grams as minted at Athens on the so-called Attic standard. The nearby mint of Aegina, by contrast, minted a drachma weighing 6.1 grams and therefore worth about 40 percent more

---

J1a   See Thucydides 8.28.4. It was presumably named after the Persian king Darius I (521–485 B.C.).

Some manuscripts of the text read "Doric stater," but this is an obvious mistake.

than the Athenian drachma. Six *obol*s equaled one drachma, and some mints, such as that of Aegina (5.47.6), produced obols and fractions of obols as smaller denominations. The reference at Thucydides 8.101.1 to coins of Chios called "fortieths" may also refer to a small denomination, but we lack other evidence to clarify this obscure term.

§4. Coins larger than the drachma also existed; the largest denomination in each weight system is known as a *stater*. Silver staters represented different multiples of the drachma in different weight standards. The mention of staters at Thucydides 3.70.4, for example, is usually taken as referring to Corinthian staters, which were equivalent to three-drachmae-each on the Corinthian standard (whose drachma weighed about 2.9 grams). The staters of Phocaea mentioned in Thucydides 4.52.2 refer to coins weighing about 16.1 grams and minted from electrum, a naturally occurring alloy of gold and silver that only a few Greek mints used. A Phocaean electrum stater was probably worth about twenty-four Athenian drachmae (sometimes a few more, sometimes a few less as exchange rates fluctuated). As I mentioned above, the Greeks also referred to Persian gold coins as "staters"; these coins weighed about 8.4 grams.

§5. People wishing to exchange different currencies had to make careful calculations of relative values, and moneychangers charged a hefty fee of about 5–7 percent for their services. As the text of Thucydides shows (e.g., 1.96.2; 3.50.2), Greeks could calculate large sums of money by using terms of Mesopotamian origin that literally referred to weights and not to existing denominations. The largest such unit was the *talent,* which meant a weight of just over twenty-six kilograms (about fifty-seven pounds), or a value in Athenian coin equivalent to six thousand drachmae. A *mina* (plural = *minae*) stood for one hundred drachmae (and therefore one-sixtieth of a talent). No mints produced coins that approached these values. Since the terms "talent" and "mina" strictly speaking referred to weights, they could be used to indicate amounts of precious metal still in bullion form (see 6.8.1).

§6. The only meaningful way to measure the value of ancient money in its own time is to study wages and prices. Before the inflation characteristic of the Peloponnesian War period, an unskilled laborer could expect to earn two obols per day. Toward the end of the fifth century that had risen to a drachma a day, which is what a rower in the Athenian fleet was paid. Since a *trireme* (see Appendix G, Trireme Warfare) warship carried a crew of about two hundred men, it cost one talent per month to pay the crew of a fully manned ship (i.e., six thousand drachmae, calculated as 30 days x 200 men at 1 drachma per day). Therefore, Athens needed at least six hundred talents to keep a fleet of one hundred triremes operational for six months.

§7. By about 425 B.C. a citizen of Athens received three obols for each day spent on jury duty. This payment seems to have been enough to make jury service attractive for men who could use the money to supplement other income. It was not enough money, however, to replace a day's pay for most workers. Food and clothing could be very expensive by modern Western standards. Enough barley to provide a day's porridge, the dietary staple, for a family of five cost only one-eighth of an obol, but a gallon of olive oil, another staple, cost three drachmas. A woolen cloak cost from five to twenty drachmae, while a pair of shoes could set a customer back from six to eight drachmae.

Thomas R. Martin
Classics Department
College of the Holy Cross
Worcester, Massachusetts

APPENDIX K

Calendars and Dating Systems in Thucydides

§1. The Modern, Western, Christian system of indicating years by assigning them numbers from a single point in time and then designating them consecutively as B.C. or A.D. obviously did not exist in the classical Greek world. Ancient Greek city-states used a completely different system based on local arrangements: each city-state identified a particular year by the name of the person who held a specified religious or political office in that particular city-state during that year. Therefore, the same year was known by a different designation in every city-state.

§2. Thucydides illustrates the complexity of Greek dating systems with his famous attempt in Book 2.2.1 to specify the date at which hostilities first broke out in the Peloponnesian War. The war began, he reports, when at Argos the priestess Chrysis was serving in her forty-eighth year, when at Sparta the political office of *ephor* (see Glossary) was held by Aenesias, and when at Athens the office of *archon* (see Glossary) was held by Pythodorus (see §5 below for Thucydides' reference to months at this point).[2a]

§3. Thucydides gave three different references to make the date of the first year of the war understandable by as many people as possible; that is, he hoped that any particular reader would be able to make sense of at least one of these three systems. To do so, of course, a reader would have needed a list that recorded in chronological order the names of the holders of the office being used as a standard of reference. By the fifth century B.C. city-states officially compiled lists of this sort, but ordinary people were unlikely to have had personal copies because they had no need of them for everyday purposes. Making correspondences between different local systems for indicating years, as Thucydides did, required research. He expected his readers to use the chronological fixed point of the first year of the war to calculate the date of other important events in his history, most notably the Thirty Years' Peace between Athens and Sparta that he says (1.87.6; 2.2.1) had been negotiated fourteen years earlier.

§4. The only non-local Greek system for indicating the dates of years was based on the celebration of the Olympic Games, which took place every four years. Each

K2a Athens selected nine archons every year. The one whose name was used to designate the year is known as *eponymous*, meaning "giving his name to."

period of four years (called an "Olympiad") was numbered consecutively, starting with Olympiad I, which was agreed to have begun in the year that we designate as 776 B.C. An individual year could then be specified as year one, two, three, or four of a certain Olympiad. As Thucydides' failure to give an Olympiad date for the opening of the Peloponnesian War implies, this system of reference seems not yet to have been in use at the time when he wrote.[4a] All he could probably do to derive chronological information from the Olympic record was to consult a list of victors in the games for a rough approximation of the time when someone like Cylon, whose victory he mentions at 1.126.3 as evidence of the man's eminence, had lived. As his imprecise dating of Cylon to "former generations" reveals, he could not hope for much precision from this source.

§5. In Book 2.2.1 Thucydides also mentions that Pythodorus's annual term as archon still had two months to run. Since Greeks divided the calendar of the year into twelve months, a reader who knew that the Athenians reckoned the year to begin around midsummer could deduce that the war had begun about two months before that season. To make matters more complicated, different city-states had different dates for New Year's and different names for the months. Thus, when in 423 B.C. the Athenians and the Spartans agreed on the date upon which an armistice was to begin, the same day had to be specified according to the differing calendars of the two city-states: the fourteenth day of the month Elaphebolion according to the Athenian calendar and the twelfth day of the month Cerastius according to the Spartan calendar.[5a]

§6. Greeks reckoned months according to observation of the changing phases of the moon, which meant their months were generally twenty-nine or thirty days long. Since twelve lunar months amounted to a smaller number of days than the slightly more than 365 days in a solar year, Greeks had to add extra days to the annual count to try to keep their cycle of months synchronized with the year and its seasons. Such days are said to be "intercalated," that is, inserted between other days.

§7. Since no uniform method existed for inserting extra days, sometimes officials would insert days into the calendar for religious or political reasons rather than merely to fill out the solar year. Thucydides reports (5.54.3), for example, that the Argives began a military expedition to invade their neighbor Epidaurus on the third day before the end of the month that preceded the month called Carneia by Dorian-speaking Greeks. Carneia was a month that Greeks of Dorian origin regarded as sacred and therefore off-limits for waging war. The Argives, who observed this custom, manipulated the calendar by repeatedly inserting another "third day before the end of the month" every day that they were in the field. That is, they kept designating each day of their expedition as the same day in the calendar. Since in this way they postponed the start of the month Carneia, they could continue to fight without committing any religious impropriety. When they returned home, they could then resume the regular progress of their calendar.

K4a The sophist Hippias, who lived from approximately 485 to 415 B.C., had compiled a list of Olympic victors, but numbering Olympiads to yield dates did not take place until the fourth century B.C.
K5a Thucydides, 4.118.12, 4.119.1.

§8. Thucydides explains (5.20.2) that he devised his own system of time reckoning to use in his history because he wanted a greater precision than reference to the names of officeholders allowed. His system divided time into summers and winters. "Winter" referred to the period of several months each year when Greek armies and navies generally refrained from conducting military operations for fear of inclement weather. "Summer" referred to a longer period that more or less encompassed what we mean by the seasons of spring, summer, and fall, when war could for the most part be conducted at will. Thucydides' idiosyncratic system made sense for a narrative like his that was organized around the rhythm of the military campaigns of a protracted war.

Thomas R. Martin
Classics Department
College of the Holy Cross
Worcester, Massachusetts

GLOSSARY

Acropolis: the top of a city, its highest point. Typically, it was the site of temples, shrines, and public buildings. Enclosed by its own set of defensive walls, it served as the ultimate place of retreat when a city's outer walls were breeched.

Aeolians: those Greeks who spoke the Aeolian dialect: Boeotians, Thessalians, Lesbians, and inhabitants of a small part of the adjacent coast of northern Asia Minor.

Agora: a Greek city's marketplace, its center for commercial, social, and political activity.

Archon: a magistrate at Athens, chosen by lot in the later fifth century. The nine archons were concerned with administering justice, overseeing foreign residents of Athens, adjudicating family property disputes, and carrying out a variety of other tasks. The eponymous archon gave his name to the civil year.

Ceramicus: the district of Athens, both inside and outside the city wall, where the potters lived and worked. It was also the site of an important and famous cemetery.

Delphic Oracle: a shrine to Apollo at Delphi where petitioners consulted the god as prophet. It was the most important oracular shrine in the Greek world.

Demos: originally, those Greeks who lived in the villages (*demes*) of the land. In Athens and other ancient Greek states the term "demos" came to mean the common people, the most numerous body of citizens of the state. They were often a political force—The People or The Many—in contrast to nobles, oligarchs, or despots. In Democratic Athens, the word also stood for the citizen body as a whole.

Dorians: those Greeks who spoke the Doric dialect and whose lives shared certain distinctive cultural, governmental, and religious features. They were located mainly in the southern areas of Greek settlement: Sicily, Peloponnesus, Crete, Libya, Rhodes and nearby islands.

Drachma: a unit of Greek currency: Six **obols** equaled one drachma; one hundred drachmas equaled a **mina;** six thousand drachmas (or sixty minas) equaled a **talent.**

Hellenes: men of Hellas, of Greek descent and Greek speaking, i.e., the Greeks.

Helots: Although Helot-type unfree laborers are known elsewhere, in Thucydides these are the lowest class of the Spartan state who lived in oppressive, hereditary servitude, and who were for the most part engaged in agriculture. They lived throughout Laconia and also in adjacent Messenia, where the Helot system had been extended by Spartan conquest, and they apparently far outnumbered their masters, who feared as well as exploited them.

Hermes: messenger of the gods, escort of the dead, and a fertility figure. This last identity is clearly signified by Hermae, stone columns featuring a carved depiction of Hermes' head at their top and an erect penis at the column's midpoint. Hermae were placed in front of homes, apparently as good-luck charms.

Homer: a poet thought to have lived in the eighth century B.C., possibly on the Ionian coast. Greeks knew him as the author of the epics *Iliad* and *Odyssey.* These works were famous and familiar to almost all educated Greeks.

Hoplite: a heavily armed Greek foot soldier. Though not wealthy enough to maintain a horse, a hoplite could afford the expense of outfitting himself with bronze armor consisting of helmet, breastplate, and greaves, a heavy bronze shield, a spear, and a short iron sword. The hoplite fought in close rank and file with his fellows, both giving and receiving support.

Ionians: those Greeks who spoke the Ionic dialect and whose lives shared certain distinctive cultural, governmental, and religious features. The Athenians believed that the Ionians had originated in Athens and had spread from there by an early colonization to what came to be called Ionia on the central coast of Asia Minor; there they founded and formed a loose league of cities.

Knights: the second rank of Athenian citizens, whose annual income was between three and five hundred **medimnoi** of grain; see **pentecosiomedimnoi, zeugitae,** and **thetes.**

Lacedaemon: the region of southeastern Peloponnesus that was governed by Sparta. Thucydides used the terms "Lacedaemon," "Lacedaemonian," and "Lacedaemonians" almost interchangeably with those used exclusively in this edition: "Sparta," "Spartan," and "Spartans."

Mede: the Greeks regularly referred to the Persians as "the Mede," or "the Medes," and to the Persian Wars as the "Median Wars," although the Medes and the Persians were distinct, but related, peoples.

Medimnos: an Attic dry measure of approximately twelve gallons. The **pentecosiomedimnoi,** for example, were Athenian citizens whose annual income equaled or exceeded five hundred medimnoi of grain.

Medism: those Greeks who submitted to the Persians, or who otherwise joined or assisted them, were accused of "Medism" or of having "Medized."

Metics, Resident Aliens: inhabitants of Athens who were not citizens. They could not own land but were liable to special taxes and military services. Many were involved in commerce.

Mina: a unit of currency worth one hundred **drachmas.** Sixty minae (plural) equaled one **talent.**

Neodamodeis: a special military class created by Sparta whose numbers seem to increase steadily in the succeeding half century (Sec. 7.19.3). Their precise status remains unknown, and although the name implies that they were made part of the citizen body, most scholars reject this notion.

Obol: a small unit of Greek currency; six obols equaled one **drachma.**

Ostracism: a formal procedure by which the Athenians could banish a citizen from Attica and other Athenian controlled territory for ten years without his incurring loss of property or citizenship. A citizen was "ostracized" if, after the Athenians had chosen to hold such a vote, he received the most votes, and a total of at least 6,000 votes (noted on shards of pottery called ostraka) were cast.

Paean: a ritual chant that Greek soldiers and sailors sang as they advanced into battle, rallied, or celebrated victory.

Panathenaea: an Athenian festival celebrating Athena's birthday with games, sacrifices, and processions (along the Panathenaic Way from the **Ceramicus** to the **Acropolis**). It was celebrated every year but with particular magnificence every fourth year (the Great Panathanaea).

Paralus: one of two special Athenian state triremes (the other was the *Salaminia*) used on sacred embassies and for official business.

Peltasts: lightly armed soldiers who fought without formation from a distance by throwing javelins or other missiles. Their name derived from the small, light shield that they carried.

Pentecosiomedimnoi: Athenian citizens of the highest economic class whose annual income equaled or exceeded five hundred medimnoi of grain (see **medimnos**). Below them came **knights** whose annual income was between three and five hundred medimnoi of grain, **zeugitae** whose annual income was between two and three hundred medimnoi of grain, and **thetes,** whose annual income was less than two hundred medimnoi of grain.

Perioikoi: In Thucydides these are people who "lived around Sparta." They paid taxes to the Spartan state and served in the Spartan army, but they did not participate in the Spartan government or enjoy the rights and privileges of Spartan citizens.

Peripoli: a special military corps, perhaps consisting of young recruits who served as a frontier guard.

Pnyx: the hill where the Athenian assembly met to conduct its deliberations.

Proxenus: a citizen and resident of his own state who served as a "friend or representative" (much like a modern honorary consul) of a foreign state.

Pythia: the priestess who conveyed Apollo's prophecies at Delphi.

Salaminia: one of two special Athenian state triremes (the other was the *Paralus*) used on sacred embassies and official business.

Spartiate: a full citizen of Sparta and a member of its highest citizen elite.

Stade: a unit of distance from which is derived our word *stadium;* the Attic stade was 607 feet long; the Olympic stade was 630.8 feet.

Stoa: a shedlike structure with one open side whose roof is supported by columns.

Talent: a large unit of currency equal to sixty **minae** or six thousand **drachmas.**

Thetes: the lowest rank of Athenian citizens, whose annual income was less than the two hundred **medimnoi** of grain; see **pentecosiomedimnoi, knights,** and **zeugitae.**

Thranitae: the uppermost bank of rowers in a trireme.

Zeugitae: the middle bank of rowers in a trireme; also Athenian citizens of middling status, whose annual income was between two and three hundred **medimnoi** of grain; see **pentecosiomedimnoi, knights,** and **thetes.**

BIBLIOGRAPHY OF
ANCIENT SOURCES

For the reader who would like to explore additional ancient sources—some more or less contemporary with Thucydides whose writings were influenced by events of the Peloponnesian War, others who wrote about the war or events immediately before or after it, or even some who lived and wrote much later than Thucydides (Plutarch, for example, worked in the second century A.D., five hundred years after Thucydides) but who wrote about the Peloponnesian War or some of its leading figures and used sources that were subsequently lost and are unavailable to us now—the following list of historians, philosophers, and playwrights may prove useful. All are available in English translation.

Andocides (c. 440–c. 390 B.C.): This is the very man whom Thucydides mentions but does not name in 6.60.2–4, who confessed to a role in the mutilation of the Hermae. In one of three extant speeches, *On the Mysteries,* he describes his imprisonment and the reasons for his decision to confess.

Antiphon (c. 480–411 B.C.): Several speeches and exercises survive. This is the man Thucydides describes as "not liked by the multitude because of his reputation for cleverness, and as being a man best able to help in the courts." Although a leader of The Four Hundred, he did not flee to Decelea with the other extreme oligarchs when the regime fell, and remained to be tried, found guilty, and executed.

Aristophanes (c. 450–385 B.C.): The greatest of Attic comic playwrights. Eleven of his plays survive; many speak directly of the Peloponnesian War, criticize Athenian policy, and satirize all parties, particularly contemporary Athenians.

Diodorus Siculus: He wrote a world history (c. 60–30 B.C.), some parts of which are preserved in full, others lost or only fragmentary. The work is not of high quality, but it is of interest to us for its reflection of other historical writers and sources that he used and that are now lost. His section on the Peloponnesian War is complete and found in his Books 12 and 13. While he clearly relies upon Thucydides for some events, much of his account comes from others, presumably a great deal from the historian Ephorus, whose work is lost.

Euripides (c. 485–c. 406 B.C.): One of three outstanding Attic tragic playwrights and poets of the fifth century, some of whose surviving plays are clearly marked by events of and attitudes connected to the Peloponnesian War.

Herodotus (c. 485–c. 425 B.C.): A marvelous historian of the Persian Wars (who describes much else besides); his work was certainly known to Thucydides, and it is probably Herodotus whom Thucydides criticizes (without mentioning his name), in 1.20. See the Introduction to this volume, II.i, ii, v; IV.i, ii.

Hippocratic Writings: A compilation of medical writings, some more or less contemporaneous with Thucydides, which may well have influenced his extraordinary clinical description of the plague (2.47–53).

Lysias: A resident alien at Athens; a manufacturer of shields during the war who, when condemned to death by The Thirty tyrants in 404, managed to escape to Megara (although his brother Polemarchus was captured and executed). He returned later to write many legal speeches that have come down to us, many of which are informative about Athenian life at that time, and one of which (*Against Eratosthenes*) describes his own arrest and escape from the tyranny of The Thirty.

Old Oligarch: The name given by us to the author of a pamphlet titled *The Constitution of the Athenians* that describes and explains the Athenian democracy and the success of its navy while criticizing the system as unnatural. The unknown author is thought to have been a fifth-century Athenian with oligarchic views.

Oxyrhynchus Hellenica: Three separate papyri containing some nine hundred lines of an unknown Greek historian were found at the site of Oxyrhynchus in Egypt in 1906. This competent historian writes of Greek history in the period that immediately followed that covered by Thucydides, and like him he arranges his material by successive summers and winters. The best section of what survives deals with the Boeotian federal constitution of 396/5. See note 5.38.2a.

Plutarch (c. A.D. 50–c. 120): A Boeotian author who wrote comparative biographies of famous Romans and Greeks to illustrate morality and personal worth or failure. Despite this moral focus, and the fact that he wrote almost five hundred years after Thucydides died, he provides interesting information, some of it in the form of personal anecdotes, and much of it drawn from sources now lost. Among many biographical depictions, he wrote about such Athenians as Pericles, Alcibiades, and Nicias, and about the Spartan Lysander, all of whom were military and political leaders during the Peloponnesian War.

Xenophon (c. 428–c. 354 B.C.): As an Athenian of aristocratic background, Xenophon took part in and intentionally wrote about events that occurred just after Thucydides' narrative breaks off. His aristocratic background and connections with The Thirty in 404–3 forced him to leave Athens for most of his adult life. While not nearly as skillful a historian as Thucydides, he provides much useful information for which he is the only source.

R.B.S.

CONCISE BIBLIOGRAPHY
OF MODERN SOURCES

All modern inquiry on Thucydides is based on A. W. Gomme, A. Andrewes, and K. J. Dover's five-volume *A Historical Commentary on Thucydides* (Oxford, 1945–1981). The *Commentary* is much more than a running guide to the Greek text of Thucydides; in addition it serves as a philologically based history of fifth-century Greece itself. More recently, Simon Hornblower has published the first installment (Oxford, 1991) of a proposed two-volume *A Commentary on Thucydides,* which is planned to update, but not to replace, Gomme et al., incorporating more recent advances in archaeological discovery and modern secondary historical and philological research. Hornblower has wisely designed his commentary to appeal to the growing number of introductory students working entirely from an English translation of Thucydides.

Both the most recent and the most accessible surveys of Thucydides in English are Simon Hornblower's *Thucydides* (Baltimore, 1986), and W. R. Connor's similarly entitled *Thucydides* (Princeton, N.J., 1984). Connor's book is the more approachable for the student, providing an empathetic and often moving account of the historian and his subject matter within a formal summary of the eight books of the history. Hornblower, in contrast, is concerned with introducing the scholarly problems that arise from the specialist's use of Thucydides. One finds within the latter's eight chapters an introduction to controversies over methodology, dating, the speeches, and Thucydides' own notion of history itself.

Literally hundreds of comprehensive articles and books have been written in the last two centuries on Thucydides in the modern European languages. Most are specialist studies of authorship, language, structure, and dating, and many of the best remain untranslated in German. However, some of this valuable work of K. von Fritz, O. Luschnat, E. Schwartz, and W. Schadewaldt can still be accessed in English through derivative criticism in F. Adcock's well-written *Thucydides and His History* (Cambridge, 1963); F. M. Cornford's widely speculative, but at times brilliant *Thucydides Mythistoricus* (London, 1907); J. de Romilly's *Thucydides and Athenian Imperialism,* trans. P. Thody (Oxford, 1963); and especially the essays by A.

Momigliano (*Studies in Historiography* [London, 1966]) and M. I. Finley (*Ancient History: Evidence and Models* [London, 1985]), which contain random though invaluable insights into Thucydides' place in the tradition of Greek historiography. Less detailed efforts also draw on the same material in placing the thought and language of Thucydides within the intellectual landscape of his times. The two best shorter summaries still remain J. H. Finley's *Three Essays on Thucydides* and K. J. Dover's brief *Thucydides* (Oxford, 1973).

Standard encyclopedias of Greek history and literature contain well-summarized entries on Thucydides as historian, philosopher, and literary artist. The four most useful and available articles are found in *The Cambridge History of Classical Literature, Vol. 1: Greek Literature*, ed. P. E. Easterling and B.M.W. Knox (Cambridge, 1985); *The Cambridge Ancient History, Vol. 5: The Fifth Century B.C.*, ed. D. M. Lewis, J. Boardman, J. K. Davies, and M. Ostwald (Cambridge, 1992); A. Lesky, *A History of Greek Literature*, trans. J. Willis-C. de Heer (London, 1966); and a brief sketch in W. K. C. Guthrie, *A History of Greek Philosophy*, 6 vols. (Cambridge, 1962–1980).

Finally, general accounts of the Peloponnesian War critique Thucydides' investigative accuracy and his overall value in reconstructing Greek history of the period. The two most engaging summaries of Thucydides as historian of the war between Athens and Sparta are found in D. Kagan's sober *The Archidamian War* (Ithaca, 1974), the first volume of a comprehensive and indispensable four-volume history of the Peloponnesian War, and G. E. M. de Ste. Croix's brilliant but often combative *The Origins of the Peloponnesian War* (London, 1972). G. B. Grundy's *Thucydides and the History of His Age* (Oxford, 1948) was written before many of the important fifth-century Attic inscriptions were published, but it remains a fascinating review of Thucydides' own knowledge about the military, economic, and social conditions of fifth-century Greece.

Victor Davis Hanson
Professor of Greek
Department of Foreign Languages
and Literatures
California State University, Fresno

ACKNOWLEDGMENTS

This edition could never have been completed without the assistance of a large number of colleagues and friends. Foremost among them is Alan Boegehold of Brown University, who not only submitted two appendices to this text, but has consistently supported my forays into the classics in many ways and for many years. Special thanks also go to Donald Kagan of Yale University, who provided encouragement at crucial moments and recommended me to others who became vitally important to the project. Among those was Glen Hartley, my agent for the book, who gave much helpful advice and introduced me to Adam Bellow, who seems unique among current trade editors for his interest in the classics. Glen also recommended Kim Llewellyn, who designed this book, and whose expertise is basically responsible for its lucid and tasteful presentation of text, notes, and maps. Stephen Morrow did the editorial trench work for The Free Press and deserves high praise for bringing the whole project together. Thanks also are due to Loretta Denner for her superb copyediting and proofing supervision.

Victor Davis Hanson of California State University, Fresno, has contributed the Introduction, an Appendix on hoplite warfare, and the modern bibliography to this volume. I am profoundly grateful for his invaluable support, advice, and counsel. George Cawkwell of University College, Oxford, also provided much indispensable counsel and assistance, particularly in examining and revising Crawley's text, but also in reviewing and commenting on other elements of the edition. Paul Cartledge of Clare College, Cambridge, contributed appendices on Sparta and the Peloponnesian League, gave much good advice, and greatly improved the many sections of text that he kindly reviewed.

Many thanks are owed to Anne Gibson, manager of the Clark University Cartography and Information Service, who drew the finished maps: her patience and professional skill were a tremendous help to me, and I believe the quality and clarity of her work is outstanding. I am also most grateful to Professor Richard Talbert, director and editor of the Classical Atlas Project, for his expert assistance in locating obscure classical sites and his general review of this edition's maps.

I wish also to express my appreciation to Simon's Rock College of Bard, its students, and its provost Bernard Rodgers; it was while teaching there that I first perceived the need for this volume. Elli Mylonas and Gregory Crane of the Perseus project gave freely of their time and educated me in the basic computer techniques that were so essential to my own preliminary design of the maps, the notes, and the text itself. My assistant Sandra Kleiner kept the project in order when I was not, conducted the search for illustration rights, and remained cool even when machine breakdowns at crucial moments threatened to overwhelm us.

I would like to acknowledge a debt to the History Department of Harvard University, which in 1958, when I was an undergraduate, set up a special tutorial course for me in ancient history. The man who tutored me, George Nadel, provided the stimulus and the scholarly background that I believe made it possible for me to return to the study of ancient history some twenty-five years later, after a career in business. In that context, I would also like to thank John B. Wilson of Oxford who provoked my interest in Thucydides' Pylos narrative and encouraged me to write about it, and Christopher B. R. Pelling of University College, Oxford, whose excellent and always sympathetic editorial assistance made it possible for me to complete the articles that marked my entry into the field.

Finally, I must acknowledge the assistance and support that I received at all times from my family. My daughter, Karen, reviewed Crawley's text and by noting terms, phrases, and constructions that seemed to her modern ear to be archaic, obscure, or awkward, provided an invaluable opening platform for revising his text. My son, Matthew, has always expressed interest in this edition and provided much assistance to my first efforts to return to the classics when I wrote articles on the Pylos campaign. My brother, David, who is also my partner in business, must be thanked for permitting me without comment or complaint to greatly reduce my time and attention to our business affairs in order to pursue this labor of love. Last but certainly not least, my greatest thanks go to my wife, Toni, who suffered through my occasional bouts of despair when I doubted whether this book would ever be completed, and endured my frequent bursts of obsessive attention to this six-year project. Her support through it all at no little personal sacrifice was more essential to the completion of this edition than any element of assistance that I received from anyone, anywhere. I am profoundly grateful to her.

R.B.S.

INDEX

Note that this index treats only the English translation, not the Greek text. Thus, abstractions, concepts, and images present in Thucydides' original version but absent in the translation are not cited.

laid waste by Thracians, 2.100.4
Anthene (Laconia), 5.41.2
Anthesterion (month of Athenian calendar), 2.15.4
Anticles (Athenian commander), 1.117.2
Antimenidas (Spartan envoy), 5.42.1
Antiochus (king of Orestia), 2.80.6
Antiphemus of Rhodes, as cofounder of Gela, 6.4.3
Antiphon (Athenian statesman)
democracy in Athens opposed by, 8.90.1
in establishment of oligarchy, 8.68.1–2
sent to Sparta to make peace, 8.90.2
Thucydides describes, 8.68.1–2
Antissa
Astyochus sends hoplites from Eresus to, 8.23.4
on Lesbos, 3.18.1–2, 3.28.3
Antisthenes (Spartiate), 8.39.1
Aphrodisia (Laconia), 4.56.1
Aphrodite, temple of at Eryx, 6.46.3
Aphytis on Pallene, 1.64.2
Apidanus river, 4.78.5
Apodotians, 3.94.5, 3.100.1
Apollo
Apollo Archegetes at Naxos, 6.3.1
Delian, Rhenea consecrated to, 1.13.6
Malean Apollo festival, 3.2.2–3
Pythaeus, temple of, run by Argives, 5.53.1
Pythian
access to all at Delphi, 4.118.1
at Athens, 2.15.4
sanctuary of Delium fortified, 4.90.1–4
statue of at Amyclae, Sparta, 5.23.5
temples
at Actium, 1.29.3
at Argos, 5.47.11
in Laconia opposite Cythera, 7.26.2
at Leucas, 3.94.2
at Malea, 3.3.3
Apollo Temenites (Syracuse)
Syracusan army refuge, 6.100.2
Syracusan forces at, 7.3.3
wall built to enclose statue and district, 6.75.1
Apollonia (Corinthian colony), 1.26.2
arbitration
Argive offer to submit to, 5.59.5
Athenian readiness to meet Spartan demands through, 1.145.1
Athens tells Sparta to submit differences to, 1.78.4
Corcyraean offer to settle dispute over Epidamnus, 1.28.1–3
by Spartans
Argos–Sparta treaty calls for, 5.79.1
Athens refuses to arbitrate Scione dispute, 4.122.4–5

Elean–Leprean dispute, 5.31.2–5
Spartan apprehension over their past refusal to arbitrate, 7.18.2–3
Spartans not submitting issues to, 1.140.2
Spartans refuse Argive demand for, 5.41.2
Spartan view of Athenian unwillingness to arbitrate, 7.18.2–3
Arcadia/Arcadians, 1.2.3
as ally of Sparta, 5.57.2, 5.64.3–5
in battle of Mantinea, 5.67.1–2
Mantinea reduces to subjection, 5.29.1
in Sicilian expeditions, 7.57.9
Archedice (daughter of Hippias), epitaph of, 6.95.3
Archelaus (son of Perdiccas), 2.100.2
archers
Athenian
at Aegitium, 3.98.2–3
at battle of Anapus river, 6.69.2
Pericles enumerates, 2.13.8
plan for use in naval battle, 7.60.4
at Sphacteria/Pylos engagement, 4.32.2–4, 4.34.1–3, 4.36.1
at Syracuse, 6.43.1
of Camarina at Syracuse, 7.33.1
in naval battle off Sybota, 1.49.1
Spartans raise force of, 4.55.2
Thracian hordes mounted, 2.96.1
Archestratus (Athenian commander), 1.57.6
Archetimus (Corinthian commander), 1.29.2
Archias
Heraclean founder of Syracuse, 6.3.2
plans to betray Camarina, 4.25.7
Archidamus (king of Sparta)
censure of, 2.18.1
gods and heroes of Plataea appealed to by, 2.74.2–3
as guest-friend of Pericles, 2.13.1
as leader of
first Peloponnesian invasion of Attica, 2.12.4, 2.19.1
Peloponnesian army against Plataea, 2.71.1
Peloponnesian forces in Attica, 3.1.1
second force to invade Attica, 2.47.2
offers protection if Plataeans accept neutrality, 2.72.1–3
Peloponnesian army moved against Plataea by, 2.75.1
speech about possible war with Athens, 1.79–1.85
speech before army at the Isthmus, 2.11.1–9
strategy at Acharnae, 2.20.1–5
Archonides (Sicel king), 7.1.4
Arcturus, the rising of, 2.78.2

Argilus (Chalcidice)
Brasidas' army takes position at Cerdylium on, 5.6.3–5
inhabitants plot with Brasidas to take Amphipolis, 4.103.3–5
will pay tribute to Athens, 5.18.5
Arginousae, 8.101.2
Arginus, Cape, 8.34.1
Argos/Argives
Agis outmaneuvers in Arcadia, 5.58.3, 5.59.4
alliance with Elis, 5.31.1–5
ambassadors sent to Athens to negotiate alliance, 5.44.1–2
at Anapus river, 6.67.1, 6.70.2
antidemocratic faction
brings about acceptance of peace treaty, 5.76.3
creates oligarchy, 5.81.2
Argive Pollis with Peloponnesian envoys to Persian King, 2.67.1
army. *See* armies: Argive
Athens and
Athenian alliance with, 1.102.4, 1.107.5
Athenians go to relief of, 6.105.1–3
Athenians hire for expedition to Sicily, 6.43.1
Boeotian decision on alliance with, 5.37.1–5, 5.38.1–4
Corinth as ally of, 5.48.2
as Dorians fighting with Athenians against Dorians, 7.57.9
economic conditions at end of Archidamian war, 5.28.2–3
envoys. *See* envoys: Argive
government. *See* government: Argos
as group in early Hellas, 1.3.3
joins allies at Olympia, 5.50.3
long walls built and destroyed, 5.82.4, 5.82.5, 5.83.1
marches against Epidaurus with allies, 5.75.5
Milesians defeat at Miletus, 8.25.1–3
negotiations with Corinth after fifty-year peace agreement, 5.27.1–3
neutrality of, 2.9.2
popular party overthrows oligarchy, 5.82.2–6
pro-Spartan Three Hundred removed from, 5.84.1
seeks alliances with Hellenic states, 5.28.1–3
against Sparta and allies, 5.58.2
Spartans march against in
year 417/6, 5.83.1
year 414, 6.95.1, 6.105.1
Spartan treaty, 5.77.1–8, 5.78.1–4
Spartan treaty proposed by, 5.41.1–3
territory of Phlius invaded by, 6.105.3
Themistocles in exile in, 1.135.3, 1.136.1

deception *(cont'd)*
unstated real goal of is to conquer
Sicily, 6.6.1
Corcyraeans cause opponents to
attempt escape, 4.46.5
by Egestaeans to fool Athenians, 6.8.2,
6.46.3–5
Hermocrates convinces Athenians to
delay departure, 7.73.2–3
in maneuvers to become leaders of the
People, 8.89.4
Plataeans accept proposal but concentrate forces for attack, 2.3.1–3
by Sparta
Alcibiades and Chalcideus deceive
the Chians, 8.14.2
Athenians dismissed without disclosing real reasons, 1.102.3
Brasidas lies to Acanthians about
forces at Megara, 4.85.7
conceal their concern over revolution, 4.41.3
confers freedom on bravest Helots
then kills them, 4.80.3–5
Pausanias' real intention is to plot
with the King, 1.128.3
Persian threat cited as pretext for
Athens to remain unwalled, 1.90.2
true mission of Spartan envoys is to
find pretext for war, 1.126.1
Syracusans dine quickly to fool Athenians, 7.39.2, 7.40.1–5
Themistocles falsely claims credit for
unbroken bridges, 1.137.4
Tissaphernes' duplicity concerning
Phoenician fleet, 8.87.1–5
defection. *See also* betrayal
of Argos from alliance with Athens,
Elis, and Mantinea, 5.81.1
of Athenian allies, 1.99.1–3
attempt to persuade Tegeans to defect
to Argos, 5.32.3
of Mantineans to Argos, 5.29.1–2
Delian games, 3.104.2–6
Delium
Athenian losses at, 5.14.1
Athenians leave garrison in, 4.96.9
Athenians prepare to engage Boeotians
near, 4.93.2
battle of, 4.93–4.96
battle losses at, 4.101.2
Boeotians and Athenians dispute over,
4.97.1–4, 4.98.1–8, 4.99.1
Boeotians use flame device to capture,
4.100.1–5
commanders speak to their troops,
4.91, 4.96.1
Hippocrates fortifies sanctuary of
Apollo at, 4.90.1–4
in plot to install democracy in Boeotia,
4.76.4–5
Delos
Delian games, 3.104.2–6

Delians expelled by Athenians from, 5.1.1
Delians returned by Athenians to,
5.32.1
earthquake at, 2.8.3
as location of early league treasury and
congresses, 1.96.2
Peloponnesian fleet reaches, 3.29.1
purification by Athenians of, 1.8.1,
3.104.1–2
verses of Homer related to, 3.104.4–5
Delphi
Corinthians propose borrowing from
treasury of, 1.121.3
Delphic god commands Athenians to
return Delians to Delos, 5.32.1
expedition against Naupactus assem-
bles at, 3.101.1
free access to all agreed during armistice, 4.118.1
oracle of
Cylon might have misinterpreted,
1.126.4–6
Epidamnus asks advice of, 1.25.1–2
Spartans ask about outcome of the
war, 1.118.3
Spartans at Ithome follow old oracle, 1.103.2
Spartans get advice about founding
colony at Heraclea, 3.92.5
Sparta and Athens vie for control of
temple, 1.112.5
Spartans fear Pleistoanax bribed priestess of, 5.16.2
spoils from battle of Laodicium sent
to, 4.134.1
Delphinium (Chios), Athenians fortify
base at, 8.38.2, 8.40.3
Demagon (one of founders of Heraclea), 3.92.5
Demaratus (Athenian commander),
6.105.2
Demarchus (Syracusan general), 8.85.3
Demeter of Eleusis, temple at Athens,
2.15.1
Demiurgi (government officials at
Mantinea and Elis), 5.47.9
democracy
in Argos, 5.31.6
Mantinea and Argos combine because
both are democracies, 5.29.1
replaced by oligarchy, 5.81.2
seeks alliance with Athens because
both are democracies, 5.44.3
Athenagoras compares oligarchy and,
6.39.1–2
in Athens
abolished in subject cities, 8.65.1
Alcibiades' view of, 6.89.4–6,
8.47.2, 8.48.1
Cleon calls it "incapable of empire,"
3.37.1
Diodotus describes the proper role
of speech and speakers in, 3.42.3–6

mutilation of Hermae thought to be
part of antidemocratic plot, 6.27.3
"nominal democracy under Pericles
is government by first citizen,"
2.65.9
opponents of call for rule of Five
Thousand, 8.92.11
Pericles on, 2.37.1–3
political faction hopes to subvert,
1.107.4–6
prudence of citizens of when in crisis, 8.1.4
put down, 8.63.3
reestablished, 8.97.1
Thucydides calls regime the "best
government in his time," 8.97.2
Boeotian faction wants to introduce,
4.76.2
Corcyraean oligarchs murdered
attempting to subvert, 3.81.4
in Samos
Athenians at Samos plot subversion
of, 8.47.2, 8.48.1, 8.49.1
the People revolt in Samos, 8.21.1
set up by Athenians, 1.115.3
Sicilian adversaries of Athens as cities
similar to Athens, 7.55.2
Thasos abolishes, 8.64.2
Thespiae, pro-democratic coup fails,
6.95.2
Demodocus (Athenian commander),
4.75.1
Demosthenes (Athenian commander)
Aetolians defeat at Aegitium,
3.96.1–3, 3.97.1–3, 3.98.1–5
Agraeans subdued by, 4.77.2
Ambraciot reinforcements defeated at
Idomene by, 3.112.1–8, 3.113.1–6
arrives at Siphae but finds it closed to
him, 4.89.1
athletic contest used to extract garrison, 5.80.3
command of
allied army at Amphilochia,
3.105.3, 3.107.2–3
fleet sent round the Peloponnesus,
3.91.1–3
forces against Leucas, 3.94.2–3
reinforcements to Athenian expedition to Sicily, 7.16.2
ships at naval battle in Great Harbor, Syracuse, 7.69.4
forces routed raiding Sicyon, 4.101.4
leads charge of light troops from
ambush at Megara, 4.67.2–5
negotiations with Peloponnesians after
Olpae, 3.109.1
persuades Acarnanians to help defend
Naupactus, 3.102.3–4
plots with dissidents to introduce
democracy to Boeotia, 4.76.1–2
plots with Megarian popular leaders to
betray Megara, 4.66.3

information *(cont'd)*

of Chian revolt reaches Athens, 8.15.1

to Cleon of Brasidas' approach at Amphipolis, 5.10.2–4

to Cleon of movements of Brasidas' troops at Amphipolis, 5.10.2–3

about conduct and personality of Brasidas, 4.108.2–3

to Corinthians of Athenian expedition, 4.42.3–4

Demosthenes informs of danger to Pylos, 4.8.3

Demosthenes knew of enemy's approach in time to obtain help from Acarnania, 3.102.3–4

Demosthenes learns of Ambraciot reinforcements, 3.110.4

enemy fleet's campfires warn Athenians of arrival, 8.102.1

to Gylippus about siege works at Syracuse, 6.104.1, 7.1.1

herald discovers Ambraciot losses at Idomene, 3.113.1–5

about influence of Thucydides in Thracian mainland, 4.105.1

informant in affair of the Mysteries and mutilation of the Hermae, 6.60.2–4

messages sent by Spartiates at Caunus to Miletus, 8.39.4

to Mytilene from Sparta about invasion of Attica, 3.25.1

Mytilene learns of approaching Athenian fleet, 3.3.5

in Nicias' letter about conditions on Sicily, 7.11–7.15

to Nicias of financial problems of Syracuse, 7.49.1

to Nicias of pro-Athenian faction in Syracuse, 7.48.2, 7.49.1

to Sparta about rebuilding Athens' walls, 1.91.1

Spartans fear Athenians at Melos will broadcast news of them, 8.39.3

Syracusans learn of Peloponnesian reinforcements, 7.2.1–2

to Syracuse about Athenian expedition, 6.32.3, 6.45.1

Tegea sends word urging Spartans to come immediately, 5.64.1

Thucydides on reliability of traditional, 1.20.1–3

insubordination

Athenian soldiers have sudden impulse to build fort at Pylos, 4.4.1

Athenians refuse to board ships, 7.72.1

authorities fear Syracusans will refuse to take up arms after naval victory, 7.73.2

Cleon learns about Torone from deserters, 5.2.3

Hermocrates calls Syracusan soldiers insubordinate, 6.72.4

Nicias complains of natural indiscipline of Athenian seamen, 7.14.2

order breaks down at Assinarus, 7.84.3

Spartan unit commanders refuse to obey, 5.72.1

Syracusans and Thurians attack Astyochus, 8.84.2–3

intelligence. *See also* disinformation; information; news; reconnaissance; signals

Aetolians aware of Demosthenes' plans, 3.96.3

of the approach of Phoenician fleet, 1.116.3

to Athenians about arrival of Peloponnesian and Sicilian ships, 8.26.1, 8.27.1

to Athenians about Spartiates and ships at Caunus, 8.41.3–4

Athenians at Eresus finally learn of passage of enemy fleet, 8.103.2

Athenians aware of Corinthian plots, 1.57.6

Athenians aware of enemy assessment of their weakness, 3.16.1

Athenians gather intelligence at Isthmian games, 8.10.1

Athenians know of preparations of enemy fleet at Las, 8.91.2

Athenians learn of enemy ships at Cnidus and Triopium, 8.35.2

Athenians learn Peloponnesian fleet is about to sail, 3.80.1

to both sides of each other's fleet movements, 8.79.3, 5

Chian slave deserters provide, 8.40.2

Chians sail to Anaia to gain, 8.19.1

Corcyraeans learn of Corinthian preparations, 1.28.1, 1.31.3

Corinthians learn of Corcyraean siege of Epidamnus, 1.27.1

Eurymedon learns at sea of loss of Plemmyrium, 7.31.3

Gylippus knows Athenian tactical plans, 7.67.2

Hermocrates knew Nicias was reluctant to command, 6.34.6

to Mytilene by messenger, 3.25.1–2

news of Athenian intentions not believed at Syracuse, 6.32.3

Nicias accurately describes Gylippus' plans, 7.12.1–3

Nicias learns of approach of Gylippus, 6.104.2

Peloponnesians learn of disturbances at Samos, 8.79.1

Potidaeans learn of Athenian demands, 1.58.1

proxeni inform Athens of Mytilenean plot, 3.2.3

Spartans knew Athenians intended to dispute their passage, 1.107.3

Syracusan exiles provide Athenians with information, 6.64.1

to Syracusans about Athenian cavalry, 6.96.1

Syracusans know Athenians winter at Naxos, 6.75.2

Syracusans know of Athenian request for reinforcements, 7.7.3

Syracusans learn Athenians send envoys to Camarina, 6.75.3

Syracusans learn of approaching Athenian fleet, 7.36.1

Syracusans learn of Athenian cargo ships, 7.25.1

Syracusans learn of Athenian decision to depart, 7.51.1

to Syracusans of Athenian grappling-irons, 7.65.1

interest(s)

Athenians say calculations of lie behind Spartan cries for justice, 1.76.2

Athenians say no one can fault a city for safeguarding its, 1.75.5

Brasidas: "It is indeed in our interests to do what we say," 4.87.1

Corinthians say Hellas will join war against Athens from fear and, 1.123.1

going to war to serve one's interests, 4.59.3

the issue is not their guilt, but our interests, 3.44.1

leave right alone and talk only of interests, 5.90.1, 5.98.1

Perdiccas departs from his natural interest, 4.128.5

public interests suffer in revolution, 3.82.8

Iolaus (Macedonian general), 1.62.2

Ionia/Ionians. *See also* Miletus; Mycale

adopt Athenian fashion, 1.6.3

Athenian colonies, 1.2.6, 1.12.4

Athenians agree to cede to the Persian King, 8.56.4

Athenians as, 7.57.2–4

Athenians remain with Ionian allies, 1.89

celebrate festivals at Ephesus, 3.104.3

Dorians defeated by, 8.25.5

Myonessus, 3.32.2

naval strength of, 1.13.6

Persian conquest of, 1.16.1

subjects paying tribute to Athens, 7.57.4

Themistocles sails to, 1.137.2

towns of listed as tributary to Athens, 2.9.4

Ionian gulf

Demosthenes and Eurymedon lead fleet across, 7.33.3

Epidamnus on the right side of
entrance of, 1.24.1
Ionian sea
on coasting route to Italy, 6.13.1
route of Athenian fleet to Sicily,
6.30.1, 6.44.1
route of Gylippus across, 6.104.1
Ionic gulf. *See* Ionian gulf
Ipnians, join Peloponnesians against
Naupactus, 3.101.2
iron. *See* metals
Isarchidas (Corinthian commander),
1.29.2
Ischagoras (Spartan commander)
in implementing Spartan–Athenian
treaty, 5.21.1
joins Brasidas, 4.132.2–3
Isocrates (Corinthian commander),
2.83.4
Isthmian festival, 8.9.1, 8.10.1
Isthmian games, 8.10.1
isthmuses, occupied for reasons of
commerce, 1.7.1
isthmuses in Thucydides
of Corinth
assembly point for Peloponnesian
invasions of Attica, 2.10.1
Athenian raid on Corinthian territory near, 4.42.2
Athenians display sea-power at, 3.16.1
hauling machines to carry ships
across, 3.15.1
Spartans haul ships bound for Chios
and Lesbos across, 8.7.1, 8.8.3–4
strategic commercial location, 1.13.1
Epidamnus located on, 1.27.1
in Laconia opposite Cythera
evacuated by the Athenians, 8.4.1
fortified by the Athenians, 7.26.2
of Leucas, 3.94.2
Peloponnesians haul ships across,
3.81.1, 4.8.2
at Methana fortified by Athenians, 4.45.2
at Miletus, 8.25.5
at Potidaea, 1.64.1
at Thapsus, 6.97.1–2
at Torone, 4.113.2
Istone, Mount
Corcyraean exiles fortify themselves
on, 3.85.3, 4.2.3
surrender and capture of Corcyraean
exiles, 4.46.1–3
Italus (king of the Sicels), 6.2.4
Italy. *See also* Croton; Iapygia;
Locri/Locrians, Epizephyrian;
Medma; Metapontum; Rhegium;
Sicily; Tarentum; Thurii
Caulonia, 7.25.2
Cumae, 6.4.5–6
Gylippus, believing Syracuse lost, aims
to save, 6.104.1–3
Halex river, 3.99.1
Hipponium, 5.5.3

Hylias river, 7.35.2
Italian allies ordered by Sparta to build
ships, 2.7.2
Italians serving with Athenians at
Syracuse, 7.57.11
Peloponnesian colonies to, 1.12.4
Petra (Rhegium), 7.35.2
Phaeax tries to enlist friendships in,
5.5.1–3
sends provisions to the Athenians,
6.103.2
Sybaris river, 7.35.1
Syracuse and Leontini supported by,
3.86.2
Itamenes (commander of foreign
troops at Colophon), 3.34.1
Ithome
besieged by Spartans, 1.101.3,
1.102.1, 1.103.1
rebel Helots from Ithome settled at
Naupactus, 1.103.2–3
Itys, outrage of, 2.29.3

javelin throwers, 1.49.1
judges
to decide fate of Plataeans, 3.52.3–4,
3.68.1–4
Judge of Cythera, 4.53.2

Kaiadas (Sparta), where Spartans cast
criminals, 1.134.5
Kestrine (borders Thesprotis), 1.46.4
knights
Athenian property class, 3.16.1
unit in Spartan army, 5.72.4
Krokyle (Aetolia), captured by
Athenians, 3.96.2

Labdalum (Epipolae)
Athenian garrison at, 6.98.2
fort built by Athenians, 6.97.5
Syracusans take Athenian fort at, 7.3.4
Lacedaemonius (Athenian commander),
1.45.2
Laches (Athenian commander)
arrives with troops to assist Argos, 5.61.1
in command of fleet at Sicily, 3.86.1,
3.90.2, 3.103.3
in command of ships sent to Rhegium,
3.86.1–4
replaced by Pythodorus, 3.115.2
Lacon (Spartan *proxenus* of Plataea),
3.52.4, 3.35–3.59
Laconia. *See also* Thyrea
Anthene, 5.41.2
Aphrodisia, 4.56.1
Asine, 4.54.4
Athenian fleet ravages in
year 431, 2.25.1
year 428, 3.7.2
year 424, 4.54.4
year 413, 7.26.2
Cotyrta, 4.56.1

and Cythera, 4.53.3, 4.54.3
fort evacuated by Athenians, 8.4.1
Helus, 4.54.4
Las, 8.91.2
Sciritis, 5.33.1
Spartans reorganize defense of, 4.55.2
Lade (island off Miletus)
Athenian ships take up station at,
8.17.3
blockade of Miletus by Athenian ships
at, 8.24.1
Laeaeans (Paeonian tribe, Thrace),
2.96.3
Laespodius (Athenian commander)
envoy of Four Hundred taken by
Paralus crew to Argos, 8.86.9
leads raids on Laconia, 6.105.2
Laestrygones (people of Sicily), 6.2.1
lakes in Thucydides. *See also* terrain (as
military factor)
Acherusian, Thesprotis, 1.46.4
Bolbe, Chalcidice, 1.58.2
Cercinitis (Strymon lake), Thrace,
4.108.1, 5.7.4
Copais, Boeotia, 4.93.4
Lamachus (Athenian general)
command of ships to Sicily, 6.8.2
killed at Syracuse, 6.101.6
loses ships at anchor in Pontus,
4.75.1–2
proposal for operations in Sicily,
6.49.1–4, 6.50.1
Lamis (founder of Megarian colony on
Sicily), 6.4.1
Lampsacus
given to Themistocles for wine,
1.138.5
retaken by Athenians, 8.62.2
revolts to Dercyllidas, 8.62.1
land forces. *See* armies
Laodicium, battle of, 4.134.1–2
Larisa (Asia), 8.101.3
Larissa (Thessaly), as ally of Athens,
2.22.3
Las (Laconia), 8.91.2
Laspodius (Athenian general),
6.105.1–2
Laurium (Attica)
Alcibiades: "Decelea will halt revenues
from silver mines at," 6.91.7
Peloponnesians ravage Attica as far as
mines, 2.55.1
law. *See also* judges; trials; Thucydides
son of Olorus: on law
Athenian
accomplice of assassin is tortured
but reveals little, 8.92.2
according to Pericles, 2.37.1–3
allies of Athens voluntarily using,
7.57.2
Antiphon best man to help in court,
8.68.1
breakdown of during plague, 2.53.4

morale *(cont'd)*
restored after victory of Point
Cynossema, 8.106.2, 5
"panics to which great armies are
liable," 4.125.1
of Spartans after occupation of
Cythera and Pylos, 4.55.1–4,
4.56.1
of Spartans rises because of Athenian
refusal to arbitrate, 7.18.2–3
Morgantina (Sicily), given to Camarina
by treaty, 4.65.1
motives
of Alcibiades to initiate revolt in
Miletus, 8.17.2
of Athens
in acquiring and holding empire,
1.76.2
of expedition to Sicily, 6.33.1–3
Hermocrates on, 4.61.3–4
of Corinth to aid Epidamnus,
1.25.3–4, 1.26.1
of Sparta
in founding Heraclea, 3.92.4–6
in Plataean affair, 3.68.4
Syracusan, 7.56.1–3
of Tissaphernes, 8.5.4–5, 8.6.1,
8.87.1–6
Motya (Sicily), 6.2.6
mountains in Thucydides
Aegaleus (Attica), 2.19.2
Athos (Chalcidice), 4.109.2, 5.3.6
Brilessus (Attica), 2.23.1
Cercine (Thrace), 2.98.1
Cithaeron (Plataea), 2.75.2, 3.24.2
Etna (Sicily), 3.116.1–2
Geraneia (Megara), 4.70.1
Haemus (Thrace), 2.96.1
Ida (Asia), 4.52.3
Istone (Corcyra), 3.85.3, 4.46.2
Ithome (Messenia), 1.101.2, 3.54.5
Olympus (Thessaly), 4.78.6
Oneion (Corinth), 4.44.4
Pangaeus (Thrace), 2.99.3
Parnassus (Boeotia), 3.95.1
Parnes (Attica), 2.23.1, 4.96.7
Pentelikos (Attica), 2.23.1
Pindus (Epirus), 2.102.2
Rhodope (Thrace), 2.96.1
Scombrus (Thrace), 2.96.3
Thyamus (Agraea), 3.106.3
Munychia (hill), Piraeus,
assembly in theater at, 8.93.1
peripoli at, 8.92.5
within walls of Piraeus, 2.13.7
music. *See also paean*
Homer's hymn to Apollo at Delos fes-
tival, 3.104.4–5
hymn sung by Athenians before fleet
sails, 6.32.1
Spartan army advances to flute-
playing, 5.70.1
Spartan war songs, 5.69.2

trumpeters in Athenian and Syracusan
armies, 6.69.2
trumpets sound for silence, 6.32.1
Mycale (Ionia)
site of Hellenic victory over the Per-
sians, 1.89.2
military maneuvers at, 8.79.1–2
Mycalessus, 7.29.2–5, 7.30.3
Mycenae, estimates of armament and
navy, 1.10.1–5
Myconus (Aegean island), 3.29.1
Mygdonia
as part of Macedonia, 2.99.4
Perdiccas gives land to Chalcidians in
territory of, 1.58.2
Thracians lay waste to, 2.100.4
Mylae (Sicily)
Athenian forces move against, 3.90.2–4
surrenders to Athens, 3.90.4
Myletidae (founders of Himera), 6.5.1
Myonessus (Ionia), 3.32.2
Myonians, join Peloponnesian cam-
paign against Naupactus, 3.101.2
Myos, 1.138.5, 3.19.2
Myrcinus (Thrace)
revolts to Brasidas, 4.107.3
sends peltasts to Brasidas at Amphipo-
lis, 5.6.4, 5.10.9
Myronides (Athenian commander),
1.105.4, 1.108.2–3, 4.95.2
Myrrhine (wife of Hippias), 6.55.1
Myscon (Syracusan general), succeeds
Hermocrates, 8.85.3
Mysteries
Alcibiades' connection to, 6.28.1,
6.53.1
information of mock celebrations of,
6.28.2
mock mysteries perceived as part of
conspiracy, 6.60.1–2
Mytilene
Athenian blockade of, 3.6.1–2,
3.18.4–5, 3.27.1
Athenian *proxeni* dissent from the
revolt, 3.2.3, 3.4.4
Athenians retake, 8.23.2–3
Cleon speaks for harsh punishment of,
3.37–3.40
Diodotus speaks against harsh punishment of, 3.41–3.48
envoys. *See* envoys: Mytilenian
exiles defeated at Antandrus, 4.75.1
exiles' schemes, 4.52.1–3
forewarned of approach of Athenian
fleet, 3.3.5
hostilities with Athens renewed, 3.5.1
initial naval defense of city, 3.4.2
march against Methymna, 3.18.1
Mytilenians sent to Athens and condemned to death, 3.35.1, 3.36.1,
3.36.3–3.49
People demand food, 3.27.3
revolts again, 8.22.2

Salaethus gives arms to the People,
3.27.2
Spartan alliance requested by, 3.9–3.14
surrender to Athens, 3.28.1

Naucleides (pro-Thebes Plataean), 2.2.2
Naupactus
Acarnanian hoplites arrive in time to
defend, 3.102.4
Athenian fleet lookout point and garrison at, 2.69.1, 2.80.4, 7.17.4,
7.19.5
Athenians retire from Aetolia to,
3.98.5
Conon asks aid against Corinthians at,
7.31.4–5
Demosthenes arrives with ships at,
4.76.1, 4.77.1
Helots from Messenia settled at
Naupactus, 1.103.3
Messenian land forces at battle of,
2.90.3–6
naval battles off, 2.83.3–5, 2.84.1–5,
2.90–2.92
rebels expelled from Ithome settle at,
1.103.3
saved by arrival of Acarnanian hoplites,
3.102.3–4
Spartan attack on, 3.100.1–2,
3.101.1–2, 3.102.1–4
naval battles. *See also* casualties: naval
battle losses; triremes and trireme
warfare
Athenians and Aeginetans, 1.105.2
Athenians and Chians off Chios,
8.61.3
Athenians and Peloponnesians
off Cecryphalia, 1.105.1
off Erineus, 7.35.3–8
off harbor of Eretria, 8.95.3–7
off Naupactus, 2.90–2.92
off Patrae, 2.83.3–5, 2.84.1–5
Point Cynossema, Hellespont,
8.104–8.106
at Pylos, 4.11–4.14
off Spiraeum, 8.10.2–3
off Syme, 8.42.1–4
Athenians and Rhegians against
Syracusans and allies, 4.25.1–2
Athenians and Samians off Tragia,
1.116.1
Athenians and Syracusans in Great
Harbor, 7.22.1–2, 7.23.2–3,
7.37.3–7.38.1, 7.39.1–7.41.4,
7.52.1–2, 7.70.1–7.72.4
Carthaginians and Phocaeans, 1.13.6
Corcyraeans and Peloponnesians at
Corcyra, 3.77.1–3, 3.78.1–4
Corinthians and Corcyraeans
in earliest sea fight in history, 1.13.4
near Leukimme, 1.29.4–5
off Sybota, 1.48.1–4, 1.49.1–7,
1.50.5, 1.51.1–2, 1.54.1–2

Scione women, 5.32.1
Toronaean women, 5.3.4
epitaph of Archidice, daughter of
    Hippias, 6.59.3
female relatives of war dead are present
    at funeral, 2.34.4
in fighting in Plataea, 2.4.2
of Mende and Scione sent to
    Olynthus, 4.123.4
one hundred ten remain in Plataea to
    bake bread, 2.78.3
Perdiccas gives sister in exchange for
    help, 2.101.5
Pericles' advice to widows, 2.45.2
Plataean women and children in Athens,
    2.72.2
under Potidaean surrender terms,
    2.70.3
and slaves work on Argive long walls,
    5.82.5
woman in Plataea gives axe to Thebans,
    2.4.4
wood. *See* timber
wounded, the. *See also* casualties
Athenians disabled by Syracusan
    harassment, 7.79.5
Athenians shamed to leave wounded
    behind, 7.75.3
Athenians take up their wounded and
    depart from Miletus, 8.27.5

Spartans disabled by missiles at
    Sphacteria, 4.34.3

Xenares (Spartan ephor)
killed at Heraclea, 5.51.2
plot with Boeotians and Corinthians,
    5.36.1–2, 5.37.1, 5.38.3,
    5.46.4
refuses to give up treaty with
    Boeotians, 5.46.4
Xenocleides (Corinthian admiral)
command of fleet to Corcyra, 1.46.2
at garrison at Ambracia, 3.114.4
Xenon (Theban commander), 7.19.3
Xenophantes (Laconian), 8.55.2
Xenophon (Athenian general)
killed fighting Chalcidians near
    Spartolus, 2.79.1–7
at siege of Potidaea, 2.70.1
Xerxes (Persian King), 1.137.3

Zacynthus
as ally of Athens, 2.9.4, 3.94.1,
    7.57.7
Athenian fleet returns to Pylos from,
    4.13.2
Demosthenes takes hoplites aboard at,
    7.31.2
hoplite reinforcements to Corcyra,
    1.47.2

Peloponnesian expedition against,
    2.66.1
Peloponnesian plan to conquer,
    2.80.1
Zancle (Sicily). *See* Messana
zeal
at commencement of enterprise,
    2.8.1
of Lesbians as allies of Sparta, 3.15.2
of parties to Spartan–Argive alliance,
    5.80.2
for Sicilian expedition intimidates
    opponents, 6.24.4
of Syracusans, 6.69.1
Zeus
Cylon follows oracle to move at grand
    festival of, 1.126.6
Elis requires Lepreum to pay tribute at
    the alter of Olympian Zeus,
    5.31.2
Hesiod killed in precinct of Nemean
    Zeus at Oenon, 3.96.1
Mantineans must inscribe treaty on a
    pillar in their temple of, 5.47.11
oracle tells Spartans to release
    suppliants of Zeus at Ithome,
    1.103.2
Pausanias sacrificed to Zeus the
    liberator at Plataea, 2.71.2
sacred Corcyraean ground of, 3.70.4

REFERENCE MAPS

X   Y

Strymon River

LYNCESTIS   MACEDONIA

BOTTIAEA

Amphipolis

Eion

Thasos

CHALCIDICE

Olynthus

Potidaea

Acanthus

Mende

Scione

Torone

A

Corcyra

THESSALY

Aegean Sea

AMBRACIA

Ionian Sea

Anactorium

ACARNANIA

Heraclea
in Trachis

Leucas

PHOCIS

OPUNTIAN
LOCRIS

Euboea

B

AETOLIA

Delphi

Oeniadae

Naupactus

BOEOTIA

Chalcis

Eretria

Thebes

Cephallenia

ACHAEA

Crisaean Gulf

Plataea

Decelea

Sicyon

Megara

Athens

Carystu

ELIS

Phlius

Corinth

Piraeus

ATTICA

Andr

Zacynthus

Olympia

ARCADIA

Mantinea

Argos

Epidaurus

Aegina

Tegea

Troezen

Hermione

MESSENIA

Pylos

Sparta

LACONIA

Melos

100 km   100 mi

Cythera

AY	Acanthus	CY	Laconia
BX	Acarnania	AY	Lemnos
BX	Achaea	BZ	Lesbos
BY	Aegean Sea	BX	Leucas
CY	Aegina	BY	Locris Opuntian
BZ	Aeolis	AX	Lyncestis
BX	Aetolia		
BX	Ambracia	AX	Macedonia
AY	Amphipolis	CX	Mantinea
BX	Anactorium	BY	Megara
BY	Andros	CY	Melos
CX	Arcadia	AY	Mende
CY	Argos	CX	Messenia
BY	Athens	BZ	Methymna
BY	Attica	CZ	Miletus
		BZ	Mytilene
BY	Boeotia		
AY	Bottiaea	BX	Naupactus
		CZ	Naxos
CZ	Caria		
BY	Carystus	BX	Oeniadae
BX	Cephallenia	CX	Olympia
AY	Chalcidice	AY	Olynthus
BY	Chalcis		
BZ	Chios	BY	Phlius
BY	Crisaean Gulf	BY	Phocis
BX	Corcyra	BY	Piraeus
BY	Corinth	AY	Potidaea
CY	Cythera	CX	Pylos
		CZ	Rhodes
BY	Decelea		
CZ	Delos	BZ	Samos
BY	Delphi	AY	Scione
		BY	Sicyon
AY	Eion	CX	Sparta
BX	Elis	AY	Strymon River
BZ	Ephesus		
CY	Epidaurus	CY	Tegea
BY	Eretria	AY	Thasos
BY	Euboea	BY	Thebes
		AY	Torone
BX	Heraclea in Trachis	CY	Troezen
AZ	Hellespont		
CY	Hermione	CX	Zacynthus
AZ	Imbros		
BZ	Ionia		
BX	Ionian Sea		

713